Principles of
EDUCATIONAL
PSYCHOLOGY

P-21

W. D. COMMINS
ASSOCIATE PROFESSOR OF PSYCHOLOGY
CATHOLIC UNIVERSITY OF AMERICA

BARRY FAGIN
ASSOCIATE PROFESSOR, EDUCATION AND
PSYCHOLOGY, UNIVERSITY OF FLORIDA

SECOND EDITION

THE RONALD PRESS COMPANY · NEW YORK

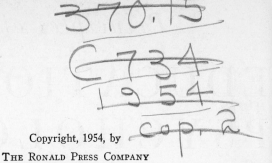

Copyright, 1954, by

THE RONALD PRESS COMPANY

———

Copyright, 1937, by

THE RONALD PRESS COMPANY

———

All Rights Reserved

2

Library of Congress Catalog Card Number: 54-6963

PRINTED IN THE UNITED STATES OF AMERICA

PREFACE

THE PAST two decades have seen profound changes in the schools and in teacher training, and the ideal teacher's role approaches that of an applied psychologist in the guidance of learning. In some respects the words of William James in 1899 pertain to our time: "The 'new' psychology has become a term to conjure up portentous ideas withal; and you teachers, docile and receptive and aspiring as many of you are, have been plunged in an atmosphere of vague talk about our science, which to a great extent has been more mystifying than enlightening." The recent self-searching, redefinition, and course-charting by educational psychologists perhaps reflect a recognition of some such state of affairs. This book is based on the belief that educational psychology should be taught as science, that is, an empirically derived discipline with unifying concepts. If removed from its empirical foundations in the interests of a "practical" approach, it will consist of fragmentary facts and opinions dished up piecemeal, and will come to resemble the "vague talk" about psychology to which James referred.

This is a textbook for courses in educational psychology. The present revision maintains the viewpoint of the first edition: the common ground of psychology and education lies in the field of mental development. The treatment of the principles of maturation, learning, personality and adjustment, measurement, individual differences, and guidance thus attempts to focus on the core of professional teacher training, which we conceive to be human development. The developmental viewpoint is particularly advantageous in deciding just what material should be selected from the complex mass of psychological facts and principles to make a distinctly educational psychology. The recent advances in learning theory, personality theory, and

iii

the social sciences, for example, seem to be most meaningful and clearly integrated as they focus on developmental problems. The extensive revision of the text has therefore particularly recognized these trends. The new material in the book reflects this development also, as evidenced by discussions of social backgrounds of child development, group processes, problems in counseling, and learning as a social process.

While recognizing that the study of educational psychology should help the teacher understand children and favorably influence his behavior toward them, we believe that this can hardly be achieved through exclusive concern with the practical problems of classroom management. The teacher who would "psychologize" educational problems must have some grasp of psychological theory. To that end, we have made a selection of old and new theoretical approaches, as well as current techniques, which seem to have the most important implications for the guidance of learning. The aim has been to present these in a consistent organization, with an organismic viewpoint.

The book is divided into five parts, with Part I providing the essential ideas and the vocabulary. The first chapter is an attempt to show that our current psychological ideas have a history and that psychological theories both past and present have influenced teachers and the general public in their attitudes toward school practice. The second chapter presents current concepts of learning and development basic to educational psychology. Part II deals with the psychobiological principles of growth and development, traces the outlines of physical, intellectual, social, and emotional development, and points up the factors that influence the development of the child as an individual. The last two sections deal with learning. Part III details the principles and facts of individual differences among pupils, how they are measured through tests and inventories or observed in other ways, and what they mean in school practice. Part IV develops the principles of the learning process: the mental processes involved, the conditions under which learning occurs, the importance of the learner's motives, the ways in which he transfers or utilizes past experiences in new situations. Part V deals with the various forms of learning, such as habits and skills, memorizing, thinking and problem solving, and personal adjustment.

The unifying concepts, it seems clear to us, are embodied in learning theory, particularly as applied to mental development. We need not be deterred, in seeking a unified approach, by unresolved conflicts between different schools of learning. To the educational psychologists, and particularly to the teacher, the points in dispute are trivial by comparison with the areas of agreement. The treatment of the learning process is systematic, based on the conviction that all learning is cognitively controlled at least to the extent permitted by the learning situation. The future teacher must somehow come to see that the learning process is lawful and therefore understandable and manageable. Whether this insight comes from a consideration of animal learning or classroom learning is unimportant. We include, both as illustration and evidence of certain points, examples of animal learning that may help the student to conceptualize important principles. Their application to human life and to schools does not require the conclusion that animal and human learning are necessarily alike.

We recognize an indebtedness to many authors, teachers, and students whose mention here would make a formidable list. In particular, our thanks are due to Dr. Henry Garrett, Dr. W. Max Wise, and Dr. Kenneth Eells, who read portions of the manuscript and offered valuable suggestions; to Josephine Senn, who typed much of the manuscript; and, for typing and other labor beyond the call of duty, to Ada Fagin.

Washington, D. C.   W. D. Commins

Gainesville, Florida   Barry Fagin

   February, 1954

CONTENTS

PART III

Individual Differences in the School

PART IV

The Conditions of Learning

PART V

The Forms of Learning

TABLES

ILLUSTRATIONS

INTRODUCTION

What Is Psychology? Psychology is a social and natural science comprising a body of knowledge and a characteristic discipline. As scientists, psychologists study behavior for one primary purpose, to give a systematic explanation of the facts. Psychological theories are framed so they can be tested by experimental methods, and they stand or fall on experimental results. The only principles of psychology are those which can be and have been verified, which give an adequate explanation of the facts of behavior. The work of the psychologist may be described something like this: he assembles and studies facts of behavior to see how they are related, proposes theories to account for the relationships, devises experimental situations by which he can test the validity of his theoretical principles, and confirms or modifies his theories accordingly.

The quest of the psychologist as scientist has one other aspect: In his explanations of behavior he seeks economy, or as it is sometimes called, *parsimony*. This means that he tries to frame fewer and fewer principles to account for more and more facts of behavior. He attempts to give an orderly account of behavior with as few principles as possible. In this sense a science is *systematic,* since the purpose is to construct a theoretical system of this character. The problems involved in theoretical psychology are serious ones, as in physics or chemistry. Since psychology is a fairly young science, systematic or theoretical problems are frequently controversial matters. There are differing points of view as to which theories give the best account of the facts.

We must distinguish, however, between two kinds of scientific approach, which are often called "pure science" and "applied science." Pure science is concerned primarily with theoretical

I

systems and their detailed verification. Applied science seeks to establish principles which help to solve practical everyday problems. The student of educational psychology must be aware of this distinction, because much of the literature in systematic behavior science, although apparently trivial from the point of view of applied science, is of crucial importance to the systematic psychologist. The two approaches are complementary rather than conflicting. Engineering (applied science) does not conflict, for example, with theoretical physics. The engineer simply borrows from physics and other sciences the principles and techniques he finds useful in practical problems. And the practical need for immediate solutions requires the engineer to go ahead independently with his more practical research.

What Is Educational Psychology? Educational psychology is applied science. It is a natural and social science whose discipline is essentially psychological, and consists of a body of principles selected from many sources. Some of its principles, but not all, come from the psychological laboratory, from experiments on men and animals. Some are borrowed from other branches of applied psychology—industrial, clinical, social, vocational. Some facts and explanations come from sociology and anthropology. All of these sciences are concerned with the solution of practical problems in the realm of human behavior. To the educational psychologist, the sole criterion in selecting from these sources is this: Does it have implications for educational practice?

Probably the most important human problem is that of educating children: what to teach, how to teach it, and with what purpose. The solution to this problem is tied up with questions of philosophy, economics, and politics, which enter into the larger problems of society as a whole. The principles of educational psychology are useful in providing *some* solutions to *some* educational problems. Psychology also helps to light the way and provide the tools and "know-how" for educational research. As applied science, educational psychology emphasizes its reliance on evidence. It is not a hodge-podge collection of vague generalizations, but is organized like any science around a few basic concepts validated by investigation. Although not a special "brand" of psychology with special laws, techniques, and principles of its own, educational psychology has typically concerned itself with the more immediate problems of the school. It thus represents a considerable body of research in its own right. The educational psychologist is a contributor to other branches as well as a borrower.

In 1949 a committee of Division 15 (Educational Psychology) of the American Psychological Association defined two purposes of educational psychology. The first is (1) "the study of behavior as it is changed or directed under the social processes of education," and the secondary goal consists of (2) "studies directed toward *how* behavior is changed and directed through education." (2)

The Content of Educational Psychology. The above-mentioned committee listed five general areas essential to educational psychology.

1. *Human Growth and Development*. This includes the general principles of growth and development, the contributions of heredity and environment, social and emotional development, theory of motivation, intelligence, aptitudes and interests, individual differences.

2. *Learning*. The nature of the learning process, the factors that influence learning, devices for motivating the learner; learning skills, reasoning and problem solving, learning of attitudes; the application of learning principles to school subjects; the transfer of learning. The guidance, direction, control, and evaluation of learning is considered to be the core of educational psychology. The learning process is the concrete expression and means of mental development.

3. *Personality and Adjustment*. These broad terms refer to the many aspects of the development of the whole child in his social and emotional adjustments as well as his intellectual growth. This area would include such topics as emotions, mental hygiene of pupils and teachers, the adjustments of exceptional children, character education, and social interaction. This area is particularly concerned with the *interaction* of the

physical, intellectual, social and emotional sides of development.

4. *Measurement and Evaluation.* The basic principles of testing and measurement, their application to the measurement of intelligence and other aptitudes, achievement, and personal adjustment; the application of the results of testing to the work of the school.

5. *Techniques and Methods of Educational Psychology.* As a scientific discipline educational psychology has developed characteristic methods and techniques for studying educational problems. Methods of research and statistical techniques are an important part of the subject.

Educational Psychology as Professional Education. Educational psychology is essential to the professional education of teachers (3). Its content consists of what the teacher needs to know about psychology to do a good professional job. The professional language of teachers, first of all, includes many psychological terms, such as intelligence quotient, percentile, needs, motive, "readiness," adjustment, level of aspiration. These concepts, as embodied in principles of learning, development, mental hygiene, and measurement, must be understood if the teacher is to read educational literature with profit. In the teacher's role of guiding the learner, psychological principles are basic. For the professional educator, an "objective experimental approach to educational problems" is more desirable on the whole than purely empirical solutions based on opinion (1). The teacher should think objectively about her own classroom problems and about educational issues, should seek scientific verification of her theories.

To some people, "theory" means something that "doesn't work in practice." When taken in this sense, theory and practice seem to be opposites. For our purpose, a theory is a belief or a point of view which has been tested experimentally and has many implications for educational practice. Our ability to apply a theory to a particular situation is the test of our understanding of theoretical principles. Educational psychology is not a collection of rules-of-thumb for teaching, but of theory; that is, of concepts, principles, methods, ways of thinking.

What the teacher does in the classroom, whether she realizes it or not, is always the result of her beliefs about human behavior, or in other words her theories. In this sense, theories of learning and development are as old as education itself.

Finally, the professional teacher possesses certain skills which are based at least in part on educational psychology. She must guide the learning of children according to established principles of learning, and maintain a classroom atmosphere conducive to the child's mental health and personal development. In helping the child to adjust to his personal problems, she must be aware of and provide for individual differences. She must select, use, and interpret various kinds of tests as a normal part of the teaching and guidance process.

REFERENCES

1. ANDERSON, G. L. Educational psychology and teacher education. *J. educ. psychol.*, 1949, **40**, 275-284.
2. NOLL, V. H., HORROCKS, J. E., & ANDERSON, G. L. Functions of the division of educational psychology of the American Psychological Association: a committee report. *J. educ. psychol.*, 1949, **40**, 361-370.
3. NATIONAL SOCIETY OF COLLEGE TEACHERS OF EDUCATION, Committee on Educational Psychology. Educational psychology in teacher education. NSCTE, *Monog. No. 3, 1953.*

SELECTED READINGS

AMERICAN ASSOCIATION OF TEACHERS COLLEGES. *Child growth and development emphasis in teacher education,* 1944.

ANDREWS, T. G. (Ed). *Methods of psychology.* New York: Wiley, 1948. Ch. 1 describes the scientific method and its application to psychological problems.

NATIONAL SOCIETY OF COLLEGE TEACHERS OF EDUCATION. *Monogr. No. 3, 1953.* Final report of society committees for determining the content or learning experiences necessary for the training of beginning teachers. Several pertinent articles by committee members appear in the *Journal of Educational Psychology* issues of March, 1948, May, 1949, and October, 1950.

NATIONAL EDUCATION ASSOCIATION. *National commission on teacher education and professional standards.* Washington, D.C.: NEA, 1948. The education of teachers as viewed by the profession.

PART I

Psychology and Education

1

OUR PSYCHOLOGICAL HERITAGE

> These ideas we inherit . . . are never static. They are either fading into meaningless formulae, or are gaining power . . . by a more delicate apprehension.—ALFRED N. WHITEHEAD, *Science and the Modern World*.

IN a sense every teacher is an applied psychologist, because his teaching is based on certain beliefs or ideas which may be called psychological. He responds to people, and to situations requiring the guidance or management of people, in terms of his beliefs about how the mind functions and how people learn. He responds differently to persons differing in age and sex as a direct result of his beliefs about sex and age differences. He has a concept of discipline, which perhaps expresses his beliefs about human motives. These beliefs, opinions, and general feelings about people actually function as psychological theories in the sense that they determine how we go about the task of managing our daily relationships with other persons. The teacher's beliefs about the behavior of children determine his educational practice. We need to ask, therefore, how these beliefs are acquired.

Probably some are acquired directly from one's parents, and many are certainly the result of one's own experience and observation; but the most important and enduring beliefs are those which are part of our cultural inheritance. By this we mean that they are so intimately bound up with our society and its institutions that they tend to be accepted without question. Many of our notions about teaching are of this kind; we did not invent them ourselves, but "inherited" them through the culture in which we were raised. If we go far enough back in the history of thought, it is possible to identify their origins; it is especially important to recognize ideas with scientific roots.

The past three or four centuries have produced many psychologists who have had considerable to say, either expressed or implied, about mental development. Their ideas have often been taken over by educators, and form many of the ready-made notions which influence the psychological thinking of the well-read person of today. These psychologists are often regarded as belonging to certain "schools" of thought, each of which contributed its share of ideas and terms to the background of educational psychology. It would not perhaps be strictly true to say that the particular concepts attributed to these schools had not been given expression before their time or that practical use had not been made of them in the classroom. But the credit for expressing them as inferences from a well-thought-out system of psychology, and so leading to their firm entrenchment in the common mind, belongs especially to the group of thinkers who scientifically sponsored them. Nor should it be said that any particular psychologist would perhaps have found all the ideas attributed to his own school wholly acceptable, especially in the summary form in which they are expressed here. But these ideas and the manner of their expression do in general represent how his more erudite and accurately expressed notions have been interpreted by others and in what form they have reached the common mind.

Association Psychology. The members of the English school of philosopher-psychologists, often known as associationists, including Locke, Hume, Mill, and others, have had much to do in the intervening years with the choice of both ideas and terms to describe mental development. Their first principle of the "association of ideas" has become at times almost synonymous with mental growth and has furnished an explanation of the school's influence on the child. It has also served at times either to justify or condemn educational methods and to suggest a new approach. The following notions concerning mind and its education can be traced back, either directly or indirectly, to this psychological doctrine.

The mind of the infant is supposedly a "tabula rasa"—a blank page. All that will ever be recorded thereon must come from impressions of the world round about. This seemed to place education in the light of a "stamping-in" process, or one of implanting knowledge in the mind of the child. It ran counter to the view of education, somewhat prevalent at the time, as simply offering an opportunity for the mind to bring its innate or self-originated ideas into play. We not only learn from impressions and experience, but experience is the only teacher. Just as the blind man, it was said, can have no image or idea of color because he has never seen one, so all knowledge must come from previous impressions.

The child received his mental impressions of things through what appeared to be a kind of photographic sensory equipment. The resulting sensations or sensory experiences became the warp and woof of mental development. Concepts or ideas were not thought to be different in kind, but were regarded as the original sensory impressions in a modified or combined form. An idea, for example, was identified with a sense image, or was thought to be a kind of faded-out sensation. It seemed logical in the light of this doctrine to stress "sense training" in the early days of schooling and to ignore at practically all ages any commonly observed distinction between "higher" and "lower" forms of mental activity. It was thought that rational learning could be explained in terms of the ultimate units of mental life—the elementary sense experiences.

Learning itself became principally a matter of combining the first sensations or their faint images in an additive sort of way. This is the principle of the *association of ideas,* according to which certain single impressions may be made to adhere to other impressions in an external, accidental union. The mind, being passive and photographic, appeared to depend upon outside objects not only for its original contents but for the manner of their combination as well. The prime reason for learning was placed in the environment and not in the child. Repetition and drill seemed to be the favored teaching methods. It appeared to be the view that if only a person were exposed long enough or often enough to anything, he could not help but learn it.

The mind of the child, with its mirror-image of reality, had supposedly a margin and a focal point. Everything before the child was thought to be represented somewhere in this field, and whether or not he could see it clearly depended merely on his readiness to reflect upon what was already contained in it. *Attention,* consequently, became a key word in education. Could or would the child cast the searchlight of his attention upon the half-hidden recesses of his mind? The great defect of the infant mind, it was said, was its inability to give attention. Teach the pupil to concentrate, by strong discipline if necessary, for his inability to do so was the only apparent reason for his not seeing what he was supposed to see. The classroom often became a kind of battleground for the conflict of wills—the will of the teacher trying to force the attention of the pupils and the children on their part rather indisposed to give this attention.

Association psychology formulated certain laws of mental growth, but as we look at these now, they seemed to refer more directly to the external manner in which experiences came to the child rather than to the nature of the mind itself. The fundamental law seemed to be that of association by *contiguity.* Two ideas would get associated or bound together in the mind, it was said, if the objects happened to be contiguous or near one another in time or space. The great emphasis placed by the associationists upon impressions and the proper presentation of these in order to bind them together gave rise to what appeared to the average person as a somewhat mechanical view of mental development. The extreme of this viewpoint was expressed in the writings of one author who said that if he were given a marble statue endowed with the power of sensation alone he could educate it.

Association psychology has had a very strong influence on educational thought. It was helpful in stressing the importance of the past history of the child, and it focused the attention of educators on mental processes. On the other hand, associationism has turned out to be an oversimplified description of the learning process because it attempted to reduce all kinds of psychological processes to one law. As an educational psychology, association psychology has two grave shortcomings: it held the external environment to be all-important in determining what the child would learn, and minimized the importance of the child's goals. Just as "attention" was the key word in associationistic education, the modern concern with the child's needs and goals makes "motivation" the key word in current thought.

The Psychology of Mental Powers. We have received another heritage of educational ideas from the "faculty" or "power" psychologists of the eighteenth and nineteenth centuries. They are represented by Wolfe in Germany and the Scottish philosopher Reid. Their teachings seemed to appeal to a common-sense view of the nature of mind and accorded fairly well with the implications of ordinary language. The phrenologists who were popular at about the same time received some support from this doctrine and in turn helped to justify it.

According to this theory, the mind was constituted of a number of separate mental powers, each of which might be trained through appropriate mental exercise. When we say that a person has a wonderful memory but is weak in observation, or that his power of attention is good but his judgment is poor, we are very close to the same notion. Each of these mental powers was supposed to grow and become stronger through exercise much after the fashion of a muscle of the body. If we wish to strengthen the muscles of our arm, we exercise the arm and not the leg or some other part of the body. Just so, each faculty or power was thought to require its own *form* of training. Education, from this point of view, could be regarded as a series of mental exercises—one to train the power of observation, another to strengthen concentration of attention, and still another to improve judgment. Such is the doctrine of *formal discipline*. How often have we not heard it said that there is nothing like mathematics to train our powers of reasoning? Or have we not frequently read advertisements for books and training courses to help us strengthen our memory?

The aim of educating the child, so it seemed, was to produce a highly trained mind, not of necessity a useful one. Knowledge and practical information were thought to come through later experience, after the mind had been first properly trained and strengthened. And as it was the strengthening of the mental powers that was the important thing, the more difficult the school tasks the better were they thought to be suited to this end. Such a view tended in many instances to keep practically useful or interesting matters out of the classroom because these apparently would not produce the show of painful effort on the part of the pupils which the more abstract and abstruse mental puzzles evoked. Effort and difficulty became in a way the standard for judging the educational value of a subject. Do we not recognize this view as akin to one often expressed or implied at the present time, that to be educationally worth while a thing must be "hard," or that one of the advantages of a "liberal" education is the superior training of the mind brought about by the forced study of abstruse and nonpractical matters?

Because the various mental powers had apparently their own rates of growth, it was thought that these could best be trained at separate ages. Memory, for example, appeared to best advantage at an earlier age than reason, so the young child might be expected to memorize but not to understand. The early training of memory would furnish the raw material, as it were, or produce a useful adjunct to reason, when this faculty came to be exercised later on. To assign the effective appearance of the various mental powers to different ages of childhood and youth could not help but make the lessons of the schoolroom rather formal matters. The belief that children have a better "memory" than adults is a survival of the power theory of mind.

In its influence on educational thought, the "mental powers" doctrine had some good features as well as bad ones. It allowed for the possibility of individual differences, that children differ in ability to learn different kinds of things. Also, the mere fact that it distinguished among kinds of mental activities was helpful in an age when individual differences in mental abilities were largely ignored.   Although the distinctions made among mental abilities were arbitrary and mistaken, from a modern perspective, the theory of mental powers thus opened up the problem of transfer for scientific study.   As educational psychology, the bad features of the mental powers doctrine are readily apparent. Its analysis of mind into powers of observation, memory, reasoning, and the like, took its cues from language usage rather than the study of mental processes.   Since we have a word for "memory," for example, it is easy to assume that there is such a power.

The theory of formal discipline, when applied to education, would make the school too adult-centered and too content-centered.   It confuses the products of learning with the learning process, and thus not only ignores the way a child actually learns but imposes on the child a régime mistakenly patterned after the way the adult *thinks* he thinks.   Training through formal discipline not only misses fire but prevents the educational transfer effect it is designed to achieve.

The Psychology of Apperception.   A reaction to the theory of mental powers is found in the writings of the Herbartians (who took their name from the psychologist Herbart), with their doctrine of *apperception*.   These students of mind spoke of mental development in terms of "apperceptive masses," groups of previously developed ideas that laid the mental setting for the hospitable reception or apperception of new ideas. They seemed to disagree with association psychology as well when they shifted the stress in learning from outside to inside the mind.   The fate of any new idea was closely linked with that which had preceded it in mental development.

In their stress upon a hospitable mental background for the reception of new ideas, the Herbartians gave first place to mental "content" rather than to mental "training."   Knowledge and organized information became the aim of, and pointed the way to, education.   When carried to an extreme this notion seemed to favor simple knowing at the expense of doing.   The person who knew something about everything but who might or might not be able to put into practice the things he knew seemed to be the logical outcome. It is likely that we still find ourselves doing homage at times to the learned pedant, and wondering that "the one small head should carry all he knows."

It has been said that the psychology of apperception centered the learning process in the teacher instead of in the child because of the rather rigid lesson plans it favored. Members of an older generation apparently miss these logically organized lessons in the classrooms of today. "The teachers," they sometimes say, "do not teach." They probably mean that teachers do not give the same amount of attention as formerly to the mere imparting of information and knowledge, or to the "teacher-control" of mental content.

The Herbartians distinguished between a *logical* and a *psychological* approach to subject matter, or in other words, between an adult and a childish way of organizing knowledge. This distinction was based upon a difference in the apperceptive masses or previous experiences of the two, and suggested that a child should not be expected to learn history or geography, for instance, in the same manner in which these subjects would be logically presented to an adult mind. Because of the difference in mental background, history for the child should begin with the study of one's own neighborhood and country. This view naturally favored bringing subject matter down to the child's level of understanding and experience, something which was not always felt so necessary as it is now.

The psychology of apperception stressed the significance of *interest* in learning. While not exactly clear as to just how interest might intervene in the process of apperceiving, the Herbartians nevertheless believed it to be very important. Without interest on the part of the learner, the new ideas could not firmly unite with the "apperceptive masses." When this doctrine of interest was carried to an extreme, it became practically synonymous with what was merely entertaining or amusing to the child.

The Herbartian theories were revolutionary in their own time, even though many of their ideas are today widely accepted and appear quite commonplace. This approach was probably the first to be based on an empirical psychology of learning.

The theories were not supported by experimental data, and were thus not "scientific" by our standards, but their formulation was aided considerably by a careful study of learning processes in children. It was largely the Herbartian doctrines that stimulated the educational reforms in Germany in the early nineteenth century and eventually made popular the beliefs that play activities are educational (Froebel's "Kindergarten") and that education should be socially useful. Another result was the emphasis on systematic *methods* of pedagogy and the teacher-centered school, which lasted well into our own time.

Psychology Becomes Experimental. Psychology as we know it in the twentieth century was generally described as the "new psychology" about 1900 because it had entered the laboratory and had begun to feel firmly entrenched there. From the first psychological laboratory, founded by Wundt at the University of Leipzig in 1879, came most of the pioneer laboratory psychologists in America: Witmer at Pennsylvania, Cattell at Columbia, Pace at Catholic University, and Titchener at Cornell. The "old" psychology's shortcomings were not necessarily held to be in what was taught so much as in the nature of the evidence they had to support it. Casual observation of common events, anecdotes, and accounts from memory were regarded as foreign to "science" and therefore were often dismissed as "armchair" methods. An attempt was made to replace these by carefully designed experiments in memory and learning as well as in sensation and perception. The hope for the future of psychology as a science lay in controlled observation and in quantitative methods of evaluating results.

Psychology from the earliest days had been considered a branch of philosophy. Now the attempt to link it with the natural sciences produced for a while some intellectual confusion. Many writers regarded the "new" psychology as a kind of "cause célèbre," as an important intellectual revolt against the speculative, rational methods of philosophy. The extreme form of some psychological theories (e.g., Watson's behaviorism) developed largely from this attitude. Of this development it was said that psychology first lost its soul, then its mind, then consciousness, and ended with behavior of a kind—the behavior of an automaton. In many respects this resulted in throwing out the baby with the bathwater, but it was probably a necessary part of the strenuous attempt of a young science to "come of age." It is now widely recognized that the study of philosophy provides essential background for questions about the nature of man, the goals of life, and human values. The study of such questions properly constitutes a field of "philosophical psychology," and is certainly basic to a philosophy of education. As professional psychologists now use the term, however, "psychology" tends to be restricted to topics and problems which lend themselves more readily to objective and quantitative methods of study. Psychology has come to be an experimental discipline, as well as a body of facts and principles supported by experimental results. Educational psychology took the same trend.

The Stimulus-Response Concept. There were other influences. Psychology took over from physiology the "stimulus-response" concept—the view that all behavior can be described or accounted for in terms of stimuli and responses. In the laboratory the terms "stimulus" and "response" had very specific meanings. A beam of light was a prepared stimulus which excited receptor neurons in the retina of the eye; acid placed on the tongue excited taste receptors; an electric shock was applied to a muscle. The "response" was any reaction to a specific stimulus. In time, the "stimulus" came to mean any object, event, or set of conditions that caused a reaction, not just a prepared stimulus. There was a tendency to describe learning in terms of reactions, or more specifically, a learned act as a *connection* or bond established in the organism between a stimulus and a response. Experimenters found that in many cases it was difficult or even impossible to predict the response from the stimulus. They found, for example, that such "intervening variables" as the kind of organism (human or animal, child or adult), the condition of the organism (hunger, fatigue), and past learning are just as important in predicting a reaction as are the stimulating conditions themselves. The attempt to reduce all psychological phenomena to "stimulus-response" terms therefore imposed considerable strain on the original concepts, and some psychologists have expressed the opinion that the "stimulus-response language has outlived its usefulness" (3).

In their study of learning and mental development, psychologists sought to correlate their findings with what was known of physiology, particularly the nervous system. They became concerned with the problem of *localization* of learning: just where, in the physiological mechanisms, does learning take place? It came to be more or less generally accepted that the organic "seat of learning" was the synapse or junction point of nerve fibers. Writers of textbooks felt called upon to include a rather minute account of the anatomy and functioning of the nervous system. This shift in viewpoint induced some writers to express their view of education in terms of training the nervous system, rather than the older idea of training the mind. Although not very helpful to educators in their practical problems of teaching, this was another aspect of the changing views of psychology.

Psychologists began to study animals. Animals of course do learn, and their learning seems at times to be so simple and direct, and so easily controlled, that animal experiments seemed to offer the best opportunity for getting down to fundamentals. Animal learning would not be complicated by such changeable human factors as interests and attitudes. Through discovering the fundamentals of learning, these experiments promised to contribute to our understanding of human development. The first results seemed to cast serious doubts on the supposed insight and instinctive foresight of animals. We are likely, it was said, to be much too "anthropomorphic" in attributing to them our own human experiences. Animal learning appeared to be quite blind; animals learned by "trial and error." To put it somewhat crudely, they learned by making mistakes and then gradually eliminating them, not because they "saw" they were wrong or had any insight into the "correct" solution, but because the wrong responses led to pain or unpleasantness. In neurological terms, the unpleasantness was held to block the synapses leading to the wrong responses and thus eliminate them. Then the tables were turned, so to speak, on the human mind. Blind "trial-and-error" learning came to be regarded as typical of human development as well. It appeared that we had not only been too anthropomorphic about animals, but even about ourselves. Such terms as "insight" and "foresight" became practically tabu in explanations of learning. Even human reasoning was thought to be basically a kind of trial-and-error process. When judged from a common-sense viewpoint, the psychology of learning came to be couched in rather strange terms. Most of these terms derived from experiments with dogs, cats, and rats.

Experimental psychology had a profound influence on the thinking and language of educators. Most important, educational psychology became experimental; its conclusions rest on objective empirical evidence. However, some ways of thinking were led up blind alleys by partial evidence resulting from the early psychologists' preoccupation with stimulus-response bonds, synapses, and restricted types of animal learning experiments. Extremist viewpoints were the result.

Some Extreme Views. As we have seen, certain trends in experimental psychology introduced new terms and new formulas to explain learning and development. Mental acts became reactions, to be analyzed in terms of stimulus and response, and learning at the physiological level was regarded as the forming of connections in the nervous system. The application of some of these assumptions, when carried to their logical (and sometimes illogical) conclusions, resulted in some "isms" which pervaded educational thought. Because these points of view sprang from attempts to be scientific and were usually expressed in ultra-scientific language, they have perhaps been more influential than they might seem to the ordinary person armed with his common-sense standard of judgment. However, they have been largely opposed from within the fold of science rather than by popular opinion.

Behaviorism. In its extreme form, behaviorism was an attempt to reduce all learning to conditioned reflexes—human and animal, verbal and nonverbal, feelings and ideas. The idea of the conditioned reflex came from the experiments of a Russian physiologist, Pavlov, with dogs. He found through experimenting that when he presented food to a dog and sounded a bell at the same time, the dog's salivation reflex became conditioned to the bell. After a number of trials, in other words, the dog would salivate at the sound of the bell alone, with no food. It was found that the animal could be conditioned to a wide variety of stimuli, and that a wide variety of reflexes could be conditioned. Some years later this concept of the conditioned reflex was taken by the "reflexologists" as the key to all learning. From this viewpoint, what we know as "thinking" was said to be of the same order as Pavlov's salivary reflex, but more complex. Learning was held to be a matter of conditioning reflexes—a process of adding to the inborn reflex equipment new kinds of external stimulation that would set off the old reflexes. Carry this one step further and we have a psychology that denied the importance and the actual existence of consciousness. Thinking became "subvocal speech"; terms like purpose, intention, and insight, which the ordinary person had always believed were intimately related to learning, were no longer used. The notion of instinct was also discarded. Soon the reflexologists rejected any kind of mental heredity, and held that mental development and education were wholly a matter of environment and training. This seemed to be getting back in a roundabout way to the idea of association psychology that learning depends altogether upon what stimulates the child and thereby gives him the material of his experience. The foremost exponent of behaviorism, Watson, stoutly claimed that if he were given any child at birth, he could raise the child to any educational level he wished. It was not clear just how this could be done; but Watson, in making this claim, was stating exactly what behaviorism implied.

The concept of conditioning provides a very useful and convenient way of understanding how certain forms of learning can occur unconsciously—how a child learns the meanings of words, for example, or fear of snakes. "Conditioning" is still a very useful term in psychology. But behaviorism, in its extreme form, is now almost a dead issue.

These viewpoints often led to extreme positions on the "nature-nurture question," or the relative importance of heredity and environment in mental development. A great deal of discussion was devoted to the question of whether certain human traits are innate or acquired. They could not apparently be both at one and the same time. They must be *either* part of man's inborn mental equipment, it seemed, and so "hereditary," *or* something added through experience. This tendency to draw a sharp line between what is inherited and what is acquired was quite unfortunate. To say that it is "human nature" to do this or that, or to say that mental disease is hereditary, implies to many persons a kind of fatalism about the trait that nothing short of a miracle can change. To say that a trait is learned, on the other hand, implies to some persons that heredity has no influence on it. There seems to be a great liking for the "either-or" classification. This approach made the nature-nurture question a source of controversy—and of confusion—in educational psychology for many years.

Gestalt Psychology and Field Theory. At the same time that behavioristic concepts were becoming prominent in America, a group of German psychologists took a completely opposite direction and came into sharp conflict with behaviorism. The original reaction, however, was against the old association psychology—not just against the methods, but against the whole approach. Association psychology thought of experience as a combination of elementary sensations, and an "idea" was therefore a compound of simple sensations. Gestalt psychology rejected the analysis of percepts or ideas into elements as completely misleading, since this kind of analysis is based on the assumption that a whole is identical with the sum of its parts. On the contrary, the Gestaltists insisted, a "whole" consisted in the arrangements or relationship among the parts; two percepts might be quite different, although containing identical parts, simply because the two sets of parts are arranged differently. The word "Gestalt" means roughly "form" or "shape";

it has also been translated as configuration, pattern, structure.

The Gestalt experimental work was a frontal attack not only on associationism, but on many of the "orthodox" psychological statements which took their meaning from associationist doctrine. Even what appear to be such obvious commonplaces as "we learn by experience," and "mental life begins with sensations," have been rejected by Gestalt psychologists as being basically unsound. These writers have claimed that a wholly new approach to the study of mind is required, comparable to the innovations introduced into the field of physics by the relativity theory. Quite apart from the merits of such a claim, it would be impossible for a respectable scientific movement of this kind to remain without considerable influence on psychology in general. The main thesis of Gestalt theory seems to be that mind and behavior had been traditionally analyzed into too many and too minute elements, and that much of significance was lost in this kind of piecemeal study. Gestalt psychologists would substitute the study of "wholes" of experience and behavior, making these more nearly comparable to the objects and acts of ordinary observation, such as table, smile, and song. They have also said that psychology has in the past placed too much stress on the "mechanics" of mind and not enough on the "dynamic" aspect.

Educational thinking has been strongly influenced by the Gestalt concepts through what is known as *field theory*. The word "field" is a term borrowed from physics, where it is conceived as a basic notion for the physical context in which an event occurs. Thus any event which occurs in a magnetic field has meaning only with respect to the structure of the field. "Field" is a difficult abstraction, but if we think of it as a "larger whole" which gives meaning to the "part" events we are not far wrong. In astronomy, the solar system is a "field" because the movement of a planet (event) can be understood only with respect to the organization of the whole system. The living organism is a "field" within which many microscopic events are taking place in such a way that the organism remains in equilibrium, e.g., maintains an optimum blood temperature. Similarly, a social institution can exhibit "field" characteristics; a family, a school, or a nation are in a sense unitary or "larger wholes" because they have qualities that are something more than the individuals who make them up. This field theory seems to be saying "experience *comes* organized; it is not compounded of parts; psychological units are complex structures, just as are organisms and other systems; do not analyze them into parts if you want to understand them."

Field theory, often called the *holistic* or *organismic* point of view, is really a broad trend in science and philosophy. It is a movement away from the "atomistic" type of thinking which tended to reduce events to elements of one kind or another. In educational circles, we are likely now to hear such expressions as "education of the whole child" or "the child is a dynamic unit." These are signs of the influence of field theory on education.

Mental Testing. The introduction of mental tests was responsible for many innovations in educational thought and practice. It is a significant fact that scientific measurement in psychology has been closely linked with the abilities, aptitudes, and traits in which the educator has also been very much interested. In fact, one of the founders of the testing movement, Binet, was induced to undertake the solution of an important practical school problem—that of trying to accommodate school subjects and methods to the needs and capacities of retarded pupils. This step was an important one in the linking of psychological tests with education.

The objective nature of scientific measurement was soon seen to demand a refined statistical treatment of test techniques and results. As a result of this, educational psychology took on the outward appearance at least of one of the natural sciences. At the turn of the century the subject matter of educational psychology was constituted largely of special phases of the more philosophical treatment of mind. With the introduction of mental tests many of these topics were replaced by others requiring the use of mathematical ratios, coefficients, and tabulations of scores. The study of mental development and education accordingly became *quantitative* as well as descriptive and explanatory.

One of the most significant results of the use of mental tests in the school was the emphasis placed on *individual differences* in the ability of the pupils. This meant, so far as it was translated into classroom practice, that all children were not to be treated in the same manner educationally or taught by the same methods. It was no longer sufficient for good teachers to know how children in general learn, say, arithmetic. They must also be acquainted with any special features of learning brought out by a comparative study of pupils of high and of low ability. Both the means available for studying such a problem and the stress laid upon it have been due in no small measure to the mental testers.

It was early claimed for mental tests that they were capable of measuring *hereditary* differences in mentality. The science of genetics, making great strides in its own right at about the same time, tended to emphasize the contribution of heredity to behavior; to speak of "innate differences" in mental ability became a commonplace in educational psychology. The slogan "democracy in education" took on a new meaning. Instead of being interpreted as equal schooling for all, it was said to mean the opportunity for each child to develop in accordance with his own capacity. A mental test, it appeared, would tell us what this capacity was.

Mental testing served as a foundation for the field of vocational guidance, always by implication at least, within the sphere of education. To be able to measure a child's abilities and aptitudes meant that we should be able to offer him good advice about his future educational and vocational training. This brought psychology face to face with the possibility of prediction in a very definite and practical way. To have formulated laws of learning or of mental development, as many psychologists have in their time attempted to do, has implied prediction of a certain kind, but nothing quite so sweeping as the mental testers thought of doing had ever been attempted before.

During the past thirty years mental testing has become big business. Starting with World War I, during which various group tests were standardized on large numbers of soldiers and economically administered to large groups, large-scale testing has found its way not only into the schools, but into industry and government as well.

Research during World War II again stimulated this trend. Tests are now so widely used in education that the professional teacher must know how to choose tests and how to interpret them.

Modern Learning Theory. Civilized man has always been curious about problems of learning. Questions about how birds learn the songs of their species, how a pigeon finds its way home, why a man forgets some things and remembers others are found in very old literature. One reason for this curiosity is that practically everyone is a teacher of something and before that he was a learner. The "how" of learning is then of immense practical significance. Everyone has a stake in it, but particularly educators because society places primary responsibility for formal learning on their shoulders. The question "How, and under what conditions, does a person learn?" is clearly the central one in educational psychology.

The teacher puts the question in a practical way. How does a child learn to add or multiply, to write or spell? What is the best way to learn to read, to play tennis, to make a dress? From the purely practical side, she would be best satisfied with some answer that described a method of teaching or learning these things. This is pedagogy, rather than psychology. The educational psychologist directs his question rather at the mental process involved in learning, and seeks general principles that explain *why* one method is better than another. We learn through practice, but what kind and how often? We learn through trial and error, but is this the only possible way to learn? We learn through insight, but what conditions make for insightful learning? We learn because we achieve thereby certain goals, but are some incentives more effective than others? He seeks answers to these questions because they are important in school practice.

The laboratory psychologist studies learning problems also, but with a different purpose in mind. Rather than undertaking immediate practical problems, he aims eventually at a unified understanding of all facts, principles, and theories. Although he may seem to be studying rats and nonsense syllables, he is really not interested in rat behavior and probably feels that memorizing nonsense syllables is a waste of time. He plans elaborately contrived experiments designed to test some particular aspect of a learning theory, to reconcile discrepancies, to modify a conclusion. It is the theory, and often some very fine points of it, that captures his interest. Very often his experiments and his findings may seem quite useless to the school man. His theories, however, may have very important implications for the work of the school.

So we have two lines of investigation in the psychology of learning, and two contributing sources: educational psychology from the practical standpoint, and systematic behavior science. The two lines are not always separate; they have almost merged at times and have always been mutually influential.

There are many theories of learning, some more important and influential than others. To show in a rather crude way how they differ, we might ask a question about Pavlov's dog: Just what was it that caused the dog to salivate in response to the bell after the food was removed? There may be several answers, depending on which theory you like:

1. (Principle of contiguity) The stimulus (bell) and response (saliva) had previously occurred at the same time together. This fact alone (i.e., their contiguity) is the sole condition for establishing a connection between stimulus and response.

2. (Principle of reinforcement) The contiguous pairing of the bell with the salivation response is necessary, but does not explain why a connection was established. The real reason is that the dog's response was rewarded (reinforced) by food and his need satisfied. Since bell and food were presented together, he was rewarded by both. When the bell is presented alone, the animal salivates *automatically* in anticipation of reward. It is the reward, the satisfied need, that established the connec-

tion between stimulus and response, not just the fact of their occuring together.

3. (Cognitive-sign principle) The reward or need satisfaction is important, but in itself does not explain. The dog had to perceive some *relation* between the bell and the reward. He salivated to the bell alone because he perceived the bell as a *sign* leading to food. His response was insightful, not merely automatic.

Although the example may seem rather trivial, it illustrates some important differences between theories. The first two are associationistic, connectionist in flavor; they explain learning as a somewhat automatic process, without giving the learner any credit for "ideas" or cognitive processes. They look upon the learner as though he were an automaton, whether animal or human; the organism does not "think" but rather moves in response to stimuli; it learns movements or responses, not ideas. If the organism is said to think at all, it has "thought habits" which are made up of simpler connections. By contrast, the third is Gestalt-like, or field-theoretical. It assumes "idea-like processes" of the organism in the role of perceiver and interpreter, rather than as a mere responder to stimuli or a complex machine made up of simple parts. Learning theories thus fall into two broad families, which can be distinguished on a number of counts as "association" or "stimulus-response" viewpoints on the one hand, and "field theory" on the other (3). The S-R approach centers around a principle or principles which explain how connections are made, how complex habits are built up from simpler habits. The favored illustrations are motor skills or movements. Field theories center around principles which explain how the relationships of a situation are perceived. The organism learns perceptually, and the favored illustrations of field theory are therefore examples of problem solving. We are reminded here of Bertrand Russell's amusing comment about learning experiments:

. . . Animals studied by Americans rush about frantically, with an incredible display of hustle and pep, and at last achieve the desired result by chance. Animals observed by Germans sit still and think, and at last evolve the solution out of their inner consciousness. (6)

Learning Theory and Education. The principle disagreements among learning theories have arisen because of certain preferences and tendencies on the part of system builders. Some have tended to explain *all* forms of learning with principles derived from simpler forms, just as the ancient Greek king Procrustes tried to fit all of his hapless citizens into one "Procrustean bed" by stretching the shorter ones and lopping off the legs of the taller ones. From the pure science point of view, the better theory is the one that is more scientifically fruitful, and this is a matter to be decided by experimental evidence.

The teacher is interested not in improving psychology as a science, but in improving teaching. Educational psychology, then, needs principles which explain practical learning problems as they are encountered by teachers. This should direct our survey of learning theories toward their points of agreement rather than their differences. The teacher might ask "What implications of learning theory, generally agreed upon by psychologists, will help me improve my teaching?" From this point of view, the points of agreement among theories are much more striking than the points of conflict, and much more meaningful to the teacher (5). Some of the implications are as follows:

1. The learner must interpret a complex situation. The teacher must be concerned with organizing the situation to the advantage of the learner, according to certain principles.
2. The learner responds to the situation as he interprets it. The teacher must be concerned with the incidental or seemingly "irrelevant" acts of the learner and attempt to understand them.
3. No learning occurs without motivation. The teacher must adapt materials and approach to the needs and goals of the learner, and must see that these needs are somehow satisfied.
4. For a successful outcome the learner must both discriminate and generalize. The teacher must enable the student to make fine distinctions as well as broad applications of what he learns, and must provide opportunities for doing so.

5. Learning is the meaningful and purposeful reorganization of the learner's previous experience. The teacher must be aware that everything the student learns, in so far as it has meaning for him, modifies or transforms previous learning.

The implications of these principles for the work of the teacher are far-reaching and of immense practical importance. They transcend a pedagogy of "teaching methods." Perhaps the chief contribution of learning theory to modern education is this idea: Concentrate on the learner, rather than the method, the materials, or the desired outcome. Understand him. Motivate him. Reward him. See things from his point of view.

The Mental Health Viewpoint. In recent years society has become increasingly conscious of mental health problems. This is reflected not only in the demand for books and motion pictures on mental health themes, but in the growing membership of national and local organizations that support "education for mental health." Clinics for the treatment of emotional disorders are becoming accepted as a normal service to the community. The emotional complexity of modern life, plus public awareness of the nature of mental illness, tends to focus popular interest not only on psychiatry and allied professions, but on the mental health aspects of education.

Psychiatry is that branch of clinical medicine that treats mental illness. It began to take fairly definite shape in the nineteenth century; in fact, most of the terms for types of mental illness come from the writings of psychiatrists of that time. Early psychologists were less directly concerned with mental illness; they studied rare and abnormal traits, to be sure, but mostly in connection with theories of mind. The first psychological clinics dealt principally with behavior problems of children, particularly those arising from school work. Usually founded under educational auspices, they tended to center around child study, the use of mental tests, and family case work.

Over a period of years psychology has shifted its attention from the "static" aspects of mind to the "dynamic" aspects. Instead of asking "What are the elements of mental processes?"

psychologists now ask "What changes in mental processes affect behavior, and how? What is the origin of emotional and motivational changes?" The development of psychoanalysis, with its exploration of unconscious motives, has contributed greatly to this trend. Much of the research in personality dynamics is being applied in the expanding area of clinical psychology. There is rather general agreement that the focus of preventive measures is on the child, since the foundations of personality are laid in the early years.

The responsibility for mental health rests squarely on the community; and the school, as an agency of the community, bears a large share of it. Today's teacher is expected to do more than teach "subject matter." In so far as possible, the school must see that Johnny masters not only the three R's and a fund of knowledge, but also the adjustments necessary to get along with himself and others in a personally satisfying way. The teacher is in a position to make these adjustments easy or difficult, to estimate how well Johnny is making them, and to obtain professional help for him if he needs it. For these reasons, educational psychology is tending to emphasize more and more the problems of mental health.

Our Heritage from the Social Sciences. The most recent development in the study of human personality has brought together the efforts and techniques of three disciplines (psychology, sociology, anthropology) in what is often called the study of "human relations"—the interrelations of the individual, society, and culture. Psychology is concerned primarily with the individual. Sociology has contributed to our understanding of the child as a member of a primary group such as the family or neighborhood, where close, face-to-face contacts form his attitudes toward himself and others. Sociologists say that the best way to understand a child is to know his neighborhood, and this is true in the sense that its customs and ways of thinking tend to become his. The teacher must therefore know how to study a community in order to understand the children in it.

Cultural anthropology has helped us to understand how cultural patterns influence personality development. We must study the individual, the anthropologists say, "against the background of a specific culture, not culture in general" (4). Studies of primitive and unusual cultures, strikingly different from our own, have made it apparent that things formerly considered "innate" or "basic to human nature" are actually learned products of a culture. If two tribes of the same ethnic group and region differ markedly in their way of life—if one shows hostile and pugnacious traits while the other is gentle and peace-loving —what are the grounds for a "combative instinct"? Yet war has often been ascribed to innate instincts. In another case, a study of Samoan culture corrected our earlier notions that the "stress and strain" of adolescence were due to physiological changes. The story of how a culture is transmitted to the child is a fascinating example of applied learning theory.

Recent Developments in Education. We have pointed out, in the foregoing account of our psychological heritage, instances in which theories and experimental results have influenced the thinking of educators. What has been the net effect of these developments in educational practice? In the *1937 Yearbook* of the National Society for the Study of Education, Gates (2) listed the "chief factors that have contributed to modify general methods" of education. He mentions:

1. New conceptions of the nature of learning.
2. New conceptions of the child as a learner.
3. Clearer recognition of individual differences.
4. New conceptions of the role of the teacher.
5. The role of the social setting.

Of these factors, the first three are clearly the contributions of psychological thinking. Learning was no longer conceived to be a process of acquiring subject-matter knowledge by means of repetitive drill and recitations, but a process of organizing one's total experience in accordance with one's needs. The needs and motives of the child became of paramount importance, and it was recognized that children differed so much in capacities, needs, motives, and "readinesses" that the older methods of cramming knowledge into unwilling heads under competitive pressure simply would not work for many children and would be destructive for some. The role of the teacher therefore changed from that of a drillmaster to that of a leader, counselor, and guide. The fifth factor listed—the role of the social setting—is largely the contribution of social science.

The problems of education are defined in the *1950 Yearbook* of the National Society for the Study of Education. It is the task of the school, according to this definition, to

1. Assay society's needs and to define the kinds of behavior which children and youth must exemplify for effective living in the American democracy.
2. Select the curriculum content and the activities which will, as they are experienced by pupils, assure the attainment of the requisite standards of behavior.
3. Skillfully organize instructional and activity programs and cause children to so interact with them that the new behavior patterns will emerge.
4. The school must evaluate this behavior with respect to the school's original objectives and re-pattern its procedures if the behavior is found wanting. (1, p. 2)

Educational psychology is expected to provide some of the principles which govern the school in its attainment of these objectives.

Many of the recent trends in psychology and in education have cooperated to produce what may be rather loosely called an "organismic" viewpoint. This is a dynamic psychology in its emphasis on inner moving forces in human behavior. It frequently refers to "wholes" and "organizations" and "dynamic relations." It is a developmental psychology in the sense that it favors explanations of mental events in terms of how they came to be rather than as to how they are constituted. It is because the organismic viewpoint offers the most promise of being able to coordinate the various scientific facts and concepts of educational psychology that we shall try to take full advantage of what it has to say concerning the important problems of mental development and education.

REFERENCES

1. ANDERSON, G. L.   Learning and instruction.   *49th Yearbook,* I, Nat. Soc. Stud. Educ., 1950.
2. GATES, A. I.   Ch. in *37th Yearbook,* II, Nat. Soc. Stud. Educ., 1938.
3. HILGARD, E. R.   *Theories of learning.*   New York: Appleton-Century-Crofts, 1948.
4. LINTON, R.   *The cultural background of personality.*   New York: Appleton-Century-Crofts, 1945.
5. MCCONNELL, T. R.   Reconciliation of learning theories.   *41st Yearbook,* Nat. Soc. Stud. Educ., 1942.
6. RUSSELL, B.   *Philosophy.*   New York: Norton, 1927.
7. WARREN, H. C.   *Dictionary of psychology.*   Boston: Houghton Mifflin, 1934.
8. WOODWORTH, R. S.   *Contemporary schools of psychology.*   (Rev. ed.)   New York: Ronald Press, 1948.

SELECTED READINGS

ANDERSON, G. L.   What the psychology of learning has to contribute to the education of the teacher.   *J. educ. Psychol.,* 1950, **41,** 362-365.

BOYD, W.   *From Locke to Montessori.*   London: Harrap, 1920.   A history of ideas about development and education.

BRUBACHER, J. S.   *A history of the problems of education.*   New York: McGraw-Hill, 1947.

GARRETT, H. E.   *Great experiments in psychology.*   (Rev. ed.)   New York: Appleton-Century-Crofts, 1951.   Gives an account of the original experiments in mental testing, individual differences, animal learning, memory and transfer of learning which contributed to the development of educational psychology.

HARTMANN, G. W.   *Gestalt psychology.*   New York: Ronald Press, 1935.   Ch. 16 discusses the application of Gestalt psychology to educational problems.

HILGARD, E. R.   *Theories of learning.*   New York: Appleton-Century-Crofts, 1948.   Ch. 1, "The nature of learning theories."

JAMES, WM.   *Talks to teachers on psychology.*   New York: Holt, 1946.   A classic which is still refreshingly modern.

MURPHY, G.   *An historical introduction to modern psychology.*   (Rev. ed.)   New York: Harcourt Brace, 1949.   For general reference.

NATIONAL SOCIETY FOR THE STUDY OF EDUCATION.   *49th Yearbook, 1950,* Part I, Section I, Basic factors underlying learning.

WOODWORTH, R. S.   *Contemporary schools of psychology.*   (Rev. ed.)   New York: Ronald Press, 1948.

2

SOME PRINCIPLES OF MENTAL DEVELOPMENT

THE educator is interested in guiding and directing the mental, personal, and moral development of the child. Psychology assists in the understanding of this course of development. Psychology does this by describing the changes in terms internal to the individual, by offering generalizations about the nature of these gradual changes, and by suggesting the psychological reasons why some educational practices may be more effective than others. The educator's perspective with respect to the whole course of change will not only suggest certain guiding principles covering the whole age-range but will frequently be reflected as well in what he attempts or wishes to do at any one stage or episode of this story of development. Even such a seemingly discrete educational activity as, say, learning the multiplication table is not without its forward and backward overtones. From a psychological point of view we could scarcely ask a child to engage in such an activity without, at the same time, keeping in mind that we are dealing with a continually maturing individual whose course of development will give personal meaning to such an activity, will affect its educational efficiency, and will provide consequences for the future course of development. By trying to coordinate both psychological fact and theory we shall first aim at gaining an over-all view of the nature of development before getting down to particulars.

The Goal-Directedness of Mental Life

Needs and Motives Basic to Activity.   Living beings characteristically show in their life processes a directiveness or trend toward a goal or end of their activity.   They always seem to be seeking or working toward some more or less final state which is the natural issue of their behavior.   The embryo, in a way, anticipates its future and responds to the conditions surrounding it in the light of these anticipations.   A similar thing seems to be as true of mental reactions as of other forms of vital activity.   It would be very difficult to understand why a living being should react to anything, out of the infinite number of objects making up the external world, unless that thing stood in some intimate relation with, or had an important meaning for, its trend of activity and the goals toward which its activity is directed.   The object may stand as an obstacle to, or as an appropriate means of facilitating, the attainment of the goal, but some such relation it must have, whether we are dealing with the dog scenting its prey, the hungry baby moving its head toward the touch of the nipple, or an Edison concerned with the physical qualities of tungsten.   Action, or activity, is prior to reaction.   The reaction is primarily an indication that the directed vital activity is being, as it were, precipitated, reformed, and reshaped by the external situation calling forth the response.

As Woodworth says:

Ordinarily a stimulus breaks in upon some activity in progress, some "incomplete reaction." . . . This activity has a trend towards some goal, immediate or remote. We have, then, not first stimulus, then activity of of the organism; but first an activity going on, next an intercurrent stimulus, and then the activity modified in response to the stimulus. (29)

Even the power of the stimulus to break in upon the activity in progress will depend upon the nature of the activity. [Earlier psychological writings have often appeared to place the greater emphasis upon the external stimulus or situation and to imply that our experience and behavior, and the changes wrought within them, are chiefly the result of the outside forces to which we have been exposed. But "the organism is not an idle machine which can be set into operation by pulling a lever; . . . it always tends some whither and always performs as it is functionally inclined" (29).

Motives and Development. The dynamic psychological sources of our goal-directed activities are commonly called needs or motives. These play such an important role in mental development because each step of the process is a kind of venture or practical "transaction" between the child with his very general behavior tendencies, on the one hand, and on the other, a relatively unknown and, at times, seemingly uncooperative physical and social environment. To profit from this transaction, or to adjust to the demands of the situation, he must become "personally involved," and it is his needs or motives that insure this. They do this through one or all of the following characteristics:

1. Motives initiate and supply the energy for activity.
2. Motives give general direction to the activity.
3. Motives sensitize the individual to the existence of relevant objectives and properties.
4. Motives sustain the activity against temporary rebuffs or diversionary influences.
5. Motives, in their successful issue, supply the personal and affective satisfactions that become the basis of new motives, dynamic tendencies, attitudes, and "expectancies."

The personal activity so indispensable for mental development grows out of the attempt to satisfy needs and motives which vary in nature and strength according to the stage of development attained. Some of these, such as hunger, or love, are so general or "primary" in nature that they may commonly be taken for granted. There are others, however, more specific, "secondary," or "derived," which cannot be as easily assumed to be present because they are likely to have a particular developmental story behind them and are distinctly the product of the child's interaction with his particular physical and social environment. It is this latter class of needs in which the educator is often most directly interested because it is to our particular social heritage and values that the growing child is to be attuned. It is often the case that the child must first be made to want the things upon which we as adults place such high value before the mental development leading to their attainment is undertaken. Much of our attempted education of the child may not be very effective unless we first succeed in bringing home to him the fact that he has need of it. Otherwise it may have no vital meaning for him, he may see no relation between it and the more general or ordinary goals of his activity. Simply being exposed to a thing will not bring about learning.

The Conditions of Learning. Learning does not occur by chance, nor does it come about through repetition. Contrary to the old adage, practice does not necessarily make perfect. Learning occurs only under certain conditions, of which "practice" is perhaps one. If such conditions could not be specified, learning would not be an orderly, understandable process, but a chance phenomenon that just "happens because it happens." We could then make no predictions about the outcome of the learner's activity or exercise any control over the learning process. The classroom teacher with no notion of the conditions of learning would be in no position to choose one method rather than another or to guide the learner's efforts.

We must distinguish at the outset between two uses of the term "learning," one which refers to the *products* of learning, and another which refers to learning as a *process*. In everyday usage the term more commonly refers to the products—the "what" of learning rather than the "how"—as in the expressions "a man of learning," "the pursuit of learning," or "a little learning is a dangerous thing." In this sense we sometimes tend to think of learning as "acquisitions" of something. This may cause us to jump immediately to the conclusion that learning is a process of "acquiring" facts or skills, and that the mind is either a kind of storehouse or an entity to which our sense impressions "adhere." The mind is neither a hopper nor a camera. These notions are inadequate for understanding the process of learning and mental development. In psychology the term "learning" refers to a sequence of mental processes which leads to changes in the learner. These changes, or modifications, consist not merely of acquiring so many facts or increasing the number of things the learner can do, but in the alterations of his motives, needs, goals, tendencies. In short, learning alters his "readiness" to think, to behave, or to feel in certain ways. Any "experience," or sequence of mental events that results in changes of this kind is called learning. In this sense, the learning process is a *modification of functional tendencies*.

A rather crude summary of the conditions of learning is given in the following statement by Miller and Dollard: "The learner must want something, notice something, do something, and get something" (27). In other words, he must have a motive which prompts a certain kind of activity. Activity (noticing and doing things) is not in itself a sufficient condition for learning; the learner must "get something." That is, the activity must lead to certain consequences which satisfy his motive. As a simple illustration, a person learns to use an umbrella when it rains when (1) he feels a need to stay dry, (2) he notices other persons using umbrellas, and also notices certain cues which he interprets as signs of approaching rain, (3) he makes a provisional trial of the umbrella during the downpour, and (4) discovers that it works to satisfy his need. He is now predisposed or "ready" to get out the umbrella whenever signs of rain appear. The effect of "practice" or repetition is this: After the sequence has occurred a number of times with satisfactory consequences, the interpretation and response may become habitual. The individual may reach for the umbrella without conscious awareness of the conditions. This is "overlearning."

There are four sets of learning conditions:

1. *Needs and readiness* of the learner. Is he ready to learn? These are motivational conditions which determine how the learner will interpret the situation, whether he will respond, and what kind of response he will make. A child who feels no need to stay dry will not notice the appropriate cues.

2. *The learning situation* provides things, persons, and events to which the learner attends and responds. In some sit-

uations these cues are distinctive and easily noticed; in others the cues are indistinct, hidden, or "embedded," and force the individual to look for them.   Unless the appropriate cues are discernible, the learner will not notice or do the right things leading to his goal.

— 3. *The interpretation and responses* of the learner are essential conditions, because no learning occurs without activity. When the learner notices cues, he interprets them according to his needs and goals.   What he does in a given situation depends on how he interprets it.   He selects or rejects certain responses because he expects that they will, or will not, lead to his goal.

4. *The consequences* of the learner's activity may be success or failure, reward or punishment, approval or disapproval. "Consequences" refer not only to external events, but to the learner's interpretation of these events.   He interprets the outcome of his actions as successful or unsuccessful, depending on whether they satisfy his needs, confirm his expectations, or result in the attainment of his goal.   "Failure" to one person may be "success" to another.   When the consequences are satisfying, the learner will reproduce the same behavior in future similar situations because he has learned, i.e., he expects the same consequences to follow from that behavior.   His original tendencies have been modified: there is now a more specific goal, increased expectations, and more accurate knowledge of "what leads to what."

Role of Motives in Learning.   From the viewpoint of the child and his background of motives, each learning situation is a *problem,* a situation in which the child's goal cannot be attained by what he already knows or can do, and which requires him to do something new.   The child interprets the outcome with reference to his own needs and goals.   The consequences of any experience are thus always personal, and will affect his subsequent behavior in various ways.   There are several possibilities:

1. If the outcome is favorable, the learner will tend, when confronted with the same or similar situations in the future, to be attentive to the same cues, to interpret the situations in the

same way, to duplicate the original behavior, because he expects this to lead to the same consequences. A certain "readiness" to action is established by the specific experience. The child acquires a degree of confidence in himself, a degree of certainty about the outcome of such situations. His "know how," in other words, includes an ability to predict the outcome of what he has done, thought, or said in that situation. When the situation is repeated, it is less of a "problem" because the child is ready to respond in a certain way. There is no reason for him to alter his behavior as long as it works to his satisfaction. The child tends to repeat the kind of behavior which he finds rewarding.

2. If the outcome is unfavorable, if it results in dissatisfaction, or does not confirm expectations, the behavior will not tend to be repeated very long if the dissatisfaction is very great. The learner is forced to pause and to seek new cues and newly recognized properties of objects and to make other "provisional tries" to meet the situation in the light of its newly emerging properties. His perception of these may not at first be very clear, his behavior may appear fumbling and at times almost aimless, but a closer view will usually show that he is trying alternative solutions. When he finally adopts a mode of behavior which results in satisfaction, this behavior will tend to become the basis of a new form of readiness, a new skill perhaps, and new clearer perceptions of things in themselves and in their relation with others. This kind of perceptual and behavioral transformation is often called "reorganization."

3. If all provisional tries result in continued dissatisfaction or failure, the learner may give up and withdraw from the situation. This is likely to happen if the essential cues or properties of the situation are well concealed from him or if he is not able, by his internally aroused mental activity, to cause these to emerge into a position of conscious "salience" from their more or less hidden "embedded" condition. If his personal expectations of success were high, he might show considerable emotional disturbance because failure is likely to be frustrating. There are various possible outcomes of the frustration. The

learner may "adjust" through different forms of self-defense by blaming others, or circumstances, in order to reduce the feeling of defeat. It may also be expected that he will tend to avoid similar situations in the future. This may entail a shift of motivation by dropping the goal appropriate to the situation, by substituting another but less appropriate goal, or by lowering his expectations of himself. He thus may get rid of the problem by getting rid of the motive. New attitudes may of course be acquired in this manner, such as dislike of certain situations and disinterest in certain activities. New self-evaluative attitudes may also ensue. The prospective learner may come to think of himself as "poor" in this or that field, which will probably mean that his interests, his intention to learn, and his "ability" to concentrate will be impaired. Thus a difficulty which may be primarily a matter of motivation in origin may become in later life interwoven in the growth of ability.

4. The outcome may lead to "stereotyped," or repeated inappropriate behavior which seems to be continued without rhyme or reason. This behavior is sometimes called nonadaptive or nonadjustive because it does not seem to attain any worthwhile goals or satisfying consequences. The learner apparently does not learn; he keeps on doing the same things and repeating the same errors without reinterpreting or trying anything new. It is a kind of failure or refusal to adjust without withdrawing from the learning situation. There is some evidence that this may occur under certain conditions:

a) An impossible or too difficult problem, accompanied by very strong motivation. It would perhaps appear more reasonable for the learner to give up, but if strong motivation continues, the nonadaptive behavior is also likely to continue. In some cases the behavior itself supplies its own motive power and becomes an end in itself.

b) "Overlearning" to the point of mechanization. This may be accompanied by a loss in the flexibility of one's goals, by a kind of hardening of "mental sets," by the retention of less mature behavior appropriate enough at the time but now no longer strictly suitable, or by inability or readiness to search for new cues or properties in a new, similar, but somewhat different situation.

c) Strong punishment during critical periods of the learning. If a hungry animal is shocked electrically at a "choice point" in a maze, his behavior may become "fixated." He will then always follow a previously learned route, which in earlier trials led to food, even though this route now no longer leads to food. It seems that strong punishment, or perhaps any strong irrelevant emotion, may interfere with an effective "cognitive reorganization" of the situation.

THE GENETIC CONTINUITY OF MENTAL DEVELOPMENT

The analogy for the concept of "genetic continuity" is taken from the field of embryology. The study of the developing embryo shows a sequence of changes that is not just a temporal one, a matter of before and after, but better described as a true generation of the later from the earlier. New structures with special properties and functions are seen to emerge from the old against the background of structure and properties of the old. Thus the stomach and the liver arise from developmental refinements of a relatively simple or primitive type of alimentary tube which, if development had stopped at an earlier stage, might be thought of as possessing a certain adequacy for the work of digestion. But of course the development of these primitive powers into special functions and special organs will make the digestive process much more efficient. The liver or stomach does not come into being through the simple growth or expansion of a mysterious liver or stomach "substance" contained in the original egg cell. The organs appear on the scene, as it were, when the stage of the organism is set for them, in response to environmental stimulating forces both within and without the organism. This stage sets limits for what can appear upon it and is far from being the plaything of the environmental forces.

In a similar way, every stage of mental development comes as an outgrowth of what has gone before. Each activity receives its vital meaning and functional utility from the fact that it emerges from a certain kind of mental or behavioral background. Nothing wholly new can be introduced from the outside into the individual. A particular mental reaction is possible only so far as the individual is prepared for it through the previous course of his development.

The continuity of present with past is not simply an identity of the two. We do not, say, merely go on thinking the same old thoughts over and over again. Each step in advance may be truly creative, but it is so within certain limits set by our earlier experiences. Our present principle offers the basis for understanding both the inventiveness of thought and action, whereby education becomes truly an achievement for the child, and the regularity and order in which this is likely to occur. It is often the natural and fundamental continuity of development that needs most to be emphasized in a practical way because it is likely to be slighted in a common-sense approach to the development of the child. It is opposed to the viewpoint called "preformism," which suggests that mental development is chiefly a matter of the unfolding of certain definite mental powers that existed from the beginning, to be merely strengthened or exercised through educational practices or use. It is likewise opposed to the view that the child has from the beginning only so many mental or behavioral units to work with, that their nature is originally and definitely set, and that education merely confirms or eliminates some of them, or introduces new objects to evoke them, or arranges or rearranges different additive combinations of them.

Readiness and Education. Because the child always brings with him, to every learning situation, certain "functional inclinations" and tendencies, even though of an ill-defined sort, it will be these tendencies and inclinations that determine his first reactions and lay the basis for the "readiness" with which the more refined and appropriate behavior is elicited. Each step in advance made by the child is brought about by his attempt to re-form or work over, to define or redefine his earlier experience and behavior so that they may become more adequate to the new situation. The cue for the child to undertake this genetic change lies in the felt inadequacy of the old experience or behavior, although he may not at first have any very clear idea of what in a detailed way is called for. This realization itself comes through reorganizing and redefining.

The development of skills and of knowledge comprises a sequence of events in which experience and behavior pass through many gradual, progressive, qualitative alterations. Consider, for example, a simple skill like using a spoon in eating. From the developmental point of view, the child's first use of a spoon and the adult's use of it can scarcely be described in the same psychological terms. For the adult, the perceived spoon is the stimulus and his manner of handling it the response. It is possible to describe the adult's mature behavior as the combination of these two, stimulus and response. But to suppose that the adult's mature behavior came into being simply by putting these two together is another matter altogether. The child at least does not seem to learn this behavior merely by putting the two together.

The original stimulus may be very different for the child from what it is for the adult, as is also the child's original response. The spoon may of course be perceived by the child as something used to bring food to his mouth, but it is probably a very vague something, without recognition of its concave nature or the fact that it must be held horizontal to keep the contents in it. Against this vague perceptive background, he usually grasps it in his whole, massive manner, with his fist closed, dips it into the food, getting some to stay on by chance, and, working mostly with his shoulder muscles, brings the spoon toward his mouth and his mouth toward it, with the result that most of the contents is spilled on the floor or up his sleeve. But this untoward result and other similar experiences bring home to the child the fact that what he is doing is inadequate, and that the spoon has certain properties, of which he is becoming aware for the first time, that must be respected. This developing insight into the nature of the spoon is expressed at the same time in his attempts to modify his muscular movements accordingly. He generates wrist and forearm action of a more delicate kind in order to keep the spoon always straight up. It is in such a manner as this that the spoon, as the adult knows it, becomes the stimulus of mature behavior with meaningful properties, and it is also in this manner that the mature response comes into being. They are both evolved from the child's original vague perceptions and behavior, at first crude and undiscriminating but transforming themselves with time into the refined and straightforward action of the mature stage. It should be apparent that unless this vague perception and behavior tendency existed at the time the child undertakes to "learn" how to handle the spoon, the desired skill could not be induced from the outside or produced by the mere mechanical repetition of a set of imposed movements. He would not be "ready" for the kind of transformation or evolution that is the essence of the development.

Sources of Readiness. What we think of as ability and its maturing, as distinct from, say motivation, is of course one of the sources of readiness. But readiness is not to be understood as a mere synonym for ability as this is empirically studied and tested in a more formal and rigid manner. We need to keep in mind, particularly in the case of young children, the possible interplay of other more dynamic factors that make the child willing and likely to undertake what is asked of him. These are perhaps more easily brought to light in the study of the child's spontaneous, rather than his "test" behavior. Thus a study of quantitative expression in children (23) shows very little relationship between what they *spontaneously* do when faced with an opportunity for the use of number and their level of ability as measured by a traditional form of the number ability test. "That which determines a child's behavior in a quantitative situation which is unstructured in the sense that no particular kind of behavior is defined as acceptable or nonacceptable by the experimenter is not only his knowledge and ability in this specific area, but also his motivation toward and his sensitivity to quantitative characteristics in that situation."

It is often difficult to break down psychologically the mentality and behavior of the younger child into such clear-cut compartments or elements as we find so scientifically useful in the study of the adult. The study of "developmental trends" with respect to school subjects and activities (18, 19, 20), including the whole repertoire of child behavior, should be very helpful here particularly before we enter upon the more analytic study of definite psychological processes and functions. Any convenient way of expressing the "maturity" of the child would also be helpful. But for a more effective understanding of genetic continuity we should not be satisfied by specifying the child's maturity in such merely quantitative terms as mental, chronological, psychological, emotional, or social age. We should try to go on to an actual qualitative description of the particular behaviors and behavior tendencies that are the immediate precursors of the new activity.

School and Reading Readiness. A promising beginning to the study of reading readiness (16) shows the importance of a many-sided approach to the problem. Among the factors that have been found to be relevant are: (1) sensory acuities; (2) development of form perception; (3) a conceptual development that would set language apart from other forms of behavior; (4) the ability to attach personal meaning to arbitrary symbols; (5) the desire to learn to read and to regard it as an achievement; (6) a simple kind of emotional stability that would allow some "concentration"; (7) a sufficient social development that would give some meaning to communication with others; and (8) a mental age sufficient at least for apprehending simple relationships.

There are probably other specific forms of readiness involved in reading as well as those that might be thought to be involved in general "school-readiness." These include: a "task attitude," a willingness or ability to set a goal for one's activity and to follow through, something that the less mature child does not have; a receptiveness to a task set by others; a certain amount of self-criticism that implies the existence of standards outside the self; the ability to compare oneself with others; the ability to distinguish the real world from a merely imaginary or desired one; a certain play cooperativeness that at least considers the presence and possible reactions of others; a certain ability to "take it" and not withdraw into himself or to the complete protection of the home if things do not turn out just right. Many of these characteristics often seem so simple to the adult that he does not realize that the child is not born with them, that he has to learn them, and that much later development is dependent upon them. Each school activity and subject has its own factors or readiness, but what they are with respect, say, to high school algebra or biology is largely a problem for future psychological study.

Learning a Continuous Process. Another way in which the continuity of development appears is in the progressive nature of learning. Nobody probably ever learned, for once and all, the meaning of a word; with more reading and experience and use of the word its meaning grows. Even a "fact," like "Columbus discovered America in 1492," changes its meaning with time so that some aspects are broadened and extended in their implications while others are reduced and perhaps forgotten. Paradoxically enough, forgetting can be part of the learning process. This can be supplemented by unconscious, internally induced changes, often vaguely referred to as maturation, so that James could say that we learn to skate in summer and to swim in winter.

Even important personal acts of choice have a long history behind them. An example of this is to be found in a study of the factors that accumulate over time to affect one's choice of occupation (10). Occupational choice seems basically to be a developmental process; it is not an isolated event or a single decision. Each succeeding step seems to be based upon a preceding one, with the process largely reversible. The process ends in a kind of compromise or final synthesis of determinants, interests, capacities, opportunities, and values.

THE NATURE OF DEVELOPMENTAL CHANGES

Both quantitative and qualitative changes appear as we follow any being from birth to maturity. The first may be referred to as "growth" and the second as "development," but whatever our terms, these two aspects of change may be distinguished scientifically.   Children may be said to grow when they show a quantitative increase in height and weight.   They may be said to develop as their bodily proportions and the balance of physiological functions change, leaving behind the qualitative characteristics of the child and taking on those of the adult.   A dwarf may be a fully developed man but not a fully grown one. A tadpole fed on thyroid extract may develop but not grow, and if fed on thymus gland it may grow to considerable size but transform only very slowly into a frog.

Many of the changes occurring in the mind and behavior of the child have a quantitative aspect and may be studied by quantitative means, particularly if we are interested in the efficiency of the child's "performance," such as his speed of computation, the number of facts or words he knows, or the difficulty of the task as determined by a comparison with the work of other children.   Many psychological studies have been concerned with such facts and we shall consider many of them later. But just now we are more interested in the qualitative changes and those seen from within the child, which are often the real reason for the more objectively shown improvement of performance.

Differentiation.   The embryologist employs the term "differentiation" when he speaks of the development of new organs of special structure and function from a more immature, primitive, ill-defined structure that, however, contains within it the potentialities of their generation.   At the psychological level we may think of differentiation as occurring when the more all-inclusive, the more general, the more massive behavior of the child is gradually replaced by the more specialized, the more discriminate, and the more refined activities of a later stage.   It is a progression from the general to the particular, from mass activity to specific response.

Differentiation of Skills.   The development of handwriting shows the kind of change we have in mind.   The primary school child commonly attacks the task of writing by bringing his whole body into play.   From this massive, diffuse approach he eventually evolves the refined movements of forearm, wrist, and fingers. A close study of the grasping responses of infants (12) shows a similar sequence. The earliest approach movements toward an object, consisting largely of crude shoulder and elbow movements, are correct, as it were, in principle, but crude in function. A kind of "palming" action appears, with the thumb and fingers relatively inactive in their own right. With time, this clawing kind of hand closure is developed into a more refined forefinger-tip grasping, and this in turn gives way to a precise thumb-forefinger opposition. The later stages differentiate from the earlier ones.

Language skills have a similar pattern of development. The child first speaks in terms of what appears perhaps to us adults as single words but which are really word-sentences, expressing in a jumbled manner information, command, emotional overtones, and object-object relationships. It is only as this crude comprehensiveness of the first attempt at speech isolates, as it were, and accentuates its implied features that he will come eventually to know and use nouns and action-words, assertive and imperative tones, interjections and adjectives, prepositions and conjunctions. It is probably similar with all skills. We must first do a thing crudely before we can do it well.

Differentiation in Perception and Knowledge. From a globular perception of the human face, the infant comes later to distinguish eyes, nose, and mouth, which are seen as particular features only after seeing the face as a whole. The child's perception of space (26) shows at first only a very vague "practical-space" quality; objects are reacted to only in relation to himself and his activity, and he neglects their relations to other objects. There follows a "subjective-space" stage in which the child begins to apprehend objects in themselves, but still largely from the viewpoint of the possibility of his acting upon them. In the later apprehension of "objective-space," the child sees himself no longer as the center of his world but only part of it, and he sees the relation of one object to another. The perception of "past" and "future" time are analogously differentiated from a vague, ill-defined "present."

The child's ability to discriminate and compare the qualities and properties of common objects is also a matter of differentiation. The example which the teacher can effectively employ with the young child in illustrating a point of difference or likeness must commonly at first be one that shows the point in a very exaggerated manner. And it is only after the first appreciation of crude differences that the more refined and subtle distinctions become possible. An analogous principle seems to work for animals in the field of sensory discrimination. If we wish to study the ability of, say, monkeys or dogs, to discriminate the pitch of musical tones, we must commonly begin with a comparison of two tones, one very high in pitch, the other very low. Only after such a discrimination is established can finer differences in pitch be effectively studied. Animal learning has been found to be more efficient when the animals are first trained on easy discriminations and when they approach the refined "test discrimination" through a series of graduated differences (22).

The child's advance in knowledge of the world, in ideas and information is not just because the objects are "there," making an "impression" on his sensory capacities, and requiring only that he become increasingly attentive to them, or that he seek out objects to fill in the recognized gaps in his own experience or awareness. It is a matter of successive acts of perception and apprehension, each complete enough for its level of maturity and generating new acts with new properties. From the first vague wholes of experience we discriminate by successive stages the things that later on come to be known as objects, qualities, and elements. The mental "elements" of adult life are the products of development and not its starting point. Most of these do not exist for the child until they come into existence for him through differentiation or emerge from the total situations of which in the beginning they were unimportant or submerged features. How far this process is carried probably varies from person to person. As James says:

We all cease analysing the world at some point, and notice no more differences. The last units with which we stop are our objective elements of being. Those of a dog are different from those of a Humboldt; those of a practical man from those of a metaphysician. But the dog's and the practical man's thoughts feel continuous, though to the Humboldt or the metaphysician they would appear full of gaps and defects. And they are continuous, as thoughts. It is only as mirrors of things that the superior minds find them full of omissions. And when the omitted things are discovered and the unnoticed differences laid bare, it is not that the old thoughts split up, but that new thoughts supersede them, which make new judgments about the same objective world. (21)

Differentiation of Emotions and Motives. Studies of emotions in infancy show their original undifferentiated character (6). A reasonable conclusion from these investigations is that all emotional responses are derived from an original, vague, general excitement. Distress and simple delight soon appear as specific forms of this excitement, depending upon the general unfavorableness or favorableness of the situation, activity, or consequences. Delight further differentiates into elation and affection, depending upon whether merely impersonal objects or other persons are involved. This process can continue more or less indefinitely, producing ever new and varied emotional experience, and ends in the refined sentiments and affective tones of adult life. The level of differentiation attained by the child at any age will determine the richness and subtlety of his emotional repertoire.

Motives likewise attain variety and maturity, partly at least, through differentiation and through changes that are closely similar. It is only in the early life of the child that we need to appeal to the relatively cruder "drives" like pleasure, pain, hunger, and so on. An activity which is at first only a part or feature of a larger cycle of behavior, in the service perhaps of one of the earlier drives, a means-to-an-end, may become a drive or end in itself, and attain a kind of independence independent of its origin, a "functional autonomy" (1). Motives can become "canalized," fixated, as it were, through first experiences, upon an object which thereafter will become an integral part of the definition of our desire and make it prepotent over the possible desires for other things that might readily have been the equivalent in satisfying the general need. Motives become "externalized" (3) by the tendency of objects or situations to take on the power to evoke behavior, freeing the individual from the original dependence upon internal affective or drive states, necessary though these may have been for the personal meaning of these objects in the beginning. The affective consequences of an act help us in the future to perceive a situation in a different light and may give it different incentive value.

Differentiation of Abilities. The original behavior of the child is so global, and of such an indefinite, generalized nature that it is impossible to isolate and identify in a satisfactory way such discrete functions as cognition, emotion, or volition. Although the germs of these are present in aspects of the original behavior, they must go through a process of emergence and accentuation before we can consistently employ such terms in describing any momentary activity of the child. In the psychological meaning of the term there are very few, or no, "innate" abilities. An ability, in the empirical sense, is a limiting readiness to perform a certain kind of task, to run, to read, to solve number problems, to discriminate musical tones. The readiness of the infant to perform any task of interest to the educator is very limited indeed. It is rather meaningless, then, psychologically, to say that education "trains" or "exercises" the original abilities of the child. It is rather that education, formal and informal, and working by way of maturation, creates abilities, or the more specialized forms of readiness. These will appear as development and differentiation proceed; they are not present in the beginning.

The empirical study of ability throughout various age levels has led a number of psychologists (2) to believe that the facts can be best understood in terms of differentiation. Preschool-age children manifest their ability in the form of a rather broad general ability, with very few forms of specialized efficiency that cover any moderately broad area of activity. At school age special abilities begin to appear more clearly, such as memory, verbal, numerical, and spatial abilities, each covering a number of similar tasks or performances with a fairly high degree of consistency. Still older children show more of this differentiation or transformation of the earlier general ability into more and more specific units of mental function.

It would be reasonable to suppose that any direction of development entered upon as the result of differentiation would show the influence of the child's physical, educational, and cultural environment. How far his formal education progresses, with its attendant uniformity and standardization of activities; whether he is a boy or girl, and so developing under different kinds of social customs and pressures; the occupation of the parents in so far as this might reflect differences in opportunity and need; cultural differences that exist between, and probably also within, nations—all these seem to have a bearing on the nature and number of abilities and aptitudes that determine the efficiency, relatedness, and predictiveness of a person's performances. One's "inherited nature," whether we speak of the part held in common with other human beings or of the part peculiar to each person, is not alone sufficient. When the forces that operate to produce differentiation in the mental development of an individual are different from what we ordinarily find, then the expected ability may not appear. Thus, if we find the savage unable to carry on abstract thinking, this does not of itself mean that we are dealing with a difference in "nature," for the ability to think abstractly is not present in either primitive or civilized man by original nature alone.

It may be permissible at times to speak of innate abilities in a figurative manner if we have in mind the possibility of the existence of some constitutional or hereditary factors that may determine the emergence or rate of growth of ability. This is a reasonable possibility and can be put to an empirical test. But constitutional or hereditary determiners of later appearing abilities are not abilities as the psychologist describes and measures them. They may be present in chromosomes, in bodily status, or in "potencies," but existing in this form they are not psychological facts at all but rather biological or metaphysical ones. Abilities and behavioral traits are always *learned*.

Integration

Integration is the process of forming new, larger, and more comprehensive wholes or units of behavior. An analogy for this taken from the field of embryology is the formation of the upper lip from the fusion of two tissue buds from the cheeks, with one coming down from the nose (the failure of fusion resulting in a hare-lip), or the formation of the adrenal gland from a migrating bud of nerve tissue and another wandering bud of primitive gonadal tissue, each fusion resulting in a new unitary functioning organ. The dynamic features of integration are best seen in the formation of our physiological "system," such as the circulatory system, or the endocrine gland system. Here we can see the subordination of each part to the work of the whole, the likelihood that deficiency in any one organ will disturb the whole equilibrium and change the activities of each of the other component organs, the relative position of dominance and subordination of different parts of the system. The whole responses which result from the integration of behavior are similarly preceded or accompanied by the differentiation of unit objects and responses, these are apprehended or combined in embracing schemes and patterns or relationships, and the properties of each unit or part activity are affected by their position in the whole.

Integration is found characteristically to occur in a number of phases of the development of skills, perception, and understanding. The beginning typist must begin with individual movements of each finger in response to single letters, but she soon learns to type by words and phrases without giving attention to the single letters or single finger movements. Those who, in the old days, began their reading in school by the alphabet method progressed to the stage where they read by words, phrases, and sentences. It was in fact due to the recognition in psychology that these were really higher perceptual units that it was thought worth while to change the method of teaching reading by introducing the child to these higher units from the start.

Integration and Association. The term "integration," has largely replaced the older term, "association," in describing learning and mental development because it is more likely to suggest certain features of change and growth which may be otherwise easily neglected. To say that the child forms mental associations or stimulus-response connections may frequently imply that development results chiefly from adding together, as it were, things that already pre-exist, and that they enter this chain-like combination without any change of properties either of the parts or the whole. Integration is a kind of synthesis, but it is more like a "creative synthesis," such as occurs in chemistry when the two poisonous elements, sodium and chlorine, combine to produce common table salt. The integration of behavior shows the following properties:

1. It is characterized by the emergence of something new and different, a new melody, as it were, showing a creativeness that gives rise to the thrill often associated with invention and discovery. Properly paced education and training has this characteristic.

2. Integration takes place with reference to some goal of action. How things will be organized or integrated will depend very much upon the purposes of the learner. In this sense knowing *how* to do something involves knowing *why* to some degree.

3. The "form" or "structure" of any organized activity is of distinct psychological importance. Practice, drill, or repeated exposure to a situation can often be without effect until the child gets the "feel" or rhythm of the act as a whole.

4. A new integration or organization is accompanied by the perception of new properties or relationships of the things so organized. Objects acquire many of their most important properties for the child by the part they play in his organized cycles of behavior. They often resist the showing of other properties until they can be disengaged from one structure or setup and "re-organized" into a new behavioral activity.

5. There are certain natural forms or principles of combination that are more efficient than others. It is not probable that anything can be "associated" with anything. There are at least

more and less efficient forms of organization which seem to vary with the maturity of the child.

6. Insight, or the Aha!-experience as it has been called, is the personal, concrete evidence that integration is taking place. Anything that we can do to further insight in the learning child will be very effective. It is particularly at the higher thought levels that the important phases of integration can be clearly seen. The decisive steps in the development of Einstein's theory of relativity, as he narrated them to Wertheimer (28), are excellent examples of progressively higher and higher levels of integration in his thinking covering many years of constant preoccupation with the problem.

The Integration of Motives. Human motives are so many and so varied that a person would likely turn out to be an unpredictable combination of unrelated strivings and self-contradictions unless some system or organization were introduced through development. The young child in fact frequently shows something approximating such a picture in his motivational life. But conflicts arise—conflicts of his desires with the physically impossible, conflicts with other people who will restrain him or whom he does not wish to offend, conflicts within himself between certain individual desires and his developing long-time goals, larger purposes, and his slowly emerging ambitions and ideals. He learns that, although most of his desires do not actually have to be completely surrendered, they do have to be made to take their proper place and position of subordination to the main goals of his endeavors. It is thus that a kind of integration occurs that is often called a "hierarchy of motives." Each child develops his own "hierarchy," some more rigid than others, some with different goals in the position of dominance, some more "realistic" than others. The combined educative and maturational factors have their influence, but it is often difficult psychologically to trace the story in too much detail. The particular story that holds for each child is one of the chief sources of his "individuality." This kind of hierarchical organization, subject to so many combinations and permutations, suggests why a study of children in terms of sin-

gle motives or "traits" may miss something of the child's whole
personality, the particular "pattern" of the combination.   Stubbornness, for example, can be a very different thing if we are
stubborn at the right time, and the desire for social approval
will have different meaning depending upon where and when
we seek it.

Some psychologists (24) write of a "hierarchy of needs" in
a slightly different sense but also with important implications.
They regard needs or motives as being organized for people in
general in a series of levels, which however do not necessarily
show a one-to-one correspondence with the actual steps of development.   This plan suggests an order of dominance of needs
in the person faced with frustration; he will seek to satisfy the
lower-level needs first.   On the other hand, if the lower-level
needs are being fairly well satisfied in general, they do not become effective sources of motivation and the person typically
acts on the basis of higher-level motivation.   This scheme
would imply that the teacher could not hope to appeal to higher-
level motives in the child if the home background or other circumstances of his development had left the lower-level ones
in general unsatisfied.   This hierarchy of needs is as follows:

1. Gratification of bodily needs.
2. Safety from possible injury, danger, and physical threats.
3. Love, affection, warmth, acceptance, a place in the group.
4. Self-esteem, self-respect, self-confidence, feeling of strength
   and adequacy.
5. Self-actualization, self-fulfillment, self-expression, working
   out one's own fundamental personality.

Abstraction

The child's cognitive mental life has its origin as a phase or
aspect of goal-directed activity in which the "response" follows
very quickly in the presence of the object or situation as he
vaguely and simply perceives it to be.   As the consequences of
his prompt behavior are not always as satisfying as he might
have anticipated them to be because he ignored some relevant
features of his surroundings, he is induced, at least the next

time, to look a little "harder" at the situation. Perhaps a momentary delay may ensue, but it is often infinitesimal because the new properties or features emerge so quickly from this second look and are so closely bound up with the obvious physical properties of the object that he can continue to respond very quickly, although now more correctly. But as time passes he must eventually "slow down." His goals become more specific; not any food will do, but just this kind; the perception of the most obvious properties of the object will not alone guarantee its adequacy, the white liquid may turn out to be buttermilk; the object may be only one among alternatives present, it may be some distance away, or standing behind an obstacle, and so he will have to decide whether he really wants it and whether it is worth the effort. As a result of such factors we find that the older child is not so quickly "triggered" into action by either need or situation. He begins to engage in "ideational" activities which may include memory, imagination, anticipation, and the awareness of less obvious object-properties, and he finds it pays him to do so before entering on a course of action. One of the most helpful mental functions in this respect is the tendency and ability to "abstract," selectively to ignore a number of object-properties and attend to one, to consider a property that he "knows" the object has but does not see, to ignore differences and to see similarities, to concentrate on "meaning" and outcome, to raise to a high level of awareness the relations of things to each other rather than the things themselves.

The Abstract Attitude. It is in the "intellectualization" of his behavior that man shows his great superiority over brute animals. The psychological study of intellectual functions in the adult has in general been more rewarding than when children have been employed as subjects. The relatively undifferentiated nature of the child's abilities has a great deal to do with this. Evidence of the development of intellectual activities is found in many areas of behavior that might not strictly be called intellectual, or perhaps even cognitive, although it may be very difficult to say just what intellectual process or function is involved at any one time. Thus a child cannot experience the emotions of joy, jealousy, or worry until he can abstractively appreciate certain subtleties of personal relations or anticipations of the future; his drawing of a man offers similar evidence when he "overdraws," as when he puts in both eyes even when the figure is seen in profile; his volitional determination and perseverance show in his ability to concentrate and to work toward remote goals. It is because of this scientifically jumbled nature of low maturity levels that some psychologists content themselves with a general description of behavior against a background of intellectual growth without trying to specify the particular internal cognitive operations that make it possible. By contrasting "abstract and concrete behavior," it is possible to summarize the over-all differences. The following points have been made as a result of a study of clinical patients whose abstract behavior has deteriorated, but they are probably also applicable to the concrete behavior of children (11):

The abstract attitude is shown in the readiness:

1. To detach our ego from the outer world or from inner experience: the concrete minded, for example, cannot handle a comb without combing the hair, cannot say, "snow is black," cannot drink water from a glass unless thirsty.
2. To assume a mental set: the concrete minded cannot set the hands of a clock even though he can tell time; if interrupted in counting letters, cannot begin again; cannot name the preceding or following day of the week.
3. To account for acts to oneself, and to verbalize the account: the concrete minded may throw balls into boxes well, but he cannot tell which box is farther; he can point to the direction of a noise, but he cannot state the direction in words.
4. To shift reflectively from one aspect of the situation to another: the concrete minded cannot shift from reciting the alphabet to the days of the week; he cannot shift easily in conversation; he cannot shift easily in ambiguous figures (or puzzle pictures).
5. To hold in mind simultaneously various aspects of the situation: the concrete minded cannot easily cross out two differ-

ent letters simultaneously, although he can cancel each one separately; when figures overlap he cannot see a space that is contained in two figures; he can put parts of a picture together according to shape but not according to feature lines on them.

6. To grasp the essential of a given whole, to break up into parts, isolate and synthesize them: the concrete minded can give only details of the picture, not its interpretation; he cannot read words if letters are separated by a space.

7. To abstract common properties reflectively, from hierarchic concepts: the concrete minded cannot state whether 7 or 4 is larger although he can count them on his fingers; he has no understanding of analogies, metaphors and proverbs; he fails on a very simple syllogism.

8. To plan ahead ideationally, to assume an attitude toward the "merely possible," and to perform symbolically: the concrete minded cannot draw a map of his walk toward his home; he cannot demonstrate how to use a key to open a door unless the door is present; he cannot demonstrate how to drink when an empty glass is used; he cannot write his name in the air; he cannot hammer on an imaginary nail.

Abstraction and Concepts. The more immediate end product of the process of abstraction is commonly called an *idea* or *concept*. It is a form of mental content and knowledge through which the child is able, as it were, to disengage his knowing from the very great singularity involved in the innumerable irrelevant details and stimuli of each event and situation. No event or object is ever identical with another, yet the general pattern, structure, or over-all "togetherness" may show a similarity in perception and this then may be abstracted as a kind of skeletal or "blueprint" outline. At first the child may know only five apples, or five matches, or five trees, but not "fiveness." He cannot add five and two unless it be five and two something. Happily, however, most children can go on to the abstraction of "fiveness" and the concept of "five."

As in other areas of development, there are levels and "genetic sequences" in abstraction. There are problems of what concepts must come before other concepts are possible, and what makes some concepts more difficult in themselves than others. A promising beginning in the study of such things has been made, but much more information is desirable. The results, generally interpreted, show at least that there is, for example, no particular "age of reason" at which abstraction suddenly appears. Also, the ability to think abstractly in any sphere of knowledge is not simply a matter of general intelligence or general mental maturity. Information, training, as well as other more subtle environmental factors, are important. The neophyte in any field of science tends to think in a much more concrete manner than he will later on. Our first attempt to understand what an electron is will probably mean that we picture it as a little ball, a concrete image, and we should probably not find it very helpful to be told that it is a "locus of energy," a very abstract term which the expert has no difficulty in handling. It is probably better to state our generalization in the form, "the course of mental development is marked by progress from the *more* concrete to the *more* abstract kind of thinking," rather than to contrast the two terms in any absolute manner.

Abstraction and Symbolization. The ability to abstract makes language possible, and the use of language, in turn, can often be taken as a good indication of the level of abstraction attained. Words get their meaning from the fact that they can be employed as signs or "symbols" either of an object or of the concept of the object. They can, consequently, become important cues in learning and they greatly aid us in summarizing and generalizing our knowledge, and in seeking and in keeping order among the innumerable items of knowledge. We can organize our concepts into higher and higher orders of concepts—as for example when we go from "dog" to "mammal" to "vertebrate" to "animal" to "living being," although we never see a "living being" in the "raw"—and we can invent or discover a word for each level of abstraction. We can, as we know, also be rather arbitrary about the term employed, as is the case with the "x" of algebra, and we can also carry the process of abstraction to such an extent or such a height (as in the case of "hypothetical construct") that we may not feel quite sure finally whether there is anything in the real world corresponding to it. The use of the symbol, $\sqrt{-1}$ is a good example of a high-level abstraction since it does not appear to have any relation to "thingness" at all, but is nevertheless basic to the mathematics underlying nuclear fission and the atomic bomb.

It has often been noted that there is a coincidental hazard to true mental development and education in the indiscriminate use of higher-level abstractions and symbols. Thinking itself often can be fun, and words and symbols have their own fascination, even when there no longer exists any necessary correspondence between the "inner world" of thought and the language symbols on the one hand, and the "outer world" and its true properties on the other. The result may be "empty" concepts, or more likely, the substitution of names, words, and verbal formulas for real knowledge. While a great deal of schooling necessarily consists in introducing the child to new language terms and to more or less arbitrary symbols and devices for communication, we perhaps do not give enough attention to seeing that the child realizes their means-to-an-end character. In cognitive development, words are not meant to be ends in themselves, although they may legitimately approach this kind of use in poetry and literature.

SOCIALIZATION OF DEVELOPMENT

Changing viewpoints about the psychological nature of the impact of society and social life upon the growing child have helped us to get a better understanding of the problem. People and their customs and cultures obviously do get involved, and in a very important manner, in fashioning the picture of the mature adult, both because man has such a long infancy and because of the complexity of modern civilized life. But at what psychological points the two meet and in what areas of mental functioning and behavior the child carries with him the after-effects of the encounter is the important problem for the psychologically minded student. Earlier writers often seem to have gotten off on the wrong foot because of two handicaps; one, a particular psychological theory of how learning and development must of necessity occur, and secondly, an assumption—often only implicit and very easy to fall into—that the chief traits and characteristics of the people we know most intimately, those of our own race, nation, and level of educational sophistication, best express the natural outcome of development, and that these would really be the universal result if only certain cultural environments were not so backward, restrictive, or limiting.

It seemed to be thought that, basically, there was an "original human nature" that could be rather clearly described in terms of psychological elements like instinct, sensation, imagination, and the like, and that what society and social life did with these raw materials was to work on them, as it were, from the outside. It might suppress the undesirable elements and confirm the good ones; it could offer many opportunities for the exercise and strengthening of serviceable abilities; it could make rewards greater or less; it could add together or associate elements in the right combinations where only chaos existed before; it could connect these elements with proper objects or occasions in the social environment so that they would be evoked at the relevant time; it could offer high opportunities for the many desirable ones to come to expression. The educational and cultural influences could, apparently, do a lot *with* human nature, and a lot *for* it, by facilitating its own development, but they did not seem to be able to do much *to* it by way of change or alteration from within. At the present time, however, human nature is not regarded as nearly so "set" as all this would imply, and it is believed that man and society, psychologically described, interact in a much closer and more organic union in development.

Anthropology and Psychology. The findings of anthropologists in their study of "acculturation" in different peoples suggest that there are many things, like the "instinct" of acquisitiveness, or of rivalry, competitive behavior, the drive to achievement and speed, which are not always constant components of human behavior. The particular culture into which the child is born induces in him a "characteristic life style," which works, as it were, from above down to produce relevant traits, tendencies, and abilities. A short summary of four cultures is as follows (7, p. 275):

Samoa: a static, unchanging, socialized way of life flattening out the great individual differences that appear among the younger children.

Zuñi Village: a thoroughly socialized Indian community, in which the impact of the culture on the child produces a co-operating being.

Kwakiutl tribe: a rank-order society in which intense competition rules the life of the tribe, and every aspect of the culture molds the child into a competing individualist.

Colvin Hollow: an American backwoods community, the complacent human and mild physical environment developing in its children poorly motivated, somewhat flattened-out personalities.

As a result, we have: "the cooperative Samoan, the sharing Zuñi, the individualistic Kwakiutl, the inert, satisfied-to-stay-as-he-is Colvin Hollow American."

Early psychological test studies of certain primitive races showed them not to be superior to civilized man in sensory capacities in spite of their refined performances in tracking game, and other skills, an expertness that had been at one time attributed to their better heredity along this line brought about through "natural selection." The anthropologist's use of the Rorschach ink-blot test in the study of different races and cultures (8) has raised many questions about how the human being "naturally" perceives. The best answer in many cases seems to be that what is "natural" in one environment is not "natural" in another. Thus we find rather basic differences where a rigid psychological concept of human nature would expect similarity, and similarities where differences would be expected.

The interaction of the individual and society in development can scarcely be regarded as leading only to products that are superimposed, as it were, upon a definite original human nature. Rather, the results of the interaction represent changes taking place within general patterns of tendencies, needs, and goal-activities, which, because of their general character and their lack of specific form and direction, are sufficiently similar in outline in all human beings for us to recognize them as belonging to the same "species." There is apparently no original nature in the sense that the child is born with a set of specific behavior tendencies already determined by heredity and ready to act in a definite fashion, and to which are added by way of accretion the results of later experiences. Human nature, when described in the psychological sense of observable behavior and behavior tendencies, is as much a product of "human environment" as it is of heredity. This does not mean, of course, that a child reared by animals, as is sometimes reported for certain "feral" children, would show only animal behavior. This inference would be based upon an equally deceptive theory that the child learns chiefly through imitation. "Imitation" is probably not a psychological process at all, but indicates only a result, evaluated from the "outside," like "making shoes."

Culture and Ability. Psychologists have recognized for a long time the importance of cultural factors in interpreting the results of their tests. It is rather a commonplace to say that each test must be standardized on the group with which it is employed, and that many tests assume for their validity a "common experiential background." This phrase may, however, turn out to be a rather vague one for practical purposes, and may be interpreted in a manner strongly emphasizing the practical importance of the principle of development with which we are now concerned. A psychological test covers both *content* and *function,* the latter referring to the mental process or activity in terms of its nature, like spatial discrimination, memory, and the like, and the former to the kind of material or subject matter contained in the particular items employed to test such a function. It would seem that the phrase "common experiential background" is often applied only to test content. It would be the same as if, in a test of the value of coins, we should make sure that our English child dealt with farthings and pennies, and the American child with cents and nickels, but ignore at the same time the English child's culture-induced tendency to make higher units by multiplying by four, two, three, twelve, while the American child has become accustomed to function in such a case on the basis of the decimal system. This is of course a trivial example, but the analogy points up the importance of considering the possibility of both culturally determined function and content before we can evaluate the success attained by those students now working to devise "culture-free tests." In the absolute sense, of course, there cannot be a culture-*free* test, a better term, perhaps, being culture-*neutral*.

That culture factors may, by differentiation, determine the appearance in children of certain functions, to be manifested with enough consistency to be scientifically measured as an ability, is not at all unreasonable. Evidence from studies on the role of learning in perception (17) shows that we can "learn to learn," that we can learn not only the specific responses expected of us but also the general kind, form, or pattern of response required, and that we usually have to learn the latter before we can meet the specific requirements of the former. Monkeys can acquire *learning sets* which will determine just what feature is to be reacted to in one situation and what in another (15), and they can quickly learn to shift the set or approach from one condition to another. These learning sets determine for the animal in advance just how the situation is to be analyzed, as it were, *this* time, before it is called on to perform correctly in response to the specific cue from among a number of alternatives, all of the same general kind that the learning set tells the animal are going to be used *this* time. It would seem reasonable to believe that cultural factors could also tell the growing child what pattern is to be employed in analyzing the situation at this or that time, what general kind of approach to have, what kind or form of response to make, and that such learning sets would be consistently retained and manifested in accordance with the customs, rewards, and values of his particular culture. From then on they could appear as special mental functions and abilities.

Even the incomplete reports of anthropologists would show us the naïveté of the belief that the young child is faced with an environment already cut up nicely into the kinds of objects, unities, and features that the mature person so readily sees. Apart from the experience of a relatively few unitary objects, like a person, hat, or tree, which are apparently present to the child in early life by reason of simple perceptual organization (but without too much meaning), by far the greater number of perceptual, abstractive, and conceptual objects and properties found in the world around us are the result of selective trends established in our analysis of the world.   Many of these can be due to distinctive cultural forces.   One anthropologist (25) writes of some of the difficulties faced by an American in trying to learn a primitive language by reason of what appear to be differences in concepts of the two peoples.   In some areas the primitive has more terms and concepts than the American, in some areas fewer; he apparently sees more in the world along some lines, and less along others.

> In Bali there is a word for what the witch does when she throws her hands up and back, which is also the word for a child who is startled by a fear of falling or for what a man does when he falls out of a tree. . . . You may look at a dog with one verb and a woman with another. . . . If a boy is in front of you with a loaf of bread and a knife, whose task has been to cut bread with that knife every night for two years, and if you don't use the verb that means "to cut in even regular slices across the loaf," but instead use any of the other thirty or so words for cut, . . . he will look at you with absolute amazement and have no idea whatsoever what you are saying. (25, p. 175)

In other areas the primitive could not answer such an apparently simple question as, "Why did so-and-so take an offering to a particular temple?"   The author comments, "The quicker you learn which areas are not articulate the better," for these vary from culture to culture.

The "Self" and Society.   Psychologists show increasing recognition of the importance of the child's "self-concept," the image that he has of himself as an individual, in the development of both normal and abnormal behavior.   While the picture he gains of himself is, in terms of psychological processes and internal activities, basically of his own making, the chief occasions for the development of this concept are to be found in the give-and-take of his interactions with other people. The child could of course arrive at some idea of himself as a definite being through contacts with the physical environment alone, but it would lack the richness that we commonly associate with human personality, so much of which is dependent upon the "role" we play, or think we play, in various social relationships. The young child early develops an attitude, not always conscious by any means, of "belonging" to this or that group, to his family, to his age or school group, to his sex group, to his athletic team, to his race and nation, to his religious and cultural groups. Belonging to these different groups carries with it certain requirements and standards of action and thought, such as "boys don't play with dolls," "your mother loves you more than anyone else in the world," "a good sport does not spike the second-baseman," "a gentleman just doesn't do those things." In thinking of himself as a member of the separate groups, he meets expectancies on the part of others with respect to him, and these create within him expectancies of himself which he incorporates in his self-concept. From some points of view, self and personality on the one hand, and society on the other, are almost correlative terms like "father" and "son."

While the child's self-concept naturally develops along many lines in accordance with the available social norms, customs, and values, we must not think that in his "interiorization" of these it is a simple process of more or less passive "imitation." As we know, the child may on occasion react violently, at least emotionally and internally, to the expectancies that others may have of him, and he must work hard at restoring order and stability in his disturbed self-concept, a goal that is commonly regarded as of supreme importance in the development of personality and character. Many psychologists think of the personal agitations and disturbances of adolescence as being primarily a matter of reconciling those aspects of his self-concept through which the individual still tends to think of himself as a child, and those aspects through which he sees himself as a developing adult.

When we think of "self-actualization" as one of the strongest motives for ambition and achievement, we should realize that the "self" involved is the one the child thinks himself to be, which of course may or may not be the one he "actually" is, or as others would describe him. The child's self-concept is in turn a product of complex social interactions.

THE PERSONAL NATURE OF MENTAL DEVELOPMENT

Mental development and learning take place as aspects of the development of the whole personality. When we isolate certain features of mind and behavior for the purposes of separate psychological study, this should always be done against a background of the realization of the interrelatedness of all developmental processes. These processes are not usually independent of each other. Motivational and socializational changes work through differentiation and integration, which in turn are usually parallel and complementary. Integration does not ordinarily occur without differentiation, and higher levels of differentiation are preceded by lower level integrations. Abstraction is likely to be going on all the while, influencing the development of attitudes, emotions, and volitional life.

The child's behavior and mental activity represent an attack upon some problem or required adjustment through the operation of various psychological factors, some clearly active in the present, others identifiable perhaps primarily through a study of the past. The principle of "multiple causation of human behavior" would imply that an act of a child can be understood in its completeness of cause and condition only when we are able to take into account such factors of personal nature as his aptitude for insight, his physiological maturity, his motives, temperament, the influence of his fellows, the general attitude of his home and social environment, and his own attitudes toward school and life.

We do not, of course, have to consider all these factors every time we seek to explain a difference in achievement between two particular children, but this does not mean that the factors presently left out of account are unimportant in the over-all story of development. It may merely mean that, for the present case, we may reasonably assume that the contribution made by the neglected factors is the same for both children, a "constant," and that other factors, the "variables," while not being as influential perhaps in affecting the absolute level of achievement, are nevertheless the significant ones when we are concerned only with differences between individuals. In many instances, however, we may find that we cannot rightly assume that certain personality factors are constant, or much the same from one child to another, and we must then widen our psychological vision to cover many more aspects of personality and development, any one of which may on occasion turn out to be of practical significance.

Developmental Tasks. Mental development is a complex process best described as *bio-social-psychological;* that is, progressive changes in behavior have a biological, a psychological, and a cultural basis. Perhaps the best way to synthesize the principles of mental development is through the use of the concept of "developmental task" as elaborated by Havighurst and associates (13, 14). This concept calls attention to certain aspects of behavior or attitudes which the child must learn if development is to proceed at a normal pace and sequence.

A developmental task, according to Havighurst, "is a task which arises at or about a certain period in the life of the individual, successful achievement of which leads to his happiness and to success with later tasks, while failure leads to unhappiness in the individual, disapproval by society, and difficulty with later tasks" (14, p. 2). We should first differentiate the terms "task," as used here, and "need." The latter is somewhat equivocal, since it easily confuses what the child wants and what the society requires of him. Because of this confusion, the concept of "needs" as an approach to educational psychology has been strongly attacked because it leads to the mistaken impression that the work of the school should center around the whims of children (5). A need, properly understood, is social as well as personal, and the needs of society define to a considerable extent the needs of the individual. The term "developmental tasks" refers to personal-social needs, but serves to define what is required of the child for wholesome development in a democratic society. Another important aspect of the developmental task is its emphasis on a *critical stage* of development at which the task must be learned. The child learns the rudiments of speech, for example, during its second year, and by age two has learned to talk. The period just preceding this appears to be crucial. Some evidence indicates that a child deprived of the normal human environment during the early years will be permanently retarded in development, since many later tasks depend upon an appropriate level of ability in language. It would appear that a normal *pacing* of development, appropriate to the critical learning period of the various tasks, is essential to future progress of the child. Educational procedures, from the very beginning of the child's life, must strike while the iron is hot if the tempering is to be adequate for the learning of future tasks. The third emphasis of the developmental task concept, then, is that of *sequence* or continuity of mental development.

Since the developmental task emphasizes what is required of the individual, we must ask whence the requirements or needs arise. First of all, the developing organism itself makes demands on the individual. The organism also imposes limits. Biological factors determine and limit at all stages what can be learned, how it can be learned, and when the crucial period of learning occurs. "Readiness" thus has an organic aspect. Secondly, society imposes demands on the individual. Cultural values often determine what should be learned and when. The culture also sets up standards for success or failure in developmental tasks. Cultural differences among nations, regions, and families must therefore be taken into account, as well as organic factors, in interpreting whether development is "normal" or "subnormal." Thirdly, the individual imposes certain demands on himself. Through the interaction of biosocial factors, the child develops a "personality," with personal motives and goals. He develops a scheme of personal values by which to order his life and to judge his relative success or failure or personal adequacy. Certain developmental tasks—such as vocational and educational choices, for example—arise from the psychological factors of personal motives and values.

The biological, cultural, and psychological determinants of developmental tasks are seen to be interrelated. To say that the organism gives rise to organic needs, society to social needs, or that the personal "self-imposed" needs are independent of these is to miss the point. For example, one important developmental task is the adjustment to an appropriate sex role. The appearance of sex organs obviously determines whether the role is to be masculine or feminine. But it is social custom which defines the kind of behavior appropriate to boys and girls, men and women. These customs provide the developing child with a scheme of personal values and motives by which to judge whether certain kinds of behavior are "manly," "sissy," or "tomboy." With biological maturity during adolescence comes a sharper delineation of sex roles, and new developmental tasks. Sex attraction has a social basis, however, as well as a biological one. Our concepts of "mature" relations with the opposite sex are greatly influenced by custom, and developing personal values determine the eventual choice of a mate. Similarly, the task of vocational choice and preparation becomes more critical during this period because sexual maturation is a sign of adulthood, because society requires behavior appropriate to one's appearance, and because the acculturated individual accepts and personalizes the social values and begins to judge himself accordingly.

The Continuity of Developmental Tasks. Some suggestion of the continuity of personal development is apparent from Havighurst's list of developmental tasks appropriate to infancy and early childhood, middle childhood, and adolescence (14). Although such lists are somewhat arbitrary and subject to further psychological refinement, they serve to illustrate the chief educational problem in development very well.

Infancy and Early Childhood. Learning to walk, take solid foods, talk, and control elimination of bodily wastes; learn sex differences and sexual modesty; simple concepts of social and cultural realities; emotional relationships, especially with parents; learning to distinguish right and wrong.   One task is purely biological: the achievement of physiological stability of the organism.

From the integration of these kinds of learnings arises the basis of personality, the first dawning of a self-concept.   Although the developmental tasks during this period do not spring from personal values or goals, and the child is not self-directive in the adult sense, experience with these tasks lays the groundwork for the formation of the self.   Erikson (9) has pointed out that the first year is the crucial one for learning a "basic attitude of trust."   Emotional relationships with parents are very important, since an attitude of mistrust and emotional insecurity developed at this time may have an enduring effect.   During the second and third years the child faces the task of learning "a sense of autonomy," or self-direction.   Failure during this period will result in an overdependent child, or perhaps a hostile and aggressive one.   During the fourth and fifth years, according to Erikson, comes the period for learning initiative and a conscience.   These successive adjustments depend of course on earlier ones.

Middle Childhood. Learning physical skills in ordinary games, wholesome attitudes toward the body, health, and hygiene, attitudes helpful in getting along with age mates; learning appropriate sex role, fundamental educational skills (three R's), and a number of abstract concepts for everyday living; learning a self-directing conscience or scale of values, a sense of personal independence, democratic social attitudes.

This period, from about six to twelve years of age, is what Erikson calls the period of "industry," and the development of a sense of accomplishment is critically at stake during this period.   The child feels a need to work at "real" socially important tasks and carry them through to completion.   The ability to do this, however, depends on the prior development of a sense of initiative.   Failure in the tasks of middle childhood can result in feelings of worthlessness or inadequacy, which are serious handicaps in learning the later tasks of adolescence and adulthood.

Adolescence. Learning mature relations with age-mates of both sexes, an appropriate masculine or feminine social role, and emotional independence toward parents and adults; learning to accept and respect one's physique; learning positive attitudes toward one's self which give assurance of eventual economic independence; how to choose an occupation and prepare for marriage; abstract concepts of law, government, economics, and social institutions for civic competence.

Adolescence, according to Erikson, is the crucial period for developing a sense of identity. The general task for the adolescent is to understand himself, to understand society, and to develop a sense of participating in it. The clarification of his future role in society is a difficult task, in view of what to him are obvious personal limitations. The key task, perhaps, is developing personal independence. This is not only a radical change from the childhood role, but is made difficult by the fact that he is judged (and judges himself) by adult standards to which he doesn't quite "measure up."

The continuity of development is seen in the fact that the success of later adjustments always depends on a dispositional state of "readiness" arising from earlier adjustments. To gain the proper perspective on such a task as vocational choice, for example, we must realize that the approach to this problem has a genetic history. We must "read backwards," so to speak, to the origins of self-doubt or self-confidence, to the groping attempts to achieve a sense of initiative and a sense of accomplishment at an earlier period. There are also developmental tasks in early adulthood, in middle age, and later maturity. Success in these is largely conditioned by the degree of personal independence achieved during the adolescent period.

The whole of educational psychology, in a sense, is concerned with the biological, psychological, and cultural aspects of various developmental tasks. The work of education consists in pacing the child, in providing experiences appropriate to his level of development. To do this properly, the teacher must keep his eye on the child's future as well as on his past. Of any task we must ask when it must be learned, and how it can be learned. How do individual differences in organic growth or physical abilities limit or facilitate its accomplishment? How do individual differences in mental ability, interests, and values affect its accomplishment? How does success or failure in the task affect subsequent mental development and personality? How does the task vary from one culture to another, or among various subcultures in our own society? What is the responsibility of the school for the accomplishment of the task, and what can the school do to help the child accomplish it?

REFERENCES

1. ALLPORT, G. W. *Personality: a psychological interpretation.* New York: Holt, 1937.
2. ANASTASI, ANNE. The nature of psychological traits. *Psychol. Rev.,* 1941, **55,** 127-138.
3. ANDERSON, E. E. The externalization of drive. *Psychol. Rev.,* 1941, **48,** 204-224.
4. BLAKE, R. R., & RAMSEY, G. V. *Perception, an approach to personality.* New York: Ronald Press, 1951.
5. BODE, B. H. The concept of needs in general education. *Progressive Educ.,* 1938, **15,** 7-9.
6. BRIDGES, K. M. B. A genetic theory of the emotions. *J. genet. Psychol.,* 1930, **37,** 514-527.
7. COLE, L. E., & BRUCE, W. F. *Educational psychology.* Yonkers, N. Y.: World Book Co., 1950.
8. DENNIS, WAYNE. Cultural and developmental factors in perception. Ch. in BLAKE & RAMSEY (4).
9. ERIKSON, E. *Childhood and society.* New York: Norton, 1950.
10. GINZBERG, E., *et al. Occupational choice, an approach to general theory.* New York: Columbia Univ. Press, 1951.
11. GOLDSTEIN, K., & SCHEERER, M. Abstract and concrete behavior. *Psychol. Monogr.,* 1941, **53,** No. 2.
12. HALVERSON, H. M. An experimental study of prehension in infants. *Genet. Psychol. Monogr.,* 1931, **10,** 107-286.
13. HAVIGHURST, R. J. *Developmental tasks in education.* Chicago: Univ. of Chicago Press, 1948.
14. HAVIGHURST, R. J. *Human development and education.* New York: Longmans, Green, 1953.
15. HARLOW, H. F. The formation of learning sets. *Psychol. Rev.,* 1949, **56,** 51-65.
16. HARRISON, M. L. *Reading readiness.* Boston: Houghton Mifflin, 1936.
17. HILGARD, E. R. The role of learning in perception. Ch. in BLAKE & RAMSEY (4).
18. ILG, F., & AMES, L. B. Developmental trends in reading behavior. *J. genet. Psychol.,* 1950, **76,** 291-312.
19. ILG, F., & AMES, L. B. Developmental trends in arithmetic. *J. genet. Psychol.,* 1951, **79,** 3-28.

20. ILG, F., & AMES, L. B. Developmental trends in writing behavior. *J. genet. Psychol.*, 1951, **79,** 29-46.
21. JAMES, W. *Principles of psychology.* New York: Holt, 1890.
22. LAWRENCE, D. H. The transfer of a discrimination along a continuum. *J. compar. & physiol. Psychol.*, 1952, **45,** 511-516.
23. MARTIN, W. E. Quantitative expression in young children. *Genet. Psychol. Monogr.*, 1951, **44,** 147-220.
24. MASLOW, A. H. A preface to motivation theory. *Psychosomatic Med. Monogr.*, 1943, No. 5.
25. MEAD, M. Experience in learning primitive languages. In *Cybernetics,* H. V. FOERSTER (Ed.). New York: Josiah Macy Found., 1951.
26. MEYER, E. Comprehension of spatial relations in preschool children. *J. genet. Psychol.*, 1940, **57,** 119-151.
27. MILLER, N. E., & DOLLARD, J. *Social learning and imitation.* New Haven: Yale Univ. Press, 1941.
28. WERTHEIMER, M. *Productive thinking.* New York: Harper, 1945.
29. WOODWORTH, R. S. *Dynamic psychology.* In *Psychologies of 1925.* Worcester: Clark Univ. Press, 1928.

SELECTED READINGS

AMERICAN ASSOCIATION OF TEACHERS COLLEGES. *Child growth and development emphasis in teacher education.* AATC, 1944.

ANDERSON, I. H., & DEARBORN, W. F. *The psychology of teaching reading.* New York: Ronald Press, 1952. See Chapter on "The concept of reading readiness."

HAVIGHURST, R. J. *Human development and education.* New York: Longmans, Green, 1953. A summary and explanation of developmental tasks in education.

LINTON, R. *Culture and personality.* New York: Appleton-Century-Crofts, 1946. A readable discussion of the influence of culture on personality development.

OGDEN, R. M. & FREEMAN, F. S. *Psychology and education.* New York: Harcourt, 1932.

WERNER, H. *Comparative psychology of mental development.* Chicago: Follett, 1948.

WHEELER, R. H., & PERKINS, F. T. *Principles of mental development.* New York: Crowell, 1932.

PART II

Human Growth and Development

3

HUMAN VARIABILITY AND GROWTH

At the very base of all problems in education is the fact of
individual differences. We know in a general way that human
beings differ in bodily shape and size, physical strength, and appearance. Teachers, perhaps more than other persons, are
acutely aware of differences in mental abilities and achievement
in their students, just as physicians are more conscious of human differences in blood temperature, glandular functions, and
metabolic rates. The basic fact is that human variability is
universal, that there are differences in *all* traits. The same generalization holds for all living things, including even single-
celled organisms. What is the extent of these differences?
What causes them? What are the practical implications of human variability, particularly in education?

Education is concerned chiefly with the growth and development of individual human beings. Growth implies an increase
in the *amount* of something—in height or weight, in skeletal or
neural tissue, in the number of things the individual can do. Do
all children grow at the same rate? Do all abilities develop at
the same rate? How much does schooling contribute to
growth? These questions imply some way of measuring growth,
and of measuring individual differences. Some idea of the nature and extent of human variability, and of the way in which
individual differences are measured, is basic to the study of any
educational problem.

The Distribution of Human Traits

In everyday life it is popular to classify people into "have's"
and "have not's" with respect to any particular trait. We are
accustomed to talk about people—and about ourselves—as

"artistically gifted" or "can't draw a straight line," as mechanically inclined or unmechanical, as musical or nonmusical. Sometimes, instead of classifying into two "boxes" we extend the scale somewhat and use three; people are athletic, nonathletic, or some place in between—"just average." We do not really believe that abilities are distributed in two or three categories, but it is a popular way of talking (and sometimes thinking), chiefly because we do not have any handy words to label finer categories.

We can assume that abilities, like physical traits, may differ in quantity among the various human individuals by very small amounts which sometimes defy measurement. There are no categories except those we invent—an amount of any given ability is best symbolized by a line drawn from zero to infinity, not by an arbitrary arrangement of intervals or boxes. When we invent categories or intervals, we do so because we lack finer measurements.

If we were to ask what percentage of people are athletic, of average athletic ability, and nonathletic, we are asking how athletic ability is distributed among these three categories. If we take high jumping ability as a measure of athletic ability, and test a representative sample of people by measuring the height of a crossbar which each individual could clear, we could lengthen and refine our scale of measurement to include a range of ability from the lowest height cleared to the highest, and to include a large number of categories or intervals of ability—a typical interval being "at least 45 inches but less than 46." If the frequencies of persons in each interval of ability were counted (frequency distribution) and the results were plotted in graphic form (frequency polygon) we would have an answer to our question: how is high jumping ability distributed in the population sampled? We could determine, in other words, the range of ability, the relative frequency of individuals at each level of ability, and whether the distribution is symmetrical. In all probability, we would find that for a large and unbiased sample the shape or contour of our distribution would, like other biological measures (e.g., neck size, spread of swallows' wings, weight of grains of wheat), closely approximate the bell-shaped curve called the *normal curve of distribution*.

Practically all measures of human traits, when so graphed, approximate the normal curve. This is very significant because the normal curve has well-known mathematical properties, with important practical implications. We should find this fact encouraging scientifically, for it suggests a mathematical treatment of human ability. The normal curve is the basis of many of the practical steps taken in devising and scoring mental tests, and in evaluating the results of their use. It also throws a great deal of light on the nature and number of the developmental causes of ability. Figure 1 shows this curve.

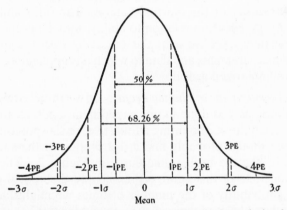

FIGURE 1. Normal Probability Curve. The mathematical relationship between the standard deviation and the normal curve makes it possible to estimate the percentage of cases falling between any two values of sigma for any normal distribution. The probable error (P.E.) is a constant fraction of the standard deviation: $PE = .6745\sigma$. In terms of probability, this means that the chances are 68 in 100 that any measure or score will lie within $\pm 1\sigma$, or 50 in 100 that it will lie within ± 1 PE. (From Garrett, *Statistics in psychology and education*.)

In speaking of human measurements, we commonly say that these have a "tendency to conform" to the normal curve. The normal curve is a mathematical one; that is, it marks the mathematical limits of a distribution showing such a tendency when an indefinitely large number of measurements are taken. In actual practice, we never make an indefinitely large number of measurements. We may measure a hundred children, or a thousand, or even ten thousand, but as this always falls short of the indefinitely large number assumed in mathematics, we do not expect exact conformity of our real measurements with the normal curve. There will almost always be found little bumps or depressions on our actual curve of distribution which will not be found on the perfectly smooth and symmetrical normal curve. But that there should be a marked tendency of our actual measurements to conform to this theoretical curve is of itself very significant. The greater the number of measurements we make, the closer and closer, as a rule, do we find our data approaching the limits of the normal curve.

Applicability of the Normal Curve. The full significance of the normal curve, in relation to ability, may be properly appreciated only after we acquaint ourselves with the different kinds of measurements and data to which it is applicable. These may be summarized as follows:

1. *Measurement of chance events.* If we threw twelve dice 4,096 times, as was done in one experiment, and recorded the result of each throw (counting a four, five, or six spot as a "success") we should probably find a distribution of the successes something like the broken-line curve in Figure 2. The other continuous line of this figure represents the theoretical or calculated probability of the number of times we might have expected, on the basis of mere chance, to get one, two, three, etc., "successes" from our throws. There are some irregularities in the actual curve obtained, and it is not quite so symmetrical as the "probability" curve, but it clearly shows a tendency to conform to the latter.

The normal curve may be employed to represent the distribution of chance events (dice throws, flips of coins, etc.) when the number of measurements or records is indefinitely large, and when the number of factors entering into these measurements (dice to be thrown, for instance, and all the circumstances surrounding each throw) is indefinitely great. This is why the normal curve of distribution is sometimes referred to as the *normal* or *theoretical probability* curve. It is an expression of what

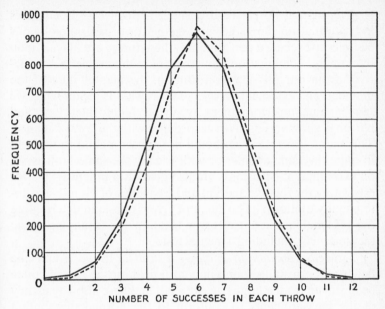

FIGURE 2. The Results Obtained in Throwing 12 Dice 4,096 Times. The broken line shows the actual number of "successes" obtained, counting a four, five, or six spot a "success." The continuous line represents what might have been expected on the basis of pure chance.

Broken-Line Curve				Continuous Line Curve			
Successes	Frequency	Successes	Frequency	Successes	Frequency	Successes	Frequency
0	0	7	847	0	1	7	792
1	7	8	536	1	12	8	495
2	60	9	257	2	66	9	220
3	198	10	71	3	220	10	66
4	430	11	11	4	495	11	12
5	731	12	0	5	792	12	1
6	948			6	924		

happens when an infinite number of factors act together, in different combinations, to produce variable results in accordance with the laws of chance.

2. *Measurement of error.* The normal curve was early employed to represent the variation in errors of judgment, estimation, and skill. Hence it is often called the *curve of error.* The name suggests that our human performances are also "chance events." This does not mean that they are the result of blind

chance, or that no personal element is involved. But it does indicate that, in the gathering together or organization of our energies to execute a performance, these forces are played upon by now this combination, now that, of innumerable factors derived from our physical constitution, the mental state of the moment, and external sources. This is what is meant when we say that human performances, even when highly intentional and personal, show variations in accordance with the laws of chance. This fact tells us why we should not expect a child to perform in quite the same manner or with exactly the same proficiency on two different occasions. It also gives us a practical rule for estimating the relative amount and frequency of his moment-to-moment variations. The curve of error is basic in determining the reasonable amount of error to allow for in any scientific measurement, including a mental test.

3. *Measurements of biological traits.* If we graph the height of corn stalks found in a corn field, or the size of coffee beans taken from a large bag, we shall find here also a tendency of the measurements to conform to the normal distribution curve. Biological events are also chance events, in the sense that the material causes of growth, whether heredity with its genes on the one hand, or environmental factors such as light, air, moisture, soil, crowding, on the other, are to be found in great variety and number. These interact, in different forms of combinations, to produce results of varying magnitude and varying frequency. Life processes are to be known only by their constancy of form amid ever-varying details.

4. *Individual differences in human traits.* Graphs such as we have in Figures 3 and 4 show close approximation to the normal curve. The variety of human beings is apparently the product of "chance" events, since most human traits are similarly distributed.

IMPLICATIONS OF NORMAL DISTRIBUTION OF ABILITY

Characteristics of the Normal Curve. A mere inspection of the normal curve, taken as typical of the distribution of ability, will suggest some preliminary notes.

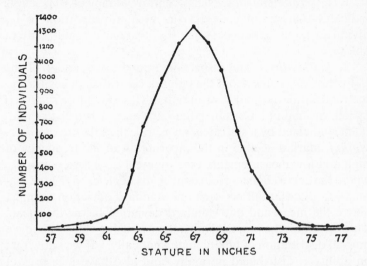

FIGURE 3. Distribution Curve for the Stature of 8,585 Adult Males. (From Frederick H. Lund, *Psychology,* Ronald Press, 1933.)

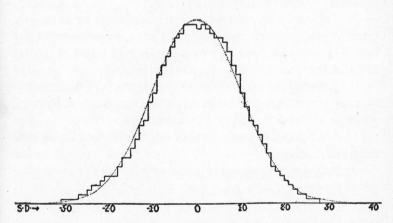

FIGURE 4. The Intelligence of Ninth-Grade Pupils. This is a composite curve for a number of ninth grades tested by eleven different intelligence tests. The broken line represents the theoretical normal curve. (From E. L. Thorndike, *The measurement of intelligence,* Bureau of Publications, Teachers College.)

1. *Central tendency.* The central hump of the curve indicates that we may expect the greater proportion of individuals to be grouped about the average or mid-point of ability.

2. *Variability.* The dispersion (spread or scatter) of the individual measures about the point of central tendency is symmetrical in the normal distribution. This spread or scatter is called variability. Certain points above and below the mid-point, indicated by a statistical measure called the *standard deviation,* mark a decline in the tapering off of the frequency of high and low measurements (see Figure 1). These points are where the curve changes from convex to concave. We note that 68.26% of cases fall between one standard deviation (sigma) above the mean and one standard deviation below the mean. This illustrates the practical advantage of being able to handle a normal distribution of ability mathematically. If we know that an ability is distributed normally, and also have measures of central tendency and dispersion (mean and standard deviation) we can predict approximately what percentage of cases will fall between any two measures on our scale.

3. *The rarity of extremes.* Extremely large or extremely small values are very uncommon. The curve approaches the base line very closely at its two extremes. In terms of mental abilities, there are few geniuses and few idiots.

We have only to add to these evident features of the distribution the fact that the curve is basically an expression of "chance" events—or events determined by a multiplicity of causes—and we should be able to point some of our inferences toward very practical matters.

The Continuous Distribution of Ability. Ability is distributed in a "continuous" manner throughout a large group of individuals. There are no breaks in the scale from the lowest to the highest point. In other words, there are all degrees of ability to be found within a large, unselected group of children or adults. This continuous variation up and down the scale means that we have not only "good," "average," and "poor" pupils, but all grades in between.

There is no natural classification of human beings on the basis of ability. Nature does not classify; we do the classifying. While it is convenient for us at times to make use of such terms as normal, bright, and dull, these have a way of beclouding our thinking on occasion. Many people seem to believe that if a child is to be classified as dull, he is thereby set off in a distinct natural class beyond a boundary line which is clearly marked by nature. They ignore the fact that his "dullness" may place him on the scale of ability only a slight degree below another child who has been classified, largely for the sake of convenience, as "normal." "On the continuous scale of ability, normals and subnormals jostle each other." We should aim at understanding the individual rather than classifying him. It is, in fact, only when some of our most rigidly classified humans, such as the "feebleminded" and "insane," are understood as mental "deviates" that they can be helped in an intelligent, practical manner.

The hump of the normal curve offers whatever scientific justification there is for Lincoln's saying that "God must love the common people, for he made so many of them." While we recognize this hump as representing average ability, we may ask, "Where does it begin and end?" or "How many children are of average ability?" "Average ability" should most certainly include those clustering around the central point of the curve. But how many? Some say one-third of all children, some say one-half, and some say two-thirds are of average or normal ability. Our scientific measurements will not of themselves give us the answer. We must depend upon other criteria for the practical validity of our class names.

We should not be surprised, then, to find that psychologists sometimes disagree on the limits they assign to, say, "normal" intelligence. If they believe that one-third of all children are to be considered average or normal, then the test limits designated for this range of ability will be from 95 to 105 IQ. If on the other hand, they decide that about 60 per cent of all children are to be designated as of average ability, then the limits will be from 90 to 110 IQ. There is no reason inherent in the nature of the test alone why the former range should be more or less correct than the latter. If there is a way of deciding which of these assumptions is more correct, it must be found in the practical use to be made of the measurements. There can, apparently, be no natural classification of children into discrete "types" of ability if the ability depends upon more than a few simple factors. Otherwise we should expect our distribution curve to show two or more well-defined peaks, or to be *bimodal,* or *multimodal* as it is more technically called. If the number of factors is small, and if these determine the result by their mere presence or absence, we may then have some justification for the strict use of "types," but their practical value may still be open to question.

It is possible, however, to consider psychological types in another way. Certain human traits may be regarded as organizations or patterned combinations of specific behavior tendencies. While each one of these tendencies, taken in itself, may manifest variability of the normal kind, their combinations may have a certain individuality about them. It might also be true that there would be a relatively small variety of such patterns, which then could be considered as types. This seems to be the basis of some of the plausible findings concerning "body types." The attempt to construct a graphic representation of the "average" man, based on the mean dimensions of each organ, will produce a rather queer looking creature. This is because such a procedure ignores the existence of certain common factors in the relative growth and proportioning of different body parts. Because of the more qualitative features of such a concept of type, we may expect it to be more closely related to personality traits than to the quantitative aspects of ability.

The extremes of ability are in symmetrical balance about the average. This means that there tend to be as many individuals at one extreme of ability as at the other, although there may be relatively few at either extreme. We are at times blind to this symmetry of the distribution of talents, and perhaps act toward children as if they can only be either average or below average. This may happen particularly if we rate skill and accomplishments by adult standards. We may well ask whether children representing the upper extremes of ability are receiving their educational due. It is, as a matter of fact, only rather recently that the educational study of the "exceptional child" has come to include the superior as well as the inferior. Exceptional children are those found at the extremes of ability, and there are as many to be found at one extreme as at the other.

Measuring the Amount of Variability. The term variability refers to the amount of spread or scatter of individual measures about the average or midpoint. Many problems in educational research, and even practical problems in the school, require some way of estimating the amount of variability within a group. We might wish to compare, for example, the variability of the fifth and sixth grades in arithmetic; that is, we wish to know which group contains the greater variety of individual ability. We might of course compare the distribution curves for the two grades. In such a case (see Figure 5) it would be clear that the flatter, less sharply humped curve shows the greater amount of individual differences in ability, or a greater "spread" about the average. This visual aid is a help in *seeing* the difference in variability between the two groups.

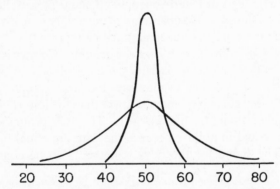

FIGURE 5. Two Distributions Differing in Variability but Alike in Area Under the Curve (Same Number of Cases) and in Mean (50).

However, it is not really necessary to draw the curves in order to make this comparison. The more usual way of doing it consists in calculating statistical measures of variability. The simplest way is to calculate the *range,* or the difference between the highest and lowest score. Although easily understood, this measure is not well adapted to exact statistical work. Since the range depends on only two scores—the highest and the lowest— it may be too easily distorted by an extremely low score or an extremely high one. It gives us information about the extreme limits, but not about the group as a whole, and this is often a grave disadvantage.

The *standard deviation,* or *sigma,* is the most commonly used measure of variability, for both mathematical and logical reasons. It is computed from *all* the measures in a group, and therefore describes the variability of the group as a whole.[1]

The importance of knowing the variability of a group can be seen from several examples.

1. *Making generalizations about the ability of a group.* When a class is said to have an average IQ of 117, we may ask whether most of the class are close to that level of ability, or whether that figure represents a wide spread from very dull to very bright. Is the group homogeneous (individuals relatively similar in ability) or heterogeneous? The mean score by itself does not tell us this. To characterize the ability of a group as a whole, both the mean and sigma must be reported.

2. *Making comparisons between groups.* Comparisons between two groups on the basis of averages alone can be quite misleading. Boys and girls may have the same average in reading ability, but some boys may be lower than the lowest girl, and some higher than the highest girl. The two groups cannot be called equal in ability, because they are not equal in *variability.* The sigma for the boys is higher. To be considered

---

[1] The standard deviation is sometimes called the "root-mean-square" of the deviations, which describes the way it is calculated. In calculating the sigma we take the deviation of each score from the mean, square each deviation, add the squares, divide the sum of squares by the number of cases to get a "mean square," and finally take the square root of the mean square. Expressed as a formula, this is $\sqrt{\dfrac{\Sigma d^2}{N}}$, in which d is "deviation" and N "number of cases." Less laborious ways of making the calculation are learned in a course in statistics. For our purpose, it is more important to understand its relation to the normal curve than to know how to compute it.

equivalent in ability, two or more groups must be approximately equal in both mean and standard deviation.[1]

3. *Comparing different abilities of the same individual.* If we wish to compare a child's ability in reading with his ability in arithmetic, we may say that he is found to be, for example, two sigmas above the mean of his grade in arithmetic but only one sigma above in reading. This is much more meaningful than to try to compare directly the original scores actually obtained on the two tests. One sigma, or any multiple of it, will always have the same significance for any two or more abilities. This is based on the assumption that the normal curve is typical of the distribution of all abilities. One reason why test scores are often scaled in sigma units and expressed as "standard scores" is that the scores are made comparable through this procedure.

The Influence of Selection on Variability. *Selection,* as a technical term, means that some extraneous factor, and not the mere possession of the trait or ability, enters in to influence the composition of the group upon which the measurements are made. Thus, if instead of measuring the height of a representative sampling of all American men, we confine our measuring to a particular locality, to a particular racial group, or to a particular social class, then our group will be a "selected" one. Selection may be, and usually is, both unintentional and unforeseen. By influencing the character of the group, it may affect the nature of the distribution. It would be reasonable to suppose that selection on the ground of racial origin (that is, by measuring the height of only those Americans of a certain racial stock) would give a distribution with a different average and of greater homogeneity than would be found in the distribution of height for all Americans.

[1] Statistical procedures for determining the *significance* of a mean difference between two groups take into account not only the size of the mean difference, but consider this amount relative to two other factors: (1) the variability of the two groups, and (2) the number of cases in each group. To say that a mean difference is "significant," in statistical language, means that it is significantly larger than would be expected by chance in the case of two groups of given size and variability.

Selection may affect a distribution in the following ways: (a) it may shift the average or central point of distribution up or down, (b) it may lessen variability or, in other words, increase homogeneity, or (c) it may make the distribution lop-sided or *skewed,* instead of symmetrical as we find it in the normal curve.

There are many ways in which education may be selective and accordingly affect the distribution of ability found within a group. The results, however, will be one of the above or perhaps a combination of them. The selective effect of grading, for example, is shown by the upward shifting of the average of ability as we go from the lower to the higher grades. This may be accompanied by a decrease in group variability. The latter point may readily be seen when we compare, for instance, the distribution of scholastic ability among ten-year-olds in general with that of a group of ten-year-olds who are all in the fourth grade. The ten-year-olds in the fourth grade will be found to be more homogeneous in ability than will the ten-year-olds in general. This is, of course, only to be expected for the simple reason that the school has certain standards for promotion.

The Causes of Human Variation. The fact that the normal curve is applicable to chance events, such as dice throws, where an indefinitely large number of material elements are brought into play, suggests that ability is due to a correspondingly large number of causative factors. There is perhaps no single fact about our personality that is unrelated to achievement in school or in life. Differing from one another as we do in numerous aspects of our physical constitution, in the tremendous detail of environmental surroundings, and in the time and place of their interactions, it should not be difficult to conceive that we have in such a setting for mental development the source of the innumerable factors postulated by the "laws of chance." These varied psychological influences cooperate, in a manner similar to the chance combinations of the dice throws, to give us our typical distribution of ability. As Moore says, "The ability of the individual of today may be regarded as due to a very great number of elementary primordial causes, each contributing a very small fraction to the individual's ability and each primordial cause uncorrelated with every other primordial cause" (2). As things seem to work out, there are many combinations of these human factors to produce average ability and relatively few of them that will produce ability of either extreme, high or low. From another point of view, we may say that the probability of finding, or creating, extreme ability or genius in a particular child is very low because the particular combination of psychological factors sought for has to be just right. It has to be one of the exceptional and unique combinations that happen only once in perhaps thousands of times. (All the dice must fall just so and no other way before the highest sum possible is obtained.) But the probability of finding or creating average ability is relatively high because there is a fairly large number of combinations, any of which may reasonably happen, to give an average result. (The dice may fall in a variety of ways to give a sum of average size.)

It would be a hopeless task for the psychologist to attempt to identify particular causes of ability if they existed only in the great profusion and independence that may at first seem to be assumed by the laws of chance. But, as Moore points out, there is order to be found in the cooperation of the primordial causes. The psychologist can then seek the causes of ability in humanly significant groupings of chance elements, such as heredity, genetically prior ability, method of teaching, motivation through rivalry, and parental attitude. Each of these in turn may show chance variability, but we do not have on each occasion to carry our analysis to the ultimate step. We can stop at any one of these agent-groupings. In the strict sense these, and not the ultimate primordial causes, are the *psychological* factors in ability.

It is, however, only because each of these psychological factors has an internal variability of its own that we can make use of the more common scientific methods for studying them as causes. A cause in the quantitative sense is a factor which, in its own variation, affects the variation of something else. This is not quite the same as cause taken in a qualitative, genetic sense. A prior mental act, an insight, a desire, a discrimination, an intention are causes of our ability in the second meaning of the term. This distinction is very necessary if we are to understand clearly not only the advantages and limitations of scientific measurement, but the validity as well of two contrasting approaches, the qualitative and the quantitative, to the study of mental development.

Variability Within the Individual. If all desirable human traits *were* positively related, the assessment of individual abilities would be an easy matter; a high IQ, or score on a general test of intelligence, could be taken at face value as an index of general superiority, and a low IQ of general inferiority. However, the test performances of many persons are uneven, with

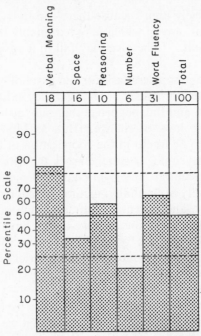

FIGURE 6. Variability Within the Individual as Reflected in Primary Mental Ability Test Scores. The profile is that of a twelve-year-old boy whose total score is at the median of his age group. The total score, however, would conceal very important differences from one ability to another. If used alone, it might underestimate some abilities and overestimate others. (SRA Primary Mental Abilities Test, Intermediate.)

some aspects of performance showing up better than others. This unevenness is called internal variability (because it occurs within the individual), or trait variability [1] from trait to trait. Thus a single test score (like an IQ) often obscures some important aspects of trait variability, since it does not tell us in what ways an individual is superior or inferior. Two children with

	Raw Score	Scaled Score
VERBAL TESTS		
Information	20	13
Comprehension	17	12
Arithmetic	8	7
Similarities	16	13
Vocabulary	49	14
(Digit Span)	10	10
Sum of Verbal Tests		69
PERFORMANCE TESTS		
Picture Completion	13	11
Picture Arrangement	30	10
Block Design	28	10
Object Assembly	22	8
Coding	52	13
(Mazes)	17	10
Sum of Performance Tests		62

FIGURE 7. Variability Within the Individual as Reflected in Intelligence Test Scores. The data above show how the same twelve-year-old boy performed on various subtests of the Wechsler Intelligence Scale for Children. His IQ scores were as follows: Verbal, 110; Performance, 103; Full Scale, 107.

the same IQ may really be quite different if we analyze their performances in different aspects of the test. The variation among the abilities of an individual is such an important factor in interpreting tests that psychologists have developed test profile

[1] "Trait variability" was the term originally suggested by Clark Hull to distinguish variability among traits or abilities within the individual from variability among individuals on a given trait. Hull also suggested some ways of measuring trait variability. "Variability in amount of different traits possessed by the individual." *J. educ. Psychol.*, 1927, **18**, 97-104.

charts, or *psychographs,* to present a clear visual picture of this variation. Figures 6 and 7 are profiles showing the variability of an individual from test to test.

When a child shows wide deviation in various kinds of mental abilities, this fact may be of diagnostic significance. If he has higher scores on nonverbal tests than on verbal tests, this may reveal a language deficiency. A person may show high ability in putting parts of an object together or working with concrete objects, and at the same time be poor in solving verbal problems. The generally superior child may have good abilities in several areas, may be outstanding in one or two, and be quite deficient in one. The generally inferior child is ordinarily poor in verbal ability, but sometimes shows outstanding ability in mechanical or manipulative tasks. These diagnostic factors pose the educational problem of making the most of the student's abilities, which is a matter of educational and vocational guidance.

Extreme unevenness in abilities also raises the question of how the child got that way. His development may have followed the direction of one or two early interests, to the exclusion of others. He may have had special opportunities for very good training in some areas and very limited opportunity in another. He may be able to improve some deficiencies to some extent through guidance and training. The diagnostic significance of a very uneven ability profile depends, in other words, on the facts of the individual's developmental history.

MEASURING RELATIONSHIPS

How can we determine the relationship between one trait and another? This can be a very practical question, as well as a theoretically important one. Normally we infer a relationship between two traits, like weight and height for example, when they "go together." The taller the heavier, we say, and the shorter the lighter. Of course immediate exceptions come to mind, and we recognize that the relationship is not one of perfect correspondence. But it exists to a degree. We may wish to know the relation between height and high jumping ability in order to know how well we can predict the ability from measures of stature. If the prediction is good, then stature is an aspect of aptitude. If on the whole, tall persons can clear a higher bar than short persons, we may put this another way and say that height is a contributing factor or "cause" of the ability. The degree of the relationship may tell us something about the relative contribution of stature to the ability.

Although the causes of individual differences are multiple and hard to isolate, a "cause" in the quantitative sense is some factor, which by reason of its own variation, influences the variation of something else. In the study of child development we want to know what factors influence the differential growth of a trait, and to what degree. We can ask about any trait, what factors comprise it, what factors can it be predicted from, what behavior we can predict from it. The method of correlation supplies some of the answers.

Correlation is a method of summarizing the relationship between two sets of data, or measures of abilities. The *correlation coefficient* (r) is a numerical index expressing the degree of relationship; it may vary from zero to $+1.0$, which expresses perfect positive correlation, and in a negative direction from zero to -1.0, which is perfect negative correlation. If the correlation between two abilities were 1.0, the amount of one could be predicted exactly from another—but such perfect correlation is never found. A correlation of -1.0 would make possible perfectly accurate prediction in reverse, so that the lowest in one ability would be highest in the other, the second lowest in one would be second highest in the other, and so on. A correlation of zero (.00) would indicate that no prediction whatever can be made of one ability from the other. Table 1 gives some typical correlations found between mental abilities, and physical and personal traits. We note that mental abilities tend to be positively correlated with one another, as do physical traits, but that correlations between physical traits and mental abilities are negative or zero. This means that a person high in one mental ability usually ranks high in another, but that the size of one's head, for example, has no relationship to intelligence. The cited correlation of $-.50$ to $-.60$ between cheating and intelligence indicates that generally (but not always) the brighter school children cheat less and the less bright cheat more. But the correlation does not tell us *why* brighter children cheat less, and furthermore does not tell us that dullness is the

TABLE 1

SOME CORRELATIONS SHOWING TRAIT RELATIONSHIPS

	Correlation Coefficients
PHYSICAL TRAITS	
Height and weight (men)	.50 to .60
Height and strength of grip	.40 to .50
Head size and intelligence	close to .00
Height of forehead and academic grades	.00 to —.15
MENTAL ABILITIES	
Intelligence and musical aptitude	—.10 to .10
Vocabulary and spelling	.50 to .60
Intelligence and school grades	.40 to .60
One school subject with another	.30 to .50
Intelligence of parents and children	.50
Verbal and performance tests (children)	.40 to .50
Intelligence and reading ability	.60
Intelligence and drawing ability	.10 to .20
Intelligence and handwriting	.10 to .20
Intelligence and mechanical ability	.20 to .50
PERSONALITY TRAITS	
Cheating and intelligence (school children)	—.50 to —.60
Introversion and college grades	.35
Self-sufficiency and dominance	.40 to .60
Neuroticism and dominance	—.50 to —.70

cause of cheating. What psychological information, then, does correlation give us?

The Meaning of Correlation. In general, a substantial degree of correlation tells us that variation in one ability or trait is associated with variation in the other. When r is .90, there is a tendency for a deviation above the mean on one test to be accompanied by a correspondingly large deviation above the mean on the other test. As r decreases in value, this tendency becomes less pronounced, and it becomes increasingly difficult to tell just how much variation from the mean of one is associated with variation of the other.

The value of r, then, gives us an index as to the amount of variation of X which is associated with the variation of Y.

When *r* is 1.0, *all* (100%) of the variation of *X* and *Y* are associated, and we may assume that the deviations on *X* and the deviations on *Y* are due to common factors; if *X* and *Y* are tests, for example, we say that the tests are measuring the same factors, no matter what the tests are called. *But the correlation coefficient is not a percentage;* when *r* is .40, it does *not* tell us that 40 per cent of the variation of *X* and *Y* are due to common factors. On the other hand, *r* can be *converted* into a percentage measure of the amount of variation which *X* and *Y* have in common. Table 2 shows how this may be done.

TABLE 2

SIGNIFICANCE OF THE CORRELATION COEFFICIENT IN TERMS OF VARIANCE *

When *r* is	.10	.20	.30	.40	.50	.60	.70	.80	.90	1.0
r^2 is	1%	4%	9%	16%	25%	36%	49%	64%	81%	100%
(% of common variance)										

* "Variance" is a technical term for variability in this connection. When r_{XY} is .50, test *X* and test *Y* have 25 per cent common variance; or, 25 per cent of the variance of test *Y* is associated with, or attributable to, the variation of test *X*.

The significance of a correlation, as well as its size, will be influenced by the heterogeneity or range of differences in the group studied. For example, we would get a high correlation between mental age and length of feet in a group of children ranging in age from three to sixteen years, but we would get a zero correlation between these two characteristics in a group of ten-year-olds because the range of differences in both ability and foot length would be much less in this group.

What is a "high" correlation or a "low" correlation? Whether an obtained *r* would be regarded as low, medium, or high depends largely on the nature of the abilities or traits being studied, and also on the characteristics of the measuring instruments. In educational and psychological testing, the terminology used in describing a positive correlation between .00 and +1.0 would generally run as indicated in Table 3.

The practical use of descriptive terms like "high" and "low" are not dependent on the size of *r* alone. If the same intelligence test, for example, were given twice to the same class and

TABLE 3

TERMINOLOGY IN DESCRIBING A POSITIVE CORRELATION

r	Description	Example
.80 to .95	Very high	Test correlated with itself, or with alternate form of the same test.
.60 to .80	High	One intelligence test with another; reading test with vocabulary test; height with weight.
.40 to .60	Substantial	Intelligence test with school grades; one mechanical information test with another.
.20 to .40	Low	Clerical ability with mechanical ability; group intelligence test with shop grades.
.00 to .20	Very low	Physical traits with mental abilities; intelligence test and handwriting.

the two sets of scores correlated .65, the r would be considered relatively "low." If we obtain a correlation of .40 between intelligence and a handwriting scale, it would not be described as "low," but as unusually high.

Uses of Correlation. The method of correlation enables us to study and measure the relative contribution of a number of factors in producing a certain trait or ability. For example, if age of children (between six and sixteen) correlates to the extent of .80 with height, we may say that age contributes 64 per cent of the variation in height found among such children. If hygienic living conditions correlate with height to the extent of .30, then this factor can be seen to contribute 9 per cent of the total variance. In comparing the two causes of growth, we may conclude that the relative contribution of age is distinctly greater. The growth of ability can be studied in a similar manner. If we took a group of fifth-grade children, measured their reading achievement, and correlated this in turn with intelligence, method of instruction, age, and physiological condition, we should probably find that these causal factors contribute in about this order to the individual differences in the group.

But correlation gives us no information about the nature of the association or influence; it does not tell us what the common factors are which produce the correlation. It does not tell us which is cause and which is effect, or whether the correlation is due to some common factors operating as causes. We cannot assume a causal relationship unless we have other evidence. It would, of course, be manifestly absurd in the example cited to say that height contributes 64 per cent of the variation in age. We may infer that the reverse is true, because we know something of the relationship between age and height, but from the correlation alone we cannot tell which contributes to which.

Some investigator (who was probably also a humorist) once reported a substantial correlation between the number of Italian immigrants entering New York and the number of forest fires in Canada over the same period; the more immigrants, the more forest fires. A true relationship, of course, does not occur by chance—there can be common (economic) factors producing both results. It would be ludicrous to assume a particular cause-relationship, i.e., that the immigrants went to Canada and set the fires. Similarly, we may find a correlation of .50 between the quality of the home and the intelligence of the children living in it. It would be a very rash person who would immediately jump to the conclusion that the character of the home surroundings influence, in a differential way, the growth of intelligence. Many other relevant data must be brought to bear on this question before we can make such a statement.

The usefulness of correlation is sometimes limited by the range of differences in the population studied, which influences the size of correlations. Thus what is found in a particular study to be the most significant factor may not turn out to be such when a similar study is carried out on a very different group of children. Thus, a study of the physical growth of children of the lower East Side of New York City might lead to the conclusion that race was more important than family in accounting for the differences found in physical size. The same kind of study carried on in another city with fewer race differences might find the opposite to be the case. The two results would not necessarily be contradictory. Both conclusions would be scientifically acceptable, but they would be applicable only to the group upon which the measurements were made, or upon similar groups.

The same thing may be said of ability. A study of reading in a school system where there was a great variety of methods of instruction in use might show "methods of instruction" to be of greater significance in the development of speed in reading than in another school system where uniformity of instruction obtained.   Our conclusions from the study of one particular group should not be extended or applied to other groups unless we are sure that the conditions are really comparable.

Substantial positive correlations show that superiority in one trait is ordinarily accompanied by superiority in the other trait, while a minus or negative coefficient of correlation indicates that superiority in one trait is ordinarily accompanied by inferiority in the other trait.   It can readily be seen that a "law of compensation," to be true, would require a large number of negative coefficients of correlation between abilities.   If to be high in one ability we must be low in another, there should be many abilities that would correlate negatively.   Such, however, has not usually been found to be the case, at least so far as the abilities that are of interest to the school are concerned.   It has rather been the unusual thing to find negative coefficients of correlation in experimental studies.   The positive coefficients commonly found have not always, to be sure, been consistently high.   And even fairly high coefficients allow for a rather large number of exceptions, in terms of individual children, to any general rule based upon them.   But if a general rule is justifiable, it must be that, in opposition to a law of compensation, superior abilities tend to be associated with other superior abilities, and inferior with inferior.   The principle has sometimes been extended, perhaps unwisely, to cover many different characteristics in such a statement as "All desirable human traits are positively related."

Partial Correlation.   Sometimes, as we have seen, the relation between two abilities or traits is accounted for not by a direct cause-effect relationship between the two but by a third factor which affects both simultaneously.   There are special cases in which we want to know whether there is any relationship between the two abilities *independently* of the influence of the third.   A classic example of this is seen in the question of the curricular value of Latin which stirred many educators a number of years ago. It was held that the study of Latin aided the development of English vocabulary, and there was evidence of substantial correlations between achievement in Latin and English vocabulary tests. This does not necessarily indicate that the study of Latin influenced the vocabulary growth, but may show the presence of a third factor (e.g., intelligence) which influenced both. It is reasonable to assume that the more able students took Latin, and that the brighter Latin students achieved better in the subject, and made higher vocabulary scores because they were brighter. The problem here is to measure the influence of intelligence on Latin achievement and intelligence on vocabulary by correlating intelligence test scores with these two abilities, and then by special statistical methods rule out or "partial out" the effect of the intelligence relationship on the correlation between Latin and English vocabulary. This is the method of partial correlation. The result in this case was a negligible correlation between Latin and vocabulary when the influence of intelligence was controlled statistically. The coefficient of partial correlation can thus be calculated to show the relation of two factors when the second, third, and so on, have been eliminated or held constant.

Methods of Control. Besides statistical controls like partial correlation, prearranged experimental controls may be used to hold constant, or eliminate the influence of, some factors in order to study another. Experimental methods are often limited by the practical demands of arranging suitable conditions. But there are instances in which the factors to be studied are easily controlled by experimental arrangements. If we wish to discover, for example, the relative influence of different teaching methods on improvement in arithmetic, we may separate a class into two comparable groups, teach each group by a different method, and compare the relative gains in arithmetic of the two groups. Or we may employ a new method of teaching one group of children, which then becomes the *experimental group*, and compare the gain with that of a *control group*, which has been taught under standard, everyday conditions. But we should note that if the two groups to be compared are not equal in the beginning with respect to some influential factors (age, readiness, previous instruction, intelligence, etc.) we would not be able, when the results were in, to say that any observed difference in gains is definitely the result of the teaching methods rather than these other factors. We must also be certain that the conditions of teaching are the same.

The more factors we try to control, the more complicated the arrangements become. How can we be sure that the groups are not different to begin with? Ordinarily this is accomplished by means of the *matched group,* by which we make sure that experimental groups and control groups are equivalent or "matched" with respect to all important factors. Two groups are equivalent if they are of equal composition (e.g., both sexes represented equally) and if the mean and standard deviation on any important factor (e.g., intelligence) do not differ significantly. One way of arranging equivalent groups is to assign students to the various groups by random methods (shaking dice, lottery, or random numbers) so that any given student has an equal chance of being assigned to either group. This allows "chance" to operate, and on the basis of chance all of the various factors we wish to control will be distributed equally among the groups. Another way of arranging equivalent groups is the *matched-pair* technique, by which each member of the experimental group is matched with a corresponding member of the control group with respect to irrelevant factors likely to be influential. Thus one member of each pair is the same in age, sex, IQ, and arithmetic ability as the other. Ordinarily, scientific experiments in psychology and education are conducted by a combination of statistical and experimental controls. Conditions of the experiment are arranged so as to control as many factors as possible, and statistical methods are used to control others.

THE MEASUREMENT OF GROWTH

We are perhaps inclined to think of "growth" as an increase in size, which we can measure directly by such means as height and weight. But the expression "growth and development" implies some change of psychological functions, which cannot be directly measured. Any improvement in mental functioning must show itself in the number and difficulty of things a child can do, in improvement in performance. It is from the performances, such as the movements the child can make, the words he can use, the correct answers he can give, the problems he can solve, that the child's maturity of development must be inferred. Just as height or weight is taken as an estimate of physical growth, so a certain kind of performance may be taken as an estimate of mental development. There are two problems here: we must select the kind of performances that will give us a good estimate of the kind of behavior we wish to measure, and we must contrive some kind of scaling procedure to give us a score. When we do this we have a "test," for a test, broadly defined, is a *sample of behavior* that yields a numerical result. In this respect, a test does not differ from measures of height or weight, except in that it samples behavior (or performances) instead of physical size.

How Tests Are Classified. The results obtained in measuring performance may be employed, so far as mental development is concerned, with either a forward or a backward reference. If we are interested in present performance so far as it may be predictive of future performance, the test so used is called an *aptitude* test. If on the other hand we are interested in disclosing the progress already made by the child, and particularly if the abilities concerned are in a special way the product of formal education, the tests of these abilities may then be called *achievement* tests.

If we are interested in neither a prediction of the future nor a demonstration of the effect of training, then we might call our tests simply "ability" tests. But such a use of this term is perhaps not very enlightening, for both aptitude and achievement tests are basically tests of ability. We sometimes find a tendency, not always clearly recognized, to give the phrase "ability tests," and also "psychological" or "mental" tests a special connotation. It then has reference to attempts to measure the more fundamental psychological functions such as visual discrimination, speed of perception, memory facility, logical reasoning, and so on. It is perhaps implied that "psychological" tests are concerned with ability in a more academic or theoretical way or with the more practical mental functions. Correlative terms, such as "educational" and "trade" tests, refer to the abilities more directly underlying accomplishment in practical life situations.

We may also have tests of *general* aptitude and of *special* aptitude. Tests of "mechanical ability" and of "musical talent" are examples of the latter. The most commonly used measure of general aptitude is the test of the ability commonly known as "general intelligence," or "general mental ability." The intelligence test, whether designed for testing an individual or a group, usually samples such functions as language usage, verbal or nonverbal reasoning, computing, discrimination of objects and pictures, and spatial visualization.

Origins of Intelligence Testing. The science of mental measurement began to take definite shape about 1900. Three key ideas or trends were mainly responsible for the development of intelligence testing. First was the concept of mental maturity, implying a process of mental development taking place from *within* the growing child—rather than mere accretion or addition, as though the mind of the child were a container for gathering and holding ideas and products of his training. This insight leads readily to the idea of a *rate* of development, which in the beginning at least was basic to intelligence testing. The second influence was the systematic study of individual differences, which began in the nineteenth century and developed rapidly through the use of statistical techniques of measurement. The third was the need for classifying pupils in terms of their abilities. This practical problem was undertaken by the French psychologist Alfred Binet, who studied those aspects of mental development so important in the school by applying the principles of measurement previously developed in the psychological laboratory. Binet's earlier crude attempts led him to believe that a kind of "general ability" could be measured through a choice of tests of "higher mental processes," and that scores on such a test might be used for classifying children with reference to one another rather than with reference to some fixed standard of superiority or inferiority.

Binet's first scale of tests was published in 1905, and consisted of thirty "tests" or test items. He learned from research what the *average* child of three, five, seven, nine, or eleven years might be expected to do on the tests. Such a scale might indicate the growth of mental ability. It might also serve to discriminate between children of the same age but manifesting different degrees of intelligence. This difference in level of mental maturity was indicated by the number of tests passed. The possibilities of his concept of "mental age"—the level of intellectual ability characteristic of an average child of any particular age—awaited one further technical refinement: expressing a child's relative ability in terms of a score. He did this by grouping the tests, assigning each one to an appropriate age group according to its level of difficulty. Now the number of items passed by any given child could be translated directly into a mental age score. The child could not only be compared with children of his own age, but inferentially at least with those of other ages. This laid the foundation for a later development, now known as the "IQ" or intelligence quotient, the ratio between mental age and chronological age.

Binet's chief contribution was his shift from the attempt to measure the "mental elements" of intelligence to measuring the child's ability to "adapt" or function in real life. This led him to devise tests of practical significance. The value of the Binet method of testing does not depend on how accurate or profound is the definition of intelligence given by Binet or any other psychologist. "Intelligence is as intelligence does"; that is, the practical value of the concept of general intelligence comes from the experimental results of testing. Intelligence is analogous in this respect to electricity; the practical use of it does not depend on defining it. The difference between high and low intelligence is discovered by its effects in life situations. Its most important features, as Binet saw them, were (1) the ability to take and maintain a definite mental set or direction, (2) to make adaptations for the purpose of attaining a desired end, and (3) the power of self-criticism. In a task requiring the child to unite the disarranged parts of a divided paper triangle, for example, the child must (1) keep in mind the goal of his activity, the figure to be formed; (2) try different arrangements of the paper triangles under the influence of this mental set; (3) judge the result of his work by comparing it with the model to decide whether it is correct. It is assumed that intelligent behavior in real life situations has these characteristics. The "performances" comprising the test are then a sample of this general ability.

The development of intelligence testing proceeded from the pioneer work of Binet. His original 1905 scale was succeeded by improved versions in 1908 and 1911. Interest in intelligence testing became world-wide during this period. A number of American psychologists translated and adapted Binet's materials for the testing of children in this country. The best known and most widely used of these early tests was the Stanford-Binet revision of 1916, based on the work of Terman and his collaborators at Stanford University. This test made the term "IQ" part of the popular language. The 1937 revision extended the range of difficulty both upward and downward, and was standardized on a carefully selected representative sample of the whole United States population (5). It is the most widely used individual intelligence test.

Developmental Scales. Instruments designed for measuring the general ability, or degree of development, of preschool children or infants fall into a special category for several reasons. First, they differ in content; tasks requiring abstraction, reasoning, computing, and verbal or pictorial discrimination are clearly inappropriate for this age group. Yet these are the abilities that constitute "intelligence" as we know it and measure it in older children. Developmental scales rely on responses that may be expected from young children, and therefore tend to sample manual performances, coordination, attention span, and simple manipulative tasks. Vocabulary responses are sampled at the upper levels of preschool age. Second, most of them are not tests, in the usual sense of the word, but *normed* *inventories;* that is, there are no "right and wrong" responses. The responses of the child are compared with the responses known to be typical of children of various ages. Thus, a three-year-old child who can do many of the things that four-year-olds can do is assumed to be precocious in development, while another four-year-old whose responses are typical of two-year-olds but can do very few of the things three-year-olds can do is assumed to be retarded in development. Third, they are more appropriately classified as measures of general maturity rather than of a specific mental function, although the various scales differ in this respect.

Growth Curves. If we plot height or weight against the age of a growing child at successive intervals, we get a "growth curve." When this is done for large samples of children of different ages, this cross section of the population gives us an estimate of the rate of growth at various ages, and of the upper limit of growth. This is a useful way of studying, for example, the differences between boys and girls. As long as we keep in mind that the curve is based on averages, that there is variability about the average of each age level, and that any individual child may vary from the average and still be "normal," the picture we get is a helpful one. However, the curve itself obscures some important data. Figure 8 shows what the growth curve for height would look like when variability about the average and sex differences are taken into account. It follows from this that any individual boy or girl may show spurts of growth earlier or later than the curve implies.

Age-Progress Curves of Ability. Just as we can picture the quantitative aspects of physical growth through the use of a growth curve, we can use a similar curve to depict quantitative increases in ability. Although such curves have been called "growth curves" and "learning curves," they are more properly called *age-progress curves,* because they show improvement with age (1). A learning curve shows improvement with practice over a short time span. The data for it are usually obtained from a group of practice periods following each other rather closely. By contrast, the age-progress curve shows improvement taking place over long periods of time. It reflects growth as well as learning; that is, improvement with age is due not only to the specific practice associated with learning, but to the more general maturing of the individual as well.

Several factors may affect the shape of age-progress curves:

1. *The nature of the ability being measured.* Motor skills, particularly if measured in terms of speed or in quality of product, show a curve indicating a decreasing rate of improvement

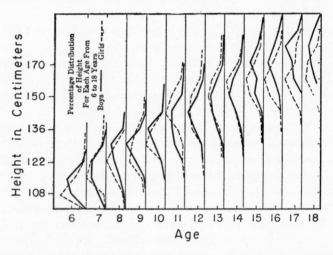

FIGURE 8. Individual Differences in Height. Distributions are shown for boys and girls from ages 6 to 18. A growth curve based on average height for each age would conceal not only the sex differences, but the considerable "overlapping" of height for successive ages. The figure makes clear, for example, that some children at age 7 approach the average height of ten-year-olds. During the teens, overlapping is greater than in childhood. (Adapted from B. T. Baldwin, *Physical growth of children from birth to maturity,* Univ. of Iowa Studies in Child Welfare, Vol. I, 1921, p. 149.)

with age. This seems to be true of the simpler mental functions, such as rote memory, digit-symbol substitution, and sensory discrimination when difficulty or speed is the basis of measurement. Even more complex activities, such as verbal or numerical reasoning, may show a decreasing rate of improvement if speed is a factor in measurement. Figure 9 illustrates this. Furthermore, a test may measure different kinds of abilities at different ages. Intelligence tests for preschool children usually are based on motor skills, while verbal abilities are tapped at the school ages. A single age-progress curve of general in-

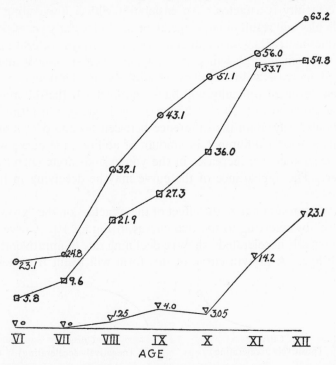

FIGURE 9. Age Differences in Reasoning Ability. The top curve represents "reasoning" or the verbal solution of thought problems. The middle curve represents the detection of logical fallacies. The bottom curve represents the ability to detect "autistic" fallacies, those involving an emotional or unconscious bias. (From T. V. Moore, *Studies in psychol. and psychiat.*, 1929, **2**, No. 2.)

telligence may conceal two or more overlapping curves for different abilities.

2. *Nature of the sample.* Curves obtained from children of different cultural backgrounds will reflect the cultural factors which contribute to differences in score. Age-progress rates

will differ in different groups, and there may be more variation about the averages in some groups than in others.

3. *Characteristics of the measuring instrument.* The tests we employ, or the way we measure the ability, may have a profound effect on the shape of the improvement curve. The level of difficulty is a factor. An easier test with a low ceiling of difficulty will result in large age increases in the early years, and smaller increases with advancing age (negatively accelerating). A more difficult test will show slow improvement at first and a rapid increase with maturity (positively accelerating). Unequal levels of difficulty will have an effect. If the difference between scores of 20 and 25 on a test is greater in terms of difficulty, say, than the difference between 50 and 55 (represents a greater difference in amount of ability), the curve will show smaller age increases in the young and larger increases later. The appearance of the curve may be deceiving in this case.

We can summarize the effect of these factors on the "growth curve" by referring to the two curves in Figure 10. Curve *N* (negatively accelerated) shows a declining rate of improvement with age. A growth curve of this form will result from tests

Curve *P*
(positively accelerating)

Curve *N*
(negatively accelerating)

FIGURE 10. Two Different Types of Age-Progress Curves. Curve *N* is typical of curves of physical growth. It is perhaps the best way to depict mental growth of functions in which speed or a physiological limit is a factor. Growth in knowledge or understanding is perhaps depicted more accurately by Curve *P,* or one somewhat similar.

of motor abilities, speeded tests, tests with a low ceiling of difficulty. Curve *P* (positively accelerated) shows an increasing rate of improvement with age. This form will result when the ability test is difficult, has a high improvement ceiling which "allows" higher scores, or when unequal units of difficulty make the younger age differences appear smaller than the age differences among older children.

We may have a tendency to suppose that the negatively accelerated curve showing "diminishing returns" with age is the more "natural" one to depict the growth of ability. We may feel that the ability curve should be similar to that of physical growth, or that it should show the effect of a "physiological limit" at the higher ages of development. While it may be reasonable to suppose that improvement is relatively greater in earlier years than in the teens due to a maturational limit, this need not be true of *all* mental abilities.

There is certainly no single growth curve of human ability. The nature of the units we employ in measuring ability will be reflected in the features of the growth curve actually found. This is why certain tests, having too many easy items for one age, or too many difficult ones for another, will not exactly parallel the findings based on other tests. Differences to be found in mental growth curves can usually be explained by keeping in mind that there are not only differences in the rate of improvement and in the age at which the maximum is attained, depending upon the nature of the ability, but that the curve of growth itself is closely related to the way in which the ability is measured.

Meaning of the Intelligence Quotient

Why the IQ? The intelligence quotient is the ratio of the mental age, as obtained from a test, to the chronological age. The mental age, as we have seen, is an "age score" derived from a test performance. The IQ, as given by the formula $100 \times \dfrac{MA}{CA}$, is then nothing more or less than a type of test score. What is its particular advantage?

Binet was aware that the whole significance of testing a child, and of the mental age obtained, depended on taking the child's actual age into account. Some children, for instance, were mentally in advance of their actual or chronological age; that is, their mental age was greater than their chronological age.

Others had mental ages considerably below the chronological. Most children had mental ages approximately the same as their chronological ages.   The differences appeared to be important. It was not enough to know the level of mental maturity attained by the child, but at what age he attained that level.   Binet himself was satisfied with only a rough comparison between mental age and actual age.   Users of the Binet tests, however, soon came to realize that some refinement in scoring was necessary. Simply to state that a child was retarded one or two years mentally, for example, did not cover all the implications contained in the measurements.

Some consistent way of expressing the relation of MA to CA was then sought.   It was found that a year's retardation in MA at age five, for instance, was a more serious matter than the same amount of retardation would be at later ages, and was actually equivalent to two years' mental retardation at ten and to three years at fifteen.   Approximately twice as many children were found to be one year retarded mentally at ten years of age as at five years, and three times as many at fifteen as at five.   The same number of children, moreover, were found to be retarded one year in mental age at five as were found to be retarded two years at ten, and three years at fifteen.   Thus the meaning of the difference between MA and CA seemed to bear a definite relation to the actual age of the child.   To express this finding, a *ratio* of MA to CA was suggested, first by Stern (in his mental quotient) and then by Terman (in his Intelligence Quotient or IQ).   Thus the five-year-old child having a mental age of four would have an IQ of ($4/5 \times 100$) 80; the child of ten with a mental age of eight would have an IQ of ($8/10 \times 100$) 80; and the child of fifteen with a mental age of twelve would also have an IQ of ($12/15 \times 100$) 80.   This identity of IQ's of the three children of different chronological ages would take into account the experimental finding that the significance of any retardation in MA was to be determined with reference to the child's chronological or actual age.

Terman found, in justification of the use of this measure, that the range of IQ's was about the same for different ages, while of course the range of MA's was not (3).   We should naturally expect to find such to be the case, if the significance of mental retardation or acceleration were a matter, not of how many years or months in MA the child was retarded or advanced, but how this amount of retardation or advancement compared with his actual age. The use of the IQ is justified whenever we wish to take the chronological age into account, and so we have in it a measure for comparing the intelligence of children of different ages.

The IQ as a Measure of Brightness. Older children are, of course, more mature mentally than younger children—the increase in MA as we go from year to year would show this—but an older child is no brighter simply because he is older. Brightness (or dullness) is a relative matter. It expresses the relation of the child's actual mental maturity to what we may reasonably expect of the average child of his age. If he is much advanced mentally over what we may reasonably expect of him, then he is *bright;* and if much below, then he is *dull.* The amount or degree of brightness or of dullness is accordingly expressed by the IQ, which is taken to mean the same at all ages. Thus an average child of five, having an MA of five and an IQ of 100 would be of the same *degree* of brightness as the average child of ten, having MA 10 and an IQ of 100, although the latter would necessarily be much more mature mentally than the former. The average child of ten would be more *mature* but not *brighter* than the child of five. Similar comparisons may be drawn between dull and between bright children of different ages. When we are interested in learning how far various children have severally progressed along the path of intellectual development, then we should compare their mental ages. The greater the MA, the greater the intellectual maturity. But if we are interested in comparing them on the score of brightness or dullness—or how they severally stand with reference to what we might reasonably have expected of them—then we should use the IQ. The greater the IQ, the greater the degree of brightness, whatever the actual ages may be. In other words, we can have dull, bright, and average children of all ages, and the IQ was originally suggested to express this fact.

The IQ as an Index of the Rate of Mental Development. Terman and others found by retesting the same children over a period of years that their respective IQ's seemed to remain about the same. Thus they had good reason to believe that the IQ not only gave a picture of the significance of any amount of retardation or acceleration in mental age so far as brightness was concerned, but it also indicated the *rate* at which a child was maturing mentally. It should be apparent that the IQ actually did indicate the rate at which the child had developed in the past, and that, with this further experimental finding, there was good reason to believe that it also indicated the rate at which he would develop in the future. If a child of five, for example, having an MA of 5 and an IQ of 100, could be expected still to have, when he reached the age of ten, an IQ of 100 and correspondingly an MA of 10, then the IQ of 100, determined at any age, could be taken as an indication that this child was developing at an average rate and that his MA would always be equal to his CA. Such a child would be one of average brightness, and would develop at an average rate. If this child of five, however, had an IQ of 80 (and an MA of 4), then his IQ of 80 (and a corresponding MA of 8) when he was ten years old would indicate that he was a dull child and that his rate of maturing mentally was considerably retarded. The bright child of five, on the other hand, with an IQ of 120 and an MA of 6, would show an accelerated rate of development, giving him an MA of 12 at ten years of age (with an IQ still of 120). The significance then of the evidence brought forward to show that the IQ remains relatively stable throughout a child's career was to make the IQ an accepted indication of the *rate* of intellectual development. If it fell much below, or much above, 100, it was taken to mean that this rate was slow or fast.

The IQ as a Measure of Capacity. The fact that the IQ determined at any age gave a reliable estimate of the rate of mental development up to that time, and that it seemed, moreover, to offer a firm basis for predicting the future rate of maturing, readily led to the supposition that the IQ was an indirect measure of intellectual capacity. We may define capacity as the constitutionally determined upper limit of mental development. Most of the early intelligence testers believed that the IQ, because of its very great constancy amid possible variable influences, really indicated a rate of development that was determined by a constitutional factor, and that the capacity or limit of development indicated by this regular rate of growth was a hereditary one. This point has developed into a controversial question of recent years, and the relevant evidence will be taken up later. It is probably sufficient here to indicate the chain of reasoning that has served to connect intelligence testing with mental capacity.

How to Interpret the IQ. It is to be noted, as a very important point in our logical orientation, that the evidence concerning the IQ has seemed to justify its acceptance as a practicable measure of three distinct features of intellectual development, viz., *brightness, rate of maturing,* and *mental capacity.* These three should be kept clearly distinct, for they really indicate concepts making different demands upon the experimental evidence offered in their support. Experimental findings may, for example, justify one of these notions to the exclusion of the others, or may corroborate one and actually disprove another. How we interpret the IQ is very important.

These features of mental development, moreover, have different practical significance for the educational psychologist. As a measure of brightness the IQ may enable him to understand how children of the same age severally profit from their school instruction and may furnish a means of indicating how the instructional methods should be modified to suit them individually. The IQ as a measure of the rate of mental development would furnish a means of predicting future progress and would suggest how a child might be guided in order that the most might be made out of his rate of maturing. The IQ as a measure of capacity would offer a basis for deciding just what are, and what are not, the significant aspects of education in bringing this capacity to fruition. Besides, it seemed to be of great importance for evaluating the relative influence of heredity and environment. Accordingly, the results of an experiment in intelligence testing should be clearly envisaged with regard to what they purport to offer: a measure of brightness, of rate of maturing, or of mental capacity.

Significance of Mental Age. It is often important to know the variation in mental age within a particular group. This knowledge can be employed both in sectioning classes and in understanding the special problems of the individual child. We must keep in mind the principle that the MA is a test score, and the IQ a test score in relation to the age of the individual. The use which may be made of MA on the one hand, and of the IQ on the other, depends upon their respective characteristics as indices of mentality and on their implications. When we ask "What kind of intelligence does the child have?" we may receive our answer in either of two forms, in terms descriptive of his present maturity, or in terms referring primarily to his future mental development. Since a child's MA and his IQ are not directly related, the size of one being no immediate indication of the size of the other, which index we shall appeal to will depend on our purpose of the moment.

Mental Age indicates the level of maturity attained by the child at the time of testing, or his *present* mental maturity. Its educational significance may be looked for in connection with the school work now actually being done by the pupil. It should offer us some explanation of the relative ease or difficulty of the work of his grade, and tell us why he may not be keeping in line educationally with the other children. It may indicate whether he has the ability to grasp certain fundamental facts or principles, and whether he really needs to put forth much or little effort in order to do so. We may also look to mental age for cues as to differences in the rate of learning, and differences in teaching methods that may be suitable for one level of maturity but not for another. It may furnish a logical basis for classifying pupils in a grade so that the different sections may be more homogeneous in their general ability.

The Intelligence Quotient, on the other hand, may be expected to show its educational significance in connection with the fact that it is a measure predictive of *future* ability. It indicates the rate of mental development which becomes of significance whenever the child's later career is in question. We may look for evidence of this in the rate of progress of the child through the school system, in the prediction of his ability to do, say, high school or college work, or to carry on the work of a vocation, and in the type of curricular offerings best suited to his particular needs.

The Mental Age of Adults. The concept of mental age in the case of children implies that mental age is an index of mental development. With older adolescents and with adults, this concept is less meaningful, because the age differences in test performance after age 15 are insignificant. In fact there is not *much* difference between age 13 and 14, and still less between 14 and 15—as compared, say, with the age differences in performance between age 6 and age 7. Almost since the beginning of intelligence testing the application of MA and IQ, which are demonstrably useful concepts for testing children, to the measurement of adolescent and adult intelligence has presented a thorny problem.

The first difficulty, of course, is the question "What CA shall be used as a divisor in calculating IQ?" In computing the IQ for adults, actual chronological age could not be used because this would lead to an artificial decrease in the size of the IQ with advancing age. Since test performance was not found to increase with age beyond a certain age point, it seemed logical to use that "certain point" as a divisor. That point would be the age beyond which the *average* person did not increase his test score, or the "final mental age of the average adult." In the early days of intelligence testing it was tentatively assumed that an MA of 16 might well represent normal adult intelligence. The extensive testing of soldiers in World War I, however, found the average soldier to have a Binet MA of less than 14. This finding provoked a great deal of discussion about the "true" mental age of the average adult.

The problem was (and is) a difficult theoretical one, and its solution depends on adequate data on the whole course and nature of mental growth. Prior to the 1937 revision of the

Stanford Binet, there was an experimental search for the most adequate divisor, or "final mental age" for computing the IQ. Rappaport, for example, tested 150 mentally subnormal children before the age of 14 and again around 19 (3). Employing 14, 15, and 16 in turn as the divisor in computing the IQ at the latter age, this investigator found that the second IQ was more similar to the first when 15 was used. Similar research with different kinds of subjects tended to lend support to 15 as the most generally appropriate divisor, and the 1937 Binet sets the mental age of the average adult at 15-0 (5).

This simply means that the average adult has about the same general mental ability, *in terms of a test score,* as the normal fifteen-year-old. It does *not* mean that the mental ability of the adult is qualitatively the same, that the "mental maturity" is the same, that the average person stops developing intellectually when he reaches the age of fifteen. There is good evidence to show that such is not the case. To say that we as a nation have the "mentality of a fifteen-year-old" is quite misleading. The terms "mental age" and "intelligence quotient" are actually quite meaningless when applied to adults. Their particular advantage, when employed with children, is that they tell us something about rate of development or mental maturity. When applied to adults, they tell us nothing about adult development.

We may ask why, if the assumptions underlying the MA and IQ do not hold for adults, the widely used Wechsler-Bellevue Adult scale employs an IQ score. One reason, according to Wechsler (6), is tradition or custom; most people expect intelligence to be expressed in IQ's. A more significant reason, however, is that Wechsler's "working definition" of the MA and IQ is somewhat different from the traditional one, and is particularly adapted to the testing of adults. When John Doe, a fifty-year-old adult, is tested on the Binet, his IQ is the ratio $\frac{MA}{15}$, or the ratio of a test score to age 15. If Doe happens to make a score of MA 15, his IQ is then 100. In other words, we are not comparing him with persons of his own age, but with fifteen-year-olds. To say that his IQ is 100, we must assume that he would have made the same score when he was actually fifteen years old. But this cannot be assumed, because the average score for fifty-year-oldsters, due to loss of speed and other factors, is less than the average for age 15. If we are not to underestimate the intelligence of adults, we must abandon, as Wechsler argued, the traditional use of MA, CA, and IQ, which forces us to compare the scores of adults with norms for adolescents.

The logic behind the Wechsler IQ extends the Mental Age, not just to some arbitrary ceiling like 22 years 10 months (the upper limit or "perfect score" on the Stanford Binet) but throughout the age span. There must be MA's from 30 to 80, decreasing with age to reflect the decline in test-taking abilities of older people. This is consistent with the definition of MA as the average score of a certain age group.

Wechsler went further in pointing out that *the CA is also a score.* The logic of comparing MA with CA to get IQ, he said, lies simply in the assumption that chronological age is an esti- mate of "the *expected* score for a certain age group." That is, we form a ratio between MA 5 and CA 5 and call it a norm be- cause we *expect* five-year-olds to get a score equivalent to the average of five-year-olds. Chronological age is therefore a kind of norm, and we should not expect the seventy-year-oldster to get a score equivalent to the average of youngsters of age 15. To estimate the IQ of the adult, we should compare his actual score with the expected score for his age. The Wechsler Belle- vue IQ is therefore:

$$IQ = \frac{\text{Score obtained}}{\text{Score expected}}, \text{ or } IQ = \frac{\text{Actual weighted score}}{\text{Mean weighted score of age group}}$$

This is the principle underlying the somewhat novel IQ score in both the Wechsler adult scale and the Wechsler Intelligence Scale for Children (WISC) (7).

REFERENCES

1. ANASTASI, A., & FOLEY, J. P. *Differential psychology*. New York: Macmillan, 1949.
2. MOORE, T. V. Formal causality and the analysis of mental life. *J. educ. Psychol.*, 1934, **25,** 401-421.

3. Rappaport, M. E. The selection of the intelligence quotient divisor for clinical cases between fourteen and nineteen years of age. *J. educ. Psychol.,* 1934, **25,** 101-114.
4. Terman, L. M. *The intelligence of school children.* Boston: Houghton Mifflin, 1919.
5. Terman, L. M., & Merrill, M. A. *Measuring intelligence.* Boston: Houghton Mifflin, 1937.
6. Wechsler, D. *The measurement of adult intelligence.* Baltimore: Williams & Wilkins, 1944.
7. Wechsler, D. *Wechsler intelligence scale for children.* New York: Psychol. Corp., 1949.

SELECTED READINGS

Anastasi, A., & Foley, J. P. *Differential psychology.* New York: Macmillan, 1949. Chs. 1, 3. An account of the methods employed in studying the nature and extent of individual differences.

Garrett, H. E. *Great experiments in psychology.* (Rev. ed.) New York: Appleton-Century-Crofts, 1951. See chapter on development of the Binet scale.

Goodenough, F. L. The measurement of mental growth in childhood. In Carmichael, L. (Ed.), *Manual of child psychology.* New York: Wiley, 1946.

Levinson, H. C. *The science of chance: from probability to statistics.* New York: Rinehart, 1950. A nontechnical discussion of the logic underlying statistics and measurement.

Terman, L. M., & Merrill, M. *Measuring intelligence.* Boston: Houghton Mifflin, 1937. A description of the Stanford-Binet scale.

Tyler, L. *Psychology of human differences.* New York: Appleton-Century-Crofts, 1947.

Wechsler, D. *The range of human capacities.* (Rev. ed.) Baltimore: Williams & Wilkins, 1951. Presents a wealth of factual data on human variability.

Wechsler, D. *The measurement of adult intelligence.* Baltimore: Williams & Wilkins, 1944.

4

GROWTH AND MATURATION

WHEN we speak of a child "developing" or "maturing," we usually refer to the improvement of such psychological functions as movement skills, sensory abilities, thinking, adapting to conditions in his environment, and emotional reactions. The tangible evidence of development is always improved performance. From one point of view these performances are the products of learning or experience, because every improvement in behavior can be traced back to situations which afforded training or practice. But mental development does not result from experience alone. If it did, the more training or practice a child received the faster would be his pace of development. This notion is quite common, but is based on a "half-truth." According to this line of thinking, the proper way to raise a child would consist of creating the best of all possible conditions and pushing, forcing, and otherwise stimulating him to greater improvement in performance, in much the same way that we grow flowers in hothouses. However, just as we cannot grow petunias as big as sunflowers through such a process, there are limits to the results we may expect in the child from developmental stimulants.

Psychological development is a complex result of the *interaction* of three sets of factors. One set we call "hereditary." These are what the child starts with at the moment of conception. Another set of factors, sometimes called "maturational," seems to regulate or control the rate of development of the child from within, the growing organism as it were setting its own pace. This internal growth principle would seem to be largely governed by the child's heredity, but not entirely so. The third set of factors, usually called "experience," consists of the stimulation the child receives from without: his training or learning. We cannot form a correct notion of child development from just one or two of these factors; all three operate together. A great deal of research with children and other organisms shows that we cannot overstress or neglect any of the three if we are to have anything but a one-sided and wrong-headed view of child education.

Some Principles of Heredity

The science of genetics does not attempt to explain the existence of living beings. It is concerned more directly with the way in which these living beings differ from one another. The early Scholastic philosophers, even while strongly upholding the doctrine of man's spiritual nature, readily accepted the possibility that heredity may influence mental traits in this manner. They not only gave place among their mental faculties to sensuous and instinctive functions arising in the racial inheritance of the animal, but even in the case of purely intellectual operations they implied at least a differential heredity. "The diversity of souls," it was said, "proceeds from the manifold commensurate relation of souls to bodies, for this soul is commensurate with this body and not with that, that soul with another body, and so on" (34). When we ask without qualification the question, Can heredity influence mental traits? there can really be only one answer.

The question of heredity is important in psychological development because heredity is what the individual starts with. At the moment of conception, the single cell contains the determiners of the organism's structure and functions, and the basis for mental traits dependent on these has already been laid down. Sex, for example, is one basis. The big question, so far as education is concerned, is whether that cell, on the basis of what it contains, can or cannot develop into a poet, a mechanical wizard, a musician, a solver of quadratic equations or problems in fractions, or a helpless human vegetable who cannot count beyond 10. The die is cast, but how does it read? Is the final outcome inevitable?

The principles discussed here make up the essentials of what every person—and particularly the teacher—should know about heredity. For some reason, popular notions of heredity have lagged considerably behind the progress of the science of genetics, and misunderstandings are widespread. One reason is that we often use the word heredity in an analogous way, as in "cultural heritage" and "social heredity," and many people talk about inheriting ideas as readily as they talk about inheriting money. To begin with, heredity means *biological* heredity and refers to organic processes only.

The Anatomical Basis of Heredity. All the inherited characters are present in the single cell present at conception. The sperm brings some and the ovum brings some; nothing of a hereditary nature is added later. The hereditary contribution of either parent to the traits of his offspring is *germinal, not somatic*. In other words, the sex or germ cells which the parent carries, and not the body (soma) cells, determine what is inherited. Both the father and mother, at the time of their own births, had in their sex organs the germ cells from which sperms and eggs were eventually produced.

At one time it was believed that the chromosomes and genes were contributed by various parts of the parent body, so that the offspring would become a "blend" in this way. Plausible though this may seem, geneticists have established the fact that the chromosomes and genes are not something the individual parent produces himself, but something which he inherited and which he passes on. Bodies are therefore said to act as "hosts," each generation of hosts passing along chromosomes and genes to the next, and contributing nothing except what they received. We know that individuals change, and the individuals of succeeding generations change, but the hereditary characters (chromosomes and genes) are not affected by behavioral changes in the individuals who carry them. A child is not the hereditary result of the parents' intelligence, personality, or physical characteristics at the time it is conceived, but the hereditary result of what the parents inherited from their ancestors.

Genes are believed to be highly complex protein molecules which operate as catalysts; that is, they produce changes in the body tissues without being changed themselves. No one has ever seen a gene or seen it work, so their functions are inferred from the results produced. The function of genes is to effect the specialization of cell growth, or the differential development of the body materials into cells of nerve, muscle, brain, blood, skin, and the like—and, deserving of special mention—the germ or reproductive cells. In other words, each gene has a specialized job to do in influencing the construction of some body tissue. One of the effects of gene action is to reproduce exact replicas of the original chromosomes and genes in each body cell, including the germ cells. As each cell splits to become two (mitosis), the two daughter cells get identical sets of chromosomes and genes. Every body cell is thus identical in heredity.

Another word about genes. They differ in their working characteristics as well as in their properties as determinants. Chemically speaking, gene functions are determined by their structure, i.e., by the arrangement of atoms comprising the protein molecules, but (by analogy only) it is possible to conceive of them as different in "traits."

. . . There are strong (dominant) genes and weak (recessive) genes; highly active genes and sluggish genes; superior genes and inferior genes; constructive genes and destructive genes; steady, dependable genes and temperamental genes; genes which will work one way with some companions, and in an entirely different way with other gene company. In fact, if we endow them with personalities, genes individually have as many different characteristics as have the people they create. (26, p. 62)

Some changes in gene or chromosome structure, called "mutations," may affect the action of genes. However, these events are very rare, and so far as human heredity is concerned, they are not subject to control. Animal mutations, on the whole, produce undesirable traits rather than beneficial ones. It is generally accepted by geneticists that there is no known convenient means whereby the behavior of the parent can influence the germ plasma.

. . . No non-hereditary trait in a person's body developed during his or her lifetime can cause the genes to change so that they will produce a similar trait in the child. And nothing that we ourselves or any scientist is now able to do can change the makeup of our germ cells in any specified direction. (26, p. 15)

From studies of inherited traits it would appear that the genes are very stable units biologically. A unit character may appear, disappear, and reappear unchanged through many generations of offspring, in spite of the varied associations or combinations that it may be found to form with other traits. The germinal complex of genes or germ plasm does not seem capable of being altered in any fundamental way by any process of breeding or selection of stock. Selective breeding may operate to eliminate some genes from the stock and preserve others, but it does not create new genes or alter the old. The end result is determined by the germinal complex with which we start in our selective breeding experiments, although it may turn out that the final product is representative chiefly of the better genes, the poorer ones having been eliminated along the way.

This principle has a very important corollary. It implies that the nature of the original germ plasm places definite limits on what we may expect to derive in the way of inherited traits from a selective breeding experiment or a eugenical program. The hereditary potencies of the genes are apparently not subject to being raised or lowered through such means.

Germinal Constitution and Environment. In popular usage, "environment" consists of our surroundings, i.e., everything except the self. Since the food we eat becomes part of the organism, we may well ask when the food stops being "environment." The scientific answer is "never." From the point of view of genetics, environment is a name for all the developmental influences except those contained in the chromosomes and genes. Even this distinction is not so simple. Consider the following questions:

1. Adjacent chromosomes in the germ cell may get twisted around each other, break off in segments, and exchange

genes in different combinations. This may affect the working characteristics of genes. Heredity or environment?

2. The influence of a gene may be affected by the genetic
environment, i.e., by the company of other genes. Heredity
or environment?

3. The influence of genes depends to some extent on the chemical composition and nutrition of the body cell they are working in. Heredity or environment?

4. After splitting, two monozygotic twins compete for food
and space to move within the uterus. One gets the upper
hand and develops faster. Heredity or environment?

The last question is the easiest to answer. No two organisms
ever share an identical environment, even in the prenatal state.
No sharp division can be made between heredity and environment in their relative effect on development. Chromosomes
and genes operate within an *intracell* environment, and every
cell has an environment of other cells, or *intercell* environment.
The germinal *constitution* or germinal complex (genes) influences and is influenced by environment from the moment of
conception.

No trait per se is inherited or transmitted by heredity. To
speak of the trait itself as being passed on, unless our expression
is only a matter of convenience for the sake of avoiding an
awkward circumlocution, is reminiscent of the first microscopist
who thought he saw a little man, or *homunculus,* in human
sperm. Common expressions often seem to imply a similar
"unfolding" of the trait contained within the germ plasm. It
is not the trait but the gene or germinal complex that is transmitted from generation to generation. What this germinal
complex will produce in the development of the individual will
depend upon its orderly interaction with an environment. That
is, a trait is the product of both the germinal determiners and
the physiological conditions of development. *Every trait is a
product of development.* We have inherited none of our human behavioral characteristics ready-made.

Genetics of Inherited Traits. We might summarize the
foregoing remarks as follows: the hereditary traits produced in

the offspring will depend on (a) the physical constitution of the gene itself as a differential factor, (b) its interaction with other genes of the germinal complex, and (c) the influence of the environment (both uterine and external) upon the trend of development in the animal, conditioned by the germinal complex.

Prediction of inherited traits is very complicated, because a single gene may influence many different traits while a number of genes operating together may produce a single trait. Some of the principles affecting the inheritance of unit characters were first demonstrated by the Austrian monk Mendel, and have since become known as "Mendelian laws." Like all laws, they can be employed as a basis for prediction, and have been very generally confirmed in accurate studies of many inherited traits. It is sufficient for their scientific confirmation in many cases, however, if it can be accurately predicted that *so many* of the offspring, or that such and such a *percentage* of the offspring, will show a particular trait. It cannot reasonably be required of the Mendelian laws that they enable us to predict with certainty the case of every single offspring. They simply are not laws in that sense of the term. Like the laws of probability in the flipping of coins, they can never give certainty of prediction for a single incident. A knowledge of ancestral traits enables us to make better predictions *in terms of probability* than we can do by sheer guesswork, but predicting the specific traits of the individual from such knowledge is impossible.

The individual offspring, from the standpoint of his inheritance, may be regarded as the product of all the traits related to single genes, and of all the traits due to the interaction of the genes. The consequent variety within a species is virtually unlimited, since the number of genes is taken to be very great. Neglecting the variability of genes for a moment (because they are transmitted in groups) and considering only chromosomes, the mathematical possibilities are astounding. A parent animal with two pairs of chromosomes, Aa and Bb, may produce four (or two to the second power) different kinds of sex cells, namely AB, Ab, aB and ab. An animal with three pairs of chromosomes may produce eight (or two to the third power) different kinds. An animal such as man, with twenty-four pairs, may produce 16,777,216 (or two to the twenty-fourth power) varieties of sex cells.

Each offspring, however, is the product of the union of two sex cells. So the possible variety of offspring is found by getting the arithmetical product of the varieties of germ cells produced by each parent. Thus in man, the theoretical possible variety of offspring would be 16,777,216 times 16,777,216, or roughly three hundred thousand billions. This would hold within one family. For these reasons, it seems safe to say that except for identical twins no single human being has ever duplicated the genetic equipment of another, at least during historic times. Heredity makes for variety as well as for similarity.

The Genetics of Ability. The few studies available which deal with the genetic basis of human ability or other complex mental traits are very incomplete. It has been suggested, for example, that feeblemindedness may be inherited as a simple Mendelian recessive, but it is now known that the hereditary basis of such a trait must be more complex than this. Careful studies of the inheritance of ability in animals, for want of more direct authentic data, offer perhaps a close analogy for many human traits. The hereditary factors in the running ability of race horses and the maze learning ability of rats are of interest.

The inheritance of racing capacity in thoroughbred horses has been studied by Laughlin (19). After developing a scale for measuring racing ability, this author applied it to predicting the aptitude of offspring of known hereditary stock. Figure 11 shows the probable distribution of racing capacity among offspring of two genetic backgrounds, one with a "Futurity Index" or promise of 110 on the scale, the other with a "Futurity Index" of 120. The form of the distribution as well as the overlapping of the progeny of the two stocks shows that many genes must be involved. As Laughlin says,

Racing capacity in the running horse involves nearly every natural resource of the animal. It is a complex function which calls on physiological and nervous quality, together with the entire anatomical structure of the individual. . . . A structural quality like stature in man, or a

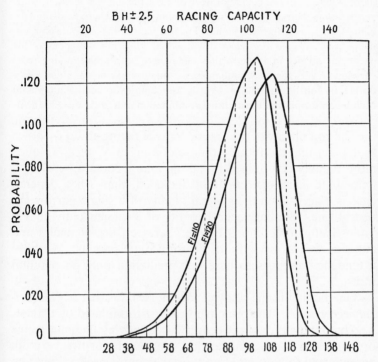

FIGURE 11. The Inheritance of Racing Ability in the Thoroughbred Horse. The curve marked "FI = 110" shows the probable distribution of racing ability among offspring of an ancestry whose "Futurity Index" of racing capacity is 110, one of the lesser grades. The curve marked "FI = 120" shows a similar distribution where the genetic promise of future racing ability among the offspring is 120, one of the higher grades. The median racing ability of offspring has been found to be higher in the latter case than in the former, but there is considerable overlapping. This is what we might reasonably expect when the genetic basis of an inherited trait depends upon multiple genes. (From H. H. Laughlin, "Racing capacity in the thoroughbred horse," *Sci. Mo.,* 1934, **38,** 310-321.)

functional quality, like racing capacity in the thoroughbred horse, far from being based upon a single or a few Mendelian genes, is doubtless the developmental end-product of a great many—possibly a thousand or more—genes. In the course of development these genes interact, some accelerating their fellows, others cancelling what otherwise would be high plus-effects in the individual. The resultant is that, keeping environment constant, the pre-selected individual offspring will possess the particular quality in an end-value somewhere on a scale ranging from very low to very high. Although such a quality may be definitely measurable, its constituent nature is vastly too complex to be attributable, in Mendelian fashion, to the additive combination of a few genes. (19)

The complexity of the genetic basis of racing ability is shown in the fact that the future promise of a given offspring is much more reliably determined by taking into account a number of immediate ancestors, collateral included, than when dependence is placed upon the general quality of a single narrow ancestral line. Similarly, the heredity of a human individual is "statistically" determined by the characteristics of uncles and aunts as well as by those of his immediate parents. We have a tendency at times to base our prediction only on parental traits.

One finding in the study of race horses was that of *"biological regression."* The principle was first formulated by Galton, who before the turn of the century was studying the inheritance of physical traits such as height. He found that two very tall parents tend to have children shorter than themselves, and two very short parents to have children taller than themselves. That is, the offspring of extremes tend to approach the average of the whole population (see Figure 12).

In a study of the inheritance of maze-learning ability in rats, Tryon (35, 36) found it possible to separate the good and the poor learners through selective breeding. Beginning with a group of ordinary laboratory animals, he measured their learning ability on a standard maze and then proceeded to isolate the good learners and allow them to reproduce. He did the same for the poor learners, continuing this selection of good and poor rats for a number of generations. Figure 13 shows the distribution of learning ability in the two stocks during the process of selection and at the end of the eighth generation of offspring.   In the latter case we find practically no overlapping of ability in the two stocks.   The nature of the distribution of

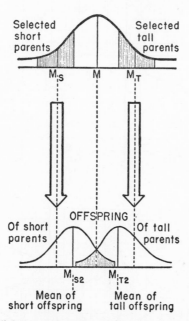

PARENT GENERATION

Selected short parents

Selected tall parents

M_S M M_T

OFFSPRING

Of short parents

Of tall parents

M_{S2} M_{T2}

Mean of short offspring

Mean of tall offspring

FIGURE 12. Filial Regression Toward the Mean. Because of the many factors operating in inheritance, offspring are more variable than their parents if the latter represent extremes in the population. The illustration shows that this variability is accompanied by a shift toward the mean of the population. The offspring of extreme parents are closer to the average than their parents. This is Galton's "law of filial regression." (From W. Etkin, *College biology,* New York: Crowell, 1950, p. 317.)

ability in both the isolated stocks and in the original animals suggests a genetic basis of "independently assorting multiple Mendelian factors" or genes.   The result of selective breeding seems to be the "gradual sorting into one race of all the genes

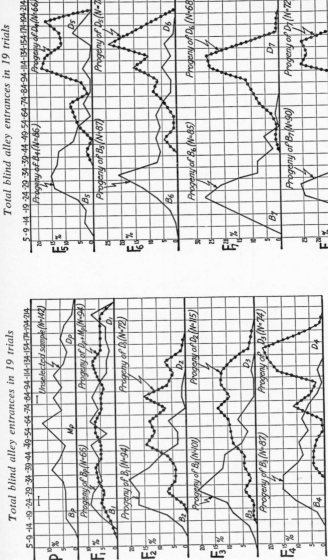

FIGURE 13. The Effects of Selective Breeding on Maze-Learning Ability in Rats. By selecting the better learners of each generation and breeding them, groups of rats consisting of the better and poorer learners respectively are produced. By the eighth generation the separation of the two stocks is practically complete. Each group, however, shows an approximation to a normal distribution of ability, suggesting a multiple gene basis of the trait. (From R. C. Tryon, "Individual differ-

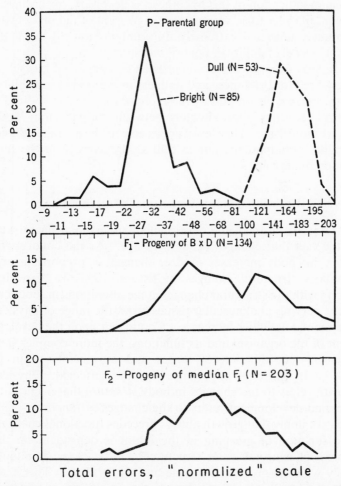

FIGURE 14. The Results of Crossing Two Strains of Rats Selectively Bred for Brightness and Dullness in Maze-Learning Ability. Relatively few of the offspring can be classified as "bright" or "dull." The F_1 generation appear to be just as variable in their performance as the F_2 rats, with the latter closer to a normal distribution. (From R. C. Tryon, "Genetic differences in maze learning of rats," *39th Yearbook*, Nat. Soc. Stud. Educ., 1940, p. 115.)

for brightness, and into the other, all the genes for dullness."
Some modification of this hypothesis is necessary, according to
Tryon, in order to account for the regression of the progeny of
extremely able and extremely dull animals toward the more
average level of ability of the original stock.

In later experiments Tryon crossed two strains of rats selectively bred for brightness and dullness in maze-learning ability.
In the *second* generation of these crosses the ability showed a
central tendency approximately between "bright" and "dull"
(See Figure 14). Very few were as able as the average of their
"bright" grandparents, nor as dull as the average of the dull
grandparents (36).

BIOLOGICAL GROWTH AND DEVELOPMENT

The term "growth and development" refers in a general way
to the fact that changes occur with age. As the child grows
older, his body increases in size, changes in proportion, and
produces structural changes in tissues. This is "growth."
Along with the structural changes come alterations in function;
as the nervous and muscular tissues grow, the range of physical
and mental activities increases. Contingent upon the development of the organism and its functions, the more complex acts
requiring coordination of senses and movements begin to
emerge and, through experience, become perfected. Physical
growth refers to the changes in body *structure* that occur with
age, and development refers to the changes of *function*. This
does not imply that growth always precedes functional changes.
The function of grasping in the infant is dependent on the
growth of neuromuscular structures, and develops simultaneously with the growth of muscle and nerve fibers. This is an
unlearned "reflex." The differentiation of abilities in handling
various objects depends partly on practice. The close relationship between physical growth and sensory-motor skills is clearly
apparent in the young child. As a consequence, we tend to
talk about "physical growth" and "psychomotor development"
as though they are the same thing, and at this stage the words

"growth" and "development" are used interchangeably with little confusion.

The Organismic Pattern of Growth. At an earlier period in scientific thought the organism was conceived to be a kind of machine, and its functions analogous to the mechanical model created by biologists from the analysis of its parts. The earlier cell doctrine in biology, for example, held the organism to be a mere aggregation of anatomical units. The earlier neurologists analyzed the nervous system into a number of isolated units called "reflex arcs." It was thus possible to think of human development as a mechanistic process of connecting together parts which had a separate unity in themselves. When development was studied in this way, some of the larger and more important aspects of development tended to escape notice. During recent years biologists have stressed the importance of the "organism as a whole," and a number of experiments with lower animals confirmed what is called the "organismic hypothesis" of development. It is now generally accepted that the behavior of developing organisms shows unity from the beginning, and develops from a unitary, coordinated "whole" (or mass activity) toward a later individuation of parts. The organismic view of development thus stresses the progressive individuation of parts *within* the whole, rather than the accretion or aggregation of originally distinct particles.

The development of the human fetus follows the form and function of other mammals during the prenatal period, and does not show distinctively human traits until nearly ready to be born. Growth begins not at birth, but at conception. With prenatal growth come corresponding changes in prenatal development. As the embryo increases in size and passes into the fetal stage, the growth of muscular and nervous tissue follows a certain pattern, which is related to a regular pattern of physical development. The details of neural growth need not concern us here, but in general a crude pattern (neural groove) in the embryo grows in such a way that the spinal cord, brain stem, and cerebrum gradually emerge. Nerve fibers grow out from the spinal cord and connect with sense organs and muscles. Growth is from the centers outward, with the main nervous pathways being laid down earlier and the local ones later. There are no movements in the embryo, and the first movements in the fetal stage (two months upward) are generalized "mass" movements; when stimulated, the fetus moves as a

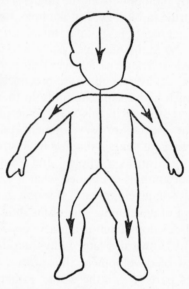

FIGURE 15. Illustration of the Principle of Anterior-Posterior Development. Growth proceeds from the head downward and from the centers outward. (Adapted from F. Goodenough, *Developmental psychology*, New York: Appleton-Century-Crofts, 1945.)

whole. The differentiated development that gradually occurs enables the fetus to respond to a stimulus in a more and more particularized manner. At later stages of development, the different parts are capable of more independent movements; a touch on the arm will provoke a specific arm movement. Still later, specific reflexes like sucking or grasping occur when the lips or palm are touched. Figure 15 illustrates the principle of *anterior-posterior development*. You will notice that there are two centers instead of one: the brain (anterior) and the spinal cord (posterior). The term *cephalocaudal* (head-tail) is also used to describe this relationship. Differentiated movements develop from the brain downward and from the spinal cord outward.

Growth is not merely an increase in size; it reveals a change in proportions. Some bodily parts grow faster than others at different stages of development, and this is reflected in the appearance of the organism at different ages. In man, the growth of the brain is remarkably ahead of the growth of the other bodily parts, as compared with the lower animals. Much of the early prenatal human growth is brain growth; Figure 16

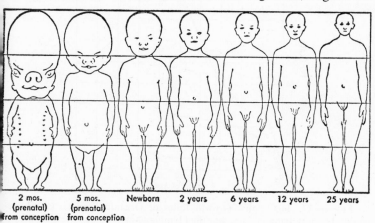

| 2 mos. (prenatal) from conception | 5 mos. (prenatal) from conception | Newborn | 2 years | 6 years | 12 years | 25 years |

FIGURE 16. Changes in Bodily Proportions with Age. (From Morris, *Human anatomy*, P. Blakiston's Son & Co., 1925, p. 17.)

shows that the head accounts for one-half the length of the organism. The newborn child has sense organs that function fairly well, but with less precise differentiation than will develop later. He responds to changes in temperature, light, sound, and to tactual stimulation adaptively, and shows a wide variety of reflexes. Growth and development up to age five is rapid. Height and weight increase, but this is less important psychologically than the development of basic motor skills. By age five the child is usually able to walk, run, jump, and handle objects almost as well as the adult, although speed, strength, and coordination will improve through the adolescent period.

Rates of Tissue Growth.   Growth curves are usually composites of the several aspects of growth; we therefore say "rates" instead of "rate" because there are different growth rates for different kinds of body tissue.   Curves of height or weight do not reveal these differences.   Figure 17 shows striking differences in rate of growth of neural, genital, and lymphoid tissue

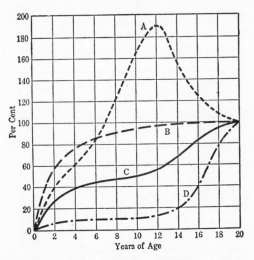

FIGURE 17.   Differential Growth Rates of Organic Tissues.   (A) Lymphoid: Thymus, lymph nodes, intestinal lymphoid masses; (B) Neural: Brain, dura, spinal cord, optic apparatus, head dimensions; (C) General tissues: Body as a whole, respiratory and digestive organs, kidneys, spleen, aorta, musculature, skeleton, blood volume; (D) Genital: Testes, ovaries, and other genital tissues.   (From J. A. Harris, *et al., The measurement of man,* Univ. Minnesota Press, 1930, p. 193.)

as compared with the body as a whole.   Neural tissue grows earlier than the others; before birth the fetal brain is the most prominent organ in size.   Neural growth continues in the postnatal period, is seen to taper off around age five, and is practically complete by age 15.   This is why motor skills develop early, and may perhaps be why the upper limit of average mental age is 15.   Skeletal growth slows down after age six and speeds up sharply at pubescence.   The relative amount of lymphoid tissue is highest at age 12, then declines, while the genital organs grow chiefly during adolescence. These facts illustrate, as well as anything, the fallacy inherent in generalizations about *"the* growth curve." Any single curve, as of height or weight, gives a relatively poor indication of physical development because various tissues mature at somewhat different rates, just as mental abilities do.

Internal Regulation of Growth and Development. There is good reason to believe that the development of a child may be largely a matter of some principle of regulation internal to the child himself. Many studies of children show regularity in the sequence of development of sensory motor skills somewhat independent of their environment.

Longitudinal studies of infant behavior, such as those of Gesell (15), show this trend. Through observation and motion picture record of many children, these studies have traced the genetic development of behavior patterns in motor skills, adaptive behavior, language, and personal social behavior. In spite of individual differences in rate of development, the striking feature is the uniform sequence of development in all children. Shirley (27), in following the development of infants from birth to the end of the second year, has shown the regularity inherent in the process of maturing. New forms of behavior or new abilities appear from day to day, but they manifest a rather definite sequence in the order of their appearance. Children show differences among themselves in the rate at which they follow this sequence, but she found only 12 per cent of reversals of the serial order established for all children. This consistency in the pattern of growth, in spite of variations in its details, brings clearly before us the significance of individual tempos of growth in these early days.

A further fact to be added to the above, as Gesell has shown, is the consistency to be found among young children in their individual rates of maturing. Not only is an advanced or reduced level of maturation likely to manifest itself throughout a broad range of activities, but the child who is retarded or accelerated at early ages tends to remain so throughout succeeding months. Figure 18 shows this in a graphic manner. While these facts do

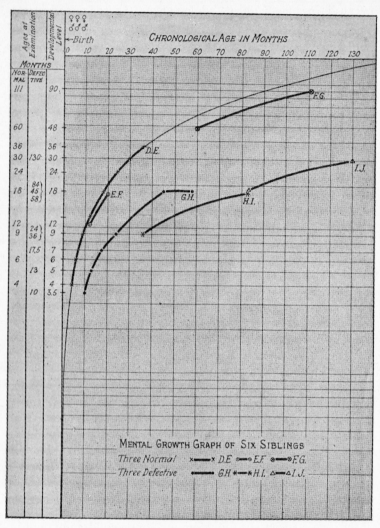

FIGURE 18. The Mental Growth of Preschool Children. These curves show considerable consistency in mental growth from month to month. The smooth, light-line curve is the theoretical curve of normal growth. (From A. Gesell, *Infancy and human growth*, 1929, by permission of The Macmillan Company.)

not of themselves prove heredity, they do seem to disprove the efficacy of the postnatal environment at least in accounting for a large share of the differences to be found among infants.

The presence of an internal regulating principle in infant development is given further support by the studies of Hopi and Navaho infants by Dennis (9). He found that the marked difference in Indian culture and child rearing practices did not appreciably affect patterns of infant development. The use of the cradle board, in which Indian infants were tightly bound during the early months, did not affect the age of walking. Although these infants walked later than white Americans, the development of walking behavior followed similar patterns. Neither was there much difference in other patterns, such as sleeping and crying. In the author's opinion, his findings confirm the view that "the characteristics of infancy are universal and that culture overlays or modifies a more basic substratum of behavior" (9).

It is possible, of course, that the regular sequence of development noted in these studies might be due to a cultural similarity in child training, rather than an internal principle regulating growth. Dennis (10) checked this with a carefully controlled study in which he restricted the activity of infants so as to minimize the role of social stimulation and practice. He reared two girl twins to 14 months, during which time they had no practice in sitting, reaching, or grasping such as other infants do. No one smiled at them, played with them, or talked to them. Instead of being retarded, both infants developed normally as compared with a group of children used as controls. The result definitely supports the inference that development is regulated from within, since "all the common responses of the first years of life may be developed autogenously . . . without encouragement or instruction, without reward or example" (10).

Heredity, Growth, and Environment. These studies prove the futility of setting off heredity and environment against one another in terms of separate bits of behavior. We can scarcely attribute to the newborn infant a certain set of special traits or tendencies, to be called his heredity, which are ready for immediate action and for receiving the "acquisitions" of experience. The neonate, it is true, does manifest inborn or congenital traits, but these as a rule are far from being specific and definite. They are the product of a previous stage of development, which in turn reflects hereditary and environmental influences, but are not to be identified in a piecemeal fashion with them. The infant's behavior is of a more general kind which is on its way to produce more highly differentiated and integrated patterns. Birth itself is but a conspicuous point of reference on the time scale marking the progress of the physiological processes underlying maturation.

Differences to be found among infants in their behavior are accordingly to be referred to a growth or maturity scale. A particular child is not to be regarded as one who possesses or who does not possess certain specific traits which other children manifest, but rather as one who has reached a point on the scale of maturity which is either in advance of, abreast of, or behind, the point reached by others. These early differences are so significant because we may regard them as the product of various individual rates of maturing, which are clearly manifest in spite of great similarity of environmental conditions. At least the variations in an infant's environment, and in respect to the abilities and traits characteristic of this early age, can scarcely be thought as extensive as those to be found in later life.

Organismic Age and Individual Differences. Different measures of growth reveal somewhat different estimates of growth rates. This is illustrated by various measures of "growth age" of the same individual over a period of time, as in Figure 19. Growth age is computed in the same way as mental age: height in inches and weight in pounds are taken as "scores," so that a height age (HA) of 6 is equivalent to the height of the average 6-year-old of the same sex, and a weight age (WA) 10 equals the weight of the average child of 10 of the same sex. The dental age (DA) score is based on the number of permanent teeth erupted; carpal age (CaA) on the degree of ossification of wrist bones, as determined by X-ray photographs; grip age (GA) on strength of grip as measured on a hand dynamometer. Figure 19 affords a comparison between these measures of biological growth and two measures of "mental growth," Mental Age and Reading Age. The average of all biological growth measures thus taken has been called *organismic age* (24).

No two individuals grow or develop at the same rate. All generalizations about "standards" for height, weight, strength, or sexual maturity are subject to modification in terms of individual differences. In Figure 19 for example, we note that the various measures of the child's growth age tend to be above the average of his chronological age group. In another child, the various measures might show a trend below average. Chronological age, in other words, is often an unreliable estimate of the child's biological maturity. Furthermore, some children fall into the category of "split growers"; that is, some measures indicate organic growth above average and other measures show retarded growth.

Individual differences in attaining puberty and physical maturity are especially notable. The pubescent period is one of rapid growth. In puberty, the gonads and ovaries mature, discharging the male and female sex hormones into the blood stream and causing the appearance of secondary sex characteristics. Differences in pitch of voice, facial and body proportions, and in boys the growth of facial hair mark the appearance of male and female adulthood. Individual differences in adolescent maturation and growth are illustrated in Figure 20. The prepubescent boy C, age 15, is smaller than D and E, who are much younger. The postpubescent boy D, age 13, is much larger and stronger than many boys older than he.

Girls generally mature somewhat in advance of boys. Sex differences in attaining puberty are shown in Figure 21, which compares the proportions of boys and girls reaching this period at various ages. In general, girls run ahead of boys at all stages in dental age and in skeletal or carpal age. Although boys tend on the whole to be heavier and taller than girls, and stronger in grip during the earlier years, girls mature *earlier* in these things relative to their own sex. That is, boys are higher in absolute amount of weight, height, and hand strength, but since WA,

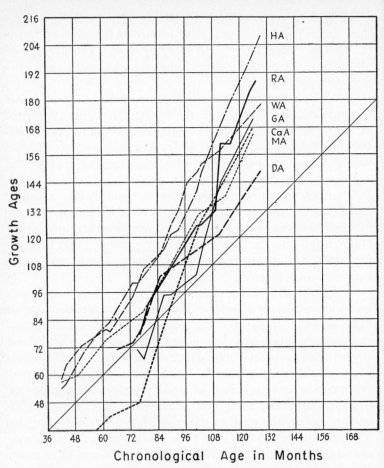

FIGURE 19. A Comparison of Different Estimates of Growth Rate for a Girl from Age 3 to Age 11. Although the various measures of "growth age" are not uniform, they indicate that this girl's pace of development is somewhat in advance of the average for chronological age (indicated by the diagonal line). Her "organismic age" is advanced. In another child, a clustering of these measures below the diagonal would indicate retardation, or low "organismic age." A very wide distribution of the various measures indicates "split growth," i.e., the individual is advanced in some respects, retarded in others. (From W. C. Olson and B. O. Hughes, "Growth of the child as a whole," in R. G. Barker, *et al., Child behavior and development,* New York: McGraw-Hill, 1943.)

HA, and GA are measured relative to the child's own sex, the measures show a higher growth age for girls than for boys. This fact is often presented as an explanation of the general superiority of girls in reading ability. In spite of individual differences in growth rates, and the fact that some children show

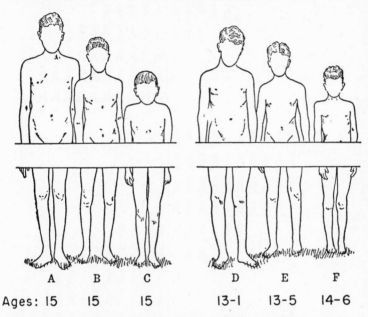

Ages: 15   15   15   13-1   13-5   14-6

FIGURE 20. An Illustration of Individual Differences in Physical Development. Boys A, B, and C are all fifteen years old. A is postpubescent, B is pubescent, C is prepubescent. In boys D, E, and F, the order of physical size and maturity is the reverse of their age order. D is postpubescent, E pubescent, and F prepubescent. (From Pressey, *et al., Life: a psychological survey,* Harper, 1939. Adapted from H. S. Dimock, *Rediscovering the adolescent,* New York: Association Press, 1937, p. 140.)

the phenomenon of "split growth," longitudinal studies of the growth of individual children show uniformity and consistency in the pattern of growth. The child in Figure 19, for example, shows at age 10 a difference of over 48 months between growth age for height (HA) and growth age based on dentition (DA). Organismic age of the child, however, is above the average for his chronological age group. Wide fluctuations of the various

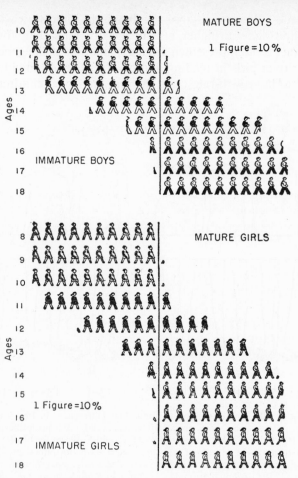

FIGURE 21. Sex Differences in Age of Attaining Puberty. (From L. L. Cole, *Psychology of adolescence,* rev. ed., New York: Rinehart, 1942, pp. 52-53.)

measures are rare for any individual. The following generalization may be made, according to Olson and Hughes: "The variability of the values for a given individual is typically less than that for a whole age group of children" (25). There is, according to these investigators, a kind of center of gravity of organismic growth which is fairly stable, in spite of lags or minor fluctuations of certain aspects of growth. We would expect a child below average in growth age to remain so in the future, and a child above average to maintain the same relative position at various ages. Growth, in other words, is internally regulated and the organism sets its own pace of development. As Gesell puts it, "each child has tempo and a style of growth which are characteristic of individuality as the lineaments of his countenance" (14).

MATURATION AND DEVELOPMENT

Maturation is the *interaction* between developing physiological functions and experience. Each stage in the development of behavior is an outgrowth of some earlier stage, not a mere addition. Experience does not supply "acquisitions" to be added to a hereditary modicum, but it works within the general patterns of human behavior to bring them to more definite, more specialized, better organized, and more highly adaptive forms. A distinction between "learning" and "maturation" is then pointless. We should not ask whether a certain act of a child is due to learning or maturation, for the latter always furnishes the background for any specific adjustment. If we wish to restrict learning to the specific adjustment itself the contrast will still be only relative, for a specific adjustment at one age becomes a general adjustment for a later age. Learning passes into maturation and maturation becomes the basis of further learning. This can happen because there are general features of the change or transformation accompanying learning which are good for other situations besides that which originally evoked it.

The rate at which changes of this kind may take place is apparently influenced by a constitutional factor. This idea seems to underlie the definition given by Courtis: (7) "Maturation is a process by which immature organisms reach a terminal state under the influence of constant forces operating under constant conditions." Maturation is not therefore mere anatomical growth and development, but a principle or mental organization which results from the interplay of organic function and experience. Maturation is often taken to be the mere unfolding of an incomplete hereditary mechanism which requires only time and the absence of inhibitory factors for it to make its appearance. Or maturation may be regarded as a simple growth of anatomical structures, which at an appointed period are thrust upon the psychological scene to influence behavior and experience in some mysterious manner. This is supposed to occur without any previous contact between such a mechanism and the sphere of experience or behavior. Such a view of development draws too sharp a line between physiological and psychological levels of behavior. It tends to look upon behavior itself as a kind of accidental adjunct of anatomical structures rather than as a dominant activity of the whole individual with its own continuous story of development from beginning to end.

The Maturation Principle. As applied to education, the principle of maturation is this: the ability to learn is limited by the degree of maturity of the child at the time the learning situation is encountered. There are practical limits, in other words, to what we can teach children of different ages, or to what they can learn. We cannot teach a newborn child to walk or talk, nor a three-year-old to multiply numbers. The level of maturity, or "readiness" to learn, is limited not only by the amount of previous experience, but by biological growth. A logical separation can be made between two kinds of readiness: that which is due to previous learning, and that which depends on organic development. When we speak of a child as not "ready" to respond to a given learning situation, we mean that he lacks the necessary ability or motivation to do so. If the lack of ability, needs, interests is the result of immaturity, we say that he lacks *maturational readiness*. In human infants, walking is learned, but it cannot be learned unless there is sufficient development of muscular and nervous tissue. Ability to talk is similarly limited by growth and development of the speech organs. The ability to discriminate between marks on a printed page is limited by the organic correlates of perception, which are too numerous to describe.

Maturational readiness is not, however, the mere result of the presence of organic structures, but a level of psychological functioning. We are dealing, in mental development, with some organizing power of the mind. Mental development shows clearly the presence of an internal, active organization of mental life and its qualitative transformation with time. The mind is not a passive receptacle for facts, impressions, and the materials of the school. While it is perhaps customary to speak of "maturational limits" or "physiological limits" as though some static condition were setting limits to performance, we must remember that the "limit" is determined from within by the dynamic nature of the living being.

There is a point here for the teacher. We do not know what the limits of mental development are, except in a very general way, for any stage of growth. In any one kind of ability, no one can distinguish between the contributions of sheer physical development and previous learning. The assumption that "reading readiness," for example, is simply a growth factor has led some teachers to sit back and wait for it rather than work for its development.

. . . The findings of child development have sometimes been interpreted by teachers and others to mean that the school's chief function is merely to provide a rich nurture for growth. They seem to assume that, if conditions are favorable, development occurs as a result of maturation or inner growth rather than as the consequence of carefully directed learning activities. For example, some have assumed that "reading readiness" or emotional and social maturity are developments which surely come with time and which one patiently waits for rather than teaches or works for. (2, p. 21)

Maturation and Training. It would not be reasonable to believe that we can explain all the mental inequalities of even very young children by an appeal to constitutional growth factors alone. Environment, practice, and training contribute a great deal. Ordinary differences in human traits are an entangled mixture of the influence of both sets of causes. It is only natural to ask, then, what is the relative contribution of each. If we compared the performances of two fully grown organisms, one of which was trained and one not, we would no doubt find that the difference in improvement would reflect the unequal training if the two were equal in ability to start with.

But with *immature* organisms the case is different.   The important question for the school is this: can we so crowd or push the training of the growing child so as to add considerably to his ability in the long run?   If so, to what extent would he outstrip another child, of equal original ability, who is deprived of this training?   And if so, how long would it take the second child to "catch up" after the training opportunities are equalized under ordinary conditions?

Studies of maturation and training attempt to answer such questions.   They ordinarily proceed by selecting two individuals or two groups, giving them unequal training or practice, and comparing their performances after a certain interval.

1. *Animal studies.*   Bird (3) studied the ability of newly hatched chicks to seize grains of corn.   He kept a group of chicks in total darkness and fed them by hand for four days, then put them with chicks which had not been restricted.   Within one day they were just as accurate as the practiced chicks.   A similar study by Cruze showed improvement with practice in all chicks, but more remarkably in older chicks (8).   He also found, however, that the chicks with the most practice, after being removed from the dark, improved the most.   Carmichael (5) raised one group of tadpoles in tapwater, and another group in a solution that immobilized them so they could not swim. When removed from the solution and placed in tapwater, the drugged tadpoles quickly caught up with the group which had more practice.

2. *Studies of twins,* based on the method of co-twin control, are perhaps more enlightening.   By making use of identical or monozygotic twins in the experiment, it is possible to equalize heredity while at the same time controlling environment. Gesell and Thompson (13, 15) submitted one of a pair of identical twins to an intensive six-week training period, at the age of eleven months, in stair-climbing, manipulating cubes, and tower building, while the other was not allowed this kind of experience.   Strayer (32) did the same kind of thing with another pair of identical twins, but for the purpose of analyzing the relative importance of vocabulary training and of maturation on speech development.   One twin was given five weeks

of practice in language usage while the other was ignored. It was concluded from both experiments that the added exercise and drill affected very little the rate of improvement in these activities. A study by McGraw (21) compared twins which were probably fraternal rather than identical. The results confirmed the findings of the other studies in certain particulars, but throw more light on the effect of early training on the child's personality as a whole. The trained twin is likely to show greater advancement in personality traits, such as courage, initiative, and activity, rather than in the sphere of abilities. This is a very important point, for it shows that it is possible even at an early age to discriminate among human traits in respect to maturation.

3. *Equated groups of children,* instead of twins, have often been used in studies of maturation and training. The design of such experiments follows a pattern like this:

Group A:	Initial test	Period without practice	Final test
Group B:	Initial test	Period of continuous practice	Final test

The two groups are equated on the basis of initial test results. One is given intensive practice, and the other none. If the two groups are equal on the final test, or even if the untrained group shows a substantial gain, this result must be a maturational effect since training cannot account for it.

A typical experiment is that of Gates and Taylor with kindergarten children (12). The children were tested for immediate memory of digits, and divided into two groups of equal ability. The final test showed the practiced group to be superior, but the untrained group showed substantial gains (Figure 22). All practice was now stopped, and several months later the two groups were tested again. Both groups showed gains over the initial test, but were now *equal* again in ability.

Jersild (17) trained children ranging in age from two to 11 in a number of mental, motor, and musical performances, as well as giving practice to improve strength of back and grip. In all cases the practiced groups improved more than the unpracticed groups. Three months after practice had ceased (neither group was trained in the interval) they were equal in everything except grip strength and singing. Even these differences disappeared after a time, although the practice effect of singing lasted longest. Again we see that the effects of intensive training, as compared with improvement due to "growth from within," are of only temporary advantage.

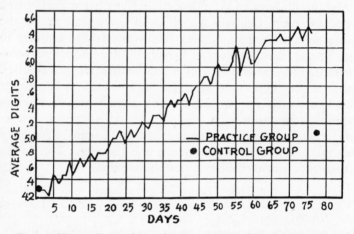

FIGURE 22. A Comparison of Improvement of Trained and Untrained Kindergarten Children in Memory for Digits. The curve shows the progress of the trained group during the training period. The large dots show the performance of the untrained group at the beginning and at the end of a period of 78 days. Some improvement is indicated here although this group had no formal practice in the meantime. After a second interval of 4½ months, not shown on the graph, during which no practice was given to either group, both groups were found to be equal again. (From A. I. Gates & G. A. Taylor, "An experimental study of the nature of improvement resulting from practice in a mental function," *J. educ. Psychol.*, 1925, **16**, 583-592.)

Maturation and Interests. A maturational effect on adolescent attitudes and interests has been suggested by a number of studies of hormone secretion. In one study (31), the Furfey scale for measuring Developmental Age was administered to a group of adolescent boys and their scores (representing degrees of maturity in interests, attitudes, goals, play preferences, etc.) were compared with the hormones secreted in urine samples (representing degrees of physical maturity). Marked differences in interests were shown between the more mature and less mature boys. Similar results are shown in several studies in which changes in interests and attitudes have been brought about by feeding hormones. This would lead us to believe that the maturation of the endocrine glands during puberty is accompanied by changes in interests as well as in behavior, although there are probably exceptions to this rule.

Maturation in School Achievement. The correlations (Table 15, p. 354) between intelligence and the various school subjects show how individual differences in general mental maturity may extend their influence into more specialized forms of achievement. The child of high IQ is also the one who as a rule makes the greater progress in his reading and arithmetic. Other school subjects may reflect these differences much less clearly or perhaps not at all. This is what must be expected, even though one credits to general mental maturity a large part of the causation of individual differences. Not all abilities are to be explained by the same factors in the same relative proportions. But our scientific studies of the past two or three decades have clearly shown that manifest similarity or difference of environment and training cannot adequately explain most instances of similarity or dissimilarity of ability. Individuals ranging in actual age from four to twenty years and above, for example, will show remarkable similarity in the extent of their general information only if they are alike in the level of general mental maturity attained. On this basis Taylor (33) compared three groups of children, a bright group from the kindergarten, a normal group from the first grade, and a dull group from an institution for the mentally deficient. They were chosen because tests showed them all to have a mental age of between six and seven. Unless we allow for the operation of some kind of internal regulatory principle in mental development, it is difficult to understand how individuals differing so widely in actual age could yet have so much in common in what they "all knew" or "all did not know." On many points of the comparison the similarities far outweighed the differences.

The loss in scholastic abilities over the summer vacation period appears to be confined largely to those subjects in which special information or techniques of work are very important. In one study (28), for example, it was shown that arithmetic reasoning ability actually increased over the vacation months while reading facility suffered no loss or change.

While such facts as these have perhaps a more direct bearing on the effectiveness of school instruction as related to age, their explanation is to be sought in terms of the same factor that largely accounts for individual differences in ability among children of the same age. It is customary, perhaps, to think of this factor as expressing itself most clearly in "general" maturity or mental age, but it should not be limited to this. In the sphere of particular abilities there are also more specific, relatively independent forms of "readiness" which give evidence of an internal regulation of their own rate of development. It is distinctly helpful to keep this viewpoint in mind, for it directs our search toward the only possible way in which heredity may make its contribution felt. Even before we have sufficient data to show that the genes may be differential with regard to ability, we can be sure that our final interpretation of all available evidence must be in terms of genetic accelerating factors in growth and not in terms of components of mental life or traits. It will be easier to attempt to draw up an intelligible balance sheet between heredity and environment, moreover, if we regard them both as the source of growth factors.

Relation of Physical and Mental Growth. The term "mental growth" is at best an analogy of physical growth. We have seen that Mental Age may be taken as a measure of "growth age" and compared with measures of physical growth. This is helpful in comparing degrees of mental and physical development, but it easily leads to a misunderstanding. Mental development is dependent upon learning, and is in fact synonymous with learning; physical growth is not. "Mental growth" refers to two quite different things: (1) the measurable *amount* of improvement in performance, such as the number of words learned or the number of problems that can be solved at different ages, and (2) the psychological organization that makes improvement with age possible. The psychological organization that makes an intelligence test score of MA 100 possible for the average ten-year-old child (i.e., his mental maturity) depends partly on the degree of biological maturity achieved. This does not mean that the contribution of experience can be ignored. If we assume that physical and mental growth are alike, we tend to attribute mental improvement falsely to a kind of hereditary unfolding of functions. Although it is common practice to describe improvement in reading or arithmetic as "growth," improvement does not occur inevitably with age, like skeletal growth, height, weight, dentition, and sexual maturity.

Older studies of the relationship between physical and mental growth were usually based on correlations between the two sets of measurements, and showed little relationship. Correlations between intelligence and such measures as height, weight, carpal index (ossification of the wrist bones), and dental age were uniformly low and insignificant. One defect in such studies, of course, is that no *single* physical measure gives a reliable estimate of organic growth. On the other hand, brighter children as a group were found to be taller and heavier than average, and mentally retarded children as a group were found to be shorter and lighter. More recent evidence tends to support the idea that "mental growth" is an aspect of biological growth, or as Olson and Hughes put it, *"achievement is a function of the organism as a whole."* These authors have shown that the Mental Age and Reading Age of most children tends to fall within the band of "growth age" scores, or in other words within the *growth pattern* of organismic age (24). Further evidence of this lies in the fact that many children who are retarded in mental age or in school achievement are also retarded in physical growth by comparison with their chronological age group. This implies, of course, that when we look for explanations of developmental lag in the retarded child, we should look first at his total growth pattern. He may be biologically immature for his age. The "retardation" *may* be only temporary. The growth difference may be evened up later, and he may catch up in achievement as well.

Reading as Growth. The importance of the maturation factor is clearly seen in the development of reading skills. Reading is perhaps the basis of all school achievement, and certainly occupies the center of the stage in the primary grades. To speak of "reading as growth" is not to imply that the ability is a natural accompaniment of increase in height and weight, or that instruction in reading is unimportant. The child *learns* to read, so reading is not a function of growth alone. But it has become increasingly evident to educational psychologists that improvement in reading is a result not only of instruction and practice, but of the *interaction* between learning and biological growth. Some children are retarded in reading because they are deficient in "reading readiness," or in other words because they are relatively immature in the abilities and motives necessary to profit from instruction. The retarded reader may be a relatively immature organism. Figure 23, for example, compares the age-for-age progress in reading of two girls equally intelligent but unequal in total maturity. Girl B lagged behind in reading ability until age 9, then improved remarkably during the next year, finally "catching up" with girl A in the tenth year. Girl B's reading age, at age 9, was below the various measures of her "growth age," but a comparison of the two girls at this age showed a difference in organic maturity of one and one-half years. This does not mean that height or weight or carpal age are the best predictors of future achievement, but it does illustrate the relation between maturation and school achievement.

It would seem that the school might gain little or nothing from redoubling its efforts to bring the immature nonreader up to "standard." Even the best remedial methods are likely to be of little avail. The principle of maturation implies that the slowly developing child sets his own pace, and it may be useless to hurry him.

Maturation and Educational Method. Inferences derived from studies of maturation have been widely applied to education. While a child is growing and developing mentally, the environment may be considered to offer him more opportunities for growth than he can take advantage of because of the fact that his general maturing is taking place at a rate largely determined by a constitutional factor. What a child gets out of his experience may then seem to depend more upon his natural motivation than upon the experiences themselves. Or, if we

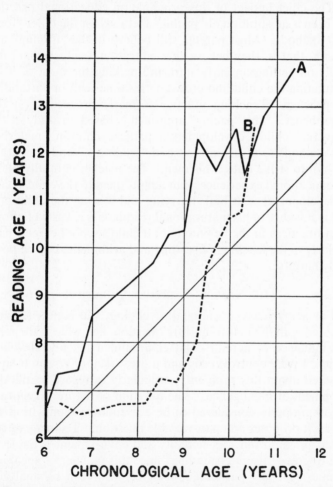

FIGURE 23. Contrasted Patterns of Growth in Reading for Two Girls of Equal Intelligence but Unequal Total Maturity. (From W. C. Olson, "The meaning of growth," in *Child growth in an era of conflict, 15th Yearbook* of the M.E.A., Department of Elementary School Principals, Lansing: Michigan Education Association, 1944.)

wish to express it a little more technically, the differential mental development of a child, in an environment that offers him more opportunities than he can profit from ("over-rich"), will be a function of his rate of maturing and not of the environment.

The chief impact of this principle on educational practice has been a substitution of "pacing" methods for the older "forcing" methods. Most parents still believe in the "forcing" approach; that is, they believe that educational achievement depends on getting an early start and making the most of it by stimulating the child and crowding his time with opportunities for practice. Teaching practice formerly proceeded on the same theory. The "pacing" approach is based on study of the individual child's developmental pattern, choosing materials and methods to fit his interest and "readiness," and encouraging him to strike out on his own. The teacher carefully plans the educational experiences, but adapts them to the child's pace of development. At best, hurrying and forcing the child at a rate in advance of his maturational readiness is a waste of effort. Such practices in the beginning of a child's school career, particularly in the teaching of reading and arithmetic, can be positively harmful.

THE NATURE-NURTURE QUESTION

For many years educational psychology was concerned and troubled with the nature-nurture question, i.e., what is the relative influence of heredity and environment in child development? Lively controversies and a great deal of research have centered about this problem, particularly in regard to the development of intelligence. The question of nature vs. nurture is now properly considered to be a pseudo-problem; in other words, it proposes an unanswerable question. To speak of the "relative" importance of heredity and environment is liable to lead to grave misunderstanding, since this manner of speaking assumes that any particular bit of behavior can be analyzed into components of the two kinds of influence. The nature-nurture question, in the form stated above, is not a sound scientific hypothesis because no amount of data can supply a satisfactory general answer. As J. B. S. Haldane put it, "the question of the relative importance of nature and nurture has no general answer, but . . . a very large number of particular answers" (16).

Trait Resemblances of Biological Relatives. Although parents and children must of necessity have a different inheritance so far as the whole germinal complex is concerned, we may nevertheless expect to find greater resemblance among biological relatives than among people taken at random. The offspring will in general stand a better chance of receiving the germinal elements producing the parental trait, and hence will tend to resemble their parents and siblings more than they resemble unrelated persons. Similarity among biological relatives in mental traits has often been cited in evidence of hereditary determination. This kind of evidence, however, is far from conclusive unless (1) it can be shown that environmental factors alone do not account for the similarity, and (2) the evidence is based on a very large number of cases, for there is no guaranty whatever on the basis of genetics that any one child will resemble his parents.

The early *genealogical studies* of certain human stocks, such as the Jukes, the Kallikaks, the Hill Folk, and the Edwards family, in which the appearance of feeblemindedness, mental disease, or talent was followed for many generations, are held at the present time to be without scientific value. They were defective on two counts: the physical and social environment was not held constant, and the methods of gathering data were not carefully enough controlled.

The *correlation of family traits* based on mental tests supplied more valuable evidence on the question of biological similarity. In general, the facts of correlation brought to light by the early studies have not needed revision. They are as follows (1):

Physical traits:

Height father-son correlation .50, height of brothers .50.

Intelligence:

(1) Biological relatives show about the same amount of relationship in intelligence as in physical traits. The correlation for both kinds of

traits in siblings is around .50. The parent-child correlation is approximately the same when the child is age 5.

(2) Children of the same family are more similar in ability than are cousins. The size of the correlation is in general proportional to the degree of kinship.

(3) The age of siblings does not seem to have much influence on the amount of resemblance they bear to each other either in general intelligence or in school achievement.

Personality:

(1) Earlier correlations of trait ratings for relatives have been as high as .50, but are of doubtful objectivity.

(2) Low positive correlations (about .15) have been reported for trait dimensions measured by tests (e.g., introversion-extroversion).

(3) Somewhat higher correlations for character traits among relatives have been found, but with a high degree of variability.

(4) Attitudes and interests of relatives correlate still higher, sometimes almost as high as intelligence.

While these findings are in accord with an hereditary hypothesis, they can scarcely be regarded as proving its truthfulness. An equal amount of similarity in respect to physical and mental traits does not demonstrate a common cause. It might be heredity in the first case and something else in the second. Unless we have the means of evaluating the effect of a common environment, we can hardly go beyond the mere fact of correlation itself. Even when studies of this kind are based upon reliable mental tests given to parents as well as to all the children in the family, a very desirable feature in itself, and even though the resulting correlations are high, this does not necessarily indicate heredity. We must first isolate the possible influences of environment. This is almost impossible to do when the related individuals are living together.

Foster-Children: Relatives Living Apart. If children are adopted into homes differing in many ways from the homes of the true parents (or from the orphanage), the resultant change in environment may throw some light on the meaning of intra-family correlations. Will the foster-child develop traits more similar to the foster family or his own family? Will the IQ change according to the quality of the foster-home environment? This question has been studied in various ways: (1) by comparing correlations of child to true parent with child-foster parent correlations, (2) by correlation of the foster child's IQ with the foster-home quality, as measured by scale of "socioeconomic level," (3) by following retests of intelligence in the foster child after placement. Several extensive studies of this kind have produced different results and conflicting interpretations.

A study by Burks (4) examined the question of the influence of the adopted child's environment very minutely. Employing dependable rating scales for home and cultural surroundings, she tried to get a measure of the extent to which these are reflected in the child's intelligence. The adopted children studied had all been taken into their new homes before they were a year old. A control group of children, living with their true parents, was matched with the foster group for variety and equivalence of home background. Burks found a correlation of .20 between the intelligence of the foster parents and their adopted children. The correlation between true parents and true children was .50, a considerably higher figure. The difference, it was thought, must be due to a factor of mental inheritance. The same kind of difference was found when the total home background was correlated with the intelligence of the child. The child in the home of his true parents seemed then to reflect his biological relationship in the amount of his IQ. The conclusion thus favored the hereditary influence as the more important.

A study by Freeman and others (11) was interpreted differently by the authors. The correlation between foster parents and adopted children in intelligence was about the same as that between true parents and their own children. This seemed to negate Burks' conclusion, particularly since children placed in "good" homes were found to have a considerably higher mean IQ than those placed in "poor" homes. However, the Freeman study was widely criticized as inadequate, chiefly because of the probability of "selective adoption." Many of the children were placed after age 4, so that prospective foster-parents might have been able to estimate the child's level of intelligence from his behavior by that age. It was suggested that the more intelligent parents might have selected the more intelligent children for adoption, and this would have raised the correlation between foster parents and adopted children. Leahy's research (19) made a point of avoiding as far as possible any influence of selective adoption, since the foster children of her study were all placed before 6 months of age. The results of the Burks and Leahy studies are in close agreement, as seen in Table 4. The

TABLE 4

A COMPARISON OF CORRELATIONS OBTAINED IN THREE STUDIES OF FOSTER CHILDREN *

Correlation of Child's IQ with:	Children in Foster Homes (Foster Parents) **			Control Children (Real Parents)	
	(Burks)	(Leahy)	(Freeman)	(Burks)	(Leahy)
Father's intelligence...	.07	.19	.37	.45	.51
Mother's intelligence ..	.19	.24	.28	.46	.51
Cultural rating of home	.25	.26	.48 †	.44	.51

* Data from Burks (4); Leahy (20); and Freeman *et al.* (11).

** The *r*'s for mother's and father's intelligence refer to foster-parent/foster-child correlations in the first three columns, and to "real parent/real child" correlations in the last two columns. With the exception of the Freeman correlation of .48 (†) the results show a relatively smaller relationship (and, presumably, effect on development) in foster homes.

Leahy study was the best controlled of the three, and therefore must be considered most conclusive.

The University of Iowa study of child placement was based on a longitudinal follow-up approach, employing successive retests of the child's intelligence after placement (29, 30). It was reported that children showed no correlation in intelligence with either foster parents or true parents at the time of placement. As the children grew older, however, the IQ's of the foster children appeared to be higher than would be predicted from their true family origins. It has been reported that even the children of feebleminded mothers performed much better on intelligence tests after some period of time in foster homes, but this interpretation has not been found acceptable for technical reasons (22).

None of the results actually permits a conclusion about the relative influence of heredity and "environment" on mental development. The home is only one aspect of environment. Such aspects as schooling and prenatal environment, among others, are left out of account. However, these studies have definitely established the fact that the home environment does influence intellectual development. For data bearing on the question of "mental heredity," we must turn to the studies of twins.

Identical Twins. These genetic duplicates are the product of a single fertilized ovum which, shortly after it begins to grow, splits into two genetically identical organisms. They are often called *monozygotic,* since they originate from one zygote (fertilized egg). Each organism, after the split, has duplicate chromosomes and therefore the same genes. Fraternal or dizygotic twins, on the other hand, originate from two separate ova fertilized by two different sperms; although nurtured and born together, they are no more alike genetically than siblings conceived and born at different times.

There is still a popular tendency to call "identical" any twins of the same sex who look alike. An illustration of the modern methods of diagnosing monozygosity may be seen in the celebrated case of the Dionne quintuplets, born in May, 1934.

How are the Dionnes known to be identical? The evidence is impressive: all five are of the same sex, the same blood group "O," the same medium brown eye color mixed with gray, the same rare eyelid pattern, eyelashes, and eyebrows. They have the same hair color (dark reddish brown and wavy), the same light and fair complexion; the feet pattern is the same, with all five having a slight "web" between the second and third toes on each foot. Their hand prints are quite similar. But the facial features are similar only in a general way, with recognizable differences. There are other differences: four are right-handed, one left-handed; four have counter-clockwise hair whorls, one clockwise; two are slightly cross-eyed and farsighted. They differ in their manner of grasping a stick (see Figure 24). But these differences, far from contraindicating their monozygotic origin, are actually evidence in favor of it. Furthermore, the differences have enabled geneticists to form a theory as to the zygotic and embryonic splitting that resulted in five organisms from one fertilized egg. Figure 25 is a diagram showing the order in which this came about. The chart shows that Yvonne, Annette, and Cecile were similar in characteristics, and they actually look more alike than the other two. Emilie and Marie, in addition to the similarity of grasping and eyesight, had slenderer faces and more sloping palates, and were the lightest and smallest at birth. The difference between these two in handedness and hair-whorls are an illustration of what is called *"mirror-imaging,"* which often occurs in monozygotes. Each twin is a mirror-image of the other, since they have duplicate traits which are laterally reversed.

Identical twins are classified as such only after painstaking investigation of their physical traits. Such investigation includes various anthropometric measurements, comparison of

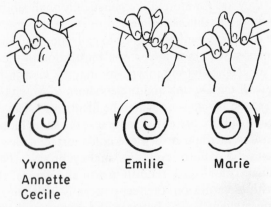

Yvonne   Emilie   Marie
Annette
Cecile

FIGURE 24. Some Physical Characteristics of the Dionne Quintuplets. (From *The New You and Heredity* by Amram Scheinfeld, Copyright, 1939, 1950, by Amram Scheinfeld, published by J. B. Lippincott Company.)

fingerprints, close examination of hair structure, and the like. Also, let us note that identical twins are not really "identical" in appearance, size, and other traits. The differences are not due to heredity, so they must be due. if the differences are noted at birth, to the prenatal environment.

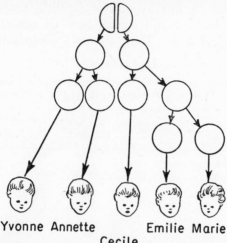

Yvonne Annette Emilie Marie
Cecile

FIGURE 25. Order of Embryonic Splitting in Development of Dionne Quintuplets. Emilie and Marie are very similar as compared with the other three quints, and are also "mirror images." This is strong evidence for the theory of embryonic splitting diagrammed above. (From *The New You and Heredity* by Amram Scheinfeld, Copyright, 1939, 1950, by Amram Scheinfeld, published by J. B. Lippincott Company. Pp. 108-110.)

Studies of Twins. Since identical twins have the same heredity, they would be the only two individuals in the world enjoying this distinction. Fraternal twins, on the other hand, must have a diverse heredity. The study of twins should enable us to compare the effect of a common heredity plus a common environment (identical twins) with that of a dissimilar heredity plus a common environment (fraternal twins).

Nature thus provides a laboratory for the study of the nature-nurture question. The two general hypotheses leading to studies of twins are these:

1. Identical twins should be more alike than fraternal twins, if heredity is an important influence. Findings of this kind therefore support the explanation that heredity is a major factor accounting for differences in development.
2. If environmental influences are important, then identical twins reared together should be more alike than those reared apart.

Concerning the first hypothesis, identical twins have been found more similar than fraternal twins on almost every kind of psychological trait. Table 5 shows comparative correla-

TABLE 5

COMPARATIVE SIMILARITIES OF IDENTICAL AND FRATERNAL TWINS IN PHYSICAL TRAITS, MENTAL ABILITIES, SPECIAL APTITUDES, AND PERSONALITY TRAITS

| | CORRELATIONS | | |
	Identical	Fraternal	Source
PHYSICAL TRAITS			
Standing height	.93	.65	Holzinger
No. finger ridges	.97	.46	"
Cephalic index	.95	.60	"
INTELLIGENCE			
Binet mental age	.86	.60	"
Otis test score	.90	.57	"
Word meaning	.86	.56	"
SPECIAL APTITUDES			
Tapping	.69	.38	"
Motor skills	.79	.43	McNemar
Mechanical ability	.69	.28	Brody
PERSONALITY			
Downey will-temperament	.31	.37	Holzinger
Neurotic tendency (Woodworth-Matthews)	.56	.37	"
Bernreuter inventory	.63	.32	Carter
Vocational interests (Strong)	.50	.28	"

tions for identicals and fraternals on physical traits, mental abilities, special aptitudes, and personality traits. We note that one-egg twins are most alike in physical traits (r over .90), nearly alike in intelligence (r .90), somewhat less alike in special abilities like motor skills and spatial relations, and least alike in personality traits and vocational interests. Presumably the environmental influence on these traits is stronger as we go down the list. If we compare the correlations for fraternal twins with the data given earlier for biological relatives, we note that they are no more alike than are nontwin siblings. Besides the traits shown in the table, identical twins have been found strikingly more similar than fraternals on such varied traits as Rorschach ink-blot responses, and the answers they give to specific questions on self-report personality inventories. Identicals are very much alike on such complex psychomotor traits as handwriting and such physiological reaction patterns as the galvanic skin reflex (6). In a psychiatric study of the twin siblings of schizophrenic patients, schizophrenia was found in nearly 86 per cent of the identical twins, while only 15 per cent of the fraternal twins had the disease (18).

In spite of such clear-cut indications of twin similarity in one-egg twins, these genetic duplicates often show marked dissimilarity even when reared together under uniform conditions. The Dionne quintuplets and the monozygote Morlok quadruplet sisters have been reported to show notable personality differences (1). On the whole, however, it is difficult to avoid the conclusion that the greater amount of resemblance shown by identical twins is to be explained on the well-grounded hypothesis that they have the same heredity. Fraternal twins, with a known divergent heredity, are apparently no more similar mentally than ordinary brothers or sisters.

Identical Twins Reared Apart. A series of interesting case studies of identical twins who had been separated at an early age and reared in separate homes has been studied by geneticists and psychologists. When located later in life, they were given many different kinds of tests and their individual life histories were recorded in detail. The most extensive study is that published by Newman, Freeman, and Holzinger, of the University of Chicago, based in 19 pairs of twins (23). (A twentieth case was reported later.) Most of the pairs had been separated during the first year of life, but in most cases were raised in homes which did not differ greatly with respect to developmental advantages.

One important aspect of the study was a careful evaluation of the differences in their environmental backgrounds, based on personal interviews, interviews with foster parents, analysis of home backgrounds and health records, school records, and other factors. Ratings of the differences in educational advantages, social advantages, and physical advantages of their backgrounds were made by five judges familiar with the data. Although a great discrepancy of actual years of schooling occurred in only two of the pairs, the range of difference in educational and other advantages as reflected in the judges' ratings was in some cases fairly extensive. Differences in advantages are accompanied by differences in IQ, usually favoring the twin with the "better" environment.

Which kind of advantages (educational, social, physical) is most strongly associated with differences in intelligence? This question was answered by correlating the environmental difference scores (ratings) with the IQ differences between twins. The results showed that educational advantage reflected the greatest difference in Binet IQ (r .79), social advantage next (r .51), and physical advantage least (r .30). The latter correlation is not significantly different from zero, considering the small number of cases. Educational advantages especially affected school achievement (Stanford Educational Age), which was highly correlated with educational opportunity.

It is of some interest also to compare the similarities of these identical twins reared apart with the similarities of identical twins reared together and with the similarities of fraternal twins. If the identicals reared in separate homes were found no more alike than fraternals, then the home environment might be considered more influential in development than the hereditary factor. This comparison was made by the investigators, and the results for height, weight, and IQ are given in Table 6. Mean differences between the twins of each group are also given. The results indicate that the identical twins reared apart are as similar in physical traits as those reared together, but less similar in intelligence. On the other hand, they are not quite as dissimilar in intelligence as fraternal twins reared together.

These data represent the best evidence we now have concerning the effect of environmental differences on mental development. The conclusions of the authors of this study are therefore of special interest. They concluded that identical twins reared apart were (1) most similar in physical traits, which are therefore least affected by environmental differences;

(2) less similar in intelligence, which is therefore assumed to be more affected by environment; (3) still less similar in educational achievement, which largely reflects environmental advantages; (4) least similar in personality, indicating here the greatest influence of environment on mental traits.

TABLE 6

COMPARISON OF IDENTICAL TWINS REARED APART WITH FRATERNAL TWINS
AND WITH IDENTICAL TWINS REARED TOGETHER *

| | MEAN DIFFERENCES BETWEEN TWINS | | |
	Fraternal	Identical—Together	Identical—Apart
Height	4.4	1.7	1.8
Weight	10.0	4.1	9.9
Binet IQ	9.9	5.9	8.2
	(Correlation between Twins)		
Height	.64	.93	.97
Weight	.63	.92	.89
Binet IQ	.63	.88	.77

* From Anastasi and Foley (1), p. 342.

The Teacher's Concept of Heredity. Our discussion should have cleared up, if they needed clearing up, some common misconceptions such as the confusion of "hereditary" with "innate," "heredity" with "resemblance," inherited vs. acquired traits, and so on. Since the teacher frequently meets with these misconceptions in relation to broad social questions, some of the implications are summarized here.

1. Heredity makes for variety as well as similarity. The variety and combination of genes may produce diversity within the family as well as similarity between families. The arbitrary notion of human "stocks" is of little help to the psychologist and misleading to the educator. "Like father, like son" as a generalization of hereditary influence has no foundation in fact. A child may inherit traits not manifested by either parent, and trait similarity is not proof of heredity.

2. Biological structure is inherited, not psychological functions. Psychological traits are not disembodied; they do have structural correlates. Mental functions are "hereditary" to the extent that they depend on biological structures.

3. Psychological traits are both hereditary and environmental. Not all environmental factors may exert an equal influence upon the development of a particular trait, and the

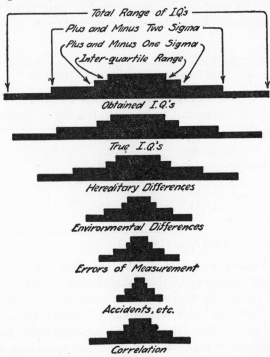

FIGURE 26. Variability of IQ's Due to Hereditary and Environmental Differences and Other Factors. This illustration is based on analysis of correlation coefficients. The top graph shows the distribution of IQ scores in a group of California children. The second graph represents the variability in IQ after the effects of measurement errors have been eliminated. The lower graphs show the statistical contribution of each factor. The bar at the bottom, "correlation," shows the joint influence of heredity and environment, since it reflects the fact that those of "good heredity" are usually raised in better home surroundings. (From F. K. Shuttleworth, "The nature vs. nurture problem," *J. educ. Psychol.*, 1935, **26**, 655-681.)

influence of any special factor may vary according to the stage of development already attained. Environmental influences moreover should not be thought of simply as modifying ones, as if the trait were somehow "set" by heredity itself, with environment entering only to modify it within rather narrow limits. The study of environmental influences has shown them to be much broader in their possible effect than this. They may produce their effect by preventing the appearance of an expected trait, by modifying the expected trait, or by inducing the appearance of a new trait that is not found outside that particular environment. In all cases the trait produced is both hereditary and environmental, and no more or less so in one instance than in others.

The teacher's attitude toward heredity should be one of respect, but not of fatalism. We should have reason to be just as "fatalistic" about environmental influences in many instances. Environmentally determined differences, once "set," may be just as resistant to any attempt to modify them as any differences determined by heredity. So while we may not be able to say in a particular instance that an ability or trait is or is not the work of the genes, it may still be possible to have a very well grounded belief that the ability or trait will or will not be altered in the future. To say that intelligence tests measure "native capacity" is not only scientifically inaccurate, but their value in assessing and predicting behavior does not strictly demand that they should do so.

The research of recent years indicates that the upper limits imposed by heredity on human development are not as rigid as was formerly believed. It seems conclusive that large differences in cultural environment can cause moderate differences in intelligence and educational achievement, and can cause greater differences in personality traits, attitudes, and interests. This does not mean that a difference in home environment, education, or social stimulation can make a genius of a moron, or a bright pupil of a dull one. On the other hand, it appears that human development is modifiable within reasonable limits, and that education can raise the general average of the mental functions we know as intelligence. Consistent with scientific findings, the most appropriate attitude of the teacher and social worker is one of moderate optimism. It must be the concern of psychologists and educators to discover and define the conditions which will enhance the development of whatever potentialities there are.

REFERENCES

1. ANASTASI, A., & FOLEY, J. P. *Differential psychology.* New York: Macmillan, 1949.
2. ANDERSON, G. L., & GATES, A. I. The general nature of learning. *49th Yearbook,* Nat. Soc. Stud. Educ., 1950.
3. BIRD, C. The relative importance of maturation and habit in the development of an instinct. *Ped. Sem.,* 1925, **32,** 68-91.
4. BURKS, B. S. The relative influence of nature and nurture upon mental development: a comparative study of foster parent-foster child resemblances and true parent-true child resemblance. *27th Yearbook,* Nat. Soc. Stud. Educ., I, 1928.
5. CARMICHAEL, L. The development of behavior in vertebrates experimentally removed from the influence of external stimulation. *Psychol. Rev.,* 1926, **33,** 51-58.
6. CARTER, H. D. Ten years of research on twins: contributions to the nature-nurture problem. *39th Yearbook,* Nat. Soc. Stud. Educ., I, 1940.
7. COURTIS, S. A. Maturation as a factor in diagnosis. *34th Yearbook,* Nat. Soc. Stud. Educ., 1935.
8. CRUZE, W. Maturation and learning in chicks. *J. comp. Psychol.,* 1935, **19,** 371-409.
9. DENNIS, W. Does culture appreciably affect patterns of infant behavior? *J. soc. Psychol.,* 1940, **12,** 305-317.
10. DENNIS, W. Infant development under conditions of restricted practice and of minimum social stimulation. *Genet. Psychol. Monogr.,* 1941, **23,** 143-189.
11. FREEMAN, F. N. HOLZINGER, K. J., & MITCHELL, B. C. The influence of environment on the intelligence, school achievement, and conduct of foster children. *27th Yearbook,* Nat. Soc. Stud. Educ., I, 1928.
12. GATES, A. I., & TAYLOR, G. A. An experimental study of the nature of improvement resulting from practice in a motor function. *J. educ. Psychol.,* 1926, **17,** 226-236.
13. GESELL, A., & THOMPSON, H. Learning and growth in identical twins. *Genet. Psychol. Monogr.,* 1929, **6,** No. 1.
14. GESELL, A., et al. *The first five years of life.* New York: Harper, 1940.
15. GESELL, A., & THOMPSON, H. Twins T and C from infancy to adolescence: a biogenetic study of individual differences by the method of co-twin control. *Genet. Psychol. Monogr.,* 1941, **24,** 1-121.

16. HALDANE, J. B. S. *Heredity and politics.* New York: Norton, 1938. Quoted by Jones, H. E., in CARMICHAEL, *Manual of Child Psychology,* New York: Wiley, 1946.

17. JERSILD, A. T. *Training and growth in the development of children.* New York: Teach. Coll. Bur. Publ., Columbia Univ., 1932.

18. KALLMAN, F. J. The genetic theory of schizophrenia: an analysis of 691 schizophrenic twin index families. *Amer. J. Psychiat.,* 1946, **103**, 309-322.

19. LAUGHLIN, H. H. Racing capacity in the thoroughbred horse. *Scien. Mo.,* 1934, **38**, 310-331.

20. LEAHY, A. M. Nature-nurture and intelligence. *Genet. Psychol. Monogr.,* 1935, **17**, 236-308.

21. McGRAW, M. B. *Growth: a study of Jimmy and Johnny.* New York: Appleton-Century-Crofts, 1935.

22. McNEMAR, Q. A critical examination of the University of Iowa studies of environment influences upon the IQ. *Psychol. Bull.,* 1940, **37**, 63-92.

23. NEWMAN, H. H., FREEMAN, F. N., & HOLZINGER, K. J. *Twins: a study of heredity and environment.* Chicago: Univ. of Chicago Press, 1937.

24. OLSON, W. C., & HUGHES, B. O. The concept of organismic age. *J. educ. Res.,* 1942, **35**, 525-527.

25. OLSON, W. C., & HUGHES, B. O. Growth of the child as a whole. In BARKER, R. G., *et al., Child behavior and development.* New York: McGraw-Hill, 1943.

26. SCHEINFELD, AMRAM. *The new you and heredity.* Philadelphia: Lippincott, 1950.

27. SHIRLEY, M. The first two years, I. *Postural and locomotor development.* Minneapolis: Univ. of Minnesota Press, 1931.

28. SISTER M. IRMINA. The effects of summer vacation upon the retention of the elementary school subjects. *Cath. Univ. Educ. Res. Bull.,* 1928, No. 3.

29. SKODAK, M., & SKEELS, H. M. A follow-up study of the mental development of one hundred adopted children in Iowa. *Amer. Psychol.,* 1947, **2**, 278.

30. SKODAK, M., & SKEELS, H. M. A follow-up study of children in adoptive homes. *J. genet. Psychol.,* 1945, **66**, 21-58.

31. SOLLENBERGER, R. T. Some relationships between the urinary excretion of male hormone by maturing boys and their expressed interests and attitudes. *J. Psychol.,* 1940, **9**, 179-189.

32. STRAYER, L. C. Language and growth. *Genet. Psychol. Monogr.,* 1930, **8**, No. 3.

33. TAYLOR, G. A. An inventory of the minds of individuals of six and seven years of mental age. *Teach. Coll. Contr. Educ.,* 1923.

34. THOMAS AQUINAS. *Summa Contra Gentiles.*

35. TRYON, R. C. Individual differences. In Moss (Ed.), *Comparative Psychology.* New York: Prentice-Hall, 1942.

36. TRYON, R. C. Genetic differences in maze learning in rats. *39th Yearbook,* Nat. Soc. Stud. Educ., 1940.

SELECTED READINGS

ANASTASI, A., & FOLEY, J. P. *Differential psychology.* New York: Macmillan, 1949. Chs. 5 and 6 on growth factors; Chs. 4, 10, and 11 review the principles and evidence on the nature-nurture question.

ANDERSON, I. H., & DEARBORN, W. F. *Psychology of teaching reading.* New York: Ronald Press, 1952. Ch. 1, "Reading as growth."

BLATZ, W. E., *et al. Collected studies on the Dionne quintuplets.* Toronto: Univ. of Toronto Press, 1937.

BURKS, B. S., & ROE, A. Studies of identical twins reared apart. *Psychol. Monogr.,* 1949, **63,** No. 5, whole No. 300.

CARMICHAEL, L. *Manual of child psychology.* New York: Wiley, 1946. Ch. 2, "The onset and early development of behavior."

COLE, L. L. *Psychology of adolescence* (4th ed.). New York: Rinehart & Co., Inc., 1954.

DENNIS, W. *The Hopi child.* New York: Appleton-Century-Crofts, 1940.

DENNIS, W. *Readings in child psychology.* New York: Prentice-Hall, 1951.

GESELL, A., & ILG, F. L. *Infant and child in the culture of today.* New York: Harper, 1943. Pt. I, Chs. 1-6, considers the interaction of inner and cultural forces. Pt. II, Chs. 7-21, describes specific patterns of behavior in early development.

GOODENOUGH, F. L. *Developmental psychology.* (Rev. ed.) New York: Appleton-Century-Crofts, 1945. For general reference.

JONES, H. E. *Development in adolescence.* New York: Appleton-Century-Crofts, 1943. A study of age changes in growth.

KUHLEN, R. G., & THOMPSON, G. G. (Ed.). *Psychological studies of human development.* New York: Appleton-Century-Crofts, 1952.

NATIONAL SOCIETY FOR THE STUDY OF EDUCATION. *39th Yearbook,* 1940. Intelligence: its nature and nurture.

SCHNEIDERS, A. A. *Psychology of adolescence.* Milwaukee: Bruce, 1952.

FILMS

Principles of Development. (17 min.) New York: McGraw-Hill. The fundamentals of growth from infancy, illustrating six principles of development.

Heredity and Pre-natal Development. (21 min.) New York: McGraw-Hill. Illustrates cell division, role of chromosomes and genes, fetal development.

Life with Baby. (18 min.) March of Time film. Patterns of growth and responses to standard tests at different ages. Photography done at Yale University Child Development Clinic under direction of Dr. Arnold Gesell.

5

INTELLECTUAL DEVELOPMENT

THE PROGRESSIVE changes taking place in the child's intelligence with age are of both a qualitative and a quantitative kind. The numerical results of testing become the basis of the study of the *growth* of intelligence, or quantitative increase in general ability. We may also regard the changes taking place within the realm of intelligence in a qualitative light, that is, in regard to the *nature* of the tasks the child becomes increasingly able to perform, and what these tell us about the genetic changes to be found within his experience and behavior. We may, for example, describe the mental maturity of the average child of five by identifying the different kinds of intellectual tasks of which tests show him to be capable. When compared with a similar description of the average child of ten, we may be able to see the character of the qualitative changes—the organizations, the discriminations, the refinements, the abstractions—that ordinarily take place during the intervening years. This should give us an understanding of the particular insights, interests, and achievements of both the five- and the ten-year-olds, so far as these are dependent upon the quality of their experience. It should also tell us, in terms of mental processes, just what is meant by "general intelligence."

THE COURSE OF INTELLECTUAL DEVELOPMENT

The Prespeech Period: Adaptive Responses. The earliest appearances of what is taken to be general mental ability are found principally in motor activities of a purposeful and adaptive sort. The neonate's responses are limited to reflexes like grasping and sucking, lateral head movements, and postural adjustments when lifted. At the age of three months the average child is able to reach for an object and carry it to the mouth. At four months he shows the beginnings of finger-thumb opposition, and a month or so later can pick up a cube clumsily and hold two cubes in his hand. At six months he has developed simultaneous flexion and thumb opposition, can lift a cup, accept a second cube when he is already holding one, and reaches persistently for objects. Motor deftness and adaptive behavior continue to develop until at 12 months he is able to hold a pencil adaptively and mark with it, and lift a cup to drink. At 18 months he can mend a broken doll and feed himself with a spoon. This gives us a picture of the progressive refinement and organization of movement, suggesting a corresponding refinement and integration of perception.

Considering perception in a rather broad sense as another sphere for the expression of intelligence, we find a similar development of differentiation and integration. At six months the child is apparently able to differentiate strangers from members of the family. At ten months he discriminates between word sounds, at one year is able to recognize common objects and is then at what Binet called the "identification stage." At 18 months he recognizes objects in a picture. His reactions to pictures pass through a number of distinct stages: (a) recognition of objects in a picture (18 months); (b) pointing out a named object in a picture (two years); (c) naming and enumerating a number of pictured objects (three years); (d) seeing simple relations and describing the picture (seven years); (e) interpreting the picture as a whole (twelve years).

Perhaps the most significant aspect of development during infancy is the perceptual foundation of language. At about 8½ months, the child attends to familiar words, says "da-da" or the equivalent; by 12 months he imitates words, and can say two or three words. From 18 to 24 months the child moves rapidly through the "naming objects and pictures" stage. The background for the development of speech appears before the actual use of language. The child very early understands gestures, facial expressions, and tone of voice. Particular sounds and words gradually take on a special meaning for him, and he is soon seen making the attempt to communicate with others. When he takes the important step toward realizing that everything has a name, he is well on the way to an effective use of language. This takes place at about 18 months.

Speech and Language Period: Early Childhood. The child's use of speech is apparently a very favorable sign of intellectual development. The mastery of language to a certain degree is the *sine qua non* of conceptual thinking and one of the best indications of a child's stage of intellectual maturity (20). Words are the counters of thought, and without a ready command of these, thinking is vague, awkward, and ineffectual. On the other hand, vague thought usually shows itself in an impoverished language.

The development of words into sentences is an interesting phenomenon. Some time after two years the child begins to make "statements about" things and people; that is, he "predicates" or uses a simple sentence form containing subject and predicate.[1] In many children this behavior emerges suddenly, yet it has a definite genetic origin. The first words are nouns, and come gradually. Toward the end of the second year comes a vocabulary spurt, and the child learns new words every day. At first his vocabulary is largely made up of "concrete" terms, but little by little adjectives, adverbs, and prepositions creep in. They do not emerge in child speech as "hooked together" sentence forms, but this does not mean that the child has not perceived relationships. He may use word-sentences, in which a single word may stand for a sentence. "Dolly" or its equivalent may mean "where is the doll?" or "the doll is broken." The ability to employ adjectives, adverbs, and prepositions, together with the use of the sentence form, is an indication that the earlier, more massive experiences are being refined and specialized.

---

[1] Predication is the essence of language. The ability to make "statements about" things distinguishes man from lower animals, makes reasoning and thinking possible, and is the foundation of human culture. Chimpanzees may learn to pronounce human words (10), but cannot be said to predicate.

The development of language influences the behavior of the preschool child in many ways. Language, more than any other kind of learning, raises the child's behavior to the human level, which is based not only on perceptual, but conceptual development. Language enables the child to (1) talk to himself and (2) talk to other people. "Talking to himself" lays the groundwork for *thinking,* not in the sense that all thinking is mere inaudible speech movements, but that it is the basic kind of "doing" that is essential for learning. Language develops the ability to respond to "reduced cues"; words stand for things. Talking to other people is the basis of socialization, for learning how to get along with others. It also facilitates the development of thinking because it disciplines his thought so that it becomes logical and communicable (6).

Evidence for behavioral changes based on language is seen in the change of play activities of children, as described by Jones (12). Under two years, children spend most of their time pulling and pushing wheeled toys, and for some time after play is devoted mostly to the integration and precision of movements essential to riding such things as kiddie cars, wagons, and tricycles. With the development of language, however, comes *role-playing.* The child is now a policeman or cowboy, or fireman, and the vehicle is a horse or fire-engine. Another development is "thought before action." Younger children are impulsive, use their muscles a great deal, get themselves into difficult situations, and solve the problem mostly by muscular effort. With language development comes deliberation, planning, and forethought, usually accompanied by vocalizations such as "I better not ride my kiddie car over there, I might get hurt." The point is that "thought before action" is facilitated by language, and should not be expected during the prelanguage period.

The child's definitions are always very interesting, both from the viewpoint of the number of words he can define as well as the form in which he expresses the definition. At the age of five he defines things in terms of use ("a chair is to sit"). By the age of eight, his vocabulary contains 3,600 words, and he defines common terms by describing the objects or by naming the substance or materials of which they are made ("a chair has a back, legs, and a seat" or "it is made of wood and you sit on it"). Somewhat later he becomes able to define words by giving the class names of the objects ("a chair is a piece of furniture"). This, with further refinement, is the stage that characterizes the adult. At ten, the child's vocabulary contains 5,400 words and he is able to name sixty unrelated words in three minutes. At twelve, his vocabulary jumps to 7,200 words, at fourteen to 9,000 and at sixteen to 11,700. At twelve, he can define abstract terms (such as pity, charity), at sixteen he can discriminate between synonyms (laziness and idleness).

The ability to apprehend relations and to orient himself in place, time, and social environment shows intellectual development in a number of ways. At three, the child knows his family name and sex. At five, he knows his age. At six, he can distinguish between right and left, morning and afternoon. By age six, the average child is well enough oriented socially and has mastered sufficient relationships through language that he is able to go to school and begin, after some elementary coaching, the difficult task of reading.

The School Age Period. The content of most intelligence tests reflects not only the central role of language in development, but much school-learning material. After age six, we begin to see the effect of the structured school-learning situation on the development of intelligence. At seven years, the child can repeat sentences of 13 words, make sentences from words like "horse, bigger, dog" and detect picture absurdities (e.g., a man sitting on the limb of a tree and sawing the limb off). At eight, he can detect *verbal* absurdities such as "Walter now has to write with his left hand because two years ago he lost both his arms in an accident." He can also name the days of the week, and tell how a mosquito and sparrow are alike. At ten, he can remember the essentials of a story about "The School Concert," and name 12 common animals. At twelve, the average child is expected to give two reasons why there should be plenty of railroads in the United States. The twelve-year-old can also infer a moral lesson from fables, after having passed through the stage of merely repeating the facts of a story. It is not until about age 15 that he can generalize these moral lessons in a satisfactory manner.

The ability to *generalize* goes hand in hand with discrimination. At the age of seven, the average child is able to give from memory the differences between common objects, such as a stone and an egg. The recognition of differences is found a year before the awareness of hidden resemblances. At eight, he can give resemblances from memory—e.g., an apple and a pear—and from this time on discrimination and generalization progress steadily. Intellectual development is particularly evident in increased ability to note essential differences and likenesses, as contrasted with those which are of a trivial, superficial, or accidental kind (19). It requires greater intellectual maturity to distinguish an egg from a stone because one is organic and the other inorganic, than to distinguish them because of shape, color, or fragility. It implies a rather mature mind to be able to give essential likenesses and differences, and when a young child manifests this kind of thinking it is a very favorable sign.

The Adult. The later stages of intellectual development, as evidenced by tests for adolescents and adults, are represented by the abstractive and relational thinking involved in analogies, comprehension, reasoning, completion, and similar tasks usually of a verbal nature. These ordinarily contain informational material of a familiar kind but put in the form of *novel* combinations. The responses are evaluated for their accuracy or truthfulness. In the past, many tests for adults were unsuitable in content because they were adapted from items that appealed to children. To assess properly the level of mental functioning of the adult, the test items must command his interest and respect. The most notable aspect of adult development in later years is the stability of the language functions and the loss of perceptual and motor speed.

Developmental Implications in Testing. Our description of the course of intellectual development makes it apparent that *intelligence may mean different things at different ages,* when the kinds of performances are compared. With what justification, it may be asked, are all these various aspects of mental development included under the single heading of "general intelligence"? Outwardly there may not seem to be much similarity between the test items for the earlier years, such as turning the head toward the source of a sound or the prolonged holding of an object placed in the hand, and the tasks found in intelligence tests for school children. We may well ask whether these can be taken as indications of the same thing.

The "intelligence" tests so far devised for the infant and preschool years are neither so consistent nor so prognostic as tests given to older children. The IQ's found for these very young children are admittedly less dependable than the IQ's of older ones. It is reasonable to suppose that these findings are affected by a number of more or less irrelevant factors, such as the great difficulty of getting cooperation on the part of very young children and the fact that failing a single test has a greater arithmetical effect on the size of the IQ than it would later on. This may account for a good deal of the variation. But, with such data as we have, we must proceed slowly in identifying the tested intelligence of the young child with that of the school child. It seems probable that different abilities are tapped by the tests at different ages. Present evidence, at any rate, shows that the prediction of future rate of development from the child's performance as an infant is not practically feasible (3).

Developmental Concept of Intelligence. An adequate definition of intelligence must be in accord with such facts of development as our short outline has suggested. There are, according to Freeman (7), other requirements which such a definition should meet. It should fit the description of intelligence based on tests for the different age levels and should harmonize with the known facts of correlation. It is probably because of the difficulty of satisfying the first requirement that some of the suggested definitions of intelligence may fit one age level very well, but seem to be rather inappropriate for earlier ages. Such descriptive terms as "abstract" or "relational" thinking hardly apply to infant behavior.

It will perhaps be most helpful in coordinating our varied facts to regard general intelligence as the level of maturity attained in the differentiation and integration of our general mental functions. This will be expressed in many different ways, depending both on age and on the more special nature of the mental operation. The mentally deficient infant will show its retarded development in the absence of taste discrimination for a bitter quinine solution. The bright infant will manifest its accelerated growth in the early appearance of the organized movement of hand to mouth. Later years will manifest differences in other spheres of mental life, in comprehension of verbal material, and in reasoning. These later mental processes need not be thought of as the same qualitative kind as the earlier ones. They resemble each other, so far as intelligence is concerned, because each may manifest the level of general mental maturity attained by the individual at the time.

The fact that most abilities correlate positively with general intelligence should also not be surprising. Special abilities may be regarded as further differentiations of general ability, effected through the agency of narrower constitutional or aptitude factors, or of specialized training material. They tend to become still more highly differentiated with the passing of time. At least it would seem so, if we can interpret in this manner the studies by Garrett and others (5) showing that the more specific abilities, such as memory, attention, and number facility correlate less closely with the central or general factor as children become older (9).

If we accept these implications, we have in the genesis of any human performance—solving an arithmetic problem for example—a certain hierarchy of developmental stages or aspects. There is, first of all, forming the basic pattern of the whole act, the general readiness for acts of such a kind, involving the insights and discriminations which are useful not only in arithmetic but in reading and history as well. This is the level of the child's intelligence. Then there is the level of the less general kinds of comprehensions and distinctions, linked closely in development, through the "number" factor perhaps and ordinary arithmetic experiences, with the more special readiness or ability for problem solving. Finally, there is the third or lowest level of readiness, arising from the child's specific information and skills involved in the very particular process of multiplying, and subtracting, and in the actual apprehension of the particular facts expressed in the problem.

The level of general mental maturity will of course be manifest in "adaptability to new situations," as some have thought to define intelligence. It will make for "good responses from the point of view of fact or truth." It will imply in the higher reaches of development "abstract thinking," and "organization of experience into new patterns," because of its differentiating and integrating character. Intelligence may also be thought of as an aptitude or power, when measured as an ability for the prediction of future growth.

GROWTH OF MENTAL ABILITIES

The measurement of mental ability at different stages of the child's growth does not tell us directly of the qualitative changes taking place within the child's developing experience and behavior. These must be approached in another way. But the study of ability and its growth can tell us many things about mental development which we should like to know for practical reasons. In planning educational work it is often helpful to know, for instance, just how difficult a task the child of a given age can do and the extent to which this mental power changes with age. We might also wish to know the effect of age changes on the number of things he can do, and the relative speed or facility with which he does them. The following questions about the growth of mental ability are pertinent to educational psychology:

1. What is the general nature of improvement? Are there any general conclusions to be drawn with reference to the growth of ability which may reflect upon the nature of mind, the part that maturation plays in development, or the mutual relations of the growing child and his educational environment?

2. Is the growth of ability regular or irregular? Does it tend to show unpredictable ups and downs, spurts and periods of

stagnation, depending perhaps upon obscure accidental circumstances?   Or do we find here sufficient regularity to be of practical service both in predicting future ability and in identifying the reasons why predictions may in some cases go awry? Is there such a thing as an individual rate of mental growth which may differ consistently or significantly from that of other individuals?

3. How are the child's abilities related to each other in their growth?   Does each tend to go its own way in development? Or are there general principles of relationship according to which superiority or inferiority in one kind of performance tends to be accompanied by a corresponding superiority or inferiority in another kind?   What does this tell us about the organization of our mental functions, and perhaps about the organization of training?

Growth in Comprehension. The positively accelerated curve, showing an increasing rate of improvement with age, is probably the correct way of depicting growth in such things as the knowledge functions.   Where it is a matter of the development of insight into relationships, organizations, generalizations, it seems that the growth of ability, as measured by the broadened field where one's proficiency may be put to the test, increases as it were in geometrical progression.   We may take, for example, the sphere of mathematical abilities.   The young school child is capable of attacking, on the basis of his limited knowledge, only relatively few mathematical problems.   But with each step in development the number of solvable problems becomes increasingly greater.   Each new principle or method understood opens up a sphere of application that is usually much broader than the corresponding field at any previous level of comprehension.   This rate of expanding the sphere of application gathers increasing momentum as time goes on. When the individual advances to the upper levels of difficulty and gains insight into the principles, methods, and relations brought to light here, there is then opened up to him practically a whole universe of tasks for him to solve.   This is the comprehensive, rather than the intensive, phase of mental growth.

Because of the relationships holding in the sphere of science and knowledge, the learning of one fact is often the "open sesame" to a large number of similar or related facts. With each advance in the capability of understanding the more hidden plans or patterns of reality, the facts of experience are brought together in larger and more embracing organizations. Thorndike says:

> Each item of information may in such cases make the acquisition of other items easier; learning some one fact may involve knowledge of a score of new facts in the shape of its relations to the facts previously learned. So knowledge may roll up like a snowball, its sum being, say, as the cube of the amount of time spent. What we may call the "knowledge functions" do, as a rule, show, to say the least, very much less of the diminishing returns from increasing practice. (21)

If we had a way of measuring the growth of ability in terms of its social significance, the last few steps to be taken, small though they might be in terms of the units otherwise employed, would perhaps not show any diminishing returns as they approached the peak of human perfection. The last fifth of a second by which the professional runner reduces his recorded time for the hundred-yard dash would be greater, from this point of view, than a reduction of five seconds earlier in his career, for it may make a champion of him. There is no reason why we should not think of the growth of mental abilities in a similar manner. The negatively accelerating curve, showing a tapering off of improvement with age, is not very well suited for depicting the comprehensive aspect of the growth of ability. And this is perhaps the most important aspect, encompassing as it does the ever broadening range of opportunities for achievement that come with each step of the child toward greater maturity. Nor would this type of curve reflect the social significance of gains in social maturity with age.

Growth in Altitude, Breadth, and Speed. There is more than a single dimension to intellectual growth. To get a clear perspective of what happens intellectually to the growing child we must think of intelligence as three-dimensional (23). (1) The *altitude* of a person's intelligence is measured by the *diffi-*

culty of the intellectual tasks at which he can succeed. We must keep in mind, of course, that we first try to rule out the possibility of any lack of special training required by the task. (2) *Breadth* is measured by the number of tasks, at any level of difficulty, that can be performed by a person who has attained that level in his mental growth. (3) *Speed* is measured by the time taken by a person in performing a task of known difficulty.

We may diagram the growth of intelligence with regard to height and breadth by drawing an inverted triangular figure such as Figure 27. The apex of the figure would represent zero intelligence and the base its maximum. Going up the figure from apex to base would represent the changes taking place with increasing age. These are of two kinds—vertical growth (altitude) and horizontal growth (breadth). The figure attempts to express in graphic fashion how the two are related.

By vertical growth we mean, of course, the successive changes in the ability of the child to solve tasks of increasing difficulty. At birth, or even before birth if the zero point must be pushed back there, the level of difficulty of the tasks performable is at a minimum. But as the child grows older he becomes increasingly more able to solve tasks of greater and greater difficulty. The stage of maturity attained by any child at a certain age will determine just where on the vertical scale of difficulty we shall locate his degree of ability. As his ability grows in this vertical fashion, that is, with respect to tasks or test items varying in difficulty and arranged on a ladder or scale of difficulty, his progress up this developmental ladder represents his advancing mental maturity.

Besides this growth of a vertical kind there is also horizontal growth. The child's ability "broadens" as he grows older. As he makes progress up the scale from level to level, there is an increasing number of intellectual tasks that he is able to perform. At the mental age of three, let us say, there are relatively few intellectual tasks that he can perform. At the mental age level of sixteen, on the other hand, the number of appropriate intellectual tasks becomes very great. The number of things into which the child can then gain insight, in which he may become interested, and for the achievement of which he would

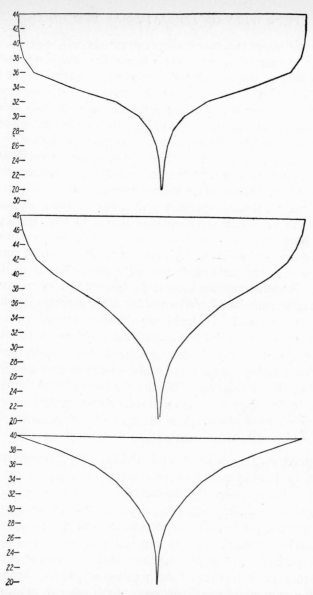

FIGURE 27. Samples of Possible Relations Between Growth in Height and in Breadth of Intelligence. Each increase in the ability to solve intellectual tasks of greater difficulty brings with it a broader range of opportunities where this ability may be put to use. (From E. L. Thorndike, *Measurement of intelligence,* Columbia Univ., 1927.)

have the requisite intellectual maturity increases with each advance in vertical growth. This is another way of saying that the world of understanding is continually expanding for the growing child, although it is rather narrow in the early years. That "the world is full of a number of things" is true only for those who have attained the upper levels of mental maturity. The world is rather circumscribed and empty for the lower mental ages. The attainment of maximum vertical growth would mean that there would be practically an infinite number of facts and relationships for one who reached the peak.

It may be noted, especially with respect to the higher levels of vertical growth, that a particular individual is not necessarily able, here and now, to perform all the specific intellectual tasks appropriate to his level. He may not be able to do so because of a lack of the particular knowledge and information necessary. We must consider these tasks, however, as "open" to him. That is, he suffers no handicap so far as his general mental maturity is concerned. He lacks only the special training or experience required. Thus the intellectual problems of the physician and of the lawyer make specific demands upon their respective training, but if these problems are to be found at the same level of intellectual difficulty the two will have an equal status in this respect. The child who gives evidence of attaining such a level of growth in the future may, moreover, look forward toward either vocation as a promising one.

Speed vs. Power in Mental Ability. The progressive increase in speed of mental operations is perhaps not such a conspicuous feature of intellectual growth as is the advance in either altitude or breadth. Quickness does, however, have a significant bearing at times upon mental work both in the school and in relation to the time limits imposed in testing. The almost universal custom of employing time limits in group tests of intelligence has in fact raised the question whether we are really measuring mental "speed" or "power." If these were found to be really different aspects of mental efficiency, it might make a difference in some of our interpretations of test results. Not all tests which have a time limit are actually speed tests, of course, even though they may outwardly appear to be. Many instances of the use of time limits are simply for the sake of convenience. If they allow 80 or 90 per cent of the children to finish all items, then the different scores earned must depend upon some other factor. A speed test is one containing items all of about the same level of difficulty and with a time limit which allows no or very few children to complete it.

Because of the importance of the speed vs. power question in assessing ability, a number of studies comparing speed of performance with level of ability have been made. When an intelligence test is administered twice to the same group, once with a time limit and then without a limit, the correlation has usually been high, but not as high as typical correlations between height and breadth. The speed-power correlation has been found to vary with the test employed, running from as low as .60 to as high as .90. This means not only that tests vary in the degree to which they measure speed, but that a "good" test should be well graded in difficulty in relation to its own time limit, so that speed does not enter into the score (4). By "speed" here we mean of course the speed of *intellectual* processes and not simple reaction time, which shows very little correlation with mental maturity. The good worker is in general the quick worker, or at least can be on occasion. While exceptions to this rule are apparently found in the "slow but sure" person, they often turn out, upon analysis, to be matters of personal preference under ordinary conditions of work, and not to be due to any inherent slowness of the mental machinery. Under controlled conditions, such as we have in testing, the slow but sure individual, provided he is "sure" is very rarely found to be as slow as we might expect from his ordinary actions.

Increase in Variability with Age. The inverted-triangle picture of the growth of intelligence has some important implications. We should expect, for instance, that the differences found among three-year-olds in the number or kind of intellectual tasks they are able to perform will tend to be much smaller than the differences found among ten-year-olds. This is because the "field" of intellectual tasks is relatively narrower at the earlier age while it is much broader later on.   There is more chance for variety to appear as the field widens.   Saying it another way, we may expect to find three-year-olds more alike intellectually than ten-year-olds.   It should be remembered, however, in this connection that a common schooling and common life interests may work toward preventing the appearance of the full amount of variety we might expect to find among older children.

The data from intelligence tests given to large numbers of children of different ages confirm this expectation of increased variability with age.   Figure 28 illustrates how the range of

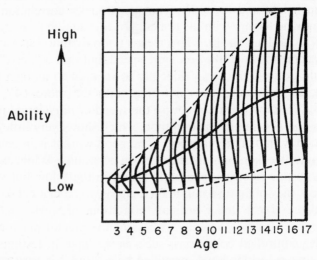

FIGURE 28.   An Illustration of Increased Variability with Age in Growth of Intelligence. The solid line shows the average of mental growth, while the bell-shaped curves show increased variability or "spread" with age and increased overlapping between successive ages. (From S. L. Pressey *et al.*, *Life: a psychological survey*, p. 169. Data from Thurstone and Ackerson.)

ability gradually increases with age.   Also, the overlapping from age to age is notable.   Some children at age eight surpass some sixteen-year-olds in ability, and some seventeen-year-olds are less able than the average child of ten.

In the higher reaches of ability we may find very great differences in the number and kind of problems that a mathematician and a historian, for example, individually solve. At this advanced stage of maturity there is an indefinite number of tasks from which to select, and each person may do his selecting without overlapping the sphere of another to any great extent. We have in this relationship of height and breadth the basis of specialization in intellectual tasks which may differ in everything except their demand upon general mental maturity.

Implications for the School. The relative lack of variety possible in the intellectual tasks of younger children as compared with older ones means that curricula and courses of study for the early grades must after all remain pretty much the same. In the higher grades there is greater possibility of variety and selection.

It is largely because of this that a wide knowledge of scientific facts and relationships is not so immediately necessary for the teacher of young children, because only relatively few of these data can be profitably employed in the setting of their intellectual tasks. The primary grade teacher is a specialist in children, rather than in subject matter. The simplification of subject matter so necessary for the early grades is often a matter of studiously ignoring the aspects and relationships appropriate only to a higher mental level. The appropriateness of "broadening" curricular offerings as the child grows older is also suggested. Specialization can hardly be expected very early in life.

It would seem that the school is better able to teach the individual of low mental maturity, young or old, how actually to solve all the intellectual problems of which he is theoretically capable than would be the case with the person of advanced mental maturity. This is because there are fewer of such problems for the lower levels. With the individual of advanced maturity, on the other hand, the school is in a more difficult position. The best the school can do in such a case is to make an appropriate selection of problems and concentrate its effort on giving the special training and knowledge required for these.

It can hardly hope to offer the special training and experience required for the actual performance of all possible tasks. Expressing this thought in another way, we may say that there is more likelihood that education will fill the capacity of the dull than of the genius. The school can hardly be expected to do as much relatively in increasing the breadth of the bright child's intelligence as it can with respect to the duller child. The school may and should *try* to do so; we are not implying that the bright child should be neglected. It is possible, however, that formal education is a relatively less significant factor in the intellectual development of the bright child. There are perhaps enough examples of eminent men to confirm this.

The Rate of Mental Growth

Some Age-Progress Curves of Intelligence. Most of our curves of intellectual growth depict what we have called vertical growth, or increase in altitude. Horizontal growth (breadth) would very probably be represented by a positively accelerating curve, showing an increased *rate* of growth with age. Here again enters the question of method in plotting curves. A "mental age curve" is a straight line. If we plot MA against CA for the average child, employing the data from such a test as the Stanford-Binet, we shall have a straight line up to the point where growth stops. This upper limit of growth was, in the early days of testing, very tentatively set at sixteen. There are good reasons for believing that this type of curve does not really represent true mental growth, and that its straightness and abrupt change of direction at sixteen are artifacts. This is due merely to the fact that a change of one year in mental age is always taken to be the same thing, whether at four or at fourteen. This is a very doubtful assumption, since most kinds of growth show a fairly rapid rate at first and then a gradual slowing up.

Would curves based on raw scores be more meaningful? Curves based on raw scores obtained from point scales or group intelligence tests may seem at first to have an advantage over the mental age curve. But the same question may be raised here. Do we know that a point earned at age ten, for example, has the same meaning as a point earned at age five? Can these points be regarded as "absolute units" of intellectual growth and not perhaps as mere artificial units of the particular test employed? The fact that group intelligence tests sometimes give growth curves very different from each other suggests that point scores cannot be accepted, for such a purpose, at their face value. Many curves of this kind, moreover, do not cover a very wide range. This is because the same group test cannot usually be given to both young and old.

It should be clear that the only meaningful way to plot an age-progress curve is in terms of an "absolute zero" and equal units of difficulty, so that the equal distances along the curve have the same meaning in regard to *amount* of ability. This has been accomplished by statistically or empirically determining a zero point and dividing up the segments of the scale into equal units of measurement. Examples of age-progress curves based

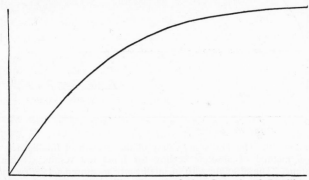

FIGURE 29. The Thorndike Curve of the Growth of Intelligence. A smoothed and extended curve based primarily on the Thorndike CAVD test. An absolute zero point was obtained statistically from expert estimate of low levels of intelligence. (From E. L. Thorndike, *The measurement of intelligence,* Columbia Univ., 1927.)

on various methods are given by Figures 29-31. The Thorndike curve is based on the CAVD intelligence tests, a battery of Completion, Arithmetic, Vocabulary, and Directions. The items were first scaled for difficulty by experimental techniques, then referred to an "absolute zero" point determined from ratings by psychologists. The Thurstone scale (24) based on Stanford-Binet scores converted into absolute scale units shows a slow rise to age 4½ or so, then a more rapid rise during the school years, and a tapering off in the later teens. The first three years were not based on tests, but agree fairly well with retests of children on developmental scales which were treated by the same statistical analysis.

The McManama curve (14) is based on a battery of verbal tests given to 2,500 pupils from age 9 to 19. Intercorrelations of the tests were high throughout the whole age range, indicating that the same general ability, or "cognitive G" was being

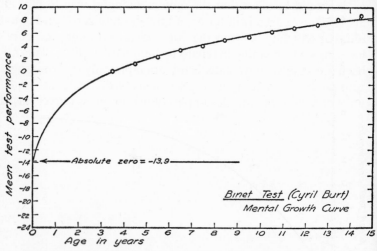

FIGURE 30. The Thurstone Curve of the Growth of Intelligence. Based upon a method of absolute scaling for Binet test results. (From L. L. Thurstone, "The absolute zero in intelligence measurement," *Psychol. Rev.,* 1928, **35**, 1936.)

measured consistently at the various age levels. The results were then scaled by the Thurstone method of absolute scaling. By going beyond this point, however, and by applying to her data the equation for a growth curve, previously determined by Moore (16) to hold for certain learning functions, McManama was able to estimate the zero point of intellectual development. This agreed closely with the zero point established by the Thurstone technique. Both determinations located the zero point approximately at birth, a finding we should expect if the methods were valid. Values for the different age levels were then calculated and expressed in terms of a common unit, the sigma of the nine-year age group. A comparison of the curves reveals the same rise to about 4½ years, acceleration and steady climb, then a tapering off.

These results were obtained with different groups, similar but not identical test materials, and fundamentally sound techniques which nevertheless differed somewhat in detail. They

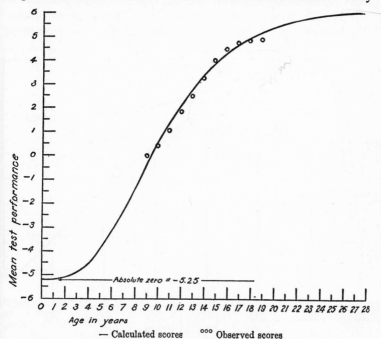

FIGURE 31. The McManama Curve of the Growth of "Cognitive G." A theoretical curve based on an absolute scaling method applied to a group test for "Cognitive G." (From Sr. M. McManama, "A genetic study of the cognitive general factor in human intelligence," *Stud. Psychol. & Psychiat.*, 1936, **4**, No. 2.)

represent therefore the best present answers to the questions (1) What is the rate of intellectual growth of various ages, and (2) at what age does (vertical) intellectual growth stop? On the latter point the findings do not coincide. The Thurstone curve shows a flattening at age 18, while the McManama curve appears to flatten at about age 25. The difference may well be due to the test materials employed, since the 1916 Stanford-Binet had a low ceiling or "top." However, these curves represent an answer based on children and adolescents. What answer is given by the intelligence testing of adults?

The Decline of Mental Abilities in Adults. The findings from tests administered to adults show that test performance not only stops gaining with age, but that it actually goes downhill steadily past a certain age range of "peak" performance. The best evidence for this comes from three well-known studies.

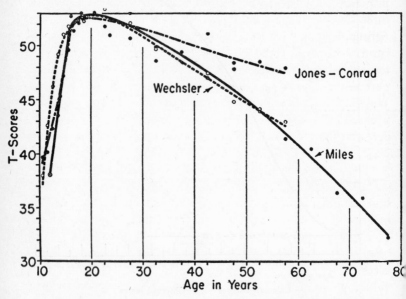

FIGURE 32. Age Changes in Intelligence Test Scores. (From H. E. Jones & O. J. Kaplan, *Mental disorders in later life,* Stanford Univ. Press, 1945, Ch. 4.)

1. Jones and Conrad (11) tested about 1,200 persons from 10 to 60 on the Army Alpha, including in their sample nearly the whole populations of a number of rural New England villages.

2. Miles and Miles (15) tested over 800 persons from ages 7 to 94 on the Otis Self-Administering Test of Mental Ability, a group intelligence test. The sample of adults consisted of

paid volunteers who were located through various lodges and clubs in California.

3. Wechsler (25), in the process of standardizing the Wechsler-Bellevue Intelligence Scale, tested 670 children and over 1,000 adults with an age range of 7 to 70. The characteristics of this sample are well known in terms of educational level, and appear to be representative of the population as a whole in this respect.

The results of all three studies are plotted for comparison in Figure 32. The "decline" shows up fairly consistently in all three sets of results, although they differ in the test employed (group *vs.* individual tests) and in the sample tested (urban *vs.* rural, age range, region). The Jones-Conrad curve shows a less steep rate of decline than the others. This may be due in part to the kind of test employed, and also the sample tested. We shall bear in mind, however, that such curves represent averages, that there is a good deal of overlapping from age to age, and that all individuals do not show the same rate of "decline."

The interesting thing about such results is that the curve of so-called mental decline in adults is very similar to curves showing a decline in such physical factors as reaction time, strength of grip, vital (lung) capacity, height, vision and hearing, and even brain weight. However, the decline is not necessarily one of *effective* intelligence, except in the limited sense that the adult is less adaptable to new tasks in which past learning is of little value. Even in this case, it is probably a matter of motivation rather than loss of ability.

It may be that the decline shown in Figure 32 is one of sensory-motor ability and of speed, rather than a decline in mental power. One set of evidence for this conclusion lies in the tests used. The Alpha and Otis tests have time limits, and many of the tests on the Wechsler not only have time limits but bonus scores for speedier performances. Next, the Jones-Conrad study revealed that all the abilities measured by the Alpha did not decline at the same rate. That speed was almost the total factor responsible for the Jones-Conrad results is revealed in a study by Lorge (13). He tested a large number of adults on the CAVD, a power test with no time limit, and the Alpha and Otis. He then arranged the individuals in age groups which were equated in scores on the CAVD; that is, each group had the same average score. As seen in Table 7,

TABLE 7

A COMPARISON OF AGE DIFFERENCES IN TEST PERFORMANCE ON SPEEDED AND UNSPEEDED TESTS *

Age Range	CAVD	Army Alpha	Otis SA (20 min.)
20-25	405	149	44
27½-37½	405	142	39
40 and over	405	128	33

* Data from I. Lorge, *J. educ. Psychol.*, 1936, **27**, 100-110.

the performance on the speed tests reflects the age differences as expected. The differences are not due to mental ability, because the groups performed equally well on the power test. From these results Lorge then computed a correction factor for speed, which when applied to the original Jones-Conrad data practically wiped out the slope of the "decline" curve. In other words, when the correction scores for speed were *added* to the scores of the New England villagers, the new curve resembled a straight line rather than a slope. Mental "deterioration" with age may be to some degree an artifact of our tests.

Individual Differences in Regularity of Mental Growth. One of the first significant facts brought to light in the study of age progress in mental ability was the apparent regularity of the process. That is, mental growth on the whole appeared to parallel physical growth. One expected irregularity was not found. The "adolescent spurt" in physical growth did seem to be paralleled by a spurt in mental growth at that period, although there were individual exceptions. Nor did girls show the superiority in mental growth that might be expected from their earlier maturity (8). There appears to be no direct constitutional effect of puberty upon aptitude or fundamental ability, although many students show improved rates of achievement at this time. Improved school progress, when it occurs among adolescents, is more probably the result of changes in motivation. Through the broadening of spheres of interested and increased susceptibility to the appearance of many social motives in particular, a rapid advance in achievement may take place at this time. There are perhaps some cases in which retarded students "catch up" in achievement at puberty, when the previous retardation was a general effect of slowed organismic growth. But age-progress curves based on large samples reveal no such general effect during the pubertal period. They indicate a fairly regular, uniform rate of growth.

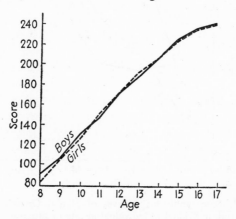

FIGURE 33. Composite Curves of Boys' and Girls' Intellectual Growth. These curves are based on mean intelligence test scores obtained from systematic "follow-up," or longitudinal studies. (From *Monogr. Soc. Res. Child Devel.*, 1937, **2**, No. 2, p. 60.)

However, these general curves are a mathematical invention. As in the case of physical growth, there are individual differences in the growth of abilities. Curves based on averages tend to obscure the differences among individuals. Many children are regular in progress, but some individuals show irregularities in rate peculiar to themselves. This is illustrated by a longitudinal study based on annual retests of 169 children over a nine-year period on four verbal tests of vocabulary, analogies, completion, and "opposites." Figure 33 shows the curves of boys and girls for the entire group and Figure 34 shows

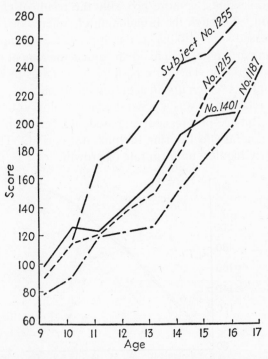

FIGURE 34. Some Individual Curves of Mental Growth. These show irregularities from individual to individual in rate of progress. Comparisons of these four children's scores at different ages might result in different conclusions about their relative ability. Some individual curves show unpredictable spurts and "plateaus," unlike the smooth age-progress depicted in composite curves. (From *Monogr. Soc. Res. Child Devel.*, 1937, **2**, No. 2, p. 61.)

some selected individual curves which exhibit variable growth cycles. Conclusions about regularity of growth must be carefully qualified:

A comprehensive and accurate statement concerning the rate of intellectual growth of different individuals is necessarily a qualified statement. Neither the simple statement that the growth curves of different individuals resemble each other and that the growth of an individual is predictable, nor the statement that the growth curves of different individuals are diverse and the growth of an individual is not predictable covers the case. It is a matter of degree. Growth curves do exhibit a certain degree of similarity, but by no means complete uniformity or even a close approach to it. (8, p. 155)

We may conclude that individual growth rates, although variable, are sufficiently similar to allow some degree of prediction. The individual who is relatively high at age nine will be high at age 13 and also at age 17, while the relatively low individual will remain low at later ages. Those in the middle of the distribution at an earlier age will probably show greater fluctuation, and these fluctuations are probably partly a matter of maturation and partly motivation.

Some psychologists have suggested that the abilities showing the greater amount of irregularity in growth are likely to be the ones that are determined more by environmental than by heredity factors. But there is no reason why the effect attributable to inheritance must be considered necessarily immutable while environmental effects may readily be modified. Rather, we might say that abilities which in general show the greatest amount of irregularity in growth are likely to be those more responsive to educational guidance.

How Constant is the IQ? This question has long been a source of controversy among educational psychologists. A good deal of evidence was accumulated during the 1930's to indicate that the predictions of IQ from one age period to another, although fairly reliable for the majority, showed a higher proportion of exceptions to the rule than was expected. Some children showed substantial increases in IQ with age, and others showed decreases. Further, it was shown that certain kinds of experience, or the lack of it, affected the changes. Perhaps the widespread interest (and dismay) provoked by these findings was due to the traditionally dominant assumption that the IQ measured something innate, that it expressed a constant rate of development, and if not strictly constant was at least very stable.

Terman's statement (1919) "that it makes little difference whether the child was bright, average, or dull, how long an interval separated the tests, or what the age of the child was at the earliest test" (20) was an expression of this point of view. Findings to the contrary raised the heredity-environment question—whether the chief determiners of intellectual growth and development are laid down in the genes or were the result of environment.

When we ask how constant or stable the IQ is, we are really raising *two* questions: (1) How well can we predict a future IQ from one taken yesterday or today? and (2) the more theoretical issue, how constant or regular is the rate of mental development? These questions are not the same, because in the first we are concerned only with *performance* on mental tests and in the second with the underlying *mental organization* that makes the performance possible.

The answer to the first question is no longer a matter of controversy. A longitudinal study by Bayley (3) at the California Institute of Child Welfare, based on testing 40 children from birth to 18 years of age, shows that in the majority of cases the IQ is not constant over this entire period. The future IQ was found to be very unpredictable from tests of infants, and in general the accuracy of prediction tends to increase with the age of testing.[1] That is, the future IQ of the individual can be predicted better from a test at age 6 than at age 4, and better still from a test at age 8. From age 6 on, correlations between successive test scores were .70 or higher, indicating that on the whole the IQ is fairly stable for school age children. However, the individual fluctuations in growth curves from age to age were so large that the term "constancy" hardly seems appropriate as applied to the IQ. Not even the performance of the group as a whole was "constant," as indicated by fluctuation of the mean score and the variability from age to age. It would seem that the prediction of future mental development from a

[1] A factor analysis of Bayley's data by P. Hofstaetter (*J. Genet. Psychol.*, in press) suggests that different primary factors or abilities may actually be measured by tests for the early years as compared to later ones.

test taken in childhood is to be approached very cautiously. The IQ is relatively stable, but not constant.

Does the stability of the IQ necessarily indicate a constant rate of development? Traditionally, the regularity of development has been taken as the only possible explanation of age-increases in score. From this point of view, "constancy of the IQ" was taken to be proof of regularity in developmental rate, and lack of constancy to be disproof. The older the child when first tested, the more accurately we can predict a later test score. But it should be clear that part of the later score consists of the earlier score, i.e., the two scores "overlap." For instance, the Stanford-Binet score of an eight-year-old consists in part of the test items he passed or could pass at age 7; his score at seven years consists in part of items passed at age 6, and so on. The older child does not lose the abilities he had at an earlier age. Why can we predict a child's future IQ (say, at age 16) more accurately from his score at age 10 than from his score at age 3? Because at age 10 the prediction of final status is based on a *larger proportion* of what will be included in the score at age 16. In other words, the score at age 10 includes more of what is present at 16 years than does the score at age 3.

An interesting study by Anderson (2), done with an ordinary deck of cards, revealed that our predictions of later scores from earlier ones could be explained largely by the proportion of "overlap" of the scores at different ages.

> . . . the numbers on the faces of playing cards were recorded after shuffling. The cards were again shuffled and the numbers that turned up were added in succession to the results of the final shuffle; the results of the next shuffle were added to the sum of the previous two shuffles, and so on for 16 shuffles. Scores for 96 cases that cumulate from the first to the sixteenth shuffle were obtained. The cumulated scores at each shuffle were then correlated successively with initial score and with final score. (2, p. 388)

Anderson then compared these correlations between initial and terminal "scores" (obtained from shuffling cards) with the correlations between tests and retests of intelligence obtained by three well-known "follow-up" studies. The correlations were about the same; actually, the intelligence correlations were a little lower! What does this mean?

> . . . The growing individual exhibits an increasing consistency of ability level, not because the "rate of growth" is constant, but because his present accomplishments constitute an ever-increasing portion of his future accomplishments as he grows older. This is tantamount to saying that at age 15 we can make a more accurate prediction of an individual's subsequent behavior than at age 2, because we know more about him at age 15. The proportional change in his behavior from age 15 to 16 is less than from age 2 to 3, and certainly much less than from 2 to 16. (1, p. 296)

According to this view, the fact that the IQ is constant enough to enable us to predict it neither supports nor excludes the possibility that the rate of development is regular or constant. Whether the developmental pace is regular or irregular, however, the changes of test score with age are certainly the result of changes in mental organization through learning, i.e., mental development. They are not due to a simple accretion of behavior.

Mental and physical growth are alike in at least one respect. Whatever regularity or constancy is noted in either is a function of certain conditions, and would not be expected to hold in the absence of those conditions. The relative stability of the IQ, as Wheeler points out, is a general principle only to the extent that the conditions of mental development are uniform:

> . . . It often happens, to be sure, that intelligence quotients remain constant over a long period of time, and for this reason the constancy of the IQ has been accepted as a general law. It is a law only because the conditions under which children develop remain sufficiently constant to produce a constant rate of mental growth. There is no reason whatever for asserting that because a child at the age of six has an IQ of 60, he must have only an IQ of 60 when he is twelve or fifteen. Such a claim violates one of the cardinal principles in science, namely, that any event is the product of existing conditions. And conditions can be changed. (27, p. 174)

Rate and Limit of Intellectual Growth. A study of both group and individual growth curves would probably justify the following conclusions concerning intellectual growth.

1. *Rate.* The "absolute zero" of intelligence is probably some time before birth. Intellectual life begins with a period of relatively slow growth, but showing a progressive increase in rate (positively accelerating), which may last for four or five years. Then comes a period, up to about the age of ten or twelve, when the growth is practically of the straight-line sort, with equal increments from year to year. The final period is marked by a progressive decrease in rate of growth. Each year now brings less advance than the one just preceding.

2. *Upper limit.* The upper limit of mental growth is probably reached between twenty and twenty-five years of age. Some evidence shows continued progress in college students at age 23. The superiority of the college group, plus the continuing education, is reflected in this finding. For the *average* person, we should probably expect a conspicuous slackening of the pace of increase in the later teens.

3. *Horizontal intellectual growth is probably unlimited.* The broadening of the sphere of intelligence, if we may take our cue from the inverted-triangle picture of its growth, does not show a practically attainable limit. Even though there may be a theoretical limit to the horizontal growth of intelligence, it would be so indefinite that the average person could not live long enough to accomplish all the things of which he is capable. Thus a person may continue to attain greater and greater wisdom with advancing years, but doing it all with the same level of mental maturity that he enjoyed when he was twenty.

4. *Regularity of individual growth.* Age progress of individuals, based on retests, show a fairly consistent rate of increase. However, there are individual differences. Regularity of mental growth does not mean absolute invariability, but it does mean that we have adequate grounds, when we know all the conditions, for a reasonably safe forecast. The older the child, the more reliable the forecast.

5. *Unreliability of early testing.* Preschool children (especially under four years) are generally found to be less regular in their tested rate of mental growth than older children. This is probably a feature of the tests themselves rather than an indica-

tion of any great difference between the growth of intelligence at early and at later ages.

6. *All children grow intellectually*. Whatever their original intellectual status, all children show growth in general intelligence with age. Children may differ among themselves in their level of mental maturity at birth, in their rate of development, and in the maximal limit attainable; but there is no group of children which manifests no intellectual progress whatever. Even feebleminded children are not such because their rate of mental growth is less than that of the normal person. Naïve parents are very often surprised at the intellectual progress of their feebleminded children, apparently never expecting anything of the sort. This sometimes gives rise to false hopes that the children will "outgrow" their deficiency. The mere existence of mental growth is of course not a good basis for such hopes because it is everywhere present and inevitable. The criterion must always be the *slow rate* of growth, and not the mere fact of improvement.

Some Controlling Factors in Intellectual Growth

Since general intelligence is an ability, or readiness to perform, it must be evident that a person could not perform in any intellectual way unless he had previously learned certain things. We should not ask the bare question whether a child's score on an intelligence test shows any effect of his experience. There would be no score whatever unless there was a previous developmental history of some kind. The real question must come down to this, "Will any experience do, just so they are human experiences and above the level of those of Romulus and Remus while they were being cared for by the mother wolf?" Or, "Will some particular kind of experience, such as we find when we go from one country to another, from one community to another, from one household to another, be more favorable for the growth of intelligence than other particular kinds? The question is not, "Does experience affect intelligence?" but "Is the individuality of experience accompanied by a corresponding difference in intelligence?"

We may illustrate these points by supposing that we have placed an average American infant with a very primitive race of people for his rearing till the age of ten. There would be no doubt that, if he were then tested by the Binet method, he would appear as below average in intelligence. This might readily be due to the kinds of experiences, common to American children, which underlie the test items and which are foreign to him. But let us suppose that our expatriated child were returned to America at the age of ten, and we allow him time for his adjustment to things American, for learning specific facts and information. What might we then expect of him when he reaches the age of fourteen? Would he lag far behind American children of his age, or would he catch up? Could it be that the environments were so different that they actually determined different *rates* of development which would continue to be different in the future? To put it another way, would the rate of mental progress become so retarded by the primitive environment that he could never again "catch up" with the average American child, or might not the handicap be largely eliminated by subjecting him to the average American environment for three or four years?

This is the fundamental question. It is not whether experience affects the growth of intelligence or whether intelligence test results are influenced by any environmental or developmental factors. This must be so in the very nature of the case. Rather we must ask whether the factors that influence the growth of intelligence are, first, more likely to be found in some environments than in others, and secondly, if this be so, whether the influence so exerted leads to a definite handicap or facilitation carrying over to one's tested ability or life adjustment in future years. These controlling influences may be summarized under three headings, as follows: Organic, educational, and socioeconomic.

Influence of Organic Conditions. We have seen that organic growth underlies dispositional "readinesses" at the various stages of development and may thus be a limiting condition. Here we do not mean mere growth in size, but development of the essential neuromuscular, sensory, and glandular functions which are basic to the activity of the child as a whole.

Anything which impedes organic growth and the proper development of these functions will therefore have an effect on tested intelligence. There is evidence that certain organic factors, such as thyroid secretion and congenital syphilis, which influence general physiological development, also influence the growth of intelligence in a differential manner. Such factors must apparently operate from an early age, and their physiological influence must be of a general nature. Thus the activity of the gonads at puberty is apparently too specialized to be reflected in the growth of intelligence. Sensory deficiencies, particularly of hearing and sight, also affect the rate of mental growth. Extensive studies of deaf and hard-of-hearing children reveal definite language handicaps, which cause a general retardation of age progress in intelligence amounting to about two to three years (17). Visually defective children tend to be somewhat below average for their age, either because the visual defect retards development or because the tests penalize these children unduly.

There is no satisfactory evidence that factors influencing one's general physical or health status—but not general physiological development—such as common infections, poor nutrition, diseased tonsils and adenoids, and hookworm, affect the rate of mental growth. Such things as these may leave their mark upon an individual's performance, but they are apparently without permanent effect upon his mental development.

Influence of Formal Education. There is evidence that many possible influences of a formal educational nature, such as the number of days in attendance at school (beyond a certain minimum of about 50 per cent), preschool attendance at a nursery school or kindergarten, the amount of money spent by a community on its schools, have no lasting effect on the long-time growth of intelligence. Some of these factors, such as preschool attendance, have a transient effect which apparently disappears after a year or two in a more common educational environment. This transient effect would perhaps not appear if a more valid test were at hand. It seems established, however, that drastic lack of school attendance will retard intellectual growth and that prolonged school progress will have an effect on test performance.

Special techniques of instruction, such as coaching for a particular test through practice on similar material, and praise and reproof, affect intelligence test scores. This is of sufficient degree, particularly with regard to coaching, as to invalidate the results of intelligence testing on occasion. However, the effect is usually so short-lived (about a year at the most) that there can scarcely be any serious question of an influence on future mental growth.

Recent and widely publicized reports of large increases in intelligence in children originally classified as feebleminded (18) have not been carefully controlled and offer no satisfactory evidence of permanent changes. Although special instructional techniques with really feebleminded children are perhaps of some value, their effect in producing permanent changes in intelligence is widely doubted.

There is ample evidence that the child who goes to school for a substantially longer time will ordinarily surpass those who left school early in tested intelligence, even though the two children were equal in ability at an earlier age. It is therefore assumed that formal schooling contributes something to intellectual growth, even "vertical growth." But again, the developmental influences underlying this improved performance are quite difficult to specify. It may be that verbal ability is improved somewhat through longer school attendance, or that the advantage gained through additional reading and vocabulary growth favors the test performance of those who remain in school. Additional schooling, even as late as high school years, does make a difference in intelligence test scores.

Curricular Influence on Mental Growth. If we now ask what kind of schooling contributes most to intellectual growth, we raise an issue about which opinions are strong and evidence is sparse. Most of the evidence, even the most recent, shows that one subject is about as good as another as far as effect on intelligence is concerned (26). It does seem that the brighter student improves to a greater extent than the less able from any kind of subject studied, which is consistent with what we know about intelligence. As a corollary of this, it seems reasonable that any school subject which requires more thinking, reasoning, or abstraction will be favorable to intellectual growth. The finding that such high school courses as algebra, geometry, economics, chemistry, physics, Latin, and French contribute slightly more to the growth of intelligence than drawing, English, history, music, stenography, agriculture, and dramatics would be consistent with this view (22). But on the other hand a minimum level of intelligence is required to master the more difficult subjects, so they can hardly produce gains in everybody. Again, it seems that the *way* a subject is taught is more important than the subject itself. Learning by rote, verbalisms, and reproduction of nonvital "facts" will produce little intellectual growth, no matter what subject is taught.

The kind of educational situation that produces intellectual differences at high school age is not usually found during the elementary period. The high school student's intellectual status, and his ability to profit from instruction, is very largely determined by his intellectual progress of earlier years. But there is very little variety in either curriculum or methods of instruction in elementary school, nor does it seem possible that the primary grades could ever have the curricular variation typical of the high school. We must have the possibility of variety, or of differential development factors, before elementary schooling can show any differential effect on the growth of intelligence.

These remarks might be made more pointed by saying that if educators undertook deliberately to raise the IQ of an ordinary child they might be rather puzzled to know just what they should do. If the child were taken from a very poor home and school environment, the chances of success would be greater. It would perhaps be necessary that he have control of the child's education from an early age. It is almost certain that if he depended upon the merit of a narrow formula, such as particular devices of infant training, of teaching or instruction, he would fail.

In summarizing, we might distinguish between the effect of schooling on vertical, as contrasted with horizontal, growth. Formal education by and large does not seem so greatly to influence the level attained or the rate of progress from level to level. But the child may through schooling realize in his actual achievement as much as possible of the horizontal growth of which one at his level of mental maturity is capable.

Socioeconomic Conditions. These are really educational in nature, in the sense that they provide environmental stimulation essential to intellectual development. The relationship between measured intelligence and socioeconomic status has been conclusively established. Table 8 illustrates, for example,

TABLE 8

THE RELATION OF MEAN STANFORD-BINET IQ's OF CHILDREN AND LEVEL OF FATHER'S OCCUPATION *

Father's Occupation	Age of Child			
	2-5½	6-9	10-14	15-18
I. Professional	114.8	114.9	117.5	116.4
II. Semiprofessional, Managerial......	112.4	107.3	112.2	116.7
III. Clerical, Skilled, Retail Business....	108.8	104.9	107.4	109.6
IV. Agricultural (Rural Owners)	97.8	94.6	92.4	94.3
V. Semiskilled, Minor Clerks, Small Business Owners	104.3	104.6	103.4	106.7
VI. Slightly Skilled	97.2	100.0	100.6	96.2
VII. Day Laborers	93.8	96.0	97.2	97.6

* Data from Q. McNemar, *Revision of the Stanford-Binet scale,* Boston: Houghton Mifflin, 1942.

the relationship between intelligence and the occupational level of the father's occupation. A similar relationship exists between intelligence and family income. This of course does not prove a cause-effect relationship. Occupational level and income are merely indications of the general "cultural level" of the home. The effect of environmental background has also been studied from other points of view: by comparing the intellectual growth of children in various kinds of homes, by measuring the effect of placing children in foster homes varying in educational advantages, by comparing urban and rural children, and following up the intellectual growth of children raised in isolated or primitive environments.

There is sufficient evidence to show that *extreme* environmental differences affect the growth of intelligence. The conditions for the appearance and durability of such an effect are about as follows: (1) The environmental difference must be a drastic one. The contrast between a mediocre orphanage and a very good home, between the best 15 per cent of homes and the poorest 15 per cent, between an upper middleclass life and a gypsy life, between the urban home of a banker and the primitive surroundings of isolated mountain regions are examples of such extremes. (2) The child must be raised in the beneficial environment for some time, and during the critical years of development (early and middle childhood). To alter the rate of development seriously, the change in environment must come early, probably before age 5 or 6. Apart from such extremes, differences in home environment appear to account for a relatively small amount of variation in intellectual growth. The effect of cultural differences on mental development is considered in more detail in the next chapter.

REFERENCES

1. ANASTASI, A., & FOLEY, J. P. *Differential psychology.* New York: Macmillan, 1949.
2. ANDERSON, J. E. The prediction of terminal intelligence from infant and preschool tests. *39th Yearbook,* I, Nat. Soc. Stud. Educ., 1940.
3. BAYLEY, N. Consistency and variability in the growth of intelligence from birth to eighteen years. *J. genet. Psychol.,* 1949, **75,** 165-196.
4. BENNETT, M. W. Factors influencing performance on group and individual tests of intelligence. *Genet. Psychol. Monogr.,* 1941, **23,** 237-318.
5. BRYAN, A. I., GARRETT, H. E., & PERL, R. E. A genetic study of several mental abilities at three age levels. *Arch. Psychol.,* 1935, No. 176.
6. DAVIS, A., & HAVIGHURST, R. J. *Father of the man.* Boston: Houghton Mifflin, 1947.
7. FREEMAN, F. N. *Theory and practice of psychological testing.* New York: Holt, 1950.
8. FREEMAN, F. N., & FLORY, C. D. Growth in intellectual ability.

Ch. in BARKER, KOUNIN, & WRIGHT, *Child behavior and development,* New York: McGraw-Hill, 1943.

9. GARRETT, H. E. A developmental theory of intelligence. *Amer. Psychol.,* 1946, **1,** 372-378.

10. HAYES, C. H. *The ape in our house.* New York: Harper, 1951.

11. JONES, H. E., & CONRAD, H. S. The growth and decline of intelligence: a study of a homogeneous group between the ages of ten and sixty. *Genet. Psychol. Monogr.,* 1933, **13,** 223-298.

12. JONES, T. D. The development of certain motor skills and play activities in young children. *Child Devel. Monogr. No. 26.* New York: Teach. Coll. Bur. Publ., 1939.

13. LORGE, I. The influence of the test upon the nature of mental decline as a function of age. *J. educ. Psychol.,* 1936, **27,** 100-110.

14. McMANAMA, SISTER M. A genetic study of the cognitive general factor in human intelligence. *Stud. Psychol. & Psychiatr.,* Cath. Univ., 1936, **4,** No. 2.

15. MILES, C. C., & MILES, W. R. The correlation of intelligence scores and chronological age from early to late maturity. *Amer. J. Psychol.,* 1932, **44,** 44-78.

16. MOORE, T. V. The analysis of association by its equational constants. In *Aspects of the new scholastic philosophy.* New York: Benziger, 1932.

17. PINTNER, R., EISENSON, J., & STANTON, M. *The psychology of the physically handicapped.* New York: Crofts, 1941.

18. SCHMIDT, B. G. Changes in personal, social, and intellectual behavior among children originally classified as feebleminded. *Psychol. Monogr.,* 1946, **60,** No. 5.

19. TERMAN, L. M. *The measurement of intelligence.* Boston: Houghton Mifflin, 1917.

20. TERMAN, L. M. *The intelligence of school children.* Boston: Houghton Mifflin, 1919.

21. THORNDIKE, E. L. *Educational psychology,* II. New York: Columbia Univ. Press, 1913.

22. THORNDIKE, E. L. Mental discipline in high school studies. *J. educ. Psychol.,* 1924, **15,** 1-22. See also 1927, **18,** 377-404.

23. THORNDIKE, E. L. *Measurement of intelligence.* New York: Columbia Univ. Press, 1927.

24. THURSTONE, L. L. The absolute zero in intelligence measurement. *Psychol. Rev.,* 1928, **35,** 179-197.

25. WECHSLER, D. *The measurement of adult intelligence.* Baltimore: Williams & Wilkins, 1944.

26. WESMAN, A. G. A study of transfer of training from high school subjects to intelligence. *Teach. Coll. Bur. Publ.,* No. 109, New York: Columbia Univ., 1945.

27. WHEELER, R. H. *The science of psychology.* New York: Crowell, 1940.

SELECTED READINGS

ANASTASI, A., & FOLEY, J. P. *Differential psychology.* New York: Macmillan, 1949. Chs. 8 and 9 review the evidence on age differences and effects of schooling on intelligence. Ch. 23 discusses the effect of socioeconomic differences on intellectual development.

DENNIS, W. *Readings in child psychology.* New York: Prentice-Hall, 1951.

DEARBORN, W. F., & ROTHNEY, J. W. M. *Predicting the child's development.* Cambridge: Sci-Art Press, 1941.

HAVIGHURST, R. J. *Human development and education.* New York: Longmans, Green, 1953. Gives account of sequential developmental tasks and factors that influence them.

NATIONAL SOCIETY FOR STUDY OF EDUCATION. *39th Yearbook,* 1940. Intelligence: its nature and nurture.

PIAGET, J. *The psychology of intelligence.* New York: Harcourt, Brace, 1950. Deals principally with thinking processes, but has many implications for study of intellectual development.

TERMAN, L. M., & MERRILL, M. *Measuring Intelligence.* Boston: Houghton Mifflin, 1937. Study of the Stanford Binet test items for different ages provide interesting illustrations of the course of mental growth.

TERMAN, L. M., & ODEN, M. *The gifted child grows up.* Stanford University Press, 1947.

6

SOCIAL BACKGROUNDS OF CHILD DEVELOPMENT

THE FACTORS that influence the child's development are difficult to specify. While we have sufficient data to indicate the
general kind of developmental factors that influence differentially the growth of intelligence, and in some cases the average
trend or amount of such influence, we are often in the rather
paradoxical situation of not being able to tell just what are the
special features of experience, training, or education to be credited with this effect. We are justified in saying, for instance,
that a "good home," or "lack of schooling," or "low cultural
level" are rather important matters, but when we become more
scrutinizing we cannot easily single out just what it is in the
home, in the schooling, or in the cultural status that merits special attention and consideration.

Many features of home life, to which we may be inclined to
attribute a possible training effect, seem to merit no special consideration in this respect. Thus the kind of books available,
playing with constructive toys, being read to, or taking trips to
stores, theatres, or the zoo, have apparently no higher correlation with mental age of preschool children than have such supposedly irrelevant factors as cleanliness of the home, having a
bed of one's own, and body height (14). The IQ's of children
of school age are as likely to reflect the income of the family,
owning their own home, taking dancing lessons, as they are to
give any evidence of the number of books in the home, the
extent of the parent's education, the amount of parental supervision, or the hours of home instruction (2). What we under-

stand, perhaps only in a vague manner, as the "general level of culture," is undoubtedly reflected in the development of intelligence. This seems to be as true of so-called "racial" differences as of individual differences.

Hence, knowledge of external conditions affecting development is meaningful to the extent that we understand how and why these conditions exercise their effect. The environment of the growing child consists primarily of people, and the dominant people during the formative period are his own parents. Since children grow up in families, and families differ in cultural level, we are concerned here with the effect of these cultural differences on child development.

Children Grow Up in Families. The development of the child must be understood with respect to the family setting. The child plays a role in the family, and the role differs according to the composition of the family, the interaction of its various members, and the way in which the stimuli or behavioral influences arising from the family pattern operate upon the child. The attitude of the family toward the child, and of the child toward the family, varies with the size and composition of the family group and with the role of each member within the group. The attitude of the child toward men, for example, will depend on the family role of the father or older brothers. The development of attitudes toward women will depend on the role of the mother. Parental attitudes toward children and their training will be affected to a great extent by the childhood role of the parents in their own families, and the way in which the parents themselves were raised. Even the term "family" means different things in different societies and varies according to subgroups of society.

Certain aspects of the family in our society are worth noting here. First, the term "family" ordinarily refers to the immediate reproductive group, consisting of parents and children. The family setting may contain members of a wider kinship group, such as uncles, aunts, or grandparents, but this is perhaps less typical. The family as a social group tends to be limited to a relatively small number of persons, as contrasted with the Chinese kinship group in which several generations are housed together in a close-knit unit. The child's world in two such contrasting groups will be quite different. Sociological changes over a period of many generations, resulting in the reduction of the family to a relatively smaller and less complex social group, have certain implications for child development. (1) The parent-child relationship is greatly intensified. The parents' attention tends to concentrate more on the children, and the child's attention on the parents. Since the child's family contacts are reduced, he is more dependent on the parents in attaining his rewards and goals. The parent-child relationship thus tends to be more intensely emotional. (2) The smaller family group, by limiting the number of social contacts available to the child, makes it possible for the parents to exercise greater control and direction over the child. It also places the burden of responsibility for training the child directly on the parents. The mother and father thus become not only the dominant models of behavior, but the policing of the child's behavior and contacts tends to occupy a much more considerable portion of their time and energy. (3) Comparisons between children tend to extend outside the family circle. Parents compare their children's behavior to a greater extent with that of children of their neighbors and associates, rather than with members of the kinship group. The net result of the family pattern, according to many social scientists, is an increased pressure on the child to conform to parental expectations, more heightened emotional conflicts between parents and children during the various developmental stages, and a greater drive toward achievement on the part of the child (1, 7). Also, there may be greater possibility of intensifying the child's feelings of personal insecurity.

The foundations of the child's personality are laid in early childhood, and are largely developed inside the family. The family circle provides the setting in which emotional relationships are developed. The child's need for love—the need to be wanted, accepted, and appreciated—is first satisfied in that setting, with the result that emotional ties are established. The child's first lessons in adjustment are also learned here. In the family setting he first becomes aware of the presence and needs of other persons, and learns to modify his own desires in order to get along with them. The family also provides the setting for the development of abilities, since the first learning situations are the result of a selection of games, toys, playmates. The family is the first audience as well, and its reactions of approval or disapproval provide the rewards which determine the lines along which the child's abilities and traits develop. In short, the early lessons are the most incisive and enduring because the child is completely dependent on the family for the satisfaction of his needs, and because the learning situations and available rewards are limited and controlled by the small social group of the family.

Correlation studies of similarity in attitudes of parents and children illustrate the social importance of the family setting in child development. Hartshorne and May (10) had school-age children mark questionnaires covering their attitudes on right and wrong behavior, and administered the same questionnaires to the child's parents and associates. A correlation of .54 was found between the attitudes of parents and their children, with the child's judgments more similar to those of the mother rather than to those of the father. This is about the same degree of relationship usually found between child and parent in physical traits and intelligence. Other correlations are offered for comparison:

Child-parents .... .54
Child-friends .... .35
Child and club leaders .... .14
Child and day-school teachers .... .03
Child and Sunday School teachers.......... .00

Another study (11) by these authors compared the character traits of 734 pairs of siblings and found intersibling correlations to be positive, ranging as high as .44 on such traits as honesty, persistence, and inhibition. In general, the attitudes and interests of members of the same family circle are found to be much more similar than members of different social groups. Since this similarity can hardly be attributed to hereditary influence, it illustrates the effect of family social interaction during the formative years.

Children and Culture. Culture is a technical term. Although in popular usage the word refers to good manners, refined taste, and higher levels of intellectual or artistic pursuits, in the technical sense "culture" is not an evaluative term. Every society has a culture, no matter how simple, and every person is cultured in the sense that he is a member of some society and participates in its culture. The culture of a society is, simply, its way of life. It consists of the ways, or *customs,* of doing and thinking, and is therefore a kind of sum total of knowledge, beliefs, attitudes, morals, laws, language, and art. From the child development point of view, the most important aspect of culture is its transmission; that is, culture is a social heritage in which he is born and to which he is reared. Culture is the way of life of the child's family—not just what the family does, but how it thinks and feels about the problems of life. Culture provides the child with a kind of ready-made pattern of beliefs and habits for adapting himself to the environment in which he must live and function.

How is the culture transmitted? Linton (12) points out two influences: (1) child rearing practices, which are important in infancy. The "right" way to rear children is determined by custom or tradition in all societies, and such customs are ordinarily unquestioned. Practices other than the customary ones are unthinkable. (2) Observation and instruction in the mores of desired behavior patterns. Adults of the society, as well as the child's age and sex peers, serve as models. The child sees what is rewarded, and he is told. Adapting through "imitation" is as important, and in many respects more important, than instruction from parents. Through these processes the child is initiated and inducted into the culture of his family, which reflects to some degree the larger cultural pattern of society. The family setting thus acts as a screen, selecting those aspects of the child's environment which it feels to be important, interpreting the child's experiences for him, and evaluating the results. The values learned by the child are the family's because he sees his experiences through the family's eyes.

It becomes clear that social learning, rather than any kind of instinct or constitutional "human nature," accounts for the principal differences in human personality development. The common expression among anthropologists is that "culture shapes the personality." This can only mean, from the point of view of learning theory, that the cultural environment provides the situations and the rewards that are responsible for the formation of some traits rather than others. In the sense that customs are techniques, we may say that society provides the behavior models from which the techniques are learned. Custom is thus truly an *invisible environment,* which becomes as much a part of the growing child as the air he breathes or the food he eats. The behavior of Zuñi school children, who when doing problems at the blackboard refrain from finishing before the other students or in any way outdoing the others, would be considered strange in classrooms in Boston or San Francisco. Anthropological evidence tells us that any white American child, if raised like a Zuñi, would not only act so, but would regard self-assertive behavior as strange.

All members of society share the same culture, but society is very complex, is split or stratified into subgroups. We therefore speak of subcultures, or differences in cultural pattern from group to group. There is thus a national culture, a regional culture, a social class culture, and a family culture. According to Young, for example, the American culture is dominated by the following beliefs: (1) belief in individual material success and national progress; (2) belief in universal literacy and education as the means of solving social and personal problems; (3) belief in the advantages and virtues of rapid movement through space; (4) belief in the virtue of constant change in most aspects of life; (5) confidence in man's ability to control and direct his destiny, both personally and socially (21). Americans tend to accept these ideas of values, and to teach them consciously or unconsciously to their children. However, the degree of importance attached to them, and the behavior through which they are expressed, will vary among regions, classes, neighborhoods, and families. The version learned by the child is his family's version, which is therefore most important to child development.

The Social Role of Language. No culture can exist without language, since culture is embodied and given form through words. Language is tremendously important in social interaction. Words are used to express feelings and to influence others, and the interplay of human relations is so dependent on the emotional tone of words that language is not only a part of the culture, but the richest expression of it. Cultural participation is dependent on learning the language, as witnessed by the popular expression "they don't speak my language." The way a person speaks, the words he uses, and the feeling-tones associated with words furnish a kind of index of social placement. We can often infer from these things a person's way of life, as indicated by the ease with which we can guess his region, his occupational level, his neighborhood, his amusements, and the kind of house he lives in. Even at the level of national culture, learning a language is practically identical with learning a culture. A person who cannot speak or understand French cannot hope to understand the French very well, because their way of life and their subtle emotional reactions are intimately bound up with their language. Language enables us to share the experiences of others, to see things as they see them, and therefore to communicate with them. This is the essence of cultural participation. Inability to understand a social group or to be understood by its members leaves us outside that group. The ability to relate one's self to others, to share their experiences, and to be accepted by them depends on initiation into the subtle meanings and feelings words have for them.

Words are powerful forces in human behavior. The power of words derives not merely from their literal "dictionary" definitions, but from the feelings associated with them. Words may be used to convey logical meanings, but are more often used to inspire, to repel, to impress, and otherwise work on the feelings of others. The power of words in motivating behavior derives from the identification of things with words; that is, a word tends to evoke the same feeling as the thing for which it stands. Linguists and semanticists have this in mind when they call attention to "the constant interplay between language and experience" (13). The word "dog," for example, differs in meaning (the emotional reactions it evokes) in different people, depending on their experiences with dogs and with the word "dog."

Language thus reflects culture itself, through its identification with the experiences by which the individual is initiated into the culture. We are aware that words are sometimes untranslatable from one language to another, because the cultural setting which gives meaning to the word in one language may have no counterpart in the other. It is said, for example, that the "gypsy" language has no word to represent "ownership," "clean," or "honest," which shows that certain cultural aspects of gypsy society differ remarkably from our own. Whether true or not, this illustrates the social role of language. Words are cultural inventions, standing for certain customs, beliefs, and values and taking their significance from the cultural setting. Culture is learned through words, but words themselves are culturally and emotionally colored by the experiences that produce them. Language development therefore plays an important part in the child's social and emotional growth, as in the intellectual side of his development.

Language development is thus associated with the development of attitudes toward the environment, and the basic foundations are laid within the family circle. The family selects, interprets, and evaluates words for the child. It supplies not only the words, but their meanings and their emotional tones. The child's view of the world is limited and modified by his family's use of language from his earliest initiation into communicative processes. Records of family table conversations, as reported by Bossard (1), show characteristic family differences in modes of expression, words used, word taboos, type of conversation, and pronunciation. These family differences are shown to be reflections of cultural differences among families.

One important factor in this interplay is the development of the attitude toward language itself.

Our material reveals highly significant family attitudes toward words and their meaning. In one of these families, with two children aged seven and nine years, there is a continuing attempt on the part of the parents to enlarge the children's semantic grasp. In the course of the family conversation, the children are asked if they understand the words used, or they interrupt to ask, for example, "Daddy, what does emphasize mean?" Both the father and the mother in this family leave the dinner table to consult the dictionary, with a statement like: "Well, we might as well find out now." In contrast, there is the family where John, aged thirteen, used the word preference, only to have his father curse him and say, "Preference, Preference, I'll Preference you. You with your fancy words. You can't high-hat me as long as I pay the bills." Then there is the family in which the child said, "I don't know what that means," to which the parent replied, "If I get the razor strap, you'll understand what I'm saying." (1, p. 184)

CULTURAL NORMS IN CHILD DEVELOPMENT

From the viewpoint of child development, the human environment is of vastly greater importance than such things as climate, geographical terrain, dwellings, or household furniture. The human environment consists of people organized and interacting in a group (society) and a distinctive way of life shared by members of the group (culture). The behavior patterns developed by the individual are the result of his interaction with human beings, who behave toward him according to established customs and beliefs. The language, behavior, and emotional responses learned by the child depend not merely on where he lives or what kind of individuals are present in that place, but on human interaction. That is, cultural influence depends on the possibility of establishing intimate contacts with people.

All human environments have certain features in common. In its broad aspects, American society is similar from Maine to California, and so is the American family pattern. The similarities are more notable than the differences. But the possibility of establishing intimate human contacts, for any individual child, is limited by the particular subculture in which he is born and reared. We must therefore be concerned, in our effort to understand the background of child development, with cultural differences within our society.

The culture of which we are least aware, paradoxically, is the one of which we are a part. In fact, we become aware of it only by contact with persons who have customs or beliefs different from our own. It has been said that the last thing a dweller of the deep sea will become aware of is the water in which he is immersed (12). Our own way of life is the most familiar and "natural," and therefore the most easily taken for granted. The individual is ordinarily convinced that his own customs and beliefs are universally accepted, or at least that they should be. He is sometimes puzzled and disturbed when he finds, through contact with persons who are "different," that his own customs are not understood or accepted. There is ample evidence, however, that people in our society are sufficiently in contact with cultural differences to be aware of cultural levels either "above" or "below" their own. This does not mean, unfortunately, that he understands the "different" subculture, that he is sympathetic toward it, or able to communicate with the members of society of whom it is typical. He may be quite intolerant toward persons who "don't speak the same language," whether they are "higher up" or "lower down" in social status relative to his own. Intolerance, whether disguised or not, is usually based on lack of intimate contact and the *inability* to establish intimate contact. In the face of cultural differences, the individual may be like the dweller in the deep sea who cannot imagine any environment except water and who is annoyed, repelled, or frightened when he encounters air and persons who breathe air. To the teacher, who encounters children from many cultural levels, a knowledge of cultural differences in child development is essential.

Some cultural subgroupings are widely recognized, such as those typical of ethnic groups, rural vs. urban society, and those associated with economic classifications such as "rich," "poor," and "middle-income" brackets. Such groupings are often roughly indicative of important differences in abilities, interests, emotional traits, and general way of life, but the classifications are not sufficiently exact to permit an adequate picture of cultural groups in our society. Recent research by sociologists in American communities, employing the concept of "social class," has resulted in a more exact and meaningful description of cultural levels in our society.

Social Stratification. The study of several American communities in different regions, such as New England, the Deep South, and the Middle West, has revealed that American society is, culturally speaking, stratified in a number of association groups, or social strata (5, 17, 19, 20). Although American society is traditionally "classless," the term *social class* is ordinarily employed to indicate these strata of cultural groupings. The term "class" is easily misunderstood in this connection, however, if we think of stratification in terms of economic competition and conflict, or in the Marxian term of "class struggle." Social classes are cultural groupings rather than economic ones. "Social class differences" are both social and economic, but social differences are the important ones for our purpose here.

The fact that society is stratified in social classes has several important aspects:

1. A social class is an *association grouping,* which means that the individuals or families with which one may associate on intimate terms, as an equal, are limited to those of the same social stratum. Intimate association is in fact the *criterion* of social class. That is, a person is said to be in the same social class as other persons with whom he can associate as an equal. The ordinary criteria of intimate association are these: persons are in the same class if they customarily eat and drink together, visit one another freely in their homes (without invitation), and are free to intermarry without disapproval of family and friends.

2. A social class is a *selective cultural grouping.* That is, individuals and families in the same class have similar customs and beliefs, values and interests, habits of thought and speech, and in general a similar way of life. They are of approximately the same occupational level, educational level, and income level. Because of such similarities they communicate easily,

recognize one another as equals, and generally regard themselves as belonging to the same group. Social class therefore represents a relatively fixed pattern of behavior, in the sense that a person can recognize, as typical or atypical of a culture standard, characteristics of his class.

3. Social class is a *status grouping*. That is, a person can ordinarily "place" himself relative to others in a hierarchy of social distance, prestige level, or relative superiority or inferiority. Investigators have found fairly good agreement between the way the individual places himself and the way others place him in the hierarchy. Status placement is therefore a relative matter, but the social scale would seem to be a cultural reality. Class distinctions in terms of status are made by the people themselves, not by sociologists. However, there is no consistency in the labels employed to designate one's own group. One investigation showed that when given a choice of upper, middle, and lower class, most individuals placed themselves as "middle." When the additional category of "working-class" was added, the largest number placed themselves in that class (3, 4). It is understandable that the term "lower" would be rejected.

4. *American society is an open-class, not a fixed-class, society*. That is, social mobility up and down the scale is possible. This differs from a strictly caste system like that of India, for example, where a person's caste is fixed by heredity, and mobility is not possible. It has been found, however, that rapid and easy mobility of the "rags to riches" variety, which is held to be traditional in our society and is often described as the "American dream," is not as common as it is supposed to be. It has been estimated, for example, that only 14 per cent of individuals in America change their social class position either upward or downward during one generation (18). Also, upward mobility is more difficult, both socially and psychologically, than popular folklore would lead us to believe. In spite of some dramatic exceptions, a person tends to remain, as a general rule, in the social class into which he was born. He usually works at about the same occupational level as his father, marries and makes lasting friendships among persons of the

same cultural level, and raises his children pretty much as he was raised himself. This is merely one aspect of the general sociological principle that changes in society are effected slowly.

5. The relative distinctness and fixedness of social class behavior patterns depends on a number of factors. The patterns may be modified slowly by population and cultural changes, education, and changes in distribution of wealth. Geographical isolation, cultural segregation, and unchanging income differences may tend to fix the pattern and make it less subject to change.

6. American society includes *color caste,* particularly in the South and as applied to Negroes. However, Negro society appears to be stratified into classes, resembling on the whole the cultural groupings of white society. The distinction between white and colored groups is primarily a cultural matter, in spite of differences in inherited factors, i.e., physical traits. Color-caste distinctions in the United States are less rigid than the caste system of India, and are probably being modified considerably with time. The chief differences between white and Negro class distributions is that over three-fourths of Negroes are in the "lower class" of Negro society (15).

The social class concept is not a recognition of snobbery based on conspicuous differences in wealth or ostentatious display, but a recognition of cultural differences underlying different patterns of social participation. People of different classes have different patterns of work and play, dress and speech, and social attitudes. These patterns comprise the entire range of social behavior, including family life, attitudes toward children, and child rearing. The fact that families of different social classes show remarkable differences in child rearing makes it possible to use fairly exact terms in identifying environmental differences rather than loose and biased terms like "good" and "poor" homes. Differences in "environment" are essentially differences in class culture, at least for white Americans.

Cultural Strata in American Society. Investigators determine the cultural stratifications in a town by interviewing large numbers of people to find out "who associates with whom," or how the families are grouped according to social participation. Afterward, the socioeconomic differences between the various "classes" are determined by objective study. It has been found, for example, that such socioeconomic differences as occupation, amount and source of income, type and location of dwelling, length of education, club and church memberships, are associated with social class groupings. But the original criterion of social class is not money, or occupation, or type of house; it is social participation. Through objective study of the cultural differences among these groupings, it has been determined that the distinctions are based not on economic factors alone, but on such things as family background, education, manners and customs, beliefs and attitudes, and moral standards.

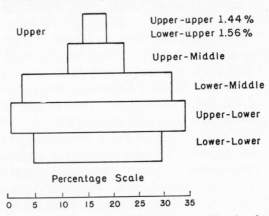

FIGURE 35. Distribution Among Social Classes. The drawing is a composite from several studies of social strata. The data from "Yankee City," a New England town, show the percentage distribution between UU and LU given above. Midwestern towns reveal a stratification into five levels, with no evidence of a distinction between UU and LU. From the scale, the percentage of the population in the LL group, for example, would be estimated at 25 per cent. The distributions shown above, however, may not hold for any particular community. (From W. L. Warner *et al., Social class in America,* p. 70.)

This is illustrated by the studies of Warner and his associates, which may be taken as typical of the findings (18). The familiar terms Upper, Middle, and Lower are used to designate the groupings, with two distinct subgroups within each category.

UPPER–UPPER CLASS

"Old aristocracy"	UU
"Aristocracy," but not "old"	LU
"Nice, respectable people"	UM
"Good people, but 'nobody'"	LM
	UL
"Po' whites"	LL

LOWER–UPPER CLASS

UU	"Old aristocracy"
LU	**"Aristocracy" but not "old"**
UM	"Nice, respectable people"
LM	"Good people, but 'nobody'"
UL	
LL	"Po' whites"

UPPER–MIDDLE CLASS

"Society" { "Old families"	UU
"Society" but not "old families"	LU
"People who should be upper class"	UM
"People who don't have much money"	LM
	UL
"No 'count lot"	LL

LOWER–MIDDLE CLASS

UU	"Old aristocracy" (older) ┊ "Broken-down aristocracy" (younger)
LU	
UM	"People who think they are somebody"
LM	**"We poor folks"**
UL	"People poorer than us"
LL	"No 'count lot"

UPPER–LOWER CLASS

	UU
	LU
"Society" or the "folks with money"	UM
"People who are up because they have a little money"	LM
"Poor but honest folk"	UL
"Shiftless people"	LL

LOWER–LOWER CLASS

UU	
LU	
UM	"Society" or the "folks with money"
LM	"Way-high-ups," but not "Society"
UL	"Snobs trying to push up"
LL	**"People just as good as anybody"**

FIGURE 36. The Social Perspectives of the Social Classes. (From Davis, Gardner, & Gardner, *Deep south*, Chicago: Univ. Chicago Press, 1941, p. 65.)

Figure 35 shows the relative proportion of individuals in each subgroup. Figure 36 shows the differences in perspective of members of different levels, based on a study of a southern town. This illustrates characteristic ways in which members of different social levels view themselves and their associates, as contrasted with the way persons of a different cultural level view them. The attitude toward persons of a given cultural level, in other words, varies according to "social distance."

The social class structure discovered by these studies is complicated, both in its composition and its functions. A composite description of the various levels, based on the studies of Warner and associates, would run about as follows:

Upper-Upper. Old family, wealth inherited, large proprietors or professional, social 400, philanthropically inclined, exclusive clubs. Children of these families seldom go to public schools. Found only in old towns, such as in New England, Atlantic Seaboard, and the South.

Lower-Upper. Wealthy, but not "old family." In style of life, resemble Upper-Upper, who serve as models of behavior. Usually more class-conscious, tend to avoid middle class socially. Dominate and control civic affairs through influence on Upper-Middle. Highest income group. Practically all upper class children go to college, mostly private colleges of "Ivy League" type.

Upper-Middle. Pillars of the community, active in civic affairs, strivers. Professional, proprietary, and managerial occupations, but less income. Property owners. Most children go to public schools, 70 per cent go to college, many to state university. Members of Rotary, school board, chamber of commerce. Value education highly, assume PTA leadership easily. Live in larger houses in better suburbs.

Lower-Middle. Clerks, salespersons, white-collar, small tradesmen, some skilled workers. Often homeowners, but no other property. Smaller or older houses; "side-streeters." Top crust of "common man." Lodge members, but very few belong to charitable organizations, or "culture-conscious" social clubs. All children go to high school, small number go to college, usually publicly supported institutions. Tend to prize education as a means of "getting ahead," often active in PTA groups.

Upper-Lower. Semiskilled, unskilled workers, with some skilled workers and minor clerks. Not property owners. Live in somewhat run-down neighborhoods, poorer and older houses. Change jobs oftener than lower middle; better reputations than lowest class. Children very seldom go to college, and do not value education highly. Do not read much; little interest in community affairs. More often than not, children are expected to attend school, keep out of trouble, and get a "good job," but are not usually encouraged to excel in school or to rise socially.

Lower-Lower. Poor reputations; described by others as lazy, shiftless, untrustworthy, lacking in sexual morality, "live like animals," much of which is exaggerated. Often unemployed, very low annual income spent mostly for food and shelter. Often on relief. Larger percentage of arrests. Live in worst sections. No ambition to "get ahead," and tend to reject middle-class virtues absolutely. In lack of social striving and rejection of pretense, resemble upper-upper class. Have no use for education, and very rarely does a lower-lower child finish high school and go to college. Receive most attention from social welfare agencies, policemen, school attendance officers.

Cultural Differences in Child Development. These association groups have different ways of life, and thus in a sense live in different worlds. The so-called "American way of life," although having features in common to all American families, is stratified into cultural patterns. These "class cultures" are transmitted to children from the beginning of life, and pervade every aspect of child development. The child is conditioned in the way of life of his family, which results in a mode of behavior suited to a particular cultural level. Since a "class" is a social participation group, there is a "social distance" or gap between the various levels. This implies a lack of communication among the various classes, or lack of a common bond of shared experiences.

The differences in customs and attitudes are much more important, in their effect on child development, than the differences in purely physical environment.[1] This does not minimize the importance of the physical setting, but merely puts it into its proper social perspective. Thus the "advantages" of being raised in a larger house in better condition in a "nice" neighborhood are clear only when we ask such questions as these: Does the child have his own room or living quarters, or does he share a small amount of space with many others? Does he have space for play, or is the household dominated by adult activities? Does the mode of living enhance or retard attitudes of respect for property, for the privacy of other persons, for pride in his home and his personal possessions? Is a separate and distinctive family life possible in the neighborhood? Does the child have opportunity for privacy and for self-expression? Can he, in the surroundings, experience a feeling of permanence, of personal security, or family solidarity? The development of such attitudes is less possible in cramped quarters of small or run-down houses, in crowded and physically unattractive neighborhoods. But, even more important, these attitudes will not develop in the child if his family and his family's associates do not have them. The difference between "house" and "home," in other words, is not primarily a physical difference in structures but a difference in the attitudes of persons living in the structures.

Class cultural differences are important in child development chiefly for three reasons:

1. The child's social contacts are generally limited to those of his own immediate family or kinship group or to those of his family's associates, and thus tend to be restricted to persons and groups within his own class culture. The opportunity to de-

[1] An indication that the static or material features of a child's home are not always too indicative of the factors affecting ability or level of mental development is found in a recent study (McGurk, F. C. J., "On white and Negro test performance and socioeconomic factors," *J. abnor. and soc. Psychol.,* 1953, **48**, 448-450).

velop customs and values different from his own group is quite limited. A child may develop friendships and associations with children from a different segment of society, but such associations are ordinarily not encouraged by parents of the higher status group. Thus John, whose father is an accountant and whose family culture is typically "middle-class," would not be encouraged to play with Joe, whose father is a day laborer and who lives "across the tracks," unless Joe's behavior conforms to "middle-class" standards. If Joe is "dirty," or uses "bad language," the association will be short-lived. If Joe makes an effort to conform to standards expected of him by John's parents, Joe's parents and associates will ordinarily think Joe is "putting on airs" and endeavor to "teach him his place." Ordinarily, Joe will think the middle-class standards strange, unnatural, and possibly affected, and will tend to reject them himself. As children become older they learn their own class culture and apply it in their choice of associates. Lasting friendships therefore tend to be confined to one's own cultural level. John and Joe, through the natural course of social interaction, would tend to drift apart without conscious intent on the part of either one.

2. The learning situations provided for the child reflect his family's class culture. The family's associations narrow the child's opportunities for learning by defining the social group with which he may associate intimately. Learning situations are therefore "class-typed," in the sense that the intimate social environment of the child is limited. The class culture is thus instilled and reinforced. He learns the speech, customs, and attitudes typical of his class culture because no other models are provided, but more particularly because this kind of behavior, and no other, is accepted and rewarded by his family and associates. The only effective rewards, in other words, are those administered by persons of his own cultural status. The child needs the approval of his parents, his kinship group, and his neighborhood peers. He learns what he is rewarded for doing. This fact influences or "molds," so to speak, not only his social and emotional development, but his intellectual development as well.

3. Class cultures differ in their attitudes toward children and toward child training. The differences are so striking and so important in their effect on child development that any generalization about mental development of "*the* child," apart from the differential effect of the class culture, tends to be misleading. It has become increasingly evident during the past few years that the study of child development cannot afford to ignore these cultural differences.

Differential Aspects of Child Training. In many essential respects, the sharpest cultural differences are those which distinguish the middle and so-called "lower" or working classes (6). Although there is evidence that the lower middle group tends to identify with the working class politically and economically, attitudes toward children in this level are typically "middle-class," and therefore resemble the top half of society more than the bottom half. In middle-class society, home ownership is much more common, employment more stable. There is less tendency to move from job to job or from one place of residence to another. This represents a pattern of stability, permanence, and continuity of the family which is less noticeable in working class society and practically absent in the "lower-lower" segment. The middle and lower also have characteristically different attitudes toward education and community responsibility, and different concepts of achievement. These differences are revealed in those phases of family life pertaining to child rearing.

Students of this problem point to characteristic differences, first of all, in the social role of children in the family, and in parental attitudes toward the child and the achievement expected of him. The upper-class pattern, according to Bossard (1), is focalized in the wider kinship group. That is, pride in the family name and history takes the form of an attitude of "possessive pride and hope" toward the child, a greater participation by relatives (particularly grandparents) in the rearing of the child, and greater pressure on the child to live up to family expectations. The child's models of behavior and achievement consist largely of relatives and ancestors. Child rearing in the class cultures below this level is centered more in the immediate family.

The middle-class pattern stresses individual achievement and success for the child, and the child's models of "success" are ordinarily outside the family. Since the middle-class family is ordinarily socially mobile, i.e., striving to maintain its social status or to rise socially, the child's achievement is often expected to reflect this. Vertical mobility depends on "making good" in school and in a higher status occupation, or on marrying someone of higher status. Family expectations for the child therefore tend to center around pressure to succeed in school, to "amount to something" occupationally, to make a successful marriage, and particularly to cultivate the class-cultural traits considered necessary to achieving these goals. Since the child is a symbol of family ambition, these attitudes are similar to the upper-class pattern. Middle-class parents, however, are less occupied with upholding family traditions than with providing for the child opportunities which they feel were denied to them.

By contrast, the child of "lower-class" culture is ordinarily not a symbol of parental ambition. Exceptions may be noted, of course, among those families which are "socially mobile," i.e., which are striving to gain higher status and therefore value the middle-class virtues. To most observers, the child at this cultural level seems to be regarded chiefly in terms of his utilitarian value in the home. The family is ordinarily occupied with obtaining the necessities of life, and economic crises occur frequently. The child is expected to work at an earlier age, not because the experience contributes to his development, but for the wage or the economic value of his work to the family. Younger children, not being economically useful, tend to be ignored as inconveniences. They learn to shift for themselves, to "keep their place," and are usually punished for being nuisances. Unlike the children of middle-class culture, they are not usually the objects of a vigorous training regime for their own development.

During the past few years cultural differences in child training practices have been increasingly studied. Although families of the same cultural level differ somewhat in the training they give their children, investigators have concluded that (1) families of the same class culture train children pretty much alike, (2) the greatest contrast in child rearing practices is between the middle and "lower" cultural strata, and (3) this generalization applies to Negro society as well as white; that is, middle-class training of white and Negro children is very similar (6).

The contrast between the two patterns of child rearing is striking in the following respects. (1) Middle-class child training is *planned and systematic*. The parents believe wholeheartedly in planning carefully almost every phase of the child's development, and the educational value of his activities and contacts is of prime importance. Toys, games, and associates are selected with care, and training the child tends to become an active program of keeping him busy with new tasks, teaching and correcting, rewarding and punishing. At the lower cultural level, child rearing is a relatively passive matter, and relatively little thought and planning goes into the learning situations provided. (2) Middle-class training is based on *exacting standards* of industry, responsibility, speech and language, cleanliness, manners, and school progress. These traits are treasured highly because their possession is very important in the middle-class culture. In the "lower-class" way of life, they are much less important factors either socially or occupationally; parents are less given to evaluating their children's behavior, to teaching and correcting, making comparisons among children, or "pushing" the child to attainment of these virtues. They may, however, teach him economically useful tasks around the home or teach him to fight, and be very exacting in standards of conduct in this respect. There are also cultural differences in standards of sex behavior. (3) Middle-class culture emphasizes *restraint* to a greater degree. The child is weaned earlier, toilet-trained earlier, and is allowed less freedom in roaming the neighborhood or keeping late hours. Restrictions concerning speech, dress, cleanliness, sex behavior, and playmates are more rigidly enforced. By contrast, the lower-class culture allows the child relative independence. His parents apparently expect him to learn through imitation and to set his own pace in growing up. (4) The middle-class training regime tends to emphasize *reward rather than punishment*. The child is rewarded for "being a good boy" by parental approval and privileges, and the rewards are systematically employed as aspects of training. Investigators have noted, on the other hand, that positive rewards are rare for the child in lower-class culture, unless absence of punishment is considered rewarding. Punishment is usually corporal rather than social, and is usually administered because the child has been a nuisance rather than because of its educational value.

Class-Cultural Differences in Abilities. It has long been known that individual differences in measured intelligence are related to such socioeconomic factors as family income, father's occupational level, and quality of the home. It should not be surprising, then, to find the same differences among children of different social class levels. In one intensively studied midwestern community, referred to in the literature by such pseudonyms as "Midwest," "Prairie City," and "Elmtown," the social status of each family was determined by the usual methods, and a variety of tests was given to practically the whole population of children aged 10, 13, and 16. Some results are given in Table 9. On the whole, they show (1) clear-cut differences in abilities between the various groups at all age levels, with some exceptions; (2) more striking differences among class levels on the high *verbal* tests, with smaller differences on the tests less verbal in content. The IQ differences among the status groups of sixteen-year-olds on the Stanford Binet, for example, were much less than the differences on the Wechsler-Bellevue Performance Scale. In the case of the Minnesota Mechanical Assembly test, the boys of the lower groups did better than those of the upper ones, reversing the trend among the ten-year-olds.

These findings support the belief that differences in ability may be largely due to cultural differences among the groups. That is, boys of lower cultural levels tend to have more experience and interest in mechanical tasks, hence this more pronounced development of ability is reflected in the tests at age 16 but not at the earlier ages. On the other hand, cultural advantages of the verbal type are more typical of the higher status levels of all ages. More recent studies have confirmed the fact that lower socioeconomic groups make consistently lower scores on tests emphasizing verbal abilities (8). The tests, in the opinion of some investigators, are so culturally

TABLE 9

CLASS-CULTURAL DIFFERENCES IN CHILDREN'S TEST SCORES *

	TEN-YEAR-OLD CHILDREN				
	Stanford-Binet IQ	Goodenough Draw-a-Man IQ	Iowa Silent Reading (Quotient)	Minnesota Paper Form Bd.	Minn. Mech. Assembly (Boys)
Lower-middle (mean scores).	114	116	99	22.5	52.5
Upper-lower	110	102	99	21.3	49.2
Lower-lower ...	91	91	88	15.7	46.9
	SIXTEEN-YEAR-OLD CHILDREN				
	Stanford-Binet IQ	Wechsler-Bellevue IQ	Iowa Silent Reading (T-score)	Minnesota Paper Form Bd.	Minn. Mech. Assembly (Boys)
Upper and upper-middle	128	118	58.0	44	46.8
Lower-middle ...	112	109	51.0	40	51.6
Upper-lower	104	102	48.9	31	48.8
Lower-lower ...	98	103	45.6	31	53.0

* Data from Havighurst and Janke (*J. educ. Psychol.*, 1944, **35**, 357-368), and Janke and Havighurst (*J. educ. Psychol.*, 1945, **36**, 499-509).

"loaded" as to favor children of higher classes and to handicap those of lower cultural levels. We cannot conclude from this, however, that our intelligence tests measure only cultural "class" differences. But it does seem clear that the abilities of children from different cultural levels develop along different lines.

What Are the Developmental Influences? The study of cultural differences among families of different socioeconomic status has revealed at least two important factors in child development. The developmental influences are seen chiefly in (1) the cultural function of language, and (2) the motivation of the child through training.

1. *Language.* We have seen that language provides the symbols which are the basis of thinking and of socialization, and that the content of our intelligence tests is largely verbal or linguistic. To the American middle class, language is a central factor. It plays an important role in class status, since the kind of language one uses is a mark of his station in life. Most middle class people actually make their living through linguistic skills, in "white-collar" jobs. Occupational skills in professional, managerial, clerical, and sales fields are chiefly skills in handling verbal symbols.

Skillful use of language is also essential to social mobility. Middle-class parents are therefore keenly conscious of language development in their children, work hard to bring it about, teach and read to them, constantly correct their words and grammar, and in general provide a "verbal environment." The environment of the child of lower socioeconomic status is of course verbal also, but differs greatly in grammar and vocabulary. Furthermore, language is less important in "lower-class" life. The child does not learn that linguistic skills are important in earning a living, for within his experience this is not so. The occupations of his parents and associates deal with things rather than symbols, and the child's vocabulary tends to be a "thing vocabulary"—concrete rather than abstract. As a consequence, unless his parents emphasize training for a middle-class way of life, he is almost certain to "stay far behind the middle-class child in the extent of his vocabulary, in the accuracy of his grammar, and in his interest in reading" (7). This lag is no doubt reflected in intelligence test performance, as well as in the development of interests.

The limitations are very real deterrents in mental development, since the developmental processes of differentiation, integration, and symbolization depend very much, at the higher levels, on language facility. In a very real sense, intellectual development *is* language development. Does this mean that children of different cultural levels are equal in "innate" capacity to acquire verbal skills, that the lack of ability is explained totally by "environment"? Probably not. We do know, however, that the child most likely to rise in status is one who performs better on tests and in school work, and he typically "takes active steps to seek out a human environment which will provide him with models of middle-class language" (7).

2. *Motivation through training.* The middle-class parents prize education and occupational achievement, since achievement is the means by which one's status in life is maintained or improved. As a consequence, the middle-class child is *pushed* up the ladder of achievement, while the lower class child is in this respect left pretty much to his own devices (7). The differences in motivation are partly due, of course, to the differences in parent-models; the child of either level will tend to acquire the motives and attitudes of his parents because they dominate his environment during the early years.

But the parents are not merely models for imitation; they are active agents in child training. Davis and Havighurst (7) point out that the middle-class child is trained to assume various responsibilities around the home earlier than the child in the "lower-class" family. He also learns very rapidly that he is expected to "make good," and that this implies doing good work in school. Since book-learning is much less important in lower socioeconomic status, report cards mean very little and parents do not push the child or plan educational sequences of tasks. The one respect in which the child of lower status assumes responsibility earlier is in working for wages. He is expected to get a job sooner, and to become a wage-earner, even if school is sacrificed. "Getting ahead" means getting a job, not getting good grades. There is not only less teaching and urging at this level, but whatever teaching occurs is not intellectually centered. The parents are more concerned with practical and utilitarian matters as defined in their way of life. Although there are undoubtedly original differences in potentiality for intellectual development among children of different socioeconomic status, these differences are affected by the kind of stimulation and training typical of different cultural levels.

SOCIAL NORMS IN EDUCATION

Cultural Differences in the School. The school cannot afford to ignore differences in cultural backgrounds and outlook among the students, but can easily do so if teachers are not keenly attentive to them. Cultural differences play important parts in facilitating or handicapping the achievement of students. At least three aspects of these are worth attention: (1) attitudes toward school work, (2) social relationships among students, and (3) teacher-pupil relationships.

1. *Attitudes toward school work.* As we have seen, educational achievement is very important in the value system of families of upper socioeconomic status, and of little importance to those of lower status. Ability to read, write, spell, type, and compute, as well as knowledge of history, literature, and science is less important to one way of life than to another. The child of lower status, even though above average in academic aptitude, would not be expected to show keen interest in the more academic subjects. In this attitude, he may actually be more realistic than his teacher. There is evidence that the greater proportion of school "dropouts," particularly beyond the eighth grade, are from lower socioeconomic groups (17). The high school, as well as the college, is selective not only with respect to scholastic aptitude but also with respect to social status (16). On the whole, children of lower status are not as ready to benefit from the typical school curriculum. They are less likely to enjoy school, to be accepted, or to establish effective working relationships with teachers.

2. *Social relationships among students.* There is evidence that class-cultural differences often determine "who associates with whom" in school as well as in the community. Contrary to the belief that children are naturally democratic and recognize no social distinctions, some studies have shown that the social status of the child's family determines a child's choice of friends and his reputation among his schoolmates. In one intensively studied community, "Jonesville," "friendship groupings seemed to follow a pattern in which children of a given social class tended to associate with others of the same class"

was determined from a sociometric study of all h-grade children in the public school. The chil- ed to name their best friends, and also to name girls with whom they did not want to associate, ...ued this information anonymously in prepared book- lets. As shown in the top row of Table 10, a striking degree of relationship between social status and social participation was found. "The lower the social class of the child, the fewer times he is mentioned as a 'best friend' and the more times he is mentioned as 'don't like to be with' " (17). When the author employed a "Guess Who" technique, asking the children to name those children who they thought were well-dressed, good-looking, or had "bad manners" or "fights a lot," the same relationship between status and reputation was found, as shown in Table 10. The data showed also that "social status factors determined not only which children received favorable and unfavorable mention but also the way in which each child casts his votes" (17). In this school, the child of lower status is more likely to be socially isolated. In another school, where a large majority of the students are of lower status, the "upper-middle" child may be isolated. The fact that friendship groups tend to be formed along class-cultural lines creates a psychological climate, in any case, which makes the social adjustment of some students very difficult. A cold, unfriendly atmosphere for the student who feels "left out" will certainly affect his attitude toward scholastic work. This poses an important problem for the school, since its goal is to further the achievement of the individual and to secure for each individual the group participation essential for democratic living. The results of such studies seem to indicate that proper social adjustment in school can be achieved only through the help of the teacher.

3. *Teacher-student relationships.* A child's progress in school depends on whether he enjoys it, and his satisfaction is determined largely by the degree to which he is able to get along with teachers. The child of lower cultural level is not only more likely to find school work unattractive and to feel rejected by his age-peers, but less likely to establish rapport with the teacher. To the child the teacher's middle-class values will

TABLE 10

RELATION BETWEEN CLASS STATUS AND REPUTATION AS DETERMINED FROM
CHILDREN'S RESPONSES TO "GUESS WHO" QUESTIONS *

	UM(6%)	LM(17%)	UL(62%)	LL(15%)
"Best friend"	64 **	37	18	15
"Well dressed"	93	33	14	3
"Good looking"	43	27	11	1
"Popular"	39	15	8	1
"Likes school"	45	15	9	3
"Clean"	44	16	8	2
"Has good time"	27	14	5	5
"Good manners"	41	15	5	3
"Plays fair"	28	11	7	4
"Leader"	41	12	5	1
"Don't like"	9	5	11	37
"Not well dressed"	0	1	11	55
"Not good looking"	2	3	10	27
"Unpopular"	1	2	6	21
"Doesn't like school"	3	3	9	28
"Dirty"	0	1	7	34
"Never has good time"	3	5	4	8
"Bad manners"	5	6	5	19
"Doesn't play fair"	4	4	5	11
"Fights a lot"	20	8	9	21

* Data from Neugarten, in Warner *et al.*, *Democracy in Jonesville* (17),
p. 80.

** The figures shown here "may be interpreted as the series of ratios
which would obtain if there were an equal number of children in each of the
four social classes."

appear unfamiliar and unreal. The child's attitudes and behavior may be repugnant to the teacher—even to the teacher inclined to be warm and sympathetic. Studies have shown that
teachers tend to rate the intelligence, manners, and other traits
of children in accordance with the class-cultural level of the
children's families (5).

Education and Social Mobility. Although upward mobility is less common than American tradition would lead us to
believe, it occurs frequently enough to keep the tradition alive.
The term "success," as commonly employed, means different
things at different levels of social status. At the lower socioeconomic levels, "success" is practically synonymous with up-

ward mobility, i.e., getting more education, making progress in an occupation carrying higher prestige. The main channels through which upward mobility is possible are education, occupation, and marriage. Schooling is obviously an important one, since it opens up the possibility of rising in occupational level and marrying someone of a "higher" social stratum. In our society, the school is widely expected to fulfill this function.

However, there are psychological barriers to upward mobility, of which the educator must be aware if he would provide guidance to the student of lower socioeconomic status who is attempting to rise.

1. The student may not have the ability required for scholastic achievement. His level of society may represent several generations of an hereditary-environmental winnowing process that leaves the least able products of society at the bottom. Class differences in scholastic aptitude, in any case, are a fact. But some children low in the socioeconomic scale do have the ability.

2. The able ones, if well integrated in "lower-class" customs and values, tend to lack the motivation. The child would not be expected to believe in the "American Dream," in education, in white-collar standards. He does not ordinarily want to rise. But there are some, poorly integrated in their own cultural level, who aspire to middle-class "success," and who have potentialities. The teacher recognizes such an individual as a "diamond in the rough," and his own associates may see him as a "snob trying to push up."

3. Even with the ability and the desires, the ambitious student will have rough going. In the first place, he may lack the economic resources to continue his education. His teachers may encourage him, and his parents not. Or his parents may encourage the schooling, but not the changes in social values and customs that schooling brings. As he tries to rise, he may be ostracized both by the group above (because he does not resemble them sufficiently) and by his own group, whose customs, manners, and language he must repudiate.

4. Some psychological conflict is almost inevitable. The change is an inward, psychological change, not just a change

in externals. The ambitious person's attitudes toward hi: ,
ents and his early associates will be sharply ambivalent; he
will both approve and disapprove of them. Attitudes toward
persons of the higher cultural level will also be ambivalent. He
must learn not to be too aggressive, but may at the same time
feel a strong need to be aggressive in order to prove his worth.
Even his self-evaluative attitudes will be ambivalent. He may
be regarded by others, and to some extent may regard himself,
as a pretender or impostor. Learning dilemmas, in the face of
which he may expect very little guidance, will confront him constantly as he competes for educational and occupational opportunities and for social status.

Social Role of the Teacher. Studies of the social participation of teachers in various communities show them to be pre-
dominantly middle-class persons (16). One writer on the
subject points out that the American teacher has come chiefly
from the "lower middle" socioeconomic level for the past one
hundred years (9). Considering the fact that the occupation
of teaching is fairly high on various prestige scales of occupations, it seems probable that many teachers may enter the occupation as a channel of vertical mobility. This means that the
most typical attitudes of teachers are middle-class attitudes,
and this affects their role not only in society, but in their special
mission of introducing children to our society and of guiding
their adjustment to it. As Warner says,

. . . Teachers represent middle-class attitudes and enforce middle-
class values and manners. In playing this role, teachers do two things.
They train and seek to train children in middle-class manners and skills.
And they select those children from the middle and lower classes who
appear to be the best candidates for promotion in the social hierarchy.
(16, p. 107)

This, of course, is not the only role of the teacher, and it is
by no means consciously defined and carried out in the school
program. Stating it in this way, however, calls attention to the
cultural standards that dominate the life of the typical school.
It is to be expected that teachers, unwittingly or otherwise, will
judge the students' backgrounds, progress, and potentialities in

terms of the customs and beliefs which they themselves feel to be "right," in terms of values they hold most dear.

The tendency to judge students of different cultural levels in terms of one set of cultural standards is not an unmixed blessing. The school completely dedicated to selecting and training children for one (middle-class) way of life serves the needs of one segment of society, while ignoring another. It helps the socially mobile student greatly, but misses many opportunities to help those who must work out their salvation in a different way of life.

Cultural differences are not only potent factors in child development, but also in the school program. As a promoter of democratic values and social solidarity, the teacher must understand the social structure of America and of her own community in order to interpret it for her students. As a guide to the young learner, she must think of the student not as a mere combination of abilities, but as a person with a social background and social goals. From this point of view, the value of the curricular subjects does not depend entirely on their utility in promoting the student's rise in class status. There is thus room for instruction in music, art, crafts, and recreational play, not because they represent middle-class values, but because they contribute to the development and satisfaction of the student at any cultural level. Vocational guidance does not consist in pushing more students into professional and white-collar jobs, but in helping the individual to attain the skills and outlook essential to the attainment of appropriate social goals, whether middle class or not. The effective school is one that treats students of different social backgrounds with warmth and understanding, but *differently,* in order to equalize as much as possible their unequal educational opportunities.

REFERENCES

1. Bossard, J. H. S. *The sociology of child development.* New York: Harper, 1948.
2. Burks, B. The relative influence of nature and nurture on mental development. *27th Yearbook,* Nat. Soc. Stud. Educ., 1928.

3. CENTERS, R. *The psychology of social classes*. Princeton, N. J.: Princeton Univ. Press, 1949.

4. CENTERS, R. *Intern. J. Opinion Attitude Research,* 1951, **5**, 159-178.

5. DAVIS, A., GARDNER, B. B., & GARDNER, M. R. *Deep south.* Chicago: Univ. of Chicago Press, 1941.

6. DAVIS, A. Child training and social class. In BARKER, KOUNIN, & WRIGHT, *Child behavior and development,* New York: McGraw-Hill, 1943.

7. DAVIS, A., & HAVIGHURST, R. J. *Father of the man.* Boston: Houghton Mifflin, 1947.

8. EELLS, K., *et al. Intelligence and cultural differences.* Chicago: Univ. of Chicago Press, 1951.

9. ELSBREE, W. S. *The American Teacher.* New York: American Book, 1939.

10. HARTSHORNE, H., & MAY, M. A. Testing the knowledge of right and wrong. *Relig. Educ.,* 1926.

11. HARTSHORNE, H., & MAY, M. A. Sibling resemblance in deception. *27th Yearbook,* II, Nat. Soc. Stud. Educ., 1928.

12. LINTON, R. *The cultural background of personality.* New York: Appleton-Century-Crofts, 1945.

13. SAPIR, E. Language. In *Encyclopedia of the social sciences.* New York: Macmillan, Vol. IX.

14. VAN ALSTYNE, D. The environment of three-year-old children. *Teach. Coll. Contr. Educ., No. 366.* New York: Columbia Univ., 1929.

15. WARNER, W. L. American caste and class. *Amer. J. Sociology,* 1936, **42**, 234-237.

16. WARNER, W. L., HAVIGHURST, R. J., & LOEB, M. B. *Who shall be educated?* New York: Harper, 1944.

17. WARNER, W. L., *et al. Democracy in Jonesville.* New York: Harper, 1949.

18. WARNER, W. L., MEEKER, M., & EELLS, K. *Social class in America.* Chicago: Science Research Associates, 1949.

19. WARNER, W. L., & LUNT, P. S. *The social life of a modern community.* "Yankee City Series," Vol. I. New Haven: Yale Univ. Press, 1941.

20. WEST, JAMES. *Plainville, U.S.A.* New York: Columbia Univ. Press, 1945.

21. YOUNG, K. *Sociology: a study of society and culture.* New York: American, 1942.

SELECTED READINGS

CENTERS, R. *The psychology of social classes.* Princeton, N. J.: Princeton Univ. Press, 1949. A study of social and political attitudes influenced by class affiliation.

DAVIS, A. *Social class influences upon learning.* Cambridge: Harvard Univ. Press, 1948.

DAVIS, A. Socialization and adolescent personality. Nat. Soc. Stud. Educ., *43d Yearbook,* Pt. I, 1944.

DAVIS, A., & DOLLARD, J. *Children of bondage.* Washington, D.C.: Amer. Council on Education, 1940. Analyzes the effect of caste and class on personality development of the Negro.

DAVIS, A., & HAVIGHURST, R. J. *Father of the Man.* Boston: Houghton Mifflin, 1947. Discusses the function of the family and its class-culture in personality development of children.

EELLS, K. W., *et al. Intelligence and cultural differences: a study of cultural learning and problem solving.* Chicago: Univ. of Chicago Press, 1951. An analysis of class-cultural differences in answering items on intelligence tests.

HOLLINGSHEAD, A. B. *Elmtown's youth.* New York: Wiley, 1949. Based on study of adolescents in midwestern town of 535 families. Pt. II, The social scene, Chs. 3-7.

KUHLEN, R. G. *The psychology of adolescent development.* New York: Harper, 1952, Ch. 4.

LINTON, R. *Culture and personality.* New York: Appleton-Century-Crofts, 1945. The viewpoint of an anthropologist.

MEAD, M. *From the south seas.* New York: Morrow, 1939. Studies of children in primitive societies.

WARNER, W. L., *et al. Democracy in Jonesville.* New York: Harper, 1951. The social structure of a midwestern town and its effect on the life of the school.

WARNER, W. L., HAVIGHURST, R. J., & LOEB, M. B. *Who shall be educated?* New York: Harper, 1944. The influence of class-culture factors on educational opportunity and teacher-pupil relationships.

SHERMAN, M., & HENRY, J. N. *Hollow folk.* New York: Crowell, 1933. Description of a contemporary American subculture.

7

SOCIAL AND EMOTIONAL DEVELOPMENT

W̲E̲ ̲M̲A̲Y̲ now consider some factors important in understanding how a child matures socially and emotionally—how he learns to get along with other people and to solve his emotional problems or conflicts, which usually involve social relationships. What are the child's needs and how are they learned? Through what channels are they gratified? What are the child's problems? What are the sources of frustration at the various stages of development? What kinds of experiences cause some traits to develop rather than others? Do the childhood traits carry over into adulthood, and if so to what extent do they affect behavior? These are critically important questions to society and the school. Some partial answers are presented here.

Emotion and Education. A practical as well as a theoretical distinction must be made between intellectual maturity and social or emotional maturity. Intellectual attainments and emotional adjustment may go hand in hand, but they are clearly not the same thing. A person can be highly intelligent and well educated, but a neurotic social misfit. The mentally dull can be well adjusted, happy citizens. Intellectual training may, or may not, help to develop a socially mature person, depending on many interrelated factors in the individual's experience. But the ability to solve intellectual problems and the ability to deal with the frustrating circumstances of life are of a somewhat different order. Emotional conflicts are complicated by unconscious needs, expectations, and fears which are often at odds with one another. Any problem situation, be it one of arithmetic or of courtship, can of course be both intellectual and emotional. When coming to grips with a problem, the individual "thinks" and "feels" at the same time. The distinction between intellectual and emotional therefore does not imply that they are easily separable in behavior or in development, but that problem situations differ in the extent to which they require intellectual abilities or traits of another kind.

Children in our society get formal and fairly standard training in the solution of intellectual problems, but practically no formal training in the solution of social-emotional problems. We train them in arithmetic, grammar, government, physical health, and occupational skills, but the skills and attitudes necessary for achieving harmony in personal life they must somehow "pick up" in other ways. As a consequence, the typical adult has at his command many formal principles for solving intellectual problems and very few for dealing with emotional problems. The popular demand for "How to be Happy" books is perhaps an indication of this.

Children in our society get a great deal of training in standards of behavior. They are taught how to behave, how to conform. Important as this is for mental health of the child, it does not guarantee that the child will be able to adapt to the changing conditions of life. As the child grows older, the social pattern to which he must conform undergoes changes. He must "act his age," conform to standards expected for his sex, and sometimes adapt his behavior to different class-culture standards. This is not easy. The child must not only learn new ways of behavior, but must learn to give up the old ones. As Preston puts it, "There can be no more futile order than 'stop being a baby.' You cannot stop being a baby. You have to give it up gradually, one step at a time" (20, p. 110).

To some persons it might appear that social maturity means doing what society expects, and that emotional maturity means keeping the emotions under control. Actually, a person might do both of these things and still be unhappy and socially ineffective. Presumably the educational ideal is that of the "mature person," and this is perhaps a psychological ideal as well. The mature person is one who achieves an emotionally satisfying life based on an effective balance between his own needs and society's demands. Mere compliance with society's demands is not in itself a mark of psychological maturity.

The development of the mature person can be hindered by an educational approach that emphasizes either social demands or individual freedom of expression to the exclusion of the other. Some teachers have apparently thought fear to be the great "prime mover" in learning, judging from past educational practice. The end, conformity, was apparently held to justify this means of motivating the child. Emotional maturity could hardly result from frightening the child. On the other hand, social maturity can hardly result from either suppressing the child's emotional life or through unrestrained emotional license. This child who always gets his own way will hardly adjust to an adult social role.

It may be impossible to specify rules and regulations for achieving the personal security basic to mental health. In a general way, however, social and emotional maturity depend on harmonizing the goals of the individual and the goals of the culture within which he must live. This is implied in the concept of education as a sequence of "developmental tasks." Education must contribute, if it is to be worthy of the name, to this developmental process. It would seem wise to make explicit here what is all too often an unstated assumption of educators: that going to school is expected to contribute to the student's welfare, i.e., to his personal security and happiness. The individual's welfare presumably contributes in turn to the general welfare of society. Seen in this light, the social and emotional aspect of education is primary, not subsidiary to the three R's.

Socialized Behavior. Behavior is "socialized" when it is in accord with the expectations of others. Most of our behavior is socialized; it is motivated, either consciously or unconsciously, by the desire to gain the approval of others. We do the things that society expects us to do, and refrain from those things which society does not expect. Many persons like to think of themselves as independent of such influences and feel reluctant to admit that their actions are organized to secure social approval. This fact merely illustrates the principle of socialization; "independence" or self-direction is itself a socially approved trait.

The desire for approval is a powerful motive, and is practically universal in human society. In other words, most of our behavior is regulated by *custom*. Our dress, speech, language, posture, gestures, attitudes, and emotional reactions comprise a social pattern which we unconsciously recognize as correct or appropriate. The only unsocialized persons are (1) very young children, (2) those mentally unbalanced or psychotic persons who have "lost touch with reality," (3) low grade feebleminded persons. To realize how important a controlling factor custom is in our behavior, we need only point out that unsocialized persons in the categories above are not considered responsible for their actions. Psychotics and idiots are usually segregated by society because they cannot play the role which society considers necessary and appropriate. The person who does not behave in accordance with the expectations of others is considered queer, immature, (in extreme cases) unreliable, or dangerous. The ability to conform, in a wide variety of particulars, to social demands is therefore a mark of maturity, adequacy, and stability.

Socialized behavior is learned behavior. The infant is not socialized, but is in the process of becoming so. From a very early age, he begins to undergo training in the customs of his society. Since social training commences early and is pursued vigorously in infancy and early childhood, the pattern of personality development is quite well "set" by the time the child goes to school. The kind of training he receives has a profound effect on the social behavior pattern produced. A child trained by Zulus will think, feel, and react like a Zulu, regardless of ethnic origin, and a child raised in an American family will show early the main outlines of the "American character." Differences in custom are important because the very meaning of socialized behavior (of maturity, adequacy, stability) differs markedly according to cultural background. The concept of the "mature person" has no meaning except with reference to a particular culture.

Emotion and Emotional Behavior. Since personality is the characteristic integration of social and emotional response patterns, the words "social" and "emotional" describe aspects of behavior which are really inextricable. It is perhaps easier to see how social responses are learned than how emotional patterns are learned, because certain traditional ways of thinking about emotions tend to get in the way. How do emotions originate? Are they instinctive or modifiable through experience? If modifiable, how? Is emotional expression a simple unfolding of a hereditary mechanism, so that people are innately "hotheaded" or fearful or affectionate? These questions are of practical concern to educators because the modification of emotional life is clearly related to personal welfare, and because emotional states affect learning. Our concept of emotion and its role in behavior determines to a large degree our attitudes toward emotional expression and our educational approach.

Psychological theories of emotion attempt to account for emotional experiences in terms of physiological events. This complex problem need not concern us here, except to note that the word "emotion" refers to three different aspects of behavior. (1) The emotional experience, or "feeling tone" of pleasantness-unpleasantness, is known only to the subject. (2) Emotion is characterized by a certain pattern of physiological events. The domination of the sympathetic nervous system during heightened states of "rage" or "fear" results in characteristic changes in pulse, blood pressure, respiration, pupil dilation, visceral reactions, etc. (3) In emotional states a person tends to express the feeling by movements, posture, or physiognomic patterns. The relationships among these three aspects have been investigated experimentally, and some of the findings are contrary to popular opinion. These findings are essential to our understanding of the principle that *emotional reactions are learned*.

The physiological reaction pattern is the same for emotions called by different names. There is not a distinctive pattern for "rage" and another for "fear"; physiologically, they are the same pattern. In this sense, emotional states differ in intensity only. We know that rage, fear, love, pleasure, or astonishment may be expressed differently. However, emotions called by different names do not have unique behavioral patterns of expression. Anger, fear, or grief may be expressed in any number of ways, and cannot be distinguished by their appearances alone. Experimental attempts to judge emotional states from facial or postural expression alone have not been conspicuously successful. You can tell whether a child is experiencing "fear" or "anger" or "sorrow" only if you know the stimulus that provokes the emotion. In this case, we may correctly infer how the child is interpreting the situation through a process of empathy; that is, by assuming that he is reacting to the situation as we would react to it. We know also that persons of different cultures express emotions in different ways. The Chinese child sticks out his tongue when surprised, and the Japanese expresses embarrassment by smiling. The various names which we commonly give to emotional states, then, have only a subjective reference.

The principle that emotional behavior is learned implies three things: (1) A person's characteristic emotional responses to certain situations are a product of his experience, or the way he has learned to interpret the situation. (2) The gestures or facial expressions for expressing emotion are the result of acculturation, as well as unique individual experience within a given cultural pattern. (3) Habits of emotional control are learned. The perception of an emotion-provoking situation is a cognitive act. Knowledge and skills can therefore reduce fear or disgust, and unpleasant situations can through learning become pleasant ones. This should make us cautious about inferring that "hot-headedness," "recklessness," or "timidity" are the result of innate or constitutional tendencies.

Genetic Theories of Emotion. The fact that no specific patterns of distinctive emotional states have been discovered may mean either (1) that there are no specific innate patterns or (2) if there are innate patterns, they are so modified through personal and social learning as to be unrecognizable. Several views of emotions have therefore been advanced, as follows:

1. *Emotions as instincts.* This view holds that emotion is entirely a matter of organic structure. The emotion is an aspect of a basic general instinct, rather than a specific pattern. Fear is thus an aspect of the basic "built in" instinct of self-preservation. The expression of emotion is uniform to the extent that the human organism is uniform. According to this theory, sex differences must be constitutional and changes in emotional expression with age must be due to age changes in organic structure. This is perhaps the most traditional view of emotions. It minimizes the importance of learning in the development of emotional behavior.

2. *Emotions as primary innate patterns.* This is the behavioristic view of emotions, and is based largely on the pioneer experiments of John Watson with young infants. He distinguished three primary or innate patterns identified as fear, rage, and love.

Fear, or emotion plus withdrawing, was provoked by two kinds of stimuli, loud sounds and loss of support. The reaction consisted of sudden catching of the breath, random clutching with the hands, sudden closing of the eyelids and pursing of the lips, followed by crying. *Rage,* or emotion plus struggling, was evoked by one stimulus, restraint of movement. The struggling reaction consisted of slashing and striking with hands and arms, up and down movements of the legs, and prolonged holding of the breath, plus a distinctive cry. *Love* was evoked by stroking, petting, and fondling, and the reaction was that of cessation of crying, smiling, gurgling, and cooing. We note here the emphasis on "specific response to a specific stimulus." These primary patterns were held to be characteristic, unlearned (instinctive) behavior patterns, basic but modifiable. Other investigators have advanced similar views regarding primary or characteristic facial expressions of emotion.

The evidence against the "innate pattern" theory comes from three sources. (1) Experiments have shown that observers cannot identify the emotional pattern unless they see the stimulus. For example, when psychology and medical students were shown motion pictures of infant reactions to hunger, sudden dropping, restraint, and being stuck with a needle, they labeled all of these responses "anger." The response to sudden dropping was called "anger" fourteen times and "fear" only five times. When the judges saw the child being dropped, however, the tendency to name "fear" was much more apparent (22). (2) Physiologically, no difference has been found between fear and rage. (3) Investigations of facial expressions of emotions show that there is no pattern of expression characteristic of any situation or emotional experience.

3. *Emotions as learned patterns.* This view holds that emotion in infants is a diffuse state of *general* excitement caused by any overstimulation. Specific patterns of emotion are differentiated from this general reaction through learning. Both the physiological and behaviorial characteristics of emotional expression, as well as maturational changes in emotional life, are accounted for by the "learning" theory of emotions.

Supporting evidence comes from careful studies of children's reactions. When nursery school children were systematically observed over a long period of time, no rigid patterning was apparent in emotional reaction among children of the same age. Under similar conditions, different children responded differently, and an individual reaction differed at various times. Progressive modifications of reactions with age and experience were noted (3). Daily records of anger in children showed anger reactions to become gradually more adaptive, or directed toward a given end (9). This would indicate that changes in "angry" behavior are products of learning, and that the characteristic pattern adopted by the child is one that works best in attaining his goals.

Human emotional behavior is thus a progressive modification of an original tendency to respond in a diffuse, general manner. Emotional reactions become more goal-directed, and like other forms of behavior, they develop out of the constant *interaction* between the genetic changes of organic growth and learning through social conditioning. Emotional development is therefore a component aspect of social development. Modes of expressing anger become socialized; the kicking and stamping of the child becomes displaced by verbal threats or name calling, and later by persuasive talking and more symbolic modes of action. Similarly, the cues for fear and the manner of expressing fear are learned. According to learning theory, any consistent pattern of emotional reaction persists because it is rewarding, satisfying, goal-attaining, or tension reducing, not because it is an innate, fixed response pattern. Emotional behavior, then, can be modified.

The Organismic View of Emotion. We may be accustomed to think of emotions as something outside of behavior and acting on it, rather than belonging to behavior as a characteristic aspect of it. This point of view is perhaps implicit when we ask such questions as: "What is the effect of anger on the behavior of a boxer in the ring? How does fear affect the concentration of a child doing problems in arithmetic?" We observe that the behavior of the speaker with "stage-fright" differs from his usual manner, and conclude that emotion is in some way interfering with or altering his normal speaking behavior. When we speak of the disorganizing effects of emotion, we are speaking from this customary point of view.

Although there is more than an element of truth in these observations, we may thus be led to certain beliefs or attitudes that cause us to distrust emotions and their expression. Some persons, perhaps because they see emotions only as *disrupting and disturbing* factors, may feel that emotions are something to be distrusted and suppressed. To some, the ideal of the "emotionally stable" person is one who has few emotions or carefully conceals them. It may be that emotional control means, to such a person, avoiding or conquering or stamping them out. This attitude may make us blind in some respects to the importance of emotions in mental development.

From the organismic point of view emotion is *purposive*. Behavior is characteristically emotional. To say that behavior is goal-directed implies that motives are states of emotional tension. Rather than saying that our emotions act on behavior, we should say instead that the purpose of emotion is to help us reach goals and to overcome obstacles in the path of the goals.

As Goldstein (11) has pointed out, we do not cry because we are sad, as common sense sees it, nor are we sad because we cry, as the classic James-Lange theory holds. Both sadness and crying are disturbing, but crying is an aid in overcoming the difficulties of the situation that produced them.

Seen in this light, fear is goal-directed because it organizes us for flight from the fear-producing situation, and anger because it organizes us for action. When the "stage-frightened" speaker confronts an audience, he is in an unfamilar and complex situation involving a threat of failure. His excitement and its physical symptoms may be regarded as a preparation for meeting the crisis. If properly controlled and utilized, his emotions may assist his delivery through heightened intensity, mental alertness, and resourcefulness. Emotional control, then, is achieved when the emotions are directed toward achieving one's goals. This is one aspect of socialization and of social and emotional maturity.

Social and Emotional Maturity. When is a person mature? He is legally mature at 21, and physically mature long before that. We recognize that legal or physical or even intellectual maturity do not guarantee psychological maturity—the ability to assume and to discharge adult responsibility in its manifold aspects. And although we may recognize the existence of "adult infantilism" and deplore the "adolescent" behavior of persons above statutory age, socially and emotionally mature behavior is quite difficult to define. Prescott lists three criteria of mature behavior:

1. A *genetic criterion* of mature behavior would demand the achievement of patterns of affective behavior that are effective in resolving physiological tensions and disequilibria and that result in a strong hedonic tone of pleasure in carrying out of fully integrated behavior.

2. A *social or cultural criterion* of mature behavior would demand the achievement of patterns of affective behavior such as are common and accepted within the population of a given area, and the avoidance of patterns of affective behavior which run counter to the mores or which arouse tension and antagonistic action in a considerable number of other persons.

3. An *ethical criterion* of mature behavior would demand the achievement of patterns of affective behavior that conform to certain basic value principles which are accepted by a given individual or population, and the avoidance of patterns of affective behavior that are contrary to these value principles in their effects upon oneself or upon others. (19, p. 98)

Prescott points out the conflict among these criteria. (1) The mores of society impose limits on the development, say, of sexually mature behavior. (2) If society is accepted as the final arbiter of maturity and children are trained merely to adjust to the *status quo* of social mores, we are faced with the problem of deciding whether mere conformity is the goal of mature behavior. (3) Ethical values differ in various segments of society, and this imposes a further difficulty. Furthermore, detailed information about the maturity of social and cultural behavior is lacking. As a consequence, there can be no fixed and immutable definition of maturity in terms of behavior patterns, for "maturity implies a considerable range of complex behavior varying from situation to situation for a given person and varying also from person to person in a given situation." However, psychologists agree on some general descriptions of social-emotional traits that characterize the mature adult from the child. They also agree on the clinical evidence that individuals lacking in these qualities will not adjust well to the adult role in society. On the basis of this general agreement, scales have been developed for the measurement of social and emotional maturity.

Willoughby (25) has given us a scale for measuring emotional maturity in adults. It is clear that he is dealing with an important aspect of personality development. Emotional maturity is taken as the degree in which a person has left behind his childish self-reference and fluctuations of emotional life and become more "realistic," "impersonal," and even-tempered. Such traits are likely to show variations independent of intelligence and other aspects of development. Examples of mature and immature behavior from the Willoughby scale are as follows:

1. The emotionally mature person
    a) chooses a course of action with reference to maximum long-time satisfaction of the entire group of persons involved.
    b) welcomes opportunity for exercise of precise or realistic thinking.
    c) welcomes legitimate association with members of the opposite sex and is not ashamed, fearful, or unduly preoccupied with the topic of sex.
    d) is clear-cut in his decisions; when it is necessary to relinquish an objective, he relinquishes or postpones it entirely; when retaining it, he retains all of it and without regret.
2. The emotionally immature person
    a) chooses his courses of action with reference to his own immediate satisfaction.
    b) characteristically appeals for help in the solution of his problems.
    c) passes rapidly from one interest or attachment to another.
    d) is jealous of his spouse; feels insecure when any other interest claims spouse's attention. (25)

Furfey (7) has devised a scale for measuring what he calls *developmental age,* "the progressively increasing and non-intellectual maturity of general behavior which shows itself in the growing child's play performances, in his fantasy life, in his choice of books and movies, in his ambitions." He finds a low correlation between developmental and mental age and a significant relation between the former and the child's social adjustment. An overprotective home environment is likely to be associated with low developmental age (16), as is also residence in an institution for children. Puberty is commonly found to lead to a definite increase in developmental age. There is apparently a constitutional factor operative here, as it has been found that the boy of the stout or "pyknic" body build matures earlier than the more slender "asthenic" child (4). Developmental age has been shown to be of considerable significance in influencing children's friendships, more important it would seem than either chronological or mental age. The play life of the child and his reading interests are also thought to be related to his social development.

Differences in social traits between adolescents and young adults are revealed in a study by Weitzman (24) with a self-report inventory given to 900 young men and women ranging in age from 16 to 24. The differences between younger and older members of this group were apparent in the degree of participation in social activities such as dances and movies, the older subjects being more moderate in this respect. The older ones also showed more foresight in planning expenditures, saving money, and looking after their health, and assumed more responsibility for their personal affairs.

In summary, we observe that the mature person has developed a balance between independence and socialization. His behavior is characterized by self-direction, and is organized around a consistent scheme of values and self-chosen goals. He shows a purposeful inhibition of immediate impulses in favor of long-range plans. Also, maturity consists in the ability to subordinate one's impulses to the demands of cooperative social living. We shall see, later in this chapter, the emergence of certain signs of social and emotional maturity at various stages of child growth and development.

INDIVIDUAL AND GROUP BEHAVIOR

The Individual and the Group. The general principle that all human behavior is socialized implies that the individual *behaves as a member of a group;* that is, he "belongs" to a social group and takes his cues from group behavior. From this point of view, the behavior of any person can be understood only in its social context or setting. However, from the psychological point of view this is an oversimplification. Every person also *behaves as an individual;* his acts are self-directed. He is a psychological unit organized about a set of needs and goals of his own, not a mere cog in a larger "group unit."

Two questions arise here in connection with the relation between the individual and the group. (1) How do the values of the social group become individual personal values, or social demands become "felt needs" of the person? (2) How does the child become socialized; i.e., how are the individualistic self-chosen acts of the child gradually transformed into acts chosen and approved by society, without losing their self-directive character? Principles of learning tell us something about this process, but the psychology of "the self" may tell us a great deal more.

The Self. It has often been pointed out that every person is really four "selves." He is (1) what he thinks he is (self-definition), (2) what he would like to be (aspirational self), (3) what others think he is (reputation), and (4) what he really is. Which of these is the real self? What he really is may be quite different from the first three, and in this sense have a kind of independent reality. But it should be clear that "what he really is" cannot in practice be plumbed or defined except in terms of the individual's self-definitions or the definition of others. Psychologically speaking, the only self which any individual experiences is his own view of himself, or his *"self-concept."*

The Phenomenal Self (23). All the things, individuals, and events in a person's experience are not equally close to his "self." He perceives some objects as unrelated to himself and some as closely related or "identified" with his self. If I own a cocker spaniel or a Buick, I will notice other cocker spaniels more readily than fox terriers, and Buicks more than Fords. If I define myself as a tennis player or aspire to be one, I will notice or identify myself with things, persons, or events which are related to the self-definition. Teachers are more likely to become "ego-involved" with a tax question affecting teachers' salaries than one affecting sewer installations, and more likely to take an interest in teachers' salaries in Duluth, Minnesota, than in Afghanistan. Self-interest operates in our perceptions. To put it another way, the external things, persons, and events become *internalized as self-symbols,* and in this way become aspects of the self. The objects of experience are said to have a self-reference. The extensions of the self into the phenomenal world of experience constitute a "phenomenal self." We may define the self-concept as follows: The self-concept includes those parts of the phenomenal field which the individual has differentiated as definite and fairly stable characteristics of himself (23). The core of the self-concept consists of the self-evaluative attitudes, or the self as perceived by the self.

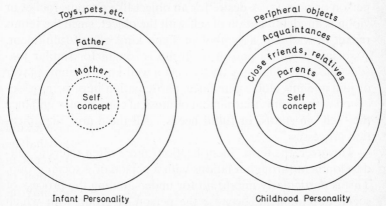

FIGURE 37. The Self. The infant self-concept (dotted lines) is vague, ill-defined, while the child's personality is more definitely structured. (Adapted from Lecky, *Self-Consistency*. New York, Island Press, 1945, p. 90.)

So far as individual behavior is concerned, the self-concept is the "real self," since it is the only self which the individual apprehends. It consists not only of what the person thinks and feels he is, but what he wants to be, because goals have a self-reference and are thus incorporated in the self. It is the self-reference or self-involvement of goal objects that explains how they function as motives. The boy who wants very much to become an engineer, for example, tends to picture himself as one, and consequently tries to act and think like one. His perception of "engineer," no matter how imperfect it may seem to his teacher or to a professor of engineering, provides him with a behavioral model and a role to play. Whther or not this causes him to work hard at mathematics depends on his perception of the goal, or what being an "engineer" actually means to him.

Identification. Through identification, the individual makes any thing, person, or event part of the self. Identification is thus the name for the act of becoming self-involved, or "ego-involved," in some aspect of his environment. We are said to identify with a person or object when we anticipate reward, or the satisfaction of some need, in connection with that person or object. A desire for an object like a tennis racket or violin is an identification of self with the object, since the tennis racket or violin is a symbol of some kind of self-fulfillment. Association with a person or group is sought for similar reasons; the individual may try to meet a well-known tennis player or join a tennis club. Similarly, participation in or being associated with a tennis tournament or musical concert may enhance the "self" in status, or fulfill needs. All these are "identification processes."

However, the term "identification" more often refers to self-development through relations with a person or a social group. This is particularly important for understanding the process of social development, because the person or group with which the individual identifies provides him with models of behavior and rewards that behavior. Through imitation, the individual learns a social role—how to think and behave so as to gain the rewards which he anticipates. The rewards consist primarily of approval of the person or group with whom he identifies. The principles governing the relation of the individual to the social group, as listed by Snygg and Combs, are as follows:

1. Individuals tend to seek self-enhancement through identifying themselves with and winning the approval of groups or individuals they believe to be important.

2. People tend to withdraw from groups whose approval they are unable to win and from groups which no longer satisfy their need.

3. Identification of an individual with a group leads him to adopt and defend the standards and behavior of the group.

4. Having adopted the standards of one group, the individual has adopted a set of standards by which he evaluates the behavior of other people and the importance of other groups.

5. Members of a group accept and approve those individuals who seem to them to be important. (23, pp. 187-189)

The same principles apply to identification with a person. Thus the boy who identifies with his father anticipates self-enhancement through the father's approval, adopts the father's attitudes and behavior, and defends them against attack because depreciation of his father is an attack on the boy's self. He also evaluates other persons in terms of the father's standards. The father-identification will terminate when the boy is no longer able to win the father's approval, or when the father's approval no longer satisfies his needs.

Internalization. This is the process of adopting the values or standards of a person or group, and making them part of one's self. Identification and internalization thus always go together. This is of tremendous importance in understanding how the child learns his attitudes toward things, persons, and events outside his skin, and particularly how he learns self-evaluative attitudes. As Preston puts it,

> If you believe that your father knows everything and is always right, then if he says, "You're a fool," you are a fool and no question about it. If one of your parents says you are slow or dumb or ugly or clumsy or bad and repeats it, you believe it because you believe the other things your parents have said. Children learn to estimate their own value in the world from the opinions of their parents. (20, p. 68)

The individual thus develops feelings of adequacy-inadequacy, worthiness-unworthiness, largely through the identification process. He not only forms and maintains identifications as a means of self-fulfillment, but also disrupts or breaks them off when they become frustrating or threatening, as an elementary matter of self-defense.

Socialization of the child is brought about through the processes of identification and internalization. The unsocialized infant is completely self-centered and self-engrossed because he does not identify with other persons. He is not able to differentiate between himself and others, and does not perceive other persons as individuals like himself. With intellectual development, and particularly with language which furnishes the symbols for differentiating himself and the others of his environment, comes the socializing process of identification.

The role of language is important in internalization, particularly through the words by which parents administer praise, prohibitions, and reproofs. The parent says "That's a good boy" and the child says "I am a good boy"; the parent says "big girls don't do that," and the child says "I am a big girl." "You are filthy" becomes "I am filthy" to the child, and "aren't you ashamed of yourself" becomes "I am ashamed of myself." Through this process the child learns the terms, and the emotionally toned meanings attached to them, for comparing himself with others, forming value judgments about himself and his surroundings, and thus acquiring a self-concept.

Informal Learning of Social-Emotional Roles. Although judgments about the self are learned informally, and not as the result of formal plan and intent of a teacher, they are often by-products of lessons in control or social conformance. They are said to be "caught, not taught." The following example, taken from Porter, illustrates the learning of a self-evaluative attitude in a toilet-training situation:

Johnny and His Mother

1. *Mother:* "Johnny, go to the bathroom. You're squirming around like a Whirling Dervish."
2. *Johnny:* "No."
3. *Mother:* "Go on! You have to go, don't you?"
4. *Johnny:* "No."
5. *Mother:* "Well, go anyway."
6. *Johnny:* "I don't want to!"
7. *Mother:* "Now go on before you have an accident."
8. *Johnny:* "I'll get a hatchet and chop you all up!"
9. *Mother:* "Why, Johnny! That's a terrible thing to say. You wouldn't really want to hurt me, would you?"
10. *Johnny:* "Yes."
11. *Mother:* "Now this is silly. You just march yourself on into the bathroom this instant." (18, p. 46)

The psychological aspects of this situation are quite complex since the mother's attitudes and statements have implications for Johnny's self-evaluation, and his defense of himself in turn provides cues for the mother's attitude toward herself. The mother's opening remark (1) implies that Johnny is irresponsible; that is, he is not able to decide for himself whether he should go to the bathroom. Why does Johnny refuse, and continue to refuse? Because his self-concept (perhaps including such feelings as "I am responsible, capable of taking care of myself") is *threatened,* and refusal to obey amounts to defending or maintaining this attitude. From this point of view, disobedience is predictable. The mother's reaction is also predictable, because Johnny's disobedience implies that she is a failure as a mother, inadequate in exacting obedience of her son. Johnny's behavior thus threatens the mother's self-concept, which we will assume includes "I am an adequate mother, capable of directing successfully my son's behavior." She defends herself from the threat by reiterating her demands (3), and the stage is set for the entire sequence. Johnny continues to resist, finally with threats of aggression, and in the end loses. Mother continues to insist, and finally crowns her efforts by forcibly taking full responsibility for Johnny's bladder control. Mother's continued insistence (3, 5, 7) provokes Johnny because it emphasizes his inadequacy, and his refusals (2, 4, 6, 8) threaten her adequacy as a mother.

The real issue is not whether Johnny should go to the bathroom, but who should decide when he is to go. Both Johnny's self-approval and Mother's are at stake. What does Johnny learn from such situations, repeated over and over? He learns that mother (and father) are unbeatable, and that they will assume responsibility, in spite of all he can do, for his most personal behavior. He learns a sense of guilt for being angry and expressing anger (mother's response 9). He may learn to feel, if such situations are varied and extensive enough, that he is incompetent and inadequate. *He learns to evaluate himself as parents evaluate him.* There is danger, of course, in generalizing from one situation. What Johnny will learn even in this situation cannot be determined, because it depends on his past learning, how he feels about himself, how sure he is that his mother loves him, how his father behaves toward him, and many other factors.

The situation described here merely illustrates that "lessons" for self-evaluation are inherent in the simplest kind of parent-child exercise in social control. Resistance and disobedience are lawful and predictable whenever the child rejects the parents' evaluation of him. We are accustomed to see the above situation in terms of what it means to the parents, not in terms of what it means to Johnny. "Getting Johnny to do what he should do" is not the same as "getting Johnny to decide for himself." The social learning conflict is not basically one of obedience-disobedience, but one of responsibility-irresponsibility. Children should not learn obedience, in other words, but responsibility. The "good, obedient" child often grows up with feelings of dependence, inadequacy, and incompetence. He grows up, but may not attain social and emotional maturity.

THE COURSE OF SOCIAL-EMOTIONAL DEVELOPMENT

As we observed previously, particular conclusions about development of the child are valid only within a certain culture. Many of the following particulars therefore apply chiefly to American middle-class behavior. In many respects generalizations can be made about Americans as a whole, because the varying patterns of American family life are after all more similar to one another than they are to those of the Chinese or the Tanala of Madagascar.

Infancy: the Prelanguage Period. In infancy physical needs and physical responses predominate. The neonate needs food and elimination, plus warmth and pleasant body stimulation, which he gets from fondling and cuddling. As the neuromuscular structures develop, so do the needs for sensory and muscular activity. At about 18 months, much of the child's activity is exploratory. He is curious, experimental, restless, and "gets into everything." He obtains intense physical satisfaction from muscular activity and from seeing, tasting, touching, and breaking things. Punishment from parents does not deter him, because the behavior itself is more rewarding than approval, and the pain and deprivation of parental punishment are of less consequence than the sensory delights of exploration and discovery.

The study of children's behavior at this period leads us to infer that one dominant need is that for self-direction and freedom of movement, which is essential to the mastery of his immediate environment. He impulsively does what he wants when he wants to; in other words he is not socialized. He does not yet perceive other persons as individuals like himself, so the needs and expectations of parents and ideas of personal property are beyond his perceptual ability.

The genetic origin of socialization, however, has its foundations here. As the child grows older, restraints are gradually imposed, and restraints are frustrating. Weaning involves a complete reorganization of his responses, his needs, and satisfactions. Physical restraints are imposed, and boundaries are marked off. The social and emotional effects of training are important because restraints are imposed by parents and particularly the mother, who is the source of most of the child's early satisfactions.

We are accustomed to think of the young infant as helpless. In some ways he is. But he is actually king of the household and rules it with an iron hand. His repertoire of responses may not be great, but they suffice to get him every attention and satisfaction he needs. As he grows older, he gradually gets disenthroned. His subjects (the parents) get more and more unmanageable, and he learns new ways of controlling them: by eating or not eating, keeping clean or soiling himself, being quiet or noisy. The very young infant cannot do this because he does not differentiate "self" and "others." As he learns to differentiate persons, he also learns to behave differently toward different people, chiefly as a method of controlling them. The child is an active learner, even at this period.

Emotional development has its origins here also. The infant is not "self-conscious," and therefore does not fear disapproval. It is frustrated by, and therefore afraid of, those events which disturb its physical equanimity or interfere with physical satisfactions. The chief fears of the infant appear to be flashing lights, noises, and other unexpected sensory events like sudden falling. When old enough to differentiate people, it will learn to fear persons associated with such events or with physical frustrations. Just as the infant fears unexpected and disturbing sensory experiences, it resists abrupt changes in routine by hostility and aggression. The young infant will often scream and struggle if tightly held. The older one will respond aggressively to abrupt weaning, and early coercive toilet training also arouses anxiety and defiance. The various forms of aggression are both means of emotional expression and means of controlling parents by punishing them.

Early Childhood: the Language Period. With the emergence of speech and language comes socialization. We have seen that language lays the foundation for social control as well as for thinking. At about two years, the child can associate things, persons, and events with spoken sounds, and can even speak a little. Language provides the symbols (terms and names) for differentiating self, various people, and things that belong to himself and others. Also, at this age the child's troubles begin in earnest, in the sense that social training becomes intensive and the parents' efforts to dethrone him from his infant kingship are redoubled. To parents, his language development is tangible proof of understanding, and the child can now be told that he is "old enough" to conform to new sets of expectations.

Social restraints are intensified, and are usually backed by systematic rewards and punishments. The child is taught not to handle his genital organs and not to soil himself; he learns the rituals of eating at table, how to behave like a boy or a girl, and to respect property rights. This kind of training is effective for two reasons: the child develops ability to differentiate, and a new set of rewards is functioning. Physical rewards are gradually displaced by social rewards (approval of parents).

Identification with parents is therefore an essential condition of socialization. The training takes time, results in predictable frustration and aggressive behavior on the part of the child, and equally predictable frustration for the parents. All situations are learning situations, and the family atmosphere is highly charged emotionally. Children develop ambivalent attitudes toward parents, who are sources of frustration as well as satisfaction, and parents develop ambivalence toward the child.

The period between ages two and four is sometimes called the "age of negativism" because the child's resistance is so fre-

quently verbalized in "No!"   It is in this highly emotional struggle between child and parental attitudes that the foundation
of future social and emotional developments is laid.   Parental
identification is basic.   From the infant, with "no clear sense of
self-identity," the child develops self-definitions: ". . . as he
grows up he must disengage himself from this universality, and
become a well-defined individual.   By the time he is five or six
years old he must see himself for what he is" (8).

Through parental identification, the child learns to see himself as his parents see him and to behave in accordance with a
self-defined rule.   If his parents see him as inadequate, helpless,
or wicked, he will behave in accordance with his interpretation
of that role.   If they see him as adequate and self-directing, he
will incorporate these feelings into his self-definition and behave accordingly.

It is helpful to think of the early social training period as
one in which the "ruling" power of the child and parent are reversed.   The child is now dethroned; the parent is all-powerful,
and the source of all satisfactions.   This reversal takes time,
and the learning process is one in which physical rewards and
social rewards (approval) are competing for ascendance.   Observations of child behavior in the home reveal this conflict constantly.   In the end, the social rewards win out and the parental
identification is fairly definite by age 4.   By age 6 the child is
fairly well socialized, and his guiding need and motive is social
approval.   Studies of children's fears during the preschool period show this gradual process of socialization.   Fears of unusual sensory events are gradually replaced by fears of the dark,
being left alone, imaginary creatures, and by age 6 some fears
of ridicule, failure, and personal inadequacy (14).   Socialized
play also shows some development from the self-centered role
("play with me") to the dawning self-concept of being a member of a group ("play with them").   The drive for social survival takes the form of what Davis and Havighurst have called
adaptive anxiety:

    . . . The desire to win this social acceptance from his parents and
older brothers and sisters (and very soon from his teachers and his playmates) becomes a major drive of his behavior.   This drive is really a

form of adaptive anxiety. It makes him anxious, first to avoid punishment, and, second, to win that approval which leads to social reward. (6, p. 38)

Middle Childhood. The period of six to twelve years is one enormous social development, usually along the lines of a pattern already laid down. Most of the lessons are already learned, but not finally. When he goes to school, the child tries out his self-concept developed within the family in the complex life of the school. If the school and the new acquaintances reward the same kind of behavior his parents have rewarded, all goes well. If not, the child faces a "learning dilemma" and a more or less difficult adjustment period involving reinterpretation, trial of new responses (often imitated from schoolmates) and reorganization. This adjustment is often complicated further by the fact that the imitation of schoolmates' behavior is sometimes disapproved at home. Identification with parents is thus often disrupted, and identifications may be transferred to other persons (usually the age peers) who provide new behavioral models and social rewards. Going to school thus opens up new patterns of variability in social and emotional development.

The drive for social acceptance and the accompanying "adaptive anxiety" is fundamentally a drive to control others in his family. The child carries over the same technique in the school. From the point of view of the teacher, the "obnoxious child" is one who has learned very well to predict and control the behavior of his parents by attention-getting tactics. They may not work in school, but they have probably worked at home. Paradoxically enough, the striving and pushing for preference in such a child does not stem from the desire to be *different,* but to conform to certain expectations which have been set up by previous training.

From the age of six onward, the child becomes more and more self-critical. At six years, he begins to form value judgments of his own behavior, to set up conscious standards for himself, and to feel more and more keenly the experiences of self-approval and self-disapproval. It is probably because of this that age 6 or so has been sometimes called the "age of reason." This self-criticism is not, however, a reasoning process. As he grows older, he is more and more aware of attitudes of others toward himself. His adaptive anxiety becomes more directed toward social approval. He has more things to worry about, and research on fears during this period shows that he worries more about things which are less likely to happen. The findings show that "apprehensions concerning the *possibility* of troubles of various kinds far exceed the *probability* of such troubles or the frequency of their *actual occurrence*" (13, p. 339).

The changes in emotional reactions are in the direction of greater social acceptance and become gradually more adaptive to the child's social experience. This is best illustrated by the social roles learned in childhood. The child learns a sex role, an age role, and a social class role. Training in all three begin during the preschool period and become gradually more differentiated during the elementary school years.

1. *Sex role.* The child learns early to avoid sex exposure, and other behavior appropriate to his sex. The boy learns not to fight girls, not to cry when hurt, not to be afraid of certain things. He learns to fear the social stigma of being a "sissy." The girl learns to express her emotions in a way appropriate to her sex, and to fear the stigma of being "unladylike." Social differentiation of the sex role progresses rapidly in the period preceding adolescence.

2. *Age role.* As soon as the child can understand language, he becomes aware of his age status. He is constantly reminded to act his age, and learns that increasing age brings increased status. He learns to avoid smaller children and not to pick on them; he evaluates and seeks the company of older children as an aspect of drive for status. Acting beyond his age is also repulsed, and his behavior thus takes on the character of age status to which he conforms.

3. *Class role.* The child learns whom he may play with, and whom to avoid. He learns from his parents the approved language, manners, customs, values, and attitudes not only of his sex and age, but also his "social class." He may learn not only that being a "snob" is "bad" but also that "snobs" are persons above him in status. Inevitably, his self-evaluative atti-

tudes take on a class character; he learns that some persons are socially "better" than he is, and that he is socially "better" than some others. He becomes accustomed to, and accepts, a set of social expectations determined by the class structure.

Adolescence. This is the "social age." During adolescence the social roles become more channelized in some respects, and new ways of social and emotional expression begin to take form. The sex role becomes more sharply differentiated with puberty. Sex interests become stronger and more patterned. Keeping company with the opposite sex is now fully approved by one's age peers. The interests of both boys and girls become more sex differentiated, i.e., develop more along the lines of the difference between men and women. Vocational interests tend to be stereotyped along sex lines, with boys wanting to be "engineers" and girls "nurses." The age-sex-class role becomes highly standardized through the emergence of the "social clique," or "gang."

Unlike the social group of earlier childhood, the adolescent group is a closely knit organization, with intense feelings of "we-ness" or group consciousness. Boys' groups usually center about a leader, and about a specialized function like fighting or sports. Girls' groups are less specialized in leadership or in activities. Being like the crowd becomes the dominant motive of the adolescent. Interests and attitudes are spontaneously standardized, and the individual must either dominate, conform to, or be ostracized by the crowd.

The fears and anxieties of adolescents reflect this striving for conformity. The adolescent has already accepted most of the adult standards of social behavior, and judges himself by them. But he has not yet learned the social skills and techniques of the adult. As a consequence the adolescent is often painfully aware of a discrepancy between what he wants and what he has attained. As compared with the relatively simple and personal fears of the younger child, the adolescent's fears are mainly social, particularly fears of social situations in which he will appear at a disadvantage (13). According to studies summarized by Cole,

The adolescents concentrated upon fear of school examinations, automobile accidents, and diseases; worry over inadequate funds, getting a job, loss of work by parents, or appearance of the home; fear of being sinful, being led astray by bad companions, or being tempted to cheat; worry over being unsuccessful, over hurting other people's feelings, over making a bad impression upon others; fear of growing up, of social incompetence, of sexual experiences, of disappointing one's parents. The causes of anger are also primarily social. Anger in adolescents is provoked chiefly by frustration of social needs, arising from social situations in which he feels embarrassed, ridiculous, or offended. He responds more by talking than by violence (5, p. 99).

Puberty brings remarkable physical changes—remarkable not only because they alter the physical appearance, but because some of these changes have important implications for social and emotional development. Increase in height and length of bones is especially notable during the pubertal growth spurt, while increase in weight lags behind. The result is a gangling, gawky appearance that seldom fails to capture the attention of parents, who never seem to get tired of commenting about it. Some adolescents (particularly girls) tend to acquire enduring attitudes of inadequacy as a result of such experiences. The common notion that adolescents are awkward, however, is not supported by what we know of neuromuscular growth and the development of motor skills. The stumbling and physical clumsiness for which adolescents are famous—in so far as it exists—is not due to lack of physical coordination, but to self-consciousness and embarrassment. An excellent basketball player may be known to his parents as "awkward."

The fact that the pubescent growth spurt occurs earlier in girls than in boys also has implications. The twelve-year-old boy may suddenly find himself "looking up" at the twelve-year-old girls of his acquaintance, and begin to feel that he is a "runt," with a consequent temporary feeling of inferiority. This is particularly true if he happens to be late in maturing. Individual differences in size and appearance, due to variation of rates of maturing illustrated in Figure 20, may become magnified in importance. These differences are quite striking in adolescence, although many of them will be evened up later.

The social adequacy of many adolescents is critically at stake, for instance, at a dance. The average differences, presented in a cold table of figures, do not give a clear picture. As Cole says of boy and girl differences in height,

. . . These differences are not large and, at the average, not important. What is important, however, is the situation at the extremes. The tallest and biggest of the girls have in magnified form the usual troubles of malcoordination and distress over being much too big. These girls are generally taller than the tallest and heavier than the heaviest boys of their age. The shortest boys are in equal difficulties; they are usually shorter than the shortest girl. (5, p. 22)

The personal sense of social and sexual adequacy is often threatened or enhanced by differences in sexual appearance, as well as in height and weight.

The development of generalized attitudes, or ideals, appears to be a characteristic of adolescence. The intellectual ability to generalize is an important difference between the adolescent and the younger child. Moral "good" and "bad" to the younger child is simply a function of reward and punishment, but the adolescent can attach concrete significance to such terms as honesty, justice, charity. He is therefore more capable of making moral decisions in terms of moral ideals, and can apply the general concept to novel situations. One important aspect of this is that he can and does evaluate the behavior of adults in terms of such generalizations, and often in doing so develops doubts and cynicism about his elders.

Adulthood. What is an adult from the social-emotional point of view? He has been defined as a "sexually mature individual who has assumed independence, who is considered by other adults to be responsible for his own behavior, and who, in our culture, is expected to compete with other adults" (20, p. 100). The criteria are, according to this definition, sexual maturity, independence, and responsibility. The ability to meet competition is the ability to get what he wants by his own efforts, not by having things handed to him. The socially immature individual is one whose methods of meeting his needs are typical of the younger age level. Social and emotional education has for its aim the development of a mature adult who can get what he needs by his own foresight and effort, without violence to the rights of others, and without being destroyed by his disappointments. Independence and responsibility are learned only in situations which permit independent and responsible activity, and which reward such activity. If they are learned in time to meet developing sexual maturity, adult adjustment should not be difficult.

For the majority, training of the child within the family is sufficient to internalize the cultural pattern of behavior in which he will work out his salvation as an adult. If the family is fairly well integrated in society and there is no great discrepancy between the early training and the situations of adult life, the transition from adolescence to adulthood is fairly successful. As Linton says, "The individual who spends his life in any society with a fairly stable culture finds his personality becoming more firmly integrated as he grows older" (15, p. 144). The transition, however, may be complicated in two ways. Inadequate early training leading to emotional immaturity is one. Drastic changes in the cultural conditions faced by the adult is another complication. "The acculturated individual can learn to act and even think in terms of his new society's culture, but he cannot learn to feel in these terms. At each point where decision is required he finds himself adrift with no fixed points of reference" (15, p. 145).

Nature of the Child's Difficulties. There is reason to believe that childhood, which tradition cherishes as the happiest period of life, is actually the most painful period for many. Most adults have probably forgotten their presocialized period and the shocks of early training. Their forgetfulness in this respect is perhaps a contributing factor to the difficulty of the conflicts experienced by the developing child. It may be well to set down here some of the sources of conflict.

1. *Immaturity of the child.* This accounts for some of the personal difficulties peculiar to the early years. He has yet to learn some of the commonplace lessons of life. The adult has long since accepted as inevitable the natural consequences of

behavior and the conditions of the physical, social, and moral world which govern these. He recognizes the futility of "kicking against the goad" and he realizes that everything must be bought at a price. But the child has to learn even these elementary principles of conduct. There is no reason in an untutored, wishful human nature why they should be regarded as necessary. Another source of the child's conflicts is to be found in his lack of perspective. Single events are likely to loom much larger and appear fraught with greater consequences to the child than when looked at from an adult viewpoint. Finally, the child's close dependence on others, who may unconsciously embroil him in difficulties not of his own making, sometimes creates problems which might not appear if he enjoyed greater independence.

2. *The immaturity of parents.* Parents may contribute unknowingly to the personal difficulties of the child in spite of their best intention to the contrary. In many cases the behavior of parents is itself based upon their inability to handle successfully their own personal problems. Excessive affection or over-devotion to the child, based perhaps on unsatisfied "emotional hunger" leading back to a lack of affection in their own childhood, or the outcome of unhappy marital relations, may make such a demand upon the child for affection that he may actually develop an antagonistic attitude. He may on the other hand form an undue attachment for the parent from which he may never be able to emancipate himself. Keenly felt parental sacrifice for the sake of the child may, if brought continually to his notice, make an unreasonable demand upon him for gratitude. He may react to this by wishing to escape from the home because he may feel unwanted, or unable to make return for the debt he is daily incurring. Parental ambitions may be projected onto the child without due regard for his own individuality of interest and aptitude. Because the parent may feel that he has "missed" something in his own life he may create a difficult situation for the child in attempting to insure that the latter shall not also "miss" it. A feeling of inferiority, because he cannot measure up to the high ideal set by the parent, may result, or the child on the other hand may never reach the stage

where he takes into his own hands the reins of his personal development.

3. *Inconsistency of training.* It is important to note that identification with parents is basic to the development of moral conscience. What is rewarded is "right"; what is punished is "wrong." What happens when the parents reward and punish the same behavior on different occasions? When one parent rewards behavior which the other punishes? When the child gets no rewards but plenty of punishment? Punishment of children often becomes an emotional outlet for parents, and is administered according to parental whim, not according to the child's needs. Inconsistent treatment lays the basis for personal insecurity and aggression, since the child never learns what to expect. The essence of socialization is learning what to expect, and learning what others expect. Under such conditions the child may find it difficult or impossible to differentiate right and wrong, propriety and impropriety. Inconsistency of early training may lead to a lack of *feeling* about right and wrong, even when in the intellectual or legal sense a person knows the difference.

4. *Parental ambition.* When parental ambition takes the form of class striving, the child sometimes becomes a pawn in the desire for social status. The child thus becomes a symbol of parental achievement, and is exposed to extraordinary pressure to fulfill his parents' expectations. Such pushing and striving often reveals itself in the child's behavior, particularly when parental identification is strong and the child's abilities are not quite up to the high level of achievement and recognition which the parents expect.

Sources of Personality Differences

We have seen that the possible variation in biological inheritance is vast. The variation of environmental factors in shaping the personality is virtually infinite. Because the most deeply rooted social and emotional traits are learned in early childhood, we look to this period for the sources of variation in personality development. The four major areas of influence are (1) physical and physiological factors, (2) social training, (3) early emotional relationships, and (4) chance factors. As we discuss these factors, it may be well to note that even same-sex siblings in the same family develop differently.

Physical and Physiological Factors. Physical constitution becomes of significance in personality development either when it affects the impression that the individual makes upon others, or when it is instrumental in giving a particular trend to the development of certain personality traits. We have, for example, certain terms in common use, such as "robust" and "petite," which refer primarily to one's bodily status but which often come by reason of this fact to be applied to the personality as well. These terms, along with such common sayings as "redheads are excitable," or "fat men are jolly," indicate that we ordinarily expect people of a certain body build or character to display certain related personality traits.

Quite apart from the scientific justification of this, it often happens that our attitude toward such people will be unconsciously influenced by our first impression of them, and that they on their part will respond by attempting to live up to the role others expect them to play. The fate of the big man or the small man in a crowd undoubtedly has much to do with the personality traits he manifests there in response to the attitude of others, often strangers, toward him. The same thing would apply to the personality of the child. As a matter of good social psychology, we can not really divorce the study of the child's personality from the traits he manifests in the group as a reaction to the attitude of others toward him, which in turn may be based at least partly upon his physical constitution.

The large, physically vigorous boy has by this fact alone a certain role assigned to him by others which he is expected to live up to in his social life. Other children will be less likely to badger him or to make him the butt of their jokes. Even the teacher may place him in the forefront when school lines or exercises are to be gone through, and perhaps expect of him as well a maturity of behavior commensurate with his physical development. It can hardly be possible that these things would not be reflected in the child's personality. A failure on his part to play the role expected of him may be just as significant. Children are quick to tag as a "sissy" the boy whose overdeveloped body belies his ineffectual behavior, much more so than in the case of the physically small child. To the teacher he may become a "big hulk of a boy" if he tends to be somewhat slow or dull. A child's personality, or an adult's, for that matter, is not something which he simply lets shine forth before men. It is in part the playing of a certain role in social life. The attitudes of others toward him, and what he believes these are, have a great deal to do with the role he plays.

Because parents react differently to physical traits, such physiological differences as metabolic rate, energy, stamina, glandular activity and rate of growth, susceptibility to sickness, and the like, may be sources of social and emotional traits. Parents may allow more freedom and place more responsibility on the "robust" child, and shelter the smaller or more sickly one. They may reject the "lazy" one whose metabolic rate is low, and pity or ridicule the "clumsy" one. Even an attitude of extreme solicitude for the child may focus his attention upon the fact that he is "different" or "weakly." Such an attitude may then influence the child's future behavior, and because of its origin in early life, it may have a rather general bearing upon many phases of personality development. Clumsiness of movement or lack of motor skill may make the child unpopular in games or ridiculed at home, with the result that he may lose confidence in himself and become retiring in social groups.

A child with a handicap may learn through his parents to compensate for it and develop strong drives for achievement. The stutterer Demosthenes becoming a renowned orator, the drive of the physically small Napoleon toward world domination, the development of the doctrine of the "superman" by a physically weak Nietzsche are classical examples of an overcompensation in the sphere of personality for a defect in the bodily organism. Parents' attitudes toward physical traits thus become incorporated in the child's self-definition and influence his characteristic role in life situations.

Social Training.   The child becomes socialized by learning a social-emotional pattern, or behavior role, which appears to be fairly well standardized according to cultural groupings. According to investigators of the customs in child training at different cultural levels, the conspicuous factors in middle-class child rearing are (1) the severity of early training in socialization and (2) the deep emotional attachment between child and parents.   As we have seen, the middle-class family commences training earlier, pushes the child harder, and has more exacting standards.   This regime is not only harder on the child, but complicates the child-parent emotional relationship.

Davis and Havighurst (6) list four traits which appear to be characteristic goals of social training and which receive greater emphasis in the middle-class training pattern: (1) self-control, (2) foresight, (3) individual achievement, and (4) responsibility.   These traits might therefore be expected to vary according to the cultural pattern of child training.

The emphasis placed on these traits will of course vary from family to family, and there are no doubt many exceptions to the "class-typing" of the patterns.   It is estimated that about 50 per cent of the population values the virtues of thrift, self-improvement, and foresight highly, while to the remainder these values are much less important (12).   The "developmental tasks" imposed by society therefore vary in timing and in relative importance according to the family's particular way of life.

Emotional Relationships.   The emotional ties between parent and child have important implications for social and emotional development.   According to some observers, emotional reactions are established even during the infant period.   Ribble's observations of suckling, fondling, weaning, and toilet training of infants led to the conclusion that "the younger the organism the more serious and widespread is the effect of frustration" of organic needs (21).   Mead's description of suckling among the Mundugumor, a primitive tribe of New Guinea, illustrates how tendencies toward violence, aggression, and pugnacity may have infantile origins (17).   Mundugumor women, she reports, "suckle their children standing up, supporting the child with one hand in a position that strains the mother's arm and pinions the arms of the child. . . . Children therefore develop a very definite purposive fighting attitude, holding on firmly to the nipple and sucking milk as rapidly and vigorously as possible. They frequently choke from swallowing too fast; the choking angers the mother and infuriates the child, thus further turning the suckling situation into one characterized by anger and struggle rather than by affection and reassurance" (17, p. 195). Weaning is abrupt and "accompanied by cross words, which further accentuate the picture of a hostile world that is presented to the child." The cultural pattern typical of this tribe is thus transmitted in part through parent-child relationships during infancy.

We have seen that between age 4 and 6 the child goes through the critical period of forming cognitive, personal identifications with parents. During this period he learns to imitate his parents, believe them, and conceal his hostility toward them. The development of moral values requires that this identification be fairly complete. In other words, he must want to be like them and want their approval in order to form permanent feelings about right and wrong. Without the identification, reward and punishment would be effective in influencing behavior only in the presence of parents, which is true of the younger child.

Apparently, then, the development of conscience depends on getting both love and reward-punishment (approval-disapproval) from the same person or persons, whether parents or parent substitutes. The rejected child may get discipline but no affection. The overprotected child gets affection, but no discipline. Either of these combinations may lead to social and emotional maladjustment. Many studies of delinquents lead to the conclusion that rejection is part of the typical pattern of development. Studies of maladjusted adults indicate that their basic insecurity often derives from a pattern of rejection, or overprotection, or inconsistency, or all three combined.

Traumatic Emotional Relationships. Early emotional relationships can be traumatic, and thus lay the foundation for a

disturbed or neurotic personality. According to Angyal (2),
"the two cardinal disturbances on which the neurosis rests consist first, in the person's *loss of mastery* over his own fate, and
second, what is rather generally accepted as a basic factor in
the neuroses, namely *anxiety*." In this view, the neurotic child
or adult is one with impaired self-determination and impaired
capacity for self-surrender and love. The basis of this impairment is a "secret feeling of worthlessness" founded on the belief
that one is "inadequate to master the situations that confront
him and that he is undeserving of love." The child who feels
worthless may become a neurotic adult.

The traumatizing conditions responsible for the individual's
self-derogation and loss of self-respect are found chiefly in the
early emotional relationships established through the parents'
training pattern. Angyal lists five common factors which account for this: (1) The overprotective attitude by the insecure
parent may cause the child to feel that the world is full of dangers with which he is inadequate to cope. The parent who does
too much for the child may be teaching the child by implication that he is incapable of doing things by himself. (2) When
the parent is too eager for the child to do well and criticizes him
excessively, he may indirectly convince the child that he is inadequate. (3) Parents who go to the opposite extreme, ex-
aggerating the child's superiority and confidently expecting a
great deal of him, may cause the child to feel worthless in another way. The child may know that the parents' picture of
him is false, and lose confidence through comparing himself
with the parents' often fantastic standards. (4) Too many
"don'ts" may create in the child the feeling that the things he
most wants are forbidden or evil, that he is fundamentally an
evil person. (5) The child treated in many ways without understanding or respect may develop the feeling that he does not
matter in an adult world, that he is worthless. The child may
tend to accept this verdict rather than blaming the parents—
perhaps, as Angyal suggests, because the child *needs* to feel that
he has "good parents" and tenaciously adheres to this idea at the
expense of his own self-evaluation.

Sex Competition. During the period of parental identification (age 4-6), while the child is developing a sex role, there is often competition between the child and the parent of the same sex for the attention and affection of the parent of the opposite sex. Boys are rivals of fathers and girls of mothers. That is, the child *feels* such competition, and the natural identification with the parent of his own sex is at stake. Boys usually solve the problem by transferring the identification from the mother to the father, thus learning the male sex role. The situation is sometimes quite delicate, particularly when there is parental dissension, or when either parent is emotionally immature and uses the child to satisfy his own needs primarily. The prominence of this conflict in psychoanalytic theory calls attention to its complex nature. Adequate learning of sex roles, and self-evaluative attitudes basic to personal security, apparently depend on the basic principle: adequate identification with at least one person who will provide both affection and appropriate training (20).

Sibling Competition. Much study and conjecture has been made of the rivalry between siblings for the affection of parents. The rivalry is held to be particularly strong between the first and second child. One study of two-child middle-class families revealed that the first child was trained more severely, and that mothers "agreed overwhelmingly that the first child was the more jealous and the more selfish, and that the second child was the happier and more generous" (6). Many authors agree that this rivalry is inevitable, and that the first child should be expected to experience some feeling of displacement and loss of parental love. That age rank results in differential development is indicated by a study of nearly 400 kindergarten children (10). The children were rated by teachers on different personality traits. After relating these to position in the family, the authors came to such conclusions as the following: (1) "Oldest" children showed slightly greater tendency toward lack of aggressiveness, self-confidence, qualities of leadership, and greater tendency toward suggestibility, seclusiveness, and introversion. (2) The "middle" children showed these tendencies in a lesser degree, while the "youngest" children were not in any way outstanding. (3) "Only" children were rated high for aggressiveness, self-confidence, gregarious interests, instability of mood, and flightiness of attention.

Adler has called attention to what he believes are the difficulties of the first or only child. He maintains that such a child leans heavily upon his parents for the satisfaction of his needs, and that, being the center at home, he often finds it a problem to adjust to the school and other situations outside the home where this conspicuous position is not reserved for him. He may compensate by developing ruses to attract attention to himself, or on the other hand he may be easily crushed by his disappointment and develop feelings of inferiority (1).

However, any generalizations about the traits of "only" children or children of different age rank must be tempered by the larger generalization about the family pattern of emotional relationships. Every family situation is unique, and the durability and significance of sibling rivalry will depend on the family pattern as a whole.

Broken Homes. The same must be said about the influence of this factor on development. Not just the fact of the broken home, but the psychological factors that cause it to break up, cause the damage. It is not dissension between father and mother, but the behavioral form it takes, which influences child development. If parents, whether living together or divorced or separated, compete for the child's affection or use the child as a tool of dominance or revenge over each other, the learning situation is unwholesome. The effect on the child, again, depends on whether a satisfying and effective emotional relationship be established early in life with some adult. Psychologically, it does not matter whether that adult is parent, foster parent, or grandparent.

Chance Factors. It is often "chance," or the coincidence of many hereditary and environmental factors, that influences parental attitudes and child-parent emotional relationships. The child's age rank or sex is a coincidence. Chance factors in heredity may determine not only physical constitution but physical resemblance. The child may look like father or mother, or bear a fortunate or unfortunate resemblance to Aunt Minnie or Uncle Ben. Not the traits, but the parents' reactions to the traits, determine patterns of identification, rejection, and overprotection. Also, two children of the same IQ will develop differently if one is the brightest in his family and the other is the dullest in another family.

The Basis of Mental Health. The present state of psychological knowledge does not permit the formulation of any hard and fast rules about mental health. There has been increasing concern among educators during recent years, however, with the mental health of pupils and teachers alike, particularly as this is affected by the life of the school. It appears to be generally agreed that an adequate concept of mental health is part of the basic professional knowledge required of every teacher. The concept of mental health is very difficult to express, and is really the subject of a book in itself. But the foundations of mental health, or ill health, are certainly laid down very early in the life of the child. The concept is therefore fundamental to our notion of social and emotional development. It would seem quite clear, on the whole, that mental health is not so precarious, nor its techniques so complicated, that a program of child training favorable to mental health needs to be placed in the care of experts.

Our concept of mental health may be clarified somewhat by the diagram in Figure 38, adapted from Preston's delightful little volume, *The Substance of Mental Health.*

1. *Heredity* provides the base, because biological inheritance determines the structure of the physical organism and lays down some of the important aspects of physical health, which serves as a foundation. As the author points out, however, it is not so much heredity as the attitude toward heredity which is the important determinant in individual cases. Unfortunate heredity is not fatal to mental health, nor does excellent heredity guarantee it.

2. *Physical condition* is important, because physical and mental health are not independent. The relation between the two is not, however, an absolute one; good mental health may exist in the poorest physical constitution. On the other hand, diseases and accidents take their toll of mental health chiefly through the attitude acquired by the person so handicapped. The damage is often wrought in the afflicted person's feelings about himself more than in his physique.

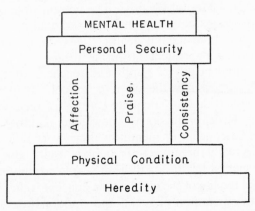

FIGURE 38. The Structure of Mental Health. (From G. H. Preston, *The Substance of Mental Health,* 20, p. 145.)

3. *The pillars*—affection, praise, consistency—represent the supports which are provided through child training during the early years. The techniques mentioned are not complicated and are within the reach of all families. Deficiency in the supports, however, collapses the structure of Personal Security on which mental health rests. *Affection* makes the child sure that he is wanted, enables him to feel "we" instead of "me." *Praise* makes him sure that he is adequate and worthwhile, and able to stand the criticisms and failures he will certainly meet. *Consistency* in training teaches him what to expect, so that the small doses of disappointment, competition, ridicule, and obedience to authority which are the lot of every child and adult become vaccinating or immunizing doses, not overpowering and de-

bilitating attacks on his security. Consistency of reward and punishment prevents overprotection, teaches the child that his actions have consequences, and teaches him what they are.

4. *Personal security,* a complex psychological state compounded of self-possession, self-respect, and self-confidence, plus a feeling of not being too different from others, is the keystone in the structure. Its presence does not guarantee mental health, but makes it more likely. Feelings of security, no matter how learned or on what experiences they are based, provide an antidote against the things, persons, or events that threaten to tip the balance in the direction of mental ill-health.

REFERENCES

1. ADLER, A. *Understanding human nature.* New York: Greenberg, 1946.
2. ANGYAL, A. A theoretical model for personality studies. In KRECH, D., & KLEIN, G. S., *Theoretical models and personality theory.* Durham, N.C.: Duke Univ. Press, 1952.
3. BRIDGES, K. M. B. *Social and emotional development of the preschool child.* London: Kegan Paul, 1931.
4. CAREY, T. F. The relation of physical growth to developmental age in boys. Ph.D. dissertation. Catholic Univ. of America, 1935.
5. COLE, LUELLA. *Psychology of adolescence.* New York: Rinehart, 1942.
6. DAVIS, A., & HAVIGHURST, R. J. *Father of the man.* Boston: Houghton Mifflin, 1947.
7. FURFEY, P. H. A revised scale for measuring developmental age in boys. *Child Dev.,* 1931, **2**, 102-114. See also Sister Celestine Sullivan, A scale for measuring developmental age in girls, *Stud. Psychol. & Psychiat.,* Catholic Univ. of America, 1934, Vol. 4.
8. GESELL, A., & ILG, F. L. *The infant and child in the culture of today.* New York: Harper, 1943.
9. GOODENOUGH, F. B. *Anger in young children.* Minneapolis: Univ. of Minnesota Press, 1931.
10. GOODENOUGH, F. B., & LEAHY, A. M. The effect of certain family relationships upon the development of personality. *J. genet. Psychol.,* 1927, **34**, 45-71.
11. GOLDSTEIN, K. On emotions: considerations from the organismic point of view. *J. Psychol.,* 1951, **31**, 37-49.
12. HAVIGHURST, R. J. *Human development and education.* New York: Longmans, Green, 1953.

13. JERSILD, A. T. Studies of children's fears. In BARKER, R. G., *et al.*, *Child behavior and development,* New York: McGraw-Hill, 1943.

14. JERSILD, A. T., & HOLMES, F. B. Children's fears. *Child Devel. Monogr.,* 1935, No. 20.

15. LINTON, R. *The cultural background of personality.* New York: Appleton-Century-Crofts, 1945.

16. McHUGH, M. *The developmental quotient of male siblings.* M.A. dissertation. Catholic Univ. of America, 1935.

17. MEAD, M. *From the south seas.* New York: Morrow, 1939.

18. PORTER, E. H. JR. *An introduction to therapeutic counseling.* Boston: Houghton Mifflin, 1950.

19. PRESCOTT, D. A. *Emotion and the educative process.* Washington, D.C.: Amer. Council on Education, 1938.

20. PRESTON, G. H. *The substance of mental health.* New York: Rinehart, 1943.

21. RIBBLE, M. A. Infantile experience in relation to personality development. In HUNT, J. McV. (Ed.), *Personality and the behavior disorders,* II. New York: Ronald Press, 1944.

22. SHERMAN, M. The differentiation of emotional responses in infants. *J. comp. Psychol.,* 1927, **7,** 265-284.

23. SNYGG, D., & COMBS, A. W. *Individual behavior.* New York: Harper, 1949.

24. WEITZMAN, E. A study of social maturity in persons sixteen through twenty-four years of age. *J. genet. Psychol.,* 1944, **64,** 37-66.

25. WILLOUGHBY, R. R. A scale of emotional maturity. *J. soc. Psychol.,* 1932, **3,** 3-36.

SELECTED READINGS

ANDERSON, J. E. *The psychology of development and personal adjustment.* New York: Holt, 1949. For general reference.

BARUCH, D. W. *New ways in discipline.* New York: Whittlesey House, 1949. Emphasizes the social-emotional aspects of child rearing.

HARSH, C. M., & SCHRICKEL, H. G. *Personality: development and assessment.* New York: Ronald Press, 1950. Pt. I, Chs. 1-10.

HAVIGHURST, R. J. *Human development and education.* New York: Longmans, Green, 1953. Social and emotional aspects of developmental tasks.

HAVIGHURST, R. J., & TABA, H. *Adolescent character and personality.* New York: Wiley, 1949. Report of a study of character development in "Prairie City." Pt. IV draws main conclusions and implications. Sharply drawn case histories.

LECKY, P. *Self-consistency: a theory of personality.* New York: Island Press, 1945. Chs. 3, 4.

MEAD, M. *Coming of age in Samoa.* Book I, From the south seas. New York: Morrow, 1939. A study of adolescent girls in a different culture.

MOWRER, O. H. *Learning theory and personality dynamics.* New York: Ronald Press, 1950. Ch. 21 discusses the implications of the parental identification process in children.

MURPHY, G. *Personality.* New York: Harper, 1947. Chs. 32, 34, 37.

PRESCOTT, D. A. *Emotion and the educative process.* Washington, D.C.: Amer. Council on Education, 1938.

PRESTON, G. H. *The substance of mental health.* New York: Rinehart, 1943. Brief, vivid, and readable account by a psychiatrist.

REDL, F., & WATTENBERG, W. W. *Mental hygiene in teaching.* New York: Harcourt, Brace, 1951. Practical discussion for teachers, dealing with everyday problems in the classroom.

SNYGG, D., & COMBS, A. W. *Individual behavior.* New York: Harper, 1949. Pt. I, Chs. 1-8 develop personal approach to behavior. Chs. 9-11 discuss implications for education.

FILMS

Children's Emotions. (22 min.) Excellent illustrations of major childhood emotions: curiosity, fear, anger, jealousy, joy. Major causes of fear at different age levels. New York: McGraw-Hill.

Social Development. (16 min.) Depicts social behavior at different age levels and shows reasons for age changes in behavior patterns. New York: McGraw-Hill.

He Acts His Age. (13 min.) Age roles from one to 15 years. National Film Board of Canada.

PART III

Individual Differences in the School

8

MEASURING ABILITIES

THE MODERN TEACHER needs to know what kinds of tests there are, how to choose tests, and how to interpret them. Competence in these professional tasks requires an understanding of certain principles underlying the measurement of ability. Since schools are the most important users of tests, the teacher must therefore be a critical appraiser of tests as well as a judicious consumer. There are three important reasons for studying the principles of measurement. One is to gain insight into the rationale of scientific measurement in psychology and education. This helps the teacher understand the purposes of testing, and what tests can and cannot do for the school. Second, the knowledge of how tests are made helps us to estimate the value of a particular test for a particular purpose. Not all tests are equally good, nor does one test fit a particular purpose as well as another, though both may be called by the same name. The principles of testing show why we should and must look for certain things in a test of ability in order to decide whether it is a "good" test or a "poor" test. Third, familiarity with testing principles helps the school make the best possible use of information obtained from tests in meeting the needs of students.

SOME PRINCIPLES OF PSYCHOLOGICAL TESTING

When confronted with the score of John Doe on X test, a number of questions immediately come to mind:

1. What does the score mean? The score is meaningful to the extent that it enables us to compare the performance of

John Doe with a group. A test always compares one person with a group. This is the principle of *relativity*.

2. How much can we depend on this score as a measure of John's performance? If the result is due in large part to accidental or "chance" factors, the score may vary from time to time. To be worth our time in giving it, the test must give about the same result each time, or in other words have a minimum of error in measurement. This is the principle of *reliability*.

3. How do we know what ability the test measures? Does it measure what its name implies? What does the result tell us about what John Doe has learned or can learn in the future—about his abilities or aptitudes? The score is valid to the extent that it enables us to make such inferences or predictions. This is the principle of *validity*.

4. How can we be sure that John Doe's score is really comparable to the group with which he is being compared? If he was tested under different conditions, or has had unequal (i.e., more or less) opportunity to develop the ability tested, we can easily misinterpret the test result. The test builder assumes that John Doe's score is obtained under conditions equivalent to those which determined variation in the group. This is the principle of *comparability*.

The Relativity of Measurement. By relativity of measurement we mean simply that we have no absolute standard for gauging the proficiency of a person. His superiority or inferiority must be estimated on the basis of how he compares in his performance with other persons doing the same thing. This is true of any human trait. A barber is adjudged to be a good barber because he is better than other barbers, and a musician is either good or poor in so far as he is superior or inferior to other musicians. There is no other way for us to estimate the significance of such traits, because we do not have any absolute scale of barbering ability or of musical ability.

To take another example: a man is a good runner if he is able to outstrip his fellows in a race—his running ability is relative to what other runners can do. It may appear at first glance that we have an absolute scale for measuring running ability when we measure the runner's speed in terms of seconds of time taken in covering a certain distance. A little thought, however, will show that this is not the case. A runner is fast not because he runs, let us say, 100 yards in 9.4 seconds, but because, having run this distance in such a time, he is then found at the head of the list of all runners. There is no reason in the nature of things why such speed should of itself mark its possessor as a good runner, because horses can run faster, and deer still faster. Such a record is good, not because it is 9.4 seconds, but because it is a good one for human beings to make. The recorded time of 9.4 seconds, instead of being really an absolute measure of running ability, is only a *means of comparison* which we may use in order to arrive at an estimate of the person's ability. Only the result of this comparison will enable us to say whether the ability is high or low, or in a word just what the person's ability is.

The estimate of mental ability is also relative. If John Doe takes a test of 100 items and gets them all right, what does it tell us? It does not tell too much about John; it tells us that the test was easy for him, but it might be just as easy for everybody. If he gets them all wrong (score 0), it still tells us nothing, except that the test was very difficult *for him*. No matter how carefully built, our test is not an absolute scale. We have no absolute scale of reading ability, or arithmetic ability, of drawing ability, or of intelligence. We know only the performances of children and it is only because we can compare the performance of a particular child with that of other children that we have a basis for estimating his ability. If there were only *one* child in the world, we could not "test" him. This placement in the group must always be the final court of appeal as to the person's ability.

To place such stress upon the relativity of human measurements may seem to separate the measurement of ability from other forms of scientific measurement. But the difference is really only on the surface. It may appear to us offhand that we enjoy the use of truly absolute units of physical measurement in our pounds, inches, or minutes, or at least we often employ them as if this were so. But a little reflection will show that even these measurements are basically relative. For after all, who will tell us just how much a pound of matter actually is, or just how long an inch is, or who can tell us of the absolute length of time measured by a minute? We are all so familiar with inches, pounds, and minutes that we employ them as if they had an absolute value, and without ever thinking, probably, that anyone might ever ask just how big a pound is. In mental measurement, on the other hand, the units of measurement are so unfamiliar that we must face their relativity at the very beginning in order to give them a clear meaning. The person who is not used to expressing length in terms of centimeters, for example, must do the same thing. He has to convert the centimeters into inches, or in other words consider the relativity of the metric scale before he can interpret it.

Scoring Tests. A "raw score" is simply a number indicating a person's performance. The most usual raw score is the number of right answers or some variation such as "number right minus ½ the number wrong" (R — ½W.) It could be the "per cent of items right," or the time required to complete a task, or the height a person can jump. Raw scores are familiar to us in the form of school examinations and numerous other ways, but they cannot be interpreted meaningfully.

We cannot directly compare raw scores obtained from different tests. Thus if a child gets a score of 65 on an arithmetic test and a score of 35 on a reading test (in terms of the number of problems done correctly), we cannot tell from these two scores alone how his ability in the first test compares with that in the second. It is only after we know how each of these scores stands with relation to what a group of the same kind of children does as a whole that we can draw any such inference with respect to the results.

Since the mere arithmetical size of raw scores is without significance, any ratios found between them are also of very little value. Thus we cannot say that a boy who does 60 arithmetic problems correctly has twice the ability of a boy who does only 30. We can, of course, say that the first boy does twice as many problems, or that his productivity is twice as great, but not that he has twice the ability.

A score cannot be interpreted as a percentage of ability, because we have no absolute measure of ability to form the denominator of the fraction necessary for finding such a percentage. The long established custom of reporting school grades in terms of percentages may at first be deceiving in this regard and incline us to believe that we may have on occasion an absolute measure of ability. But school grades are relative to what experience has taught us can be achieved by the average child of a particular grade.

Norms and Derived Scores. We must then have some means of converting these first or raw scores into an *Index of group placement* before they can be interpreted as measures of ability. This means that a test must first be given to a large group of individuals before we can discover what their respective abilities are. *Norms* or standards established in such a fashion for a test offer us this basic means of comparison. When, the raw score is converted into an index of group placement, it becomes a "derived score," as it is often called. Following are the various kinds of derived scores most commonly employed in mental measurement:

1. *Age scores,* an index of placement within an age group, derived from age norms. These scores are commonly employed for those abilities showing a tendency to improve with age, or at least throughout the school years. Thus we have our "mental age," "educational age," "subject age." A mental age of 8-2 means that the child's test performance is equal to the average score of children whose age is 8 years, 2 months. An IQ, being a ratio of mental age to chronological age, is thus derived from age-scores.

2. *Grade scores,* for placement within a grade group. These scores are of particular value when used for school subjects. A grade score on a reading test of 5.5, for example, means that the child's performance in reading is equivalent to the average reading performance of children who have completed 5½ grades of school.

3. *Percentiles* (*or centiles*) *and percentile ranks* enable us to locate the individual within a group of his fellows by indicating the percentage of the group that obtained scores lower than his. Thus, a percentile rank of 90, derived from a particular raw score, means that 90 per cent of the group had scores lower than this and only 10 per cent achieved higher scores. To facilitate this kind of comparison, the distribution of scores obtained by the norm group has been divided into hundredths, and there are thus 99 division points or percentiles. For convenience we can divide the distribution into quarters by 3 quartiles, into fifths by 4 quintiles, or into tenths by 9 deciles, depending on whether we want to express the relative score in a range of 1-4, 1-5, or 1-10. Percentile ranks, in a word, are finer divisions of decile ranks. Such indices of ability are of particular value when adults are tested, since age or grade scores are not appropriate, and are preferable also for high school students.

4. *Standard scores* (*sigma scores*) make use of the standard deviation or sigma of the distribution of ability as the unit of measurement. The sigma score is the difference between an individual's raw score and the mean score of the group, expressed as a ratio of the standard deviation of the group, or $\frac{\text{Raw Score} - \text{Mean}}{\text{Sigma}}$. Like all derived scores, the standard score is the individual raw score converted into other terms; in this case, the score is expressed as a deviation from the mean *in terms of sigma units* of the distribution, or in terms of units which enable us to compare the position of the score relative to the norm group. That the sigma score is an index of group placement must be evident when we remember that it depends upon the mean and standard deviation of the group as a whole.

There are several varieties of standard scores, depending on what arbitrary value is assigned to the mean and the standard deviation. But any standard scale can be interpreted readily if we know what values have been assigned to the mean and to the standard deviation (which are usually given in the manual for the test) because we can then place the score relative to the norm distribution. The basic principle is the known percentage of cases between any two sigma-points on the base line under

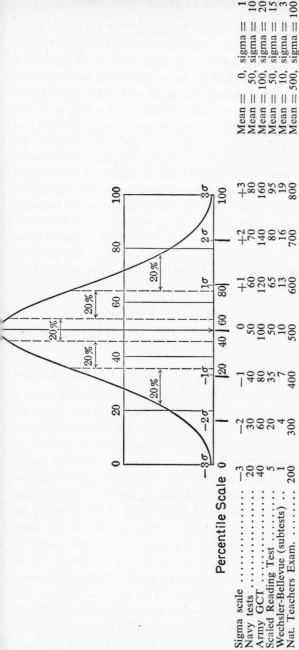

Sigma scale	−3	−2	−1	0	+1	+2	+3		Mean =	0,	sigma = 1
Navy tests	20	30	40	50	60	70	80		Mean =	50,	sigma = 10
Army GCT	40	60	80	100	120	140	160		Mean =	100,	sigma = 20
Scaled Reading Test	5	20	35	50	65	80	95		Mean =	50,	sigma = 15
Wechsler-Bellevue (subtests) ..	1	4	7	10	13	16	19		Mean =	10,	sigma = 3
Nat. Teachers Exam.	200	300	400	500	600	700	800		Mean =	500,	sigma = 100

FIGURE 39. A Graphic Illustration of Standard Scores in Relation to a Percentile Scale. The figure illustrates that standard scores, although appearing to differ in absolute amounts, may be interpreted with reference to a percentile scale if we know what amount has been assigned to the mean and standard deviation. The figure also shows the fallacy of assuming that percentile differences are equal throughout the scale. To assume that the difference between percentile ranks of 10 and 20 is the same as that between 40 and 50, for example, we must assume that the scores fall into a rectangular distribution, like that superimposed here on the normal curve. We readily see that percentile scores must be interpreted with respect to the normal curve, rather than the rectangular distribution. Compare, for example, the position of the 20th percentile in the rectangle and the same rank in the base-line scale. (Figure from H. E. Garrett, *Statistics in psychology and education*, p. 159.)

the normal curve. Referring to Figure 39, we see that a score one sigma above the mean (whether expressed as 60, 120, 65, 13, or 600) is equivalent to a percentile rank of 84 because it is higher than 50 per cent of the cases below the mean plus 34 per cent of the cases between the mean and "plus one" sigma.

Standard scores have certain advantages for test users because through them the raw scores on any number of tests can be "equated." For example, if we have norm distributions for ninth-graders on a spelling test, a reading test, and an arithmetic test, and ninth-grader John Doe has raw scores of 84, 39, and 76 on the three tests, conversion of these numbers into standard scores enables us not only to compare his scores with the norm group, but to compare the three scores with one another. We may find that his score of 39 in reading is a much higher score than the 76 in arithmetic or 84 in spelling. We can also make these comparisons if we know the percentile ranks of these scores.

Standardization of a Test. The practical significance of any of these derived scores as measures of ability will depend upon the amount of care given to the establishment of the norms upon which they are based, or as we may say, upon the *standardization* of a test. If we rely upon these scores to give us a satisfactory index of group placement, we must usually know a good many things about the nature of the group for which the norms have been determined. Does the group furnishing the norms really represent the group whose name it bears? In other words, does a fifth-grade norm really represent the ability of fifth-grade children in general? Does an educational or mental age of twelve really represent the ability of the average twelve-year-old? Would a percentile rank of 90 in a test for college students or adults still be representative of the same degree of ability if all college students or all adults were included in the group upon which the norms are based? That the ideal implied in these questions is not always realized is often due to inadequate sampling. This may be because the original group furnishing the norms was too small, introducing too great a chance of error. Or it may be that the original group was selected, perhaps unintentionally and on some other grounds than the mere possession of the ability to be measured.

The Principle of Reliability

A test is a sample of a person's behavior, or of his ability to solve problems. In testing intelligence, it is not possible to include in the test *all* the performances which exhibit intelligent behavior, so the test builder selects a variety of problems which constitute a sample of such abilities. The assumption is that we can form an estimate, from the sample taken here and now, of the larger scope of the person's abilities—or an estimate of the extent to which his behavior at other times will be "intelligent." The estimate is in the form of a score. The score is never a perfectly accurate estimate; there are always errors when we take a sample. The errors affect the reliability of the test, which by definition is the *consistency* with which it measures something. The reliable test, whatever it measures, gives us about the same result for the same individual on different occasions.

Error and Measurement. Every experimental or scientific measurement contains an error. This is just as true of the most refined laboratory measurement in physics as of mental measurement. When, however, the error is relatively small, particularly with reference to the purpose for which we wish to employ the measurement, as it sometimes is in physics or engineering, we may choose to ignore it. But it is always there if we but look for it. The measurement may be correct to the "nearest" sixteenth of an inch, or to the "nearest" thousandth of an inch, but it can be correct only to the "nearest" something or other. Only after the question of error is directly faced and its size known can the measurements themselves be evaluated.

What we should like of course in mental measurement is to obtain a measure of a person's *true ability*. The amount by which we deviate from such a measure in actual practice is our experimental error. There are a number of reasons, to be found both on the side of human nature and in connection with the techniques of testing itself, why we cannot find a person's true ability on a single occasion. However ideal we may think our present conditions for testing are, our subject will not do quite the same on another occasion presumably just as favorable. Sometimes, because of this, the obtained score is a little higher than it should be; at other times it is a little too low. If we could test our subject on about a thousand or more different occasions, these *accidental* sources of error would tend to cancel each other, and we might then take the average of these thousand tests as the person's true score; but it is not practicable to do such a thing. The reliable test, however, gives us a *good* approximation of an individual's true score.

The *sources of error* in measurement, in general, lie in the methods of selecting and constructing test items, or in the way abilities are sampled. Thus if the sample of items is too small, error in measurement is increased; a long test is more reliable than a short test. The kind of item, the language in which items or instructions are phrased, the time limits imposed, and a host of other factors may contribute error. Another general source of error lies in the subjects taking the test: their motivation, distractability, and sometimes age and sex differences, since a test may be reliable for persons of a given age, sex, or cultural background but unreliable for another group.

Estimation of Error: Coefficients of Reliability. The coefficient of reliability is a coefficient of correlation, and may be obtained through a number of different procedures:

1. By the *retest method,* the same test is given to a group on two different occasions, and the correlation between the two sets of scores is calculated. The result is an estimate of how *stable* the test score is, and is therefore sometimes called the "coefficient of stability" (2). The interval between tests must be planned so as to prevent or minimize practice effects, as opportunity for practice will lower the correlation.

2. *Retest on equivalent forms* of the same test is a variation of the first method. The alternate form given after the interval differs with respect to items or problems included, but is as similar as possible in "make-up" and level of difficulty. The correlation between the two sets of scores is an estimate of

equivalence of the two forms, but gives us no direct information as to the accuracy or reliability of either form.

3. *The split-half method* makes use of a correlation between two halves of the test. For each individual two scores are obtained, one on the odd-numbered items and one on the even-numbered items (odd-even method). This is in a way similar to the equivalent forms method, since the odd and even scores may be regarded as scores on duplicate forms of the same test, each one-half as long as the whole test. Reliability coefficients obtained by the second or third method may therefore be called "coefficients of equivalence" (2).

Standard Error of Measurement. The standard error of measurement tells us how much we may expect an obtained score to be above or below the true score. It is derived from the coefficient of reliability of a test.[1] The larger the coefficient of reliability, other things being equal, the smaller will be the test's error of measurement, and vice versa. The advantage of computing the standard error of measurement lies in this: it gives us the range, in units of test score, within which the individual's true score probably lies. If John Doe makes a raw score of 58 on a reading test with a standard error of measurement of 12, the chances are about 68 in 100 that his true raw score is between 46 and 70, i.e., within a range of scores from −12 and +12 points from his obtained score. To put this another way, we might say that if John took the test again under the same conditions, the chances are two to one that the second score would not be lower than 46 or higher than 70.

It should be clear that the error of measurement is a very important consideration when the variability of the group is small, when there are small differences in true ability among the persons being compared. Very few tests can distinguish reliably between the ability of the best student and the next best,

---

[1] The formula for calculating the standard error of measurement is as follows: $SE_{meas.} = \sigma \sqrt{1 - r_1 I}$. We subtract the coefficient of reliability from 1, take the square root of this difference, and multiply the result by the standard deviation. The somewhat less widely used "probable error of measurement" is a constant fraction of the standard error of measurement. $PE_{meas.} = .67\ SE_{meas.}$

but tests can usually distinguish between the higher, the middle, and the lower students when (1) the "spread" of ability is fairly large, and (2) the test is fairly reliable.

Any comparison of the test scores of individuals requires that we keep the standard error of measurement in mind. Our purpose should be to know the relative rankings of the true abilities of students, and not just the relative size of the obtained test scores. Test scores always involve an error. In some cases this error may be as large as the difference in scores between two individuals we wish to compare. The apparent difference in scores is then meaningless. If the error is small compared to the score difference, we may be assured of a real difference between the two individuals. It is never enough to find a difference by testing. The significance of the difference itself must be determined by comparing it with the error of measurement.

Standards of Reliability. What is an adequate coefficient of reliability? How high must it be for us to judge that a given test is reliable enough for our purpose? The answer to this depends on the purpose for which we use the test. The general principle can be stated as follows: A test of ability should have a reliability coefficient of at least .90 if the scores are to be used for individual diagnosis or prediction. This is seen to be a principle of common sense, when we realize that the degree of reliability tells us how much we can rely on an individual's score as an estimate of his ability. An unreliable test is one in which a person of given ability has a wide range of possible scores, and we can determine very little from his obtained score. To take a hypothetical case, if John Doe takes an "intelligence test" having a reliability of .50 and gets a score of 100 IQ we may conclude from our study of the error of measurement on the test that his real IQ lies somewhere between 80 and 120— but so does that of over 80 per cent of the general population. This would be a reasonable guess on the basis of probability alone, without giving the test. But if his question is "Do I have what it takes to go to college?" what are we to say about the test result? The answer ranges from "Certainly not" to "Yes, by all means." The only honest answer could therefore be "I don't know."

Factors Affecting Reliability. One important condition of a reliable test is its length. In general, we can safely assume that no very short test is reliable. We can clearly see the fallacy involved in estimating a child's intelligence from a one-item test requiring him to identify a donkey, or in a test of American history consisting of "Who shot Lincoln?" Such "tests" are poor devices because chance may largely determine whether *one* item is answered correctly or incorrectly, but as more items are added chance plays a less and less significant role in influencing the score. Any test can ordinarily be made more reliable by increasing its length, up to a certain limit. For this reason, a longer test is generally preferable to a shorter one.

In general, any factor or condition which enables chance to affect the score decreases the reliability. The type of test item is another factor. In an alternative response test, such as the "true-false" type, reliability tends to be lower than with the multiple-response variety where a larger number of possible answers reduces the probability of a correct response by chance. The recall type of test item accordingly seems to enjoy still greater reliability. As we might expect, the more objective the scoring and the less dependent this is upon the person doing the scoring, the more reliable will be the test. "Catch questions" have been found to lower reliability. A poor choice of words or of sentence construction in phrasing the items tends to lower reliability. Short items are usually better than long ones, probably because they are more readable.

Personal factors also influence reliability. Cronbach's experiments with what he calls "response sets" show that reliability is affected by individual differences among test-takers in tendency to guess, working for speed vs. working for accuracy, and the like (3). When the individual is "set" for accuracy rather than speed, reliability is increased. A tendency to guess, of course, decreases reliability.

The reliability of a test will often vary with the group which takes it. A reliability coefficient of .95 obtained with adults will not necessarily be as high for adolescents, and the same holds true for many such age and grade differences. Thus it is reported that the Gates Reading Survey Test, although reliable for most grades, was found unreliable for third graders, who found it difficult and consequently resorted to guessing (2).

TEST VALIDITY

When we ask "Does the test really measure what it is supposed to measure?" we are raising the question of its validity. We come here to what may be called the "pragmatic sanction" of a test. Does it work? Does it prove itself as a test of that particular human trait or ability it is supposed to measure and for which it is named, such as intelligence, reading, motor ability? This is the hurdle that every technique and method of measurement in psychology must pass before it can gain scientific recognition. Most of the painstaking work that must be done before a test is acceptable is concerned with whether it really measures the ability or trait that we expect it to measure. The chief aim in testing is validity.

The validity of a test is not a matter of opinion, or of its appearance or nomenclature, but of evidence. This implies that the test user should be able to appraise its value in objective results. He should never feel that he is forced to depend solely upon the opinion of this or that particular psychologist—however valuable his opinion may be as opinion—as to just what a test measures. Such an attitude would tend to place mental measurement off in a field by itself, apart from other sciences where hypothesis and opinion, although most surely having a value as instigators of experiment, certainly do not constitute the final court of appeal. Again, human nature being the highly complex and variable thing that it is, it is particularly in such a field of study that hypothesis, opinion, and prediction are most apt to go awry.

The Practical Need for Validation. A psychological test may not really measure what it seemingly professes to measure for a number of reasons.

1. The name of the test may lead us astray. The same word, "intelligence," for example, does not always mean the same thing to different people. Some confusion may naturally result. This can happen because the average person usually gives very little thought to defining many of the concepts employed in psychology. He may have only a rather vague notion of the matter. Having in mind some particular example of what he regards as a manifestation of the trait or ability, he may immediately jump to the conclusion that the "intelligence" test, for example, must measure just this kind of mental performance. Each person is likely in such a case to set up his own criterion of what the test should be expected to do. The two common fallacies to which naïve test users are subject are the "jingle fallacy" (6)—that two tests of the same name measure the same ability—and the "jangle fallacy," which assumes that tests of different names necessarily measure different abilities.

2. Psychological traits are difficult to define. There are concepts in every science which are very difficult to define even by those who have given a great deal of thought to the matter. We may think of electricity and physics in this connection. It need not be surprising that psychologists as well may not always be in perfect agreement in their first definitions of certain abilities or traits. The use of a convenient name for a test, taken perhaps from our everyday language, is usually to be regarded as only tentative and without any very serious implications. The objective experimental data on the validity of such a test furnish the only satisfactory means for enabling both the novice and the expert to determine just what a test—whatever its name—can reasonably be supposed to measure.

3. There are probably no "pure" tests of a single ability. In the construction of a test, no matter how carefully it is done, the instrument becomes contaminated with certain irrelevant or inconsequential matters which creep in to conceal or obscure the basic objective. Thus a person who wishes to devise a test of the ability to solve arithmetical problems may easily, if he is not aware of the danger beforehand, make use of such difficult words in phrasing the problems that his test in the final analysis turns out to be more a measure of the child's ability to read

than of the ability to do the arithmetic involved. The ease with which irrelevant factors have been found to creep into a test, quite surreptitiously, has taught the expert to be exceedingly wary about the supposed validity of any measuring scale unless fortified by experimental findings. What a test "looks like" is a very poor criterion to rely upon.

4. What the test measures may not be useful. Even though we may be justified in assuming that a given test measures a real ability, it may measure a function that is not practically worth while. It is not enough to measure something, even accurately. This "something" must also have a practical bearing upon other things in life.

Determining the Validity of a Test. There are many ways of determining validity. Before discussing them, let us draw attention to the fact that validity has two meanings in current use. Super (9) distinguishes between what he calls "internal validity" and "external validity." Internal validity is a kind of rational or logical validity; a test is said to be internally valid if its content is reasonably "pure" and consistent with the logical purpose of the test author, if the items are homogenous and each item correlates well with the total score (internal consistency.) Internal validity is thus similar to reliability, and is called internal because the evidence of this kind of validity is entirely within the test. The internally valid test is one that measures something which is logically specific and measures it consistently through every item of test content. This kind of evidence is of course not sufficient in itself to make clear the practical value of the test.

Practical usefulness of a test must be determined from external evidence of validity—the test's relation to some performance *criterion* outside or independent of the test itself. Thus the external validity criterion of an intelligence test might be some measure of school progress; of a mechanical aptitude test, some evidence of success in mechanical work; of a sales aptitude test, the dollar volume of sales made. Such external criteria are difficult to find and "pin down" and are also difficult to measure. Most test authors would agree that it is easier to

construct an "internally valid" test than to determine and measure a criterion of "successful" performance which is in itself
valid, reliable, and stable enough to serve its purpose in "testing the test."

For example, suppose we want a test to predict academic
performance in school. What is a good criterion of school performance? Grade averages? But grades are often not reliable,
because of the peculiar grading habits of teachers. The grade
a student gets depends often on such irrelevant things as which
teacher grades him, how he is examined, what school he is in,
and the like. Shall we then use standardized achievement tests
for a criterion? In many instances, the school curriculum does
not stress the types of content included in the tests, and we are
thus not measuring the student's progress in that particular
school. Shall we use a consensus of teacher's ratings? But
teachers may not agree among themselves, any more than they
do on grades. Shall we use the number of school years passed
successfully, or how long the student remains in school? The
"pass-fail" standards differ among schools, and some students
drop out of school for financial reasons rather than failure in
scholastic work. However, school grades are among the "best"
criteria available, and are widely used as external evidence of
validity. The questions raised above are merely examples of
the doubts that can be raised about a "good" criterion. It is
similarly clear that the criterion of sales ability suggested (value
of sales in dollars) depends on such variable factors as the kind
of commodities sold, the territory of the salesman, and the like.
Yet this is relatively easy by comparison with external criteria
for teaching ability, for example. There are many kinds of
criteria of "success" in any field of endeavor, and the selection of
a suitable and useful one is a complex undertaking.

Techniques of Validation. *Internal validity* may be determined in three ways: (1) by logical analysis of the test content,
to discover whether or not it corresponds to an exact definition
of the trait we wish to measure; thus a test of "mechanical ability" may be found, on analysis of its tasks, to measure manual
dexterity alone, with speed of arm and wrist movements pre-

dominant and with such factors as coordination or fine finger dexterity not sampled; (2) by statistical study of its items to determine its "internal consistency"; or (3) by determining whether the test scores show a normal distribution, on the reasonable supposition that most human traits are normally distributed.

External validation includes a variety of techniques, some based on correlating the test scores with an external criterion of performance, some based on the study of group differences, and some based on correlation with other tests.

1. Correlation with other tests or measures of ability is a useful preliminary device for determining what the test measures. Low or zero correlation should be found between two tests measuring widely different abilities; a substantial correlation between manual dexterity and intelligence would be suspect. A test that purports to be a measure of "social intelligence" as a separate trait should not be highly correlated with "abstract intelligence." On the other hand, the fact that one test of abstract intelligence correlates highly with another is at least partial evidence of its validity.

2. Studying group differences in test scores often yields evidence of test validity. Thus if machinists make significantly higher scores than shoe clerks on a test of mechanical ability, the result supports validity of the test: if there were no difference or if shoe clerks scored higher, the test would be a very doubtful one for the purpose intended.

3. Correlation of test results with some independent criterion of the ability supposedly measured by the test is usually the most satisfactory standard by which to judge validity. The independent criterion may be school grades, ratings by teachers or supervisors, measures of success in life situations, performance or achievement tests of various kinds. The correlation coefficients obtained from such studies are usually called *validity coefficients*. A high correlation will usually not be found between any one test and a criterion of "success." Consequently, satisfactory results in predicting a "success" criterion from tests usually involve a preliminary selection of several tests which appear to be promising as predictors. This selection

of tests is usually called a "trial battery" because the tests are to be tried out as predictors and the less successful of them are usually rejected.

The Use of Tests

The Principle of Comparability. To compare an individual's score with a norm group, we must be sure that the score is really comparable with respect to the conditions that produced it. The scientific value of mental testing depends, finally, upon whether those taking the test work under conditions, both internal and external, which are constant for all concerned. It can hardly be supposed that we could compare, without further ado, a score obtained by a boy who was not interested and who did not try with that of another who was interested and who did try. Nor can we directly compare the scores of different children when persons giving the test have differed very much from one another in their method of administering it. Again, we cannot assume, without good evidence on the point, that environmental differences have no effect on the score. Such things as these, along with other similar ones, are the types of factors that must be satisfactorily controlled before we can feel confident of the *comparability* of performance.

How stringent must be our requirements in order to assume comparability? It is evident that, the human personality being what it is, both internal and external conditions can never be absolutely the same for any two individuals. An insurmountable obstacle would be placed in the way of measurement if we had to wait upon the satisfaction of such a stringent requirement. In actual practice, however, it is sufficient if the conditions surrounding the test situation are *relatively* constant; that is, if they are comparable, first in regard to those factors and influences that are known to be the ones most likely to produce appreciable variations in the score and, secondly, in regard to the allowable variation in the score. It would be of no practical importance to hold rigidly to absolutely unvarying conditions of temperature, noise, lighting, time of day, and the like, if their effect on test scores had been shown by experience to be negligible. Some of our errors of measurement may be due to such factors, but when the test is shown to be highly reliable under ordinary standard testing conditions, we may be sure that the errors are small.

Administering Tests. Why must persons who administer tests have special training? Because the experienced or trained mental tester is prepared to hold down disturbing influences and to safeguard the comparability of performance. What has often seemed to the novice an unreasonable inflexibility in the method of administering a test, such as being required to follow the printed directions word for word, and to observe the time limits closely, represents one of these justifiable safeguards. The requirement of strict adherence to the published directions for administering a test is not always fully appreciated by the beginner. Prior to becoming acquainted with any psychological testing, he may be intrigued and mystified by the thought of mental measurement, but after seeing a test administered he may be somewhat taken aback by the apparent simplicity of the whole thing and say to himself, "Why, any one can do that." The real question is not, *Can* any one do that? but *Will* he do that, just that and nothing more? Will he modify or slight the directions here and there either because he has not mastered them or because he thinks they really should be modified a little? If he does, the question whether he *can* give the test is beside the point. The fact is, he *does not* give the test, because in introducing a new idea or two or in slighting an old one, he does not preserve the comparability of performance.

Effect of Motivation on Test Performance. Possible differences in the strength of interest and motivation with which individuals approach a test may seem at first glance to offer a serious obstacle. But this turns out in actual practice to be not nearly so serious as might be imagined. While there would be appreciable differences in the results obtained under weak motivation, on the one hand, and under strong motivation, on the other, it so happens that, as we pass beyond what may be regarded as a certain level of fairly high motivation, there is relatively little to be gained from a further increase in the strength of incentive. It is moreover a relatively easy matter, in the ordinary school situation, to see to it that the children are working at this critical level of motivation. At least we can usually tell when they are not and discount our results accordingly. With very young children, however, it is usually necessary for the tester to come face to face with the testee in order to evaluate properly the influence of motivation. It is for this reason that most tests for younger children are "individual" ones. It is also largely because of the importance of motivation that an individual test is recommended before taking any step that may seriously affect a child's educational career.

But how can we be sure that the testee has done his best? This question is relatively unimportant. It is more necessary that the test performances of children be comparable than that they be maximal. The reason for this should be clear in the light of what we have already seen, since the basis of scientific measurement is a relative one. It is not then necessary for us to be certain that each child has first demonstrated the ultimate of his capacity before we accept our test result as a satisfactory estimate of his relative performance. Experimental studies of the effect of motivation and continued practice on performance, moreover, show rather clearly that our tested individuals usually preserve their same relative ranking, even though each one individually should be brought considerably nearer to the level of his maximal performance.

It would seem then that nothing in particular is to be gained, so far as the main purpose of testing is concerned, by demanding that each child have the opportunity of performing under optimal, and perhaps humanly impossible, conditions. This is why certain misgivings as to the value of a test, based upon the suspicion that the children did not do quite so well as they might have done if the teacher could have modified the explanations a little or if the time limits could have been extended ever so little, show a misunderstanding of the nature of scientific measurement of ability. It must always be a question of finding out what our children can do under rigidly controlled conditions, for in no other way can we be sure of the comparability of performance. What we might get in the way of scores, outside this strict regulation, would be scientifically without meaning.

At first glance it may seem as though many tests are too difficult for the children to whom they are to be given. Although there may be many items or problems the child of a certain age or grade can reasonably be expected to do, it is a common thing to find along with these many others quite above this average level. Here again the point of testing may easily be missed. A good test is one that expressly includes items of such difficulty that even the superior child cannot succeed with all of them. If a test seems too "difficult" it should be remembered that it is made so intentionally, and it will be a poor one if it is not. The reason for this should be plain. We cannot be sure that our subjects work under comparable internal conditions unless we carry each one, in the test, beyond the point he can reach with ease. There must be a certain pressure exerted upon the child, either in the way of difficulty or of time limitation, because effort can affect the quality of performance. It is only in such a way that we can be at all sure that each child is putting forth a similar degree of effort. We cannot hope for comparability of performance if all the tasks are easy ones.

Again, we should have no basis for the relative ranking of individuals taking the test if they all made perfect scores. This would merely show that their proficiency was above the upper limit of our test. We should then know very little about their ability, because we could not rank them relative to each other. The "difficulty" of a test, instead of being an example of unfairness or of some impossible ideal of accomplishment, is as a matter of fact a practical necessity if we accept the principles of comparability and relativity in mental measurement.

Requirements of a "Good" Test of Ability. We may give our principles of mental measurement a practical cast in speaking of the requirements a test has to meet to be considered a "good" one. These requirements give practical hints for choosing tests, administering them, and interpreting them. The requirements of a good test are as follows:

1. *Objectivity,* in the method both of administering and scoring, so that the subjective factor or personal bias of the tester may be ruled out or at least reduced to a minimum. The objectivity of a test, attained through explicit directions for giving, taking, and scoring the test, is necessary for the comparability of performance. Objectivity also serves to reduce the error of measurement, and makes the test more reliable.

2. *Reliability,* or consistency on the part of the test in giving the same score to the same person on two different occasions. As mentioned before, however, the degree of reliability required of a test will depend on the purpose in view. Kelley (6) has offered tentative suggestions on just this point. They are worth quoting, not only as a safe practical guide to the use of tests but also as a concrete illustration of the relationship existing between requisite reliability and purpose. The six general purposes for which tests are employed and the requisite reliability (expressed as the coefficient of reliability) for each purpose are, according to this author, as follows:

(1) The measurement of the general group (grade or school) accomplishment and an estimate of the probable future general group success in school work. The test should have a reliability of .50.

(2) The measure of a school group in some specific subject and an estimate of the future group promise in the same or a closely related subject. Reliability should be .50.

(3) The measurement of the relative differences in achievement of the group in two or more scholastic lines and an estimate of the significance of such differences. Reliability should be .90.

(4) The measurement of the past general scholastic success and the future promise of an individual. Reliability should be .94.

(5) The measurement of the success of an individual in a specific school subject and an estimate of his future promise in the same or a closely related subject. Reliability should be .94.

(6) The measurement of differences in the individual of abilities and accomplishments in several scholastic lines and an estimate of the probability of persistence of differences, of the sort revealed, in future school work or vocation. Reliability should be .98. (6, p. 28)

3. *Validity,* or some evidence that the test at hand really measures what it purports to measure, giving due regard to the

worthwhileness of the function, its proper interpretation, and the exclusion of irrelevant and inconsequential matters. The coefficient of validity is a quantitative expression of the satisfaction of this requirement. There are, however, as indicated before, other experimental approaches to this question, all with the aim of having the test "prove itself." Internal evidence of validity (within the test content itself) is desirable, but not sufficient to determine the test's practical value. Some evidence of its relationship to an independent criterion is usually essential.

4. *Standardization.* Adequate norms must be available for the test if we are to feel confident of the accuracy of our "group placement" of any particular individual. Both the size and nature of the "norm group" upon which the norms have been based are important in determining whether norms are comparable for our purpose. A "good" test provides adequate descriptions of norm groups; the more we know about the group used for comparison, the better our interpretation of scores will be. A standardized test is of little value unless we know exactly what the standards of comparison are.

5. *Discriminative Capacity.* The test should enable us to discriminate between individuals who may be very close together on the scale of ability. It should also cover a fairly wide range of ability so that we shall be able to identify both the very inferior and the very superior: it should have both a "low floor" and a "high ceiling." Practically, this means that there should be no or very few zero scores, no or very few perfect scores; there should be a wide range of possible scores, and the test should yield a fairly normal distribution. Discriminative capacity also implies a low error of measurement, or high reliability. We should also be careful to note how much the speed factor (in a time limit test) contributes to the "spreading out" of scores. Unless we are particularly interested in measuring speed, the "good" test for our purpose is one whose discriminative capacity depends on mental "power" rather than speed.

School Achievement Tests. Achievement is a general term describing something a person has done or can do. More precisely, it refers to skills or knowledge which are definitely manifested in behavior and which have some social value. Achievement ordinarily has a past reference, and implies something already learned as a result of certain experiences. The ability to read, write, or throw a baseball is called achievement. Socially undesirable abilities like fighting or stealing are not ordinarily called so. An "achievement test" measures the outcome of instruction or experience. Examples are a test of reading ability, an arithmetic test, or a performance test in running a lathe. Since various kinds of achievement are goals of education, the progress of students in school is evaluated in terms of achievement.

The purpose of school achievement tests is the evaluation of instruction. The practical work of education is very largely a matter of preparing the child for knowing, doing, saying, and thinking those things upon which we, as a nation and a cultural group, place a high social value. The achievement test is designed to measure the effectiveness of teaching methods or of the curriculum in attaining these goals, and to identify those students whose educational experiences have resulted in success or failure.

The question of validity for an achievement test raises some special problems, because the purpose of the test is not so much the prediction of future achievement, as in aptitude testing, but the assessment of present achievement. It has no criterion of external validity, except this: an achievement test is valid to the extent that it measures what the teacher or the school *intends* to teach. Since there are many different purposes in teaching, and many methods and curricula adapted to different kinds of students, an achievement test may be valid for one school and invalid for another, valid for one class and invalid for another. When selecting any test, we should not ask "is it valid?" but "valid for what?" In the case of achievement tests especially, we must ask whether the test is valid for our specific purpose in teaching. Let us illustrate this point:

1. An achievement test in American history emphasizes items of political and military history. Is the test valid for a class in which the teacher emphasizes social and cultural

changes, but pays relatively scant attention to the details of wars and political events?

2. How valid is a test of geometrical reasoning problems (such as land surveying, building construction, etc.) for students whose training in geometry consisted entirely of learning step-by-step proofs of theorems?

3. Would we be justified in using a test in civics designed for students in large cities in a southern rural school where the teacher stressed local problems of government?

These are of course questions of comparability, because we are asking how comparable are the educational experiences of the population on whom the test was standardized and the educational experiences of the group for whom the test is being considered. They are also questions of validity, because we are asking how well the test content measures what is taught in the specific situation.

Achievement tests are of almost infinite variety, but can be roughly classified as follows:

1. *Subject matter tests.* These are tests of information in various subject matter fields, usually calling for factual knowledge and understanding of technical terms and processes. Standardized tests are available for practically all levels in a variety of fields from English and mathematics to cooking and woodworking.

2. *Diagnostic tests.* The purpose of these is not simply to measure general achievement, but to discover weak points in achievement. The best examples are those which test for complex abilities like reading and arithmetic. Diagnostic reading tests, for example, yield not only a general score of reading ability, but separate scores for vocabulary, rate, story comprehension, and paragraph comprehension. A diagnostic test in arithmetic is scored to show up weaknesses in fundamentals like multiplication, division, fractions, decimals, and the like. But "diagnostic" tests do not diagnose; they reveal symptoms. The teacher is the diagnostician who must discover "why" from close study of the individual pupils.

3. *Tests of educational development.* Although available in subject matter fields, this type of test is designed primarily

to test reasoning, interpretation, and application of principles rather than familiarity with facts and terminology (correlations between "knowledge of facts" and "application of principles," incidentally, have not been found high) (5). Since most authorities state the aims of teaching to be the cultivation of interpretive skills, such tests are more appropriate for evaluating the outcomes of instruction. An example of a test battery designed to measure the broader aspects of development in subject matter fields is the Iowa Tests of Educational Development, measuring interpretive skills rather than factual knowledge.

There is no hard-and-fast distinction between educational development tests and what we have called "subject-matter" tests, because many achievement tests partake of the characteristics of both, i.e., test for both knowledge of facts and understanding of principles. But to the teacher trying to choose between tests or interpret the results of tests, the distinction is an important one. Some recent educational development tests are designed to measure critical reasoning and interpretation as such (apart from traditional curricular categories) on the assumption that if principles of logical thinking or inference are directly taught in the classroom, there should be tests for evaluating this kind of achievement.

Evaluation Through Testing. The effects of standardized achievement testing on school practice can be (and have been) bad as well as good. If inappropriate (and therefore invalid) tests are used to evaluate teaching, teachers may tend to emphasize in their instruction what the tests measure, regardless of the needs, readinesses, and individual differences among students. Thus the test content may determine the teaching and curricular practices, rather than the other way around. In many instances standardized testing programs have been criticized for this reason. The principle of validity, as applied to achievement testing, implies that tests should be selected which are appropriate to the purpose of instruction, whatever that purpose is. The valid achievement test is one which measures reliably what we want it to measure, or in other words is consistent with our purpose in instruction.

Aptitude Testing. "Ability" commonly refers to something a person can do here and now. "Aptitude," on the other hand, usually has a future reference, and in the general sense has been defined as "a condition or set of characteristics indicative of ability to learn something" (13). This is a fairly adequate explanation of what we mean by such an expression as "aptitude for law," since the term refers to a constellation of traits (physical, intellectual, motivational, temperamental) which, taken together, indicate some promise of attaining a certain level of achievement. It is so general, however, that "aptitude for law" may be one set of characteristics in one student and a different set in another. It does not help us to specify even the minimum essentials of what it takes to be a lawyer.

But we must know precisely what we are measuring before we can construct an aptitude test to measure any specific ability. In order to study an aptitude scientifically, we must be able to identify it in a variety of persons and study its effect in a variety of situations. From the point of view of mental testing, then, an aptitude is an ability which is (1) *specific,* so that it can be named, identified, and described; (2) of *unitary composition,* so that as far as possible it can be identified as a relatively distinct ability and not a conglomerate of various unrelated abilities, interests, and achievements (e.g. "mechanical aptitude" is not unitary); and (3) *predictive of facility in learning* some kind of activity (9).

Measuring aptitude is a matter of predicting future achievement from present performance. There are two ways of inferring which of the earlier appearing abilities are the important predictors. First, we may measure the characteristics associated with the later achievement, and infer from them what the earlier abilities must have been. This "reading backward" in the history of development is quite difficult to do, since we always must be able to evaluate the effect of motivation and special opportunities, as distinct from ability. Second, we may use the longitudinal or follow-up approach by testing the earlier appearing abilities and later studying their relationship to subsequent achievement. Either of these approaches presents a difficulty: the more mature ability we may wish to predict from the earlier test is often the emergent integration of a great deal of learning and may really have no parallel in the behavior of children. For these two reasons—the need for specific and unitary measures of ability, and the fact that the composition of an ability is affected by maturational changes, abilities have been subjected to a great deal of analysis.

THE ANALYSIS OF ABILITY

How many kinds of mental ability are there? Some teachers might maintain that there is only one ("general intelligence"), that there is simply a gradient of brightness-dullness, that the bright students can learn anything better than the less bright. Others might insist that there are many different kinds of abilities, and that a high degree of one kind tells us nothing about the degree of other kinds of abilities.

The problem of classifying abilities has many practical aspects, as well as aspects of theoretical interest. For one thing, the construction and use of achievement and aptitude tests depend on knowledge about the kinds of abilities. If there is only one important mental ability, we need only one kind of test to measure it. If many, we need many kinds of tests to assess properly the abilities of students and to plan their educational experiences.

The Classification of Abilities: Factor Analysis. A statistical method for sorting out human abilities is called *factor analysis*. Although it may become very complex mathematically, we do not need to be mathematicians to follow the kind of thinking underlying it. A grasp of its nature and purpose will help us to understand the way relationships among abilities are studied, as well as some modern developments in test construction. Factor analysis is really an extension and refinement of the statistical manipulation of correlation coefficients, as in partial and multiple correlation, and follows the same logic.

A positive correlation between two tests of ability can indicate that they are measuring common factors. When a number of tests have high intercorrelations, we may assume that they are measuring to a large extent the same kinds of abilities, or in other words the same factor is entering into all the tests.   By the same reasoning, a number of tests having very small or zero intercorrelations have little in common, and the tests are assumed to measure as many factors as there are tests.   Factor analysis is an exact mathematical method of reducing a table of intercorrelations to a minimum number of separate factors, or "lowest common denominators" of the table.   It is generally found that most mental abilities tend to be related in some manner.   It is also known that a number of abilities tend to "hang together" to form special groups, or in other words show a higher degree of relationship among themselves than with other abilities outside the group.   There are also some abilities not related to any other.

Hence we may think of three kinds of factors: general factors, group factors, and specific factors.   A *general factor* is one which is found in all mental abilities measured, or which is common to all tests in a given set.   All the tests are then said to be "saturated" or "loaded" with the factor.   The general factor is sometimes called *g,* which accounts for the fact that most tests of mental ability tend to be positively correlated.   A *group factor* is one which is found in several tests which thus "hang together" to form a cluster or group; such tests having a high loading in one factor will be highly intercorrelated, while tests in which the group factor is not present may be found to belong to another group.   A *specific* or *unique* factor is one present in a single test.   Figure 40 shows the relationships among factors in a set of hypothetical tests.

Abilities are classified psychologically, then, not on the basis of their apparent similarity or a similarity of names by which they are commonly known, but on the basis of their statistical correlations and the nature and number of factors necessary to explain these relationships.   Abilities are classified in the same way as the tests that measure them.   Tests having a high loading of a common group factor are classified together, whether they appear superficially similar or not.

Primary Mental Abilities.   We have seen that the techniques of factor analysis are useful in reducing a large number

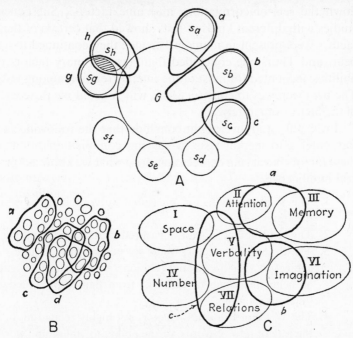

FIGURE 40. A Graphic Comparison of Three Theories of Mental Ability. These theories attempt to explain the correlations among abilities. (A) Spearman's two-factor theory conceives of each ability as divisible into *g* and some factor specific to the task. The mental tests (ellipses) overlap the general factor *g* to varying degrees, since they vary in the extent to which they are "loaded" with *g*. (B) The "community of content" theory conceives an ability to be a sample of many independent abilities (small circles) which may combine in various ways and thus enter a great variety of tasks. (C) The illustration of multiple factor, or group factor theory, shows seven hypothetical intellectual factors with three hypothetical tests superimposed. The tests "draw upon" the factors to varying degrees, and test intercorrelations will depend on the amount or "weight" of the common factors entering into the tests. These hypothetical factors, of course, are merely illustrations of the many that could be postulated. (From J. P. Guilford, *Psychometric methods,* New York: McGraw-Hill, 1936, p. 463.)

of tests into a minimum number of factors or abilities measured by these tests. These procedures were used in developing devices for measuring "primary" mental abilities, the term used by Thurstone (12). Thurstone administered 56 tests to a large group of subjects, intercorrelated the test results, and broke down the sets of correlations into nine factors. Subsequent studies with different kinds of tests showed that certain of these factors were present in many tests, since they continued to appear, and Thurstone concluded that seven primary factors or abilities accounted for most of the intercorrelation among tests. The next step was to construct tests which could measure each of the factors separately.

From this study we might conclude that the following factors enter into mental tests in varying combinations, or that these factors in varying degrees comprise what we know as "general intelligence."

1. The V (Verbal) factor, measured by vocabulary or word meanings.
2. The N (Number) factor, measured by tests of computing.
3. The S (Spatial) factor, tested by items which require the subject to visualize spatial relations, or to identify a figure as being the same or different from figures presented in different rotations.
4. The W (Word Fluency) factor, not highly related to V, is the rate of flow of words, or the ability to "think up" words rapidly.
5. The R (Reasoning) factor, testing the ability to abstract patterns of letters or objects presented in series or groups.
6. The M (Memory) factor consists of rapid rote memorizing.
7. The P (Perceptual) factor is measured by tasks which require rapid perception of likenesses or differences in the form of objects or figures.

The construction of such tests probably marks a major step forward in mental measurement, but the empirical validity of the tests still needs further study. Many persons believe, with Thurstone, that the profile of primary mental abilities gives more information about a child than does a general IQ. On the other hand, there is too little evidence of just what educational progress or behavior the scores can predict. Consequently no practical interpretation of profile differences is possible. Future research may indicate that they do have empirical validity, or may substantiate Kelley's concern that some are "mental factors of no importance" (7).

How primary are the "primary abilities?" The logic behind factor analysis does not imply that they are indivisible entities like chemical elements, or that they behave like elements in entering into various compounds of ability. Primary abilities are definitions of group factors, and a group factor is simply a basis for kinship among a number of specific abilities. Actually, the correlations among the various primary ability tests are themselves positive, ranging from .15 to .54 (11). This may imply a more comprehensive "second order" factor common to them all, or in other words general intelligence. Nor should we conclude that these factors, and only these, represent the fundamental human abilities. A study of tests used for the selection of Air Force cadets during the war revealed 28 factors, including 5 spatial factors and 8 different reasoning factors (4). Some were so unclear that they were difficult to name.

Some Theories of Mental Ability

Which Abilities Are Fundamental? The notion that any practical human ability is a composite of general functions is commonplace. For example, we may think of a highly specialized ability to play tennis in terms of such functions as strength, speed, alertness, agility, coordination. These are presumably put together or organized through practice with the materials of tennis into a smooth, integrated performance. The notion of a *general* athletic ability would imply that a person superior in strength, speed, agility, and coordination should with practice excel in any *particular* activity to which these simpler functions are fundamental. Does this general ability exist? If so, of what discrete functions is it composed? How can these simpler processes be measured? Psychologists have asked these kinds of questions about mental ability or intelligence. They have asked how it is manifested, what fundamental abilities or mental processes comprise it, and how these processes can be measured.

Fundamental abilities are those identified with the more general mental functions and measured with test materials taken

from common experience.   Because these simpler mental processes may affect the speed, accuracy, and efficiency of the more
highly specialized activities of everyday life, they may be regarded as aptitudes.

Theories of mental ability are then attempts to answer the
question "What are the fundamental human aptitudes?"   Since
many different kinds of tested abilities have been intercorrelated
and analyzed, a theory of mental ability is really an attempt to
explain, in terms of such mental functions, the known facts of
correlation.   The facts may be summarized briefly as follows:

1. There is a general tendency for practically all abilities to be
   positively correlated.
2. Abilities may be thrown into groups on the basis of a high
   correlation found between members of each group.
3. Most, if not all abilities, show a positive relationship with
   general intelligence, though of varying degree.

The Mental Powers Theory.   In the earlier days of psychology, particularly during the last century, it was rather widely
held that the mind was constituted of a number of innate "faculties" or "powers."   These mental powers were identified by
such names as discrimination, concentration, judgment, and
memory.   They were assumed to be fundamental units playing
a part in many mental activities.   It was also assumed that they
could be trained or strengthened through appropriate practice.
The memory power, for example, could seemingly be strengthened by memorizing.   If there were such powers, then all activities manifesting the same power should be uniform and highly
correlated.   Tests of memory should be highly intercorrelated,
if the theory holds, and so should tests of discrimination.   But
we should expect zero or negative correlations between memory
and discrimination.

When put to the test of scientific measurement, this theory
of innate mental powers was not confirmed.   The principal experimental findings in opposition to the theory, which led to its
being discarded, were as follows:

1. High correlations were not found uniformly to exist between performances of the same "facultative" kind.

2. High correlations were found to exist between performances of supposedly different facultative kinds, higher in fact than between performances that were supposedly manifestations of the same mental power.

Neither did this theory explain very satisfactorily the correlation of most abilities with intelligence. The "mental powers" can scarcely then be considered as discrete, innate, fundamental abilities. The use of the word "faculty" may be defended as a qualitative term, that is, when referring to a particular *kind* of mental process or activity, such as imagining and remembering, but it apparently has no direct claim to quantitative implication (1).

The Community of Content, or Multifactor Theory. The scientific view which took form in the early twentieth century as a substitute for the mental powers theory is usually associated with the name of Thorndike, who was its most prominent and forceful exponent. Its origins were in experimental psychology, and thus it was based on a "mental reaction" hypothesis. There are, according to this theory, not mental powers, but only mental reactions or responses to stimuli, and there might be as many of these as there were psychologically distinguishable stimuli. An ability was to be regarded then as no more than a convenient—convenient for both logic and measurement —bundle of these independent reactions.

What is "community of content?" According to the theory, the same reactions might enter into the constitution of many differently named abilities at one and the same time. Thus ability A might be constituted of reactions "a, b, c, d, e," and ability B of "a, b, f, g, h." Because of this partial *identity of content* ("a" and "b" being components of both), we should expect the two abilities A and B to show a certain amount of relationship. The reason for the experimental finding of positive coefficients of correlation between different abilities was then assumed to be that the same elements, the reactions, could be found in the make-up of these various abilities. The degree of relationship, moreover, would be in proportion to the number of elements or reactions which the two abilities had in common. Thus a higher correlation might be expected between Latin and French than between Latin and German because in the former case there would be a greater number of words and word-roots in common, and the mental reactions to these would accordingly be the same. Low correlations would be found when, as in the case of spelling and arithmetic, there would be relatively few reactions or elements in common.

The "community of content" theory regards the growth of ability as principally a matter of acquiring the appropriate individual mental reactions, or "connections." In the words of Thorndike, "The gist of our doctrine is that, by original nature, the intellect capable of the highest reasoning and adaptability differs from the intellect of the imbecile only in the capacity for having more connections of the sort described" (10). The mere summation of these reactions would be ability. There might be constitutional reasons why these necessary reactions would be acquired more readily by one individual than by another, but these reasons would most likely be based on the number and kind of nervous connections existing in the brain. The theory seems loath to attribute any psychological unity to ability, this being in all cases reducible to a summation or average of a number of independent mental or physiological reactions.

Thorndike's multifactor theory made at least two important contributions to the study of ability. (1) It brought into clear relief the popular fallacy of assuming a natural kinship of mental performances called by the same name (e.g., that all "memory" performances should be highly related because we have a common name for them). (2) The theory also stressed the influence of environment and training in producing a relatedness of abilities quite apart from some underlying, common mental power. If differential abilities develop as a result of mental reactions to stimuli, as Thorndike maintained, the same individual reactions may be developed from different performances. Thus ability in history and ability in literature may show a general tendency to run parallel because of environmental or accidental relationships. Again, an assumed special "athletic ability" may show only the influence of social pressure in inducing a child to spread his activity and practice over a large group of culturally related games. The innate constitution of the human mind is not the only thing that can account for the relatedness of mental activities. Our cultural and social attitudes, including our educational biases and practices, may also produce high coefficients of correlation.

The multifactor theory of ability, however, has a number of features which make it unacceptable to many psychologists. (1) It seems to overemphasize the environmental aspect of the growth of ability by giving the dominant place to stimuli, specific reactions, and "identical elements" in subject matter. Constitutional factors underlying differences in ability seem to play a negligible role in the theory. (2) The factor of maturation seems to be slighted and is in fact, according to such a theory, difficult to understand as a practical concept. (3) The explanation of a general mental ability, for which there is strong evidence, appears unsatisfactory. The theory actually seems to deny the possibility of a general or common psychological factor when it describes such an ability as an average or combination of many independent or particular reactions. It seems to hold that no abilities are really fundamental.

The Two-Factor Theory. The two-factor theory of mental ability was proposed by Spearman (8), who attempted a definitive answer to the question: How many fundamental abilities are there and what is their nature? Unlike Thorndike's approach, which was primarily bent on attacking and destroying the then prevalent notion of "mental powers," Spearman's theory was based on a scientific groundwork of factor analysis.

A person's ability, as measured by any mental or educational test, is accounted for by a general factor (g) and a specific factor (or factors). The test result is determined partly by the g factor, which is common to all his mental performances of whatever sort, and partly by the s factor, or factors which are *peculiar* or specific to the performance measured by the test. The first factor is called g simply because it is "general," in the sense that all abilities depend at least partly upon its influence. The second factor (or factors) is called s because it is "specific" to abilities of a certain kind.

While g influences all abilities, it does not do so in the same degree. A person's success in some mental tasks may depend to a very great extent upon g and very little upon s, while in other performances the reverse may be true; g is often loosely interpreted as being synonymous with "general intelligence," since it influences all abilities. Strictly speaking, it is rather a postulated factor to account for correlations among tests, not a mental operation.

Although Spearman's two-factor theory may be reminiscent of the power doctrine of mind, there are a number of differences to be found between them. The Spearman factors are approached originally in an empirical manner, leaving the task of their identification and description until each has first been experimentally isolated. They are not, moreover, to be necessarily identified with mental powers or processes, a difficulty encountered in the older view.

The Multiple-Factor Theory, or the "primary abilities" theory proposed by Thurstone, like Spearman's, is based on factor analysis. Unlike the two-factor theory, it does not rely on a general factor to explain the correlations among tests, but on multiple or group factors. The group factor is conceived to be the basis of a kind of family of closely related abilities. What we know as general intelligence, according to this view, is really a composite of several group factors, each group factor known as a "primary" mental ability when separately measured. The multiple-factor theory does not necessarily deny the existence of general intelligence. The theory merely holds that since there are techniques for separating "general intelligence" into a number of components, the plausible and efficient thing to do is construct tests for measuring the different components as separate abilities. When this is done, it may be discovered that two persons with the same "general intelligence" score actually differ greatly in the various "primary" abilities that make up the score.

The chief differences between the two-factor and multiple-factor theories of ability are these: (1) the theories are based on different techniques of factor analysis, and therefore describe the factors underlying a set of correlations in different ways; (2) they account for the intercorrelations among tests differently, one in terms of *g* and the other in terms of group factors; (3) they differ in their practical approach to mental measurement, the two-factor theory insisting on the scientific usefulness of measuring general intelligence as a basic ability, and the multiple-factor approach emphasizing the measurement of its components.

It is safe to say that the original question proposed by Spearman (the nature and number of the fundamental abilities) has not been finally settled by factor analysis. Instead, factor analysis has revealed how enormously complex the question really is. Cronbach's simile is an apt one: "The factor analyst may be compared with the photographer trying to picture a building as revealingly as possible. Wherever he sets his camera, he will lose some information, but by a skillful choice he will be able to show a large number of important features of the building (2, p. 208).

The Effect of Learning on Ability. The specialized abilities which show up as "primary" are probably developed differentially through the learning process. Thurstone's definition of primary mental abilities as "different media for the expression of intellect" (12) is certainly not incompatible with this viewpoint. Superiority, mediocrity, and inferiority in the various primary abilities are no doubt influenced in large measure by differences in training, cultural background, and interests. The various learning "capacities" have not yet been adequately defined, even with the help of factor analysis. If we raise the question: "To what extent can the ceiling of ability be raised by specialized training?" the answer must certainly be "to an unknown extent." There is not at present any adequate quantitative definition of the ceiling of ability, nor is there likely to be in the near future.

REFERENCES

1. COMMINS, W. D. What is faculty psychology? *Thought,* 1933, **6,** 48-57.
2. CRONBACH, L. J. *Essentials of psychological testing.* New York: Harper, 1949.

3. CRONBACH, L. J. Further evidence on response sets and test design. *Educ. psychol. Measur.,* 1950, **10,** 3-31. See also Response sets and test validity, *Educ. psychol. Measur.,* 1946, **6,** 475-494.

4. GUILFORD, J. P. (Ed.) AAF *Aviation psychology report No. 5.* Washington, D.C.: Government Printing Office, 1947.

5. JUDD, C. L. *et al. Education as cultivation of the higher mental processes.* New York: Macmillan, 1936.

6. KELLEY, T. L. *Interpretation of educational measurements.* Yonkers: World, 1927.

7. KELLEY, T. L. Mental factors of no importance. *J. educ. Psychol.,* 1939, **30,** 139-142.

8. SPEARMAN, C. *The abilities of man.* New York: Macmillan, 1927.

9. SUPER, D. E. *Appraising vocational fitness by means of psychological tests.* New York: Harper, 1949.

10. THORNDIKE, E. L. *et al. The measurement of intelligence.* New York: Teach. Coll. Bur. Publ., Columbia Univ., 1927.

11. THURSTONE, L. L., & THURSTONE, T. G. *Factorial studies of intelligence.* Chicago: Univ. of Chicago Press, 1941.

12. THURSTONE, L. L. *Primary mental abilities.* Chicago: Univ. of Chicago Press, 1938.

13. WARREN, H. C. *Dictionary of psychology.* Boston: Houghton Mifflin, 1934.

SELECTED READINGS

CRONBACH, L. J. *Essentials of psychological testing.* New York: Harper, 1949. Excellent general reference. Ch. 1-5 for basic concepts. Ch. 9 describes the function of factor analysis in measurement.

FREEMAN, F. N. *Theory and practice of psychological testing.* New York: Holt, 1950.

GOODENOUGH, F. L. *Mental testing.* New York: Rinehart, 1949.

LINDQUIST, E. F. (Ed.). *Educational measurement.* Washington, D.C.: American Council on Education, 1951. Shows how individual measurement can improve educational processes (Pt. I). Pt. II is concerned with construction of achievement tests; Pt. III with measurement theory. Articles by leaders in field.

NATIONAL SOCIETY FOR STUDY OF EDUCATION. *45th Yearbook,* 1946. Pt. I, The measurement of understanding. Articles on achievement testing.

SUPER, D. E. *Appraising vocational fitness by means of psychological tests.* New York: Harper, 1949. General reference on aptitude testing, with excellent summaries of research on validity of tests.

TRAVERS, R. M. W. *How to make achievement tests.* New York: Odyssey Press, 1950. A practical book for the teacher.

9

THE PRACTICAL ROLE OF INTELLIGENCE

The aim of intelligence testing is a practical one. The first successful attempt to measure intelligence grew out of a practical school problem, and the tests have at all times been referred back to the school situation for their ultimate value and meaning. Apart from their worth as instruments of research in studying the theoretical problems of mental development, the educator is concerned with their importance in the ordinary activities of life. When the educator speaks of mental development he usually has in mind the "ability to learn." While this is only one aspect of the whole growth process, it is a very important one. Although educational objectives have been broadened to include many features of the child's mental life, the central core of mental development still seems to be, in line with the scholastic traditions of the past, the intellectual growth and development of the child. It may be nice to know the child's IQ, but why? What practical difference does it make in what the child can learn, the rate at which he can learn it, what he is taught, and the way the teaching is done? What problems in school practice arise from individual differences in intelligence? Since the teacher is also concerned with the vocational and social adjustment of students, what is the role of intelligence on the job and in society?

This chapter is therefore chiefly concerned with the external validity of intelligence tests—the kinds of behavior, adjustment, or development that may be predicted from their results. The real nature and promise of the tests is best revealed in the facts uncovered through their use and through years of research.

We shall begin by asking what kind of behavior they are expected to predict, and examine some of the asumptions underlying the concept of the IQ and practical "working definitions" of intelligence.

Some Practical Definitions of Intelligence. Practical definitions of intelligence are for the most part vague. The vaguest of all was that given by one eminent psychologist who, when pressed for a definition, said: "Intelligence? Why, that is what the intelligence tests measure." Although seemingly facetious and useless, this statement calls attention to the fact that it doesn't really matter what they measure if they are useful for predicting behavior. The intent of the definition is to emphasize external validity.

Intelligence has sometimes been defined as the "ability to learn" or to profit from experience. While this is also vague, it seems to correspond to a mental quality which we often refer to in characterizing the behavior of others, particularly children. Intelligence as "learning ability" is likely to be misleading, however, if we accept the amount of learning achieved as direct evidence of the degree of ability. In ordinary life, factors of interest and motivation form such an integral part of the background of learning that it is difficult to keep the motivational factors distinct from the factor of aptitude.

Another type of definition emphasizes adjustment, or the adaptation of the individual to his environment. It stresses the individual's ability to vary his behavior to meet new conditions and new problems, or to reorganize his behavior to cope effectively with the changing conditions of life. The more intelligent individual, from this point of view, is not just one who is more educable in the formal sense, but one who has a greater variety of responses, who can deal more effectively with a greater variety of situations, who is more "creative." According to this definition, we might expect the more intelligent persons (as ascertained from our tests) to do better work in school and to stay in school longer, to achieve greater vocational success or eminence, to get along better with people in society. Is there any evidence for these beliefs?

Intelligence and Learning Ability. Intelligence test scores are not to be taken as independent of past learning, since the assumption underlying the test is "equal opportunity to learn" or comparability of background. To what extent do intelligence tests predict future learning, independently of motivation? This question must be largely answered by the results of laboratory studies of learning, since in "real life" situations motivation cannot be held constant or ruled out as an influence. Experimental studies, in which motivation was controlled, show in general that intelligence represents a common factor in most if not all forms of learning. The effect of intelligence on ability to learn, however, varies with the nature of the learning tasks. The range of experimental evidence attesting this is fairly broad, with general conclusions as follows:

1. *Verbal learning.* The correlations between intelligence and memory for verbal materials are generally positive, from close to zero to as high as .60 to .70. The correlations are generally lower with rote memory tasks, such as nonsense syllables and memory span for digits, and higher when meaningful material is employed. Correlations between mental age and learning have been practically always higher than between chronological age and learning (16).

The question of whether intelligence tests measure ability to learn verbal materials in school has been a controversial one, with many studies of this type showing little relationship. Definite conclusions have been difficult to draw, however, for two reasons. For one thing, differences in motivation of students were often not effectively controlled. Another is the ambiguity of the concept "ability to learn," which may refer either to the amount of material learned or to the difficulty of the material learned. From the nature of tested intelligence, we should expect it to be related to the level of difficulty of the learned material; that is, students of lower intelligence should be limited in their ability to grasp difficult concepts. On the other hand, the ability to learn and remember a certain amount of fairly easy material would seem to be largely a matter of motivation rather than intelligence. A recent study by Tilton (28), for example, showed substantial correlations between IQ and an achievement test in history which was limited to the more difficult items.

2. *Perceptual-motor learning.* Laboratory studies of the learning of finger-mazes, mirror drawing, substituting digits for designs, and other similar skill performances show positive, but usually low, correlations between intelligence and facility to learn. More correlations have been found below .50 than above. When tasks are complex or more difficult, correlations are larger; smaller correlations are found with simpler tasks. Comparisons of groups differing in MA and IQ show that the more intelligence learn tasks requiring skill more readily. Single learning tasks may separately show low correlations with intelligence, but when several learning tasks are combined to produce a single score, a higher correlation between intelligence and learning is found. Thus Garrett, in a multiple correlation study, obtained a multiple R of .53 between scores on the Thorndike Intelligence Examination and eight measures of learning, although each of the learning tasks separately had little in common with intelligence (10). Since intelligence correlates very low with mere speed of response, the higher correlations between intelligence and perceptual-motor skill tasks would seem to be due to abilities of mental organization which are reflected in intelligence scores.

3. *Reasoning or problem solving.* Intelligence tests are usually successful in selecting those of superior ability in solving laboratory "thought" or puzzle problems involving reasoning, inference, or abstract relations. Correlations are practically always positive, ranging from very low to as high as .70 or .80 (16).

McGeogh (16) lists five principles which apparently govern the relationships found between intelligence and facility of learning. All of these are concerned with the kind of learning or the kind of material involved in the learning tasks. In general, we may summarize experimental results as follows: intelligence is more related to, and presumably required in a higher degree, in tasks which are (1) more meaningful and (2) which require manipulation of symbols, which (3) are more difficult and complex; (4) which require a greater amount of discovery, or insight into new relationships; and (5) in tasks which require the least amount of gross movement or muscular responses.

TABLE 11

The Relation of IQ to Ability to Perform Simple Tasks *

Approximate Minimum IQ Required	Time or No. Trials to Learn	Task or Occupation
10–20..........	15 trials	Fetch and carry a single object, e.g., chair
	1 day	Pick up stones, trash, etc., from lawn or walk
	3 days	Pull up *one kind* of weed from garden
21–25..........	6–8 days	Scrub floors or dust
	16 trials	Carry out standardized simple errand
	3 days	Pick *one kind* of fruit or vegetable
	5 days	Pick *two kinds* of fruit or vegetable
	8 days	Saw wood
	5 days	Plant *one kind* of vegetable
	5 days	Sort and hang up clothes
26–30..........	7 days	Do simple hand washing
	11 days	Do general cleaning
	18 trials	Do dishwashing
	18 trials	Tend chickens
31–37..........	8 days	Wash clothes by hand
	6 days	Pare and wash potatoes
	19 trials	Darn stockings, do simple crocheting
	18 days	Milk cow
	17 days	Do hand ironing
	52 trials	Make beds
38–44..........	14 days	Do sheep herding
	34 days	Do simple cooking
	29 trials	Do simple hand sewing and mending
	25 trials	Wait on table
45–55..........	19 days	Help around farm
	29 trials	Do shampooing
	113 days	Do simple dressmaking
	9 days	Embroider
	65 days	Paint barns, etc.
	89 days	Do simple carpentry
60–70..........	19 days	Plow
	25 days	Do general farmwork
77.............	11 days	Do general housework

* Data from M. Vanuxem, "Education of Feeble-Minded Women," *Teach. Coll. Contr. Educ.,* 1925.

An interesting example of how these principles apply to the learning of simple everyday tasks in estimating the levels of intelligence required is seen in Table 11. The data are taken from a study of the mental maturity required to learn simple tasks performed by inmates of an institution for feeble-minded women. A glance down the list reveals that the tasks vary in complexity, difficulty, and meaningfulness in relationship to the level of IQ required. One possible exception is the item "Plow," unless the management of horses and harness is subsumed under this task.

INTELLIGENCE IN SCHOOL ADJUSTMENT

Binet's intent in constructing the original intelligence scale was to measure abilities of practical educational importance— to sort out efficiently the quick and the slow learners. Success in school came to be the criterion of validity for intelligence tests, and this aspect of intelligence testing has been so widely studied that the term intelligence is practically synonymous with "scholastic aptitude." The role of intelligence in the school has several aspects: (1) It plays a part in determining the child's rate of progress in school, and what grade level is attained; (2) intelligence is related to scholastic achievement in elementary school, high school, and college; (3) differences in intelligence have implications for methods of teaching in the classroom.

The Rate of School Progress. The question "What grade level is most appropriate for a child of a given degree of intelligence?" is an ancient and difficult one for educators. Since children of the same chronological age may differ widely in mental age and ability to learn, we are concerned with the problem of *grade placement*—placing the child in a learning situation appropriate to his ability, educational readiness, and motivation. Intelligence is not the only factor in determining this, but it is clearly an important one.

A related question is "What is the minimum level of intelligence required for successful school work in the various grades? This is not an easy question to answer, but it is a practical one.

It would be of great practical value if it could be shown that a child whose test rating was below a certain critical score would be unable to succeed, say, in the work of the first grade, in academic high school work, or in some specific subject such as elementary algebra. Ever since the development of the original Binet scale, it has seemed reasonable to educators, as it did to Binet, that pupils can and should be classified somehow on the basis of mental age.

Table 12 shows the relation of mental age to grade place-

TABLE 12

MENTAL AGE NORMS FOR GRADES ONE TO NINE *

| | Mental Age Norms (Average MA) | | |
Grade	Beginning	Mid-Grade	End
1	6–6	7	7–5
2	7–6	8	8–5
3	8–6	9	9–5
4	9–6	10	10–5
5	10–6	11	11–5
6	11–6	12	12–5
7	12–6	13	13–5
8	13–6	14	14–5
9	14–6	15	15–5

* After C. M. Louttit, *Clinical psychology*, Harper, 1947.

ment for schools having six years as the entering age. The table assumes that the average adult MA, or the "final mental age of the average adult," is 14, which is approximately correct. In terms of IQ, an MA of 14 is equivalent to 100 IQ, or $100 \times 14/14$. The data in the table indicate, in a general way, what the appropriate grade placement is (on the basis of mental age only) for pupils of different intelligence.

The work of each grade is, as we know, adapted to the ability of the average child of a certain age, or in other words to that mental age. If a child is retarded in his mental development, as indicated by his IQ, he will reach the required mental age only after a relatively long period of time, and if he is accelerated mentally he will attain that level comparatively quickly. We may expect him, when he reaches the grade in question, to be over-age or under-age accordingly. Thus, if sixth-grade work is adapted to an MA of twelve, the average child (IQ 100) will be ready for this when he is twelve years old, and so will tend to spend only one year in each of the first five grades. The dull child of IQ 75, on the other hand, will not attain MA 12 until he is about sixteen years old, and so he will tend to be held back in school until his mental maturity more nearly approaches the level required for the sixth grade. Again, the bright child of IQ 125 will tend to be carried forward through the early grades at an advanced rate because he will have the mental maturity suited to sixth-grade work when he is about nine years old.

What is to be expected of a child whose IQ is 50? Assuming for the moment that the IQ is constant, this child will have an ultimate adult IQ of 50 also, or in other terms an adult mental age of 7. But MA 7, in terms of grade level, is adequate for first grade work and no higher. The child with 50 IQ will therefore probably never succeed in the first grade, is not educable through the ordinary school procedures, and ordinarily should not be started in school. Special education by specially trained teachers is indicated, if any at all.

Let us apply the same reasoning process to the case of the six-year-old child whose IQ is 60. His mental age is a little over four. He may "get by" in the first grade, but will be a "slow learner." When he reaches chronological age 14 (again assuming the IQ to be constant) his mental age will be 8, which according to the table is appropriate to the difficulty of the third grade, and certainly no higher. This child may "hang on" until the fourth or fifth grade as a slow learner, but he will never make the grade scholastically, even if kept in the fifth grade until he is fourteen, or for that matter until he is twenty.

A child of IQ someplace in the 80's may reach the seventh or eighth grade as a slow learner with special help; but again assuming the IQ to be constant, his ultimate MA will be in the neighborhood of 12 and he will never be able to do academic high school work. The middle range of IQ's, often described as the "normal" or "average" range of 90 to 110, includes the greater percentage of the school population. The lower level,

representing an ultimate mental age of 12 or so, will have difficulty in high school work, while the upper level will represent
the successful high school graduates.

The foregoing statements about intelligence in relation to
grade placement and school progress are not, however, cate-
gorical. They involve the assumptions that the IQ is reasonably accurate, that his IQ is not going to change, that the school
curriculum at various times and places is constant, and that
special training or special environmental factors will not affect
his rate of development. These assumptions can *not* be made
in every individual case. On the whole, however, the data in
Table 12 do show the general relationship between intelligence
and school progress, and most of the results of educational research bear them out. Most studies of the minimum levels
of intelligence required for satisfactory school work have been
able to settle upon a practical lower limit of probable success,
although not one that would suffer no exceptions. Thus, as a
conservative estimate, an IQ of 90 is ordinarily regarded as the
minimum required for the academic course in high school,
while an IQ of 100 represents a similar requirement for college
work.

The attempt on the part of the school to adjust courses and
methods of instruction to the ability of the pupils, and the fact
that low ability may be compensated for, to a certain extent,
by desirable motivational traits, means that the question of
minimal intellectual requirements is essentially one of statistical probability. Where the nature of the school course demands its own particular insights and quality of response, this
probability may approach close to certainty. Thus one study
found that algebra, with its characteristic symbolism and generalizations, makes much more definite demands on intelligence
than does high school English. Learning to read seems also to
represent the taking of a critical step in mental development.
First-grade children with a mental age below six and a half are
apparently very seriously handicapped in beginning reading.

Terman's early study of the distribution of IQ's throughout
the various elementary grades (25) led him to draw some interesting conclusions concerning the child's rate of maturing in-

tellectually and his rate of progress through school. He found that children of low IQ were usually found in a grade below that appropriate to their actual age and that the lower the IQ, the greater the degree of retardation. Children of high IQ on the other hand were not infrequently found to be accelerated in age-grade status, the amount of acceleration reflecting, to a certain extent, the child's relative brightness. He noted also that, if MA were taken as the index of ability to do the work of a particular grade, the dull child was found to be less retarded than he should have been, and that the bright child should have been accelerated even more than he actually was.

The Problem of Grade Placement. Even though we might expect mental age to be closely predictive of the ability to do the work of a particular grade, there are reasons why we should not expect to find exact correspondence between mental age and grade placement. Lack of the required intelligence is an important cause of school retardation (over age in grade); but it is not the only cause, nor is it to be considered (except in clear cases of mental deficiency) as a self-sufficient cause. Physical disabilities such as neurological disorders, poor vision and hearing, and personality disturbances have been found to account for retardation. Sickness, absence, changing schools, poor home background, and attitudes of parents are often important contributing factors. Specific subject disabilities (especially reading) often cause retardation in general scholastic achievement.

Again, school promotion policies affect grade placement. The wide practice of "social promotion"—the tendency to promote on the basis of chronological age so that the child will remain in the company of his age group—facilitates social and emotional development of the child and is usually justified on that basis. There is some evidence (not conclusive) that it facilitates intellectual development as well—or in any case does not deter it. Because of this trend toward "social promotion" in the schools, the problem of grade placement has received less attention than it did formerly. As a consequence, most of the studies showing the relationship between intelligence and retardation date back twenty or thirty years. For better or for worse, grade placement is receiving less and less attention from educators.

Follow-Up of Gifted Children. Another indication of the prognostic significance of intelligence is to be found in the Stanford study of gifted children. A large group of children all of IQ 140 and above (mean IQ 150) were located by a systematic search in larger California cities and tested in 1922. They were subsequently followed up in 1928 (5), 1936–38 (26), and twice during the 1940's (27). These students were in the top one per cent of general intelligence in the school population. About 80 per cent of the group were found to be accelerated in the elementary grades and to have graduated from high school about a year in advance of the normal age. In school progress the typical gifted child was accelerated by 14 per cent of his age, but in actual mastery of the school subjects (as shown by achievement tests) he was accelerated by more than 40 per cent of his age.

School achievement continued high through high school and college, and was generally consistent with the IQ's obtained in 1922. Subject failures in high school were extremely rare; during high school the group as a whole earned from four to eight times as many A's as the average student, nearly 75 per cent of all grades earned by gifted girls being A's, while half of the boys' grades were A. In the senior year of high school, the average score of the gifted group was at the 90th percentile of 12th grade students on the Iowa High-School Content Examination. Most of them went to college. Over 69 per cent of the men and 66 per cent of the women graduated from college. They received higher grades, more academic honors, and more graduate degrees than any other group used for comparison. The number receiving Ph.D. degrees was several times larger than would be expected from a representative sample of college graduates. Those of IQ 170 and above were superior in educational achievement to the group as a whole.

Acceleration in grade placement (below normal age in grade) is often assumed to be detrimental to the child's future mental development. "Pushing" a precocious child is said to be a kind of "hot-house" treatment, the assumption being that the child will later not be able to stand the rigors of a normal climate. There is also a widespread opinion, frequently encountered among professional educators, that the accelerated child will be socially retarded because of his reaction to the age difference between himself and his peers. The Stanford study, however, indicates that whatever bad effect on social development may result from acceleration in adolescence is temporary, since in adulthood the gifted group was found to be as well or better adjusted than a group of "normals" (27). The acceleration of gifted children can actually result in an extraordinary economy of time in attaining a given level of achievement. An interesting study by Hollingsworth and Cobb (14) reports a comparison of the achievement of two groups of superior children. One group had a mean IQ of 165, while the mean IQ of the other was 146. Table 13 expresses the results in terms

TABLE 13

TIME SAVED BY THE HIGHER IQ GROUP IN ATTAINING VARIOUS LEVELS OF ACHIEVEMENT *

Test of Achievement	Months Saved by Higher Group (IQ 165)
Word meaning, Stanford achievement test	16
Paragraph meaning, Stanford achievement test	15
Sentence meaning, Stanford achievement test	14.5
Nature study and science, Stanford achievement test	14.5
Addition of fractions, Monroe diagnostic test	13.5
Long division, Monroe diagnostic test	13
Multiplication of whole numbers, Monroe diagnostic test	13
Spelling from dictation, Stanford achievement test	12.5
Language usage, Stanford achievement test	11
History and literature, Stanford achievement test	9
Arithmetic computation, Stanford achievement test	7.5
Arithmetic reasoning, Stanford achievement test	7
Subtraction of whole numbers, Monroe	6.5
Short division, Monroe	6
Multiplication of fractions, Monroe	5
Multiplication of decimals, Monroe	3.5
Addition of whole numbers, Monroe	0.0

* After Hollingsworth and Cobb.

of "months saved" by the brighter children in reaching a certain level of scholastic attainment. Reading shows the greatest difference in learning time saved, and some of the arithmetic skills the least.

Studies of School "Dropouts." Pupils with lower intelligence scores tend to leave school earlier. This fact can be conclusively established only when all students are tested at the time of entrance, since comparisons of school "dropouts" and graduates based on later tests may simply reveal the differential effects of schooling on the intelligence test scores. Follow-up studies of beginning pupils are not subject to this possible limitation, for intelligence is measured before the period of training starts. An example of the latter is a study by Mitchell (17), which gives a summary report on over a thousand high school students covering a period of ten years. At the time of admission to school the pupils were given a group intelligence test, and the IQ scores were later checked against the academic records. Table 14 shows the number and percentage of dropouts

TABLE 14

NUMBER AND PERCENTAGE OF PUPILS DROPPING OUT OF HIGH SCHOOL AT VARIOUS IQ LEVELS *

IQ	Number Admitted	Number Dropping Out	Percent Dropping Out
128–	7	0	0
116–127	112	4	3
104–115	284	23	8
92–103	435	131	30
80–91	267	168	63
68–80	41	27	66

* After Mitchell.

classified according to IQ. Those with lower scores tend to drop out in much larger numbers. Figure 41 compares the distribution of IQ's of the dropouts with the distribution of IQ's of all students. The median IQ of the dropouts is about eight points lower, and it is evident that they represent a substantial "mound" at the lower end of the distribution. Another follow-up study (21), made in 1930 on individuals who had been

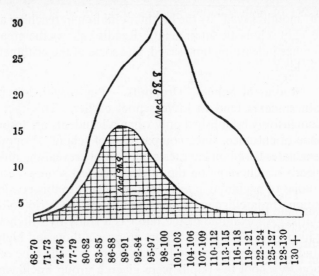

FIGURE 41. Distribution of IQ's of High School Pupils Leaving School Before Graduation. The large graph represents the total number of pupils admitted to high school over a ten-year period. The shaded graph represents the IQ's of those who dropped out of school before completing the course. (From C. Mitchell, "Prognostic Value of Intelligence Tests," *J. educ. Research*, 1935, **28**, 577-581.)

tested in school in 1917, found an early IQ average of 105 for those whose schooling had not gone beyond the ninth grade, an average of 111 for high school graduates, and an average of 116 for those who went to college.

A number of studies of college students have also indicated that intelligence is a selective factor discriminating between graduates and dropouts. The relation between intelligence and withdrawal is perhaps not so marked in college as in high school, because the economic factor is more important and because differences among institutions is also a significant factor. The mean ACE Psychological Examination scores of entering freshmen in over 300 colleges as reported in published annual norms, for example, reveal notable differences in the average intelligence of different student bodies.

Again, both high school and college curricula differ with respect to the level of ability required. In one national study

(29) of high school curricular differences in intelligence test scores, the median IQ for boys enrolled in technical schools (college preparatory) was 114, while the medians for those enrolled in general high schools were 106 (academic), 104 (commercial) and 92 (trade courses). Norms for the Graduate Record Examination, a test used for the selection of graduate students, indicate differences in mean "Verbal Ability" scores for college graduates with different college majors. This does not necessarily mean that different curricula *require* different degrees of ability, but it does seem to indicate that intelligence is a factor in the selection of the college major field.

The Selective Factor in Education. In summary, the facts indicate that the school system is in general selective with respect to intelligence. As we go from the elementary school through high school to college, we find a progressive increase in the average IQ. There can hardly be much doubt that the selective elimination of the duller students has a great deal to do with this. We cannot assume, however, that the educational advantages of remaining in school are not in any way reflected in the differences in intelligence of children in and out of school, or at various educational levels. Schooling does make a difference in test scores. However, it is safe to say that the effects of schooling account for only a small fraction of the differences we have discussed here. The character of school work, as it becomes progressively more abstract with each step up the educational ladder, would seem to place a greater premium on the possession of superior intelligence in high school and college.

Correlation Between Intelligence and School Achievement. The most commonly used criteria of school achievement are scores on standardized achievements tests and school grades. Correlations between intelligence and standardized achievement tests usually vary with the subject matter content of the tests; the scores on an entire battery of achievement tests, however, will often correlate as high with intelligence as one intelligence test will correlate with another. Despite the relationship between intelligence and school progress discussed previously, correlations between intelligence and school grades have not been particularly high. In general, they are higher in elementary school than in high school, and higher in high school than in college.

A sample list of correlations between Binet IQ and elementary school grades taken from a study by Burt (6) is given in Table 15. These are in fairly good agreement with more re-

TABLE 15

CORRELATION OF INTELLIGENCE AND ELEMENTARY SCHOOL SUBJECTS *

Subject	r	Subject	r
Composition	0.63	Arithmetic (computation) ..	0.41
Reading	.54	Writing	.21
Dictation	.52	Drawing	.15
Arithmetic (problems)	.55	Handwork	.18

* After Burt.

cent studies, particularly as to the ranking given the different subjects according to the amount of relationship shown. Dictation or spelling shows a wide range of correlations with intelligence, the median being about .50. All correlations are likely to vary from study to study for a number of reasons. The age range of the children studied and the reliability of the school grades account for some of the variation, while differences in content and in method of teaching the subject are also a factor.

It would seem, however, that certain kinds of school learning are by their very nature more closely related to intelligence than are others. Whenever a particular subject is one that requires understanding rather than memorizing, or is of a more abstract nature, intelligence test scores will usually reflect the pupil's relative proficiency. This same principle holds for both the high school and college level, but it is very difficult to generalize concerning actual courses. These may differ widely in nature, although retaining the same name, as we go from one institution to another.

Various summaries of correlations found between intelligence and high school grades have indicated a range of r's from about .30 to .80, with most of them tending to center around .50 (24). Similarly, the range of correlations obtained in college is about .20 to .70, with the modal *r* about .40. It would seem that the higher we go on the educational ladder, the smaller the correlation between intelligence and grades received. This does not mean that intelligence is a less significant factor at the higher educational levels. If we recall that a restricted range of test scores will have a diminishing effect on the correlation obtained, we may conclude that the progressive shrinking of correlations is due to the selective elimination of the less able students. This results in a decreasing range of ability at higher levels, with a corresponding effect on the correlations. Also, as the range of ability decreases through high school and college, factors other than general intelligence play an increasingly large role in determining achievement. Special aptitudes, motivation, interests, and other personality traits are perhaps likely to gain in relative importance as the student approaches his college years.

The Role of Intelligence in the Classroom. Individual differences in intelligence have implications for the kind of learning situations provided by the school, the kind of treatment given by teachers to different students, and the standards used in judging the efforts of students. Knowledge of the conditions of learning makes it clear that the teacher cannot treat all students alike. Some consideration of the characteristic differences of bright and dull children may help to emphasize the necessity of differential treatment.

The Slow Learner. In terms of IQ, the slow learner may be roughly characterized by a range of IQ from 75 to 90 (1). Composite descriptions of the "typical" dull child in this range give us in concrete form the main facts linking low intelligence with school adjustment. Some of these symptoms of subnormal intelligence show an indirect relationship and others are perhaps more or less accidental, but they are all fairly common in occurrence (2). The subnormal child usually comes to school from a home background below the average cultural level of the community. His previous record of development is likely to show that he was retarded in learning to walk and to talk, and at school age he may still give the appearance of being somewhat slow in speech and in childish skills. He has considerable difficulty with reading, his retardation in this subject remaining with him throughout his school career. Once the fundamental number concepts have been grasped, he may develop a fair amount of skill in adding, multiplying, and so on, but he is relatively poor in doing individual arithmetic problems. The dull child's vocabulary is usually limited and he has difficulty in expressing himself in written or oral composition, his sentence structure and thought content being particularly noticeable for their undeveloped character. He is unimaginative in the ordinary sense of the term, his interest being given very largely to concrete materials and objectives. He usually begins to show loss of interest in school work as the upper grades are reached and is less conscientious than the ordinary child in avoiding tardiness or absence from school. If he obtains work outside of school hours, this tends rather easily to encroach upon both the time and effort he should give to his studies.

The dull child is perhaps more likely than the average pupil to develop into a disciplinary problem for one reason or another. He commonly shows less foresight and seems to profit less from his mistakes. He finds it difficult to give prolonged attention to any abstract matter, and his goals of interest are too circumscribed to motivate him strongly over long periods of time. The subnormal child is likely to be rated below average in character and conduct by his teachers, particularly as he approaches the higher grades. His emotional life is often lacking in those sentiments to which the teacher may commonly appeal in motivating the more inspirational school work and appreciations.

The Mentally Gifted. Children of IQ 130 or above come from families which as a rule are of higher than average social status. They are usually accelerated in school progress and are not conspicuously one-sided in their development. They have the same kinds of interests as other children of corresponding mental age, although they are likely to spend less time in play than the average child. Gifted children commonly have a large number of hobbies, making more and larger collections, for example, particularly of an historical and scientific nature. They do well in reading in school and are inclined to read extensively outside school for their own enjoyment. Their reading tastes are broad and mature. They prefer the more abstract school subjects and develop refined literary and poetic appreciations. The bright child is commonly creative and imaginative as shown particularly in his composition work. Character rating scales rank him high as a rule in emotional stability, trustworthiness, leadership, and social adaptability.

Gifted children in high school are found to engage in extra-curricular activities extensively and are often selected by their classmates for positions of honor and responsibility. They have more lofty ambitions and rather definite plans about their future. It has been found that teachers are able to identify gifted children in only about 50 per cent of the cases, often mistaking the mental maturity of a child for brightness or perhaps basing a judgment on good behavior, or pleasing appearance. Contrary to popular opinion, the bright child is usually above the average of his age group in height and weight.

Implications for Methods of Teaching and Guidance. Much can be done to adapt both courses and methods of instruction to individual differences in ability. Enlightened educational guidance will therefore involve an understanding of the general nature of intelligence and the future educational promise of the child. When faced with the problem of deciding, here and now, which of two alternative methods is preferable for the bright or dull pupil, we need exact empirical information on how the bright and dull react to different kinds of classroom situations.

Two kinds of studies are valuable here. One type is concerned with the characteristic differences in errors made by bright and dull pupils. There is some evidence that the errors of brighter children are usually due to carelessness in details, while those of duller children are caused by inability to generalize. Another type of study is based on experience in teaching homogeneous groups (22). A summary of some important practical points on method based on experience in teaching the brighter (A's) and duller (C's) pupils of a junior high school grade is given in Table 16.

TABLE 16

A COMPARISON OF SCHOOL LEARNING ABILITIES IN PUPILS OF HIGHER AND LOWER IQ *

Higher IQ's	Lower IQ's
Gain through instruction of abstract nature.	Gain through concrete instruction.
Thrive on comprehensive, general questions.	Need definite and detailed questions.
Assignments take less of teacher's time.	Assignments must be detailed and definite.
Assisted by analyzing and outlining.	Such procedures more likely to confuse.
Take readily to reference material.	Not apt to use reference material.
Will profit from note-taking.	Notes of doubtful value. Need direction.
Work on own responsibility.	Need constant supervision and guidance.
Learn readily by generalization.	Depend more on rules, imitation, analogy.
Need few primary examples to generalize.	Need many examples, much explanation.
Apply generalizations readily.	Have difficulty in making applications.
Drill plays little part in learning.	Drill plays larger part.
Dislike drill and repetition.	Often persevere in drill work.
Better at planning than execution.	Better at executing than at planning.
Teacher should be "amiable but stubborn" critic.	Teacher should extend sympathetic encouragement.

* After Ryan and Crecelius (22).

The less intelligent are not just slower learners; they seem to be a different kind of learner. What seems to be reflected here is a basic difference in the ability to organize one's experience in comprehensive plans, a difference in quickness of insight, in the ease of thinking in abstract terms, and in the facility to make use of one's knowledge in a practical way. All these have, at one time or another, been pointed out as being essential features of intelligence.

INTELLIGENCE AND VOCATIONAL ADJUSTMENT

Of what use are intelligence test scores to the vocational guidance counselor? How is intelligence related to vocational success? Since intelligence is a selective factor in education, and school is the stepping stone to entrance into many occupations, the degree of intelligence is an important determinant of the level of occupation which a person may enter. In general, the higher level occupations (professional, subprofessional, managerial) require more schooling or more intelligence, and the lower levels (semiskilled, unskilled) require less. Such questions as "What is the minimum level of intelligence required for the various occupations?" and "What is the average intelligence of persons in various occupations?" are pertinent. Such information as we have, although incomplete, is of considerable value in understanding the practical role of intelligence, since occupational adjustment is an important phase of life adjustment.

There is evidence that intelligence is related to vocational choice. A number of studies have shown that the more intelligent students tend to choose occupational objectives more appropriate to their abilities (24). Also, there is a positive relationship between the level of vocational choice and intelligence; the more able intellectually tend to aim high and the less bright to aspire to a somewhat lower level. The findings with respect to vocational choice are not unexpected. The more intelligent might be expected to have better understanding of their abilities in relation to job requirements, hence make more suitable choices. The higher occupational status of the parents would probably also have an important influence here. Those with less intelligence do not aspire to high vocational levels as often as the more able, but since many social influences impel the individual to aim high, many do choose goals beyond their ability.

Some studies of employment during the depression of the 1930's revealed that while the more intelligent did not obtain jobs more easily, they did on the other hand tend to hold their jobs longer. In the occupations studied, the less able were generally laid off earlier in the depression, the more able at a later period (19).

Minimal Intelligence Requirements for Occupations. A number of studies (3, 30) have determined the mental age levels required for simpler jobs. The data shown in Table 11 are illustrative. For the most part, such information was obtained by persons supervising the training and job placement of feebleminded individuals of known mental age. The lists of jobs by mental age level therefore indicate what jobs have been held successfully. Thus handling garbage is appropriate for MA 5, while sewing machine operation requires MA 8, and sign painting requires MA 10. Since the determinations were not made by careful job analysis, they are not very reliable. In fact, different studies assign the same job titles to different mental ages. These data are of some value in guiding individuals of limited mentality, but of little other practical significance. Even less is known of the minimum intelligence requirements for higher-level occupations. Broad approximations can be made from various studies in the occupational validity of tests, but minimum levels cannot be stated exactly in terms of test scores.

Several classifications of occupations with respect to intelligence have been made through ratings by vocational experts. In these the consensus of a number of raters is used to estimate the average intellectual requirements of occupations. Typical of this approach are the *Minnesota Occupational Rating Scales* (20), which include ratings of about 400 occupations. The occupations selected were classified with respect to six degrees of "abstract intelligence," defined by the raters as the ability to understand and manage ideas and symbols. Table 17 compares the ratings of a few sample occupations on intelligence and also on mechanical, social, artistic, and musical abilities.

The Distribution of Intelligence Within Occupations. The Army Intelligence Test in World War I made possible a comparison of the intelligence level of men engaged in a wide variety of occupations throughout the country. This informa-

TABLE 17

LEVELS OF ABILITY REQUIRED FOR A FEW SAMPLE OCCUPATIONS *

Occupation	Aca-demic Ability	Mechan-ical Ability	Social Ability	Cler-ical Ability	Musi-cal Ability	Artis-tic Ability
Accountant, auditor ...	A **	D	D	A	D	D
Artist, advertising	B	D	C	D	D	B
Professional athlete	C	C	C	D	D	D
Carpenter	C	C	D	D	D	D
Mechanical Draftsman .	B	B	D	B	D	C
Journalist	A	D	B	B	D	D
Linotype Operator	C	B	D	B	D	D
Executive, Manufacturing	A	C	B	B	D	D
Church Organist	B	D	C	C	A	D
Poultry Farmer	D	D	D	C	D	D
Clergyman	A	D	A	C	C	D
Surgeon	A	A	B	C	D	D
Teacher, Primary	B	D	B	C	D	D

* Data from Minnesota Occupational Rating Scales (20).
** Level A, highest decile; B, 75–90 percentile; C, 25–75 percentile; D, bottom quartile.

tion was published in 1922 by Fryer (9), who arranged the occupations into a hierarchy of job titles on the basis of the mean scores obtained. Similar studies were made with scores on the Army General Classification Test in World War II (23). Figure 42 shows the distribution of test scores within a number of occupations. The occupations are ranked according to mean ability. Some important characteristics of these distributions should not escape our notice:

1. There is notable *overlapping* of ability from occupation to occupation. There is some overlapping of the highest ranking and the lowest ranking occupations; for example, some cooks made higher scores than some accountants. This is not surprising, for there are various levels of required ability in each occupation. It requires more intelligence to manage the Waldorf cuisine (a high level position in the occupation of "cook") than to post figures in a ledger (a low level task for accountants). Thus there are opportunities for both high and low ability in any one occupation. The overlapping effect was also present in World War I data.

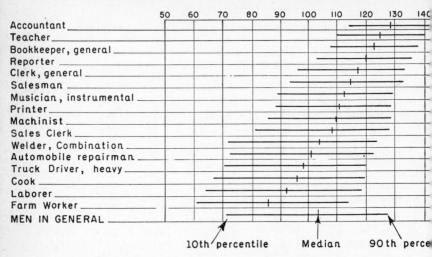

FIGURE 42. The Distribution of Army General Classification Test Scores in Various Occupations. These data are selected from a list of 227 occupations which included over 81,000 white soldiers, a random sample representing about 1.6 per cent of army personnel. Attention is called to the overlapping of scores between occupations, and to the increased variability at the lower occupational levels. This would indicate a selection effect in higher level occupations. (Data from Stewart, 23.)

2. The sample of occupations is inadequate, particularly in the professional occupations. Enlisted men only are represented in the data. Lawyers were drafted into enlisted ranks in large numbers, as were accountants; but physicians and engineers, on the other hand, were usually commissioned from civilian life and are not represented.

3. The data give us information about the relationship between intelligence and occupation attained, but none about the relationship between intelligence and success within the occupation. The information is useful, as Super says, "in ascertaining approximately the occupational level at which an individual is most likely to be able to compete without undue strain and, at the same time, with sufficient challenge to make the work interesting" (24, p. 94). But there is still the practical problem, for any individual of average ability, of deciding between an occupation of high prestige in which his ability will rank low, or

an occupation of lower prestige in which his ability will be among the highest.

4. The ability rankings of the occupations were very similar to those found for World War I. It would appear that in our society the distributions of intelligence among occupations are fairly stable, and that intelligence is therefore one selective factor determining occupational level. This conclusion is confirmed by longitudinal follow-up studies.

Intelligence and Vocational Achievement: Follow-up Studies. A typical follow-up study is the one by Procter (21). He ascertained the vocational levels attained in 1930 by those students who had been given the Army test in 1917. Table 18

TABLE 18

MEAN IQ AND OCCUPATIONAL STATUS THIRTEEN YEARS AFTER TESTING *

Occupational Level (1930)	N	Average Years Schooling	Average IQ (1917)
I Professional	130	17.3	115
II Semiprof., Managerial	565	14.0	108
III Skilled Trades	228	12.0	104
IV Semiskilled	12	10.8	99
V Unskilled	10	9.4	97

* Data from Procter, 21.

shows the results, revealing a general trend of relationship between intelligence and occupational level, which in turn is related to the amount of schooling obtained. The "rank of occupation" is based on the Barr scale of vocational status.

The Stanford follow-up of gifted children sheds additional light on the relationship between intelligence and vocational achievement (29). The 1945 data on the occupations of children of high IQ tested in 1922 reveal that 71 per cent of the men were in professional, semiprofessional, and managerial occupations, while only 7 per cent were in semiskilled or slightly skilled occupations. Their income was 70 per cent above that of employed males in general, while the income of employed gifted women was 82 per cent above that of employed women in general. The average income of the gifted was also substantially higher than the income of college graduates in general, for both men and women. There was no direct relationship between the 1922 IQ and income, but a comparison of those individuals with IQ of 170 or above with the total group indicated that men in the high group made a better showing in occupational status. This did not hold true for women.

Some of the individuals whose occupational achievement was greatest, however, were only "mediocre (as compared with the gifted) in intelligence." A comparison of two groups of gifted men from the sample—the A-group rated most successful in over-all achievement, and the C-group rated least successful —showed that the A's were only slightly higher in 1922 IQ, but came from family backgrounds of higher socioeconomic status and were rated higher (as children in 1922) on emotional stability, social adjustments, and various personality traits. This seems to indicate that intelligence is less of a factor in the achievement of a highly selected group than are favorable background and personality. The differences in vocational success of these two groups were, of course, related to differences in educational achievement; the two groups were very similar in school progress during elementary school, but began to differ in achievement in high school and even more so in college.

Some evidence which confirms, but less conclusively, the relationship between intelligence and vocational success is found in the studies of the intelligence of famous men, as reported in the Stanford Genetic Studies of Genius (8). This was a kind of "follow-up in reverse"—an attempt to estimate the childhood IQ's of 300 eminent men of previous generations. Biographies of such men as Leibnitz, Mill, and Goethe were searched for indications of early mental performances to compare with the tasks now employed in intelligence tests for children. Estimates were then made of the probable IQ's, which ranged from 100 to 200 with a mean at 135. The results of the study, even after liberal allowance is made for sources of error, tend to show that the genius of adulthood was foreshadowed in the accomplishments of youth and that intelligence tests, if they had been in use at the time, might have predicted fairly well general level of adult attainment.

Intelligence and Success Within Occupations. Comparatively little work has been done in ascertaining whether the more intelligent within a given occupation are more "successful," i.e., make more money, gain more prestige, get promoted sooner, and the like. Although this is often popularly assumed, there is no evidence to support it. Some studies made many years ago showed no relationship; for instance, a correlation of —.10 was found between intelligence and individual success in a group of business executives (4). Studies of the relationship between intelligence and sales ability gave similar results.

It appears that factors other than intelligence are more likely to be found responsible for success of the individual within a single occupational group. This may be especially true for most higher-level occupations; a certain level of intelligence is required to complete medical school, but the more intelligent physicians may not be the most successful. In the lower-level occupations, it is possible to have too much intelligence for a job, leading to dissatisfaction and relative inefficiency. After reviewing all pertinent research, Super concludes:

1. People tend, in so far as circumstances permit, to gravitate toward jobs in which they have ability to compete successfully with others.

2. Given intelligence above the minimum required for learning the occupation, be it executive work, teaching, packing, or light assembly work, additional increments of intelligence appear to have no special effect on an individual's success in that occupation. This . . . *may not apply to more strictly intellectual jobs such as those in research or to some kinds of teaching,* but only to those in which personality and interest are peculiarly important.

3. In routine occupations requiring speed and accuracy . . . intelligence as measured by an alertness rather than a power test is related to success in the learning period, and in some vocations after the initial adjustments are made. (24, p. 103)

For a group representing the higher intelligence levels, such as college students, an individual's general mental ability will tend to be less of a differentiating factor in vocational success. A general relationship between intelligence and vocational status may still be expected to hold, however, as evidenced by the follow-up studies.

INTELLIGENCE AND PERSONAL-SOCIAL ADJUSTMENT

We have seen that one type of definition of intelligence stresses adjustment, i.e., intelligent behavior is variable and adaptable according to the changing conditions of life. Such a view would lead us to expect more intelligent individuals (those with higher test scores) to be better adjusted personally and socially, to manage their daily lives happily and efficiently without being a nuisance in society. To what extent is this supported by empirical data? The studies most pertinent here are those dealing with intelligence and social conduct, and the follow-up of gifted children.

Intelligence and Conduct. Studies of juvenile delinquency have indicated that delinquents are on the average rather low in IQ. On a priori grounds, intelligence might be considered a significant factor in juvenile delinquency, since the child of low intelligence has as a rule less foresight, is less likely to be critical of suggestions received from others, and is less able on his own initiative to remedy an unfortunate situation. Normal mentality, on the other hand, would seem to offer something of a safeguard against unfavorable home and neighborhood surroundings. Low intelligence is therefore usually held to be a secondary contributing factor in delinquency, the social background factors being primary. Thus Burt (7) ranked intellectual disabilities sixth in order of importance, below such other contributing factors as defective discipline, "specific instincts," emotional instability, morbid emotionality, and a family history of vice and crime.

However, the fact that delinquents are chiefly from the lower social levels has led some writers to question whether there is any direct relationship between intelligence and delinquency.[1] "Juvenile delinquency" is actually a legal term, defined as the violation of laws by persons below a statutory age limit. A

[1] A recent study of 500 delinquents by the Gluecks (11) suggests that low intelligence is not an important factor. However, these boys, although "matched" with nondelinquents on a number of factors, including general intelligence, were significantly lower than the nondelinquents on the Wechsler Verbal Scale.

person who is not caught or who is not formally accused of law-breaking is therefore not a "delinquent." But juveniles of the higher social classes who break the law do not get apprehended or charged, because of family influence and other reasons, as often as those of lower classes. The data, it is argued, do not reveal a relationship between intelligence and delinquency, but merely the expected relationship between intelligence and the social class origins of delinquents. This view is supported by studies such as that of Lane and Witty (15). They compared the IQ's of delinquents, not with the population in general, but with the IQ distribution of nondelinquents from the same social classes, and found the intelligence of delinquents and nondelinquents to be about the same. Perhaps the most appropriate conclusion is that the more intelligent are less likely to appear in court and in institutions for juvenile delinquents. Studies of adult criminals (18) show no definite relationship between criminality and intelligence, although the type of crime may reflect the intellectual level of the offender.

Evidence of a relationship between intelligence and minor behavior problems is sparse. Haggerty (12) studied the incidence of problem behavior in public school children and found that both the bright and the dull children were rated by their teachers as problem cases more frequently than pupils with IQ's around 100. The more intelligent children, however, were in general guilty of less serious forms of misconduct, whereas the low IQ's were guilty of more serious offenses. A higher percentage of the dull pupils, moreover, were involved in some form of misbehavior. Studies based on objective tests or ratings of character, such as the investigation by Hartshorne and May (13), commonly report a small but positive correlation between intelligence and desirable character traits. Those of higher levels of intelligence, for example, are found to take advantage of opportunities for deception less often than those of lower levels for any single age group.

Personal-Social Adjustment of the Gifted. It is often popularly assumed that "geniuses" tend to be mad or queer, and that very bright children often grow up to be maladjusted, unhappy social deviants. The evidence from the Stanford follow-up studies reveals the adjustment of the adult gifted to be generally favorable or superior in most respects (27). It was pointed out earlier that their acceleration in school did not have a permanent effect on successful social adjustment, although it may have caused in some cases temporary shyness or isolation while they were in school. A comparison of the "most successful" and "least successful" (A's and C's) revealed that these two groups differed rather markedly in social adjustment as well as achievement, with the A's showing superior emotional stability, marital happiness, and personality traits. However, the two groups did not differ in intelligence.

For the gifted group as a whole, there was a smaller incidence of juvenile delinquency, mental illness, and alcoholism than would be expected in the general population. The rates of suicides and divorces were normal. "Marital happiness" scores of the gifted group on a specially devised test were slightly higher than those of a control group of average intelligence and education. The number of avocational interests and hobbies are believed to be much higher than for people in general. A comparison of those individuals whose IQ was 170 or above with the total group showed no differences in personal, social, or marital adjustment. No relationship was found between childhood IQ and social adjustment, but a specially devised "Mastery of Concepts" test of intellectual ability administered in 1940 showed a positive relationship with social adjustment.

The Teacher's Concept of Intelligence. At this point it may be well to raise the broad question of what intelligence tests measure in a practical way, and what individual differences in this respect should mean to the teacher. We shall first do well to keep in mind a few points of distinction based on the professed nature of the tests themselves. They profess to measure a general mental ability, not special aptitude or talent. Neither do they profess to measure the entire mentality of a person, including his temperament, interests, and attitudes. And, since these other traits are of the utmost importance in a person's total life adjustment, intelligence tests do not aim to measure or predict the quality of actual accomplishment in life. At most, intelligence should be considered *aptitude* for life achievement, in so far as this is affected by the level of general mental maturity.

From our review of research, we cannot help but conclude that intelligence plays an important practical role in school adjustment and vocational adjustment. Whatever the tests measure, the results seem to indicate certain limits to (1) the level of difficulty of problems a person can solve, (2) the level of educational achievement he can reach, and (3) the occupational level he can attain. On the other hand, these limits are vague and cannot easily be marked off in terms of scores and IQ's. Considered as an aptitude, general intelligence should be regarded unequivocally as a test of ability to succeed in school. In our culture, the level of education and occupational level are so interdependent, and so closely related to social status, that the role of intelligence in society must be considered a fairly substantial one.

Yet it seems that the tests do not measure *all* the abilities important in life adjustment. It is apparent from factorial studies that they are heavily weighted with a verbal factor, and this is particularly true of the commonly used pencil-and-paper tests. This does not mean that the tests are poor. On the contrary, they have proved to be of considerable value for predicting performance in a wide range of practical life situations. Verbal ability is important in our society. Too little of it, in our culture, may make it difficult or impossible to get the kind of training and the kind of job which society as a whole considers important. A serious lack of it may mark one as socially incompetent. A high degree of verbal ability, on the other hand, enables a person to get along fairly well even when he is relatively deficient in numerical, spatial, motor, or mechanical abilities.

But on the whole, the abilities measured by intelligence tests play a less important role outside of school than they do in school. The teacher is probably more likely to place too high a premium on scholastic aptitude rather than too low. She may mistakenly equate success in school with success on the job, and equate failure in school with failure in society. She needs to know that high aptitude for running a lathe, repairing an automobile, operating a florist shop, selling merchandise, painting signs, or tuning a piano is not closely related to aptitude for reading or algebra. There are many practical abilities, including the ability to get along well with people, that are not revealed in intelligence test scores but which society values in one way or another. It should not be surprising, then, that many of our so-called "dull normals" attain more than ordinary success in business and in the community.

REFERENCES

1. BAKER, H. J. *Characteristic differences in bright and dull pupils.* Bloomington, Ill.: Public School Publ. Co., 1929.
2. BAKER, H. J. *Introduction to exceptional children.* New York: Macmillan, 1944.
3. BECKHAM, A. S. Minimum intelligence levels for several occupations. *Pers. J.,* 1930, **9,** 309-315.
4. BINGHAM, W. V., & DAVIS, W. T. Intelligence test scores and business success. *J. applied Psychol.,* 1924, **8,** 1-22.
5. BURKS, B. S., JENSEN, D. W., & TERMAN, L. M. The promise of youth: follow-up studies of a thousand gifted children. *Genetic studies of genius,* III. Stanford Univ. Press, 1930.
6. BURT, C. *Mental and scholastic tests.* London: King and Son, 1921.
7. BURT, C. *The young delinquent.* New York: Appleton, 1925.
8. COX, C. M. Early mental traits of three hundred geniuses. *Genetic studies of genius,* II. Stanford Univ. Press, 1926.
9. FRYER, D. Occupational intelligence standards. *School and Society,* 1922, **16,** 273-276.
10. GARRETT, H. E. The relation of tests of memory and learning to each other and to general intelligence in a highly selected adult group. *J. educ. Psychol.,* 1928, **19,** 601-613.
11. GLUECK, S., & GLUECK, E. *Unraveling juvenile delinquency.* New York: Commonwealth Fund, 1950.
12. HAGGERTY, M. E. The incidence of undesirable behavior in public school children. *J. educ. Res.,* 1925, **12,** 102-122.
13. HARTSHORNE, H., & MAY, M. A. *Studies in deceit.* New York: Macmillan, 1928.
14. HOLLINGWORTH, L. S., & COBB, M. V. Children clustering at 165 IQ and children clustering at 146 IQ. *27th Yearbook,* Nat. Soc. Stud. Educ., 1928.

15. LANE, H. A., & WITTY, P. A. The mental ability of delinquent boys. *J. juv. Res.,* 1935, **19**, 1-12.

16. McGEOGH, J. A. *The psychology of human learning.* New York: Longmans, Green, 1942.

17. MITCHELL, C. Prognostic value of intelligence tests. *J. educ. Res.,* 1935, **28**, 577-581.

18. MURCHISON, C. *Criminal intelligence.* Worcester: Clark Univ. Press, 1926.

19. PATERSON, D. G., & DARLEY, J. G. *Men, women and jobs.* Minneapolis: Univ. of Minnesota Press, 1936.

20. PATERSON, D. G., GERKEN, C. D'A., & HAHN, M. E. *The Minnesota occupational rating scales.* Chicago: Science Research Associates, 1941.

21. PROCTER, W. M. Intelligence and length of schooling in relation to occupational levels. *School and Society,* 1935, **42,** 783-786.

22. RYAN, H. H., & CRECELIUS, P. *Ability grouping in the junior high school.* New York: Harcourt, Brace, 1927.

23. STEWART, N. AGCT scores of Army personnel grouped by occupation. *Occupations,* 1947, **26,** 5-41.

24. SUPER, D. E. *Appraising vocational fitness by means of psychological tests.* New York: Harper, 1949.

25. TERMAN, L. M. *The intelligence of school children.* Boston: Houghton Mifflin, 1919.

26. TERMAN, L. M., & ODEN, M. Status of the California gifted group at the end of sixteen years. *39th Yearbook,* I, Nat. Soc. Stud. Educ., 1940.

27. TERMAN, L. M., & ODEN, M. *The gifted child grows up.* Stanford Univ. Press, 1947.

28. TILTON, J. W. Intelligence test scores as indicative of ability to learn. *Educ. psychol. Measmt.,* 1949, **9,** 291-296.

29. U.S. Office of Education, *Bull.* 17. Washington, D.C., 1932.

30. UNGER, E., & BURR, E. T. *Minimum mental age levels of accomplishment.* Albany: Univ. of State of New York, 1931.

SELECTED READINGS

ANASTASI, A., & FOLEY, J. P. *Differential psychology.* New York: Macmillan, 1949. Chs. 16 and 17 contrast the extremes of ability and review pertinent research.

HOLLINGWORTH, L. S. *Children above 180 I.Q.* Yonkers, N.Y.: World Book Co., 1942.

LOUTTIT, C. M. *Clinical psychology of children's behavior problems.* New York: Harper, 1947. Ch. 7, "School retardation."

POFFENBERGER, A. T. *Principles of applied psychology.* New York: Appleton-Century-Crofts, 1942. The role of intelligence in adjustment, pp. 282-304.

STODDARD, G. D. *The meaning of intelligence.* New York: Macmillan, 1943.

SUPER, D. E. *Appraising vocational fitness by means of psychological tests.* New York: Harper, 1949. Ch. 6, "Intelligence." A summary of research.

TERMAN, L. M., & ODEN, M. *The gifted child grows up.* Stanford University Press, 1947.

10

PERSONALITY AND SCHOOL ADJUSTMENT

N EXT TO physical traits, differences in personality, or "characteristic styles of behavior," are perhaps the ones we are most aware of in other persons. Popular usage defines personality in terms of social attractiveness, which provides the frame of reference for talking about "good" or "poor" personality and the emphasis on improving it. The factors that make for social attractiveness, however, are difficult to define, since a wide variety of very different people are likable.

The popular concept of "personality" is not very helpful to the teacher in determining her behavior toward students, since it may lead to regarding students as relatively attractive or repulsive, to liking some and disliking others. In her professional work the teacher must be a student of personality, must attempt to understand persons and their motives in order to interpret their behavior, and use this knowledge to the pupil's advantage. With this purpose in mind, it seems best to regard personality as those factors or traits, other than ability (but not necessarily independent of it), that influence the child's adjustment to other people, the way he faces difficulties, and the bearing these have on achievement. Personality factors, in many respects, seem to be even more important than abilities in determining how the child gets along in school and how he will get along in life.

Personality Defined. A meaningful short definition of personality is "the characteristic style of behavior." According to this, individual differences are revealed through characteristic posture, gestures, speech, attitudes, ways of solving problems, and the like. However, we may wish to place more emphasis on what is behind all this, or the person's motives, and on the many factors in his past history that make him unique. A more comprehensive definition is:

. . . Personality is the entire mental organization of a human being at any stage of his development. It embraces every phase of human character: intellect, temperament, skill, morality, and every attitude that has been built up in the course of one's life. (40, p. 333)

Personality Differences

The ways in which people differ are of almost infinite variety. As a "whole," personality makes systematic study very difficult. Any expression of individual differences, however, may be defined as a *trait*. Traits then are what we must study. In total, we may say that traits make up the distinct individual, make his characteristic style of behavior. But the distinctiveness of individual personality, of course, depends not on traits in isolation, but traits in the context of other traits. When we study a certain trait, we must abstract it or lift it out of context, and when we do so the distinctive meaning of the trait is to some extent lost. "Cheerfulness" is a trait in the abstract. But we recognize different individuals as noisy cheerful, quiet cheerful, infectiously cheerful, annoyingly cheerful. It is the way these things are put together in the person, together with the basic motives underlying his cheerfulness or sadness, that make the characteristic integration or distinctiveness of the individual. And the whole of personality, at least from the point of view of the classroom teacher, is more important than its parts taken separately.

There are thousands of traits in the abstract, or at least we have thousands of trait names. All cannot be equally important, and many of them must be related. It is therefore better to think of personality in terms of basic traits, or basic themes in behavior.

Basic Personality Traits. We commonly distinguish between superficial traits and those basic underlying traits which motivate or "explain" the superficial behavior. Take "laziness," for example. Lazy behavior may be due to fear of failure, insecurity, timidity, geniality, cautiousness, lack of interest, or inadequate glandular function. Laziness may be, and usually is, the result of a complex combination of such underlying motives. We also recognize that the opposite kind of behavior —call it "industriousness"—is often the result of some of the same motives; thus a person may be industrious and work very hard because of basic insecurity or fear of failure. Again, it is not any single trait, but a characteristic integration of attitudes, interests, and abilities that causes a person to be "lazy" in some things and "industrious" in others, on some occasions, and in the presence of some people. The basic motives underlying behavior may show this to be quite consistent.

A basic personality trait has three characteristics: (1) It operates as a *motive* or functional tendency, in affecting many different aspects of behavior; it determines how a given situation is interpreted, what cues are noticed and responded to. (2) It is an *enduring,* relatively permanent characteristic which is revealed as a kind of "theme" in many different kinds of activity. (3) It is said to have *dimensions;* that is, the trait varies in amount from one extreme to another.

A trait "dimension" implies that there are varying degrees of a trait like "cheerfulness," for example; a person is not *either* cheerful or sad, but some place along a line from extreme cheerfulness to extreme sadness. The dimension is usually conceived as bipolar, with the extremes as the poles. Table 19 shows examples of the bipolar nature of personality traits.

Certain personality traits are sometimes described as temperamental, and a certain combination of them as a *temperament.* When we use the word temperament, we imply that the traits are *constitutional,* i.e., they are determined or influenced by the physiological make-up of the organism, and presumably are the result of innate or hereditary factors. It is not known which personality traits are constitutional and which are the primary result of learning, and it is therefore difficult to use the word temperament accurately. While all traits show the effect of learning, it is probable that some of them are influenced by

TABLE 19

SOME BASIC TRAIT DIMENSIONS ILLUSTRATING BIPOLARITY *

Positive	Negative
1. Easygoing, genial, amiable	Inflexible, cold, hostile
2. Intelligent, independent, reliable	Stupid, unreflective, frivolous
3. Emotionally stable, realistic, steadfast	Evasive, emotionally changeable, excitable
4. Dominant, boastful, self-assertive	Submissive, self-effacing, modest
5. Cheerful, sociable, talkative	Unhappy, depressed, seclusive
6. Sensitive, tenderhearted, sympathetic	Hard-boiled, unemotional, cynical
7. Thoughtful, cultured, esthetic	Boorish, uncultured, coarse
8. Conscientious, responsible, painstaking	Slipshod, impulsive, irresponsible
9. Cooperative, carefree, kind	Reserved, cautious, secretive
10. Vigorous, persistent, strong-willed	Languid, slack, ineffective
11. Hypersensitive, excitable, impatient	Phlegmatic, tolerant, calm
12. Friendly, trustful, enthusiastic	Suspicious, hostile, frustrated

* From H. E. Garrett, *Psychology,* New York: American Book Co., 1950. After Cattell (12).

constitutional factors. There is known to be a relationship between the activity of endocrine glands, for example, and behavior. "Character" has an ethical connotation. Any personality trait can be a *character trait* from the moral or ethical point of view. "Honesty" might then be regarded as a character trait.

Some Familiar Trait Dimensions. Some trait names are so familiar that we almost immediately tend to classify behavior in terms of them. Many have become an essential part of popular language and thought, but are often misunderstood and loosely used. We shall discuss here those trait dimensions which have been most thoroughly studied and which most commonly appear in "tests" of personality.

One of the best known traits is *extroversion-introversion,* which distinguishes between the "turned inward" and the "turned outward" person. The following three aspects of the trait have usually been emphasized in defining it: (1) the direction of interest and attention toward things, persons, and events outside of one's self, *versus* attention directed inwardly toward one's thought or feelings; (2) ease of adapting or adjusting to social conditions *versus* difficulty in doing so; and (3) a marked tendency toward overt or "open" behavior, *versus* a marked tendency toward covert ("hidden" or secretive) behavior.

The introvert child is more likely to be shy and retiring; he is rather sensitive to criticism or teasing, and tends to be suspicious and bear grudges. The extrovert, on the other hand, brings whatever quarrels he has with others out into the open. He is apt to be overactive, talkative, and boisterous in the classroom. Each of course has his good points. The extrovert child feels free to express his enthusiasms and appreciation and is stimulated by the presence of others to put his "best foot forward." The introvert, although more often in the background, is usually a self-sufficient and consistent worker on protracted and less colorful tasks. These are comparisons of extremes. Most people are neither introvert nor extrovert, but *ambivert* in the sense that most of their behavior is some place in the middle between the two extremes.

Many scales have been devised for the measurement of extroversion-introversion, and intensive study of such measurements indicates that the trait is not at all as simple as our description of it may imply. Systematic factor-analysis studies of various trait-dimension scores from personality inventories indicate that the trait of introversion breaks down into at least three aspects: social, thinking, and public or "platform" introversion (27). It would therefore seem appropriate to think of extroversion-introversion as covering at least three dimensions: sociability-shyness, "practical thinking" *versus* self-preoccupied thinking, and ease in public speaking *versus* public self-consciousness. It seems clear from the research that even more subtraits are involved. Moreover, there is evidence that the behavioral expression of extroversion-introversion in men differs from that of women. Some of these subtraits may be influenced by constitution, but there is probably no such thing as a general extroverted or introverted "temperament."

Another familiar trait dimension is *dominance-submission,* or ascendance-submission. The dominant or ascendant individual is one who tends to "dominate his fellows in various face-to-face relationships of everyday life" (1). He would thus tend to get others to do what he wants rather than go along with the wishes of others, to resist or overcome the opinions of others, to deal easily with high pressure sales tactics, and the like. The extremely submissive person, akin to the Casper Milquetoast of comic-sheet fame, shows behavior at the opposite pole.

Other common trait dimensions are *self-confidence-inferiority, masculinity-femininity* (distinguishing between behavioral traits more "typical" of men-women) and neuroticism (well adjusted *vs.* maladjusted). Various scales have been constructed for the measurement of such traits, but as in the case of introversion, many such measures have been found to be related to one another.

Measuring Personality Traits. Although personality as a whole is complex and probably immeasurable as such, psychologists have been able to adopt a practical approach to measurement by defining personality as a *pattern of trait dimensions.* With such a definition, it is possible to proceed to the construction of measuring devices. There are three commonly used devices for measuring traits:

1. *The self-report inventory,* in which the subject marks a sheet to indicate whether a certain kind of behavior describes him or not, how he would react to certain imaginary situations, and the like. Such subjective reports are obviously easy to control, and are open to considerable distortion by the person taking the inventory.

2. *Behavior rating schedules,* in which the subject's behavior in a variety of situations is observed, described, or rated by someone else. Such devices may result in either "controlled" ratings, if the situations and observations are carefully standardized, or "uncontrolled" if either the situations or observa-

tions are not standardized. Situational tests are considered more valid than self-reports, but are prone to subjective errors on the part of persons who do the rating.

3. *Projective techniques,* which are special cases of situational tests in which the situation is "unstructured," i.e., so novel or unusual that the test subject gets no cues or hints as to how he is expected to respond, and is thus unable to control his responses. The Rorschach ink-blots, the "thematic apperception" tests in which the subject looks at a picture and tells a story about it, and finger painting or drawing are examples. Projective techniques are attempts to assess the whole personality, but as a rule do not measure trait dimensions. They are said to be "self-expressive"; the individual projects or "reads into" the situation his characteristic values and basic traits.

Factor Analysis of Traits. It has been estimated that there are about 18,000 words in the English language which describe behavioral traits. On the assumption that whatever exists is measurable to some extent, it would presumably be possible to discover the behavioral correlates of the names and to devise 18,000 measures, but they would overlap one another. Even allowing for the fact that many of these words are synonyms, and that many others are so alike that we could not discriminate the behavior presumably associated with them, many such measures are possible and many have been attempted. Just as psychologists have been interested in reducing the various measures of mental ability to basic factors, they have also been concerned with the reduction of various trait dimensions to a small number of fundamental or "primary" traits. The twelve traits listed in Table 19 are the final result of such a systematic analysis by Cattell (12).

A similar series of studies by Guilford started with various types of self-report inventories or questionnaires (19, 20). The factor analysis resulted in thirteen factors as follows:

S. Social introversion: shy, keeps in background on social occasions

T. Thinking introversion: introspective, reflective, meditative

D. Depression: often "blue," worries over possible misfortunes

C. Cycloid tendency: frequent shifts of mood (ups and downs)

R. Rhathymia: happy go lucky, carefree

G. General activity: tendency to engage in overt activity

A. Ascendance-submission: social leadership or dominance

M. Masculinity-femininity: similarity of responses to those of men or women

I. Inferiority: lack of self-confidence

N. Nervousness: irritability, jumpiness

O. Objectivity: viewing self and surroundings objectively, not taking things personally

Co. Cooperativeness: accepting things and people as they are, tolerant, not fault-finding

Ag. Agreeableness: not quarrelsome, belligerent, or domineering

Self-report types of personality inventories were later constructed to measure these factors.[1] Like the primary mental abilities, the various personality factors were found to be correlated as measured on the inventories. A subsequent factor analysis of the correlations of actual scores resulted in a reduction of the original 13 factors to four, which were called drive-restraint, realism, emotionality, and social adaptability (25).

A more recent factor analysis of personality traits by Thurstone resulted in the identification of seven "primary" trait factors, namely: a pressure for activity, masculinity-femininity, impulsiveness, dominance, emotional stability, sociability, and reflectiveness.

Factor analysis studies are obviously useful in identifying and defining the traits measured by inventories and behavior ratings. However, it is very doubtful that "primary source traits" have been uncovered, in the sense that personality as a whole can be described in terms of them, or that the development of personality traits proceeds from them as a kind of core. "Primary traits" have the same limitations as "primary abilities"; they may be economical descriptive terms and nothing more. The important implication of factorial studies is this: we

[1] Guilford Inventory of Factors STDCR, Guilford-Martin Inventory of Factors GAMIN, Guilford-Martin Personnel Inventory I.

should approach with caution the interpretation of the results of personality inventories. There is probably no phase of psychological testing in which the "jingle" and "jangle" fallacies are more misleading. We have seen that a test with a single trait label may actually measure different traits, and tests of different trait labels may measure the same trait.

The Use of Personality Inventories. Some psychologists would question whether personality inventories of the "self-report" type have any great practical value. This opinion arises from many fruitless attempts to find relationships between trait scores and other variables, and the doubtful validity of the self-report technique for studying personality. The validity of such inventories is certainly questionable on both counts. On the other hand, the results of research show that they are useful in showing group trends, and for the identification of personal problems. The personality inventory may be of some use in the school within the limitations of the following general principles:

1. The inventory should be used as a screen, not as a diagnostic instrument.

2. Scores on the inventory do not necessarily indicate an *amount* of something, as does an intelligence test score. A "poor" score may indicate that a student needs further attention and help, but a "good" score does not necessarily indicate favorable adjustment. Decisions or judgments by a counselor should never be made on the basis of scores alone.

3. The principles of relativity, reliability, validity, and comparability apply to the wise selection of personality inventories. Norms should be based on a group comparable to the one being tested, and the test user should have evidence of its reliability and validity for the purpose he has in mind.

4. To get dependable results, the testing situation should be carefully structured to encourage the subjects to describe themselves truthfully. This requires careful thought and planning on the part of the examiner as to how the results will be used as well as how the test situation will be approached.

Interests and Attitudes

The Nature of Interests. Interest is an emotional attitude of "like-dislike" accompanied by attention to the object of interest. There are thus two bipolar dimensions involved in an interest: (1) the feeling tone of like-dislike, and (2) the dimension of attraction-aversion. When we are "interested" in anything, person, or event in our environment, we are attentive to a high degree, we feel attracted to the object, and we experience satisfaction in its attainment. We may try to uncover the student's interests by asking him, of course, and he may tell us whether or not he likes arithmetic or baseball. This is not always too meaningful because of the problems involved in interpreting a self-report. In general it is a poor way to try to discover vocational interests, or those that might have an aspect of permanence about them. We could ask a child, "Would you like to be an automobile mechanic?" but a simple answer would hardly allow us to infer whether or not he should consider this trade as a career. We may not know what meaning the term "automobile mechanic" has for him—whether it is a symbol of high status or low status, whether he has adequate knowledge of the occupation, or what alternatives he is comparing it with. Many studies of such "expressed interests" by students indicate that the occupations they name as possible careers are often unrealistic, with a highly disproportionate number choosing professional, managerial, and "white-collar" job titles. Such a choice is more often than not merely a status preference, and not indicative of any "basic" interest trends. The fact that students frequently change their choices has often been offered as evidence that "interests are unstable." This may be true of expressed interests, but we probably should not expect such statements of students to be highly realistic or reliable. Such reports are seldom trustworthy. Some more suitable criteria of interest, based on our definition, are these:

1. *Attention and learning*. The student is interested, by definition, in the things he pays attention to voluntarily. Since he tends to remember things to which he is attentive, what he remembers is a good indication of interest. An individual who

says "I like baseball" but shows little knowledge of the rules, teams, players, or jargon probably has little interest in the game. On the other hand, the response "I dislike baseball" from a person well informed on the game would not indicate lack of interest, but perhaps a preference for other unnamed activities. One example of a memory test employed to measure interests is an experiment by Super and Roper (36), who tested the vocational interests of students by means of a recall test of details of different pictures which were projected from film strips. An achievement test, according to the same principle, may reveal interests.

2. *Preference or choice*. A valid test of interest is the way a person spends his money or his time. A person who spends more money on books than on sports equipment probably has more literary interests than athletic interests. For preference among several alternatives to serve as an interest criterion, however, the alternative must be equally available. The preference criterion is the most widely used in inventories of vocational interests.

3. *Duration or persistence*. Usually the activity which persists over a long period of time does so because it is satisfying, and thus *satisfaction* is the real criterion here. A duffer may play tennis for years, week in and week out; we would infer satisfaction, and interest.

If expressed interests in certain occupations do not change, we may infer that they are fairly stable. Even here, the motive may change over a period of time. At age 12, "interest" in becoming a physician may be a vague desire for status; at age 16, it may be also a liking for science in school, plus the desire to help other people; at age 21, it may be these plus a genuine desire to do medical research. Similarly, a person who continues in an occupation (when change is possible) may be assumed to have interest in it, although the reasons for entering it and remaining in it may be quite different. It is possible however that some persons may continue in their occupations, originally selected for sound reasons, simply because they feel compelled to defend the original choice and not because of continuing satisfaction.

Interests are emotional attitudes, and are thus similar to other trait dimensions of personality. To be sure, "expressed interests" or simple statements of liking-disliking are hardly in this category; but *interest patterns* of the type measured on vocational interest inventories are found to be fairly stable and enduring aspects of personality, akin to motives (14). This finding, in the opinion of one writer,

. . . suggests that major trends in interests cannot be influenced by relatively superficial experiences. Specific interests, directed toward isolated objects or activities, can perhaps be influenced by these experiences, but those factors determining the general interest patterns of a person form a complex of physiological, maturational, and social conditions extending over a long period of time. (10, p. 68)

Interests and Abilities. The relationship between interest patterns and other personality factors is attested by a growing body of research; persons of different interests have been shown to differ in varying degrees on such basic personality traits as extroversion, sociability, and masculinity-femininity.

The relationship between interests and ability, on the other hand, is surprisingly less clear. On a priori grounds, we should assume a relationship to exist for two reasons: (1) High ability in some activity should lead to success and satisfaction, thence to increased interest, while low ability should lead to failure, dissatisfaction, and loss of interest; (2) high interest in an activity should tend to persist and become stronger when ability is high, since superior ability will ordinarily lead to more satisfying consequences. We would thus expect a high degree of relationship between literary interests and ability in reading and writing. On this kind of reasoning, Strong has maintained that "interests reflect inborn abilities" (34). But correlations between interests and measures of ability have been almost uniformly low; some relationship exists, but not much. In any case, we cannot assume that scores on interest inventories are indirectly measuring abilities, or that abilities directly influence such scores.

Measuring Interests. Vocational interests are most commonly measured by self-report inventories, in which the subject marks a sheet to indicate his likes, dislikes, and preferences. This approach is based on several assumptions: (1) that such responses are fairly stable or constant, and there is evidence that this is generally true; (2) that the subject will give a truthful description of his likes and dislikes, and he usually does in most situations; (3) that the pattern of scores obtained is stable and meaningful enough to predict future likes and dislikes in occupational and educational pursuits. The purpose of interest testing is to predict satisfaction; the test of validity for an interest inventory is how well a high score predicts a liking for an occupation or a certain field of study. Conversely, low scores should be associated with dislike or dissatisfaction. The best known interest inventories are the Kuder Preference Record and the Strong Vocational Interest Blank, which illustrate two different approaches to interest measurement.

The Kuder Preference Record measures the frequency or consistency with which a person chooses activities in a given field or category of interest. Kuder decided upon nine interest fields worthy of measurement: Mechanical, Computational, Scientific, Persuasive, Artistic, Literary, Musical, Social Service, and Clerical. He added a tenth field (Outdoor) in a later form of the test. Activity items were constructed for each category and are presented to the subject in groups of three, with instructions to mark the one he likes best and the one he likes least. For example:

(Mechanical)	*a*)	Build bird houses
(Literary)	*b*)	Write articles about birds
(Artistic)	*c*)	Draw sketches of birds

Scores are determined by the frequency of choice of items in the various fields, and thus give a quantitative description of the kinds of interests the person has. Figure 43 shows a profile of Kuder scores. They do not measure the absolute *amount* of interest he has, because the forced choice technique involves only a relative comparison of preferences in the various fields. The profile will not reflect any difference between one boy who is intensely interested in a variety of activities, and another who

has very little interest in any, even if they make the same preferences.   The face value of the scores means very little; in interpreting scores, only high scores (above the 75th percentile) and
low scores (below the 25th percentile) can be assigned definite

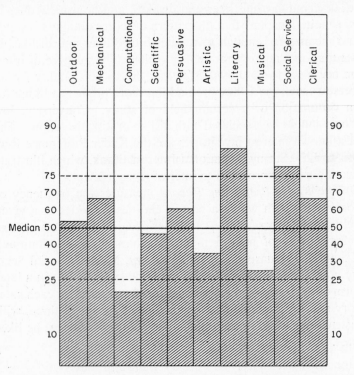

FIGURE 43. A Profile of Scores on the Kuder Preference Record. The
interest pattern here is "literary-social service," since the student tended to
choose these items very consistently. "Clerical" and "mechanical" might be
regarded as a secondary pattern, and considered in combination with the
higher scores. On the basis of these scores, what occupations might the student consider, and which should he probably avoid?

meanings.   The reason for this is that high and low scores reveal consistent tendencies to choose or to avoid certain interest
fields, while "average" scores can be obtained by chance, i.e.,
by marking the items at random.   The Kuder Preference Record has been administered to men and women of many different

occupations, and the results have shown consistent differences in interest patterns among occupational groups. The individual's interest profile is thus useful in vocational and educational counseling, and as a device for provoking the student to think about his interests and the part they play in his choice of training and career.

The *Strong Vocational Interest Blank,* also a self-report inventory, differs in some essential respects from the Kuder Preference Record. It attempts to measure the resemblance of a person's interests (likes and dislikes) to the interests of persons in certain occupations. One's score on an occupation, like Physician or Lawyer or Social Science Teacher, indicates the degree of resemblance between his interest-attitudes and those of members of these occupations.

The fact that there are "families" of occupations whose members have similar interests is important, since the value of interpreting the Strong profile is not limited simply to the occupations listed. For example, Group V includes educators, social workers, and personnel workers, and is called the "Social Welfare Group." There is no specific score for "Social Worker," but such persons as social workers, most teachers, and clinical psychologists have been found to make generally high scores on the Group V occupations. The individual score on an occupation is therefore less important than the general trend of the profile, as indicated by the occupational group in which the person scores high or low. For most effective interpretation, the Strong Blank should therefore be scored on all occupations in order to yield a profile. Follow-up studies over a long period have shown that the measures of interest are related to the kind of occupation chosen, the tendency to stay in the occupation *versus* the tendency to change occupation, and degree of vocational satisfaction (34).

Factorial studies of interests reveal a certain consistency in the group factors found. Thurstone's factor analysis of the Strong Blank (39) resulted in four factors which he named Science, Language, People, and Business. A similar analysis of the Strong scores of high school youths found similar broad groupings of interest at these ages (13).

Attitudes and Their Measurement. If we define "attitude" as a set or tendency or predisposition to feel and act in a certain way, all personality traits, interests, and emotional reactions may be regarded as attitudes. "Inferiority" and "extroversion" are attitudes toward the self, and toward things, persons, and events in relation to one's self; interest in baseball is an attitude, and so is fear of the dark. When we come to the measurement of attitudes, however, psychologists make a practical distinction, and the term attitude is used in a very specific sense. The best way to make clear this special meaning is to show the practical distinction between "interest" and "attitude." Interests are ordinarily measured, as we have seen, in terms of like-dislike. Attitudes are measured in terms of *approval-disapproval*. A person may dislike baseball, but at the same time approve of it as an amusement, say, for his son or his neighbors. When we measure an attitude, then, we usually measure the extent to which a person is "for it" or "against it." Unlike the opinion poll, the attitude scale treats a single opinion as a single test item, having by itself little or no reliability. On the principle that a longer test produces a more reliable measure, the attitude scale contains many items (opinions) which reflect a general attitude.

When is an attitude scale valid? This would depend on the purpose of the scale. If the purpose is to measure expressed opinions for their own sake, then the attitude scale is *assumed* to be a valid measure of beliefs (internal validity). External validation is essential if we wish to use an attitude scale to predict a person's behavior in everyday life from his responses on the scale. This is more difficult, because a person may approve of churches but not attend, may have a favorable attitude toward studying but not study.

Attitude scales have been specially designed to measure industrial morale, race prejudices, and attitudes toward democracy, capitalism, war, schools, and the like. "Generalized attitude scales," such as those developed by Remmers (30), are useful in measuring the individual's attitude toward any number of things: an institution, a school subject, a national or racial group, a person, or an occupation.

In the school, attitude scales may serve an especially useful function in evaluating the effect of educational experiences. We can, for example, use "before-and-after" attitude measures to determine the outcome of certain instruction on tolerance toward Negroes, literary appreciation, scientific open-mindedness, attitudes toward government, or study habits. In this respect attitude scales are similar in purpose to achievement tests. They have also been widely used to evaluate the attitudes of students and teachers, as well as attitudes of the taxpayer toward the school.

SOME FACTORS ASSOCIATED WITH PERSONALITY DIFFERENCES

Sex Differences (2). What differences between males and females have been revealed by research studies of basic personality traits, interests, and attitudes? Many of the findings are in agreement with popular opinion or stereotypes, and some are not. In regard to basic trait dimensions, males have been found to be more aggressive or dominant than females; this seems to be true at all age levels from nursery school age through adulthood. Boys and men are more emotionally stable or less "neurotic"; the evidence for this statement lies in the greater frequency in girl children of such nervous habits as nail-biting and thumb-sucking, and the sex differences in "neuroticism" scores on personality inventories for adolescents and adults. A study of introversion-extroversion by Heidbreder (21) showed no sex differences, but revealed that the signs of introversion in college men and women were not the same. The introverted male was more outspoken, self-sufficient, introspective, conservative in dress, and more retiring socially. The feminine signs of introversion were "ups and downs" in mood, difficulty in decision-making, sensitiveness, impulsiveness (works by fits and starts) and "shrinking" in the face of a crisis. Sex differences in basic traits are difficult to evaluate, and probably more suggestive than conclusive.

In interests and attitudes, sex differences are somewhat more clear. The findings of Terman and Miles (37) and Strong

(34) show men's interests to be typically mechanical, scientific, computational, adventuresome, and risk-taking, while the interests of women tend to be literary, artistic, musical, to be centered in people rather than in things, generally more "qualitative" than "quantitative." There is relatively very little overlapping in the interests of men and women, at least by comparison with personality traits.

In social attitudes, girls apparently tend to conform more closely than boys to the standards and norms of the group. It is perhaps for this reason that in general girls have been found to rate higher than boys in reputation for desirable social traits. It has been found, for example, that teachers report a greater number of undesirable behavior traits in boys than in girls (41). Conclusions about such ratings are difficult, for the ratings are undeniably influenced by the feminine tendency toward conformance, as well as the teachers' tendency to be influenced by it. Again, the greater tendency of females toward social orientation, or interest in people, plus the "conforming" attitude, may explain why women make higher scores on "neuroticism." They are more interested in what other people think of them and are more restrained in deviating from what is expected; as a consequence, they are more easily hurt by social slights and adverse criticism, are more apprehensive of social situations, and thus show more "neurotic" symptoms.

Some cautions are necessary in making generalizations about sex differences in personality. (1) Most of the differences are probably not primarily biological, but rooted in cultural learning. Boys begin to learn masculine traits, and girls feminine ones, at a very early age. (2) Stereotyped generalizations about the differences between boys and girls or men and women are usually misleading. The fact that there is some (often large) amount of overlapping between the sexes on personality traits means that there is a large number of exceptions to any generalization we can make. The teacher must always treat individuals as individuals. On the other hand, attention to sex differences is necessary to the teacher who would be understanding, tolerant, and influential in motivating children.

Cultural Differences. Since social and emotional traits, interests, and attitudes are learned, we should expect that persons of different social-cultural backgrounds would show differences in personality. The traits of the individual are to a large extent a reflection of the subculture to which he belongs, and can therefore be understood only in their cultural setting. Studies of personality through self-report inventories and other means tend to substantiate the expected differences. A study by Gough (18), for example, compared the inventory responses of high school seniors of high socioeconomic status with those of low status, and found the former to be more self-confident and socially better adjusted, to report fewer fears and anxieties, and to be less introverted. These findings are confirmed by other studies. It would appear that class differences in personality are rooted in the experiences of early childhood.

Constitutional Factors in Personality. The idea that personality differences are influenced by physiological or anatomical factors is a very old one, and is fairly well rooted in popular thought. Thus Shakespeare's Julius Caesar is made to say of Cassius:

> Yon Cassius has a lean and hungry look;
> He thinks too much; such men are dangerous.

And in answer to Antony's "Fear him not, Caesar; he's not dangerous" Caesar rejoins "Would he were fatter!"—seeing in Cassius' leanness such traits as keenness of observation and dourness.

The tradition that fat men are jolly and lean men are dour has had its counterpart in the scientific investigation of body type in relation to personality or temperament. There can be no doubt of the link between emotional traits and the functioning of the glands of internal secretion. Excessive thyroid secretion, for example, is often found to be accompanied by excitability and emotional disturbances. Also, it has been found that hyperthyroidism tends to predominate in thin people and hypothyroidism in fleshy people. Hence the belief that the relationship between endocrine glands and personality is really only one aspect of a general relationship between physique or constitution and personality. The most prominent advocate of this view, Sheldon, states the hypothesis as follows:

> . . . Glands probably determine personality only in the same sense that the long bones and the short ones, and the gut and the muscle and the skin, and the rest of the structures of the body determine personality. It seems a more reasonable hypothesis that the physique as a whole consists of a patterned organization of elemental components which all together produce the observed aspects of the individual personality. (32, p. 232)

Sheldon has developed reliable techniques for classifying physique on the basis of three components called endomorphy, mesomorphy, and ectomorphy. These components are best described in terms of their extremes. The physique in which endomorphy predominates tends to be spheroid, with a central concentration of mass and prominence of the visceral region. Dominant mesomorphy is characterized by heavy muscle and bone, with the body approaching a square in shape. Dominant ectomorphy is found in the "long-thin" individual, whose physique is characterized by linearity, fragility, and delicacy. Most individuals, of course, are "medium" blends of these components. The extremes are relatively rare.

Research into the relationships between body build and personality traits has resulted in some consistently positive but rather small correlations. The consistency of these results would seem promising for further investigation with more refined measures of personality.

Individuality and Individual Differences. The study of "individual differences" does not of itself offer us a direct approach to the individuality of the child. There are several reasons why we must draw a distinction between (1) the individual as an example of various trait differences and (2) the individual as a whole. The reasons:

1. *Individual differences are studied analytically.* We miss thereby the opportunity for seeing these traits and abilities in relation to one another, and as they operate and interact in the working individual. The "case" studies of the psychiatrist or of the clinical psychologist are an attempt to remedy this defect

by offering a panoramic or whole view of the personality of the child.   They are, in a way, a kind of psychological biography.

Besides the various distinguishable traits and abilities, there is something in the way these are found in combination, and in the manner of their complementary relationships, that determines the total energy and achievement of the individual. Taken separately, each trait or ability of a child may be found to depart so little from the standard or norm that we cannot reasonably assume that there is anything significant here.   But when we consider the particular combination of these traits, we may then find the explanation for which we have been searching.

2. *Traits showing greater variation are more often studied.* The techniques of measurement are best suited to those traits or abilities in which all or most children show differences.   There may be other traits, however, which practically all children possess to an extent sufficient for most purposes, so that our attention is not drawn to the influence of these traits on achievement.   It is only the exceptional situation that directs our attention to the presence or absence of a certain trait, attitude, or interest.   We can ordinarily assume that by far the great majority of children come to school with the attitude of "wanting to learn."   And because this attitude is so common we do not usually have to bother about it.   But if, in an exceptional instance, a child should be infected with the parental attitude that "all book-learnin' is useless," we should then find sufficient evidence of the importance of this otherwise inconspicuous factor.

3. *Many important traits are difficult to measure.*   Many human traits, undoubtedly significant either in themselves or in combination with others, are not yet capable of refined measurement.   The inspiration received from learned and enthusiastic teachers, for example, remains unmeasured.   Techniques of measurement may in the near future be extended to such traits and other important aspects of personality.   But it is as a matter of fact only rather recently that "personality" tests and attitude scales have been thought practicable.   The availability of our scientific methods of study has then in a way tended to restrict our view of the individuality of the child to those aspects of

mind for which we were scientifically prepared to show individuality. Even if the child were given all the tests and inventories we think important, the "sum total" of these measurable traits could hardly give us the needed picture of the individual child.

4. *A genetic approach is needed* for the proper understanding of individuality. It is not enough to ask what trait differences are the important ones, but how the trait differences develop. "Personality differences" mean different things at different ages, and manifest themselves differently in the various stages of development. Some mental traits, aptitudes, or aspects of personality may be regarded as being primary, causative, or limiting in their influence. General mental maturity is certainly primary. Others, because they may ordinarily be found rather constant or because they must be considered only in the exceptional case, have more of the character of a secondary influence, and may be regarded as facilitating, inhibiting, or compensatory. In their true genetic setting within the individual, they may be found on occasion to outweigh the former in practical significance.

Every individual is unique. It is possible to regard him as a product of his "multiple group membership," having some traits typical of his sex, and others typical of his age, home, neighborhood, race, national background, social class, religion, region, and the like. From the point of view of "individual and group differences," he is a composite of the contributing influences of all these factors which modify his biological inheritance. These factors are important, but the way in which they are put together in the personal history of the individual is of the utmost importance. His personality and achievement may depend upon so many different factors, now some, now others, now this combination, now that, that each person may become as it were a law unto himself. General knowledge, interest, motive, home surroundings, neighborhood, temperament, physical condition, and attitudes may all have a bearing on a person's accomplishments. And since every individual's history is unique, pure luck or coincidence probably plays a part in the way his experiences are arranged.

PERSONALITY AND ACHIEVEMENT

The Role of Personality in School Achievement. Do personality traits influence achievement in school? Super has called attention to the limitations of the usual approaches made in studying this question (35). The *clinical* or case history approach, he says, is useful in stimulating speculation but proves little because of the subjective nature of such reports. Thus a report observing that the retardation in school of mentally normal children was associated with shyness, laziness, sensitiveness to criticism, day-dreaming, hypochondriacal fears, and the like, may not be trusted because of the absence of proper controls in the observations made. The *psychometric,* or measurement approach, is often equally inconclusive because the instruments for measuring personality are imperfect, although objective. An example of the psychometric approach is a study by Gates (17), who correlated the results of achievement tests and measures of social and emotional maturity and concluded that low and high degrees of social and emotional maturity showed no difference in school achievement. The result may have been due to a defective measure of emotional maturity. "The end result is that our current knowledge of the role of personality in education and in work is impressionistic or, when quantitative, superficial" (35, p. 483). With these limitations in mind, we may go on to illustrate some of the relations between personality and achievement which are widely accepted as important.

Undesirable emotional attitudes often explain why a child with average or above average intelligence may fail conspicuously in school, especially in such subjects as reading and arithmetic. The school psychologist may uncover emotional factors, either in connection with the home or the school, which act to set up resistances or inhibitions, or otherwise handicap the child in his work. Through remedial teaching based upon a knowledge of these emotional handicaps, the child usually responds in a manner to indicate that the true cause of the disability had been correctly diagnosed. Some cases reported by Blanchard illustrate this point very clearly.

. . . Peter, who had an IQ of 93, and a reading age of 9-10, was very poor in his arithmetic. Although he was better at problem solving than he was at computation, his arithmetic age was only 8-5. His errors were very unsystematic, and he was able at times to do the more difficult problems while failing on the easier ones. These inconsistencies made it appear that the difficulty was not due to lack of aptitude for number work, and led to an investigation of Peter's home in order to search there for a possible cause. When this matter had been gone into, it was found that Peter's mother had not only taken all the fun out of arithmetic for him, but had created in the child an adverse emotional reaction to the subject. She had done this by trying to stimulate him through appeal to fear. "If you get this wrong," she would often say while supervising his home work, "I'll whip you." Arithmetic consequently had become a very unsavory subject for Peter, and what was more serious, it was always approached in a state of mental confusion, the common result of fear. On the basis of this information, a teacher was given the task of undertaking remedial instruction with the boy. She introduced arithmetic problems into the games Peter and she played in order to "condition" him positively toward the subject. Peter readily showed his ability to handle these problems, unless he chanced to fall back into the attitude of thinking of them as "arithmetic." As long as he did not regard them as part of this "fearful" school subject, he got along very well. By the end of three months even this tendency was pretty well broken, with the result that his arithmetic age was raised to 9-6, close to his reading age. (11)

A second child from Blanchard's cases with an IQ of 133, placing him well above the average in general mental ability, was found to be exceptionally poor in reading. A search for possible emotional factors disclosed the fact that the boy's father was much too critical of him while helping him at home with his reading. A dislike and distrust of his ability to read was generated in the child. Neither the mother nor his teacher displayed any confidence in the child's ability. The detrimental effect on reading could be corrected only by treating parents and teacher as well as child.

Although instances of this kind do not perhaps form a very large percentage of ordinary school difficulties, they may at times become of great significance, particularly if the disability happens to be in reading. The ability to read has an important practical bearing on the grading of the child in school, and if he tends to be unduly deficient in this, he may find his general ability underestimated by both parents and teachers. The child himself may then come to believe in his reputed lack of ability. The feeling of inferiority so engendered may not have any serious effect upon the development of the personality as a whole, particularly if the child finds means of compensating through success in athletics or in work outside the school. But he is likely thereby to lose interest in his schoolroom activities.

Statistical studies of social, economic, and personal characteristics in relation to reading ability showed reliable correlations between superior reading ability and desirable scores on such measured traits as self-confidence, persistence, and concentration of attention, as well as personality adjustment in general (23). Reading difficulties are frequently related to emotional problems (16, 26).

Personality Factors in Life Achievement. Evidence of the influence of personality traits on over-all life achievement is shown in the Stanford follow-up study of the gifted. In 1922 these children had been rated on various traits by their teachers. In 1940 each was rated again on a number of traits by himself, his wife, and his parents. On the basis of general life achievement, they were then classified into groups. As we have seen, the difference in *intelligence* between the "most successful" (A) group and the "least successful" (C) group was insignificant. But the contrast in personality ratings was clear. All three sets of ratings—by self, wife, and parents—"showed considerable agreement in rating the A's far higher than the C's on Perseverance, Self-Confidence, and Integration toward goals" (38, p. 351). A's were also rated higher on "Absence of inferiority feelings," and the wives' ratings reflected results favorable to A's on "Happiness" and "Good nature." In ratings made by the field investigators "the A group greatly outclassed the C group in Appearance, Attractiveness, Alertness, Poise, Attentiveness, Curiosity, Originality, and to a somewhat lesser degree, in Speech and Friendliness." The final conclusion of the authors is this: "Everything considered, there is nothing in which the

A and C groups present a greater contrast than in drive to achieve and in all-round social adjustment" (38). That the personality traits were the effects or by-products of successful achievement, rather than causes of success, would be contra-indicated by the finding that similar differences in personality traits had been found during childhood in 1922, eighteen years before.

The Role of Interests in Achievement.   The student's inter-est in school work is at least partly determined by his abilities. He must be able enough to enjoy some feeling of success in order to maintain interest and satisfaction in school tasks.   The belief that ability is the primary determining cause of interest—that interest in doing a thing naturally follows from the ability to do it well—might lead us to minimize the importance of interests in the development of abilities.   But the relation between in-terest and ability, we must believe, is not so direct and straight-forward as such a simply expressed explanation of the correla-tional findings would suggest.   We must keep in mind what ordinarily intervenes in the life-history of a person between the childhood appearance of aptitude and its adult fruition in achievement.   It is probably true that the possession of aptitude to achieve in some particular field generates a corresponding interest, but this interest does not develop *in vacuo* as a natural and necessary consequent of ability.   Unless the able student knows that his performance is superior or that it does really indi-cate an aptitude, and unless his ability gains for him recognition from others, the corresponding interest will very probably not develop.

Ability or aptitude then seems to generate interest through the interacting social situation.   Narrow interests on the part of teachers themselves, or for that matter on the part of the whole school system and its aims, may tend at times to prevent the individual aptitudes of children from attaining the social expression and recognition necessary for the development of corresponding interests.   On the other hand, when the school offers a wide variety of opportunity for the expression of desir-able personal tendencies, through the broadening of curricular offerings, and when teachers understand and accept the possibility of variety in interests and achievement, education would seem to be conducive to an ideal combination, throughout life, of interest and ability.

While it is doubtful that interest can "add a cubit to one's stature" so far as some of the more fundamental aptitudes so far studied are concerned, it is very probable that, in that genetic interval between aptitude and achievement, interest would be indicative of the urge to greater accomplishment and would actually result in such. We know that this is true of specific forms of motivation and of the influence of definite goals of achievement.

Measured interests (e.g., Strong, Kuder) are generally assumed to show the direction in which a person's abilities are likely to develop, or in what field his achievement is likely to bring greater satisfaction. A measure of ability (e.g., general intelligence) is taken to estimate the level to which his abilities will develop, or the level of achievement which is possible. We may therefore inquire, as we did about intelligence, whether the results of interest inventories have been found useful in predicting educational and vocational choices, satisfaction, and achievement. Some conclusions of Carter, based on his review of a decade of research on this matter, are as follows:

1. The vocational interests of high school students are incompletely developed, but they are highly individual, definitely patterned, and much more reliable and permanent than earlier studies would indicate. The changes which take place as time goes on are orderly and to some extent predictable.

2. The best interest inventories are useful in the prediction both of educational choice and of vocational choice and satisfaction. They are much less useful in predicting educational success (scholarship) or vocational success. In predicting vocational success, interest inventories are sometimes effective within a given occupation. (14)

Interests in Life Achievement. Strong's follow-up studies indicate a relationship between one's interests and eventual satisfaction in college and in occupations (34). That such satisfaction is an important factor in life achievement is shown by the differences in interests of the "most successful" and "least successful" of the gifted men studied by Terman (38). A comparison of the scores made by these two groups on the Strong Vocational Interest Blank, administered in 1940, revealed that the A's ("most successful") were significantly higher in occupational level of interests, and made a large number of higher scores on the scales for different occupations, particularly those above the skilled labor level. When the A's and C's were compared on scores for the occupation in which they were engaged, the A's generally scored higher. The A group was well adjusted occupationally, while the C's were for the most part vocational misfits who were more frequently unemployed, changed jobs frequently, reported that they had drifted into their jobs, and expressed job dissatisfaction. The Strong results were probably therefore a reflection of those factors which made for good or poor occupational adjustment. Furthermore, the A group apparently had a wider range of interests than the C's, as shown by their greater number of hobbies and higher self-ratings of interests in various fields. Let us note again that the two groups did not differ significantly in intelligence as children in 1922. On the other hand, they did differ in family backgrounds. More than three times as many A fathers had graduated from college, and more than twice as many A fathers were in professional occupations. "The important point here," say the authors, "is that the educational tradition was stronger in families of the A group" (38).

Attitudes and Scholastic Success. Many psychologists would maintain that "attitude is more important than aptitude" in both school and life achievement. This does not imply that very low aptitude can always be compensated for, but does recognize that large differences in motivation are more important in determining success or failure than small differences in aptitude.

What attitudes are important in school work? A study by Herriott controlled the effect of intelligence in order to study the effect of attitudes alone on scholastic success (22). Two attitudes emerged as important. One, called the "evaluative-nonevaluative" attitude, showed that the more thoughtful student who appraises carefully the text and instructor's thinking is more successful than the student who accepts what he is told without appraisal. The second, or "persevering-vacillating," shows the importance of maintaining a purpose in spite of difficulties, as opposed to fluctuation in opinion and purpose. These were found positively related to college grades, over and above the contribution of scholastic aptitude itself. Both of these attitudes are no doubt related to interest factors, although this was not specifically studied.

Lecky (24) makes some astute observations of the role attitudes play in such specific deficiencies as arithmetic and spelling. He makes the point that the intelligent student may be deficient in spelling not because he cannot learn, but because he *will* not learn, owing to a self-evaluative attitude, or self-definition, of "poor speller."

Let us take the case of an intelligent student who is deficient, say, in spelling. In almost every instance poor spellers have been tutored and practiced in spelling over long periods without improvement. For some reason such a student has a special handicap in learning how to spell, though not in learning the other subjects which are usually considered more difficult. This deficiency is not due to a lack of ability, but rather to an active resistance which prevents him from learning how to spell in spite of the extra instruction. The resistance arises from the fact that at some time in the past the suggestion that he is a poor speller was accepted and incorporated into his definition of himself, and is now an integral part of his personality. . . . If he defines himself as a poor speller, the misspelling of a certain proportion of the words which he uses becomes for him a moral issue. He misspells words for the same reason that he refuses to be a thief. That is, he must endeavor to behave in a manner consistent with his conception of himself. (24, pp. 103-104)

Such an attitude would explain why a person misspells a consistent proportion of words per page, misspells English words but not French, and why (according to Lecky's experience) he learns to spell very rapidly after the attitude, or self-definition, changes. Persons who "do not have a mathematical mind" may also be victims of their own attitude. Intelligent persons who "cannot" learn arithmetic and complain of inability to concentrate on it are often convinced that trying is useless and have no intention to learn. For such persons, drill is less important than counseling or other experiences that will lead to a change of attitude.

PROBLEMS IN SCHOOL ADJUSTMENT

Feelings of Insecurity and Social Inadequacy. Clinical studies of children suggest that some of the more serious of the childish conflicts result from a loss of the sense of security or a destruction of the feeling of social adequacy. The maintenance of personal morale requires that we be able to set an appreciative value upon our own existence and endeavors. The foundation of mental health is a feeling of worthiness and adequacy. For this the child is dependent on his acceptance as a worthy member of the group to which he belongs, on the esteem in which he is held, and on the implied or expressed appreciation of his efforts. This seems to be of particular importance in childhood, before strong idealistic goals of endeavor are set up. Adults may be able to withstand social disapproval to some extent, but a child cannot except in very small doses. Following are some of the ways in which the child's feeling of social adequacy may be destroyed or jeopardized:

1. Harsh criticism or sarcasm. Nothing he does seems to be right. The adult may be judging from his own standards without regard to the maturity of the child. The child may not be able to make use of the "adult discount" of criticism, and is forced to accept adverse or belittling remarks at their face value, with consequent feelings of inadequacy.

2. Physical defects or inferiority, particularly if unfavorable attention be often directed toward them. To be made to feel "different" from other children is often synonymous with being made to feel inferior.

3. Undue restrictions and discipline. The child may come to the conclusion that it is wholly an adults' world, or that nothing he wants to do is ever right. This may often conflict with the development of a sense of responsibility or destroy personal initiative.

4. The doubt of parentage, or a belief that he is an "unwanted child," may destroy the child's sense of security and cut him adrift from the more intimate social world of which he is supposedly an esteemed member.

5. Obstacles to achievement too great, or holding up to the child ideals which are so far beyond his ability that even a modicum of success is impossible.

6. Loneliness, in which there may be very little opportunity for social stimulation or social recognition.

7. Misunderstanding of childish motives. When motives are read wrongly by adults who do not appear to understand the rather harmless nature of many childish misdemeanors, a feeling of strong guilt or of inferiority may result.

Adjustment of the Child's World to Reality. The child tends to construct an ideal or wishful world which sooner or later comes into conflict with reality. If the two are so antagonistic that no compromise is possible, or if the demand for a change in his world of thought is too sudden, a serious internal conflict may result. The following are some examples of this source of difficulty.

1. The destruction of cherished beliefs. Various forms of disillusionment, such as that found in connection with Santa Claus, with the all-powerfulness or impeccability of parents, with the realization of being an adopted child, may, if these are brought home to the child with a great degree of suddenness or decisiveness, destroy some of the dominant values in his personality development. A sense of loss may be created, which the child will sometimes attempt to resist by clinging tenaciously to the threatened beliefs, bringing him into further conflict with reality.

There is a similar source of difficulty for early youth when the broadening of scientific knowledge forces a serious revision of some of the earlier beliefs accepted up until then as matters of fact. Disillusionment can be at times a serious matter in the development of personality, and it is likely to become so if it results in loss without the creation of compensating values. The startling "debunking" methods of some teachers of modern science have been shown to create at times personal difficulties and conflicts in some of their students. Much of the disillusionment is perhaps necessary as a first step toward sounder values, but such a finding should lead us to pause and ask ourselves whether this may not be done too suddenly or without constructive compensation. "Knowledge for knowledge's sake" is after all an abstract ideal that may ignore the close relationship existing among all aspects of mental development.

2. Conflict of customs, ideals, and morals. The child may find, in certain types of communities, that the accepted life values vary a great deal from person to person, or from house to house. He may consequently have difficulty in reconciling the new with the old. It is significant, in this connection, that a large percentage of juvenile delinquency has been found to be associated with certain neighborhoods known as "delinquency areas." These are characterized by an unstable social environment, by mobility of the population and polyglot mixture of racial groups, with the attendant confusion and breakdown of customs and traditions.

3. Inability to reconcile all behavior tendencies. The growing child may be very much disturbed by the outcropping of tendencies to conduct very much at variance with his tendencies at other times. The lack of understanding of the nature or of the complexity of his own motives may create difficulties for him, particularly if he has no way of knowing that similar tendencies are likely to be found in all children of his age or condition. Unless he sees how human motives can be organized around worthy goals, whatever their apparent crudity, and that other individuals in whom these tendencies apparently do not appear, at least on the surface, have succeeded in doing just this, he may feel that his ideals of conduct are practically impossible of realization. The persistence of conscious direction which is necessary for the satisfactory integration of his personality may then be wanting.

Problem Behavior. The maladjustment of the personality is variously expressed in childhood, as has already been indicated. As noted by the teacher, these expressions may extend from the less troublesome manifestations such as nail-biting, stuttering, queerness, flightiness, and isolation, to the more conspicuous ones of delinquency, intractability, antagonisms, bullying, truancy, and hysterical illnesses. Many of these develop into "problem-behavior." As Baker and Traphagen point out, children manifesting such behavior are often accused of deliberate meanness, whereas in most cases the underlying cause is to be found in some internal conflict (8). These authors have devised a comprehensive "behavior-scale" which may be employed both in gauging the seriousness of the problem-behavior and in diagnosing its causes. These are classified as: Personality and Social Factors; Home Atmosphere and School Factors; Parental and Physical Factors; and Health and Physical Factors. The order given has been found to be indicative of their relative significance, from high to low. Table 20

TABLE 20

Rank Order of Apparent Importance of Selected Items of Detroit Behavior Scale *

Rank Order	Item	Rank Order	Item
1	General behavior	11	Interests or hobbies
2	Attitude toward school	12	General home atmosphere
3	Discipline	13	Recreational facilities
4	Personality type	14	Playmates or companions
5	Pity, sympathy, etc.	15	Parents' attitude
6	Initiative and ambition	16	Parents' social adjustment
7	Anger, rage, etc.	17	Nervousness
8	Social type	18	Ideals of home
9	Attitude toward home	19	Excitement, shock, etc.
10	Scholarship	20	Family recreation

* After Baker and Traphagen (8).

shows a ranking of a selected few of the sixty-six individual items of the behavior scale. The "rank order" given in the first column indicates how well the particular item has been found to differentiate between a group of "behavior" children and a normal group. This may also be taken as a reflection of its relative causal influence. Although some of these items may be further analyzed psychologically, it is interesting to note that many factors referring to the home are included in the first twenty. Intelligence, not given in the table, was found to rank twenty-first in importance.

The results of another study describe for us some characteristic attitudes of the school-age problem child:

> Thinks school does not help children; thinks one cannot be happy in school; does not like to go to assemblies; thinks only "sissies" obey the school rules; thinks that good marks do not mean much.
>
> Thinks his teacher does not understand him; that she promotes only pupils she likes; that she likes to preach to the class; that he is often punished for things he did not do.
>
> Likes to play by himself; thinks a boy is a "sissy" if he speaks to a girl; thinks one should not belong to clubs in schools; thinks other pupils make him bad; is teased by his classmates; does not like to go to parties; gets "sore" when he loses in a game; gets tired of play quickly; wishes he had friends.
>
> Cannot make himself do the right thing; stammers and stutters when he has to recite; usually falls or stumbles over things; likes to show off in class; wishes he were somebody else; worries a great deal about school; thinks he will never amount to anything.
>
> Wishes he were a baby again; thinks his brothers and sisters do not like him; does not like to visit his relatives; thinks he does not get a fair deal at home; often punished by his parents; is very much afraid of father or mother; is ashamed of his parents; thinks he is a stranger at home; thinks his parents do not understand him. (29)

The Teacher's Appreciation of Problem Behavior. Wickman (41) asked a number of teachers to make a list of any conduct of children which they thought undesirable and to rate the various samples according to what they regarded as their relative seriousness. He then had several psychiatrists and mental hygienists rate the same traits in the order of seriousness. The difference in rating is very interesting, showing that the teacher stresses efficient control of the school situation while the psychiatrist favors integration of personality and adjustment. Following is the ranking given by the teachers, going from most serious to least serious:

1. Immoralities, dishonesties, transgression against authority.
2. Violations of orderliness in classroom, lack of application to school work.

3. Extravagant, aggressive personality and behavior traits.
4. Withdrawing, recessive personality and behavior traits.

The mental hygienists rated the traits as follows, from most to least serious:

1. Withdrawing, recessive personality and behavior traits.
2. Dishonesties, cruelty, temper tantrums, truancy.
3. Immoralities, violations of school work requirements, extravagant behavior traits.
4. Transgressions against authority, violations of orderliness in the classroom.

The fact that the traits placed last in importance by the teachers are placed first in seriousness by the psychiatrists, along with the other reversals of order, might incline us to believe that the teacher (largely by force of circumstances) tends to take too narrow a view of mental development and the educative process. Some of the author's conclusions should be at least very challenging to the thoughtful teacher, and to the interested layman as well:

Teacher's reactions to the behavior problems of children are largely determined by the direct effect which the behavior produces on the teachers themselves. In so far as the behavior attacks the teacher's moral sensitiveness, personal integrity, authority, and immediate teaching purposes, it becomes recognizable as a problem in behavior; in so far as behavior is agreeable to teachers, respects their authority, fits in with their teaching purposes as well as their ethical beliefs, it is considered desirable behavior.

Attacking types of conduct are regarded by teachers as the most undesirable forms of behavior, while many unhealthy tendencies of withdrawal and dependency are not recognized as symptomatic of maladjustment.

The usual treatment of behavior disorders in children is directed toward the undesirable behavior which is the symptom of maladjustment, instead of toward the underlying causes that produce the maladjustment. (41)

In another study, teachers seemed to stress undesirable personality traits, including regressive behavior, rather than violations of school regulations and disciplinary offenses (28). The fact that these teachers were enrolled in a course in child psychology at the time they were asked to submit case studies of maladjustment in children suggests perhaps their superior insight into behavior problems.

Student-Teacher Relations. The interaction between the teacher and students in the classroom poses some problems in human relations. The teacher and students bring to the school different interests, attitudes, and values—vastly different outlooks on the world, people, the school and what it stands for. The interaction is thus to a large extent a clash of personality differences—not necessarily fights or quarrels, but difficulties in communication. The extroverted teacher may not appreciate or understand the introverted child, and the introverted teacher may be sympathetic toward the shy children and ignore (if possible!) or disapprove of the extroverts. The English teacher with literary-artistic interests may not "reach" the mechanically minded boy who is in turn puzzled or bored by her strange outlook on life. The important point is that students "catch" these things, and the personality of the teacher may thus become an important factor in stimulating or inhibiting learning, regardless of instructional skill.

Many discussions of the "teacher's personality" consist of statements about the desirable qualities the teacher must have. A typical list would run as follows (31): Fairness, kindness, good-natured or pleasant, sense of humor, patience, inspiring, good personal appearance, sociability, interest in work, strong character, sympathetic, politeness, neatness, dignity, intelligent, broad-minded, etc. Faced with such a list, any teacher might well have feelings of inferiority! But no one can doubt their importance in the classroom. On the other hand, these terms lack precision, since the way a person defines or judges fairness, kindness, sense of humor, good appearance, politeness, or broad-mindedness (to take a few examples) is itself a personality characteristic. The teacher of a given sex, age, or social background can be expected to think, feel, and act differently from another who differs in these respects. All kinds of people are teachers. Whether a given teacher will impress any particular student as congenial or kind or inspiring will depend on the personality and background of both teacher and student. It may thus be quite meaningless to describe the "ideal teacher" by a list of descriptive adjectives.

The effective teacher is one skilled in human relations. This is essentially a matter of understanding the child and of making one's self understood, as well as giving the child the feeling that *he* is understood. Conflicts are perhaps inevitable because the teacher's background and point of view differ markedly from those of students. Successful human relations in the classroom consist in dealing with these problems so as to contribute to the growth of the student. The successful teacher is not required to be a saint, a prophet, a genius, or any idealized kind of personality. To succeed, she need only be aware of individual differences in ability and motives, accept these differences, and allow for them. The ineffective or harmful teacher is one who cannot do this, because she is a poorly adjusted and rigid person, or will not because of certain rigid notions about human behavior which cause her to reject and disapprove of her pupils.

The contrast drawn by Anderson (5) between "dominative" and "socially integrative" behavior by teachers illustrates the difference between poor and successful teacher-student relations. Teachers may solve conflicts with students through domination by dictating what is to be done and riding roughshod over the spontaneous inclinations of students as to how it is to be done. This is an inflexible approach. The "socially integrative" approach is flexible because it allows the child to "be himself," allows for interplay of individual differences, and makes it possible for the individual spontaneously to adapt his behavior to the desires and purposes of others. This approach thus encourages the growth of students. Says Anderson: "If understanding is possible only to the extent that others are free to express themselves, be themselves, then accepting others as they are is not only a good psychotherapeutic technique, but a highly desirable educational technique as well" (4). Research has demonstrated (6) that the socially integrative type of human relations has "mental hygiene value" to the extent that it produces spontaneity and initiative in the behavior of students.

The Adjustment of Teachers. The adjustment problems and mental health of teachers have been receiving increased attention during recent years. Although most investigations along this line have been chiefly concerned with the effect the teacher has on students (3, 6), there is also some suggestion that the teacher's personality traits affect the way she evaluates the behavior of students. Clark (15) found significant relationships between teachers' scores on the Guilford-Martin inventory and the degree of annoyance shown by teachers to such pupil behavior items as "Doesn't pay attention to class discussion," "Crowds ahead of others in line," "Wears dirty clothes," and "Is impolite to other pupils." Some types of pupil behavior were more annoying to teachers with good mental health, and other types were annoying to teachers whose adjustment was less satisfactory. It would be expected that differing modes of adjustment between teacher and pupil might have a profound effect on human relations in the classroom. Stagner remarks that "despite courses in educational psychology, teachers often are deplorably insensitive to the emotional problems of their pupils. The child is perceived as another source of frustration, rather than as a human being trying to adapt to inner needs and external pressures. Even at the college level one sees little awareness of student personalities" (33). Insensitivity or positive attitudes of rejection by teachers can do untold harm in the classroom. All that has been said of maladjustment or immaturity of parents applies equally to teachers. The emotionally insecure child with poor home adjustment is not only more likely to be a "problem child" in school, but is exposed to double jeopardy at the hands of the poorly adjusted teacher. Anderson, as a "psychiatrist who discusses the teacher," points out that the "maturity and integration of the personality of the teacher have now come to be considered among the most importance qualifications for that individual who would maintain the mental health of the classroom and guide in the all-around development of the personalities of the individual pupils" (7).

The most effective way of sensitizing teachers to children's problems appears to be the child-centered approach, through which individual children are studied in the context of home environment and play situations. Baruch has shown that focussing the attention of teachers on the child's emotional problems, through child-study procedures, leads not only to better understanding of children but improved self-understanding on the part of the teacher. In her study, the teachers showed attitudes of rejection, excessive moralism, and "discipline" in the beginning, but the shift toward the adjustment viewpoint helped teachers and pupils alike (9).

REFERENCES

1. ALLPORT, G. W. A test for ascendance-submission. *J. abn. soc. Psychol.*, 1928, **23**, 118-136.
2. ANASTASI, A., & FOLEY, J. P. *Differential psychology*. New York: Macmillan, 1949.
3. ANDERSON, H. H. Domination and social integration in the behavior of kindergarten children and teachers. *Genet. Psychol. Monogr.*, 1939, **21**, 287-385.
4. ANDERSON, H. H. Domination and socially integrative behavior. In BARKER, R. G., *et al., Child behavior and development.* New York: McGraw-Hill, 1943.
5. ANDERSON, H. H., & BREWER, H. M. Dominative and socially integrative behavior of kindergarten teachers. *Appl. Psychol. Monogr.*, 1945, No. 6.
6. ANDERSON, H. H., & BREWER, J. E. Effects of teachers' dominative and socially integrative contacts on children's classroom behavior. *Appl. Psychol. Monogr.*, 1946, No. 8.
7. ANDERSON, V. V. *Psychiatry and education.* New York: Harper, 1932.
8. BAKER, H. J., & TRAPHAGEN, V. *The diagnosis and treatment of behavior problem children.* New York: Macmillan, 1935.
9. BARUCH, D. *Understanding young children.* New York: Teach. Coll. Bur. Publ., Columbia Univ., 1949.
10. BERDIE, R. F. Interests. In *Encyclopedia of psychology*. New York: Phil. Library, 1946.
11. BLANCHARD, P. Attitudes and educational disabilities. *Ment. Hygiene,* 1929, **13**, 550-563.
12. CATTELL, R. B. *Description and measurement of personality.* Yonkers: World Book Co., 1946.
13. CARTER, H. D., PYLES, M. K., & BRETNALL, E. P. A comparative study of factors in vocational interest scores of high school boys. *J. educ. Psychol.*, 1935, **26**, 81-98.
14. CARTER, H. D. Vocational interests and job orientation. *Appl. Psychol. Monogr.*, No. 2, Stanford Univ. Press, 1944.

15. CLARK, E. J. The relationship between the personality traits of elementary school teachers and their evaluation of objectionable pupil behavior. *J. educ. Research,* 1951, **45,** 61-66.

16. Clinical studies in reading. *Educational Monographs,* I, *Supp.* 68, 1949.

17. GATES, A. I. The nature and educational significance of physical status and of mental, psychological, social and emotional maturity. *J. educ. Psychol.,* 1924, **15,** 329-358.

18. GOUGH, H. G. The relationship of socio-economic status to personality inventory and achievement test scores. *J. educ. Psychol.,* 1946, **37,** 527-540.

19. GUILFORD, J. P., & GUILFORD, R. B. An analysis of the factors in a typical test of introversion-extroversion. *J. abn. soc. Psychol.,* 1934, **28,** 377-399.

20. GUILFORD, J. P., & GUILFORD, R. B. Personality factors S, E, and M, and their measurement. *J. Psychol.,* 1936, **2,** 109-127. See also *J. abn. soc. Psycho!.,* 1939, **34,** 21-36, and 239-248.

21. HEIDBREDER, E. Introversion and extroversion in men and women. *J. abn. soc. Psychol.,* 1927, **22,** 52-61.

22. HERRIOTT, M. E. Attitudes as factors of scholastic success. *Univ. Illinois Educ. Res. Bull. No.* 47, 1929.

23. LADD, M. R. The relation of social, economic, and personal characteristics to reading ability. *Teach. Coll. Contr. Educ.,* 1933, No. 582.

24. LECKY, P. *Self-consistency: a theory of personality.* New York: Island Press, 1945.

25. LOVELL, C. A. A study of the factor structure of thirteen personality variables. *Educ. psychol. Measmt.* 1945, **5,** 335-350.

26. LYONS, N. T. Relating the reading program to individual differences. *Elem. School J.,* 1949, 389-394.

27. MOSIER, C. I. A factor analysis of certain neurotic tendencies. *Psychometrika,* 1937, **2,** 263-286.

28. PECK, L. Teachers' reports of unadjusted school children. *J. educ. Psychol.,* 1935, **26,** 123-138.

29. PINTNER, R., MALLER, J. B., FORLANO, G., & AXELROD, H. The measurement of pupil adjustment. *J. educ. Res.,* 1935, **28,** 334-346.

30. REMMERS, H. H., & BELL, S. E. Generalized attitude scales. *J. soc. Psychol.,* 1934, **5,** 298-312.

31. *Review of Educational Research,* 1931, I, No. 2. Teacher personnel.

32. SHELDON, W. H., *et al. The varieties of human physique.* New York: Harper, 1940.

33. STAGNER, R. *Psychology of personality,* 2d ed. New York: McGraw-Hill, 1948.

34. STRONG, E. K. JR. *Vocational interests of men and women.* Stanford Univ. Press, 1943.

35. SUPER, D. E. *Appraising vocational fitness by means of psychological tests.* New York: Harper, 1949.

36. SUPER, D. E., & ROPER, S. An objective technique for testing vocational interests. *J. appl. Psychol.,* 1941, **25,** 487-498.

37. TERMAN, L. M., & MILES, C. C. *Sex and personality: studies in masculinity and femininity.* New York: McGraw-Hill, 1936.

38. TERMAN, L. M., & ODEN, M. *The gifted child grows up.* Stanford Univ. Press, 1947.

39. THURSTONE, L. L. A multiple factor study of vocational interests. *Pers. J.,* 1931, **10,** 198-205.

40. WARREN, H. C., & CARMICHAEL, L. *Elements of human psychology.* Boston: Houghton Mifflin, 1930.

41. WICKMAN, E. K. *Children's behavior and teacher attitudes.* New York: Commonwealth Fund, 1928.

SELECTED READINGS

ALLPORT, G. W. *Personality.* New York: Holt, 1937. For general reference.

BAKER, H. J., & TRAPHAGEN, V. *The diagnosis and treatment of behavior problem children.* New York: Macmillan, 1936. Based on a discussion of 66 items (possible causes) known to be significant in the diagnosis of behavior maladjustments.

CAMERON, N. *The psychology of behavior disorders.* Boston: Houghton Mifflin, 1947. Chs. 4, 5, 6.

CRONBACH, L. J. *Essentials of psychological testing.* New York: Harper, 1949. Pt. III contains chapters on personality testing.

ENGLISH, H. B. *Child psychology.* New York: Holt, 1951. Shows in a vivid way how teachers and parents can study children for understanding. Emphasis on techniques.

JERSILD, A. T. *In search of self.* New York: Teach. Coll. Bur. Publ., Columbia Univ., 1951. Explores the role of the teacher in promoting self-understanding of students.

NATIONAL SOCIETY FOR STUDY OF EDUCATION. *49th Yearbook,* 1950. Pt. II, The education of exceptional children.

STRONG, E. K. JR. *Vocational interests of men and women.* Stanford Univ. Press, 1943.

SUPER, D. E. *Appraising vocational fitness by means of psychological tests.* New York: Harper, 1949. Chs. 16-18 on vocational interests.

THORPE, L. P. *The psychology of mental health.* New York: Ronald Press, 1950. Chs. 16 and 17 on the school and mental health.

11

PROVIDING FOR INDIVIDUAL DIFFERENCES

THE FACT that students differ greatly in abilities, needs, and motives raises some important problems in the school. The popular but inaccurate concept of "mass education" implies that the curriculum and the teaching methods should be more or less standardized. The school may aim at a kind of standard product, with a certain level of competency in the three R's and a certain standard knowledge of history, government, and geography. In this familiar pattern of education there is real danger that the school may be run for the advantage of the teachers, with emphasis on "covering the material," and that some individuals will be lost sight of in the process. It is certain that students profit unequally from classroom procedures, and that the educational process has always resulted in a number of "waste products" who do not make the grade. If the aim of education is to develop the abilities and traits of each individual for adequate adjustment to a way of life in society, the school must be concerned with the child as a whole individual. It must provide for individual differences.

Even if the school were to aim at a standard product, it could not afford to treat all individuals alike. They are unequal in learning abilities, and teaching must be adapted to these inequalities. All cannot be motivated in the same way, because all are not equally rewarded by the same experiences. Individuals differ in needs; one may need help in making friends, another needs help in studying, another needs skilled help in planning a career, and another needs help in adjusting to a poor home situation. The teacher must treat students differently in order to equalize the opportunities of benefiting from the work of the school, if for no other reason. The school guidance program, designed to meet individual needs, is based on the idea that education is an individual process of development. Guidance, as a general term, includes all those provisions made by the school for assessing the abilities and traits of the individual child, for gathering information that will assist the teacher in understanding him, and for adapting the work of the school to his needs. This chapter is therefore concerned with certain practical problems which individual differences impose on the school, and with some techniques of guidance.

Pupil Differences in Ability

Variability Within the Classroom. The scatter of ability within a school grade can become a very practical matter. It may reasonably be supposed, for example, that it would be easier to teach a class of children who were fairly like one another, or homogeneous, in their ability than a class containing a great variety of individual differences. The variations in ability within a school grade are usually found to extend from the norm for that grade both upward and downward to the norms for other grades, one, two, three, or more years higher or lower. It is not at all unusual to find, say in the fifth grade, and in regard to most subjects, some pupils who are not inferior to the average seventh-grade child and some who are not superior to the average third-grade child. The average teacher who is assigned to a fifth grade is often attempting to teach a range of five or six grades of ability. We cannot of course make a universally valid statement about the range of ability, because the extent of this will depend upon a number of things, including the particular ability (reading, writing, etc.) we are considering, and the rigidity of the grading or promoting system in vogue in the particular school system. We may say, however, that in practically all cases the range of ability within any grade is greater than might be expected. Never can we take it for granted that the grade in which a child happens to be located is always a good index of his ability. There is actually a greater difference between individual pupils in the same grade than between the averages of successive grades.

An overlapping of ability from grade to grade is a consequence of the scatter of ability in each grade. The amount of overlapping may be spoken of in terms of percentage. Thus it is not uncommon to find that 10 to 20 per cent of the pupils of a particular grade are superior to the average child in the next highest grade, and the same number inferior to the average of the next lowest grade. From 5 to 10 per cent are superior and inferior respectively to the average of the two grades above and two grades below. A small percentage of fourth-grade pupils would be found more able than the average of sixth-graders, and a small percentage of the latter below the average of the fourth grade. The overlapping of ability in the grades, if graphed, would look something like Figure 44. Kelley (8) found that in general the norm for one grade is separated from the norm of the next highest, or of the next lowest, by about .9 sigma for a grade. The statistically minded may convert this, by use of statistical tables, to estimates of overlapping in terms of percentage.

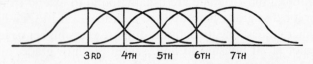

3RD   4TH   5TH   6TH   7TH

FIGURE 44. Overlapping of Ability in the Grades. (From Gast and Skinner, *Fundamentals of Educational Psychology*, by permission of Benj. H. Sanborn & Co.)

The pupils within a single grade are usually found to be more homogeneous in some abilities than in others. They are less homogeneous, as a rule, in intelligence or general mental ability than in the special scholastic abilities. We might of course expect this if the children are promoted mainly on the basis of these scholastic abilities. Even in these, however, there is considerable variation, depending on the subject. The children of an ordinary grade are probably more alike in spelling, history, and geography, for example, than in such subjects as reading and arithmetic (19). This in turn will probably depend upon whether it is a high or low grade, and upon the emphasis and adequacy of the methods of instruction. Some interesting facts about a school system may be disclosed by studying the relative variability within the grades in different subjects. Thus a school system that places great emphasis upon arithmetic in grading and in teaching would tend to show greater homogeneity, within a grade, in arithmetic achievement than in some of the other scholastic abilities.

As increased recognition was given to the scatter of ability within grades, and to the overlapping of ability from grade to grade, the traditional methods of planning curricula and evaluating pupil progress were seriously challenged. If progress from grade to grade is determined by achievement, we should expect the grades to be fairly homogeneous with respect to ability, but heterogeneous with respect to chronological age. Some years ago it was common to find sixteen-year-olds, for example, in the fifth grade along with pupils ten and eleven years of age. As social and age groupings were taken into account in grade placement, however, the schools went through a transition period in which confused grading procedures existed throughout the school system. From a study of levels of ability in New York State high schools in 1932, Coxe (3) suggested that the schools were "relinquishing grade standards of achievement but have not as yet made adequate provision for the wide range of achievement in each grade." The traditional approach in curriculum building was to provide courses and syllabi for successive grades on the assumption that higher grades represented higher levels of ability. Each grade was treated, in other words, as though it were homogeneous. It is now increasingly recognized that the professional problem of teaching is to select and present educational materials suitable to different levels of ability in the same grade (11).

The Question of Homogeneous Grouping. It has often seemed reasonable, in view of the apparently large variations in ability to be found in the typical school grade, to "section" classes according to levels of ability. The more homogeneous classes would presumably result in more effective teaching and learning. This was thoroughly tried and studied in many places a number of years ago, but the results, even when measured in terms of pupil achievement, were generally disappointing. According to one survey of such studies, "experiments fail to show consistent statistically or educationally significant differences in the achievement of pupils of homogeneous groups and pupils of equal ability in heterogeneous groups" (13). Most of the experiments were too short, and did not allow for the application of different teaching methods or curricula for different levels of ability. Furthermore, there is some question whether the type of standardized achievement tests used to measure educational "gains" during the experimental period are really valid for measuring the outcomes of instruction. These studies did, however, show that the whole problem is much more complex than it appears to be. Whatever advantages might result from homogeneous grouping depend on the school subject, on the methods of teaching employed, and even on the teachers themselves. The educational gains are very difficult to assess, even with modern experimental designs and statistical methods. Homogeneous grouping appears to benefit slower learners more than the bright pupils.

One outcome of the studies in homogeneous grouping was the concept of the "enriched curriculum" for gifted children. A pioneer study by Gray and Hollingworth, for example, involved a comparison between two groups of very bright children, one group being enrolled in a "special opportunity class" while the other was not. The special class devoted only half time to regular school subjects, and spent the remainder in such "extras" as conversational French, English composition, music, and following their interests in such fields as biography, history of civilization, science, and mathematics. At the end of three years, they were equal in ordinary school achievement to the control group, who had given full time to the regular school program. The advantages of homogeneous grouping for gifted children appeared to lie not in gains in the ordinary subjects, but in an "enrichment of scholastic experience with additional intellectual opportunities" (5).

Whatever advantages might result from homogeneous grouping are offset by disadvantages, from the point of view of the school as a whole (11). Apart from gains in knowledge and skill, what attitudes might result from sectioning? There is evidence, first of all, that students will be aware of the grouping and the basis on which it is done, no matter how carefully the school might attempt to conceal it. The groups will inevitably show age differences, with the younger and smaller ones separated from the older ones. The bright students may think of themselves as a kind of élite group, and the less bright as the "dumbbell class." (Also, since ability is related to socioeconomic status, the ability groups reflect differences between relatively privileged and underprivileged economic groups. Such grouping will result in a social stratification within the school which, many believe, brings about undemocratic attitudes and makes wholesome social participation in group life very difficult. ᵂAlso, the stimulation afforded the brighter students may be offset by the relative lack of incentive for those students segregated into a group of lesser ability.

Individual Differences and the Curriculum. Since students differ in needs, interests, and abilities, it seems evident that no one standard curriculum can meet the needs of everyone or result in equal educational benefit to all. Curriculum building is educational science, and depends on the principles of educational psychology if the curriculum is to be adapted to students. In the elementary grades there is perhaps more agreement on what to teach than on when to teach it. In secondary and higher education, provisions are more commonly made for differences in interests and vocational opportunities, and this imposes a necessity on the student for choosing a curriculum. It also requires the school to furnish the guidance necessary to wise choice.

The question of when to teach a particular subject can best be answered by information about its level of difficulty and the ability of students to master it. At what mental age, or at what grade level, should we expect children to add numbers giving sums over 10? When children are taught simple addition at the various primary grade levels, we find that the proportion of children who can do this increases from grade to grade, or increases with mental age. At some level, all children will be able to do it. One rule of thumb used by curriculum builders is this: When 75 per cent of the pupils of a given grade or mental age have learned satisfactorily, that particular age or grade level becomes a kind of standard. Addition to sums over 10 was thus determined to be in the vicinity of MA 7-7, because 75 per cent of the pupils could do it at that level. This is then thought to be the appropriate level at which to teach it. If introduced earlier, it will require more teaching time if the majority of children are to learn it satisfactorily. The standard of 75 per cent is of course arbitrary, there being no psychological reason for this figure. Educators must determine what percentage is desirable or necessary. It should be clear that some children will be able to do this at chronological age six, while others may not be able to master it by age 10.

By similar quantitative methods it has been determined that MA 6-5 to 7 is required for normal progress in reading, and lists of frequently used words for spelling have been classified for different grade levels according to level of difficulty. In arithmetic, children of MA 8-9 can learn multiplication of numbers with products under 20, but multiplication of numbers with products over 20 are not adequately learned (by the 75 per cent standard) even at MA 10-9. Plane geometry is probably easier to learn than algebra, as Judd pointed out years ago, but algebra is nevertheless taught first, and probably too early to most students.

Adapting the curriculum to individual differences requires the school to vary the materials of instruction. It is probable, for example, that the elementary reading materials are more suitable to the interests of girls than of boys. The teacher must be an astute observer of her pupils' interests, as well as a judicious appraiser of text materials appealing to a wide variety of interests and to various levels of ability. Educational objectives for the class as a whole can be supplemented, as need be, by objectives of each individual. The aim here is improvement of the individual, not comparison of one individual with another.   Experiences can be provided the child who is deficient in reading, for example, by careful selection of suitable materials.   The brighter child can be stimulated by larger amounts of work of greater difficulty and appealing to his unusual interests, in order to offset the boredom that must inevitably result from routine work below his level of ability.

The School Guidance Program

The purpose of school guidance is to provide for individual differences by meeting individual needs, and in this way to maximize the educational advantages for all.   It emphasizes the study of the student not only to help the teacher understand him, but ultimately for the purpose of helping the student to understand himself.   Good teaching always emphasizes the study of children, because such study is basic to individualizing instruction; the excellent teacher, particularly in the primary grades when the child has little self-direction, is always a student of children.   Such child study occurs spontaneously and informally.   The term school guidance refers chiefly, not to the informal observation of children typical of all school work, but to the planned *systematic* study of the individual and to the provisions for making use of the information gained.

Studying the Individual.   Systematic study of the child which leads to understanding his behavior requires training in psychological techniques.   This does not mean that the teacher must be a psychologist, nor does it mean that the teacher's attitude should be abstract and analytic, as that of a psychologist would be.   Rather, the study should result in a practical evaluation of his abilities, interests, background, and personal traits for discovering ways of providing experiences suitable to his needs.   The process is partly quantitative, because it employs psychological tests which yield information not obtainable in any other way.   But no summary of test scores is sufficient in itself to understand the individual; information about his personal history, his home life, his feelings—often gained through interviews with him and his parents, or through observation—is necessary to understand the quantitative scores.   We need to know not only what traits he has, but in so far as possible why he has them. Tests will tell us that John Doe's IQ is 109, that he is higher than 80 per cent of his class in reading, higher than only 30 per cent in arithmetic. Casual observation may tell us that he is rather shy, and his mother may remark that he dislikes school. These facts together with many more from other sources, plus some shrewd hypotheses or "hunches" by the teacher, may together form a picture of John and his world that may be useful in helping to meet his needs. The interpretation of data about John is as important as collecting it.

Techniques of Studying Students. The methods of gathering data about the individual include first of all testing, which we have already considered. Tests by themselves, however, do not constitute a guidance program; even the interpretation of test scores must depend on information from other sources. Among the supplementary techniques of getting useful data are (1) systematic observation, (2) self-reports, (3) behavior rating scales, and (4) sociometric techniques. All of these can be used in the school without highly specialized training or elaborate paraphernalia.

1. *Systematic observation* differs from that of the casual sort in several respects. Just as a test has been described as a sample of behavior, so any behavior of a child may be considered a sample that reveals something about his behavior as a whole. Systematic observation is disciplined and has a plan, the purpose of which is to make the observed sample an adequate and meaningful one. Strang (17) mentions several principles involved in observing students: (1) Observe the whole situation, since the student may be responding to aspects of it which escape our attention. He may be silent in one class, but very active in another more to his liking. He may be timid with a group of strangers, but quite at ease with his own "crowd." (2) Select one student at a time, rather than a number to observe at once, so that the less obvious aspects of his behavior are not submerged by the more obvious behavior of others. (3) Focus on the more regular or routine activities, such as the classroom or playground, rather than unusual ones. The more typical be-

havior may be expected in typical situations, not atypical ones. Unusual situations may involve more strain, fright, or tension and reveal apparent shyness, nervousness, or crankiness not particularly typical of behavior in general. (4) Make observations over a period of several days, to allow for daily ups and downs in mood. Since the teacher wishes to get information about basic, prevailing patterns of behavior, these principles help to put her on guard against snap judgments based on too small a sample, inaccuracy in observing, or personal bias. Observations may be further systematized through techniques of recording and collating them in the form of the *anecdotal record*. Through such procedures, the members of a school staff observe and record objectively certain anecdotes which have value in understanding students, and systematically evaluate and interpret them.

2. *Self-reports* consist of questionnaires, personal history blanks, and other such devices which are filled out by the student and become part of his student record form. They have the advantage of being adapted to local conditions, and when well prepared yield useful information about students' family background, home conditions, hobbies, and special interests. Personality and interest inventories are also in this category, although usually in scorable form. One self-report used in many schools is the student's personal *autobiography,* or life history sketch, which is usually written as an assignment in the English class and becomes part of his record. When approached properly, the autobiography is rich in helpful information, since it enables the teacher to gain insight into the way the child sees his personal world. It is often as revealing in what it leaves out as what it says. Still another type of self-report yielding information about how the student perceives himself and his problems is the *problem check list,* of which the Mooney Problem Check List and the SRA Youth Inventory are examples. These are a series of verbal statements indicative of problems in various areas. The student checks those items which he feels to be typical of his personal problems. Like all self-reports, the validity of these devices depends on the student's willingness to report his problems accurately; they are

generally helpful in locating the types of problems which the student feels to be important.

3. *Behavior rating scales* are devices for rating the various aspects of behavior. They are valuable in directing the attention of teachers to aspects of behavior which might otherwise escape notice. The Haggerty-Olson-Wicksteed Behavior Rating Schedule is one such device for rating the behavioral traits of children. The recently developed Fels Parent Behavior Rating Scales are promising attempts at methods of rating the behavior of parents, home atmosphere, and other aspects of the home environment relating to the behavior of children (2). The scales provide for rating such factors as warmth of parent-child relations, democratic practices in the home, intellectuality (modes of intellectual stimulation by parents), indulgence, conflict, and restrictiveness. The Fels Scales are particularly valuable because knowledge about these psychological factors in the family setting is just as significant as the behavior of children in school, and very often provides the key to understanding the latter. It would seem to be particularly useful to visiting teachers, in directing their attention to certain aspects of the home, and to teachers who interview the parents of problem children.

4. *Sociometric techniques* are very useful devices for studying the social interaction of students and the individual's social role in the class group. How do the other students react toward the individual? Do they accept him readily or reject him? Is he an active participant in group activity or a social outcast? How does he tend to be characterized by others? Sociometric techniques help to answer these questions somewhat more meaningfully than direct observation, and help the teacher to identify those students who need help in making friends and adjusting to the group. Two types of devices are useful in the school: (1) the sociogram and (2) the "Guess Who" technique.

The *sociogram* is a chart depicting the relations among individuals in the group. Its general purpose is to discover "who associates with whom" in the class, or which members like and esteem which other members. This information is obtained from written answers to a question such as "Who are your three best friends" or "Name the three members of the class you would like to work with on a committee." If possible, the question should be one that leads to a practical outcome, or deals with a really meaningful situation. Thus the second question just mentioned should elicit more valid responses than the first, particularly if it poses a situation in which the student will really

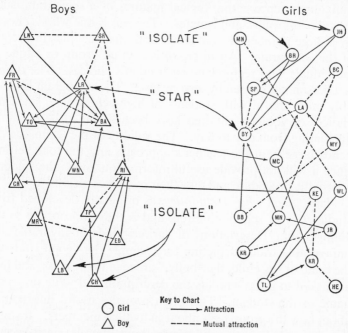

FIGURE 45. Sociogram of the Seventh Grade, Public School 181, Brooklyn. Represents the preferences of pupils for one another. Such a diagram helps the teacher to determine which students need help in social adjustment. (From J. L. Moreno, *Who shall survive? Foundations of sociometry, group psychotherapy and sociodrama*, 1st ed., 1934, p. 41; 2d ed., 1953, p. 160; published by Beacon House, Inc., Beacon, N. Y.)

be assigned to a committee consisting of members of his choice. A similar question actually used by Moreno (10), the leading investigator in sociometry, directed the students to name the two persons they would most like to sit beside them in class. The question must be chosen and stated with care. Students are asked to write down the names of persons in rank order of preference on a small card, and to write his own name on the card. The teacher then collects the cards and makes a tabulation showing who chose whom and the rank order of each choice. From these data the sociogram itself is plotted, as in Figure 45, which depicts the choices by means of arrows. By tracing and studying these arrows, the teacher can identify those individuals representing typical features of a sociogram, such as stars, in-groups, and isolates. The *star* is one who is chosen by a large number of individuals and thus occupies the center of the sociogram. An *in-group* is a small group or clique of individuals who reciprocate each other's choices. The *isolate* is a person not chosen by anyone else. The sociogram is probably more useful with students of high school age, since the choices of younger children have been found to be unstable, fluctuating from day to day. The validity of the technique depends largely on the teacher's approach and the total setting, since it will not provide useful information unless the students accept the procedure and take their responses seriously.

The *"guess who" technique* was originally developed from studies (7) of school children, and is thus appropriate to the younger set. Descriptions of various kinds of favorable and unfavorable traits, depicting for example the "good student," the timid or shy child, the "bully," are read to the class, and they are asked to guess who fits the description and write down the name of the student. This often provides useful information about how the group feels about individual members. It sometimes reveals how the child feels about himself, since he may write down his own name as fitting the description.

Evaluating Individual Achievement. We should attribute scholastic progress to the total working personality, and not simply to the interaction of educative materials or method and some one or two mental traits or abilities. Achievement, expressed in the most summary form possible, is always a matter of aptitude, motivation, and opportunity. From the negative side of the picture, we may sometimes identify certain "limiting" factors, such as low intelligence or poor physical condition. Positive achievement, however, is based on a totality of personality factors operating in a favorable environment. The total working personality is the product of the interaction of many mental traits and tendencies. Any particular pattern or combination of these traits, apart from their single value, may be fortunate or unfortunate. Only a study of the individual himself and his achievement can give us this insight.

A leading principle of guidance, and of education in general, is that the student should be achieving up to the level of his ability in a course of study appropriate to his needs. The first function of a guidance program is to find out whether he is, and if he is not, to discover why not. The answer may be that the school work is not appropriate to his needs, that the total personality pattern is not favorable, or that some aspect of his environment needs improvement. The first diagnostic step, however, is to determine his level of achievement in relation to his general ability or scholastic aptitude. Achievement may be measured by his grade point average, or by means of achievement tests. The best way of estimating his general ability is by means of the intelligence or scholastic aptitude test. But the results of the two measures must be seen in relation to each other.

One useful technique for evaluating individual achievement is afforded by the *scatter diagram*, or bivariate frequency distribution. We may take two sets of scores like those in Table 21 representing scholastic aptitude and achievement, and plot them in a scatter diagram like that in Figure 46. It will be noted that the middle interval on both variables, scored in heavy black lines, represents the average interval containing the mean. In estimating the achievement of each student in relation to his ability, we may now compare his deviation from the class mean of achievement and his deviation from the class mean of scholastic aptitude. John Black is considerably above the mean on both (upper right quadrant) and is therefore presumed to be achieving in accordance with his ability. Richard White's achievement is low, but so is his scholastic aptitude (lower left); if the latter score is a valid estimate of his ability, we may assume that Richard also is doing as well as we can expect. But Mary Brown (lower right) appears to be achieving grades far above the level we would expect from her scholastic aptitude

TABLE 21

A Set of Scores on a Scholastic Aptitude Test and Achievement Test

Name	Schol. Apt.	Achiev.	Name	Schol. Apt.	Achiev.
1. Frank Allen	88	12	16. Peter Rossi	132	88
2. John Black	138	85	17. Thomas Sage ...	78	54
3. Mary Brown ...	89	88	18. Grace Scott	100	39
4. Ada Cooper	110	75	19. Mary Scott	96	35
5. Eileen Dent	134	69	20. Marian Shaw ...	95	52
6. George Gray ...	130	30	21. Edward Shea ...	117	62
7. John Hope	118	40	22. Hattie Thompson	122	79
8. Myrtle Keane ..	95	28	23. Walter Todd ...	60	28
9. Wayne Lewis ...	73	38	24. Martha Todd ...	89	37
10. Harry May	86	70	25. Charles Van Horn	104	46
11. Ann O'Brien ...	112	50	26. Henry Wagner ..	100	79
12. Bert Patterson ..	87	49	27. Leo Waite	102	60
13. Carl Peters	100	69	28. Richard White ..	67	23
14. Irene Quinn	128	57	29. May Wills	103	53
15. Lillian Reed	85	30	30. Ruth Young	90	60

score. She would be designated an *overachiever,* at least if her aptitude score is valid. George Gray (upper left) is an *underachiever,* since his position in the diagram shows a high level of ability and low achievement. Overachievers are relatively rare, but underachievers are common in school.

The scatter diagram provides useful information for the differential treatment of these students. Nobody worries about John; he is doing well. But a further study of George Gray, the underachiever, seems warranted in order to discover the personality or environmental factors that seem to be defeating him. Much can be learned from personal interviews with him, his parents, and other teachers; from his scholastic and personal history, and other sources. What can we do about Richard, the boy low in aptitude? First of all, we must make sure that his mental ability is really low. We may give him other tests of general ability—a "power" or unspeeded test, to make sure it was not lack of speed that produced the low score in the first place—or he may be given a nonverbal test. We might arrange to have an individual test administered rather than a pencil-and-paper group test. Having ascertained that Richard is too low in aptitude to meet high academic standards, the sensible thing to do is lower the standards—for him. We can design special courses for him, suitable to his ability, or through special planning set up realistic educational goals that he can reach. In so doing, we try to get his active participation and evaluate his progress in the light of his ability. The alternative is continued failure and frustration for Richard. We should note here that

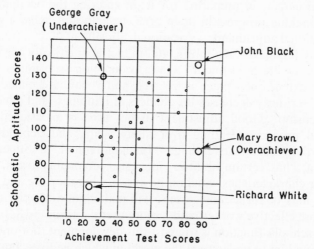

FIGURE 46. Bivariate Frequency Distribution of Scholastic Aptitude Scores and Achievement Test Scores. This "scattergram," or "correlation diagram," is a graphic aid in interpreting the test scores in Table 21 and evaluating achievement in relation to ability. If the "dots" are kept anonymous, this device is useful also in discussing test results with students.

our treatment of George Gray, the underachiever, differs, both in approach and techniques, from the treatment of Richard White. The low grades of the underachiever are a symptom of poor *personal* adjustment. The low grades of the slow learner are a symptom of poor *curricular* adjustment. Mary Brown, the overachiever, is also a cause for concern to the teacher and counselor. We must again verify that her ability is as low as the test seems to indicate. If it is, we can be reasonably sure she is achieving her grades through extraordinary efforts and also perhaps through the kindness of teachers as a reward for her efforts. If so, her grades may overestimate her real scholastic achievement. Our concern with Mary is that her educational ceiling is probably limited more than she realizes, and that she may set up unrealistic educational and vocational goals beyond her level of ability.

Vocational Guidance. The purpose of vocational guidance is to assist the individual in choosing an appropriate occupational career, in preparing for it, in entering the occupation, and making progress in it; in brief, to help him make a good vocational adjustment. Vocational adjustment plays a tremendously important role in life, and in fact is practically coextensive with life adjustment. One's occupation determines to a large extent one's place in society, and vocational maladjustment seriously decreases his chances of happiness and effective citizenship. Good adjustment in this area is a basic educational process extending over many years, and depends on growth in self-understanding. "Each individual," as Super has put it, "has certain abilities, interests, personality traits, and other characteristics which, if he knows what they are and how they may be turned into assets, will make him a happier man, a more effective worker, and a more useful citizen" (18, p. 1). The school's function is to assist this development, not only by helping him to understand the world in which he lives, but also by helping him to acquire accurate and useful estimates of his abilities, plus the interests and attitudes essential to finding his place in society. From this point of view the entire work of the school, not just that narrow aspect dealing with occupations and vocational training, is vocational guidance.

Vocational choice is not an easy matter of making logical selections on the basis of economic considerations. Like other problems in goal-setting, it involves various emotional conflicts, constant revaluation of one's experience, and gradual alteration of attitudes toward self and society. Some sources of conflict are these: Parental pressure; a vague awareness of the class status and prestige value of occupations which applies social pressure to "make good"; self-doubts, often caused by adverse comparison between the adolescent and mature members of occupational groups to which he might aspire; lack of information, often taking the form of oversimple, stereotyped concepts of occupations; unrealistic estimates of one's abilities; a foreshortened time perspective, which makes it difficult for the adolescent to make long-range plans. These factors usually operate together, often making the problem of vocational choice a difficult emotional conflict.

Many high school students need instruction in how to think about the vocational choice problem, as well as occupational and educational information. Not only are they plagued by self-doubts and pressures like the above, which need to be brought to the surface of awareness and recognized as common aspects of the problem, but they often feel compelled to make a choice too early and too specific. The student planning to go to college may, for example, make a general but perfectly adequate choice consisting of "some professional occupation in the technological field" rather than a pin-pointed choice of "mechanical engineer." The student not going to college can aim at "retail sales," "a clerical occupation involving computing," or "a skilled construction trade," leaving a more precise choice until faced with the actual necessity of planning a campaign to get a job. The student needs to think in terms of occupational families in relation to his own abilities, interests, and opportunities. This can often be accomplished through classroom instruction.

The *field-level concept* of the occupational world, described by Hahn and Brayfield, is a very useful one for providing the student with a map of occupational opportunities in relation to his own abilities and interests. Their definitions of "field" and "level" are as follows:

> The term occupational field, as used here, means a broad area of occupations which are related to each other with reference to the abilities, aptitudes, and vocational interest patterns necessary for success. The term level may be defined as the general ability or aptitude of an individual to meet complex situations and to master abstract ideas and concepts.
>
> "Field" indicates the direction in which an individual should go; "level" indicates how far he is likely to progress. (6, pp. 23-24)

MECHANICAL FIELD   MECHANICAL-SOCIAL FIELD

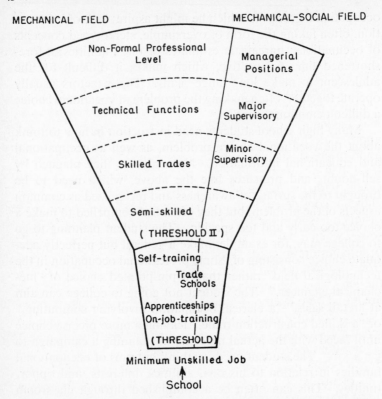

FIGURE 47. Occupational Levels in the Mechanical Field. This "job-funnel" diagram shows potential levels for individuals without professional training who must go directly into routine jobs from school. The "thresholds" call attention to the fact that routine entry jobs enable the beginner to "get his foot in the door." Future progress depends on his mechanical and "social" aptitudes, plus proper motivation. A clear picture of his prospects will help the school dropout to shorten his floundering period to a minimum. (From M. E. Hahn and M. S. MacLean, *General clinical counseling in educational institutions.* New York: McGraw-Hill, 1950, p. 78.)

Since level is defined in terms of level of general ability, the term "professional level" would refer to occupations requiring high mental ability and arduous academic training. The "unskilled level" at the other extreme refers to occupations requiring but low level of general scholastic ability and little or no academic schooling. An occupational field is defined in terms of interests and special abilities. It is thus possible to categorize occupations as belonging to such fields as mechanical, clerical, sales, artistic, musical, computational, and so on. Each field is thought of as divided into a number of levels, as illustrated by the "map" of the mechanical field in Figure 47.

Vocational problems of students may be generally identified as choice problems. The student (1) may have no choice, (2) may have an inappropriate choice, or (3) may have made an appropriate but tentative choice requiring confirmation. An appropriate choice would be one appropriate in both field and level; that is, supported by his level of general ability and consistent with his interests and special abilities. A vocational choice is considered inappropriate when it requires much more or much less than the level of general scholastic ability he possesses, when it requires special aptitudes in which he is deficient or a pattern of interests or personal traits remarkably different from his own, or when it requires training (academic or on-the-job) which he cannot obtain. Usually such unwise choices are based on pressure from his family, misinformation, romanticized wishful thinking, suggestibility, and a general lack of self-understanding. Many unwise choices stem from unstated assumptions that he can enter any occupational field and that the best choice is one in which (he has heard) the pay is high, jobs plentiful, and his future assured. The student who has made no choice should not necessarily be urged to do so. He may not be psychologically ready to do so, either for lack of maturity or because he has not arrived at a stage where a specific choice is necessary. He may, on the other hand, need information, both about himself and about opportunities. Very often this information is sufficient incentive to make him psychologically ready to think about these things. In all cases students need sufficient information about themselves and about occupations to recognize the difference between an appropriate and an inappropriate choice. When this is the case, the student is usually mature enough and well enough informed to work out his vocational problem in his own way.

The vocational guidance program in school, even when well planned and carried out through classroom group instruction, needs to be supplemented by individual vocational counseling. Opportunities must be provided to the student for talking over his problem with a competent, well-trained counselor skilled in test interpretation and the interpretation of occupational requirements. A vocational choice problem is seldom, if ever, limited strictly to the mere matching of abilities with jobs. On the contrary, the choice of a career is a critical phase of personal adjustment, and the student brings along with him his personal problems, his feelings about himself and his school work, his family and his station in life. These are definitely part of the problem and cannot be left out of the picture. Vocational counseling does not therefore differ from other kinds of counseling, and the vocational counselor must be a skilled general counselor.

Guidance Through Group Activities. One of the most difficult problems of the school is that of facilitating the social adjustment of students. The student's motives in going to school are largely social. He needs to feel that he "belongs," that he is accepted by the group. The dissatisfied or underachieving student, with little interest in school, is often one who feels "left out" or is unable to relate himself effectively to any peer group. It would appear from some studies (9) that continuation in school, as well as academic achievement, depends on the degree of social acceptance enjoyed by students. School "drop-outs" seem to be significantly more numerous among those who do not "fit in" in the social sense.

The adverse effects of poor social adjustment can be a serious obstacle to the work of the school. The effective guidance program therefore promotes activities which will enable each individual to participate in appropriate social groups. This end is best achieved by providing a range of "co-curricular activities suitable to the range of abilities, interests, and social backgrounds of students" (4). When properly managed from the educational standpoint and coordinated with class work, group activities may be of high educational value.

Children with Handicaps. Children with handicaps are first of all children, and have the same needs and problems that other children have.   By reason of their handicaps, their problems are often more difficult and complicated and their needs are less easy to meet through the ordinary school procedures. The school guidance service therefore makes special provision for (1) the identification of handicapped children, (2) the assessment of their particular abilities, assets, and deficiencies, and (3) treatment, both medical and educational.   "One of the greatest obstacles," says Baker, "to a better and more complete program of education for exceptional [handicapped] children arises from the widespread notion that they are a class separate and distinct from normal children" (1).   There is too common a tendency to segregate and forget about them, to assume that their needs are met adequately by food, clothing, and shelter, and to leave their educational needs to take care of themselves. Many families conspire to hide crippled children because of shame or ignorance.   If the handicapped are to become useful, self-supporting, and well-adjusted members of society, the schools must adopt exactly the opposite approach, and are increasingly doing so.   There is evidence that the proportion of handicapped persons in society is increasing, for the simple reason that improved medical services enable many, who years ago would have died, to go on living.

Persons with handicaps may be roughly categorized as follows:

1. The *physically* handicapped, including orthopedics, cardiacs, extremes of growth disorders, those with lowered vitality due to malnutrition or disease, and certain hereditary disorders.
2. The *mentally* handicapped, or mentally deficient.
3. The *sensory* handicaps, including the blind and partially seeing, the deaf and hard of hearing, various visual and hearing disorders.
4. *Speech* disorders and defects.
5. *Neurological and psychogenic* disorders, such as epilepsy and other nervous-motor disorders, neurotics and psychotics.

The identification of most handicaps in school is not difficult, but very often poor eyesight, poor hearing, and general low vitality are overlooked as causes of poor school work or inadequate behavior. Conditions such as post-encephalitis are often at the root of problem behavior. Some conditions, such as speech and hearing defects, may not be recognized as remediable. The school health service is therefore an important guidance function. Through a combination of medical, psychological, and social work, children with handicaps are being increasingly studied to determine (1) to what extent they can benefit from the ordinary school procedures; (2) what modifications can be introduced into teaching methods or curriculum to meet their needs; (3) what can be done to reduce the effect of their handicaps through surgery, by means of orthopedic appliances, eyeglasses, hearing aids, or through specialized training; and (4) what plans can be made for their successful vocational adjustment. This usually requires the marshaling of all the resources of the community. The school can assist with the identification and referral of these children, as well as provide the special educational services that make satisfactory adjustment possible.

THE GUIDANCE OF PERSONAL ADJUSTMENT

The effective guidance of adjustment requires a certain minimum understanding by the teacher of the following things: (1) a recognition of *individual differences* in ability, interests, and personal traits, and the uniqueness of the individual; (2) a recognition of the fact that the adjustment process is one of *interaction* between the individual and other persons, notably the teacher's, and that the latter's attitude plays a considerable part in the process; and (3) an awareness of the fact that adjustment is a *learning* process, and is thus regulated by the principles of learning. The individual with an adjustment problem—whether in the area of educational, vocational, home, social adjustment to schoolmates, sex, or legal delinquency—is a person with a motive, a "felt difficulty" due to obstacles or conflicting attitudes, and a tendency to vary his behavior to meet the obstacles.

The Guidance Approach. The general approach is to attempt to understand the problem by studying the individual in order to discover some basis for offering help. We are well aware that often a word of encouragement or advice may help the person with a problem, but more often than not such a procedure is useless or wide of the mark because we have no real understanding of the problem. Before we can do anything to help we must find out "what's wrong." Studying the individual may involve the use of tests and inventories, interviewing him, his parents, and his teachers, and observing his behavior. The information about the pupil is not just accumulated, but is arranged in a pattern which helps us to understand the problem. Such questions as these are pertinent:

1. What motives does he have? What are his goals, i.e., what satisfaction does he anticipate from their attainment? What situations is he responding to? What is the relative strength of his drives, or his degree of tension? What basic needs are not being met?

2. What are the obstacles? Are they "real," or the result of misinterpretation on his part? Is the conflict caused by misinformation, which can be cleared up by factual knowledge, or does it lie deeper in his emotional experience?

3. How is he reacting to the problem? Is he angry, upset, afraid, or is it a complex emotional state? Does he have rapid changes in mood? Is he trying various kinds of behavior at various times, or is his attitude rigid or "fixed?" Are these adjustments working to his satisfaction? What are the reactions of others (parents, teachers, classmates) toward his behavior and are their reactions satisfying or aggravating to him?

4. What means can be provided for meeting his needs more effectively? What kind of information would help him? Can his problem be reinterpreted for him, to help him see certain aspects to which he is now blind? Who should do the interpreting, and under what conditions? Will changing the situation help (changing teachers, class group, home environment) and is it possible to do this? Is the process of readjustment a considerable one requiring skilled direction and treatment (psychiatrist, clinical psychologist) or one the teacher can cope

with? Is he resourceful enough to work out his own problem with encouragement and a little guidance, or does he expect someone else to solve the problem for him? How will he react to suggestions for help—apathetically, resentfully, or with an overdependent attitude?

The guidance approach, as depicted in questions like those above, first lays great stress on the needs and characteristics of the individual which differentiate this particular student with this particular problem. This requires us to see it from his point of view. The approach which prompts us to "label" or classify the individual ("this is a case of . . .") is not a guidance approach. Secondly, we note here a concern for personal interaction with the effect of other persons' attitudes and behavior on the individual, and the effect of his behavior in turn on theirs. This is one reason why personal adjustment problems are difficult; neither the problem nor the individual "stays put," so to speak, but both continually change shape.

Some General Guiding Principles. Our general purpose is to understand the problem and the forces playing on the individual. What the guidance counselor does is of course determined entirely by his view of the situation. Some guiding principles in seeing an adjustment problem correctly are as follows:

1. Distinguish between the problem and the student's behavioral symptoms. When we describe the problem as daydreaming, extreme shyness, depression, excessive crying, stealing, or worry, we have the wrong angle; these are symptoms, or ways of reacting, not the problem itself. This behavior may be a problem to the teacher, but not to the student. The point is important, because this wrong view often causes us to treat the symptom instead of the problem. For example, if we say "John Doe's problem is lack of study, which is causing him to fail," the solution immediately appears to be one of getting him to study and perhaps showing him how. The effective solution is certainly buried much deeper than this, and certainly has something to do with *why* he is not studying. Most of our wrongheaded approaches to guidance are the result of not making this distinction.

2. Distinguish between the outsider's (our own) view of the problem and the student's version. Our aim is always to understand it from his point of view, not our own. What meaning is he assigning to the things, persons, and events in his situation? When we place the stress on the outsider's view, we are likely to assume that the problem is trivial. It is not, from his point of view. We are distinguishing here between what is called the *internal* (his) and *external* (ours) frame of reference (12). The latter causes us to respond by cheering him up, blaming him, treating it lightly ("it isn't as bad as all that"), taking sides with him. We tend to respond by approving or disapproving, assuming that he is either "right" or "wrong." We may be inclined to conclude that the parent is right and the child wrong, or vice versa. This is misleading and ordinarily useless. The student's view of the situation may be "wrong," but it is the only view he has. Our immediate attempt to classify his view as right-wrong or his statements as facts-errors means that our perceptions are in the external frame of reference and that we are missing the point: the problem lies in the internal frame of reference, in the individual's meanings and feelings.

3. Distinguish between a need for information, and indecision stemming from a motivational conflict. A boy's vocational problem, as he puts it, may involve a choice between studying medicine and going into his father's sand and gravel business. Information about his aptitudes and interests and about either occupation may be helpful, but not the critical issue in such a decision. The problem may be one of need for status (physician) *vs.* fear of offending the father, or fear of academic failure (physician) *vs.* immediate economic security. It may be (and probably is) even much more complex. A person with a personal adjustment problem usually needs clear information about the demands of the situation, and information about his resources, his assets, and his liabilities. But his attitudes toward the "facts" are more crucial than the facts themselves, particularly if his attitudes are ambivalent or conflicting. For this reason, information or advice may sometimes not help him much.

4. Differentiate between a serious problem, requiring competent professional treatment, and the kind of problem with which the school can deal. This is not a matter of classifying educational-vocational problems as "school" problems, and personal-social problems as requiring psychiatric treatment. The seriously maladjusted or nonadjusted person may be preoccupied with a vocational problem (which is symptomatic of more serious difficulty). Also, the student who is depressed because he is not making friends may be helped by joining school clubs and participating in more social affairs. One index of the problem's seriousness is the degree of emotional tension, which often shows itself in the behavioral symptoms. The adequate guidance counselor in school is one who can distinguish accurately between the less serious and more serious disturbances, and refer the more serious ones to the proper professional practitioner.

5. A fifth important principle is this: we usually cannot hope to get a good description of his problem from the individual himself. He often cannot tell us what his motives are, because he does not know. Because the person in a problem is usually confused, he cannot state just what the source of frustration is, especially if it involves motivational conflict. Even if he knew, he would probably not tell anyone, because such things are often not socially acceptable. In an interview, or even an informal conversation, the individual has his guard up. What he says is usually a careful selection of words designed to make the best possible impression, or an expression of the feelings which dominate him at the moment. This, again, is the factor of social interaction, which is important in the counseling interview.

Individual Counseling.   Since most problems in adjustment involve highly personal details, the guidance of adjustment frequently takes the form of individual counseling. The counseling interview is a private face to face relationship between two persons, one of whom has a personal problem. The purpose of the counselor is to facilitate the solution of the problem, and ordinarily this means providing a situation in which the counselee can clarify for himself the situation and his attitudes toward it. (The primary purpose is *not* to clarify it for the counselor.) Problems of personal adjustment, like other problems, are usually reacted to by mental "self-talking" or self-instruction, in which the problem-solver uses language to run off symbolically a number of alternative responses and to anticipate the consequences of each response. As in other problems, this kind of activity helps the individual to clarify the problem. The particular advantage of talking to a counselor instead of to one's self is that the presence of the other person may serve as a stimulus to self-exploration, and the necessity of communicating with the counselor helps to "objectify," or get out into the open, his feelings. This facilitates self-recognition. A student counselee once expressed this by saying "I don't know how I feel until I've said it."

The counseling interview is thus a special kind of learning situation, the purpose of which is the counselee's self-exploration and self-recognition through self-expression. The chief concern of the counselor, in setting up this situation, is to "get the [counselee] to talk about matters important to *him*" (14). This means, first of all, establishing a feeling of *rapport*—a term for feeling at ease, a feeling of being understood, a feeling of confidence and trust in the counselor. Effective rapport also implies that the counselee feels able to say or do what he wishes in the counseling situation, without any fear of being blamed, scolded, tattled on, or reported to the school authorities.

The counselor tries to establish, in so far as possible, an atmosphere of permissiveness, or freedom of self-expression. The primary aim of getting the counselee to talk thus implies that the counselor is primarily a listener rather than a talker, and speaks only for the purpose of encouraging the counselee to talk, to clarify what the counselee has said, and to help the counselee say what he cannot say without help (14). What does the counselor listen for? His purpose, of course, is to understand the problem as the counselee sees it, and he therefore pays particular attention to the meanings and feelings expressed: how the counselee feels about the problem (confusion, cocksureness, aggression, helplessness), how he feels about himself (feelings of guilt, inferiority, self-defensiveness, confidence), how he feels toward others, including parents, teachers, classmates, and any other person mentioned. The counselor will note what the student says easily, and what he says with difficulty; there is a difference in emotional tension involved here. The counselor pays particular attention to those things which the student avoids mentioning, since these often furnish clues to aspects of the problem he has not considered. Also, what he leaves out may indicate sources of emotional conflict which he avoids on purpose; for example, the student who talks about his mother all the time and never mentions his father may be unconsciously pointing to a disturbed personal relationship with his parents.

In summary, the counseling interview is a special type of learning situation which facilitates self-expression and exploration of one's attitudes. The distinctive "psychological climate" of the counseling situation affords (1) maximum opportunity for self-exploration, and (2) a minimum need for self-defense (12). The particular value of individual counseling is that a similar situation is hardly possible in ordinary life.

Communication in Counseling. The counseling relationship is basically one of interaction between the counselor and counselee through verbal communication, and this interaction is complex because of *semantic* factors, or the way language is commonly used to express meanings. The counselor must be especially skilled in communication. He must pay attention to the *intent* of what the counselee says rather than the *content* of what he says; that is, he is concerned more with the feelings expressed than he is with the meanings of the words (14). This may require some explanation.

Language may be used in three ways: (1) *To express something objective* in order to communicate facts or relations about events outside one's skin, such as the statement "It is raining outside," or "a triangle has three sides"; (2) *to express one's self* or one's feelings, as in the statement "Today is a beautiful day"; the latter, although seemingly a statement about the weather, may actually be a statement about one's feelings.

Translated, it may mean "I feel wonderful today!" To make this clear, let us ask whether the truth or falsity of "Today is a beautiful day" can actually be tested by objective tests, quite apart from someone's feelings about it. We must agree that it cannot. (3) Language may be used *to impress others* with what we say, by using words to influence their attitude toward us or toward something. Thus we may say "Today is a beautiful day" with the intent of cheering someone up. We might say "the rainfall to date is 10.8 inches above the national average," with the intent of influencing another's attitude favorably toward our stock of knowledge. Neither of these, in *intent,* is a factual statement about the weather, as it seems to be.

In a counseling situation, as in ordinary life, the counselee (or the counselor, for that matter) may use language in any of these three ways. The counselor's particular function is (1) to be aware of the intent of his own language, and never to use language merely to express his own feelings; (2) to listen for the *intent,* as separate from the *content,* of what the counselee says. The latter practically always uses words to express his feelings and to influence the counselor, but does it (as persons do in ordinary life) by disguising his intent in terms of logical, objective language. That is, he makes statements whose content appears to be factual and objective, but whose intent may be to express feelings or to influence the counselor.

He does not label his intent. He does not say "Now I'm going to show you that others are picking on me," but recites "facts" about Teachers X and Y giving him unjust grades, about classmates X and Y who snub him, about his father who treats him harshly. He does not say "Now I am going to make a play for your sympathy," "Now I am going to try to get your goat," "Now I am going to indulge in some wishful thinking or daydreaming," "Now I am going to cover up and defend myself," because he is actually not aware of any such intent. He merely expresses the way he feels. Consider the following excerpts from counseling interviews:

I'm afraid I'm taking up too much of your time.

My brother seems to get along much better in school than I do and makes more friends.

This school is a lot like being in jail.

You can't get any place without going to college, and I haven't the grades to go to college. Besides I'm not sure that I want to.

Nobody ever got any place in life by being good in algebra and French and things like that. They're a waste of time.

What's the matter with me anyway? I have a lot of friends, but no real *good* friends.

I guess I'm the type that just doesn't get elected to office.

What feelings are being expressed, and what is the intent of these remarks? As given, it is possible only to conjecture; but the skillful counselor can, by alert orientation to the *context* in which they are said, the tone of voice, the gestures and attitude of the speaker, make inferences which help to understand the problem and how the student is reacting to it. The constant temptation to treat what the counselee says as "right" or "wrong," as fact or error, results from the wrong kind of orientation (external frame of reference), and ordinarily leads to arguing with the speaker, pointing out where he is wrong, agreeing or disagreeing. His statements are essentially attitudes, "non-facts" or feelings which are at the core of his adjustment problem, and require understanding. Individual counseling therefore requires a great deal of skill, which is partly a matter of art, and partly a matter of schooling and practice under supervision.

Counselor Attitudes. Porter (12) has named five basic attitudes which may motivate the counselor:

1. A *probing,* questioning, leading, discussion-provoking intent or attitude.
2. A *teaching,* interpretive, "pointing out" attitude or intent.
3. An *evaluative,* corrective, suggestive, moralizing attitude or intent.
4. A *supportive,* sympathetic, reassuring, tempering, easing attitude or intent.
5. An *understanding,* comprehending, appreciating attitude or intent.

The first two of these approaches, characterized by an active attempt to "find out what's wrong" and to instruct the counselee toward a better way of seeing his problem, has one advantage and several disadvantages. The chief advantage lies in its being time-saving and economical. But the value of information, advice, and interpretation based on "superior" insights of the counselor depends entirely on the extent to which the counselee can accept and assimilate what he is told. As we have seen, the "ready-made" solutions of the counselor may not fit the limited perceptual experience of the counselee, and may not be very helpful to him. The counselor's interpretations may often be based on a woefully inadequate comprehension of the student's view of his adjustment problem, his personal meanings, and feelings.

The disadvantages of this approach are several. First of all, the counselor assumes most of the responsibility, which puts the student in a more or less dependent position. Second, the counselor may do most of the talking, leaving the student little opportunity for self-expression. Third, the counselor's probing questions may be psychologically threatening to the student, putting him on the defensive and causing him to "clam up," rationalize, or justify himself. This may hamper the student's self-understanding. Thus the probing and teaching approaches, even when outwardly warm and friendly, run the risk of damaging rapport and inhibiting the self-understanding which they hope to bring about.

The third, or *evaluative* approach, puts the counselor in the position of a judge, evaluating the adequacy or inadequacy of the student's interpretations, the truth or falsity of his statements. He may praise or approve desirable attitudes and ignore those he finds blameworthy, or he may praise and blame alternately. This approach, in so far as it is corrective, is usually combined with the teaching, interpreting, "pointing out" procedure. The one advantage this offers the counselee is a means of criticizing his own point of view. This is more than offset by the disadvantages: he may not accept or assimilate the criticism, may be placed on the defensive and develop a feeling of not being understood. Again, it places maximum responsibility on the counselor, and does not facilitate self-exploration or self-discovery.

The fourth, or *supportive* approach, is one of overprotection on the part of the counselor. When the student is especially upset or depressed, expresses feelings of confusion and helplessness, or indulges in feelings of self-belittling and self-accusations, the counselor naturally feels a tendency to "tone down" these feelings or to offer him reassurance and support. Such statements as "It isn't really that bad, is it?" "I think you are underestimating your abilities," or "All black clouds have silver linings," are examples of this sort. Strong expressions of hatred or bitterness (toward parents or school, for instance), of fear and anger often upset the counselor and cause him to tone them down by pointing out the brighter side or by "pep talks." In such a mental state, the student does often require support. But reassurance has a temporary effect at best, and this kind of approach also has other disadvantages.

The effect of easing or temporizing the student's undesirable feelings is to make clear to him that "you should not feel this way" or possibly "you should not express your feelings so strongly." This ignores the problem; it had better be recognized that the student *does* feel that way, and that his feelings are essentially part of the problem. Therefore even reassurance may tend to make the student somewhat defensive, to inhibit freedom of expression, and to make him feel that he is not really understood. The free expression of feelings often relieves tension through a *cathartic,* or purging, effect and clears the way for a more objective or rational view of one's difficulties.

The counselor attitudes cited above, and the approaches motivated by them, are based on certain common assumptions. It is first assumed that the counselor "knows best"—that he can define appropriate goals for the counselee and also the means of attaining these goals. Whether this is true or not is at least an open question. The counselor may have superior wisdom and insight, but his views may be simply beyond the reach of the student with a different set of values, a limited time perspective, and inadequate experience. In any case, the insight of the counselor does not often get transferred to the student through words. Second, it is apparent that the help given to the student through these forms of communication depends on his readiness for assimilating them. A third assumption is that the responsibility for what goes on in counseling belongs almost entirely to the counselor and that the latter's function is to devise techniques for manipulating the counselee toward his own point of view. These are, in other words, *counselor-centered* approaches. Both their value and their limitations are measured by the extent to which they assist or restrict the counselee's self-expression, self-exploration, and self-discovery, leading to better forms of adjustment.

The fifth counselor attitude mentioned by Porter, namely the understanding, comprehending, appreciating attitude or intent, is basic to what is called a *client-centered* approach. It is favored by some counselors as offering the most suitable "psychological climate" for inducing the changes of attitude essential to personal adjustment, and for facilitating growth in responsibility and self-confidence. Its purpose is to create a warm, friendly atmosphere in which the counselee is nevertheless forced to take the initiative in exploring his problem, and is allowed to do so without any need for being defensive. The counselee chooses his own goals and the means of attaining them. He is allowed literally to "be himself" at all times, to work out his own problem and to make his own decisions.

This may seem to abrogate all of the functions which tradition assign to the role of the counselor, leaving the latter nothing to do. What, we may ask, is the role of the counselor? The answer: to understand, to comprehend, to appreciate. This, however, is *not* a passive role. The counselor's activity consists in paying strict attention to the feelings expressed by the counselee, and responding to them in such a way as to *reflect* the feelings expressed. The intent of every counselor response is to recognize and accept the feelings expressed, by either (1) showing that he understands, or (2) responding as though to ask "Is this the way you feel?" or "Is this what you mean?" The following excerpt will serve as an example:

A girl of 15 is giving her version of a hair-pulling fight in the school bus, in which she has been named the aggressor by the bus driver and by the victim (an upper-middle-class girl of the same age).

Student: (resentfully) She was sitting next to me all spread out with one of her books in my lap and I told her to move over. She just looked me up and down so I pushed her over.

Counselor: You felt pretty annoyed with her.

Student: I sure did. She's so uppity and nasty, treats everybody like dirt and acts like she's better than you. I get mad every time I think about it.

Counselor: I gather you're still pretty angry with her.

Student: She's lucky she didn't lose *all* her hair. Anybody who treats me that way is going to get it good. I'm as good as she is. Everybody else takes it from her but not me. It makes me sick.

Counselor: You feel that she just has to be put in her place, is that it?

Student: Everybody always sides with her. The teachers do and (bus driver) and the boys—I guess you do too. I don't see what's so wonderful about her.

Counselor: It just seems as though everybody is against you.

Student: I can take it. But it makes me pretty mad sometimes.

Counselor: (understandingly). I see.

Student: It's just like my brother says. You got to look out for yourself, nobody else will. (Talks about her older brother, and some scrapes he has been in.) If you don't put up a fight, somebody's going to walk all over you.

Counselor: I see. As I get it, you feel that it's pretty important to protect yourself, and that comes before anything else.

We note here that every response of the counselor was a tentative reflection of the counselee's meaning or feelings, without "parroting" the same words. None of his responses implied what the student ought to do or not do (evaluative), what she ought to think (interpretive), or how she ought to feel (supportive).

This type of procedure appears to place an unusual amount of faith in the student's ability to guide himself. In the opinion of some counselors, this belief is not misplaced. Many others find the basic attitude difficult to accept. In any case, the client-centered approach requires arduous training, and the chief stumbling blocks to its successful use appear to be the basic attitudes of the counselor himself.

There is no client-centered "method" but a psychological approach expressed in the following hypothesis: "Reorganization of the disturbed personality will take place more readily when external intervention is at a minimum and self-exploration is at a maximum" (12). Without complete acceptance of this point of view, the practice of so-called client-centered "methods" is an empty and meaningless gesture. In the words of Rogers, "Client-centered counseling, if it is to be effective, cannot be a trick or a tool. It is not a subtle way of guiding the client while pretending to let him guide himself. To be effective, it must be genuine" (16).

The selection of a counseling approach need not involve a narrow choice between counselor-centered *vs.* client-centered. In the broad sense, any approach is "client-centered" if it is well adapted to the needs of the individual and his adjustment problem, and if it aims to help the student help himself. Hence, as Sister Annette Walters puts it, "If the student is emotionally upset, he is encouraged to express his feelings and emotions. If he is in need of information and advice, and is emotionally as well as intellectually ready to receive it, it is given to him" (20, p. 231).

REFERENCES

1. BAKER, H. J. *Introduction to exceptional children.* New York: Macmillan, 1944.
2. BALDWIN, A. L., KALHORN, J., & BREESE, F. H. The appraisal of parent behavior. *Psychol. Monogr.,* 1949, **63,** 1-85.
3. COXE, W. W. Levels and ranges of ability in N. Y. State high schools. *New York State Dept. Educ., Bull.* 1001, 1932.
4. DOUGLASS, HARL. *Teaching in the high school.* New York: Ronald Press, 1948.
5. GRAY, H. A., & HOLLINGWORTH, L. S. The achievement of gifted children enrolled and not enrolled in special opportunity classes. *J. educ. Res.,* 1931, **24,** 255-261.
6. HAHN, M. E., & BRAYFIELD, A. H. *Job exploration workbook and occupational laboratory manual.* Chicago: Science Research Assoc., 1945.
7. HARTSHORNE, H., & MAY, M. A. *Studies in service and self-control.* New York: Macmillan, 1929.
8. KELLEY, T. L. *Interpretation of educational measurements.* Yonkers, N. Y.: World Book Co., 1927.
9. McLENDON, I. R. Unpublished Ph.D. dissertation, Ohio State Univ., 1948.

10. MORENO, J. L. *Who shall survive?* (2d ed.). New York: Beacon House, Inc., 1953.

11. The grouping of pupils. *35th Yearbook,* Natl. Soc. for the Study of Ed., 1936.

12. PORTER, E. H. JR. *An introduction to therapeutic counseling.* Boston: Houghton Mifflin, 1950.

13. ROCK, R. T. A critical study of current practices in ability grouping. *Catholic Univ. Educ. Res. Bull.,* 1929, **4,** Nos. 5 and 6.

14. ROETHLISBERGER, F. J., & DICKSON, R. *Management and the worker.* Cambridge: Harvard Univ. Press, 1939.

15. ROETHLISBERGER, F. J. *Management and morale.* Cambridge: Harvard Univ. Press, 1947.

16. ROGERS, C. R. *Client centered therapy.* Boston: Houghton Mifflin, 1951.

17. STRANG, R. *Educational guidance: its principles and practice.* New York: Macmillan, 1947.

18. SUPER, D. E. *Appraising vocational fitness by means of psychological tests.* New York: Harper, 1949.

19. VAN WAGENEN, M. J. A comparison of the mental ability and school achievement of bright and dull pupils. *J. educ. Psychol.,* 1925, **16,** 186-197.

20. WALTERS, SISTER ANNETTE. In BROUWER, P. J. (Ed.), *Student personnel services in general education.* Washington, D.C.: A.C.E., 1949.

SELECTED READINGS

CURRAN, C. A. *Counseling in Catholic life and education.* New York: Macmillan, 1952. A text for college courses in counseling, with excellent material on the role of counseling in the school.

ECKERT, R., & MARSHALL, T. O. *When youth leave school.* New York: McGraw-Hill, 1938.

FROEHLICH, C. P., & DARLEY, J. G. *Studying students.* Chicago: Science Research Associates, 1952. A complete guide for the school guidance program.

GARRISON, K. C. The psychology of exceptional children. (Rev. ed.) New York: Ronald Press, 1950.

NATIONAL SOCIETY FOR STUDY OF EDUCATION. *52d Yearbook,* 1953. Pt. I, Adapting the secondary school program to the needs of youth.

PINTNER, R., EISENSON, J., & STANTON, M. *Psychology of the physically handicapped.* New York: Crofts, 1945. Presents conclusions carefully drawn from research.

STRANG, R. *Educational guidance: its principles and practices.* New York: Macmillan, 1947. Contains excellent instruction on how to observe children.

SUPER, D. E. *Appraising vocational fitness by means of psychological tests.* New York: Harper, 1949. Chs. 20, 21.

The following books present a consistent point of view with regard to theory of counseling:

CURRAN, C. A. *Counseling in Catholic life and education* (cited above).

LECKY, P. *Self-consistency.* New York: Island Press, 1945.

PORTER, E. H. *Introduction to therapeutic counseling.* Boston: Houghton Mifflin, 1950.

ROGERS, C. R. *Client-centered therapy.* Boston: Houghton Mifflin, 1951.

SNYGG, D., & COMBS, A. W. *Individual behavior.* New York: Harper, 1949.

PART IV

The Conditions of Learning

12

THE LEARNING PROCESS

LEARNING was described in Chapter 2 as a process or sequence of activities leading to a modification of functional tendencies. Learning is not then a special kind of mental activity like seeing or willing or thinking. It is the change or transformation taking place within these and other mental processes. If we ask the student trying to solve a geometrical problem to describe what he is doing in terms of mental activity, he will say that he is thinking, first of this, then of that, and so on, until at last he thinks of the correct solution. The learner can of course look back over this change once it has come to a successful issue, and know that it has taken place, that but a short time ago he did not see the solution and now he does. But there is not a special mental process over and above the "thinking" itself that the learner brings into play and which is called learning. Learning has various forms, which are merely classifications of the activities of the learner (memorizing, thinking, social and emotional behavior) or of the products of learning (habits, skills, attitudes, interests). But all forms of learning show the same characteristic processes by which the learner organizes his activities.

This chapter attempts to specify the essential conditions of learning, and to show that learning *anything* is an outcome of the conditions. It should make clear what is meant by saying "the learner must want something, notice something, do something, and get something" (3). It should answer some very practical questions: Teaching requires the use of problems, but what is a problem? Why do students make so many "boners?" Why do they learn so many things the teacher does not intend?

Why do some lose interest?   How much help should the teacher give, and what kind?

Learning and the Learner. Learning does not occur by chance. The outcome of any behavior depends on antecedent conditions within the learner, conditions in the learning situation, and the consequences of what the learner does. When we talk about the psychology of the learner, we are concentrating on *him:* what he brings to the situation, how he interprets the cues, what he does, and what changes the outcome brings about in his mental organization. From this point of view, the learning process is an active, purposeful organization of the learner's activities. We are not here concerned with learning as "acquisitions" of information or habits, nor with connections between stimuli and responses, but with the basic tendency of the learner to organize activity to satisfy his needs.

It is the whole organism, the whole individual, that acts, reacts, and learns. If we make learning broad enough to include animal as well as human learning, or if we do not narrow our perspective by limiting it to rote memorizing, we shall find clear evidence of four of its distinctive characteristics. First, there is the fact that the learner is "tending somewhither," that he is ready to persist and "blunder through" if need be to the attainment of some *goal* object or state. Secondly, his behavior is *variable* within rather wide limits as long as it is not inconsistent with the attainment of the goal. Stereotyped behavior is the antithesis of learning. Again, this variability resolves itself into greater *directness* toward the end-state, with a consequent small expenditure of time and energy. Finally, all this takes place within the *conditions* imposed by the situation to which the learner is adjusting. Some of these conditions may be represented by sensory stimuli, or cues to action, others by the temporal or spatial arrangement of these rather than their own inherent characteristics, others by reason of their similarity to or difference from present or previous objects, and still others by reason of attributes which depend on the previous life-history of the individual. There is the further fact that the situation may vary in many obvious particulars from time to time and yet the individual will show, or continue with, his adjustment to the situation as long as it is of a certain general "kind."

Interaction in Learning.   In general, the products of learning are mental changes within the learner, or modifications of his tendencies.   This implies that we can never talk about the products without some reference to the processes that produced them.   We may distinguish three kinds of changes: (1) *cognitive* changes, consisting of knowledge or ways of seeing or apprehending things; (2) *motivational* changes in motives, goals, and interests; and (3) *behavioral* changes, which unlike the first two are outwardly apparent to the observer.   Behavior refers to the movements or speech of a person.   Changes in knowledge or motives cannot be observed directly, but are inferred from what the learner does as a result of these changes. Cognitive, motivational, and behavioral changes all occur together in learning, and are *interactive;* that is, they exert an influence on one another.   Consider, for example, the person learning to swim.   From a demonstration by others, he knows that swimming consists of certain movements.   This knowledge leads to motivational changes (interest or goal) which leads him to such behavioral changes as talking about swimming or actually getting in the water or trying to imitate the movements. Similarly, the knowledge that somebody drowned may lead to fear of the water (motive) and avoiding the water (behavior). Personal knowledge of the tricks of swimming, gained through experience, heighten the interest and decrease the fear, and also lead to behavioral improvement in skills and coordination.

In common usage, the word "learn" is often restricted to knowledge or information, and to behavioral skills like speaking, handwriting, and driving a car.   These are not the only products of learning.   *Attitudes* are also learned.   In general, an attitude is a motive—a "set" or disposition to feel or act in a certain way.

Attitudes are often confused with information.   The child who says "my father is very strong" states it as a matter of fact or information, rather than as an attitude of dependence.   The adult just as easily states as facts that prize-fighting is brutal, that football builds character, or that Chinese are dishonest, and supports the statements with items of information.   But these are attitudes, or "non-facts"; they must be distinguished from the learned information that supports them.   A more accurate (but rarely encountered) statement would be something like this: "I have had certain experiences which cause me to dislike prize-fighting, to like football, and to distrust Chinese.   I have therefore tended to acquire and remember certain facts which are consistent with these attitudes."

"Learning" thus encompasses all aspects of behavior, as well as information and skills.   Interests, goals, personality traits, emotional reactions—by whatever names we call them—are produced by and modified by the learning process.   That is why, in discussing any single learning event, we must be concerned with the learner, and his predispositions.   Furthermore, we must be aware that he learns many attitudes toward himself, and toward things and persons, which are not intended. The student in the classroom not only learns the "facts" of history, but attitudes about historical events, about his abilities, and about the teacher and school.

Nearly everything we learn affects the conditions of learning something else.   If "everything depends on everything else" learning would seem to be so disorderly as to defy any attempt to make sense of it.   But the fact that learning is a process also implies a kind of order or regularity in the sequence of events that make it up.   Hence learning is *lawful,* and to some extent predictable; it is not a series of unrelated events, but a sequence of related and interacting events.   The principles or "laws" of learning are statements about the relationships.

Some Aspects of Learning.   Learning is so fundamental a concept in psychology that the word has acquired a number of meanings.   Some other words like "development" and "adjustment" refer to certain aspects of learning.   This is sometimes confusing to students, and we need to clarify the ways in which the word "learning" is used.

1. *Learning as change in behavior.* The word behavior, as we have seen, refers to activities which are observable to the outsider, so learning involves "outward change." Some writers refer to this as a change in *performance.* Ordinarily it means improvement in performance, but not necessarily, because the resultant performance may not always be better or more valuable. Errors and undesirable habits are also learned but do not constitute improvement.

2. *Learning as change in experience.* "Experience" refers to inner processes such as feeling, thinking, imagining. "Inward change" of this kind is not directly observable by the outsider, but may be inferred from changes in behavior or performance. Here again, learning does not necessarily mean improvement, as undesirable feelings and attitudes are learned as well as desirable ones. Historically, learning has often been considered as a separate faculty or power, over and above the mental processes themselves. Thus a child may sometimes be said to "learn" the multiplication table and to "reason" out an arithmetic problem. This is misleading. Remembering, thinking, reasoning, and feeling are all modifications of experience and are therefore forms of learning.

3. *Learning as an aspect of mental development.* Mental development, or "mental growth," usually connotes improvement—better skills, more socially adequate knowledge or abilities, more desirable attitudes characteristic of "maturity." Development means progress with age, and refers to changes in children's behavior and experience in terms of levels of maturity. The development point of view attempts to explain how the past interacts with the present to produce successively higher levels of performance. The principles of mental development are principles of learning, however, because they are "laws" of psychological change. Thus, when we use the term mental development, we are referring to a special aspect of learning as "improvement of behavior and experience in the direction of greater maturity."

4. *Learning as adjustment.* The process of adjusting is that of adapting one's self to conditions or situations, or relating one's self more favorably to the environment. Note "favor-

ably"—again it connotes improvement. Adjustment means becoming more adequate, acquiring better control of a situation, overcoming obstacles. Adjustment may involve acquiring a skill, altering an attitude, or gaining knowledge and understanding; all of these changes comprise learning. *Adjustment* is therefore a special aspect of learning which means "alteration in behavior or experience resulting in more adequate adaptation to situations." Maladjustment is also learned, but refers to less adequate adaptation.

5. *Learning as an active process.* It is a commonplace that we "learn by doing"—that no learning takes place without activity. This is true, but there is an unfortunate tendency to give "activity" a narrow interpretation, to restrict its meaning to skeletal movements or manual activity alone. There are some things (like swimming) that cannot be learned except through movements. On the other hand, activity includes such mental acts as perceiving, thinking, imagining.

6. *Learning as an unconscious phenomenon.* By unconscious we mean simply "unaware." Many modifications of our experience and behavior occur without our being fully aware of them or aware of the conditions under which the changes occur. Learning is usually a conscious process in remembering, acquiring specific information or skills, and problem solving. The learner can ordinarily give a fairly good account of his mental activities in such tasks, and is aware of his reactions at various stages of the process as well as the results. The learner can rarely give an account of how or why he acquired certain attitudes, likes, dislikes, or fears because he is not and was not aware of the conditions under which they were learned. The learning of infants is probably unconscious (we say "probably" because there is no way of proving it) and much adult learning is also. Many habits and attitudes are acquired without conscious intent or conscious purpose on the part of the learner. This does not mean that learning is unmotivated, but only that the learner is often not aware of the motive. Unconscious learning may not be the characteristic form of human learning, but a surprisingly large number of our tendencies are acquired without our conscious control.

THE LEARNING SEQUENCE

Learning is a sequence of mental events or conditions leading to changes in the learner. This sequence takes place in a "problem situation," or one in which the individual is forced by reason of his own goal-seeking tendencies to vary his behavior. As a sequence of events, we might look upon the learning process as follows: (1) The individual has *needs* and is therefore in a state of *readiness* to respond. These are antecedent conditions within the learner. (2) He meets a learning *situation,* or problem. A new interpretation is required because previously learned responses are not adequate for reaching the goal and satisfying his need. He encounters something new or unexpected, and must search for a different response. (3) He *interprets* the situation with reference to his goals, and tries a *response* or responses which seem to satisfy his need. The way he perceives the situation and the response he makes depends both on his "readiness" and on external conditions of the situation. (4) If his response leads to desired goals or satisfaction, he will tend to interpret and respond to similar future situations in the same way. If not, he keeps on trying and reinterpreting until satisfying *consequences* are attained. The end-result, change in the learner, depends on satisfying consequences; these are products of conditions of readiness and certain conditions in the situation. The learning process is the whole sequence. Need alone does not result in learning, nor does mere exposure to a situation. Even a problem situation does not produce changes in the learner unless his activity has consequences important to him.

Needs and Readiness. All learning is motivated. An organism acts to satisfy needs. Without need there will be no activity, hence no learning; a rock cannot learn. Need determines whether or not the learner will act in a given situation. By need we mean a state of dissatisfaction in the learner, and the motivated activity is therefore a striving for a more satisfactory state of affairs. In general, the more intense the dissatisfaction, the more active will be the behavior of the learner.

The term "need" encompasses not only such organic needs as those for food, water, oxygen, sleep, and sex activity, but the so-called "acquired needs" which are derivatives or modifications of these.   Human organic needs become modified through learning into a complex multitude of acquired needs.   Need for food may become a need for American cooking, for sirloin steak, or even for steak with a certain kind of sauce.   There are about as many acquired needs as there are nouns and verbs to express them.   Needs of the learner refer to any generalized motives, including such social motives as need for affection, approval, mastery, and the like.   In the socialized human being, most needs important in learning are modified social motives. Since no two individuals have the same experiences, needs vary with individuals.

How will a person respond in a given situation?   Response is largely determined of course by the nature of the situation, but there are factors in the learner which are often controlling. These factors can be summarized by the term "readiness," meaning that the learner has a predisposition to respond or act in a certain way.

By readiness as a predisposition, we mean that the learner has certain *expectations* of "what is likely to lead to what," and these expectations are learned from past experience.   He is set to respond in a certain way, because he expects something.   The child who has seen others swim thus expects that certain movements will keep him afloat.   We may say that the learner has a goal, with some idea or expectation of what will lead to the goal; in other words, he has interests.   Part of the readiness of a child for swimming is certainly his observation that ability to swim leads to approval of parents and other persons, especially those of his own age.

The learner's expectations also control his *attention;* that is, they determine what aspects of a given situation he will notice or respond to, and the kind of response he will make.   Thus the person "interested" in learning to swim will note the detailed differences in movements between better and poorer swimmers, while another will perhaps notice only that some splash more than others or wear different suits.   The boy acutely conscious of his inability to swim will perhaps be more attentive to the age of persons who can swim, particularly of persons around his own age. Expectations also determine the learner's degree of alertness, as well as the details he will notice.

Instead of talking about "aspects of situations" which attract attention, we may call these attention-getting aspects *cues*. A cue can be anything the learner notices, sees, hears, touches, or smells—in short, any stimulus. It serves as a sign or symbol leading to a goal, to satisfaction of need. The things, persons, and events comprising a learning situation are thus said to differ in "cue value." What is significant in a situation to one person is insignificant or unnoticed by another whose goals and interests are not related by previous learning to the cues. "Readiness" therefore means readiness to interpret or respond to available cues.

The Learning Situation. The learning situation is always a *problem,* from the point of view of the learner. A problem situation is one in which the learner's goal cannot be attained by responses he already knows, and which requires him to do something new. If his fountain pen runs dry and he has some ink, he simply fills it. In this he learns nothing new, but simply "runs off" a habit already learned. But if he has no ink and no pencil, he must try something new and may learn, for example, a new source of ink or a new substitute. To put this another way, if the learner never had to vary his responses, he would never learn anything.

We acquire information and skills, in other words, only because they contribute to the solution of a present problem or an anticipated future problem. The fact that learning goes on continuously indicates that the learner is constantly facing problem situations in which habitual interpretations and responses do not "work" in the attainment of his goal. Learning situations thus involve a "felt difficulty."

What is a "good" learning situation? In general, it may be described as one which provides appropriate cues and thus brings out the right responses. The conditions of the adequate learning situation are these:

1. It must *provide cues suitable to the goals* of the learner. It must "fit" his state of readiness, or in other words must be interesting to him and appropriate to his abilities. The most suitable cues are those which the learner expects.

2. It must *provide distinctive cues*. The appropriate cues must be noticed. They must therefore stand out from the background of the entire situation so the learner may distinguish the important ones from the unimportant ones. This often depends on contrast. Important visual cues must be more vivid or colorful than less important ones; important auditory cues must be either louder or softer than others.

3. *Combinations of cues should be grouped or patterned.* If the "right" interpretation or response depends on noticing a number of specific cues together as a whole, grouping will help. If the specific cues must be noticed one after another in sequence, the situation should make the sequence noticeable. The learning situation must be organized, as far as possible, so that relationships among cues are readily apparent. In many complex situations, this amounts to giving the learner a kind of map or outline which will keep him from getting lost in the details of the situation.

4. *Inappropriate cues must be indistinct.* This requirement, of course, follows from the others, but it needs special emphasis. A child familiar with long-haired dogs and short-haired cats may call a fox terrier a "cat," responding to the familiar cues of size and coat. A teacher complains that children who learned long division first and short division later always use the long method, even when they are given problems more easily done by the short method. In both of these examples, a present situation contains cues to which a specific interpretation and response was learned in the past; the cues are "false leads," but so distinct that they determine the learner's response. Somebody once said, for example, that he had no trouble calling a general or a bishop by their correct titles, but in spite of himself always called Senator Jones and Dr. Smith "Mister." The distinct cue for "general" or "bishop" is of course his dress. When appropriate and inappropriate cues are equally distinct, the learning situation has all the charac-

teristics of a puzzle. Inappropriate cues must be eliminated, buried, or hidden if the learner is to do something new without a prolonged period of trial and error and search for new cues.

Good teaching practice always takes advantage of these principles. They are also crucial principles which help us to understand behavior, since an individual always responds to a situation as he interprets it. When the learner makes a wrong or ludicrous response, we ask "To what cue is he attending?"

In any situation, the individual will perhaps learn something, but what he learns will be appropriate to his needs and readiness. The well-known "boners" which teachers deplore and humorists treasure are usually instances in which the student responds to cues which are appropriate and distinct to him, but not apparent to the teacher. The student who said filet mignon was an opera, defined hamlet as a little pig, and said that Denver is just below the "o" in Colorado was responding to distinct and familiar cues. Boners like the student's claim that "the climate of Bombay is such that its inhabitants have to live elsewhere" and "the equator is a menagerie lion running around the earth through Africa" are ordinarily blamed on the stupidity of the learner, but are often due to cues given unintentional distinctness in the learning situation.

Interpreting the Situation. The way the learner interprets the situation depends on (1) his past learning, or "readiness" to interpret the cues, which is a matter of information, skills, and personal goals; and (2) the way the learning situation is arranged or organized to make the appropriate cues distinctive. Interpretation is easy or difficult, depending on the learner's readiness and the distinctness of the cues.

Interpretation is cognitive, but is strongly influenced by motivational factors. Thus it is often said that a person sees in things, persons, and events what he wants or expects to see. We find it easy to see defects in persons of a particular political party, race, religion, or region toward which we have a negative attitude, and difficult to see defects in persons whom we favor or like. We pay attention to, and remember, those details which are related to our goals, and ignore those which are not.

Our motives very often distort our perceptions. For example, an experiment found that poor children overestimated the size of various coins more than children from wealthier families. For both poor and rich children, "the greater the value of the coin, the greater the constant error of overestimation" (1). Adults underestimated the size of pennies, nickels, and dimes, but overestimated quarters and half dollars. As advertisers well know, our perceptions are also distorted by suggestions appealing to desires for prestige, popularity, "sex appeal," and other motives.

Interpretation depends on three kinds of cognitive processes: differentiation, integration, and symbolization.

1. *Differentiation* is discriminating, or perceiving differences among cues. The learner differentiates when he becomes aware of the details of a situation, and "separates out" certain cues as having distinct meanings. An "undifferentiated" situation is vague, confusing, and results in aimless or random responses. Increased awareness of details is thus a kind of analyzing or breaking up the situation into separately perceived parts. The child has a low level of differentiation; he does not discriminate between nickels and dimes, calls all men "daddy," and all furry animals dogs. With continued experience, the different details become more distinct. Thus the learner, because of past experience, is more "ready" to differentiate familiar situations than unfamiliar ones. Differentiation is involved in learning to swim or type or hit a baseball, as well as in learning to speak and to name things correctly.

2. *Integration* is the process of perceiving likenesses or relationships among cues. Most learning situations not only require us to notice separate details, but to figure out the meaning of a number of separate details occurring together. When the learner interprets multiple cues as having a meaning by reason of their "togetherness" he is integrating. Integration is then the recognition of a cue pattern, or relationships among cues. What pattern does the reader recognize in the following words? WOOD-FELT-WIRE-KEY-HAMMER-BOARD-STRIKE-PEDAL-SHEET-NOTE-SOUND. Perhaps none, unless he is a musician. As soon as "music' is mentioned, most persons immediately think of

"piano." The integration makes all the words jump together into meaningful relations. This may happen when "pedal" is introduced, and the probability increases with each of the last three words.

Integration is not necessarily a reasoning process, a painstaking comparison of relationships among a number of details. Consider, for example, how the kinship of mother and son is immediately recognized because they look alike; the total similarity is recognized first, before we are aware of details. Consider how a strange town you have never before visited may seem "familiar"—again the rapid integration of multiple cues. At a simple level, integration occurs constantly and without effort.

Integration and differentiation are complementary processes. The beginning swimmer who suddenly acquires the "feel" of keeping himself afloat has integrated a pattern of differentiated arm, leg, and body movements. Integration makes further differentiation possible, so that the swimmer develops new movements and reaches higher levels of integration. The difference between the thrashing dog-paddler and the smooth, precise motions of the experienced swimmer is a difference in level of integration, as is the contrast between the child's counting and the adult's multiplication of large numbers.

3. *Symbolization.* A symbol is a sign—something that stands for something else. We have already noted that cues function as signs or symbols in the learning situation, and therefore the interpretation of cues involves symbolic processes or symbolization—sometimes called the "higher processes." We said that any thing, person, or event may have cue value (function as a symbol for the learner) and that the cue value is acquired by learning. Thus a milk bottle may be a cue for lunch, going to the store, bringing in the cows, feeding the baby, watering the flowers, public health slogans, or the solution of a problem in plumbing or mathematics, depending on the learner's "set" and the situation in which the milk bottle appears. It is said that Newton's laws of mechanics resulted from the cue of an apple falling on his head—a reminder of our tendency to think symbolically.

The commonest cues in human learning are *words,* because a word can stand for countless things, persons, and events. Words like loyal, obey, enemy, approve, and the like, enable us to "generalize" and get order or meaning from complex situations, whether the words are spoken, written, or merely "thought." Gestures operate in the same way. The human environment is remarkably characterized by words and gestures, which give us most of our cues. It is clear that the processes of differentiation and integration are made easier by the acquired cue value of words.

The more words we know, the easier it is to make distinctions and to generalize, i.e., to see deeper relationships or similarities among things and events that appear superficially to be unrelated. Words are also logical traps which often fool us and "tie up" our thinking, because we have a tendency to confuse words and things—to assume that two things called by the same word must be alike, or that two different words must stand for two different things. But in general, symbols like words, gestures, and mathematical symbols are tremendous short cuts to interpretation.

Language plays the most important role in learning and teaching. Language enables us to manipulate symbols "mentally," as we do when we plan or reason, and thus facilitates planning or *foresight* of consequences. In a problem situation, the learner can "act out" imaginatively (mentally talking to himself) a great many alternatives without actually trying any, and can select an appropriate one in terms of foreseen consequences. He says "If I do this, X will happen and Y will not."

Reasoning is the process of selecting or abstracting various elements from our past experience and combining them into an essentially new pattern to solve a problem. Reasoning involves the interpretation of cues from past experience and from the problem situation, the comparison of two sets of cues for relationships, and the symbolic manipulation of alternatives. It is a mental talking to one's self, and therefore involves abstraction, some kind of language, and foresight.

All learning is to some extent cognitively controlled (2), or involves understanding to a degree. The role of understanding, however, is often overemphasized by teachers who expect too much of the learner by assuming that he wants to achieve clarity and "get to the bottom of things." Rather, he wants to satisfy immediate needs, reach immediate goals. Some learning is relatively blind; evidence from learning experiments shows that even adults produce correct responses repeatedly without being aware of the relationships involved. Learning situations should be set up so as not to overtax the learner's capacity or readiness to understand. However, the general principle is that the more adequate the interpretation, the more adequate the response and the more adequate the learning.

Behavioral Responses of the Learner. By "behavioral responses" we mean the outward, visible movements of the learner. Assuming that some kind of interpretation has occurred, what does the learner *do* in the situation? What determines whether he will say this or that, perform one movement or another, exert himself, laugh, cry, go to sleep, or swear? Since a response is a means to an end, what the learner does is selective; it does not occur by chance. Of all possible responses, all are not equally likely to occur; some are more likely to occur than others because of habit. Psychologists sometimes use the term *response hierarchy,* indicating that responses are arranged in a sequence of "probability of occurrence," with stronger habitual responses at the top of the hierarchy and weaker ones further down (less likely to occur). "Habit" may therefore be one controlling factor.

The second factor is interpretation; the learner always does the most appropriate thing in terms of his expectations and foreseen consequences. It may seem paradoxical to say that the response may be mere habit, and in the next breath to say that the learner always does the most appropriate thing. Are not habitual responses often inappropriate? Yes, but inappropriate "running off of habits" occurs when the situation is misinterpreted, or when the learner is confused. "Right" interpretation reduces the possibility of mere habit-responses.

If the situation is well interpreted the learner's behavior will be less variable, or more precise in terms of the demands of the situation. Responses are goal-directed, to the extent that the learner interprets the situation in relation to his expectations (4). He does something because he expects something. In explaining behavior in problem situations, psychologists have used the term *provisional try* as an alternative to the "running off of habits," which is said to characterize trial-and-error behavior. "Provisional try" implies that the learner is making a "genuine attempt at discovering the route to the goal" (2).

It is important to note that insightful interpretation, or perception of a "correct" means-end relationship, usually follows a period of fumbling and false starts. In other words, the sequence is usually interpretation of cue, inadequate response, reinterpretation of cues, further response, search for cues, another response, and the like. What the learner does becomes part of the situation, because what he does (his tries, his movements, his words) produces new cues. Behavioral responses are said to be cue-producing in the sense that they make the learner aware of cues which he previously missed. Words, gestures, and other bodily movements, although sometimes apparently inappropriate or "off the track," thus frequently help the learner to reinterpret the situation and achieve solutions. We must remember that sometimes very "odd" behavior has cue-producing value for persons.

The learner always makes a whole response to the whole situation. "Whole situation" here means not the physical situation as it exists, but the situation as interpreted by the learner. This is another way of saying that he does what seems to him at the moment to be the most appropriate thing. This principle alone makes it possible to understand a great deal of behavior which seems perverse, wicked, or stupid—without attributing perversity, wickedness, or stupidity to the behaver.

Consequences to the Learner. Every act of the learner leads to consequences for him. He achieves the goal, or he does not; he has feelings of failure or of success; his needs are satisfied, or dissatisfaction continues; his expectations are confirmed or disappointed. Those responses leading to "success" tend to become a part of the learner's response repertoire; that is, they become more ready for use in a similar situation, or more habitual. They are sometimes said to have been "reinforced" by the consequence, which means that they are more likely to occur when the learner finds himself in a similar problem. On the other hand, those responses which led to "failure," punishment, or disappointment will tend to be avoided.

Changes in the learner are changes in readiness to do some things and to avoid others. The oftener his expectations are confirmed or his behavior rewarded, the more automatically he tends to behave when the situation is repeated. The responses are learned to a high degree of precision. He becomes "blind" to other cues, and his attention thus becomes "grooved." Un-rewarded or "punished" responses are discontinued if they consistently fail to satisfy the individual's needs.

The learner himself, however, interprets the outcome. He is the sole arbiter of success or failure, satisfaction or dissatisfaction, because his needs are personal needs. One person's success may be failure to another. Usually the approval of others is rewarding, because it has acquired cue value which makes it so. But even social approval may have a punishing effect. A gold star or word of praise from the teacher may serve as a cue for annoyance or punishment for the "tough boy" from the other side of the tracks, who might in this way lose the respect of his peers. Success to one person may be failure to another who expects more of himself. Thus one student may be happy with a C grade while another complains bitterly about a B. A child's personal satisfaction in thumb-sucking may counterbalance the punishments inflicted by parents, so the behavior continues.

VARIABLES IN THE LEARNING PROCESS

In the sequence of conditions and events we have described —need, readiness, problem situation, interpretation, response, reward—some change in the learner will inevitably result. We can say in general that a well motivated learner, in a situation that requires or permits purposeful, goal-directed activity and satisfying consequences, will learn. But what happens if his expectations are not confirmed? What if the situation is vague, if the learner misinterprets it and does the wrong thing? How is the individual's "readiness" altered when inappropriate behavior leads to feelings of failure? All situations are not equally clear, all learners do not have the same tendencies, and the "success" of the outcome is relative to the individual's goals. Our attention is thus called to variables in the learning sequence, resulting from individual differences among learners and certain characteristics of learning situations. The important thing to grasp is that what happens is an outcome of the conditions, not mere chance. If we understand the conditions of the learner and the situation, we may be able to predict the outcome. If we can alter the conditions appropriately, we can often control the outcome.

Because the conditions of learning vary from person to person and from one situation to another, different persons may learn different things in the same external situation. In the same classroom "lesson" one student may learn to reproduce what the book says about the hypotenuse of a right-angled triangle, another may learn a good way to lay out a tennis court, a third may learn a new way to keep from being called on. A fourth may conclude that he is "no good at math," and a fifth may develop a dawning idea of a vocational goal. All those outcomes are lawful, or in accord with learning principles. The differences in outcomes are due to the variables in motivation, in the way the situation is presented and apprehended, in the goal-seeking activities of the learners. The outcome varies according to the motive, the situation, and the consequences because all of these factors contribute to, or impose limits on, the way in which the learner organizes his activity.

Learning Dilemmas. A learning dilemma (3) is a problem situation in which a familiar response no longer leads to a familiar goal. The learner knows very well that response X will lead to goal Y, because it always has in the past. Since he has always been "rewarded" for the behavior, he has learned it very thoroughly and a high degree of expectancy has been created. The animal has always found food at a certain place in a maze, and now finds the path blocked. Mother has always come when the child cried, but crying no longer produces this result. The French student has learned that "il y a" means "there is" but is stumped by "Qu'est-ce qu'il y a?" The teacher finds that a previously successful method does not produce desired results with a new group. The salesman's tried and true techniques fail in the new territory. The "show-off" pushy child who has gained attention and approval at home finds that this gains him no friends at school. The old timer's good stories and jokes are no longer appreciated. These are learning dilemmas. The familiar situation is altered somewhat, or the problem is presented in a different way, so that the customary behavior is no longer appropriate or satisfying.

The "dilemma" refers of course to the mental state of the learner. The immediate effect on the learner is confusion, because the familiar cues are now "red herrings" and he is blind to the new ones. A search for new cues and reinterpretation is required. But reinterpreting may be quite difficult, particularly when the changed situation resembles the familiar one and the learner cannot differentiate the details.

The individual is more likely to be vexed or emotionally disturbed in the learning dilemma than he would be in the completely new, unfamiliar problem. The situation may appear conducive to thinking and reorganization, but when the goal-drive is strong this is not likely to occur right away. There are three possible end-results of the learning dilemma:

1. So-called "trial-and-error" behavior, which eventually leads to a more appropriate interpretation and response. He tries one thing after another. At first his efforts may appear to be vague and aimless, but this apparently random behavior may actually represent goal-directed "provisional tries." Sometimes the learner appears to muddle through and finally to hit upon a more satisfactory response by mere luck. The salesman's new approach or the teacher's new method is found to work better, but he cannot tell exactly why. Although apparently not insightful, this successful adjustment depends to some extent, at least, on the ability to differentiate the new situation from the old. To put it another way, the learner will not

vary his behavior in a given situation unless he perceives some change in what the situation requires.

2. Withdrawal from the situation, or giving up. This occurs usually after he has "tried everything," and has become satiated with trying. Although the outcome is not successful, *some* learning nevertheless occurs because withdrawing involves some changes in the learner. He gets rid of the problem by altering his motive. A change of goals, new interests, altered attitudes and self-definitions are the result.

3. Nonadaptive or nonadjustive behavior. The individual may continue to respond inappropriately and fail to reinterpret. Apparently no learning occurs, because the behavior becomes a kind of mechanized repetition of responses which do not lead to any goal. This type of behavior is so unusual that it is considered "abnormal."

The learning dilemma is an important aspect of education. As long as the individual gains rewards by what he is doing, he will not vary his response or learn anything new. A person will not learn a better method of swimming if dog-paddling or the side-stroke works to his satisfaction. The child who uses long division when short division would work needs to be placed in a learning dilemma. In one case, a child was retarded in learning to talk because the mother was adept at understanding the child's gestures. When the mother placed the child in a dilemma by pretending to be stupid in interpreting the gestures, the child learned to talk in order to satisfy its needs (3).

The Essentials of Learning. The learning process is one of continuous organization and reorganization. From this point of view, the essentials of learning are those conditions which determine the organizing activity of the learner. These are as follows:

1. *Motivation of the learner.* Needs are the basis of learning. The motive is not related to learning merely as a facilitating accidental circumstance. It is not something that may be present or absent, but an absolutely indispensable something, a *sine qua non* of learning. Motive is indispensable to learning because it represents the antecedent, dynamic background out

of which emerge both the original behavior and its modification. Animals do not learn in the absence of an active need such as hunger, thirst, or avoidance of pain, and the speed of learning is usually proportionate to the strength of the need. Similarly, human beings do not learn unless some need arouses activity.

2. *Structured situation.* Instead of thinking of the environment in terms of discrete cues to which we react, we must regard an effective situation as a pattern of objects or forces, which depends upon the relationships holding among them. It is these relationships which influence our apprehension of the situation and our reaction to it. Learning cannot then be understood as the linking up of a response to a particular physical stimulus, for in a pattern of configuration a particular detail or element can vary, and yet the situation may remain fundamentally the same. Thus in the oft-quoted example a melody may be played now in one key and now in another, remaining all the while the same melody. It is the tones in relation to one another and not the discrete physical sounds themselves which we perceive and to which we effectively respond. Even when we make a response to a particular detail of the situation, it is always made to that detail in relation to other details.

3. *Purposeful activity.* Purposeful or goal-directed activity is not random, but follows a meaningful pattern. Behavior is not a chain or time series of discrete reactions, but as a meaningful act it has a certain plan by virtue of which it gets its significance for the individual and its appropriateness to the situation. The dog that hurts a foot will walk on three feet. His walking is not like a circuit of bridges which is thrown out of use when any one of them caves in. It is a total act which has an underlying scheme of organization and details to be fitted into it. If one of these details or bits of behavior is eliminated, the whole is not thereby destroyed. A pattern of behavior has as its basis a unity of organization in the service of a goal-activity. It has an appropriateness of detail which is in proportion to the clearness of apprehension of the demands of the situation and of the means of attaining the goal. As learning progresses, behavior and situation change together. The situation becomes more clearly perceived as to its important features while the pattern

of behavior is more and more clearly defined. There is a close natural connection between knowing and doing, and it would appear to be unwise to attempt to divorce one from the other, at least in the early days of learning.

The individual not only initiates his activity but contributes the modification of behavior which results in learning. Stimuli have no direct power to modify behavior. They represent merely the external conditions to which the learner must conform in attaining the goal of his activity. Stimuli, standing in certain relations one to another, furnish the pattern or plan of the situation to which the organism must conform. Simultaneous stimulation, instead of being directly effective in learning, is only one of the means by which the patterns of certain situations are made evident to the individual.

4. *Satisfying consequences.* A motive or need is not only accompanied by a certain amount of tension in the learner which must be resolved, but has as well a relation to the goal of activity. Learning becomes possible only as the goal is apprehended, and as this goal is given a meaningful setting among earlier needs. The activity of the learner is for the sake of attaining a goal. This is the important matter. Consequences must be satisfying and goal-tension reduced, if any modification is to occur. This does not mean that consequences must be pleasurable. It is more or less irrelevant whether the attainment of the goal brings pleasure or pain in the narrow sense. The point is that we learn, and tend to "store up" for later use, those forms of information and behavior which have been found effective. To say that consequences must be satisfying, then, means that the learner must have some means of discovering that his activity is effective.

The Guidance of Learning. The conditions of learning give us hints for managing and controlling the process. This control, which is the essence of teaching, is exercised by (1) motivating the learner, (2) providing appropriate situations or experiences, (3) teaching interpretive skills, (4) providing for appropriate practice, and (5) providing suitable consequences to the learner.

Individuals vary in what they bring to the classroom: differences in intelligence, goals, expectations, interests, self-evaluative attitudes, tastes, prejudices, and other predispositions. These cannot be ignored either in the materials of classroom instruction or in the teacher's approach. The development of interests and goals is an important aspect of teaching. A child's apparent "inability" to learn, in spite of much drill and repetition, is not infrequently due to the fact that he may not see what good will come of it. Studying children, their backgrounds and goals and interests, is not just an amusing hobby but an essential requirement of the teaching process. Incentives of whatever kind must be related to the immediate goals of the students.

"Problems" are the most effective learning experiences, as long as they are appropriate to the abilities and interests of students. The teacher should ask herself, before planning a class session, what kind of experience she wants this to be and what kind of behavior it should produce. On some occasions she may wish to provide distinct cues, to reduce fumbling and false interpretation. This amounts to demonstrating the solution of problems. At other times, she may wish to provoke thinking, and force the students to look for cues. In any case, the approach must be suitable to the range of differences in abilities and readiness of students.

Skills in interpretation need to be taught to most students. Cues are often missed; the student often cannot "pay attention" because he does not know what to pay attention to. High school students often need to be taught how to read—how to recognize and search for the cues deliberately provided by authors of textbooks. In any situation, the student needs to know what to look for, what to expect, how to recognize it. This is an important aspect of school assignments.

Providing suitable consequences is in many respects the key to the art of teaching. It is often the most neglected. Much careful and lucid teaching is ineffective because the student feels he is "not getting anywhere" in terms of his immediate goals. He must know not only just what is to be done, but what good will come of it if he does it. The general principle is to provide the kind of reward or recognition that will satisfy his needs. If genuine effort goes unrewarded or unrecognized, it should not be expected to continue. When the student learns from a situation something the teacher does not intend, such as "algebra is really a matter of luck," "flattering the teacher will get me somewhere," "keep quiet and you won't get called on," or "I can get by without working," it is usually because some behavior has been unwittingly rewarded in terms of his immediate goals.

The guidance of learning is not a matter of the classroom alone. The classroom provides the principal learning situations where the student's interpretive skills are observed, but not the only ones. The principles of learning supply hints for observing and understanding students not only in class, but on the playground and elsewhere.

REFERENCES

1. BRUNER, J. S. Social value and need as organizing factors in perception. *Amer. Psychol.,* 1946, **16,** 241.
2. HILGARD, E. R. *Theories of learning.* New York: Appleton-Century-Crofts, 1948.
3. MILLER, N. E., & DOLLARD, J. *Social learning and imitation.* New Haven: Yale Univ. Press, 1941.
4. TOLMAN, E. C. Social learning. In STOLUROW, L. M. (Ed.), *Readings in learning.* New York: Prentice-Hall, 1953.

SELECTED READINGS

BODE, B. H. *How we learn.* Boston: Heath, 1940.
HILGARD, E. R. *Theories of learning.* New York: Appleton-Century-Crofts, 1948.
HUMPHREY, G. *The nature of learning.* New York: Harcourt, Brace, 1933.
NATIONAL SOCIETY FOR STUDY OF EDUCATION. *41st Yearbook,* 1942. Pt. II, The psychology of learning. See especially chapters by G. W. Hartmann, The field theory of learning and its educational consequences; K. Lewin, Field theory of learning.
NATIONAL SOCIETY FOR STUDY OF EDUCATION. *49th Yearbook,* 1950. Pt. I, Learning and instruction, chs. 1 and 13; also Section III, chs. 9-12.
WHEELER, R. H., & PERKINS, F. T. *Principles of mental development.* New York: Crowell, 1932. Chs. 13-19.

13

LEARNING AS PERCEIVING

LEARNING processes are fundamentally a matter of perceiving. The individual learns as he comes to apprehend a situation in a new light, as objects assume new properties and "means-to-end" relations, and as he becomes increasingly able to discriminate between relevant and irrelevant procedures. This requires a *reorganization* of the situation, a shift in value for the learner of the total situation and of the separate objects which constitute it. The original behavior often appears as a means of "clarifying" the situation rather than a mere practicing of correct reactions. Later behavior becomes more precise, economical, or specialized as the learner perceives the relation of his activity to his goals. We must give first place, then, to a perceptual overview of the situation from which the behavior issues as a natural consequence. This will be as true of "motor" learning, or the development of skill, as of any form of higher learning.

Since learning is a matter of organization, some learning is made difficult by situations which do not favor organization, or which favor the wrong kind. Some learning is relatively "blind" or "stupid" because the situation does not permit any other kind of learning. Problems are often difficult to solve because irrelevant details obscure the solution. What the learner notices and does supplies him with a number of cues which must be organized into some pattern, plan, theme, or arrangement. He must grasp this plan or pattern as a whole, else he will come out at the end of the process with only snatches of information or bits of meaningless action. The important thing is not merely to have the child learn a fact or a bit of behavior, but

to ask in what setting we wish him to learn it. We are concerned, then, with such questions as these: How do learning
situations vary in clarity, cue distinctness, intelligibility? How
do these variables help or hinder the learner, and what effect do
they have on the outcome? How does the learner organize his
perceptions? What is the function of practice? What factors
contribute to economy in learning?

THE STRUCTURE OF LEARNING SITUATIONS

All situations are potentially learning situations, but they
vary in the way they are put together (structure) and the degree
to which appropriate cues are apparent. Learning situations
are therefore more or less meaningful, more or less restricting
on the learner's responses, and more or less facilitating in the
production of understanding. To make this clear, we shall
contrast three types of learning situations which have been
widely studied by psychologists. Out of these three types have
arisen most of the concepts and terms of learning, even those
terms employed by educators. They represent three classic
prototypes, namely, (1) the simple conditioning experiments
of Pavlov, (2) the "trial-and-error" experiment typified by
Thorndike's cat in a puzzle box, and (3) the experiments in insightful learning associated with Kohler's chimpanzees.

The Forced-Cue Situation: Conditioning. Pavlov, the
Russian physiologist, showed that it was possible to produce a
flow of saliva in a dog by "conditioning" this reflex to the sound
of a bell. Offering meat to the animal normally evokes the
salivary reaction. Pavlov found that when he did this in association with the ringing of a bell he was able, after a number of
repetitions, to cause the salivary response to be transferred from
the meat as a natural stimulus to the bell as a new or "conditioned" stimulus.

It appeared to a number of psychologists that the "conditioning" of a "reflex" furnished definite evidence in support of the
synaptic and connection-forming theory of learning, and that
the conditioned response could be taken as the typical model
of all learning (27). It has since become more and more ap-

parent that the conditioned response type of learning is a product of this particular kind of learning situation, and not typical of learning in general.

The learning pattern is imposed or "forced" by the situation. Let us note first of all that the dog (see Figure 48) is strapped

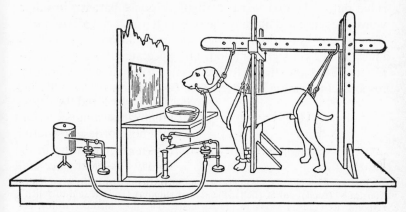

FIGURE 48. Conditioning: The Forced-Cue Learning Situation. The dog cannot escape. To satisfy his need (hunger) he learns to respond to carefully selected cues which are *imposed* on him by the experimenter. Forced learning of this kind is often blind and stupid. Superstitious reactions, emotional traits, and many desirable and undesirable responses are learned in similar situations. Meaningless "rote learning" may be likened to conditioning. (From R. M. Yerkes & S. Morgulis, The Method of Pavlov in Animal Psychology, *Psychol. Bull.*, 1909, **6**, 257.)

in a harness and is not allowed to escape. The dog must therefore select and organize its responses according to this particular situation. Since the dog is hungry and is permitted no freedom, hunger becomes the paramount need. Other needs or tensions (e.g., the need for freedom, need to explore) may be present but are not allowed to operate. This controls or restricts the animal's response "set" to stimuli having to do with food. One cue (the bell) is made distinct and all other cues are reduced. (The experimental situation endeavored to eliminate all distracting sights and sounds by keeping the dog in a sound-proof room, out of sight of the experimenter.) Only one type of reward (food) is allowed to occur. The conditions were all staged to permit his natural response (salivation) to become conditioned, i.e., to become attached to a substitute (bell) for the natural stimulus (food). The constant pairing of the conditioned and unconditioned stimuli thus reduced the experience of the animal to a single repetitive pattern (bell-food). Other forms of perceptual and behavioral activity are ruled out. The dog learns a single response pattern, in other words, because it is literally the only pattern he can learn in this "forced-cue" situation. Under these conditions, the bell is interpreted as a sign for food, an expectancy becomes established (24), and the bell thus comes to elicit a preparatory response (salivation) by itself (see Figure 49).

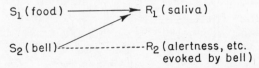

FIGURE 49. The Conditioned Response. After many paired presentations of S_1 (food) and S_2 (bell), the second stimulus (bell) is said to "elicit" response R_1 (saliva) when presented alone. The dog, in other words, responds to the bell as a sign of food.

Similar types of situations have resulted in similar types of learning. A pigeon enclosed in a box into which a grain of food is ejected at regular intervals has been found to develop a specific response to anticipation of food (21). The pigeon, however, when allowed a little more freedom in responding, developed and repeated its own anticipatory response. Different pigeons did different things, one flapping its wings, another pecking at the floor, a third walking in a particular pattern, and the like. This has been termed "superstitious" behavior because of its analogy to human behavior of the same sort.

Conflict situations have been set up experimentally in which animals were required to discriminate between two conditioned stimuli. In one of Pavlov's experiments, dogs were put into a situation in which a circle flashed on the wall was always accompanied by food and hence called for salivation, while an ellipse did not. When the dog was placed in a situation in which a stimulus was presented which could not be distinguished as either elliptical or circular, it developed marked behavior disturbances. Behavior disturbances have since been developed in sheep, rats, and pigs by conditioning techniques employing electric shock. These disturbances have been called *experimental neuroses*. They are analogous to human conflict situations which call for antagonistic but mutually exclusive responses (like the stage-frightened musician who can neither play well nor flee the stage). We note here that the conflict is induced not only by requiring impossible discriminations, but by the fact that the experimental animals cannot escape.

The stimulus response pattern learned through conditioning is an arbitrary one. There is no intrinsic relationship between bell and food, except that forced by the situation. For the most part, arbitrary relationships learned through simple conditioning do not last very long unless occasionally reinforced; that is, the bell-food pattern loses its "sign significance" unless the bell does at least occasionally lead to food.

A number of facts show that conditioning is not a simple matter of connecting a stimulus and response by repetition (24). In the first place, there must be a *need,* and it must be the strongest and most active in the organism. The dog's hunger must be strong enough to dominate other needs, or conditioning will not be too effective. Many facts suggest that the animal organizes the stimuli into a perceptual pattern, and responds to the bell as a *sign* for food. He salivates because he anticipates or expects food. If, for example, during the conditioning trials the bell is sounded after the food is given, conditioning will not ordinarily occur. Again, it has been determined that the conditioned response will become "extinguished" after a time if no food is given. This suggests that you cannot arouse anticipation time after time without reaffirming, so to speak, the dog's expectancy that the bell leads to food. Many experiments in the conditioning of infants and adults suggest that the psychological correlate of conditioning is "anticipation" or "expectation" (10).

In short, the evidence is abundantly clear that even within this simple conception of learning, the organism responds as a whole to the situation as given. The learned response is one of cognitive interpretation to the extent permitted by the situation.

Examples of Conditioning in Human Learning. So far we have been talking about animals. Much human learning is a product of situations similar to the one described above, and thus can be conceived as following a "conditioning" pattern. A wide range of experimental evidence attests that almost any kind of response can be conditioned to almost any kind of stimulus situation, provided the learning situation is rigidly enough controlled. The important point here is that the relation learned is an arbitrary one, and that one stimulus or situation may be arbitrarily substituted for another. Hence it happens that "conditioning" usually offers a sufficient basis for understanding how human beings make arbitrary "associations." Let us consider a few examples.

1. *Rote learning.* It is entirely arbitrary that "cat" should stand for the animal known by that name. Hence the child learns to respond to the word cat, as to the appearance of cat, by repeated pairings of the sight of the animal and the sound "cat." Figure 50 shows in diagrammatic form how this can

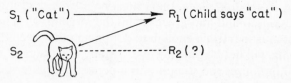

S_1 ("Cat") ⟶ R_1 (Child says "cat")

S_2 ---------- R_2 (?)

FIGURE 50. The Learning of Simple Words Through Conditioning. Paired presentations of S_1, the sound "cat" or "kitty" (parent says cat) and the appearance of the cat (S_2) result in the child's response "cat" to the appearance of the animal (R_1 response to S_2). Originally, the child could respond "cat" only in imitation of the parent (R_1 to S_1). The conditioning concept accounts very well for the child's first use of words.

occur. Thus the mysterious power of words in calling forth human emotions is no mystery, when we consider the tremendous variety of situations involved in the acquisition of language. It is common knowledge, for example, that words can induce salivation, or nausea, or feelings of fear or anger. (The learning of abstract concepts, of course, would impose considerable strain on this simple explanation of learning.) Similarly, the child learns through conditioning situations to respond "eight" to the sight or sound of 2×4, or "ninety-six" to 8 × 12. Number relationships, of course, are not really arbitrary, but learning the multiplication table is not insightful, at least in the early stages. Most of what we know as rote learning appears to occur in a situation very similar to the "forced" situation typical of conditioning.

2. *Irrational emotional responses,* as well as many that appear "rational," are matters of conditioning. Examples are fear reactions to words, sounds, sights, and other events. In this case the emotion gets evoked by a stimulus or situation that substitutes for the original emotion-provoking situation, and often persists because the behavior accompanying it is rewarding or tension-reducing. Thus a child bitten by a white dog may develop fear of anything white. Avoiding white objects (particularly white animals) reduces tension and therefore the emotional response to "white" is continually reinforced and "built up." This situation, which is similar to conditioning, keeps the response from coming under conscious control.

3. *Learning by "imitation"* often follows a conditioning pattern. A mother who shows fear reactions at the sight or sound of cats can unintentionally "teach" a child to fear cats by the same process that the child learns the meaning of the word cat.

4. *Superstitions* or compulsive behavior are often the product of conditioning. Knocking on wood may become a "sign" for warding off danger in the same way that the pigeon adopts a wing flapping or pecking response to produce a grain of corn. The reinforcement of the superstitious response is caused by the fact that the response is anxiety-reducing, and thus rewarding.

Learning through conditioning may not be typical of all human learning, but the fact remains that much human learning results from this type of forced-cue situation. The learning situations of human infants are very similar to the dog strapped in the harness, because their responses are limited and they are not free to select or control the cues in their situation or the kinds of rewards available. As Garrett points out, instances of maladaptive and stupid learning are often the result of conditioning:

In many cases, conditioned responses seem to be forced upon the learner, who acquires them almost involuntarily. As a consequence, conditioned-response learning is sometimes definitely maladaptive and from the social point of view hampering and even stupid. (5, p. 143)

The Hidden-Cue Situation: Trial and Error. The second type of learning situation is a puzzle in which the cue or cues necessary for solution are hidden, and the learner must try a number of responses until he finds the "right" one. Some of the early experimenters with this type of situation concluded that learning activity was typically a random kind of behavior, that errors were necessary for learning, and that successes were stamped in and errors stamped out through purely fortuitous "connections" in the nervous system. Although traditionally called "trial-and-error" learning, the more appropriate term would be "trial and success" because it is the successes that lead to learning, not the errors. Since the early experiments, it has become more apparent that trial and error is not a necessary characteristic of learning, but is often the result of a particular kind of learning situation.

This differs from the conditioning situation because it permits more freedom to the learner and places more emphasis on his motive in learning. The cues and responses are not forced by the experimenters, but are selected by the learner. Let us consider the cat in the problem box, illustrated in Figure 51. To learn how to escape from the box, the cat must "see" the latch as a means of opening the door. This is a means-end relationship. In Thorndike's original experiments, and many similar ones, it was discovered that the cat in trial after trial released the latch by "chance" and gradually reduced the time required to escape. But he did not become aware of the latch as a release mechanism. There was no sudden drop in the amount of time required to escape, which would have been typical of insight. There was no discovery, but a seemingly blind, random reproduction of efforts that somehow became more economical. It was "learning without awareness."

A human learning situation conducive to trial and error is the stylus maze situation which the subject must learn blind-

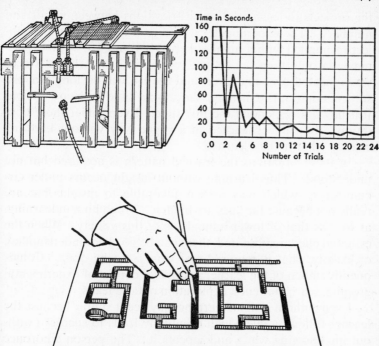

Time in Seconds

FIGURE 51. The Hidden-Cue Learning Situation. The drawing of Thorn-dike's puzzle-box above shows the door-opening mechanism which the animal could "accidentally" trip by moving or thrashing about in the box. The situation prevented the cat from "seeing" the relation between his movements and the door. Even under these conditions, the animal learned slowly through "trial and error," as shown in the learning curve. Another hidden-cue situation is the pictured stylus maze which the learner does blindfolded. If the blind were removed, what effect would this have on the learning curve? (Thorndike illustrations are from H. E. Garrett (5), pp. 146-148. Stylus maze picture adapted from N. Munn, *Psychology*, New York: Houghton Mifflin, 1946, p. 110.)

folded. The "correct" pattern is an arbitrary one, not a pattern of logical relations. Since the learner is in contact with only a small part of the maze at any time, the possibility of insightful learning is sharply limited. Another illustration of relatively blind learning is a situation used by Thorndike which required the subjects to learn arbitrary associations between words and numbers. The experimenter would read a word, and the subject responded with a number between 1 and 10. The experimenter would then say "Right" or "Wrong." A list of words was repeated over and over, and the list was so long that the subject could not remember the second time he heard a word just how he responded the first time. Even under these conditions, the subject learned in a vague way without knowing exactly what he had learned.

In these situations the learned pattern is acquired but not understood. Thus learning without insight occurs under circumstances which may appear favorable to insight, but are really not because the cues are hidden. Much human learning, as well as that of lower animals, is of this variety. When the essential cues are obscured, there can be no clear understanding of exactly what is required and what is to be done. Consequently, much of the learner's activities consist of experimental groping, search for cues, exploration of false leads.

Even without insight, learning may occur simply because the learner follows a cue which eventually leads to success (without his knowing why) and repeats it. The person who once solved a mechanical puzzle will thus try the thing that originally put him on the right track ("if I can get the pieces into that same position again") even though he does not know why this led to the solution in the first place. The student attempting a problem in arithmetic may try everything he knows until he arrives at the "right" answer given in the book. The next time he gets a similar problem, he will try the "successful" expedient first. He has "learned," in the sense that his behavioral processes have been modified and his attempts at solution are more economical. But he may not know, in literal truth, what he is doing.

Imitative social learning of the trial-and-error sort is very common even among adults. One person's actions are imitated by another because they seem to be successful. The young salesman imitates the approach and manners of the successful old timer, or even the widely different tactics of different salesmen. The person attempting to rise in social status imitates (usually not with insight) the language, dress, or manners of the social group to which he aspires. The "matched dependent" and copying behavior of the follow-the-leader variety described by Miller and Dollard (16) appears to be a kind of trial-and-error learning. In social learning, the cues provided by others are often not consciously demonstrated or made distinct. Some cues, therefore, tend to be followed blindly.

The Causes of Trial-and-Error Behavior. Trial-and-error learning is of course somewhat blind and often appears stupid and superstitious. It usually is. The reason, however, is not that humans are naturally blind and stupid learners. The reason is often to be sought in the limitations imposed by the learning situation.

Let us distinguish here between two sources of trial-and-error behavior. (1) Trial-and-error responses occur sometimes because of certain conditions in the learner. Even when the essential cues are quite open and evident, he may not "see" them. He may lack the necessary capacity or experience, which explains the child's crude trial-and-error responses in acquiring a skill like driving a nail, sawing wood, or writing with a pen. A lack of essential knowledge or familiarity would explain the sixth grader's trial-and-error in solving a problem in geometry. A mistaken point of view, or "set," may put the learner on the wrong track. Too strong motivation, provoking a bustling, pell-mell activity instead of a cautious and thoughtful approach, may cause trial-and-error. The young child's attempts to organize responses to new situations are characteristically of this type. The child's development is better described as "approximation and correction" because it is always purposive and never totally blind. (2) Trial-and-error learning also occurs in situations in which the cards are stacked, so to speak, against purposeful organization. It is the second aspect that we are concerned with here.

The fact that behavior is always a "total response to total situation," including the first stages of learning, does not of course square with the ordinary concept of random activity and pure "trial-and-error" learning. When it seems plausible to describe behavior as one of trial and error, it is not such "in the sense of a perfectly aimless and chaotic response, but only in the sense of discovering within the matrix of a behavior at first crudely and incompletely defined, a pattern that can be felt as adequate" (17). Our patterns of behavior have very different degrees of crudeness or refinement, efficiency or awkwardness, but this usually is a matter of the way in which the details find their appropriate place in the total pattern or are differentiated out of it. The fact that behavior is always pointed toward a goal and that special movements are only means to an end would imply that particular movements can arise only because of their relation to the total act as their reason for being, and certainly not independently or in spite of it.

The trial-and-error concept of learning has sometimes been extended to imply that we learn only by making errors and then eliminating them. Errors are not necessary for learning. We do not need every time to do the wrong thing before we can do the right thing, and learning is essentially a matter of doing the right thing. We do not arrive at the right way merely as a last resort or as a means of escape from our mistakes. While errors are not necessary for learning, they do usually have an indirect relation to it. They may at times serve to delimit the field for us in a striking way, particularly if they are clearly apprehended as errors.

Insight is possible only in learning situations which are arranged or structured so that the essential cue patterns are apparent. When the essential tool, word, principle, or other cue is obscure or buried in the situation, trial-and-error is predictable. The hidden-cue situation is preferable to the forced-cue situation (conditioning), since it permits the learner more freedom, allows personal motives to operate, and permits personal activity. That is, it allows the learner some selection in discovering relationships rather than having them forced on him. In brief, the hidden-cue situation is more favorable to insightful discovery than the forced-cue situation. But the possibility of discovery is limited by the availability of cues, in both animals and man. It is for this reason that the best examples of insightful learning have been those experiments, largely inspired by

Gestalt psychologists, in which all cues and experimental arrangements are open to observation.

The Open-Cue Situation: Insightful Learning. The classic example of insightful learning is Kohler's chimpanzee "Sultan." Faced with the problem of obtaining a banana beyond reach, the caged ape devised a raking tool by joining two short sticks found in his cage. In this situation, all cues are open to inspection, all aspects of the problem are clearly "given," and nothing is hidden. The solution requires understanding of the relations between the parts, the perception of stick-as-a-tool-to-reach-the-banana. The problem requires organization by the learner, but there is nothing in the situation that hinders the organization. Such a solution may be far from simple, because the meaning of the cues may be concealed owing to misapprehension of the learner. Appropriate "readiness" is required. But the situation permits and is favorable to insight, or learning through understanding of the relations. Insight is the perception of a whole pattern of relationships of cues to a goal. The most efficient, permanent, applicable, and generally useful learning is of this kind.

Insight, of course, does not occur automatically, but like other psychological acts has a genetic history. Of the following conditions for insightful learning, we note distinctions between those which depend on the learner and those which depend on the arrangements of the situation itself.

1. Insight depends on the learner's capacity, maturity, and previous experience. A cat or dog cannot solve the stick-banana problem, because they are not by nature adapted to manipulate sticks as tools. We can think here also of certain requisite levels of intelligence and mental development. Older children can achieve insight more readily than younger children. Relevant past experience is necessary and useful. However, experience does not produce the solution by itself, out of "habit." Some experience with sticks as tools would be required for adequate perception. But the animal which had used a stick exclusively to "poke" might not perceive the stick as a "rake."

2. Insightful learning depends on the way the situation is arranged. To be readily perceived "together," the two pieces of stick should be presented together. Insight would be hindered if the sticks were at opposite corners of the cage, and still further hindered if one were covered by a pile of hay. Further, if one stick were presented as a support for a box and the other as a hook to suspend a basket from the side of the cage, "togetherness" would be less apparent and so would relations between them. In this case, the two sticks are said to be "imbedded" in different wholes. Imbeddedness is a special factor serving to obscure the cues, which must be seen in a *total pattern*.

3. Insightful learning often depends on the activity of the learner. In the course of fumbling and search, which may be characterized as trial-and-error but is actually purposeful and meaningful (provisional try), the learner changes the arrangements of the situation so that a meaningful pattern becomes apparent and insight occurs. This often appears to be blind luck, but is actually brought about through genuine, if misdirected, tries of the learner. In this way, insightful learning sometimes occurs in the "hidden-cue" situation previously discussed. Need induces a perception of vague purpose or goal, which through activity becomes a clear expectancy, and finally a genuine insight.

4. Insightful learning is "transposable." This means that a solution achieved by insight can be readily repeated in a similar situation or a new situation without fumbling or search. It has been found that the chimpanzee "which has learned with insight to obtain a banana with a stick will *search* for a stick when a banana is placed out of reach in a new situation. Having reacted to the more abstract relationship of stick-as-a-tool-to-obtain-banana, it is not disturbed by a slight change in the situation" (10, p. 194).

The term insight is thus a descriptive term for that kind of learning in which a pattern or relationship is discovered and understood. Insight does not explain learning, and is not itself easily explained or predicted by mental processes. But the experimental evidence, with animals and humans alike, indicates that the chief obstacles to insightful learning, other than blind reproductive tendencies on the part of the learner, are in the characteristic structure of the learning situation itself.

Implications for School Practice. Comparison of the three situations just described have certain implications for teaching.

First of all, the way the classroom learning situation is arranged influences the interpretation and responses of the learner. The teacher places more or less emphasis on needs and goals of the learner, permits him more or less freedom to follow his own bent, and attempts, through the relative clarity of the cues selected, to provide more possibilities for insightful learning.

Some blind learning must go on in school, and is justified on the grounds that it raises levels of readiness by making responses available for later, more insightful learning. Rote learning of the multiplication table is a good example. Multiples of numbers must be known to facilitate higher-level problems solving. Dates in history are another. Knowing the dates of important events is essential to a proper time perspective, which is one purpose in teaching history. Learning to spell is mostly a matter of establishing arbitrary connections, but some "rules," if committed to memory, facilitate spelling. The "forced-cue" situations involved in drill and recitation are not altogether undesirable. The danger is that such learning may be overdone: that the teacher may plan such learning not just for the purpose of establishing levels of readiness, but as an end in itself. Forced-cue drill situations may be the *only* ones provided. This not only makes school a dull place, but places a premium on blind, useless learning—on educational "hokum." By restricting the learner's motives and spontaneous activity, we may actually achieve less economy in learning.

Purposeful organization does not appear unless the conditions of the situation permit it to appear. Why do students "forget" in school? Overemphasis on the "forced-cue" situation discourages purposeful organization in relation to vital needs of the learner, and encourages purposeful forgetting. The student sheds useless learning as a duck sheds water.

Assuming that situations are arranged so as to produce insightful learning (as they often are in the classroom through demonstrations and problems), consider the differences between hiding or "imbedding" the cues and putting them in plain sight. Contrast the blindfolded learner in the finger maze and the learner with a complete view of the maze, a visual map. In the latter case, the learner can see the goal and just how each step leads to it. School learning situations can be contrasted likewise:

Skilled teachers are well aware of differences between situations in which understanding is arrived at easily and those in which it is achieved with difficulty—even though the same ultimate steps are involved and the same end-stage reached. In the favored arrangement the problem is so structured that significant features are perceived in proper relationship, and distracting or confusing features are subordinated. Some mathematics teachers make problem-solution difficult to grasp because they go through derivations step by step without an overview of where the steps are leading or what the articulating principles are. They teach the necessary operations, but the final insight eludes the students because of the manner in which the proof is arranged. (10, p. 191)

The more restrictive the learning situation, and the less it permits organization by the learner, the more "superstitious" (less insightful) is the learned behavior. In the forced-cue and hidden-cue situations, the response pattern is acquired gradually by repetition. It can be reproduced in the same form, but is highly stereotyped and does not transfer to new situations. Conditioned responses and other forms of blind learning do carry over to other situations, but are often applied inappropriately and ineffectively.

Learning can be more or less purposeful, meaningful, and applicable. Teaching is essentially the guidance of the learner from the known to the unknown. Some teaching is ineffective, not necessarily because the situation is externally faulty, but because too much is taken for granted about what the learner "knows." Familiarity with a word does not guarantee comprehension of a concept, since the meaning is limited by the situation in which the word was learned. The ability to give a step-by-step proof of the area of a right-angled triangle from the hypotenuse and adjacent angle is not sufficient evidence of comprehension. The difficulty with most ineffective teaching, on the whole, is that (1) insightful knowledge is often assumed rather than verified, (2) insight is expected to emerge, somehow, from situations which are not favorable to it, and (3) blind and stupid learning is not recognized as such and is often rewarded. In the face of growing experimental evidence that insightful learning is to a large extent controlled by the arrangements of the situation, the role of the teacher is to work for insight rather than to drill and wait for it.

Perceptual Organization

The tendency toward organization exists within the learner. We have seen that motives organize his acts, within the limits imposed by the situation, into a purposeful pattern arising from personal needs. We now come to a further analysis of "learning behavior" that deals with other aspects of our general principle: all behavior, as well as all learning situations, is patterned. The organismic conception of learning does not mean that we must give up all idea of analyzing behavior and be content with a vague summary expression such as "the organism as a whole." But the kind of analysis it favors will be directed away from the search for independent elements or movements, and toward the identification of internal factors which organize and direct particular responses. The details of behavior are part of a whole determining tendency. As Perry put it, "The central feature of this conception of human behavior is that general state of the organism which has been termed a determining tendency. The organism as a whole is for a time preoccupied with a certain task which absorbs its energy and appropriates its mechanism." The individual not only initiates his activity, but he interprets the cues, responds by action, interprets the consequences, reinterprets and alters his responses. Through this continuous process, the individual himself contributes the modification of behavior we call "learning."

Levels of Readiness. The concept of "readiness" provides the setting for understanding the influence on learning of what

Bentley (2) called "the antecedents of behavior." These are the individual's mental set, disposition, attitude, and represent as it were an active gathering together of relevant mental forces in anticipation of a particular reaction. There is perhaps no influence reflected in the development of the child's personality which is not also reflected in his learning sooner or later. These influences are brought to bear on a present task through the antecedents of behavior, which in their effective guidance of action make learning a matter of personal achievement rather than a passive, impression-making process.

Learning is a matter of genesis or development. There is always something pre-existing out of which the learned act emerges. Thus the first trial of a learner is an expression of a pattern of behavior which represents his best planned attack upon the situation so far as he is able to apprehend the situation and organize his behavior. His further progress is an outgrowth of this. This first trial in turn is an outgrowth of his previous attitudes, tendencies, dispositions, and comprehensions. These dynamic antecedents of the act are of equal importance with the situation in determining what shall emerge from the interaction. Indeed sometimes they appear to be of greater importance. Thus our illusions, our getting off on the wrong foot, our biased interpretations, our jumping to conclusions are conspicuous examples of what these antecedents will do in the way of preparing the background for the emergence of a particular mental change.

The organization manifested in learning takes place on the background of certain levels of perceptual readiness, which may be distinguished as follows:

1. *Need.* First there is the level of the "drive" or general goal-activity. This is a state of general tension or dissatisfaction. In the terminology of Woodworth (26) this is "the mechanism for a consummatory reaction . . . [which] acts as a drive operating other mechanisms which give the preparatory reactions." As a first step toward the preparatory reactions, the individual is made more susceptible to objects and activities relevant to the satisfaction of the need. Hunger predisposes the organism to notice and respond to signs leading to food, but

thirst predisposes it to notice things leading to water. A child with a felt need for completing a task in arithmetic will be predisposed to react differently, in the same class situation, from the child who has a strong need for status. The general tension induced by need is thus the basis for the more particularized mental "sets" or goals. Awareness is not important here, since it may be absent or at a very low level.

2. *Purpose.* Next we have the level of the mental set, particularized goal, or objective. When the individual is able to formulate this consciously it becomes his "purpose." Awareness of the situation plays a part here, but only a very vague apprehension is required. The hungry child who starts out after the jam on the shelf need only realize that it is a go-after-the-food situation. The child with deprived feelings of status need only have a vague apprehension of devices for getting the teacher's attention. Whereas the state of need, or general tension, is simply a predisposing tendency, the purpose level is one of increased awareness, or a level of noticing and responding to things in a vague way as means to an end.

3. *Expectancy.* Our third level is one of general pattern tendencies, involving a clear perception of means leading to a goal—a high level of awareness that these particular actions will lead to this particular goal. A goal-expectancy consists of the tendency to perceive the situation as one of a general kind similar in broad outline to others experienced before, and the tendency to *anticipate* in behavior any further moves by a general behavior adjustment in accord with the nature of the perception. Our child seeking the jam will recognize the situation as one calling for reaching or climbing and will be prepared to act accordingly. This is the level of the learner's general insights and general attitudes of response, which determine the nature of any further steps taken. It is here that we find evidence justifying a principle of readiness in learning. As Ogden says (17): "All change in the direction of learning is attributable to a dispositional readiness . . . quite as much as to the precise nature of the objective or of the focal aspects of the behavior." This dispositional readiness has a previous history of development which could be traced in a similar manner.

Learning and development are thus sequences of activities which cause certain expectancies to become established, not because they lead to pleasurable outcomes in the narrow sense, but because they are apprehended as leading to goals.

4. *Specific insights.* Finally we have the level of the specific insights and specific behavior. The child may suddenly or after some preliminary trial and error get a chair and climb upon it, thereby attaining his objective. This is what, from a certain restricted point of view, may be regarded as the learning, although the act itself may have a long genetic history. The importance of the role played by the preceding level of readiness means that, by the proper "pacing" of tasks appropriate to the growing maturity of the child, we may have learning taking place with little or no trial and error. Say Wheeler and Perkins:

. . . Theoretically, if the degree of stimulation is adequately controlled, the child should be able perfectly and easily to solve each new problem the first time it is attacked. When he must resort to trial and error or to a random procedure, it is evident that he is not ready for the problem and that the conditions under which he is being forced to learn are not adequately controlled. (25)

The importance of the distinction between such levels of readiness and awareness is now rather widely recognized.[1] Motives not only have an organizing influence on learning, but are themselves progressively modified through learning so as to pro-

[1] In Tolman's terminology, the hunger drive of the rat in the maze produces what he calls the "immanent determinant" of purpose. He speaks of four kinds of "immanent determinants" intervening between stimuli and behavior: purposes, cognitions, capacities, and behavior-adjustments. The last includes "what mentalists would call awareness and ideas" which may substitute for or act as "surrogate for animal behavior" (23). Thorndike described three aspects of behavior besides that indicated by the level of "want." According to his statement, a person is moved by some want to enter upon a course of behavior consisting of (1) very general features, such as a set toward gratifying that want, the exclusion of irrelevant thoughts, etc.; (2) more special features, such as maintaining a certain posture or routine of movement, the direction of effort toward a series of tasks, etc.; (3) very special and detailed features such as occurrences of identifiable situations and the responses to each (22). Hull's "pure stimulus acts" and "cue-producing" responses, and the concept of "fractional anticipatory goal responses" are basic to his principles of the goal gradient and the habit-family hierarchy, and thus appear to be comparable distinctions (11)

duce more precise and specific responses. The level of motivation, by determining and limiting the response the learner is able to make, always influences his perceptual organization.

The Selection of Responses: Primacy, Recency, Intensity. First experiences and first acts in a series tend to be especially remembered. This is the principle of *primacy*. Also, recent experiences tend to be more vivid than earlier ones, hence more easily remembered. This is the principle of *recency*. The principles of primacy and recency seem, to a certain extent at least, to be subsidiary to the more general principle of motivation. When we first approach a task we are usually "fresh," and our interest is keener. Fatigue, mental confusion, and discouragement have not as yet entered in to arouse competing motives and weaken our original drive. The end of the task may also be characterized by stronger motivation than we find in the middle of a long performance. Studies of maze-learning in animals show a general tendency for errors near the goal to be eliminated first. This seems to be due, partly at least, to increase in motivation as the goal is approached, an explanation suggested by the fact that the animals move faster as they near the exit leading to the food. It is perhaps true as well that we remember recent events more easily because the original motive for remembering them has not been weakened through competition with other needs. More remote events were probably connected with motives which long since may have ceased to function. Outlived motives tend to carry with them into oblivion the behavior and experiences to which they gave meaning.

Primacy and recency are thus both subsidiary to a principle of *intensity* or vividness, which is a motivational principle. When motivation is high, a cue leading to a goal tends to be vivid or especially distinct, and thus to become established in relation to a response. We tend to remember things that serve our purpose. In a particular situation, the reason the learner tends to make one response rather than another lies in his state of motivation. It is rather misleading to say that he reproduces the most recent response, or the first response in a series, simply because it was last or first.

Perception of Relations.   Our concept of the learner as an active organizer, rather than a passive responder to stimuli, implies that a stimulus in itself has no power to evoke any particular kind of behavior.   A person's reaction to what he sees, hears, feels, or smells depends on the setting in which he perceives these things.   Things, persons, and events are perceived in relation to other things.   The learner's activity can best be understood as a "perception of relations" rather than as a "response to stimuli."   There are many different kinds of relationships among the events of experience.   We call attention here to a few of the more prominent ones.

1. Causal relations, as when X is seen as the cause of Y: This switch causes the light to go on, this latch releases that door.
2. Means-end relations, when X is seen to lead to Y.   This is sometimes called a "sign-relation."   Pavlov's dog thus perceived the bell as a sign of food.   "If . . . then" relations between events (if X, then Y) are characteristic of superstitions as well as of logical reasoning.
3. Spatial relations, as when X and Y are seen to be in the same direction, or close together, or distant.   These refer to relations among objects in space.   A rat in a maze, or a stranger finding his way in a new town, are said to be perceiving spatial relations.
4. Temporal relations, as when two events are seen to be related in time, i.e., together, apart, or in a certain sequence.
5. Part-whole relations, when an object or event is seen to be part of something else, constituting a whole.   A tone is perceived as part of a melody, a word as part of a sentence.
6. Individual-group relations, when an individual thing, person, or event is seen to belong to a group or class on the basis of similar characteristics.   A person is seen as Irish or Negro, male or female.   A rowboat and battleship are seen in relation to common features.
7. Ordinal relations, when two or more objects are perceived in some sort of rank order of magnitude.   The relationship is *more than—less than*.   This may be a special case of spatial relations, as in "bigger than," "farther than," or of

time relations. It may involve any dimension, e.g., louder than, heavier than, etc.

8. Opposites, as in black-white, north-south.

To say that our perceptions are "patterned" does not imply that the perceptions come first and are then organized into a pattern of relationships. Rather, the pattern is immediately perceived as a whole. In this sense, experience "comes organized." Even when the percept is reorganized, a detail becomes part of another whole through a shift in the total meaning. This is illustrated by our perception of ambiguous figures, as in Figure 52. Organization of experience is an integrated pattern

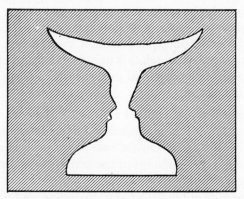

FIGURE 52. An Ambiguous Figure. This illustrates the principle that a "field cannot be experienced simultaneously as figure and ground." When the white portion emerges as figure (is seen as a vase) the "noses" lose their identity as noses. As the black and white surfaces function alternately as figure and ground, the details shift in significance. Rubin's vase figure from G. W. Hartmann, *Gestalt Psychology,* Ronald Press, 1935.)

of many kinds of relations. The various relations are not discrete or independent in experience. Causal relations, for example, may be inferred from spatial, temporal, and means-end or sign relations.

A pattern or configuration is thus the unit of mental organization, and consists of a set of relations holding among a number of sensory events. We perceive things as having membership in a pattern, as being part of a whole. Thus Kohler's chimpanzee perceived "stick" as having membership in the pattern "stick-as-tool-to-obtain-banana." The pattern-membership aspect of our perceptions explains not only why we organize things into logical relationships, but also how our perceptions and memories may become distorted. Why would a Mr. Kelly, for example, be remembered as red-haired when he is not so in fact? The controlling factor in memory here may be a fictitious class attribute, a part of the original perception pattern: Kelly might have been originally perceived as "an Irishman." A child may draw a rowboat with a smokestack. Children often attribute causal relations to objects perceived in the same spatial or temporal setting. The moon climbs up in the sky, as the child may apprehend it, *because* "it gets smaller and whiter" (or vice-versa). Many of our superstitions and conditioned reactions are examples of the same phenomenon, even though we "know" that no causal or logical relation exists. No detail of a person's experience can be understood except in relation to the whole, or perceptual pattern.

The Nature of Perceptual Patterns. An organization, as we see it most clearly exemplified in a living being, has two sets of distinctive features. On the one hand, it manifests a *unity amid variety,* a coordination of the activity of the parts which depend upon their interdependence of function. In the second place, an organism tends to resist disruption and when forced to undergo a modification it manifests a trend toward a *stable end-state or equilibrium.* Patterns of behavior as true organizations also show these features of unity and trend toward stability. To speak of learning situations and behavior as "patterned" implies that activity is directed toward discovering and developing meaningful relations among the events of experience. As learning proceeds, new relations are perceived and new patterns emerge, from which come meanings, insights, understandings.

Analyzing a pattern or configuration into elements destroys the pattern, and the parts as analyzed out become something different. An analysis of spoken and written language into words and parts of speech merely according to form may make words very unreal and formal things for a child, unless they are perceived in their vital relations to other words. Concentrating our attention upon some one detail of a skilled act, like hitting a tennis ball, destroys the balance of the pattern and makes us awkward. To see why this is so, let us consider some characteristics of learning patterns.

1. A pattern or configuration is a whole, i.e., more than merely the sum of the analyzed parts or elements. We cannot "see" the operation of a steam engine from a mere study of the parts, nuts, bolts, and rods, as separate and unrelated things. We cannot learn to play the piano by practicing first one finger and then another. The pattern depends upon the way in which the parts hang together, how they stand in relation to one another, the form of their union. It is so with a melody, with the perception of a square, with the driving of an automobile, and with the language we use. Meanings depend upon patterns.

2. Parts are features of the whole; they have no separate identity as long as they are integral parts of a pattern and before they individuated. One child could spell 'Richard" but he could not spell "rich." The Binet tests show that the average child under eight or nine cannot name sixty words in three minutes unless he employs sentences, although his "vocabulary" may contain three or four thousand words. We often find ourselves unable to perform some separate act or movement, although we may find no difficulty in doing it when it is only a feature of a larger whole. We may not be able to recall the fourth line of a poem until we have run through the first three.

3. Parts may vary in many ways and there may still be no change in the pattern. Once a child clearly apprehends the pattern of relationship of subject and predicate in a sentence, he may behold the same pattern in practically any sentence despite great variation in the words employed. We usually have no difficulty in identifying the sun in a picture although it may differ very much in both color and brightness from the real sun. The more skillful a person is, the less is he handicapped by wide variations in the material with which he works. Patterns thus exhibit "unity amid variety."

4. Patterns are transposable. What the child learns for one situation he learns for all situations which he apprehends under the same pattern. Patterns resist disruption in new circumstances.

Some Examples of Pattern in Learning. Even the relatively simple types of learning characteristic of experiments with lower animals show that the learner reacts to, and learns, a pattern or configuration. This is not reserved exclusively for the more difficult forms of learning carried on in human thinking. Goldfish, reacting positively to one of three lights, bright, medium, and dim, continued to make correct responses as long as this step-wise relationship held, even though the absolute intensity of the lights was changed consistently (18). Rats also react to two lights on the basis of the relation "brighter than." In Kohler's well-known experiment, hens were trained to eat from the darker of two gray papers. Food was placed on two gray papers next to each other, but the hen was allowed to eat only from the darker of the two. When the trained hen was transferred to another problem setup, where the "dark" paper of the previous experiment was set beside a still darker one, the hen chose not the same "dark" paper but the still darker one. The hen had learned to respond to the relation "darker than," not to a specific shade of gray (13, 12). Another experiment showed that hens would choose, from two figures of equal size, the one that appeared to be smaller because of its position (Jastrow illusion). The choice of a figure which was only subjectively smaller is a very clear case of the operation of a patterned situation (20). Human idiots, in discriminating the size of boxes, made the choice on the basis of relative, rather than absolute, size. Changing the boxes made very little difference as long as the same ratio of size was maintained (4). A response to patterns, rather than to discrete stimuli, is the rule.

That learned behavior is a pattern, a whole determining its parts and not just a chain of fragments, is shown by experiments in animal learning which demonstrate the *transposability* of learned behavior, even the simplest kind. None of the following examples of animal learning can be accounted for as an ordinary result of "practicing correct responses" or of "exercise in avoiding errors."

1. Blodgett studied what he called "latent learning" (3) by allowing some of his rats to roam more or less at will throughout a maze. He offered them no reward of food for getting out, as a result of which they showed very little improvement in threading their way through the maze during the first seven days. At the end of the run on the seventh day the rats were fed. The following day's trial showed remarkable improvement, almost as great in fact as if the rats had been running for food on each of the preceding seven days. Thus it did not seem to make much difference whether the animals spent the learning period just exploring the maze, or whether they spent the time in exercising correct responses. They had somehow learned the maze pattern, even though their performance at first did not show it. It is difficult to understand this "latent learning" unless we regard it as a matter of perceptual discrimination, or "insight."

2. An experimenter had rats run past a closed door in a maze (the path to the food), down a blind alley six feet long, and only after they had done this would they find, on their return, the door to the correct pathway open. After they had learned to do this, he then put them in the maze and left the door open from the outset. Five of the nine rats went immediately through the opened door without going down the blind alley first, which they had apparently learned to do. The other four rats eliminated the profitless excursion down the blind alley after only a few trials. Apparently the "getting there" was the thing learned by the animals. They would take the long way if they had to and the short way if they could. The learning was not an invariable lock-step of movements (9).

3. Another experimenter had his rats run through the maze for the first four trials and then had them swim through the same maze flooded with water. He found that the rats took up their learning of the maze while swimming at the point at which they left off running. They did not have to learn the maze all over again. Since the actual movements made in swimming are different from those of running, it was not apparently the particular kind of movements that were learned, but the total pattern of the maze. Having learned

a means to an end, they could substitute another means. Learned behavior is thus transposable (15).

4. Experiments on the effect of injuries to the nervous system on learning lead to a similar conclusion. Rats whose cerebellum or spinal cord had been injured could not go through a maze in the manner they had learned to do, but could still do so without error. If they could not walk at all, they could still "roll through." One of the rats, because of a brain injury, could not make a required left turn. Nevertheless he reached the goal by making a sufficient number of turns to the right (14).

5. Harlow's experiments with monkeys (8) also show the importance of patterns of experience in learning. In a discrimination experiment he trained monkeys to expect a food reward under a circle rather than under a square. A monkey so trained continued to choose the circle as long as the food appeared there. If on just one occasion the animal found no food under the circle, he shifted to the square on the next trial and continued to choose the square as long as he was rewarded. The monkeys could be trained to shift their responses readily in accord with changed conditions; as Harlow put it, they "learned how to learn," or acquired a learning set or expectancy. If the learning were a simple habit built up through repetition, we would not expect the animal to shift his response so easily.

Organizing Through Differentiation. Differentiation, previously discussed as perceiving differences among cues, is now seen to take on new meaning. It is the emergence of a feature or detail of the original pattern from its setting to become a new and particularized whole. This is what happens for example when, without requiring even the turn of head or eyes to see it, someone calls our attention to a particular article of furniture, a chair, in the room where we happen to be. Previously this chair was but part of the general background, a feature of the whole room. But as soon as we become disposed to perceive it through the mental preparation induced by the spoken suggestion, the chair emerges from its position of subordination to become a new whole of perception. It is no longer a detail of the room, it becomes the new center of the whole setting. Learning shows similar transformations and reorganizations.

Differentiation is equally applicable to our patterns of behavior. The learner comes to know details, to recognize qualities, to perform discrete movements, to act in certain partial ways, whereas in the beginning he would have vaguely seen, he would have been wholesale in his action, he would have ignored the "fine points," and would have run "rough-shod" over the whole situation. The reason for differentiation is the reason for any change in learning—need, goal, motive. As James put it, "All things fuse that can, and nothing separates except what must." The "must" refers to the advantage that will accrue to the learner.

Differentiation implies that particular responses are products of development, the course of which is from total response to particular response. Subject matter becomes a reasonable objective in education only after differentiation has been carried a good way—only as certain fields of activity, certain objects, certain kinds of tasks, certain classes of things have become differentiated from the first large, massive pattern of the young child. The reason why the learner at first tends to group so many unrelated things together in a confusing way is due not to the presence of general ideas or notions but to the absence of notions of particulars. The course of learning is from vague, crude, awkward patterns of perception and action to discriminated objects, details, and properties on the one hand (differentiation), and to generalizations, insights, and skillful action on the other (integration).

Integration and Insight. Integration is the organization of more or less discretely perceived things or actions into a new meaningful pattern which then contains them as features or details of itself. Thus when we learn to type, we organize the movements of the fingers for the individual letters into units of words and phrases. This is not just a chain of separate movements, for the typist *thinks* words and phrases (not letters) and types them as he thinks them. Again, the apprehension of the principle of the lever in operation is due to the integration of the perception of the bar, fulcrum, and loads in their dynamic interrelations as a workable unit. Just as differentiation gives us things and their qualities, so integration gives us the larger plans of action and understanding.

Integration always takes place with reference to some goal of action, or in other words, always with reference to a need, which for the time being at least is obstructed in its satisfaction. The things which the child learns to use as tools, for instance, are integrated into his patterns of action and understanding in order that he may obtain his satisfactions. Through integration things and actions take on new meanings and new uses, they leave behind their discrete thing-character to become means of achievement.

When integration or differentiation takes place suddenly and in a well-defined manner, we often speak of it as insight. There is not only foresight of some kind of a goal but also insight into the dynamic relations of the details of the whole situation. Insight is the *felt* aspect of organized behavior. Insight does not always have to be correct so far as results are concerned. There can be right and wrong insights. The wrong ones often give rise to what are called "clever" errors. Köhler's ape was guilty of a clever error when he tried to reach an overhanging banana by holding a box half-way up the side of a wall while he tried at the same time to climb on top of it. We can easily find examples of such clever errors in all forms of learning. The more stupid errors, which may still be the result of wrong insights, often give the outward appearance of haphazard trial and error.

The so-called "laws of association," where plausible, are special cases of the principle of integration. Ideas are "associated" not by the production of any bonds between them as separate things, but by being integrated into new patterns of experience. As Ogden says:

Whenever a number of more or less discrete perceptions enter into a configuration they become joined by virtue of their membership in a whole; the members are therefore held together, not by the external agency of an associative "glue," but by the transformation which they have undergone in losing something of their individuality and becoming members of a single pattern. It is then the pattern and not the individual contents that constitute the memorial residuum. (17)

Thorndike's principle of *belongingness,* by which he explained how a "connection" between two things is more easily learned if they both belong to the same situation, is also subsidiary to the principle of integration. "Belongingness" is membership in a pattern. Two things can belong together only when they are members—interacting, reacting, complementary—of a larger whole, a pattern or configuration.

Precision and Economy in Learning. Precision is the change within a pattern of experience or behavior toward greater clearness and definiteness, greater directness and economy, greater stability and strength. It is the psychological expression of what appears to be the still more fundamental principle of *"parsimony,"* which states that organisms "approach a needed object or state of affairs by the shortest route or most economical means functionally possible" (1). As perceptions become better differentiated and more highly integrated, learned behavior becomes more precise. The characteristics of precision are these:

1. The process of precision works toward greater *clearness* and *definiteness* in the sense that the pattern becomes well marked off from other patterns. This is accompanied by the awareness that we know distinctly what we are about. The child who has learned his arithmetical computations with precision goes about his task in a business-like way, he knows when he is multiplying and not dividing, and as each step is gone through he takes up the next one directly and surely. The edges of the pattern are not furred by a sense of insecurity, and marginal errors are very much reduced. Most students fail to carry their learning to speak a foreign language to any high stage of precision. They do not "think" in the language, that is, the patterns of the foreign tongue are not sufficiently marked off from those of English, the foreign words are sort of appendages to the English words, and there is often a continual and confused jumping back and forth between the two tongues. When on the other hand learning is brought to an advanced stage of precision, it becomes relatively easy for us to turn from doing one thing to doing another. And this is accomplished with no

confusion of the two. Each is well delimited from the other. There is no overlapping of the patterns of behavior.

2. Greater *directness* and *economy* become evident in many ways during the acquisition of precision. The speed with which the learned act is carried through increases and the mental effort that it costs is considerably reduced. There is also an increase in the subordination of the details of the act to the purposes of the pattern as a whole. We become less conscious of particular movements as they become more "goal-integrated." The skilled typist loses awareness of the movements of the particular fingers and thinks almost wholly of the words to be written.

3. Greater *stability* and *strength* are attained because the principle of parsimony implies a working toward limits that are stable. When the learning reaches this limit it tends to become "set." This suggests the real meaning of the "setting" of behavior. It is a matter of approaching a stable limit, and has nothing directly to do with the wearing of "pathways" in the nervous system. Precise behavior is not likely to show much variation from time to time as long as the situation remains essentially the same. By the very fact that it has reached this stage of stability it is less likely to break down when the conditions of the act are slightly changed. The beginning pupil must for instance hold his arm, his pen, and his paper just so before he can write, while the older student is little handicapped by minor changes in posture.

By "strength" we mean the relative ease with which the precise pattern of experience or behavior is remembered or reproduced. This follows because of its stability. It had originally been worked out as the most satisfactory and economical plan, so there is no need on future occasions to look for another solution. It is profitable to regard our "remembered" behavior as the recognized limit of the operation of the principle of parsimony.

The process of precision is in a way analogous to what has sometimes gone under the name of "short-circuiting" in learning. It has often been noted that a child, in learning to dress himself, to write, or to operate a typewriter has progressively made his performance more direct and economical by apparently "dropping out" of his behavior a number of superfluous activities and by passing directly from essential to essential. This "selection" of the correct responses, their connection, and the "elimination" of the incorrect, useless responses have been supposed to take place by some kind of a short-circuiting of impulses in the nervous system. In one fell swoop a "unit" of response, with its nervous and muscular arc, is supposed to drop out of the behavior. The analogy usually given is that of the short-circuiting of an electric current.

It is true that sudden shifts of behavior take place very often in learning. But while this may be looked upon by the observer as a kind of short-circuiting and eliminating of unit responses, it is not to be described as such from the standpoint of the learner. The important psychological event is not a synaptic short-circuiting but a sudden insight which renders the eliminated activity no longer useful or meaningful. In fact, the most conspicuous instances of these shifts of behavior, including even exact reversals of the original procedure, just cannot be explained by synaptic short-circuiting. A new insight, a new plan of attack, a new "hypothesis" may lead to such a change in behavior that there must also be a "long-circuiting" into totally *new* behavior and nervous arcs.

Even in cases where precision is attained gradually instead of suddenly, the short-circuiting concept is not acceptable. Rabaud, for instance, in his study on "how animals find their way about" (19), shows that bees, in returning to their hive, follow at first an angular path that is made so by their flying first toward one distinct landmark after another. Successive flights only gradually and symmetrically lead to a shortening of the path followed to the hive. There is a "shortening of the circuit" of behavior but not a "short-circuiting" of it. The principle of parsimony operates with respect to the whole act or pattern of behavior as a unit.

Precision and Repetition: The Function of Practice. It is in connection with the process of precision that repetition and drill may make their contribution to learning, which they do in a somewhat indirect manner. Because of the minute differences and variations that always exist from one situation to another, it must be realized that after all it is never the specific response (in its full particulars) that is repeated but only the goal-activity. We *repeatedly* try to attain the same goal in our learning and in doing so we have the advantage of a number of opportunities for selecting the correct response in case we did not succeed the first time. Thus repetition may make the conditions of learning more favorable for the operation of insight. There is ample evidence, however, that learning may occur in the absence of repetition, which cannot then be essential. The so-called law of "exercise," which stated that frequent exercise of a response may of itself account for the appearance of the response in the learned act, is not actually a learning principle except in a limited sense. Practice, or exercise, establishes the conditions through which *other* principles are effective.

After the initial integrative steps of learning have taken place, continued practice or "over-exercise" may contribute to the precision of the pattern. This is apparently because it takes time for the effects of this genetic process to become apparent. This can be shown in other mental operations, such as in the perception of a figure. By exposing a line figure tachistoscopically for only a fraction of a second, we find that a number of repetitions is necessary before the perception becomes precise, that is, clear, detailed, and stable. Thus by altering the conditions of stimulation, as by shortening the time of any one exposure, we can make repetition necessary for perception.

Although repetition is not essential to perception, we may, as in the case above, so alter the conditions of perception that it will on occasion become necessary. In a similar manner, repetition must not be thought essential to learning. But owing to the fact that precision takes time, repetition is often demanded by the conditions of learning. In ordinary perception, where the data are simultaneously present, we can continue looking until we see, that is, until the organization is completed. In learning, on the other hand, especially in the case of skills, when one part of the event is over before another part comes on the scene we have to take another look before we can see clearly. Repetition then becomes necessary. The practical need of repetition and drill depends on a number of factors: (1) the maturity of the learner, (2) the complexity of the task, (3) the intensity of motivation, (4) the presence of fatigue, (5) the degree of precision required, and (6) the necessity for detailed and permanent retention.

Learning as Problem Solving. If we wish to grasp the significant facts of learning as a whole, we could not perhaps do better than to regard this activity as "problem solving" in the broad sense of the term. There is no separate mental activity known as learning, for it really represents a personal attack upon the resolution of some obstacle which bars the individual's progress toward a goal. Hence it manifests itself in all forms of mental life. The individual must take an active role, for he is bent on finding and working out the best method of expressing an idea or performing a movement. His continued practice has as its goal a modification of his behavior, a complete transformation at times, toward the most economical, efficient, and expeditious manner of attaining his objective. Naturally, then, the learner must be motivated. There must be some personal reason why he should undertake these steps, and there must be some understanding of their appropriateness and relevance to the main goals of his interest.

Since learning is a matter of organizing one's responses in the direction of a goal, the good learning situation is one which favors the right kind of organization. The materials, the sensory discriminations, the ideas must be made to fit into a broad theme or plan if they are to make sense to the learner. This accounts for the advantage of "bird's-eye views," schematic drawings, diagrams, summaries, and outlines, which serve to emphasize the plan of organization.

The chief function of practice is to improve the understanding of the learner. This may require actual movement where skill is involved, but movements are ancillary to insight. We are perhaps often tempted to take the outward actions at their face value and to believe that they have an importance in their own right. Movements do not get "linked together"; they are subsumed or appropriated by a scheme of understanding and are employed effectively only in this manner. Nor must we suppose that after the first glimpse of understanding we can then hand the drill work over to some mechanical stamping-in process. Practice and drill, as second, third, and fourth steps in learning, must be motivated just as the original step taken by the child had to be. They should be surrounded with aids to understanding, if less intensive perhaps yet equally pervasive. If the plan of organization and refinement could be grasped at once there would be no need for drill. But because we do need to learn things which are difficult of comprehension or extremely specific and detailed, we cannot do without practice. But practice is for the sake of insight and not for the sake of itself.

Some learning is difficult because of limitations on the part of the learner. He may be immature in either a general way or with respect to the specific kind of task. It is always the previously developed stage of his maturity from which each new activity emerges and in relation to which it receives its setting. Excessive drill work is an indication that the learning required is too far above the level of maturation attained by the child or that he has not first been prepared in a general way for the specific task. Learning is mental development made specific by a particular problem. Nor does learning arise through purely random activity on the part of the child as he approaches a learning task. Haphazard activity indicates that learning is not taking place and cannot take place until it is supplanted by bringing the child's maturity of insight to bear upon the task at hand. The first step then is a very important one.

The course of mental development is from more general ways of doing and thinking to specific actions and ideas. The young child is clumsy, not because he is positively given to missteps; his knowledge is vague, not because he is culpably careless of his errors, but because the first steps toward skill and knowledge are naturally wanting in completeness and detail. They are made so with further learning but they are not so in the beginning. It is putting the cart before the horse to insist upon a detail of movement or insight appropriate only to an advanced level of maturity and to try to have these combined by the child in a mechanical fashion. The child is no longer taught to write by having him first practice formally the vertical lines, loops, and other "elements" of adult writing. The natural course of learning does not favor this. We may be reminded here of the distinction drawn by the Herbartians between the logical and the psychological approach to subject matter. The difference hinges on the maturity of the learner. It is not as if there were two wholly different methods of mental operation. The logical approach is for mature minds, mature discriminations, interests, and integrative plans. The essence of the psychological approach consists in having due regard for the child's level of maturity and in attempting to raise this level through the specific problem of the learning task.

REFERENCES

1. ADAMS, D. K. A restatement of the problem of learning. *Brit. J. Psychol.*, 1931, **22**, 150-179.
2. BENTLEY, M. *The field of psychology*. New York: Appleton, 1924.
3. BLODGETT, H. C. The effect of the introduction of a reward upon the maze performance of rats. *Univ. Calif. Publ. Psychol.*, 1929, **4**, 113-134.
4. DOLL, E. A., & ALDRICH, C. G. Simple conditioning as a method of studying sensory discrimination among idiots. *J. gen. Psychol.*, 1932, **7**, 104-143.
5. GARRETT, H. E. *Psychology*. New York: American Book Co., 1951.
6. GENGERELLI, J. A. The principle of maxima and minima in animal learning. *J. compar. Psychol.*, 1930, **11**, 193-236.
7. GUILFORD, J. P. The role of form in learning. *J. exper. Psychol.*, 1927, **10**, 415-423.
8. HARLOW, H. F. The formation of learning sets. *Psychol. Rev.*, 1949, **56**, 51-65.
9. HIGGINSON, G. D. Visual discrimination in the white rat. *J. exper. Psychol.*, 1926, **9**, 337-347.
10. HILGARD, E. R. *Theories of learning*. New York: Appleton-Century-Crofts, 1948.
11. HULL, C. L. *Principles of behavior*. New York: Appleton-Century, 1943.
12. KOFFKA, K. *Growth of the mind*. New York: Harcourt, Brace, 1924.
13. KOHLER, W. Optische untersuchungen am schimpansen und am haushuhn. *Abhandl. d. k. Preuss. Akad. d. Wissenschaften,* 1915, Nr. 3.

14. LASHLEY, K. S. *Brain mechanisms and intelligence.* Chicago: Univ. Chicago Press, 1929.
15. MACFARLANE, D. A. The role of kinesthesis in maze learning. *Univ. Calif. Publ. Psychol.,* 1930, **4,** 277-305.
16. MILLER, N. E., & DOLLARD, J. *Social learning and imitation.* New Haven: Yale Univ. Press, 1941.
17. OGDEN, R. M. *Psychology and education.* New York: Harcourt, Brace, 1926.
18. PERKINS, F. T., & WHEELER, R. H. Configurational learning in the goldfish. *Compar. Psychol. Monogr.,* 1930, **7,** 1-50.
19. RABAUD, E. *How animals find their way about.* New York: Harcourt, Brace, 1928.
20. REVESZ, G. Experiments on animal space perception. *British J. Psychol.,* 1924, **14,** 386-414.
21. SKINNER, B. F. Superstition in the pigeon. *J. exper. Psychol.,* 1948, **38,** 168-172.
22. THORNDIKE, E. L. *et al. The psychology of wants, interests and attitudes.* New York: Appleton-Century, 1935.
23. TOLMAN, E. C. Theories of learning. In Moss, F. A., *Comparative Psychology,* New York: Prentice-Hall, 1934.
24. TOLMAN, E. C. A stimulus-expectancy need-cathexis psychology. *Science,* 1945, **101,** 160-166.
25. WHEELER, R. H., & PERKINS, F. T. *Principles of mental development.* New York: Crowell, 1932.
26. WOODWORTH, R. S. *Dynamic psychology.* New York: Columbia Univ. Press, 1918.
27. WOODWORTH, R. S. *Contemporary schools of psychology.* New York: Ronald Press, 1948.

SELECTED READINGS

BLAKE, R. R., & RAMSEY, G. V. (Eds.). *Perception: an approach to personality.* New York: Ronald Press, 1951. Chs. 4-6 discuss the relation of perception and learning.
GARRETT, H. E. *Great experiments in psychology.* (Rev. ed.) New York: Appleton-Century-Crofts, 1951. Contains chapters on experiments by Pavlov, Thorndike, and Kohler.
HARTMANN, G. W. *Gestalt psychology.* New York: Ronald Press, 1935. Chs. 10-12, 16.
KINGSLEY, H. L. *The nature and conditions of learning.* New York: Prentice-Hall, 1946. For general reference.
LEWIN, K. Behavior and development as a function of the total situation. In CARMICHAEL, L. (Ed.), *Manual of child psychology.* New York: Wiley, 1946.
MOWRER, O. H. *Learning theory and personality dynamics.* New York: Ronald Press, 1950. Chapters 9 and 10 contrast "condition-

ing" and "problem solving" and argue for a two-factor theory of learning.

SHERIF, M., & CANTRIL, A. H. *The psychology of ego-involvements.* New York: Wiley, 1947. A wealth of material on the perceptual aspects of social learning.

TOLMAN, E. C. *Purposive behavior in animals and men.* New York: Appleton-Century, 1932.

14

LEARNING AS GOAL ACTIVITY

SINCE motivation is the first condition of learning, all problems in learning and teaching center around meeting the needs of the learner. In the broad sense, a motive is anything that energizes and directs behavior or conduct. Since learning involves changes in motivation as well as changes in knowledge, and learning is a continuous process, motives are constantly undergoing change. They become more channelized or specific through development, and become attached to specific goal objects. What is the relative effect of various forms and degrees of motives? Which is more effective, reward or punishment? Since motives involve emotional tension, what is the relative effect of learning at various intensities of emotion? Do emotions organize or disorganize behavior? These questions must be answered by the results of psychological research. They are of both theoretical and practical interest, and have therefore been investigated both in the laboratory and the school.

The purpose of experimental studies of motivation is not to tell us whether learning with a motive is superior to learning without one. Some motive is always present as the basic determiner of behavior. We turn to these investigations rather for an understanding of the relative value of different forms of motivation and of the most desirable methods of inducing mental activity. Prescott said some years ago that "the whole concept of learning now held by educators seems to be sadly lacking in insight about the role of motivation . . ." (23). This is a very practical matter in teaching. Does the teacher get the best results by concentrating on what is to be learned and the manner of presenting it, and ignoring its setting in the dynamic mental life of the child? Can we assume, without any special attention being given to the matter, that the pupil is sufficiently well motivated merely because he comes to school and is apparently ready to learn? Or, may not the child be energized in different ways with respect to what is to be learned and with different degrees of profit to himself and to the teacher? Another practical problem is whether certain kinds of motivation may be beneficial so far as immediate results are concerned and yet of little value, or perhaps detrimental, in the long run.

SOME VARIABLES IN GOAL SETTING

Goal-directed activity is partly dependent on the characteristics of the goal which the learner sets for himself. The "end-state" which the learner anticipates may be more or less clearly perceived. The anticipation may be more or less keen, depending on the person's perception and "set." The ability of a goal-set to organize behavior depends on whether the goal is (1) intrinsic or extrinsic, (2) immediate or remote, (3) vague or precise, or (4) high or low in level of aspiration. We may describe the learner's goal in degrees of such dimensions as these.

1. *Intrinsic vs. extrinsic goals* (11). The relationship between the learner's activity and his goal is said to be *intrinsic* if his activity is functionally related to the goal. The boy who reads about the methods Eskimos use in building igloos in order to build a mud igloo for himself is involved in activity intrinsically related to a goal. Personal use of the igloo is a goal intrinsic to the tasks of reading about igloos and building one. The reward (personal satisfaction in using the igloo) is also said to be intrinsic to the task.

The activity-goal relationship is said to be *extrinsic* if it is artificial or arbitrary. Reading about methods of building igloos for the purpose of passing an examination, or impressing others with the knowledge, is an example of an extrinsic relationship. Activity is here a means to an end, but the end is an artificial incentive.

In general, intrinsic goals would seem preferable as motives, because the activity is in a sense self-rewarding. Many artificial incentives, imposed and administered through authority of the teacher, are of little value when they have no relationship to the needs of the learner. The danger of extrinsic and artificial incentives, administered by the teacher, is that the student's activity becomes organized toward satisfying the teacher, and not otherwise meaningful. When artificial incentives are removed (as they are outside the school situation) the work itself may not be continued because it is not self-rewarding.

2. *Immediate vs. remote goals.* To understand motivation properly, we must recognize that goals are arranged in a kind of hierarchy. Any immediate goal may be not only an end, but a means to another more remote goal. School grades may be a means to college, a college degree to entry in medical school, a medical degree to the practice of medicine, and so on. There is usually a series of intermediate goals. An immediate goal, although extrinsic to the task, may be intrinsically related to a more remote goal. Thus getting an A in algebra may be really meaningful in relation to the goal of becoming an engineer. Attainment of an intermediate goal often brings feelings of keener anticipation of a more remote goal, which is rewarding in itself.

In general, immediate goals appear to be more effective organizers of activity than remote goals. The more remote the goal in time or space, the more vague it appears to the learner. Young people, particularly, lack the experience necessary to a well-developed time perspective, and therefore rarely foresee and plan for distant goals. Motivation thus requires some provision for rewarding efforts here and now, so that the relation between the immediate goal and the more remote one is not lost.

3. *Vague and precise goals.* Goals may be clearly or vaguely conceived, and may be psychologically well defined or poorly defined. Well defined goals have the advantage in motivation, because the learner's expectancy is then very definite and effective in organizing behavior. Under some conditions, vague goals are easier to satisfy. Wanting a "high grade" is less precise than wanting an A. A student may vaguely hope

for an A, but be satisfied with a B. Coming close to a goal may thus in some cases be satisfying.

4. *Level of aspiration.* This is the level of the goal the individual sets for himself. It may be high or low or any place in between. Many variables in motivation enter here. Cautious persons characteristically set low goals, thereby insuring "success." Bolder ones set high goals and run greater risk of "failure."

SOME PRINCIPLES OF MOTIVATION

The Intention to Learn. It is sometimes said that conscious, active self-direction, or an intention to learn, is a basic law of learning. If we take learning in the broad sense, this is not strictly true, for there is fairly good evidence of learning without awareness or intent on the part of the learner. This is true of conditioning, of the "hidden-cue" situation described earlier, and in general of all learning situations in which the nature of the task is not made explicit. In situations where means to the goal are readily perceived, however, the favorable effect of an active intention or will to learn has been confirmed by a number of experimental studies.

While it seems that "need," whether conscious or not, is more fundamental to learning, "intention" usually implies the operation of one of our more highly differentiated needs. It is then an aspect of "readiness." The will to learn commonly indicates the presence of full insight into the nature of the goal and points to a highly integrated activity on the part of the learner, two factors of undoubted importance in learning.

The intention to learn also affects the permanence of learning. One study, for example, investigated the influence on memorizing of the intention to retain for permanent use (2). Two different forms of instruction were given to the subjects before attempting to memorize a Chinese-English vocabulary. One instruction was to memorize for temporary retention and the other to memorize for permanent retention. Although the differences found were rather small, the authors believed they had sufficient evidence to show that the intention to memorize for permanent use actually brings about, with the same expenditure of effort, a longer lasting retention of the material than does the intention to retain for only a short period of time. We may have here a very important suggestion for the motivation of school work. Those who study merely to pass examinations may succeed in doing it, but their later life may give very little evidence of the effort which this cost them.

In view of such experimental results as we have referred to, it would seem reasonable that some psychologists should come to believe that the first and essential law of learning is the "will to learn." Although it would seem that the concepts of need and activity are theoretically more basic, the emphasis implied in the "will to learn" represents a step in the same general direction. The practical application of the principles of learning to the classroom would not be changed in any material way.

The "will to learn," however, will receive different emphasis according to the maturity of the student. For the older student or adult, arousing an intention to learn represents, as it were, merely the focalizing of his energies on a task, the significance of which is already appreciated. The young child on the other hand lacks the more general goal-activities and attitudes which would furnish the personal setting for the act. We cannot suppose that a mere desire to learn would have the same relative importance here as later. To depend on this alone would run counter to other principles of good motivation.

Accepting the Task. Defining the task facilitates learning by enabling the learner to know exactly what is expected and how to evaluate the outcome. This is a case of adequate *structuring,* since it provides more definite cues, makes the relations of means to end apparent, and provides knowledge of results. Adequate task definition helps to engage the learner actively, instills in him both an expectancy and the intention to learn, and facilitates his awareness of what is being learned. His activity then gives him a feeling of progress and success. Early experiments in work and fatigue (32) showed that when a worker was simply told to go ahead and work as hard as he could, without being given any specific objective, he accomplished much less than did another worker who was given a set task to perform, who was allowed to observe his results, and was moreover advised to notice the amount of work he accomplished. In the latter case the amount of fatigue was also reduced. A specific task acts by way of defining the goal and channelizing the individual's energies.

In setting a task for students, the teacher should not say merely "do this" but "notice this, try that, compare these." The student is always entitled to ask (but very seldom does, although he may feel this way) "What am I supposed to learn?" The unstructured task brings only a feeling of futility to the would-be learner. We can more actively engage the learner by telling him exactly what is expected, how to go about it, and how to evaluate his progress.

The Goal Gradient Principle. Motivation increases with progress toward the goal. Animals in a maze will run faster as they near the exit to the food. Also, the correct responses at choice points (right or left turns) closer to the goal are learned sooner than those further away from the goal. Our emotional life illustrates the same principle. Fears of impending threats are stronger than more distant ones. Tasks and problems contain many cues which are interpreted as leading to a goal, reward, or solution. The cues with the greatest "sign value" thus acquire a kind of secondary reward value by association with the goal. The effect of *almost* attaining the goal is therefore often rewarding, or interpreted as "success."

In school learning, the distant or vaguely conceived goal is not usually effective. The problem of motivating students therefore "suggests the necessity of searching for and assigning school tasks that have very specific and definite demands" (4). All teachers know that students will study for a test to be given tomorrow rather than one to be given a month away. The use of frequent quizzes and examinations, which has in general been found to be advantageous, gives the school tasks a more specific temporal setting. Tests and quizzes, however, may unfortunately at times be set up as the main objectives of learning instead of remaining incidental to the general aims of education.

The principle of the goal-gradient implies the necessity for providing learning situations that appeal to and satisfy the immediate goals of the learner.

The principle of *least effort* is related to the goal gradient principle. The learner always takes the shortest route to the goal. This is illustrated by the animal in a D-maze (so called because of its general shape); the animal learns the shorter path and takes the longer only when forced to do so. Cheating in examinations is an example of "least effort." From the point of view of learning theory, cheating is predictable when the task-motive is the narrow and specific one of passing the test, in the absence of more comprehensive or desirable motives. Highly competitive situations, with overemphasis on such a specific goal, would thus ordinarily lead to more cheating.

Students frequently demand formulas and short-cut approaches, and are impatient with roundabout ways of solving problems which the teacher considers necessary. For instance, students are satisfied with the simple method of dividing fractions by inverting the divisor and multiplying, without knowing why it works. Very often, intermediate steps are necessary for adequate learning. When the roundabout way is chosen, the cue value of intermediate steps must be clear to the student as a means to the goal. As a means of circumventing the principle of least effort, which operates when the task is oversimple and "getting the answer" the all-important goal, the successful teacher carefully selects problems which cannot be solved by the simple method. This frustrates the learner and thus puts him in the problem situation which forces him to think.

The Principle of Closure. Incomplete tasks set up tension, which carries the learner's activity forward to completion. In the laboratory, it has been found that when a person is given a number of tasks and is allowed to complete some but is interrupted in others, he later recalls the interrupted tasks much more readily than those he completed (33). The better memory for the incomplete tasks is said to be due to the goal-tension which carries over after the tasks are interrupted. This would imply that interrupted study would be favorable to active engagement of the learner when the study situation is next encountered. In other words, it is better to interrupt a study period at a good "beginning point" rather than at an "ending point."

The principle of closure also explains why a direct question is a more intense stimulus to learning than narrative statement. This is perhaps due to the fact that a question is more pointed in its direct significance. It is characteristic of the very nature of a mental task or problem that it has the outward appearance of a question or challenge about it. Facts presented merely as facts may lack this essential for learning. This seems to be but a particular instance of the general principle of motivation that a mental activity which is manifestly incomplete tends to carry forward to its own completion. As Symonds says:

> Any movement initiated in an attempt to reduce tensions set up has its own drive to completion. Regardless of the nature of the tension or of the process set in motion to relieve it there is a drive toward *success*. I have found in studies of the adjustment of school children that the drive toward success, whatever the nature of the activity, is the most potent of all drives. In every individual there is a drive, strong or weak as it may be, to the successful completion of what one undertakes. (27)

The motive for the execution of a task may seem to inhere in the task itself, although it must derive originally from the more general motives or dispositions of the individual. When these more general dispositions are present, as we may often assume them to be, it becomes unnecessary to go out of our way to bring in extraneous influences to give "interest" to the task. Most mental tasks, when appropriate to the maturity of the well disposed student, are interesting in themselves. The fault may sometimes be found in presenting these, in building up to them and in making them clear and specific.

Integration of Motives. There are, as we know, many kinds and sources of motives, which may interact sometimes by conflict and sometimes by cooperation. Both of these possibilities are of interest in the study of learning. When two sets of motives conflict, the personality is divided against itself and efficiency suffers. The adverse effect of distraction is to be explained partly on this basis. When, however, motives which may be integrated toward the attainment of a desired end are utilized at one and the same time, facilitation of learning may result.

Studies in animal psychology have as a rule shown that a combination of motives is more effective for learning than when only one is utilized. The same thing is true of human learning. But we should not expect to attain this result unless the motives to be combined are such as may be built into an effective organization without conflicting details. That is, when multiple motives are appealed to, some of them should not lead to "side-issues" which may inhibit the effective performance of the task at hand. Effective motivation would therefore involve the enlistment of the total personality. The learner's activity is more purposefully organized, and learning more effective and meaningful, when it satisfies the more vital needs of the learner. Hence the importance of intrinsic relations between the acts of the learner and their consequences.

Level of Aspiration Studies. The original studies in level of aspiration, as done by Hoppe (13), were simple but cleverly conceived experiments in throwing darts at a target. They were designed to investigate the relation between "success" and the level of the goal the subject sets for himself. Before each turn at dart-throwing, the subject was asked to estimate the score he expected to make. With repeated trials, it was discovered that the level of aspiration was ordinarily raised or lowered according to the individual's previous performance. In other words, as he increased his actual score, the goal he set for himself tended to go up; if he did not show improvement, and particularly if his performance fell below his goal level, the goal level itself tended to come down.

It was also found that the individual tended to raise his goal after "success" more than to lower it after "failure." This finding shows that the experience of success and failure is not a simple function of the result of the activity, but depends on (1) the goal the individual sets for himself, (2) the *relation* between the level of aspiration and the result, and (3) the amount of self-reference, i.e., the recognition by the learner that the result was due to his own personal performance. The learner thus has his own definition of a "success zone," which operates as a personal standard of success and failure.

Real psychological failure or success is possible only within this zone of uncertainty, where both failure and success are possible. There was a tendency to avoid setting much too difficult goals (beyond the learner's capacity), or too easy goals, which would insure a cheap but unsatisfying kind of "success." Thus a result outside the zone would be interpreted as neither success nor failure. However, profound individual differences were reported. Self-protective persons set goals they could always reach, the bolder ones set high goals which invited greater risk of "failure." With some, repeated failures not only did not result in a lowering of goal level, but in higher goals. This calls our attention to what may be called a variable in "realism" of goal setting.

A realistic level of aspiration is one in the vicinity of actual performance. The general tendency is to set the goal level a little above the level of performance, so that (as Browning put it) the person's reach slightly exceeds his grasp. The unrealistic goal is one beyond the person's capacity, or one not "anchored" to the level of his past performance. Subsequent studies in this problem have revealed that social motives influence level of aspiration; that is, the individual often takes his cue in goal setting from his knowledge of other persons' goals.

Individual differences in discrepancy between goals and performance appear to be stable personality traits. Also, experiments with school children have shown that success or failure in one kind of activity may displace the level of aspiration in another activity, upward or downward. Experiments with young children show that repeated successes induce a high level of activity in originally "passive" children, while the originally active ones can be reduced to passive conduct by failure (15). This is interesting in view of the emphasis which an extremely puritanical theory of human nature has sometimes placed upon the importance of failure and "hard knocks" in the broad setting of the problem of human learning.

The experience of success and failure, relative to the personal goals of the learner, has been found to regulate learning to a considerable extent. An interesting study by Sears (26) investigated the effect of success and failure in arithmetic and reading on the subsequent level of aspiration of students. Students who had been successful set realistic goals, slightly higher than their level of performance. In other words, they expected improvement, but their goals were in line with their demonstrated abilities. The academically unsuccessful children tended to set unrealistic goals, which were either too low or too high. This would indicate that they either (1) expected nothing of themselves and did not expect to try, or (2) they expected too much, which prevents any experience of success. Holt (12) has raised the question whether the student's level of aspiration under such conditions is a matter of real ambition or a form of defensive behavior. That is, the student who sets unrealistically high goals may be simply doing this to restore his damaged self-esteem. He may take satisfaction in the symbolic value of high aims, even without any realistic expectation of achieving them. Teachers may often encourage this kind of behavior, under the mistaken notion that it represents real ambition. Children are not motivated to do better work by tasks that are too difficult for them (5).

The implications of studies of level of aspiration for the work of the school are clear. The important principle is that success and failure depend on self-involvement in school tasks, and the setting of attainable goals. The teacher must therefore select and assign tasks which relate to the immediate goals of students and which are within the success-failure zone. Individual differences are important here, because the critical zone of difficulty varies for individual students. A task can be too easy for one student and too difficult for another; consequently, there must be a balance of tasks suitable to individuals of varying degrees of ability.

A further implication of great importance is the stress placed on experiences of success-failure rather than motivation through reward and punishment. The experience of success and failure is relative to the individual. Failure, as we have seen, is often disruptive. We may well question whether *any* student should ever be allowed to "fail" in the subjective sense. Rather, the purpose of the teacher should be to teach the student how to set realistic goals. This can be achieved only through the student's personal experience in goal setting and his enjoyment of success. Urging the student to set goals beyond his ability, whether academic or vocational, may do him mischief. For some students who set unrealistically high goals, effective motivation will actually involve lowering the level of their aspirations in order to enjoy attainable success.

Psychology of Achievement and Success. We may summarize all of the foregoing principles of motivation in one statement: *the learner's activity is aroused by a goal and sustained by a feeling of progress toward the goal.* The feeling of achievement is attained when a person becomes aware of a goal toward which his activities are directed, when he sees that these are appropriate to the attainment of the goal, and when he sees that with each change in his behavior he is approaching more closely the desired objective. Anything which contributes to producing an insight of this kind may reasonably be expected to increase the motivation of the learner and to make of him a more efficient one.

Goal setting involves immediate and remote goals. The distant future is not very real to school children, and their taste of success and failure is therefore involved in the here-and-now, the immediate task. This explains why they are so easily frustrated, why disappointments are so bitter and success so sweet, and why they are so apathetic to goals they are logically supposed to have (according to adult logic) but which are too remote to be experienced personally. It is the teacher, not the pupil, who must be concerned with the relationship between the immediate goals and experiences and the more remote ones which have meaning for the adult. This characteristic lack of time perspective (7) in youngsters implies that successes are effective in sustaining present activity, and that failures are not. Thus there is psychological substance in the old adage, "nothing succeeds like success."

To view learning according to success and failure does not contradict the possibility of control through rewards and punishments, but it puts the emphasis where it ought to be—on what the learner is trying to do. Success can be defined psychologically only in accordance with the learner's goals. . . . True success may be defined as reaching a goal, although there are partial success experiences along the way, as in the sense of progress toward the goal or getting into the goal region. The teacher can help maintain the success experience by capitalizing upon the sub-goals along the way and by avoiding so narrow a definition of goals that they are attainable by only a few. (11, p. 51)

The class in which students compete for "rewards" is thus inferior, for purposes of motivation, to one in which each sets his own personal goal.

Success and Level of Maturity. Since personal achievement is relative to the background of abilities and appreciations of the person facing the task, the appropriateness of the task is an important factor in arousing a sense of achievement. It has often been noted that most of the disciplinary problems in school arise from among those pupils who are likely to lack the stimulation resulting from the feeling of accomplishment. These are the children who find the ordinary classroom work either too easy or too difficult for them. The dull child will perhaps not be able to envision either the goal or his progress toward it. The bright child on the other hand may find the goal so close to the level of his present ability that he will not believe it worth while to put forth his best effort to accomplish so little. It may be recalled in this connection that the efficiency of the learner increases, up to a certain maximal level, with the difficulty of the material. There are perhaps many bright children who are stimulated to achievement only when they are promoted to a higher grade, one closer to their level of mental maturity.

More perhaps can be taken for granted in the case of mature students in respect to their drive toward success. They are already inured to the spirit of work and are affected by the added incentive of avoiding a socially recognized failure. These traits will often carry them over relatively long periods of time, during which no improvement seems to occur, with very little letdown in motivation (29).

Motives as Organizers

How do motives organize behavior? A motive is a predisposing tendency to seek out and select experience which will satisfy needs. The learner's motive governs his attention, his expectations, and his activities. Can we therefore generalize as follows: "the more intense the motive, the more effective the learning?" There is no such general answer. For example, can you not recall a situation in which being "keyed up" by an intense need made you overanxious and flustered, unable to concentrate? A need or a goal-set is accompanied by a degree of emotional tension. Under some conditions, emotions enable us to organize our behavior more efficiently. Under other conditions, they may be distracting or paralyzing. Different degrees and different kinds of motives produce different results, depending on the learner, the situation, and the consequences.

Attention and Distraction. The detrimental effect of distractions arises because of a conflict of motives which divide the energies of the individual. Sensory distractions are irrelevant stimuli which are so insistent in their demand upon the worker's attention that they may definitely influence his performance. An analysis of attention will show that it depends upon two sets of factors intimately related to our life of motives.

1. *External factors.* First, there is the nature of certain external objects or stimuli, which through some of their conspicuous characteristics appeal to very fundamental human needs and force their perception upon us. Thus loud noises, flashing lights, moving objects, and startling events force themselves upon our attention by reason of some of the influences which have often been spoken of as factors of advantage. These factors may be regarded as being of biological significance to the individual, for they are likely to be found in situations which are sources of possible danger to the organism. Thus a grazing deer will notice or give attention to the slightest moving object even when seen out of the corner of the eye, because such a movement may carry a threat to its very existence. Loud sounds, again, are likely to be associated most often with danger. We should probably find it very difficult to concen-

trate on a geometric problem if some one outside our room should shout "Fire." This word would touch off a latent but very strong need for self-preservation.

Distractions are ordinarily due to perceptions of this kind. They cannot be brought into the organization of our activities toward our main goal and yet are insistent enough to demand some sort of response on our part. It has been found that distractions, below a certain strength, may be resisted by directing our efforts to the task with increased energy or by trying to disregard the distracting stimuli. In the latter case the quality and quantity of the work usually suffer, as they do still more when the distractions are so insistent that mental confusion and emotional block result. In the former case, efficiency has been found at times actually to increase in the presence of distractions, owing apparently to the more highly stimulated activity of the individual in performing the work. We may also "adapt" to the distractions, which then fall into the background of our perceptions and cease to be the important influence they previously had been. Even in this case their presence seems to increase the amount of work done. But this causes increased tension throughout the body, and probably also greater fatigue.

2. *Internal factors.* The efficiency of the individual is, as we know, likely to be affected by various conditions of work, such as seating and lighting arrangements, temperature, humidity, and mental and muscular fatigue (22, 8). These factors, in common with external distractions, may exert a detrimental influence on efficiency through their connection with fundamental organic needs. Thus excessive humidity, interfering with proper skin functioning, or muscular fatigue resulting from sitting too long in one position, call at the physiological level for their correction and thus divide the organism's energies.

It may be noted, however, that complete organic quiescence is not required for most efficient mental work. It has been said that "attention is tension." Attentive behavior is usually accompanied by various subdued muscular tensions throughout the body and in the absence of these, as in sleep, mental activity also ceases. However, when physiological tensions are increased to such a degree through environmental conditions that these require irrelevant and isolated responses on the part of the worker, mental efficiency may be expected to suffer.

Attentive behavior is well motivated behavior directed toward a specific task. It is for this reason that attention makes for economy in learning. When a need is strong and the objective is seen in relation to this, the teacher usually has no difficulty in getting the child to "pay attention" or "concentrate" upon the work at hand. There are large differences among children, however, depending partly upon the level of mental maturity attained, which will be reflected in the energy and effort they give to a task leading to the remote satisfaction of even a strong need. Children must ordinarily be faced with the prospect of more immediate satisfactions, owing to their restricted foresight. The specific goal of some educational activity, which may be very apparent to the adult, may not be foreseen by them and their willingness to pay attention suffers accordingly. In general, the less mature the child the more immediate must be the satisfaction of his needs in order to produce strongly motivated behavior. This is why the "ability to concentrate" is so limited in young children. The problem of voluntary attention at practically all levels of mental maturity reduces to this question: how remote may the satisfaction of a need become and still be effective in stimulating the learner to undertake an organization of his activities with respect to this distant goal?

Motives as Emotional Tensions. Motives are emotional tensions which arouse, sustain, and direct behavior. We are accustomed to think of emotions as disruptive rather than organizing, as shown by such common expressions as "blind with rage," "paralyzed with fear," and the like. On the other hand, mild feelings of delightful anticipation, fear, or annoyance usually stimulate activity and give it direction. Emotions, then, may either assist or disrupt the purposeful organization of behavior which is typical of learning. Leeper (14) has advanced the view that all emotional responses are inherently organizing and motivating. He points out that emotion does often disorganize our responses, but that this effect is exceptional rather than characteristic, and occurs under only two conditions: (1) when the emotion is *extreme,* in which case our perceptions are less clear and our responses poorly integrated. Thus a boxer in great rage becomes less skillful. (2) When there is emotional *conflict,* that is, when the emotion conflicts with some other motive. In the case of a musician with stage fright, for example, the stage fright itself would produce flight—a purposeful and well-organized act. The musician's poor coordination, which prevents him from turning out a smooth performance and thus attaining his goal, is due not to the emotion but to the conflict between two motives, fleeing and playing well. Hebb (9) has criticized this view as oversimple in explaining *all* emotion, asking "But if there were no conflict at all, would there be any emotion?" The latter maintains that there is still, in spite of the logic of Leeper's motivational theory of emotion, some necessity for thinking of some emotional states as disturbing and disruptive.

For our purpose here, the important principle is that emotion does not imply a simple unitary state which is always or even usually disruptive in effect. To say that "motive is the basis of learning" certainly assumes that a motive or need is accompanied by tension that is emotional in character, and that an ordinary amount of tension induces a level of expectancy or attention which facilitates learning. It seems best to conclude, from our present state of knowledge, that emotion serves to organize the responses of the learner except when it is extreme or when we have severe emotional conflict. Emotional reactions may be considered disruptive and disorganizing when they fail conspicuously to solve personal problems, i.e., when they are nonadjustive.

The child's emotional reaction to repeated failure or to threats of punishment is bound to be disruptive. The teacher must try to prevent this not only because it interferes with the learning of school subjects, but because of its possible lasting effect on the child. On the other hand, mild emotional reactions to failure and disappointment may be educationally helpful if they result in more realistic goal setting. Our chief aim in education is to provide success experiences. This is the only way to maintain the natural curiosity and spontaneity of the child, and to develop the persistent goal activity characteristic of maturity.

Motives as Generalized Needs. The self-reference of goals implies that all goals are related to one fundamental need for self-enhancement or self-fulfillment. This need may take many different forms, but at least three seem to be paramount in importance: the needs for mastery, for affiliation, and for status.

1. The *need for mastery* is the intrinsic task-motive. The need to complete, and to succeed in, a given task accepted by the learner is apparently basic to human activity. This is the "problem-solving" attitude which accounts for the much praised virtues of perseverance and patience. Many biographies attest that the need for completing tasks and solving problems may motivate human activity in the absence of economic or social reward. The goal is a kind of self-symbol. Ego-involvement in the need for mastery would seem to be self-expressive; the artist paints, the poet writes, and the scientist formulates and tests theories. Such expressive behavior is by no means rare in students, although it may reveal itself more often outside the classroom than inside. These activities may often seem to be ends in themselves, but their end is self-fulfillment. The activity is thus highly organized, spontaneous, and self-rewarding.

2. The *need for affiliation* is the human need to belong to a group. Its genetic origin may lie in the fact that the human infant is helpless and dependent on its parents for survival. Identification with the family, and later with groups outside the family, is an important and necessary development. The need is satisfied through a personal feeling of "we-ness." The importance of this need in goal setting is that group goals become individual goals, and there is a need to participate in group activity. The rewards are administered by the group, in accepting or rejecting the individual.

Herein lies the most elementary fact in the motivation of students. The student goes to school, and participates in school learning activities, largely because everybody else does. Teachers may feel this motive to be somehow less worthy than an intrinsic interest in reading or arithmetic, but group participation fulfills a basic human need. It should hence be the teacher's primary concern that the child be well related to the group. He must "feel we." This is not only the foundation of his personal security, but the foundation of his attitude toward school work itself. Sometimes half the work of the first grade is spent (and justifiably so) in establishing appropriate group feeling in the youngsters whose only previous affiliation has been that of the family. Poor morale, at all levels of school life, is ordinarily a result of frustrated need for affiliation. And poor morale disorganizes learning activity.

3. The *need for status* in the group is the need for prestige, recognition, and approval. We have seen that as the child becomes socialized, gaining recognition and approval of his parents becomes an important goal. To maintain status in the eyes of parents, he must also gain the recognition of his age-peers, and usually of his teachers. He soon learns that approval begets approval, and that often disapproval begets disapproval. In our culture, deplorable though it may be from an ethical standpoint, the desire for status often becomes an end in itself. The status drive may be an important factor in learning to imitate. An experiment reported by Miller and Dollard showed that children tended to imitate according to the "prestige of models." In generalizing from this principle, the authors say:

The particular social conditions under which imitative behavior is most likely to occur, and in which, indeed, it may be predicted, seem to be, in general, those of hierarchy or rank with regard to specific skills and social statuses. It is true of learning in general, as well as of imitation in particular, that the superordinated teach the subordinate and the latter learn from the former.... The reason why imitation occurs in these situations is clear. Superordinated persons recognize the cue stimuli which designate the nearness or presence of important goals. The subordinated, seeking these goals, often find it easier to depend upon cues given off by the activity of the leaders. The superiors can act as models and critics to aid their inferiors in perfecting the desired habits. (19, pp. 183-184)

Needs and goals are thus complicated phenomena. They have all sorts of dimensions, and in any learning activity various motives play a part. We should begin to see that the learner cannot give us an account of them, other than an oversimple, nonpsychological one, and he should not be expected to do so.

EFFECTIVENESS OF VARIOUS MOTIVES

The principle of motivation implies that the learner's activity arises from personal need, and that well-differentiated goals help to organize and channelize his activity through higher levels of awareness, or readiness. Effective motivation also requires that his activity be sustained through satisfying consequences, i.e., his acts must lead to feelings of "success." Failures are effective to the extent that they cause the learner to change his goals, alter his responses, try something new, or otherwise reorganize his behavior so as to bring about eventual feelings of success. Consequences facilitate learning, in other words, through *response selection,* i.e., establishing patterns of interpretation and response. Occasionally throughout this book we have used the term "reward" in this connection, as in the generalization "rewarded behavior tends to be repeated, and unrewarded behavior tends to cease." This is easily misunderstood. "Reward," in the narrow sense, oversimplifies the explanation of why learning occurs. If we grasp clearly the principle of psychological success and failure—that is, that success and failure depend on degrees of self-involvement—it becomes apparent that reward or nonreward is not automatic in its effect, but depends on the interpretation given to it by the learner.

Consequences modify behavior by (1) establishing patterns of responses as *appropriate* to the situation; the learner perceives that his activity leads to the desired goal. This may be dimly or clearly perceived, but some level of awareness is usually present; (2) by establishing, through repeated activity, more *precise* patterns of behavior, enabling the learned acts to become more refined and definite, more direct and economical, and more stable. Since patterns of behavior are transposable, they become available for use in new situations.

The Principle of Effect. It is often said that when a particular response is followed by a "satisfying state of affairs," that response will tend to be repeated, whereas an "annoying state of affairs" will tend to prevent the repetition of the response. This is in substance the "law of effect." If we make "satisfying" and "annoying" states of affairs broad enough to include "success" and "failure" and if we think of them as issuing from the completed act rather than being connected with particular units of the response, the law of effect may be regarded as loosely descriptive of what occurs in learning. But if we employ these terms in a restricted sense as applying to certain kinds of satisfaction and annoyance such as "pleasure" and "pain," the law of effect becomes relatively unimportant. In fact, there is evidence that all learning will take place in opposition to the law of effect when given this interpretation. Experiments have shown that the subject will learn, and without any apparent detrimental effect as well, when he is punished for every correct response (21).

When a motive, such as hunger, is one which ordinarily leads to "satisfaction," the law of effect will seem to hold. The law of effect is a special case of the law of motivation. The attainment of the goal will sometimes give pleasure, sometimes not, depending upon the nature of the motive dominating the behavior. Reward and punishment may have an indirect influence on learning by being incorporated through anticipation into the motive of the act. This leads to a change in the nature of the goal. The burnt child avoids the flame because the pain gives new meaning to the fire, not because the unpleasant aftereffect has some kind of backward influence upon the original act of reaching. The aftereffect of the reaching changes the goal and motive, and only secondarily the response.

When we come to apply the law of effect as an explanation of how certain part responses get incorporated into the whole act, we not only find actual instances of violation of the law, but we must look to other factors to explain any apparent validity it seems on occasion to have. The fundamental reason for this is that the law of effect was originally devised to fit a piecemeal view of behavior and that it undertook to state how an aftereffect of a "connection" could influence this particular bond.

When we realize, however, that it is the whole individual that learns, we must refer any aftereffects to the total act of behavior, including its perceptual basis. Tolman and others (31) offer a "disproof of the law of effect and a substitution of the laws of emphasis, motivation and disruption." Their experiment required human subjects to learn to choose between successive pairs of holes by running through them in a certain serial order with a metal stylus. A group of subjects who received an electric shock on the correct responses actually learned faster than a group punished for incorrect responses. This, it would seem, is contrary to the law of effect, for which the authors would substitute the principle of *emphasis:*

Whatever emphasizes a difference between the correct and the incorrect holes will facilitate learning. And this will be in part the "correctness" of the correct holes as contrasted with the "incorrectness" of the incorrect holes. But it may be also either punishment applied to the correct holes . . . or punishment applied to the incorrect. . . . And the striking thing is that, for some reason, punishment on the correct holes seems to be more "emphasizing" than punishment on the incorrect holes. (31)

Thus aftereffects may not only alter the nature of the goal but they may give new meaning to the part responses in their setting in the total goal-activity.

The nineteenth century associationists had a theory of learning which held that the important effects were pleasure and pain, comfort and discomfort, pleasantness and unpleasantness. It was said that "we are propelled by pleasure and repelled by pain." This was a *hedonistic* theory, holding that pleasure as such caused certain acts to be repeated while unpleasantness caused acts to be discontinued or avoided. McGeogh has termed this a theory of *"affect."* Although effect and affect have often been confused, it is now generally understood that the principle of effect does not involve hedonism. McGeogh's statement (1942) makes this clear:

The effect meant in the law of effect is a consequence, a result of an act; it may also be pleasant, unpleasant, or indifferent to the individual, but this is secondary. The primary fact is that there is a state of affairs, whatever its psychological classification, which happens as a result of, or at least after, an act. This state of affairs may be symbolic, as a spoken word, or it may be primarily sensory, as the hitting of a stylus against the end of a blind alley, or it may be complexly perceptual and conceptual, as when in social or rational situations one recognizes the consequences of acts or thoughts. The fact that the *law is one of effect, not of affect,* renders pointless much of the discussion that has raged about it. (17, pp. 576-577) (Italics ours)

Some Forms of Reward and Reinforcement. Thus by satisfying consequences we mean an effect which is *congruent* or in harmony with the learner's needs and goals. Dissatisfying consequences are those which are incongruent, out of harmony with, or irrelevant to his goals and what he is doing. This is a matter of the learner's interpretation. The individual does not seek pleasure as such, but unity of organization. Since there are different kinds of motives, there are different kinds of rewards. Food rewards hunger; symbols of status reward a need for status; symbols of affection reward a need for affiliation; completion of tasks and solution of problems reward the need for mastery. Any event which solves a conflict or problem for the learner is thus said to be rewarding or reinforcing; that is, it serves to establish appropriate and precise response patterns. Following are some terms which illustrate different aspects of reward and reinforcement.

1. *Knowledge of results* enable the learner to know whether he is "right" or "wrong," whether he is on the right track, whether he is improving. Such cues, some of which are provided by the situation and some by the learner's activity, are rewarding or satisfying.

2. *Tension reduction* is an important aspect of social and emotional learning. Any event that reduces hunger, sex drives, fear, anxiety, feelings of frustration is a reward, whether in itself pleasurable or painful. The activity of the learner which brings about such an event is therefore reinforced through tension reduction, and tends to be repeated in similar conflict situations. If such learning is relatively "blind" (i.e., the learner does not perceive clearly the relation between his activity and the event that reduces his fear), he will tend to repro-

duce the learned response inappropriately, in situations in which it will not be effective. Superstition and certain forms of neurotic behavior are thus due to inadequate differentiation. But this behavior is rewarding in the sense that it reduces tension.

3. *Task completion* is rewarding. Since a task often involves a number of subgoals as well as an ultimate goal, knowledge of results is rewarding for the subgoals. Feelings of success thus sustain activity through task completion.

4. Punishment, under some conditions, is rewarding. This may appear paradoxical. However, punishment of a wrong response, such as a mild shock or reproof, furnishes "knowledge of results"—a sign that the learner is on the wrong track. Such a punishment is rewarding in the sense that it enables him to vary his behavior and thus attain the desired goal. Similar mild punishment of a "right" response is also rewarding, since it is a sign leading to a goal. The paradoxical effect of reward and punishment, which is a matter of experimental fact, has led most writers to abandon both terms in favor of the more inclusive term *reinforcement*. The reinforcing effect of reward and punishment, however, lies in their role of fulfilling the expectations of the learner.

Writers on learning often talk about reward as a tangible or external event, which of itself brings about learning. This is rather misleading. Reward is an experience of success, and can only be understood from the point of view of the learner. Consequences are rewarding to the extent that they are related to what the learner is trying to do. Reward is thus the perception of a relation between the learner's activity and his goal.

Some Factors Governing Effect. What factors make consequences more or less effective in learning? This question has been extensively studied. We shall generalize here some of the more important findings.

1. *Knowledge of results* makes a definite contribution to learning efficiency. Experiments have covered a wide variety of mental activities, and in most instances the rate of improvement has been found to be increased. Studies carried on with

school pupils have employed such devices as graphs of progress and individual learning curves to bring home to the children the fact of improvement. One review (20) of the problem states that "the findings of the studies are almost unanimously in favor of the contention that knowledge of the progress of learning is an effective stimulus. It would be difficult to find another group of experiments in which there is as great agreement among the conclusions." Heidbreder (10) has shown that the same principle holds in the sphere of reflective thinking. Partial success in the formulation of hypotheses to solve a problem spurred the thinker on to formulate new hypotheses, and even the later step of verification was influenced favorably by the success which was partially realized.

2. *Intrinsic rewards* are in general more effective than extrinsic. First, we have seen that motivation is more effective when various needs and goals are integrated toward the attainment of a desired end. Extrinsic or artificial incentives introduced into a task may lead to "side issues" which are distracting. This is illustrated in a study by Mace (16) which introduced indirect incentives of penalty and reward into a learning task based on an aiming and a dart-board test. His conclusions are as follows:

> The performance of any task is controlled by some specific intention.
>
> To introduce an extraneous penalty or reward evokes a secondary reaction, which may be either facilitating or inhibiting.
>
> This secondary intention seems to be often detrimental in skill, especially if introduced before full mastery has been acquired.
>
> Incentives should be intrinsic to the task—there should be no distinct or conflicting purpose—no arousal of secondary objectives.

In view of the above result we may well raise the question whether the use of extrinsic motives or indirect incentives in connection with school work really enters into an effective organization with motives of a "long-distance" sort which we hope to be the prime basis of the child's development. It may be that many of them do, but some of them on the other hand may give rise to side issues which contribute either very little or perhaps only transient stimulation to the main purpose of the work, or which in the final analysis may actually conflict with this.

Laboratory studies of extrinsic rewards and punishments illustrate very well the influence of these on efficiency. Rock (25) could find no evidence of a facilitating effect of money rewards on code-learning and ball-tossing. The results obtained in this experiment differed somewhat from those of an earlier experiment by Thorndike and Forlano (28) employing children from six to sixteen years of age. In this case the addition of a monetary reward for learning increased efficiency up to a certain point. When the monetary reward was made relatively large, there was found to be a decline in the rate of learning. Studies employing punishment show in general the same effect. When an extrinsic motive is appealed to, it is often capable of supplying energy to be utilized in the learning task, but when the strength of this motive is unduly increased, it may actually become detrimental to efficiency.

However, motives which are only apparently extrinsic may become relevant to a performance through the setting given them in the total personality. An extrinsic subgoal may lead to a more remote but intrinsic goal. There is thus "no automatic solution to the problem of motivation by stating a preference for intrinsic over extrinsic relations between task and goals" (11).

3. *Vivid consequences* are usually more effective than less vivid ones. Consequences have cue-value; that is, they are signs leading to goals. The more novel or striking cues are more distinct, and thus more effective in motivating the learner. The special case of pain, such as a mild shock, has its effect on learning through the vividness and distinctness of the cue. The so-called laws of primacy and recency are also related here. Instances of fears learned on a single occasion, and other forms of "one-trial" learning, are also explained by the extraordinary vividness of the experience.

4. *Repetition* of reward and punishment is ordinarily more effective than a single occasion or a few occasions. In animal learning, the strength of a habit is ordinarily directly related to the number of reinforcements. Repetition has the effect of

making the signs leading to the goal more distinctive, in both animal and human learning. One extremely vivid experience, however, may be just as effective in learning as twenty or thirty practice sessions. The value of repetition, again, is subsidiary to the principle that consequences must be relevant. The story of the boy who was given a corrective exercise in writing "I have gone" fifty times after school, and then left a note for the teacher stating that "I have went home" is very much to the point.

The effectiveness of consequences depends in general on their place in the total setting, as interpreted by the learner. All of the above principles are applicable, but they are interrelated. There is thus no formula for motivating students. The successful teacher is one who is convinced that motivation is important and sees that every student experiences some kind of success, each in his own way.

Experiments in Reward and Punishment. The influence of punishment and reward, as productive of pain or pleasure, has been the subject of a number of studies in animal learning. The "conditioned reaction" technique, whether employed with animals or with young children, has made extensive use of these incentives. From the results of experiments on animals, we may conclude that learning is more rapid when both reward and punishment are employed than when either one is used singly. When it comes to a comparison of the relative effectiveness of the two, however, it is more difficult to determine this, although many experiments have seemed to favor punishment.

What may be regarded as a crucial experiment in the effect of punishment on learning was done by Estes (6). This was a study of the effect of punishment (electric shock) in eliminating a bar-pressing habit in rats which had learned to press the bar in order to obtain food. The "bar" is a small lever provided in a device known as the Skinner box. The details of the experiment need not concern us here, but the findings are quite interesting. First, the habit of pressing the bar was not eliminated more rapidly in rats which were shocked than in rats which were not shocked. Second, it was found that shock when administered *every time* the rats pressed the bar, deterred them from responding. But after the punishment was removed, the bar pressing habit was almost as strong as it was in the first place. Figure 53 compares three groups of rats who in the

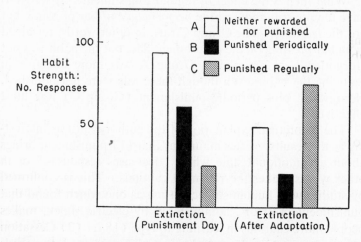

FIGURE 53. Comparative Effect of Unrewarding and Punishing Consequences on Habitual Responses of Rats. Before the punishment day the habit strength, or number of bar-pressing responses, was equal in the three groups. On the punishment day, regular punishment is seen to have a greater deterrent effect than periodic punishment, while the (A) unrewarded group maintains a relatively high rate of response. But this is a temporary effect. After adaptation (a period of no opportunity for bar pressing) the group which had been regularly punished (C) responds oftener than the other groups. This shows that regular punishment has a temporary effect only, and is less effective in breaking habits than absence of reward. (Data from W. K. Estes, 6.)

beginning were equal in habit strength (number of bar pressing responses per period).[1] On the "punishment day" Group A was neither rewarded with food nor punished by shock; Group B was not rewarded, but was punished periodically; Group C was punished regularly. Note that while the unpunished Group A showed some extinction of the habit, Group B showed greater extinction, and Group C the greatest amount of extinction.

[1] Actually, the habit strengths were not equal, but were equated by statistical methods.

Note further that after the punishment was discontinued (adaptation period) the deterring effect of regular punishment (Group C) is almost entirely eradicated, and this group now responds oftener than the other two.

What then is the effect of regular punishment? It seems to have temporarily reduced the *performance* of bar pressing, but not the *learning*. The Group C rats, in other words, refrained from bar pressing on the punishment day, but the habit was not "forgotten." Nonreward in Group A was more effective in reducing the habit, even though these rats were not punished. Nonreward, plus periodic punishment (Group C) was most effective.

The theoretical explanation of the author is just as interesting as the results. Estes maintains that (1) punishment brings about an emotional state which "decreases responses," or in other words makes the rat more cautious. This is confirmed by studies with human subjects, such as one which found that punishment of errors, administered by electric shock, makes people more cautious in learning to type (18). (2) Cessation of punishment is itself rewarding or reinforcing and thus tends to cause resumption of the response.

Practical Role of Reward and Punishment. The disadvantages of punishment should be clear. Whatever its effect in eliminating errors or undesirable behavior, the effect is temporary at best. Extinction of undesirable responses is mainly an effect of nonreward; that is, unrewarded responses are extinguished more permanently than punished ones. Punishment may actually prevent effective learning, first because of the inhibiting emotional state which it brings about, and secondly because the emotional state itself actually tends to preserve an undesirable response tendency. This latter point deserves special attention. In the case of the rats, the tendency toward bar-pressing would be effectively eliminated, according to the theory, only if the rat were allowed to press the bar repeatedly, without reward. Elimination of the habit, in other words, amounts to learning that the response will not be rewarded, and it will take a number of trials to learn this. But if, because of shock, the rat refrains from bar-pressing, he will not learn that the response does not lead to food.

The implication for human learning is that a child punished for temper tantrums may temporarily refrain from them, but will not in this way learn permanently that temper tantrums are ineffective. It is for this reason also that punishment is seldom effective in reducing the tendency toward nail-biting or thumb-sucking. Such habits usually disappear rapidly, however, when the child becomes more socialized and finds they are not re-warded socially. According to this theory, what effect would frequent and severe punishment have on learning? The result-ing emotional state would tend to inhibit not only the response which is punished, but other activity as well. It is difficult to devise punishment for a specific response which will not "spread" to other activities. We see here the disruptive or dis-organizing effects of emotion on learning.

While punishment may alter behavior, the results of punishment are less predictable than the results of reward. Reward says: Repeat what you have done. Punishment says: Stop it! But the punishment does not tell what to do, and the result may be simply emotional upset. (11, p. 49)

What purpose, then, does punishment serve in learning? (1) Punishment may be useful in reducing or preventing an undesirable response. However, to be effective in this respect it must be continued, since by itself it produces no lasting effect. (2) Punishment appears to be most effective when used in com-bination with reward. That is, the suppression of an undesired response through punishment may be helpful in making it possi-ble to reward some other (alternative or substitute) response which is more desirable. The consequences of reward and punishment thus set up cues which enable the learner to differ-entiate between good and bad. Punishment by itself does not enable him to differentiate. (3) To be effective, punishment must be given in such a way that the learner can distinguish which specific response is being punished. The learner must note that *this particular response* is the one being punished. Thorndike's comment on this point, in discussing the ways of improving results to be obtained from punishment, is particularly lucid:

The first is to try to make sure in each case that the punishment belongs to the behavior in question. If it cannot be its direct after-effect, means should be taken to recall the occurrence and to make clear and emphatic connection in the punished person's mind between the impulse to that behavior and the expectation of the punishment.

The second is to forestall the punishment in cases where the want which led to the offense can be satisfied innocently. A large fraction of punishments is used to counteract the otherwise satisfying consequences of certain behavior. Some of this behavior is really innocent and desirable and should not be punished at all. It was for example sheer folly to make children of five to ten sit still for hours in school and to punish them if they fidgeted. Some of it can be obviated by the provision of an innocent outlet. (30)

Because the source of human motives and their interaction is much more complicated than in lower animals, owing to the role of language and symbolic reward, it is often dangerous to generalize from animal to human learning. However, much of the experimental work in human learning confirms the implications of the foregoing theory of reward and punishment. Thus one report of a code-learning experiment showed that the results of punishment by electric shock were both "incentive and disruptive." (24) That punishment may be disruptive is due to the fact that it is likely to be irrelevant to the main goal-activity, and by setting up side issues in behavior, it is likely to interfere with the organization at hand. This may happen especially if the motive of avoiding punishment becomes stronger than the drive toward the main goal of the task. It then becomes a question of competition between diverging motives. Studies of maze learning in human subjects show similar results. One experiment (3) found that learning with punishment is superior to learning without, when judged by every criterion except that of time taken per trial. This would seem to indicate that punishment makes the performer more careful and cautious, and affects the learning through this change. The second study has an interesting comment to make with reference to the nature of the task performed. If the task and the methods of work are fairly simple, punishment is effective; but if the task and methods are complex, it is more difficult to arrive at any generalization.

A significant conclusion is that punishment is likely to have a "disruptive" effect when the learning is tested for "delayed retention." That is, while punishment may at times produce quicker learning in the beginning, it may sometimes be accompanied by aftereffects which interfere with the retention of the learned task. If this be so, it becomes important, when we are thinking of employing punishment as an incentive, to ask ourselves whether we are working for more immediate results or for more lasting ones.

REFERENCES

1. BOOK, W. F., & NORVELL, L. The will to learn. *Ped. Sem.*, 1922, **29**, 305-362.
2. BOSWELL, F. P., & FOSTER, W. S. On memorizing with the intention permanently to retain. *Amer. J. Psychol.*, 1916, **27**, 420-426.
3. BUNCH, M. E. The effect of electric shock as punishment for errors in maze learning. *J. compar. Psychol.*, 1928, **7**, 343-359.
4. CHAPMAN, J. C. Persistence, success, and speed in a mental task. *Ped. Sem.*, 1924, **31**, 276-284.
5. CHILD, I. L., & ADELSHEIM, E. Motivational value of barriers for young children. *J. Genet. Psychol.*, 1944, **65**, 97-111.
6. ESTES, W. K. An experimental study of punishment. *Psychol. Monogr.*, 1944, **57**, No. 263.
7. FRANK, L. K. Time perspectives. *J. soc. Philos.*, 1939, **4**, 293-312.
8. GHISELLI, E. E., & BROWN, C. W. *Personnel and industrial psychology.* New York: McGraw-Hill, 1948.
9. HEBB, D. O. *The organization of behavior.* New York: Wiley, 1949.
10. HEIDBREDER, E. An experimental study of thinking. *Arch. Psychol.*, 1924, No. 73.
11. HILGARD, E. R., & RUSSELL, D. H. Motivation in school learning. *49th Yearbook,* Nat. Soc. Stud. Educ., 1950.
12. HOLT, R. R. Level of aspiration: ambition or defense. *J. exp. Psychol.*, 1946, **36**, 398-416.
13. HOPPE, F. Erfolg und misserfolg. *Psychol. Forsch.*, 1931, **14**, 1-62.
14. LEEPER, R. W. A motivational theory of emotion to replace "emotion as disorganized response." *Psychol. Rev.*, 1948, **55**, 5-21.
15. LEWIN, K. *Dynamic theory of personality.* New York: McGraw-Hill, 1935.

16. MACE, C. A. The influence of indirect incentives upon the accuracy of skilled movements. *Brit. J. Psychol.,* 1931, **22,** 101-114.

17. MCGEOGH, J. A. *The psychology of human learning.* New York: Longmans, Green, 1942.

18. MCTEER, W. A study of certain features of punishment in serial learning. *J. exp. Psychol.,* 1931, **14,** 453-476.

19. MILLER, N. E., & DOLLARD, J. *Social learning and imitation.* New Haven: Yale Univ. Press, 1941.

20. MONROE, W. S., & ENGELHARDT, M. D. Stimulating learning activity. *Univ. Illinois Bur. Educ. Res. Bull,* 1930, No. 51.

21. PETERSON, J. Learning when frequency and recency factors are negative and right responses are painful. *Psychol. Bull.,* 1931, **28,** 207-208.

22. POFFENBERGER, A. T. *Principles of applied psychology.* New York: Appleton-Century, 1942.

23. PRESCOTT, D. A. *Emotion and the educative process.* Washington, D.C.: Amer. Council on Educ., 1938.

24. REXROAD, C. N. Administering electric shock for inaccuracy in continuous multiple choice reactions. *J. exp. Psychol.,* 1926, **9,** 1-18.

25. ROCK, R. T. The influence upon learning of the quantitative variation of aftereffect. *Teach. Coll. Contr. Educ.,* 1935, No. 650.

26. SEARS, P. S. Levels of aspiration in academically successful and unsuccessful school children. *J. abn. soc. Psychol.,* 1946, **36,** 398-416.

27. SYMONDS, P. M. Human drives. *J. educ. Psychol.,* 1934, **25,** 681-694.

28. THORNDIKE, E. L., & FORLANO, G. The influence of increase and decrease of the amount of reward upon the rate of learning. *J. educ. Psychol.,* 1933, **24,** 401-411.

29. THORNDIKE, E. L., & WOODYARD, E. The influence of the relative frequency of successes and frustrations upon intellectual achievement. *J. educ. Psychol.,* 1934, **25,** 24-250.

30. THORNDIKE, E. L. *et al. The psychology of wants, interests, and attitudes.* New York: Appleton-Century, 1935.

31. TOLMAN, E. C., HALL, C. S., & BRETNALL, E. P. A disproof of the law of effect. *J. exp. Psychol.,* 1932, **15,** 601-614.

32. WRIGHT, W. R. Some effects of incentives on work and fatigue. *Psychol. Rev.,* 1906, **13,** 23-34.

33. ZEIGARNIK, B. Uber das behalten von erledigten handlungen. *Psychol. Forsch.,* 1927, **9,** 1-85.

SELECTED READINGS

HILGARD, E. R., & RUSSELL, D. H. Motivation in school learning. Ch. 3 in *49th Yearbook,* Nat. Soc. Study Educ., 1950.

KINGSLEY, H. L. *The nature and conditions of learning.* New York: Prentice-Hall, 1946.

LEWIN, K. *A dynamic theory of personality.* New York: McGraw-Hill, 1935.

LEWIN, K., *et al.* Level of aspiration. In Hunt, J. McV. (Ed.), *Personality and the behavior disorders.* New York: Ronald Press, 1944.

McGEOGH, J. A. *The psychology of human learning.* New York: Longmans, Green, 1942. Chapter 7, Learning as a function of motive-incentive conditions.

TOLMAN, E. C. *Purposive behavior in animals and men.* New York: Appleton-Century, 1932.

YOUNG, P. T. *Motivation of behavior.* New York: Wiley, 1936.

YOUNG, P. T. *Emotion in man and animal: its nature and relation to attitude and motive.* New York: Wiley, 1943.

15

LEARNING AS A SOCIAL PROCESS

To THINK of learning merely as an individual process is to over-look the influence of social groups on the individual and the interaction among group members. The mere presence of others affects our behavior in learning situations. There are group goals as well as individual goals, and the motive of the individual often stems from his identification with a group. The "success" or "failure" of the learner, as he interprets it, is usually a matter of meeting his social needs. Our view of the role of motivation in learning would therefore be quite incomplete without some knowledge of the part played by the presence of others, by group affiliations, by competition with others, by social motives in general. In this discussion, we shall take advantage of recent work in social psychology referring to "group processes" or "group dynamics." On the whole, this research seems to show that group relations establish a kind of social-emotional "climate" which profoundly affects the learning situation and its outcome.

SOCIAL MOTIVES IN LEARNING

Most human motives are social. That is, they are learned through identifications with social groups and are the products of interpersonal relations. Social motives, such as the need for affiliation and status, provide very strong incentives for learning. As soon as a child becomes aware of the existence of other persons around him, a number of social needs arise to influence his behavior. Dennis has pointed out that "something resembling an in-group–out-group distinction is very fundamental in children's perception" (9). The child's reaction to strangers, for example, can hardly be accounted for as a conditioned response; he does not need to have unpleasant experiences with strangers in order to fear strangers. The differences between individual and group behavior are so striking that some psychologists have been inclined to believe that there must be a "group mind" over and above the minds of the individuals comprising the group. This is scarcely a tenable theory, but it does serve to stress the importance of social influences.

The mere presence of a group will modify a person's reaction to a situation. The earlier experiments on group effects seemed to indicate: (1) that the presence of fellow workers tends to increase speed and accuracy of mental work; (2) that the increase is more pronounced in work involving overt physical movements than in purely intellectual tasks; (3) that in adults there is no improvement in constancy of attention or in quality of work performed; (4) that logical reasoning is poorer in the group situation, but that this reasoning is expressed in a larger number of words; and (5) that such improvements as are produced by the presence of a group are greatest for the least able workers, and least for the most able (12). For the practical purposes of motivation, however, it is necessary to consider in detail certain features of "group" activity, which will indicate the nature of the motives involved and the variation among individuals in their response to these motives.

Group vs. Individual Motives. We may ask whether the mere presence of others while one is working will of itself, without an appeal to such specific motives as rivalry, competition, and the desire for recognition, alter the rate or quality of individual work. One experiment suggests that it is the amount of "social participation" in the group that brings about the change. Griffith (14) studied the influence of the seating arrangement of students in a classroom upon the grades received by each during the course. Since the students were seated alphabetically, we should expect no influence of selection on the basis of ability. He found nevertheless that students in the front seats received poorer grades than those sitting in second or third rows, and that those sitting in the back row were distinctly poorer than the average fourth-row student. Although it is not an easy matter to single out the factors which may account for this, the author concludes that the variation found "seems essentially to rest upon the varying degrees of social integration among the members of the group." Dashiell (8) would emphasize the importance of the arousal of a spirit of competition before group effort can become apparent. He found that a mere "co-working" but "noncompetitive" group had no influence on individual speed or accuracy. It is apparently not enough that we be "in" a group but not "of" it.

The influence of different social motives is likely to change as the child grows toward maturity. Greenberg (13), working with children from two to seven years of age, studied the influence of competition and rivalry in respect to their relative strength as incentives. Two of the conclusions are of interest to us. (1) Competition was found less effective with children of these ages than the prospect of some tangible reward, such as a chocolate bar. (2) Rivalry or competition may be effective only when the child is somewhat familiar with the learning task. It would apparently not serve when something wholly new was to be taught. Another aspect of the relation of social motives to maturity is contained in the general finding that duller children seem on the whole to be more highly stimulated by group activities than are the brighter. There is some indication that bright children may tend even to be inhibited (1). It would perhaps be difficult to explain this difference without an appeal to personality traits.

There are apparently differences in the susceptibility of individuals to social stimulation. Thus, Burri (5) found with some of his subjects that the recitation of memorized material was adversely affected by the presence of others, whether or not the other members of the group gave any attention to the recitation itself. The group may have an inhibiting effect as well as a stimulating one, particularly if the social situation is one where the individual has to put himself forward or even remotely become subject to possible criticism. Ekdahl (10) confirmed this finding for free association. In the case of those such as stutterers, who are very susceptible to the inhibiting influence of the group, it was found that they are much more successful in giving associations when alone. Some subjects, by reason of temperament, may be "overstimulated" or affected by irrelevant emotional reactions in the group situation and their efficiency thereby impaired. When competition is expressly made the motivating force, it appears that most subjects speed up their work appreciably (39), but the quality of the work may suffer. Older children appear to respond to competition better than younger children, and girls better than boys.

The question may be raised whether the child will be more strongly motivated when he is working for the good of the group than when working on his own behalf. The answer to this question has been found to depend partly at least upon the nature of the group. Sims (31) and Maller (25) found that the individual child is in general more strongly motivated when working for himself, but the second author noticed that working for one's sex against the opposite sex was at times a stronger motive. Teams chosen by the children themselves were more effective in arousing competition than the usual classroom method of pitting one group against another. Maller arranges the motives studied in the following order of effectiveness, from most to least effective: (1) work for one's sex, (2) work for oneself, (3) work for one's team, (4) work for one's school class, and (5) work for an arbitrary group chosen by the teacher. It would seem that the degree of identification with the group is an important factor. It is for this reason, probably, that competition among small groups is more effective than among large groups.

The importance of group identification is illustrated strikingly by level of aspiration studies. These show that the child sets his personal goals relative to a group norm. Anderson and Brandt (2) studied the levels of aspiration of fifth-graders. In this situation, each child knew the group norm, his own relative standing in the group, and his own previous score. He did not know, however, the scores of any other individual children, and no other child in the group knew his. There was thus no "competition" among individuals, and a minimum of "pressure" through group opinion.   Under these conditions, the children's goals "tended to converge on what for the group was mediocrity," i.e., near the group norm.   However, the average performance of this group showed better improvement than that of a control group who did not know their scores or relative ranking.   Hilgard, Sait, and Magaret found, in another level of aspiration study (16), that those with previous scores above the group norm tended to lower their goals, and those below the norm tended to raise them unrealistically on future trials. These authors concluded that "group pressure" is effective in explaining this only to the extent that "the desire for social conformity is somehow internalized."   This is similar to Sears' conclusion that level of aspiration is set with respect to "the perceived social norms" (29).

Social Effects of Competition.   Competing with others depends for its effectiveness on the need to outdo others, to strive for recognition or status in the group.   Apart from any tangible gains in achievement that might result from a competitive learning situation, we need to examine its total effect on the learner and his relations with the group.   (1) In the first place, we may ask whether the kind of behavior it produces is really socially desirable.   An overemphasis on winning for the sake of winning, on beating somebody else, on being "better than" others would certainly seem to place school learning in the wrong social setting.   It may reward this kind of motive to the exclusion of others, and tend to underemphasize the intrinsic importance of school achievement itself.   (2) Again, we need to ask how the rewards are distributed.   In the competitive situation, there are only a few "winners" and many "losers."   Success is limited to a few, and failure is the lot of the majority.   This tends to produce feelings of anxiety in all students who really want to win; the keener the motive, the greater the anxiety and the keener the disappointment to the loser.   For the student limited in academic aptitude, the only effective adjustment is to give up the goal and stop trying.   The competitive situation may thus defeat its own purpose for the majority who cannot win.   (3) What is the effect of competition on social relations in the group? On the whole, it would appear to be divisive rather than integrative. The successful competitors tend to become a kind of "elite" subgroup, and this may carry over to social relations in general. Since the chief emphasis is on winning and consequent prestige, the child who does not get prestige one way will get it another. Johnny may not be recognized as a "leader" in the classroom, but he is on the playground. With different kinds of social values competing for ascendancy, Johnny may easily become a troublemaker in class and a bully elsewhere. The competitive emphasis, in the end, may make the classroom an aggregation of anxious, frustrated individuals working against one another instead of a cohesive social group working cooperatively toward common goals.

At best, the rewards introduced in the learning situation through individual or group competition are extrinsic "side issues." When viewed in their total setting, i.e., the social situation, these incentives are seen to have by-products which are anything but favorable. We may very effectively teach the child under such conditions that his activity is worth while only to the extent that it "pays off" in the attention, approval, or prestige it gets him, or in other words, extrinsic rewards. Piting group against group may also pay off in more achievement, but the rewards may again be extrinsic to the learning situation we wish to create in the classroom.

Praise and Reproof. There have been several important studies on the relative effect of praise and reproof as incentives in educational settings. Briggs (3) found that teachers, reprimanding and encouraging the same pupils on alternate days, and measuring the results with objective tests, produced better scores among the pupils after commendation in 87 per cent of the cases. Hurlock (17) notes some differential effects of praise and reproof. Praise was found to be universally effective in stimulating better work. Reproof, on the other hand, was actually detrimental in some instances to the efficiency of the poorer students. The bright child responded better to reproof than did the dull, but not so well as he did to praise. Publicly expressed ridicule or sarcasm (4) has been found to be detrimental to the quality of work. The adverse effects of sarcasm and of "razzing" (19) are perhaps due to two principal factors, the undermining of a sense of achievement, and the production of an "emotional block" or arousal of irrelevant emotional reactions with the consequent division, as it were, of mental effort. We may reasonably expect greater inefficiency to result when, under social pressure, a conflict of motives results, one of which leads to an emotional response which cannot be easily integrated with the learning task.

A later study suggests that the effect of praise and reproof is dependent on personality factors. Praise was found more effective with "introvert" children in the primary grades, but reproof was more effective in motivating "extroverts" (36).

Dynamics of Reward and Punishment. An interesting and penetrating analysis of the dynamic factors in reward and punishment situations has been made by Lewin (20, 21) through his *topological* psychology. Borrowing his techniques from the geometric concept of topology, he represents through diagram the individual in his psychological life space, being attracted or repelled by the objects within his perceptual field and being moved by the psychological forces of his environment. The attractive or repellant aspects of objects are termed *valences,* which are positive or negative and are represented diagrammatically by plus or minus signs. The forces acting upon the individual are termed vectors, and are indicated by arrows. A simple example of a topological sketch is given in Figure 54, which illustrates a simple choice situation involving two alternatives.

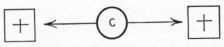

FIGURE 54. Diagram of a Simple Choice Situation. The child is attracted equally to two goals.

Lewin has clearly distinguished through diagrams the differences in motivational aspects of the simple interest situation and the conflict situation. In the interest situation (Figure 55) the child simply moves toward the doll. If prevented by an

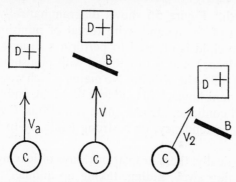

FIGURE 55. Diagram of the Interest Situation. The child is attracted to the doll (D). A barrier (B) may prevent her from reaching it. For instance, the doll may be on a shelf out of reach. The child would then tend to try a roundabout solution by "going around the barrier." If the barrier were a parental prohibition, the child might try to "get around" the parent psychologically. Diagrammatically, this would look the same as standing on a chair to reach the doll. (Figures from G. W. Hartmann, *Gestalt psychology*, Ronald Press, 1935, p. 211.)

obstacle (Barrier, B) the child simply moves around it but in a constant direction toward the goal. In the conflict situation, the child is acted upon by two opposing forces of approximately

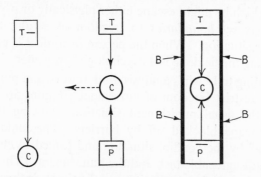

FIGURE 56. Diagram of the Conflict Situation; "Command with Threat of Punishment." The child is repelled by the unpleasant task (T) but is threatened with punishment (P) unless he does it. In this conflict situation the child would tend to escape or "leave the psychological field," as shown by dotted arrow. This must be prevented by barriers (B), either physical or social. Diagrammatically, the child is "boxed in" the conflict situation, which requires "policing" (II). (Adapted from Hartmann, *op. cit.,* and K. Lewin, 22.)

equal strength. Figure 56 shows diagrammatically the conflict situation of "command, with threat of punishment." In this case, the child is ordered to perform a disagreeable task (negative valence) and is threatened with punishment (negative valence) unless he does it. No matter which way he moves, the threat of punishment will tend to follow him, and the conflict situation will continue. Under these conditions, the child will have an escape tendency, or a strong tendency to "leave the field."

Psychologically, there are various ways of leaving the field, such as running away, hiding, taking up another task, or in some way deceiving the adult who gives the order. Means must be taken to prevent the child's slipping out of the situation. Psychological fences must be erected to keep him enclosed. These are called "barriers." Barriers may be physical ones; that is, the child may be locked in his room or forbidden to leave the room. They are ordinarily social, since they involve a threat of disapproval. Verbal hints such as "you're a big boy" or "don't be a sissy," and more direct threats of parental or group disapproval, are of this order. Barriers impose psychological forces which "press in" on the child, preventing holes through which he might escape either physically or psychologically. They set *boundaries* to freedom of action; this is a prison-like situation. When the person in conflict is prevented from leaving the field, he is a psychological prisoner.

According to Lewin's analysis, both reward and punishment situations restrict freedom of movement. Figure 56 is a diagram of the usual punishment situation, showing the tendency to escape blocked off by barriers. The child (C) is "walled in" by the conflict situation and forced to choose between the disagreeable task and the punishment. The barriers are usually imposed by authority, and the situation thus requires constant, vigilant "policing." In the reward situation (Figure 57) the conflict looks a little different. The child (C) seeks the reward (R) but to obtain it he must pass through (T) by performing the unpleasant task. There are no boundaries to the field, because there is no tendency to escape the field.

There may be, however, a tendency to move toward the reward through a devious route, thus avoiding the task. Consequently, barriers (B) must be erected around the reward to prevent this. Thus policing is also required in the reward situation, and this

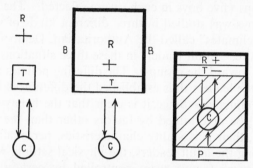

FIGURE 57. Diagram of the Reward Situation. In order to gain the reward (R) the child must accomplish the unpleasant task (T). To prevent the child from by-passing or "going around" the task, barriers (B) must be erected around the reward to block off this attempt. The barriers are ordinarily social rather than physical; restrictions against cheating in examinations are an example. The diagram at the right depicts the situation which combines both reward and punishment. This holds, for example, where the child is rewarded for his work and punished for failure to do it. Antagonism between teacher and pupil, and ambivalence toward the teacher in her dual role, often results from such situations. (From Hartmann, *op. cit.,* p. 217.)

is also somewhat restricting. It is less prisonlike, however, than the punishment situation. The pure "interest-situation" is not restricting at all, since freedom of movement is allowed in circumventing obstacles and there is no conflict. According to Lewin, the reason why rewarded activities often become eventually attractive, and activities controlled by threat of punishment become disliked or hated, is the difference in the amount of restriction required in the two situations.

GROUP PROCESS AND MOTIVATION

Some experiments in social psychology emphasize very forcefully that the motivational effect of reward and punishment, praise or reproof, must be interpreted in the light of the total social setting. One of the most significant in this respect

was the study done by Lewin and others of the effect of "social
climate" on the behavior of children (23).

From a number of schoolboys who volunteered for membership in a club devoted to making theatrical masks, a number of
small groups (five boys in each) were selected. The behavior
of these boys was studied in three different kinds of situations
or "social climates" called the Authoritarian, Democratic, and
Laissez-Faire. Adult leaders in these three situations behaved
differently toward the groups. The differing policies and techniques of the leaders thus established the differences in atmosphere or "climate." Since it is clear that the behavior of the
boys could be determined by factors other than the situation
itself (e.g., their personality characteristics, personality differences among the adult leaders, the physical setting, work procedures), these factors were controlled by certain arrangements. The groups were carefully matched for social and emotional traits, and always met in the same physical setting. The
groups and leaders were shifted about systematically to control
the effect of personality factors. Observations were made constantly of the social interaction among the group members.
Stenographic records of conversation and interpretive accounts
of behavior were kept, and motion picture films were taken of
the facial and behavioral reactions of boys transferred from one
situation to another.

The Influence of Social Climate on Behavior. Differences
in atmosphere were created by three different degrees or types
of leader control (24). The differences in control should be
compared point by point.

AUTHORITARIAN: 1. All determination of policy by the leader.
2. Techniques and activity steps dictated by the authority, one at a time, so that future steps were
always uncertain to a large degree.
3. The leader usually dictated the particular work task
and work companion of each member.
4. The dominator tended to be "personal" in his praise
and criticism of the work of each member; re-
mained aloof from active group participation except when demonstrating.

DEMOCRATIC:

1. All policies a matter of group discussion and decision, encouraged and assisted by leader.
2. Activity perspective gained during discussion period. General steps to group goal sketched, and where technical advice was needed, the leader suggested two or more alternative procedures from which choice could be made.
3. The members were free to work with whomever they chose, and the division of tasks was left up to the group.
4. The leader was "objective" or "fact minded" in his praise and criticism and tried to be a regular group member in spirit without doing too much of the work.

LAISSEZ-FAIRE:

1. Complete freedom for group or individual decision, with a minimum of leader participation.
2. Various material supplied by the leader, who made it clear that he would supply information when asked. He took no other part in work discussion.
3. Complete nonparticipation of the leader.
4. Infrequent spontaneous comments on member activities unless questioned and no attempt to appraise or regulate the course of events. (24, p. 487)

The important difference is thus the degree of dominance or control by the leader. In the first situation, control was autocratic: he took complete responsibility, and told the boys what to do, how to do it, and with whom to work. In the second, he exercised control by encouraging discussion directed toward group goals, but the group made the decisions about what was to be done and how it was to be done. In the Laissez-Faire situation, he did nothing and took no responsibility. A comparison of the actual behavior of the three kinds of leaders is given in Figure 58. The club activities were equated by arranging to have the Democratic clubs meet first and decide what they would do. The Authoritarian leader then dictated the same activities to his clubs. The Laissez-Faire clubs were then given the same materials as the other two, and allowed to do what they pleased.

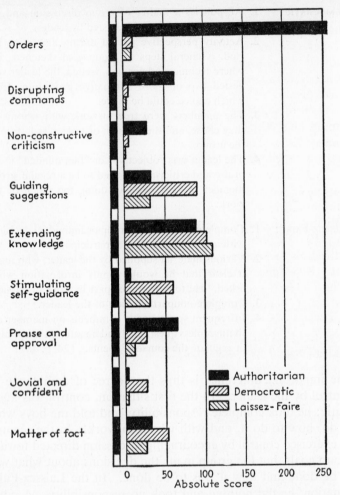

FIGURE 58. Comparison of Behavior of Average Authoritarian, Democratic, and Laissez-Faire Leaders. (From Lippitt & White, 24, p. 498.)

The analysis of behavior showed the "autocratic" group to be much more tense and hostile, with expressions of hostility "about thirty times as high in the autocratic group as in the democratic group" (21). The autocratic situation also showed less group cohesiveness, less tendency to work together. In the democratic group, cooperation tended to develop spontaneously. As expressed in language, the democratic group showed 47 per cent more feeling of "we-ness," while the autocratic showed 27 per cent more "I-ness." The feeling for group property and group goals was better developed in the democratic group.

A further analysis of these differences has been made by Lippitt and White, the other two investigators in these experiments (24). They attribute the disruption and lower morale in the authoritarian group to such factors as the following:

1. *Restricted space of free movement,* with resulting frustration of the need for autonomy and general dissatisfaction. The situation is restricting because it involves barriers and policing, with praise and reproof being administered by authority. It should be noted that the authoritarian leader was not unfriendly; he merely gave orders and saw that they were carried out. But the situation was "prisonlike" psychologically. When interviewed, the boys complained of the leader "He was too strict," and "He didn't let us do what we wanted to do." Resistance was not usually overt. In some cases, in fact, the boys gave up their desire for self-direction and independence, and identified with the leader as a master workman trying to get the work done.

2. *Frustrated need for sociability.* It is interesting to observe that the boys did not talk among themselves much, even though conversation was not forbidden. The repressive influence of the situation tended to "carry over" from the commands concerning the work to the total situation. As the authors put it, dissatisfaction with *one* aspect of the situation (lack of independence and sociability) made them dissatisfied with all of it, including the group itself and the work on which it was engaged.

3. *Opposition to the leader and his goals.* The boys felt an opposition to, or disinterest in, the goals of the adult leader. This amounted to a lack of personal involvement in the task at hand, making masks. Psychologically, they made a clear distinction between "what *he* wants to do" and "what I want to do," implying a clear opposition between the two. The im-

plication for motivation is clear: the personality is divided against itself, and the "heart" is not in what the hands are doing. None of these effects were apparent in the democratic situation.

What of the laissez-faire situation? Disruption, disorganization, and dissatisfaction was even worse than in the authoritarian climate. The situation here was restricted in a somewhat different way, but more aggravated. Autocratic controls did not, at least, interfere with the task-completion goal, but even that was frustrated in the laissez-faire situation.

> . . . the boys in the laissez-faire situation became dissatisfied with their own lack of efficiency and of solid accomplishment. They wanted to accomplish things, and they wanted the satisfaction of accomplishing them cooperatively as a harmonious working group. Both needs—the workmanlike need and the social need—were frustrated in laissez-faire. (24, p. 503)

They were dissatisfied by the disorder and uncertainty of the situation. Those who wanted to work were prevented from doing so by others who did not. Some rather desperate but pathetic attempts to plan are revealed in the records, but dissension prevented their fruition. The frustration caused by idleness and lack of common goals resulted in aggression, which caused more frustration to those who were "set" to carry out tasks. "Mutual interference proved to be a highly effective disruptive force." Thus the differences in motivation appear to have been generated by the situation, or "social climate."

Climate and Discipline. Any conclusions drawn from the studies of social climate just described have obvious psychological implications for school discipline and motivation. The climate in the three situations differed in two major respects: general atmosphere of permissiveness, and the kind of communication possible. The two are related.

1. *General atmosphere.* The difference here is in a continuum between the two extremes of "restrictive" and "permissive." We may illustrate this as follows:

Restrictive (Extreme)	Authoritarian	Democratic	Laissez-Faire	Permissive (Extreme)
	∧	∧	∧	

The authoritarian situation was most restrictive, because the group was told what to do, and was never asked. They could participate only by identifying with the leader, "giving up" their self-direction, and carrying out commands. Some were unable to do this, and developed aggressive feelings. Some conformed and carried out the tasks whether interested or not. In this situation, neither the aggressive nor the submissive boy could learn (a) self-direction or (b) how to cooperate with a group. Neither self-direction nor cooperative behavior could take place (or, at least, it was limited) or be rewarded by the group. (Praise and reproof were administered by the leader.) In other words, the situation restricted both the responses and the rewards available, and reduced individual participation.

At the other extreme, the laissez-faire situation was most permissive. The group was almost never told what to do and was not regulated. Their activities were not directed into useful channels, and their needs for doing so were frustrated. They could not learn self-direction here either because the situation, although "free," did not permit self-directed activity to be rewarded at all. There could thus be no cooperative behavior either, because there was no agreement on self-chosen goals. (Defective communication is a factor here, as it is in the whole situation.) Laissez-faire, although free enough to permit any kind of response, was actually restrictive because neither self-direction nor cooperation could be rewarded. We are reminded here, as G. K. Chesterton once said of anarchy, that "freedom" always requires a complement. Anarchy sets us "free" but not free to attain desired goals.

The democratic situation was permissive *within limits*. Free discussion was not only permitted, but encouraged and channelized, by direction of the leader, toward common and mutually satisfying goals. This "structuring" by the leader permitted both self-directive and cooperative behavior to appear and be rewarded through group participation.

2. *Communication.* In the authoritarian situation, communication was almost exclusively "down the line" of authority; that is, it consisted mostly of orders and commands from the leader to the boys. Communication in the reverse direction

(i.e., "up the line" from boys to leader) was pretty well limited to asking questions, occasional unheeded and unrewarded suggestions, and complaints. This is similar to the communication picture of the autocratically run school, business establishment, or factory. The boys (perhaps because of their youth, and recognition of the difference in age-grade status between themselves and the leader) tended to be apathetic and more inhibited in talking among themselves when the leader was present. When he was absent, they expressed resentment, hostility, and aggression toward one another. In other words, they expressed feelings which had been suppressed, and their communication was not organized toward getting the work done.

In laissez-faire there was apparently a breakdown in communication, in spite of the freedom to talk and plan. There were spontaneous attempts to form plans, and some partial progress in this direction, but these discussions soon degenerated into hostility, disorganized horseplay, and idleness. This induced frustration and further disruption of group activity. Communication "broke down" in the sense that it did not further mutual understanding. (Effective communication is not just talk, but leads persons to understand one another.) Excerpts from the stenographic reports of the group meetings show that disruption occurred because there was no effective way of identifying and clarifying misunderstandings. Disagreements were not "talked out" and directed toward mutual agreement, but resulted simply in group dissolution. No provision was made for participation by all members. One boy who felt "out of it," for example, developed hostility toward the others and became a major disruptive influence.

Communication in the democratic situation was the paramount concern of the leader, and was directed toward solution of disagreements as well as participation by all members. It thus facilitated mutual understanding, smooth and harmonious interpersonal relationships, and brought about an effective basis for group activity. Every boy was able to identify with the group, and thus subordinate his own desires to group goals without loss of status or loss of personal self-direction. Each could "be himself."

Some generalizations are possible from the above analysis. (1) Which situation provides the most effective discipline in terms of the outcomes of learning? The task is more attractive when desired by the group, and more attractive for the individual who identifies with the group. When these conditions obtain, we have the "interest situation" in which policing is not necessary. (2) Effective group atmosphere and effective communication are roughly the same thing, since "open channels" of communication are essential to harmonious and satisfying group activity. (3) There is no such thing as uncontrolled freedom. Freedom is a double-edged weapon. Absence of control leads to anarchy, which frustrates individual needs and thus restricts individual freedom. (4) Effective leadership is not chiefly a matter of "personality" but of intra-group relationships. We may be inclined to think of the natural leader as one who assumes autocratic control, but the autocrat under some conditions may not be effective. The techniques of leadership, at least under small group conditions, lie in facilitating the solution of disagreements through effective communication, and prompting individual participation in the group.

Psychology of Leadership. "Leader" is a general term for a person who can motivate others, and "leadership" a term for the techniques or behavioral qualities through which this is accomplished. The earlier psychological studies of leadership were greatly influenced, if not initiated, by the study of autocratic, democratic, and laissez-faire types of control. They studied small groups, and generally concluded that permissive, member-centered types of leadership which permitted group participation brought the most favorable results.

However, recent research has tended to modify these conclusions in some respects (32). First, there is evidence that the size of the group makes a considerable difference in the favorable or unfavorable reaction of its members to the type of behavior displayed by the leader. The member-centered type of leadership may be more favorable for small groups, but as groups become larger the members expect firmer control from the leader and appear to be more tolerant of leader-centered direction. Also, there is evidence that the effectiveness of different types of leadership depends on the attitudes of group members. Some persons value status and power highly in leaders, and thus expect this type of behavior and prefer strongly directive leadership. In one study, for example, teachers in four school systems who marked a scale showing preferences for various characteristics in an "ideal" school superintendent showed a considerable demand for directive leadership. Teachers who were in "status-attitudes," placing greater value on power and influence, showed this trend more markedly (30). Other studies show similar results. Of course, this is no proof that such leadership is more effective from the social point of view. Recent research should make us cautious about drawing political implications from studies with small groups (32). It is unfortunate, in a way, that the terms autocratic, democratic, and laissez-faire were used in Lewin's original study, because they may tempt the uncritical reader to all sorts of hasty conclusions about government and economic affairs.

For the school, however, the issue seems clear. The teacher works with relatively small groups, and group motivation is an important problem. Further, she works with children in varying stages of social and emotional development. We know how the different types of leadership function in the adult-child situation. If the child is to develop qualities of leadership in school, there must be opportunity for this type of behavior to emerge. This implies a situation in which he is free to express himself, to exercise some influence over the decisions made, to make mistakes, to participate in the give-and-take of interpersonal relations leading to decisions that affect him. The school must then provide some such situations. We need not define "leadership" exclusively in terms of autocratic control by the teacher. We may need to give room in our thinking to a somewhat different concept of leadership: not the absence of control, "laissez-faire" or classroom anarchy, but student participation. There is evidence that classroom management through "teacher-pupil planning" is effective in motivating students, assists their social development, and produces satisfactory educational achievement.

Teacher-Student Relations

The teacher, by reason of her position, must assume responsibility for what happens in the classroom. She defines the goals, provides the learning situations and the rewards, and thus assumes control. With regard to teaching practice, the question is not one of whether the teacher should exercise control, or even how much control she should exercise, but rather "What kind of controls are more conducive to learning and development?" From the point of view of social psychology, this question raises the problem of teacher-student relations, i.e., the ways in which the teacher's attitudes and values affect the students, and how those of students affect the teacher. Whatever approach the teacher takes, it is based on her beliefs about what children are like, what they ought to learn, and how they ought to behave.

The most effective relations would seem to be those that result in a minimum of conflict between the teacher's standards and the student's standards. While this may be difficult to achieve (teachers and students do not have the same values) it does not follow that discrepancies in standards necessarily result in a relationship of opposition: teacher versus class, with both trying to win. Nor is the situation of autocratic dominance intrinsically necessary, with the teacher over the class, policing and enforcing. Some recent studies of social groups suggest the possibility of other kinds of human relations in the classroom.

In democratic society as a whole, differences in goals need not result in division and disunity. They may instead be worked out harmoniously so that a common goal, mutually satisfactory to dissident groups, may be agreed upon. For this reason, what we know as "group processes," or social interaction among individuals united in a common purpose but differing in views, is being increasingly applied to education. In many schools, the classroom is seen to be a laboratory for learning human relations, as well as a place for acquiring academic knowledge and skills.

Teacher-Centered or Student-Centered. Whatever the teacher does, it affects the attitudes and feelings of students toward themselves as individuals and as members of the group. To make this clear we might contrast two different class situations.

In the first, which might be called "teacher-centered," the standards of achievement are set by the teacher not with respect to the level of ability of individual students, but somewhat rigidly. The emphasis is on covering the ground, learning the material, meeting the standards. Those who meet the standards are made to feel adequate; those who do not feel inadequate. The rewards are administered by the teacher. Since students are unequal in ability there are varying degrees of success, and some students may feel that their total worth is being judged entirely in terms of school achievement. Again, the student is likely to value the achievement itself somewhat less than the teacher does. The tasks are done, not because they are interesting in themselves, but to please the teacher or to escape the teacher's disapproval. In short, the situation works to (1) make the child less secure, (2) make his feelings of security dependent on the teacher's reactions, and (3) put the burden of enforcing the standards on the teacher. The student reactions are predictable. Some children work hard, become deferential and polite and obedient. They may become known as "teacher's pets," and may be somewhat ostracized in the group. Others may become passive, overdependent and shy, fearing to displease the teacher or attract attention in the class. They are nonparticipants in the social sense. Still others may rebel or defy the teacher, become sullen, or set out to undermine the teacher's influence. The latter individuals may form tightly knit social groups within the class, united by mutual sympathies and common cause against the teacher and her allies. The class may thus split apart into antagonistic subgroups. Or, if it coheres as a group, it may be united against the teacher. Teachers also react in different ways. One teacher may ignore the opposition and "steam roller" it into submission; she achieves her own goals to the detriment of the children's social maturity. Others may wheedle or coax, resort to "emotional blackmail," or ally themselves with one group or another. This situation may be called teacher-centered because the teacher's rigid standards and the teacher's needs always come first, because her role consists in manipulating the students' activities to her advantage rather than theirs.

In a "student-centered" situation, the teacher sets standards of achievement in keeping with the abilities, needs, and interests of the individual.[1] This means that she concentrates above all on seeing that every child enjoys the full taste of success, each in his own way. She fits the tasks to the individual, rather than forcing all into the same tasks with a uniform standard of achievement. This involves (1) providing a range of tasks suitable to the range of abilities, (2) providing a variety of activities suitable to the variety of interests found in the class, and (3) providing a social climate or atmosphere which gives the child some measure of control over what he does and how he does it. The atmosphere is not one which insures that each child "gets his own way." This would amount to simple abdication of the teacher role and surrendering control to the students, which the teacher cannot do. Rather, the atmosphere is one in which all the individual's achievements are treated with attention and respect merely because they are important to him. The student-centered situation may be achieved at times through teaching as a "group process."

Teaching as a Group Process. √The effective teacher is a skilled group worker, one who can utilize the principles of group dynamics to the advantage of her students. "Group process" is a general term referring to the procedures through which a group of individuals approaches, attacks, and solves a common problem. Since the individuals are agreed on the end but not on the means to achieve it, the group process is sometimes called an "end-means" process. √It is a process of communication; that is, the procedures consist of thinking, suggesting, planning,

---

[1] A study by Sister Mary Amatora Tschechtelin (38) is of some interest here. She found that the self-appraisals of children and self-estimates of their school progress are not closely related to the appraisals made by teachers. This would seem to imply that the teachers' standards, from the point of view of the pupils, would be regarded as somewhat "unrealistic."

deciding, acting, and evaluating as a group. This implies an opportunity for free face-to-face communication, leading to a consensus of decision and action./ We may regard the group process as a group learning situation, and consider the group as the "learner" rather than the individual. This is valid not in the sense that there is a "group mind," but in the sense that there is a group goal, conflicting or varying views on means of reaching it, and a necessity for group action. "The goal of group processes is group productivity, that is, getting something done which could not be done by a single individual" (27).

The principles of the group process rest on the results of psychological research. Four characteristics of group behavior are held to be essential to effective group action (27):

1. A democratic atmosphere, or one which is permissive rather than punitive. All members must feel free to voice an opinion, to suggest, to disagree without fear of being ridiculed or losing status. The group interaction necessary to arrive at common decisions depends on a voluntary, spontaneous, cooperative effort, to which this atmosphere is conducive.

2. Communication must be goal-directed, not aimless conversation. It is aimed at establishing a consensus, not a mere majority vote. Group decision by majority vote means practically that the majority is coercing a minority, and that the defeated minority may in the end attempt to block action. The purpose of communication is not to win an argument, but to be understood and to understand others. The group process is not a debate, but an attempt to clarify viewpoints.

3. Morale and discipline is group-centered. The emphasis is on *We*, not *I*. Morale in the group, or group cohesiveness, is in fact sometimes measured in terms of the We/I ratio—a proportion of conversational "We's to I's." In the highly cohesive and effective group, even disagreements are we-centered; that is, emphasis is not on "I do not agree" but "this won't work to our advantage." The suggestion of a member is judged according to its contribution to the group goal rather than as an expression of his individual goal.

4. Leadership is shared. Any member can be a "leader" by making a contribution. Leadership is not a matter of posi-

tion or of dominance, but of membership in the group. A member may assume leadership in the discussion, relinquish it, pass it to someone else.

Although this may seem strange and "unworkable" as a teaching process, the value of group-centered teaching may be clearer as we think of its effect on teacher-student relations. In the classroom, the teacher becomes a member of the group. As such, she may propose a problem, state her views, and encourage students to state theirs. In other words, she may assume leadership. She may also give up the leader's role when one student or another assumes it. Like any member, she may contribute remarks to keep the discussion goal-directed. As a member of the group, her influence is not lessened or restricted, but simply directed toward helping the class agree on decision and action. The teacher in the member-centered class, it has been said, works *in* the group, not *on* it. By her very presence and influence as a group member, she may thus help to establish a democratic atmosphere, assist the group in arriving at a consensus, establish a feeling of "we-ness" or group solidarity, and help the group to discipline itself. By sharing leadership and encouraging all students to assume it, she does not lose control but enables students to participate in the exercise of control. Whatever we may think about this kind of student-teacher relationship, we must admit that in this situation the student is not motivated by fear of the teacher and has no reason to oppose her. Teaching as a group process prevents overdependency on the teacher, and also prevents the students from lining up against her. Nor does it permit the students to control the teacher.

An example may help to illustrate the "member" role of leadership:

Miss G, a chemistry teacher, got along well with the class most of the time. But she always dreaded "dangerous" experiments, such as "The Preparation and Properties of Chlorine," because someone in the class usually, apparently through carelessness, would get too large a dose and have to be taken, choking and coughing, to the nurse's office. Mr. K, another chemistry teacher, almost never had any trouble with "dangerous" experiments. Miss G and Mr. K seemed, for the most part, well matched with respect to strictness, knowledge of chemistry, amount of planning shared with pupils, and the like.

Miss G always introduced the chlorine laboratory activity by saying that it was dangerous and frequently resulted in someone being overcome; that under no circumstances must anyone use larger quantities than the directions called for; that if the flame was turned too high, they would be unable to handle the volume of gas produced. Mr. K introduced the laboratory work with the question, "What are some of the points of special caution today?" and then calmly joined in the discussion from time to time. (35)

From the "group process" point of view, Miss G provided no leadership at all, since she contributed nothing to a consensus or group decision. She merely expressed anxiety, and by her directions to the class inferred a lack of confidence in their judgment. She seemed to imply that the group could not discipline itself, and allowed them no opportunity for doing so.

An Evaluation of Group-Centered Teaching. Those who favor the group-centered approach in teaching believe strongly, and not without reason, that it contributes more to the student's personal development. Democratic behavior, they maintain, can be learned only through living it. As well as providing a laboratory for democratic action, the classroom thus becomes a place where the student can try out his own social concepts, learn how he affects others, learn to contribute to group action and thus learn self-confidence. Since the procedure enables both the individual and the group to set their own goals, school learning may become more spontaneous.

Many of these beliefs should be described as tenable hypotheses at the present time, rather than established scientific principles. However, some of the hypotheses have been supported at least in part by experiments. The research program of the Human Dynamics Laboratory at the University of Chicago looks promising in this respect, since it is exploring the dynamics of individual adjustment in relation to the group process. A study by Withall (40), employing a scale for measuring "social-emotional climate," concluded that "the teacher-class interaction pattern does influence the students' feeling of anxiety and his orientation to the learning pattern." The results of

Flanders (11) indicate that this reaction was reflected in the galvanic skin reflex as well as in verbal responses of students. Rehage (28) compared the educational achievement of two matched eighth grade classes in social studies, one of which was taught by learner-centered methods and the other by the traditional teacher-centered approach. Achievement in the two groups was equal. Other studies, summarized by Thelen (34), further confirm the belief that teacher-pupil interaction affects the learning of certain social attitudes and human relations principles. They also seem to show that the interaction between pupils can usually be affected by the teacher-pupil relationship in class.

On the other hand, there is little reason to believe that group-centered teaching is the only worthwhile educational practice, or that it is the most effective for all purposes. Certain characteristics of the group process itself show its limitations, as Corey has pointed out (27). The goals must be such that group activity can lead to their attainment; that is, they must make sense to the members and meet their needs as individuals. The group process aims at achieving unity in general purpose and takes advantage of diversity (i.e., individual differences) in ways of achieving the purpose. But in order to motivate the group members the goals must be accepted, appreciated, and desired by the individuals. "Group process, then, is not a panacea, nor is it a pattern into which all educational work must be forced." Such procedures as teacher-pupil planning and other group activities, by their very nature, cannot meet any and all needs in all circumstances. Much education must therefore be individualistic. There would appear to be no reason why courses may not be prescribed for individuals who are willing to accept the prescription as the best means to an end they really want. Also, the principle of "least group size" enunciated by Thelen (34) seems to indicate that the student's feeling of participation is related to the size of the group. Class size imposes very real limits on the effectiveness of group-centered teaching. With large classes, the group approach may be quite impossible.

The Teacher's Values and Interpersonal Relations. The social adjustment of the child in school is the result of interaction between his personal desires and needs and the motives of others. In other words, adjustment involves not merely the immediate gratification of the child's desires, but adapting those desires to the demands of society. The school, with its rules and regulations and its population of age peers, is to the child a kind of sample of society in general, particularly of that adult society which the child finds so mystifying and to which he is presumably being trained to adjust. The teachers are representatives of adult society, typifying to a greater or less degree its customs and standards. From this point of view, adjustment to the teacher is an important educational process. And it is often a difficult one for the student, because teachers represent different kinds of values.

By "value" here we mean the teacher's personal concept of what is important—those attitudes and beliefs about the worth of things which function as motives. To make this clear we shall discuss teacher personalities in terms of the "value-types" proposed by the German educational philosopher, Edward Spranger (33). Spranger felt that personality could best be interpreted through an understanding of the personal values most dearly held. He described six fundamental values, each typifying a kind of personality in which a given value operates as a dominant motive: the theoretical, esthetic, economic, political, social, and religious.[1]

1. The *theoretical* person is one whose highest value is truth or knowledge. He tends to adjust to most problems by seeking the facts and weaving them into systematic relationships. The progress of the individual and of society would be measured by this standard; the theoretical person believes the chief evil of society to be ignorance and the chief remedy to be education which stresses information, facts, intellectual understanding of principles. Knowledge thus tends to be the greatest end, as well

[1] A sample for measuring the relative strength of these values through expressed references has been developed, called the Allport-Vernon Scale of Values. See P. E. Vernon and G. W. Allport, "A test for personal values," *J. abn. Soc. Psychol.*, 1931, **26**, 3-11.

as the means to all ends. We find him quoting such maxims as "knowledge is power." In education, the theoretical person is more often found in college teaching, particularly in the sciences.

2. To the *esthetic* person, the most significant value is beauty, harmony, elegance of form and color. Esthetic experiences are most highly valued, and artistic, literary, and musical interests are high. Ugliness in any form is painful, and society's ills would perhaps be most commonly attributed to ugliness. The esthetic "type" evaluates people not by their stock of information, as would the theoretical person, but by their taste and degree of refinement. As Keats put it, "Beauty is truth, truth beauty,"—that is all he knows on earth and all he needs to know.

3. The highest values of the *economic* person is efficiency and economic well-being which motivates him constantly to seek maximum results with minimum effort, and to evaluate results in economic terms. He is perhaps found oftener in business than in education, but frequently crops up among members of school boards and sometimes even in the ranks of teachers. We recognize him as the "practical man," for whom education must somehow pay off in economic betterment. As a teacher, he would stress the utilitarian value of school subjects and place great store by methods. He abhors waste of time or energy, and evaluates people in terms of their efficiency.

4. The *political* person centers his values around discipline, order, control. He stresses self-discipline quite as much as discipline for others, takes delight in exercising control over others as well as himself, and finds disorder or disobedience particularly distasteful. He is fond of quoting, and making up, rules and regulations and is often a genius at organizing people and events to this purpose. Spranger felt that the "political" type tended to gravitate toward politics and military life, which may be more typical of Germany than the United States. For every Bismarck, however, we can think of a Theodore Roosevelt. For some reason, the teaching profession attracts a fair number of this value type. They range from excellent adminis-

trators to ordinary martinets (from General Martinet, French drillmaster of the reign of Louis XIV).

5. The *social* person stresses kindness and warmth in human relations as the highest value, tending to center around a "brotherhood of man" concept and abhorring greed or cruelty as the source of all evil. He is particularly sensitive to injustice to others, quick to favor the "underdog," and evaluates persons for the degree of kindness they show to others. Many educational reformers have been of this stamp—Pestalozzi and Montessori, for example, resembling social archetypes. On the whole, teachers are probably represented most frequently by the social personality, as are other occupations of the social welfare type. Elementary teaching, particularly, seems to attract and hold persons motivated to meet the needs of children for individual guidance, even at great personal sacrifice.

6. The *religious* type, as Spranger saw it, might better be called the *philosophic* or speculative. The religious or philosophic value does not stress so much the formal aspects of religion, but the integration of all values into a meaningful scheme or philosophy. This type of person is tremendously concerned with the meaning of life, and seeks to order all experience into a comprehensive framework. As a teacher, he would presumably be very much concerned with the development of a philosophy of life in his students, and be most upset by evidence of moral inconsistency in students or in educational practice. He would probably be most likely to stress character education through inculcation of moral and religious values.

No person is assumed by Spranger to be motivated exclusively by one kind of value. They are all equally human values, and none is assumed to be better than others (unless it be the religious or philosophical, which stresses integration or balance of values). The motivation of any one teacher will probably reflect all of them to some degree, with perhaps one or two dominating. When any one is carried to an extreme, the result may be an unfortunate imbalance: the religious or philosophical person may become a fanatic, the esthetic may be a dilettante, the social person a "busybody," etc. Such one-sided persons may be found in schools, each advancing his own particular value scheme and judging the curriculum, school practice, fellow teachers, and above all the behavior of students, according to a one-sided view. This may lead to particular problems for the adjustment of teachers, as well as that of students. A personal value scheme sets up certain behavior patterns which the individual holds intellectually and emotionally to be the "right" ones. Thus his personal version of "good" or "bad" behavior, and of the worth of persons, may be highly colored emotionally by personal values.

ATTITUDES, INTERESTS, AND IDEALS

It has always been taken for granted that the school should foster development of desirable attitudes, interests, and ideals, and there is abundant evidence that good teachers and good schools have always done so. But, like other learning, these changes do not "just happen" by chance. Can the acquisition of knowledge, per se, develop desirable attitudes? Does, for example, a knowledge of chemistry and physics inspire development of the scientific attitude, or a tendency to think scientifically? Does a knowledge of the processes of government develop the attitudes basic to the "good citizen"? These questions are basic. Art and literature are taught to develop cultural appreciation of their forms; history, to cultivate an appreciation of our cultural heritage; religion, to inspire ideals of charity and sanctity and morality. Sports are justified through the supposed development of ideals of fair play and courage, and the whole life of the school is a laboratory for the development of vocational interests. Whether the battle of Waterloo was won on the playing fields of Eton or not, such claims and expectations have always been made of the school. Should such learning be treated as incidental, to be initiated by personal identification with teachers, or should it be planned for and if so how?

The Life-Career Motive. To the mature adult, vocational interest or the life-career motive is an all-important determiner of the traits and information he acquires, because this motive defines his social role. Guthrie considers occupation an important index of personality:

More information is conveyed about a man when we name his calling than when we attempt to name the vague qualities that constitute
extroversion or dominance or indecision. When we know that a man
is a professional soldier, we know much about his skills and abilities,
his style of thinking, his carriage, his opinions, his ambitions. We know
this because we know the conditions of life to which he has had to adapt
himself—what he must have learned. . . . There are people who have
acquired with their occupation the manner fitted to the occupation, the
deference of the waiter, the aggressive good-fellowship of the YMCA
secretary, the air of "being in the know" of the practiced lobbyist, the
bedside deportment of the physician, the ready classroom omniscience
of the high school teacher, the air of decision and authority practiced
on the bench, the habits of qualification of the college professor. (15,
pp. 61-62)

School children have not yet learned these patterns, because
they have not been in situations requiring such mature modes of
adjustment. It is impossible to bring to bear on every moment's
work, particularly with young children, motivating influences
as deep and persuasive as the life-career motive of the adult,
but the efficiency of school work may be improved as these patterns develop. There is some evidence, for example, that college students with definite vocational goals do better academic
work than students who are undecided, even when they have no
advantage in intelligence (26).

However, vocational interests and attitudes have their genetic origin through the preschool and school years through the
processes of identification and internalization. This process
has been explicitly detailed by Carter (6). Like all developmental sequences, the development of vocational interests is a
slow adjustive process revealing progressive stages of readiness.
Studies of pupils' vocational choices reveal unrealism and immaturity even into the late adolescent period. But they also show
that occupational information, carefully selected according to
the adolescent's immediate needs and readiness, can further the
development of the life-career motive and thus make the school
tasks more meaningful than they might otherwise be. In fact,
the properly organized school curriculum provides such information. By structuring adequate learning situations, the

teacher of almost any subject can develop in the student a better understanding of the world of work. Carter has pointed out that "the central problem in vocational choice appears to be one of developmental psychology."

In their adjustment to the world of work, young people reveal many aspects of a slow, blundering adaptation to major requirements of the culture in which they live. From the standpoint of education and psychology, it appears that individuals must be shaped and changed and adapted throughout their lives if optimum adjustment is to be attained. It is evident that the greatest service can be rendered to young persons by starting them correctly and by giving them the essential information and advice, *selectively,* with proper regard for their individuality. This seems to require a firm basis in empirical facts concerning human desires and the manner in which individuals grow and develop with reference to the occupational world. (7, p. 7)

The life-career motive, like other forms of readiness, is something the school must work for, not wait for. Teaching for the development of interests boils down to a very simple principle, which was stated by William James as follows: "Any object not interesting in itself may become interesting through becoming associated with an object in which an interest already exists" (18). Good teaching thus requires us to start with the child's present interests, and lead him along to the development of new ones. Although simple in theory, this kind of teaching demands the utmost inventiveness and versatility on the part of the teacher.

Ideals. An ideal is a concept, or abstract idea, which motivates behavior and conduct. (We sometimes think of "ideal" as something desirable but hardly attainable; in this discussion, the word is not used in this way.) Ideals symbolized in such words as charity, courage, loyalty, patriotism, friendliness, and "will power" often serve as abstract models of behavior, and as such motivate many attitudes toward particular things, persons, and events.

An ideal therefore exercises more or less cognitive control over behavior, by establishing a motivational set to respond in a certain way. The extent to which an ideal serves as a motivat-

ing force, however, depends on (1) the degree of self-involvement or emotional coloring, or how "deeply rooted" it is in the
personality, and (2) the meaning assigned to the concept. The
ideals of "democracy" or "sanctity," for example, could hardly
be expected to result in willingness to hire qualified Negroes or
strict honesty in business unless the personal meaning of these
concepts extends to such concrete applications. Since an ideal
is a generalization from the particulars of experience, it takes
its meaning from the personal experience of the individual, not
from the dictionary definition. The fact that ideals have personal meanings explains in large measure why persons do not
always "practice what they preach."

We must therefore stress the development of ideals through
provision of meaningful experiences rather than by defining
words. What does this imply for the teaching of an ideal, say,
like "democracy?" Experiences must be provided for its concrete application; the student must learn a personal democratic
role by actually discovering that a certain kind of "democratic"
behavior is effective in satisfying his needs. This does not mean
that a habit will be strengthened through practice and later
transferred to adult life. (That is the theory of formal discipline.) The concrete experience is genetically basic to the formation of a very complex concept. School work in history,
civics, and other social studies provides important information
also, but it seems improbable that learning of this kind will by
itself result in a motivating ideal. The teacher's role is to provide the appropriate situations and the cues; it then immediately
becomes apparent that the teacher herself must have a thoroughly integrated concept of democracy, which she can apply
accurately to hundreds of situations. The development of such
a clear concept is not easy, as illustrated by the present problem
of arriving at a working notion of democracy in international
relations.

The sources of ideals are numerous. One helpful source
is reading, particularly biographies. The lives of saints, poets,
statesmen, and generals have had varied and strong influence
on readers. Personal relationships with parents, teachers, and

other persons provide models for imitation and concrete experiences which can, and often do, become conceptualized. So (obviously) do plays, movies, comic strips, and television. Ideals internalized and developed through such experiences exercise a pervasive influence on character education. The teacher can make the most effective contribution to the development of character by displaying, in her own person and conduct, the embodiment of desirable ideals.

REFERENCES

1. ANDERSON, C. A. An experimental study of social facilitation as affected by intelligence. *Amer. J. Sociol.,* 1929, **34,** 874-881.
2. ANDERSON, H. H., & BRANDT, H. F. A study of motivation involving self-announced goals of fifth grade children and the concept of level of aspiration. *J. soc. Psychol.,* 1939, **10,** 209-232.
3. BRIGGS, T. H. Praise and censure as incentives. *School & Society,* 1927, **26,** 596-598.
4. BRIGGS, T. H. Sarcasm. *School Rev.,* 1928, **36,** 685-695.
5. BURRI, C. The influence of an audience upon recall. *J. educ. Psychol.,* 1931, **22,** 683-690.
6. CARTER, H. D. The development of vocational attitudes. *J. consult. Psychol.,* 1940, **4,** 185-191.
7. CARTER, H. D. Vocational interests and job orientation. *Appl. Psychol. Monogr.,* 1944, No. 2.
8. DASHIELL, J. F. An experimental analysis of some group effects. *J. abn. soc. Psychol.,* 1930, **25,** 190-200.
9. DENNIS, W. Cultural and developmental factors in perception. In BLAKE, R. R., & RAMSEY, G. V., *Perception, an approach to personality.* New York: Ronald Press, 1951.
0. EKDAHL, A. G. The effect of attitude on free word association time. *Genet. Psychol. Monogr.,* 1929, **5,** 253-338.
1. FLANDERS, N. A. Experimental research toward a theory of instruction, III. Personal-social anxiety as a factor in experimental learning situations. *J. educ. Res.,* 1951, **45,** 100-110.
2. FOLSOM, J. K. *Social psychology.* New York: Harper, 1931.
3. GREENBERG, P. J. Competition in children. *Amer. J. Psychol.,* 1932, **44,** 221-248.
4. GRIFFITH, C. R. A comment upon the psychology of the audience. *Psychol. Monogr.,* 1921, **30,** No. 136.
5. GUTHRIE, E. R. Personality in terms of associative learning. In HUNT, J. McV. (Ed.), *Personality and the behavior disorders,* I. New York: Ronald Press, 1944.

16. HILGARD, E. R., SAIT, E. M., & MAGARET, G. A. Level of aspiration as affected by relative standing in an experimental social group. *J. exp. Psychol.*, 1940, **27**, 411-421.

17. HURLOCK, E. B. The value of praise and reproof as incentives for children. *Arch. Psychol.*, 1924, No. 71.

18. JAMES, W. *Talks to teachers on psychology*. New York: Holt, 1899.

19. LAIRD, D. A. Changes in motor control and individual variations under the influence of razzing. *J. exp. Psychol.*, 1923, **6**, 236-246.

20. LEWIN, K. *A dynamic theory of personality*. New York: McGraw-Hill, 1935.

21. LEWIN, K. Experiments on autocratic and democratic atmospheres. *Social Frontier*, 1938, **4**, 318.

22. LEWIN, K. Field theory and learning. *41st Yearbook*, II, Nat. Soc. Stud. Educ., 1942.

23. LEWIN, K., LIPPITT, R., & WHITE, R. K. Patterns of aggressive behavior in experimentally created social climates. *J. soc. Psychol.*, 1939, **10**, 271-299.

24. LIPPITT, R., & WHITE, R. K. The social climate of children's groups. In BARKER, R. G., *et al.*, Child behavior and development. New York: McGraw-Hill, 1943.

25. MALLER, J. B. *Cooperation and competition*. Teach. Coll. Contr. Educ., Columbia Univ., No. 384, 1929.

26. MARSHALL, M. V. The life career motive and its effect on college work. *J. educ. Res.*, 1936, **29**, 596-598.

27. NATIONAL EDUC. ASSOCIATION. Group processes in supervision. Assoc. for Superv. & Curric. Devel., Washington, D.C.: NEA, 1948.

28. REHAGE, K. J. Experimental research toward a theory of instruction, IV. A comparison of pupil-teacher planning and teacher directed procedures in 8th grade social studies. *J. educ. Res.*, 1951, **45**, 111-115.

29. SEARS, P. S. Levels of aspiration in academically successful and unsuccessful school children. *J. abn. soc. Psychol.*, 1940, **35**, 498-536.

30. SEEMAN, M. In *Leadership in American education*, GRACE, A. G (Ed.). Univ. of Chicago Press, 1950.

31. SIMS, V. M. The relative influence of two types of motivation on improvement. *J. educ. Psychol.*, 1928, **19**, 480-484.

32. SMITH, M. B. Social psychology and group processes. *Ann. rev Psychol.*, 1952, **3**, 175-204.

33. SPRANGER, E. *Lebensformen*. Halle: Niemeyer, 1927.

34. THELEN, H. A., *et al.* Experimental research toward a theory of instruction. *J. educ. Res.*, 1951, **45**, 89-136.

35. THELEN, H. A., & TYLER, R. W. Implications for improving instruction in the high school. *49th Yearbook,* I, Nat. Soc. Stud. Educ., 1950.
36. THOMPSON, G. G., & HUNNICUTT, C. W. Effect of repeated praise and blame on the work achievement of introverts and extroverts. *J. educ. Psychol.,* 1944, **35,** 257-266.
37. THORNDIKE, E. L. *et al.* The psychology of wants, interests, and attitudes. New York: Appleton-Century, 1935.
38. TSCHECHTELIN, SISTER M. AMATORA. A study in teacher personality. *J. educ. Res.,* 1951, **44,** 709-714. See also, A diagnostic teacher-rating scale, *J. Psychol.,* 1950, **30,** 395-399, and *Child Dev.,* 1952, **23,** 75-80.
39. WHITTEMORE, I. C. The influence of competition on performance. *J. abn. soc. Psychol.,* 1924, **19,** 236-253.
40. WITHALL, J. Experimental research toward a theory of instruction, II. The development of the climate index. *J. Educ. Res.,* 1951, **45,** 93-100.

SELECTED READINGS

ANDERSON, G. L., *et al.* The school as a learning laboratory. Ch. 13 in *49th Yearbook,* Nat. Soc. Study Educ., Pt. I, 1950.
CUNNINGHAM, R., *et al. Understanding group behavior of boys and girls.* New York: Teach. Coll. Bur. of Publ., Columbia Univ., 1951. Describes practical ways of studying groups and applying the principles of group processes to teaching.
HARRIS, D. B. How children learn interests, motives and attitudes. Ch. 5 in *49th Yearbook,* Nat. Soc. Stud. Educ., Pt. I, 1950.
LEWIN, K. *Dynamic theory of personality.* New York: McGraw-Hill, 1935. Chs. 3-5.
LEWIN, K. Group decision and social change. In NEWCOMB, T. M., HARTLEY, E. L., *et al., Readings in social psychology.* New York: Holt, 1947.
ROGERS, C. R. *Client centered therapy.* Boston: Houghton Mifflin, 1951. Chs. 7, 8, and 9 discuss group centered therapy, leadership and administration, and student centered teaching.

16

THE TRANSFER OF LEARNING

IT IS commonly assumed that the educational value of school learning extends to many life activities; that is, it has "transfer value." Perhaps the basic idea of education is that what the child learns in school will "transfer" and be helpful to him later on. There can scarcely be any argument about the transfer of training in a general sense and so far as fact is concerned. But we may enter upon a reasonable discussion as to just how education derives its transfer value. Does the learning that the child carries on in school assist him in doing later only those things that he has learned in school, or the same general kind of things, or does it really assist him in doing nearly everything that he will be called upon to do? The answer to this question will have a very important bearing upon just what we are going to ask the child to learn while he is in school.

Along with the extension of knowledge and science there arose a great variety of subjects and subject matter and a number of alternative methods of teaching these. Educators might then more freely exercise a choice of courses and methods. It soon became clear that the principle of choice must be founded ultimately upon a study of the educable subject, the child, upon the way his mind develops, and upon the psychological effects of training. This is more than a mere theoretical problem, for many of the educational changes of the more recent past are due to a revision of the older ideas about the possibilities of education and the transfer of training.

From the viewpoint of the educational psychologist the problem of the transfer of learning reduces to the following questions: How and to what extent does learning one thing facilitate the learning of something else? To what extent does school learning carry over to situations outside the classroom? What conditions are necessary or helpful for the occurrence of these two kinds of transfer?

SOME THEORIES OF TRANSFER

Theory of Formal Discipline. When the learned men of the time first became aware of the problem and expressed themselves concerning it, they apparently came to the conclusion that the psychological justification of education could be found in what has been called the doctrine of "formal discipline." This theory implied that the important thing in educating the child was the form of training, the kind of mental activity brought into play, and not the knowledge or content of the training. Knowledge and experience were of course recognized at their true value in the world, but it was largely assumed that these came with age and wisdom, and that it was much more important for the young child first to have his mind "strengthened" instead of acquiring smatterings of information. First discipline the mind into formal robustness, they said, and the individual will be then much better prepared to acquire for himself the useful aspects of experience and knowledge.

This educational theory was closely connected with the *aculty* or *power concept* of the mind. Thus memory, attention, reasoning, concentration, judgment, and imagination came to be looked upon as the names of unitary abilities or powers which were the same no matter what material they worked upon. What was needed then in education was to find the kind of exercise or discipline that would train each one of these powers most effectively.

It was commonly supposed that the disciplinary subjects such as mathematics, algebra, Greek, and Latin gave "fibre, facility, strength and adaptability" to the human mind. The study of German contributed, it was said, to the "upbuilding and strengthening of the scientific intellect." Arithmetic, if well taught, could be depended upon to produce "habits of attention, argumentative sequence, and satisfaction in truth" to a greater degree than might be found to be the case with any other subject suited to the same age of childhood.

Kingsley has called attention to the report of the "Committee of Ten" of the National Education Association in 1892, which illustrates very well the thought of the time. This committee, formed for the purpose of making recommendations for the improvement of teaching in secondary schools, laid great stress on mental training in its report. These excerpts are indicative:

> The principal end of all education is training. In this respect history has a value different from, but in no way inferior to, that of languages, mathematics, and science. The mind is chiefly developed in three ways: by cultivating the powers of discriminative observation; by strengthening the logical faculty of following an argument from point to point; and by improving the process of comparison, that is, judgment.
>
> As studies in language and in the Natural Sciences are best adapted to cultivate the habits of observation; as mathematics are traditional training of the reasoning faculties; so history and its allied branches are better adapted than any other studies to promote the invaluable mental power which we call the judgment. (23)

We note there that the stressed value of history has nothing to do with its utility, but with its supposed contribution to the development of mental strength and keenness. In this view, the school subjects were conceived to be gymnastic exercises for building mental muscles, or whetstones for honing the mind like a knife.

The evidence against the assumptions of "formal discipline," starting with the experiments of William James, is not only formidable but conclusive. Correlation studies, as we have seen, showed very little consistency among manifestations of the same (supposedly) mental power, and showed further that the "faculties" were not unitary. It seemed logical to infer that the content of the mental activity is more important in education than the kind of mental activity involved. When put to experimental test in training experiments, of which there were multitudes, the formal discipline theory was completely exploded as an explanation of transfer. James found, after practicing memorizing for 30 days in Milton's *Paradise Lost*, that his ability to memorize was slightly impaired. At first he was quite surprised to learn this, and thought that fatigue was to blame. Carefully controlled studies, his own as well as others, have shown that memorizing as such does not make the memory stronger. Nor did the other "powers" fare any better when put to experimental test.

A number of studies of varied merit have dealt with the measurable effects of training in the "disciplinary" school subjects such as grammar, arithmetic, Latin, and geometry. They have usually been interpreted as indicating that the value of training in these subjects is very largely limited to other material similar in nature. The best known is Thorndike's study on mental discipline in high school studies, (34) purported to show that high school studies in general contributed little to mental growth as measured on intelligence tests. Some qualifications of this conclusion might be made, in view of the fact that vertical growth only was measured, that there was no control group not in school for comparison, and that the unit used in reporting the amount of growth was deceptively small. Figuring the growth in percentage instead of score points, Jordan (15) suggested that the best combination of courses might be credited with contributing an increase of about 60 per cent to a year's normal growth. The principal conclusion, that high school subjects contribute unequally to intellectual growth, seems most reasonable. And on the whole, there is no merit in mental training exercise as such. Learning has no value apart from what is learned, although we must keep in mind that a number of things can be learned from one experience.

The Identical Elements Theory. Most early experiments showed a transfer of improvement from one task to another, while others did not. It appeared that when there was close similarity of materials and content, transfer was large; when the two tasks were dissimilar, no transfer was noted. The reason for this, according to the theory proposed by Thorndike and others, was that the two situations showing transfer contained "identical elements." The amount of transfer was said to be in proportion to the number of identical elements common to both.

To say that transfer of improvement is due to "identical elements," is not at all the same as saying that the two situations are "similar in content." The notion of identical elements goes back to association psychology. As we saw earlier, this view held that mental development was a matter of combining discrete mental events (sensations, images, feelings) into larger functions through learning. Learning is the "connecting" of stimuli and responses. This view of learning and development is by analogy a kind of "mental chemistry," in which elements combine to form another substance. The term "identical" comes from the assumption that the elements of mental life had an independence of mental life in combining and recombining, somewhat independent of the function of the organism as a whole. Transfer could not be said to take place through "similar" elements, because this would imply a kind of extra "similarity-seeing function," beyond that represented in the elements themselves. It was held that training affected only limited neural units of response. Thorndike formulated the theory as follows:

A change in one function alters another only in so far as the two functions have as factors identical elements. The change in the second function is in amount that due to the change in the elements common to it and first. The change is simply the necessary result upon the second function of the alteration of those of its factors which were elements of the first function, and so were altered by its training. ... By identical elements are meant mental processes which have the same cell action in the brain as their physical correlate. (33)

When we come to apply this theory to concrete instances of transfer, we find it plausible only in relatively few cases. It is in general satisfactory, at least from a practical viewpoint, to say that practice in addition transfers to multiplication, because of common elements, the particular number combinations to be found in both tasks. But there are many instances of transfer which do not fit the theory so well. If the elements are thought to exist in the external situation, then it can rather easily be shown that transfer may take place even though the elements of the two situations differ widely. A melody played in two different keys and with the individual notes totally different is perceived as the same melody. If on the other hand elements are taken as mental reactions, specific reactions to specific situations, there is also much transfer that cannot be explained on this basis. As Thorndike himself says (33): "The experimental results have tempted certain writers to proceed too far toward the absurd conclusion that all practice is utterly specific in its effects—confined absolutely to just the particular situations that were met in the special training and to just the particular habits that were formed."

The difficulty inherent in the concept of element arises from the attempt to employ it is an explanation of transfer and to give it at the same time its traditional meaning. Some writers ignore apparently the latter problem and use the term simply to refer to similar *behavior* on the part of the individual in two different situations. Thus, when it is found that a person employs the same method in attacking related problems, it is sometimes said that the transfer takes place through the common element of method. But this is simply a restatement of the fact; it does not explain how the person comes to use the same method on the second occasion. What induces him to respond in the same manner is the important thing psychologically, not the mere fact that he does so respond. Even a method of work is not an element in the traditional sense of the term. It is only when the concept is expanded to include a number of recognized agencies of transfer, such as ideals, attitudes, and generalizations, not covered by the original use of the term, that the term itself may be given a reasonable interpretation. But it is just these broader forms of awareness and behavior to which the concept "element" is traditionally opposed and which could not readily be explained in terms of elements. The phrase "identical elements" seems at best to be an example of poor terminology and when interpreted in its historical meaning it represents an unsatisfactory theory.

Theory of Generalized Experience. The view that the most important instances of transfer are the result of generalized experience has been championed by Judd (16) in opposition to the identical elements theory. The oft-quoted experiment of Scholckow and Judd will illustrate this viewpoint. These authors studied the effect of teaching some boys the principles of light refraction while learning to hit a target under water. Although these boys were found to be no better in their first few trials than an untutored group, they showed a definite superiority in a second series of attempts. This, according to the authors, was the result of the original explanation given in refraction, through which the pupils were able to "generalize their experience." Says Judd:

> If there is any one who asserts that mathematics or Latin or science will train the general powers of discrimination or observation or reasoning, that person is wrong. If, on the other hand, any one asserts that all training is particular, that the mind is made up of many independent special modes of thinking, that person is just as wrong as his opponent.
>
> There is no guaranty in its content that any subject will give general training to the mind. The type of training which pupils receive is determined by the method of presentation and by the degree to which self-activity is induced rather than by content. (16)

In spite of its definite merits in stressing the necessity of self-activity in learning as opposed to the "atomism" of the identical elements theory, the theory of generalized experience has some weaknesses of its own. The term "generalization," ordinarily referring to a special abstractive mental act, does not cover all cases of transfer without extending its meaning unduly. The child who forms the past tense of "go" as "go-ed" shows transfer, but is probably unaware of a general principle. The same may be said of Dallenbach's six-year-old child (18) who when given examples of the opposite of "good" and "big" could go on to give the opposites of other words such as black, long, and fat.

Many writers professed to accept the generalization theory, but proceeded to translate "generalization" back into identical elements, usually by referring to "specific language habits" (30). The mere fact that the same language may be employed on two different occasions, however, does not explain how this comes about. What gives the language habits their applicability? Others preferred to talk about "general elements" common to two situations (15). The tendency, apparently, was to hold on to the word "element" and to imply that it existed in the learning situations, which somehow accounted for the transfer effect.

The real question, of course, is this: Just what, psychologically, is an element? In association psychology, it was clearly an element in "mental chemistry," as Woodworth calls it. If not that, then "element" refers only to the similarities in content, method, or principles which enable the learner to apply to a second situation what he learned in the first. That is what "identical element" has gradually come to mean, and nothing more. The learner must perceive the similarity.

Transfer as a Function of Relations. McGeogh (19) has pointed out the inadequacy of both the identical elements theory and the generalization theory, as formulated, in accounting for all the facts of human learning. However, enough is known of the basic conditions of transfer to state that the carry-over of old experience to new situations depends on learned relationships between the antecedent and subsequent activities. He apparently feels that such a statement synthesizes the two theories.

The elements called "identical" are general to the degree that they extend beyond the situation in which they were originally learned; they are identical only in the sense that they belong to the same class of events. Generalizations are also common to both training and test situations and are, then, as identical as the features subsumed under a theory of identical elements. Each theory emphasizes as basic to transfer certain relations between the training and the test. The two theories are not mutually exclusive and readily become parts of a more general interpretation that *transfer is a function of the relations between the activities from which and to which transfer occurs.* (19, p. 439) (Italics ours)

Whether we call these relations identical (similar) or general factors may be of no consequence. The choice here is a matter of which terminology is more suitable. One thing is certain: the relations accounting for transfer must be learned, i.e., must be perceived by the individual. It is only when these relations are regarded as patterns of experience, rather than discrete elements subsisting in the old and new situations, that we may attain a consistent theory of transfer.

PATTERNS OF EXPERIENCE IN TRANSFER

The most significant things in the world round about, as apprehended by us, are not elements in any ordinary meaning of the word but the relations holding between things. A person's wealth depends upon whether he possesses more or less than the average amount of goods, the significant size of an object is relative to other objects or to our own powers, and the meaning of a thing is distinctive of where it is found and who does the finding. This may be said not only of the inferred properties of objects but of the more immediately given facts of perception as well. Objects are always seen against backgrounds which influence their apprehended qualities. They are usually found in perceptual combinations with other objects, the resulting whole of apprehension influencing the psychological nature and meaning of each. The forms of awareness which reflect these functional relations may be called *patterns of experience*. They can contain "discriminable parts" but they "operate as unitary wholes."

It thus becomes possible to understand how, besides specific experience and specific response (specific in content and specialized in action), there can be generalities in mental life, generalities in the forms of awareness, tendencies, attitudes, mental sets, and dispositions. These, because they are based upon relationships and not upon the specific nature of any particular situation or element within it, must be considered general in the sense that they can be derived from any one of a number of situations—similar only in the relationships involved—and in turn applicable to any number of other situations in which these same relationships hold. Motion, for example, as an apprehended pattern of experience, may be derived universally and applied universally, where there may be no community whatever of the elements of the situation, the things moving. We know that "moving pictures" do not move, but are universally perceived as motion if the rate of succession is fast enough. Optical illusions, like the one shown in Figure 52, illustrate strikingly the changes in patterns of experience that occur even when the object is constant. The sensory stimulus remains the same, but the meaning to the observer changes according to the context in which it is perceived. The change is not the result of eye movements. Patterns are perceived in a context, and it is the context that determines the meaning.

It is to such patterns of experience that we must look for the possibilities of transfer, for what we really learn is to react to a situation as representing a certain general kind. We react to the particularity of the situation only secondarily as it were, only as our tendency to react to it in a general manner must be modified in detail to fit the special contingencies of the situation. What is transferred is a disposition to a certain maturity of response for which the individual is prepared through the previous course of his development.

Experimental Evidence of General Mental Functions. A considerable body of experimental evidence has accumulated to show that "the discovery of a general principle enables the learner to solve not only the problem in a single situation, but in any number of different situations which are governed by the same principle. The generalizations which carry over from one situation to another are thus very numerous, and they facilitate learning" (19). In other words, the individual learns *meanings* and responds to meanings, and this appears to be a basic factor in human learning. One of the classic experiments in meaning-response was done by Moore (21). He measured reaction times to words for both meaning and imagery, and his subjects reported that the first thing they were conscious of was the meaning of the word, while the awareness of some kind of image was secondary. This was ascertained not primarily by simple verbal reports, but by the difference in reaction times by which they responded to an awareness of meaning vs. awareness of image. Later experiments have shown that subjects can apprehend some kind of meaning from a word flashed on a screen for so short an interval that the word cannot even be "seen." Meaning-responses, then, are primary and immediate.

This applies to social learning as well. Cantril's experiments (8), in which he set himself the problem of determining the relations between general dispositions and attitudes on the one hand and specific mental content and specific reactions on the other, came to a similar conclusion.

The normal course of comprehension involves, first, the *general* comprehension of the meaning of the word. Subsequent to this general comprehension there is frequently some form of specific reference in immediate introspections, while in the delayed introspections, the meaning always becomes particularized in a form of reference. (8)

Cantril found, for example, that a person's general "evaluative" attitude, whether he is socially or aesthetically minded, influences the speed of his reaction to specific terms, taken from related fields. The socially minded individual will respond to "friend" more quickly than to "statue" while the opposite tends to be true of the aesthetic person. It was also found that a more vivid understanding of another's personality followed from a description given in general terms than when very specific terms were employed. General impressions were likewise more easily recalled. Errors made in the recall of specific items were often indicative of a correct general impression even when they were wrong as to fact.

Cantril's conclusion that "general determining tendencies are more constant and enduring than specific content" indicates that patterns of experience, besides being generally applicable to diverse situations, are actually more meaningful and longer lived than the particular experiences from which they were derived or to which they may be applied. This is the meaning of the term "readiness" as used in education, since readiness refers to a determining tendency, deriving from the integration of the child's past experiences, which predisposes him to respond to situations in an organized way. It is the generalities, or general attitudes of our mental life, that determine what we do on specific occasions.

What Can Be Transferred. We may now ask in more concrete terms what psychological processes, functions, or patterns are the basis of transfer. This will summarize a great deal of what we already know about learning from previous chapters.

1. *Perceptual patterns,* such as those of motion, brightness, melody, circle, are applicable to any number of situations in

which there may exist no elements whatever in common, but in which the same patterns or relationships of reality hold. Transfer as a psychological fact is implied in the very origin of percepts and ideas.

2. *Experiences and abilities of instrumental value* may be transferred to another situation. The reading of words helps in the integrative reading of sentences. The knowledge of Latin words may assist in the understanding of English words derived from the same root.

But transfer will not take place simply because of the existence of common elements in two situations. The mental processes corresponding to the common elements vary in nature according to the whole situation. Thus, spelling words in a list is not the same as spelling them in a sentence, writing in a copybook is not the same as writing for a composition, adding five and two is not the same thing wherever or whenever it is done. The amount of transfer from Latin to English may be very small unless there is the awareness of a relationship between the two languages.

Breaking up an act of skill into artificial parts or elements and training specifically on these usually produces very little transfer effect. This is because the whole act is something different from the mere sum of the "elements," and because the relationships upon which the pattern of the whole act is based are excluded from the awareness of the learner by such a procedure. While experiences and abilities of an instrumental value are potentially transferable, they actually become so only when the learner can *integrate* them into another performance through the medium of more general forms of awareness, insight, and the realization that they may be employed with profit. They are not then transferable because they are common elements but because the learner becomes aware that he can use them as instrumentalities.

3. *Methods and techniques* of work may be transferred, but the degree of transfer depends on how they were originally learned. Woodrow's well known experiment (37) in the transfer effects of two methods of training is of the utmost importance to the work of the school. He compared the learning of

prose, poetry, vocabulary, and a few other things in groups of subjects who learned them under different conditions. A *trained* group was instructed in the nature of efficient learning. The group was not only given practice, but was taught how to learn and why. A *practice* group spent the same amount of time on practice alone, but were not told how to learn. They memorized as best they could without any formal instruction.

The results showed that the group trained in the technique of memorizing was definitely superior to either of the other groups in a test series. The group that had the practice without the instruction was very little, if at all, better than the control. Woodrow says, "The experiment shows that in a case where one kind of training—undirected drill—produces amounts of transference which are sometimes positive and sometimes negative but always small, another kind of training with the same drill material may result in a transference, the effects of which are uniformly large and positive."

Similar experiments in the transfer of arithmetic reasoning (36), methods of critical analysis of word meanings (20), methods of outlining and organizing subject content (29), and methods of solving simple reasoning problems (39, 17) all show a transfer effect of methods, depending on how the methods are taught in the first place. The last two studies (Waters, Katona) shed some light, also, on the most effective way of teaching for transfer. In these experiments, students who were shown how to do problems were able to transfer very little to the solution of other problems. When the students were told the principle on which solution depended, they were able to transfer even more to later problems than those who were "shown." But those who gained the insight through their own efforts—that is, by discovering the principle through doing several problems unaided—not only learned faster than the others but showed the greatest transfer to later problems as well.

These experiments agree in showing that the conscious recognition of guiding principles has definite transfer value. It is not the "elements" of similarity that enable us to transfer methods or techniques, but the conscious formulation of a general principle. The formulation in words may be helpful, but is probably not necessary.

4. *Organizations of knowledge in the form of generalizations,* and the comprehension of principles and relationships are transferable patterns of experience (19). The experiments just cited are illustrations of this. They also suggest that the way principles are taught or learned influence the amount of transfer. Even the drill subjects, like arithmetic computation (25) and spelling (13) have been shown to profit in transfer effect from teaching methods emphasizing comprehensive schemes of organization. It is of some interest that high school chemistry students may transfer generalizations of scientific principles to new situations (3). In this experiment, students given training in applying principles of kinetic theory showed slightly more ability in applying other scientific principles than students not given this instruction. This gives at least some support to the possibility of a transfer value of high school science to scientific attitudes in general, but this of course depends on how science is taught. Knowledge of the general principles of light refraction, if thoroughly taught, proved more helpful in such a task as hitting a submerged target than when instruction was incomplete (14).

The ability to generalize and to transfer these generalizations is not limited to students of high intelligence. An interesting study by Peterson (26) investigated this with school children, employing principles deriving from the general law of the lever. He found that "when grade in school is held constant . . . there is no relation between intelligence scores and the ability to solve problems involving a general principle." It was found that children could deduce the principle of moments of force in balancing the lever from demonstrations, and further that differences in intelligence do not account for this ability to generalize.

5. *Ideals* of behavior and conduct may also transfer. Here again however their greatest transfer value lies in raising them to the level of awareness, and in arousing the realization that there are many instances in ordinary life to which they are applicable. An experiment on the transfer of neatness in school

work (4), for example, found that insistence on neatness in arithmetic papers had no effect on language or spelling papers. Here there was no concern with neatness as a general ideal. Ruediger (28), in repeating the experiment, attempted to make an ideal out of the objective of neatness by insisting upon it in written papers in one school subject and by giving talks to the children on the general value of neatness. Although no mention was made of the objective during classes in other subjects, there was a general gain in neatness of work.

6. *Attitudes* may transfer. Since an attitude is a general determining tendency, it governs a wide range of perceptions, interpretations, and responses. This is implied in Allport's definition (1) which considers "attitudes as broad, generic determinants of behavior." Thurstone (35) has shown how a particular experience such as seeing a movie may influence a child's attitude toward other races in a measurable degree. Particular academic courses in college have also been found to produce more liberal attitudes toward a number of social problems. A summary of such research by Sherif and Cantril (31) illustrates in a wealth of theoretical and experimental detail that attitudes furnish "frames of reference" or contexts to which all social perceptions are referred. The ideals and attitudes learned in the school are thus of primary importance.

Negative Transfer. It has often been noted that practice in one task may interfere with learning another task. The conditions under which this negative transfer takes place sometimes resemble those of positive transfer. It seems, in the case of negative transfer, that the situations are similar enough to apply an old pattern of experience and yet this old pattern, without modification, is not strictly applicable. This is not really negative transfer psychologically, but only negative so far as results are concerned. The old pattern of experience is applied to the new situation, but without justification in terms of results. Thus, in learning to spell it has been found (9) that bright children, who are more apt at generalizing, fall into characteristic errors because of this very ability. They are likely to spell phonetically ("condukter" for conductor) while the dull child is more likely to err in a nonphonetic fashion (e.g., "condimsler" for conductor). The spelling of the bright child shows transfer, but because of the vagaries of the English language, a phonetic principle does not always work.

It is thus clear that in certain instances there is nothing in the way of transfer that can substitute for specific practice and acquaintance with the demands of the particular task. Again, in cancellation experiments it has been found that practice in cancelling "6's" helps in crossing out "D's" but not "2's" (24). There is apparently a maximum amount of similarity between tasks beyond which transfer leads to interference. This is very probably because of the difficulty of discrimination within a certain mental set.

Interference or negative transfer is sometimes shown in the development of skill. Thus learning to drive two different makes of automobiles with different gearshifts may be expected to lead to a certain amount of interference, at least in the middle stages of learning. This is due to the fact that the process of precision has not been carried far enough in either case to lead to a proper differentiation or discrimination of one action from the other. This appears with further practice, as a result of which the driver may turn from one make of car to another with very little confusion. Similarly, the expert in foreign languages has apparently very little difficulty in turning from one tongue to another, while the person who has not carried his learning very far may show confusion and interference.

The experiment of Dunlap (11) is interesting in this connection. His tendency to type "hte" for "the" might be looked upon as interfering with the tendency to type the word correctly. By practicing the erroneous form he was able thereafter to type "the" without error. The explanation seems to be that the two tendencies (to type "hte" and to type "the") had not been clearly differentiated one from the other. He was able to bring about complete differentiation by practicing the wrong form. When such a stage was reached, he could type either one he pleased without any confusion or interference of the two tendencies.

For the full value of transfer and for the avoidance of interference, the inherent relationships of situations should be apprehended as similar, but there should also be a discrimination of the situations so far as they may differ in detail. In actual practice it is always a matter of nice balance between the two. The lack of necessary discrimination may really produce negative transfer in results, but psychologically there is only one kind of transfer, the positive. There is always a subsuming of new situations under previous patterns of experience, but this may be either adequate or inadequate so far as present results are concerned.

TRANSFER AND TEACHING

Generality and Conditions of Transfer. The facts of learning and development appear to indicate this conclusion: transfer is both a necessary and sufficient condition for human development. As McGeogh put it, "after small amounts of learning early in the life of the individual, every instance of learning is a function of the already learned organization of the subject; that is, all learning is influenced by transfer" (19). It is probable that all levels of perception are influenced by transfer, at least to some extent. Transfer is the basis of concept formation, thinking, and problem solving: insights, as we have seen, are transposable. What we term originality, inventiveness, or creativeness is the behavioral form that transfer takes. Transfer is not a special mental function, or even a distinguishable form of learning, but a fundamental characteristic of insightful learning. There can then be no argument about whether transfer of school learning can take place, but only a concern about the conditions which facilitate insightful learning.

Transfer is largely achieved through the apprehension of general factors (principles, methods, attitudes) which in human learning are symbolized by language. This is why language plays such an important role in human development. However, it has been clearly demonstrated that the person who learns a general principle will not necessarily apply it wherever it is applicable.

We may say that the transfer of past learning to new situations arises from (1) a similarity of contents, (2) similarity of techniques, (3) similarity of principles, or (4) a combination of these. But the similarity between old and new must be perceived by the learner. Whether he will perceive similarity depends on how he is taught and how he learns. Since the patterns of experience through which alone transfer is possible are very often of such a nature that they are not immediately apprehended, they must be expressly raised to the level of awareness in the learner's mind. The fact that a principle of science is, as a matter of fact, the basis of a particular demonstration or experiment in the classroom is of itself no guaranty that the pupil will apprehend the present instance as an illustration of the principle. He may carry away with him no knowledge whatever of the general principle as such. He may remember the experiment merely as a particular incident in his school life, never attaining the stage where the general principle is either understood or capable of being formulated. There could in such a case be no question of transfer because the only means of making transfer possible would be absent. Transfer is possible from school learning, but not automatic.

Some school subjects are admittedly more "difficult" than others; that is, the fundamental relationships can be grasped only by the brighter students. The tendency to "water down" or simplify courses by lowering the instruction to the level of the less intelligent has often had unfortunate results. By ignoring basic principles and relationships, there have been eliminated the only means by which such a subject could have transfer value. Some subjects and some forms of instruction may have considerable transfer value for certain students and very little or none at all for others. The nature of the subject, the character of the instruction, and the ability of the pupil are all factors of importance.

One additional aspect of transfer is important here: learned generalizations are not forgotten, as are the specific materials learned. Some experiments by Katona (17) tested the ability to learn and remember certain techniques involved in tricks with playing cards and match sticks. In these studies he compared the performance of a "memorizing group" which was taught to memorize details of doing the tricks, and an "understanding group" whose method of instruction favored the learning of general principles or schemes of understanding. The latter group was not only able to transfer the learning to new tricks based on the same principles, but remembered how to solve the trick problems over a longer period of time. It is also illustrated in some experiments by Bunch (6, 7) who found that mere retention of combinations of numbers "faded" rapidly with time, but that transfer effect (based on insight into relationships) was not forgotten. The result implies that learning which permits cognitive insight into relationships is likely in the end to be more useful than mechanical, associative learning.

Teaching for Transfer. The transfer of various school subjects has been intensively studied. (For a summary, see the Encyclopedia of Educational Research, 1950.) Although some subjects are found to have greater transfer than others, the results as a whole confirm Jordan's conclusion, as follows:

> The transfer effect from any mental function to any other mental function, or from a school subject to any other subject or to life itself, may be substantially modified by conscious effort in that direction. Of this, there is no doubt. Once we have determined our objectives for the teaching of any subject we can proceed with some assurance that they will be attained. If teachers, for instance, in their teaching of Latin keep their eyes ever single to the developing of an English vocabulary, then the transfer effect in this direction can be trebled. To obtain from geometry that precision in thinking, that feeling of hesitancy in making unsubstantiated statements, that rigor of proof . . . these matters must be learned as other things are learned. (15)

The role of the school is to make insightful learning and transfer possible, not simply to teach specific skills and knowledge for specific future use and to hope vaguely that transfer will occur.

The problem of teaching for transfer is that of teaching concepts and generalizations of wide applicability, and guiding students in applying them. In short, this means teaching students how to think. Some teachers say that it is impossible to teach children to think. If this means that we cannot build up a kind of power or "thinking-muscle" through exercise, they are quite right. But although the theory of formal discipline has been demolished, the fact of transfer generalizations or patterns of experience remains. The number of concepts and generalizations actually attempted in school work is tremendous. In fact, it is possible that too many concepts are taught, too hastily taught, and possibly taught at the wrong stage of development, to make transfer possible (5). The following points are therefore pertinent:

1. Abstract concepts (like nation, citizen, latitude, tense, fraction, poem, energy, rate) are very complex psychologically, considering their genetic origins and the many situations necessary for their differentiation, integration, and precise use. This is also true of concepts learned through everyday nonschool experience, such as law, duty, business, love, friend, marriage. If we ignore their psychological complexity, we tend to touch only words and to be satisfied with the student's reproduction of words. We can never be sure that the child's use of a word carries the same meaning for him that it does for the teacher. In fact, we can usually be sure that it does not. Meaningful generalizations depend on concepts, of which words are only symbols—puffs of breath and marks on paper. Consider these: "Democracy depends on the legal right and duty of the citizens to vote"; "What is good for business is good for the nation"; "A fraction is a ratio between two numbers." These statements depend on accurate formation of difficult concepts for their intelligibility and their critical, selective application (or transfer) to concrete situations.

2. Learning generalizations is a matter of problem solving, and they are learned in no other way. Here again, let us repeat that the student learns only what he needs to learn, what leads to the attainment of his immediate goals. He "can not solve a problem he does not have" (32). If his goal is to satisfy the teacher, and he knows she is satisfied with words, he will learn words. Are the generalizations about democracy, business, and practices related to immediate student needs and goals? What goals? If so, they can be learned at the level of

his needs, but not otherwise. They may transfer later to other situations related to higher goals, but not unless they are comprehended in a manner consistent with his level of development.

3. Teaching for transfer therefore involves a careful selection of the concepts to be taught, a pace of instruction adequate to maturational level, and many problem situations in which to differentiate adequate meanings. We must also recognize that all children will not comprehend at the same level. The guidance of learning requires these things. But this implies neither that "all teaching is telling and showing," nor that the student should be left to himself to make his own discoveries. Moore has put the matter succinctly:

It does help the student if you give him principles to solve his problems, and point out to him ways in which his previous training will be helpful. If all students were left to discover all their principles, few would make much progress in learning. But one should not go to the other extreme and never give the student any exercise in discovering and formulating principles in virtue of his own ingenuity. (22)

Transfer and Educational Philosophy. The educator's philosophy of his calling depends to a considerable extent on the theory of transfer he holds. A strictly utilitarian philosophy of education, the view that students should be trained to do these specific things which they will do in later life, appears to dominate present school practice. This is largely an expression of the identical elements theory of transfer. In the wave of curricular changes that followed the earlier experiments in transfer (which, by the way, were often misinterpreted by educators) much good was thrown away with the bad. When it was concluded that mental development would be as well favored by one school subject as another, no subject apparently having a very broad general effect, early specialization and narrow vocational preparation supplanted the more rigorous "disciplinary" curriculum. As Poffenberger says:

Interpreted more narrowly and less critically [the theory of identical elements] tended to vocationalize education, to eliminate the so-called culture studies and to furnish an individual with the tools needed only within his chosen occupation, providing no background for growth, for meeting changing social patterns nor for the enjoyment of his increasing leisure. (27)

During the past few years, increasing recognition has been given to the fact of transfer and to the learning conditions that facilitate it. This has been a corrective influence for the narrowly conceived doctrine of identical elements. It is becoming more evident to educators that emphasis on narrow skills actually prevents maximum transfer value for the work of the school. But education appears to be at an in-between stage, since school practice lags behind development of theory. The present school curriculum often resembles an expression of the identical elements theory. There are also vestiges of the theory of formal discipline still present in the schools, and particularly in higher education. According to Anderson and Gates (1950) "much of the confusion existing in education today comes about because of failure to reconcile an educational philosophy and the generally accepted facts concerning transfer" (2).

REFERENCES

1. ALLPORT, G. W. The composition of political attitudes. *Amer. J. Sociol.,* 1929, **35,** 220-238.
2. ANDERSON, G. L., & GATES, A. I. The general nature of learning. *49th Yearbook,* I, Nat. Soc. Stud. Educ., 1950.
3. BABITZ, M., & KEYS, N. An experiment in teaching pupils to apply scientific principles. *Science Educ.,* 1939, **23,** 367-370.
4. BAGLEY, W. C. *Educational values.* New York: Macmillan, 1911.
5. BROWNELL, W. A., & HENDRICKSON, G. How children learn information, concepts, and generalizations. *49th Yearbook,* Nat. Soc. Stud. Educ., 1950.
6. BUNCH, M. E. The amount of transfer in rational learning as a function of time. *J. comp. Psychol.,* 1936, **22,** 325-337.
7. BUNCH, M. E., & McCRAVEN, V. G. The temporal course of transfer in the learning of memory material. *J. comp. Psychol.* 1938, **25,** 481-496.
8. CANTRIL, H. General and specific attitudes. *Psychol. Monogr.,* 1932, No. 192.
9. CARROLL, H. A. Generalization of bright and dull children. *Teach. Coll. Contr. Educ.,* Columbia Univ., No. 439, 1930.
0. DORSEY, M. F., & HOPKINS, L. T. The influence of attitude upon transfer. *J. educ. Psychol.,* 1930, **21,** 410-417.

11. DUNLAP, K. A revision of the fundamental law of habit formation. *Science,* 1928, **67,** 360-362.

12. GATES, A. I. & TAYLOR, G. A. An experimental study of the nature of improvement in one mental function upon efficiency of other functions. *J. educ. Psychol.,* 1925, **16,** 583-592.

13. GATES, A. I. *Generalization and transfer in spelling.* New York: Teach. Coll., Columbia Univ., 1935.

14. HENDRICKSON, G., & SCHROEDER, W. H. Transfer of training in learning to hit a submerged target. *J. educ. Psychol.,* 1941, **32,** 205-213.

15. JORDAN, A. M. *Educational psychology.* New York: Holt, 1933.

16. JUDD, C. H. *Psychology of secondary education.* Boston: Ginn, 1928.

17. KATONA, G. *Organizing and memorizing.* New York: Columbia Univ. Press, 1940.

18. KREEZER, G., & DALLENBACH, K. M. Learning the relation of opposition. *Amer. J. Psychol.,* 1929, **41,** 432-441.

19. McGEOGH, J. A. *The psychology of human learning.* New York: Longmans, Green, 1942.

20. MEREDITH, G. P. Consciousness of method as a means of transfer of training. *Forum of Educ.,* 1927, **5,** 37-45.

21. MOORE, T. V. The temporal relations of meaning and imagery. *Psychol. Rev.,* 1915, **22,** 177-225.

22. MOORE, T. V. *Cognitive psychology.* New York: Lippincott, 1939.

23. NATIONAL EDUC. ASSOCIATION. *Report of the committee of ten on secondary school studies.* New York: American Book, 1894. Quoted from KINGSLEY, H. L., *The nature and conditions of learning,* New York: Prentice-Hall, 1946.

24. NEWKIRK, B. H., & GUNDLACH, R. H. Transfer of training in the cancellation experiment. *J. educ. Psychol.,* 1929, **20,** 291-294.

25. OVERMAN, J. R. An experimental study of the effect of method of instruction on transfer in arithmetic. *Elem. Sch. J.,* 1930, **31,** 183-190.

26. PETERSON, G. M. An empirical study of the ability to generalize. *J. gen. Psychol.,* 1932, **6,** 90-114.

27. POFFENBERGER, A. T. Psychology and life. *Psychol. Rev.,* 1936, **43,** 9-31.

28. RUEDIGER, W. C. The indirect improvement of mental function through ideals. *Educ. Rev.,* 1908, **36,** 364-371.

29. SALISBURY, R. A study of the transfer effects of training in logical organization. *J. educ. Res.,* 1934, **28,** 241-254.

30. SANDIFORD, P. *Educational psychology.* New York: Longmans, Green, 1928.

31. SHERIF, M., & CANTRIL, H. *The psychology of ego-involvements.* New York: Wiley, 1947.

32. SNYGG, D., & COMBS, A. W. *Individual behavior.* New York: Harper, 1949.

33. THORNDIKE, E. L. *Educational psychology (briefer course).* New York: Teach. Coll., Columbia Univ., 1914.

34. THORNDIKE, E. L. Mental discipline in high school studies. *J. educ. Psychol.,* 1924, **15,** 1-22. See also, 1927, **18,** 377-404.

35. THURSTONE, L. L. The measurement of change in social attitude. *J. soc. Psychol.,* 1931, **2,** 230-235.

36. WINCH, W. H. The transfer of improvement in reasoning in school children. *Brit. J. Psychol.,* 1923, **13,** 370-381.

37. WOODROW, H. The effect of type of training upon transference. *J. educ. Psychol.,* 1927, **18,** 159-172.

38. WOODWORTH, R. S., & THORNDIKE, E. L. The influence of improvement in one mental function upon efficiency of other functions. *Psychol. Rev.,* 1901, **8,** 247-261.

39. WATERS, R. The influence of tuition upon ideational learning. *J. gen. Psychol.,* 1928, **1,** 534-539.

SELECTED READINGS

BODE, B. H. *Modern educational theories.* New York: Macmillan, 1927.

GARRETT, H. E. *Great experiments in psychology.* (Rev. ed.) New York: Appleton-Century-Crofts, 1951. See chapter on Thorndike and Woodworth experiments on transfer of learning.

HARTMANN, G. W. *Educational psychology.* New York: American Book, 1941. Pp. 310-319.

JORDAN, A. M. *Educational psychology.* (3d ed.) New York: Holt, 1942.

JUDD, C. H. *Psychology of secondary education.* Boston: Ginn, 1927.

KINGSLEY, H. L. *The nature and conditions of learning.* New York: Prentice-Hall, 1946.

McGEOGH, J. A. *The psychology of human learning.* New York: Longmans, Green, 1942. Ch. 10.

MOORE, T. V. *Cognitive psychology.* New York: Lippincott, 1939. The transfer of training, pp. 473-493.

PART V

The Forms of Learning

17

HABITS AND SKILLS

Habits and skills are motor aspects of mental processes. Like other forms of learning, they reside in the organism as a whole and not merely in its particular members. Habits and skills involve refined and precise movements, or neuro-muscular processes, which are mediated through brain functions. The term habit ordinarily refers to behavior so well learned as to be highly automatic. But skills which exhibit a high degree of precision are also "automatic" in the sense that we are able to carry them on without conscious direction. Speech, handwriting, typing, swimming and other athletic skills, dancing, drawing, sewing, and using tools are examples of "psychomotor" learning. And, for that matter, so are nail-biting and thumb-sucking. In the work of the school, all teachers are concerned with psychomotor learning in one form or another.

Habit Formation

Habit, a term derived from the old "habitus" (*sese habere*) originally referred to the readiness in which a person "held himself" to perform a certain act. In this sense, it was a kind of disposition, tendency, or attitude. At present the term is more often applied to the act itself which the person does "from habit." This change has not been altogether favorable to the understanding of habit because it has tended to divorce the act from its personal setting.

Since habit is a product of learning, it was often used to distinguish a learned act from one that is unlearned, or instinctive. It was thus customary to include under the heading of

615

habit all sorts of learned acts, and to refer to "thought-habits," for example. The ancient meaning of habit as a state of readiness would be consistent with this use of the term. In present use, however, habit is ordinarily restricted to coordinated muscular movements. Habit has lost much of its former significance in psychology because of the change in our ideas concerning the sharp line of division to be drawn between heredity and acquired behavior. We now find that it is impossible to be at all specific about a human act and to say that it is strictly one or the other. The best we can do is to say that a habit, such as the "maze-habit," a "speech-habit," or a "work-habit," is an action for which either specific training was given or whose development may be fairly easily followed in terms of experienced situations. Other actions, for which we may not on occasion be able to single out any particular developmental cause or for which no explicit training was required, may be just as truly learned. Our ability or inability to identify the developmental circumstances and perhaps to control these does not mean that there is any real psychological difference between the two.

The statement is sometimes made that all "learning is habit formation." This in itself is rather meaningless, unless we have in mind a particular notion of the nature of habit-formation, in which case it is liable to be very misleading. If it is supposed that a habit is merely an isolated action, set off by some sensory cue and running to completion in a thoroughly automatic fashion, the above statement cannot be thought true. The error is not in the identification of learning with habit-formation but rather in the inadequate explanation of habit itself. If we accept the ordinary view that habit depends merely upon a physiological fixity of response, the statement is hardly acceptable.

How Habits Are Learned. The origin of a habit, as has often been noted, is usually found to lie in an earlier voluntary insightful act, of which the habit itself was a conspicuous feature, or perhaps less often an accidental feature. It represents in origin a differentiation of the early crude patterns of behavior effected by the attempt to adjust to some experienced situation

Thus a habit is a feature of the total response to the demands of some situation, at least as these were originally apprehended. The habit will remain "fixed" as long as the corresponding situation is viewed in the same light, and thus results in satisfaction for the individual. For many forms of learning, as for instance in the development of skill, the individual becomes more discriminating as time goes on and he views the situation as requiring finer and finer adjustments. But with habit it is usually different. It will not change because the situation does not change for the individual.

When the situation does not change, we encounter, as a positive cause of the habit, a certain "inertia" of previous stages of development which tend to carry the habit into execution. It is in this respect that repetition and custom build up a strong propelling force and give the habit a certain amount of independence. We find an analogy for this in the organic differentiation of body tissue. Once having entered upon a certain line of specialization, it tends to resist any diversion into other channels. Only a great display of energy can usually do this, but an infection, for example, or constant irritation, will make the tissue young again and more ready to be influenced by external forces.

This independence of habit, however, is never complete. It never loses its connection with the setting which gave it birth. When the setting changes it is also changed. As Ogden has remarked, he will reach for his watch in its customary pocket only when he is wearing his business suit. When he is dressed in formal clothes, demanding a shift in the watch-pocket, he will not make the error of looking for it in the wrong place, in spite of the fact that it is "habitual" for him to do so. If, while dressed in formal attitre, he should lapse into very informal conversation with close friends, he is likely then, however, to reach for the watch in the wrong place. The total situation has changed, and with it the background of readiness for the specific act.

Because habits represent an action based upon a previous insight into a situation, and because there is not sufficient motive for a reorganization of behavior suited to the demands of the new situation, they often contain a distinctly "personal" element. We are commonly found to differ from one another in the nature of our habits, less so in our skills. The present situation does not call for just this particular action or mode of action shown in the habit. The person might do any number of things and yet he does just this. This means that the situation appears to him differently from the way it does to others, and accordingly evokes a different response. Habit may often be regarded as the *preferred* way of viewing a situation and of responding to it. It represents something of a self-determined value and may be opposed to the true value of the situation. We have an approach here to habit through personal attitude and mental set.

Why Habits Persist. The "fixity" of habit is not so much a matter of the "setting" of certain parts of the nervous system or particular synapses. It involves all the factors that play upon the apprehension of the conditions to which the individual is adjusting. The embarrassed girl graduate walking awkwardly across the stage to receive her diploma and the nervous speaker with his high-pitched voice are suddenly breaking habits which, if years and repetition count for anything, should be well "ingrained." New factors are introduced to alter the setting of the act, and it accordingly changes with them. In this case the changes arise in external circumstances, but a change in motivational life may also bring about an altered perception of the situation and a corresponding change in behavior. We should perhaps be able to do better if we could make the "old dog" understand that it was to his own advantage for him to learn the new "tricks."

Breaking Habits. When an undesirable habit, such as nail-biting or faulty articulation, occurs as an incidental feature of a larger whole of behavior, it is sometimes difficult to check. This, however, may still be done by attacking the total setting of the act. The nail-biting that is due to nervousness or timidity can often be eradicated by looking to the personality adjustment of the child. Mispronunciations will sometimes be easily corrected by helping the child improve his perceptual discrimination of the right and wrong forms. Slovenliness of speech is indicative at times of crudeness of general behavior. The child who patterns his personality after the gangster will hardly change his speech before he changes his ideals.

The essential fact about a change in habits is that a new organization of behavior is required. A felt need of change is the first step. This, however, must ordinarily be followed by practice on the desired form, but always as a feature of the total act, in which it is to be substituted for the old. Drill, for example, on the correct pronunciation of words when taken singly, is not nearly so effective as when these are employed in their natural setting of spoken sentences. In fact the practicing of errors isolated from their context has been suggested as being of greater value. Its chief merit seems to lie in the fact that we bring about the complete individuation or isolation of the erroneous tendency from the total behavior pattern in which it was formerly swallowed up. By so doing we destroy its "membership-character."

Education and Habit. Unless we take habit in a very broad sense, we can scarcely identify the work of education with habit-formation. A good deal of habituation is required in life, but it is of the essence of habit that it harks back to an outlived past. When habits are useful, this may be very desirable, for it enables us to take advantage of the solution of earlier problems in a ready form in attacking new ones. When they can be incorporated into broader behavior patterns, they become of very great value. But if habits are understood as specific responses to specific situations, and if made the main objective of education, they would force us to live continually in the past which gave them birth. This may do for the aged, but we expect young people to keep the "problem-attitude." It would be more correct to say that the work of education is to further maturation, if we must choose between the more general aspects of mental development and its more specialized forms of expression.

A very appropriate sphere for habit-formation in education would seem to lie in early practice in the use of a foreign language. Peculiarities in pronunciation may apparently be grasped as well through imitation as through any of the higher forms of insight. The different muscular sets and tensions required for vocalization may be learned with less interference in early life and seem to be well retained.

DEVELOPMENT OF SKILLS

The Nature of Skill. A skill is a refined pattern of movement or performance based upon and integrated with the perceived demands of the situation. A skill is never a mere serial or temporal arrangement of individual and discrete movements. It is a unified and organic whole, into which the physically separate movements fit as features or details of the total act. These details receive their significance from just this relation to the whole and derive their right to existence from it. That this whole or pattern is psychologically prior to the details must be evident when we recall, with James, that "no one ever performs an act the *same* way twice."

There can be no set, stereotyped order of individual movements that would carry a person successfully through the ever-varying occasions upon which a skill is manifest. The precise details of an act of skill are something about which we can be the least certain in advance, because they are either ever changing or ever liable to change to meet new conditions. Pear (16) has well brought out this important point, namely, that in true skill the detailed movements and performances are always modifiable in the service of the general goal of the whole act. In the light of this goal and of the attendant conditions, the act takes on its pattern or form as a whole. He says,

Skill is clearly ability, but a particular kind. . . . A man who can run need not be skilled in running. But if he has learned to move his legs well, to regulate his breathing, to sprint at a particular lap, to adjust himself to different lengths of race, different classes of competitions and different competitors, he possesses skill in running races. . . .

Skill therefore implies discrimination of the situation and graduation of the response. But to this should be added . . . the ability to integrate responses, and in the highest skills, to substitute, instantaneously, if necessary, one type of integrated response for another. (16)

The refined nature of an act is probably its most distinctive note. In nicety of detail, in the "timing" and proportioning, and in the flexibility and facility of the act of the expert, we obtain a picture of the results of the process of refinement that has gone on from the very beginning. This is very different from the crudely organized and executed attempts of the beginner. So far as the general nature of the goal is concerned, they may outwardly be regarded as the same act. But the skillful person has generated out of his first crude attempts, through successive stages of refinement, the well-balanced, highly detailed and expeditious approach that leaves no doubt about the difference. This refinement does not come through the mere addition or elimination of separate movements but from the progressive attempts to reach the goal in the most direct way possible, with due regard for the conditions under which the goal is to be attained.

Analysis of Skill. It is possible for an observer to analyze an act of skill into separate movements through space or time of various members of the body. This may be done in a piecemeal fashion just as we should perhaps describe the action of a complicated piece of machinery. There can be no objection to such an analysis as long as we recognize it for what it is—an observer's account of the action in terms of purely physical units, units of space-time relationship. But it will not do to suppose that the act of skill is simply the arithmetical sum of these arbitrarily determined physical movements. The same bodily movement may vary internally according to the relations in which it stands with other movements in the make-up of the total act. "Walking" or moving the feet may be a very different thing psychologically when we are walking on a level surface and when we are walking uphill or with a heavy load on our back. While to the movie-camera the movement of the feet may appear the same, it is not so from the viewpoint of the individual. Analysis of a skill into elemental or part movements is very liable to lose sight of the form or pattern character of the whole act, based as it is upon the dynamic interplay and relations holding between the physical units. A part movement may be modified his needs or even supplanted altogether in the interest of the complete skill-act.

It may appear at times that we acquire skill by "putting together" many separate movements or performances. A plausible logic of the situation might be that if we build up a skill through the addition of separate performances, then we may later analyze the act of skill into these component parts. Once, however, a part movement is taken into an act of skill, it is no longer independent. The *integration* of individual performances into a new total act rigidly regulates, controls, and even modifies in their internal characteristics these part movements once they are integrated into the new act. These new relations of the part movement, its control and regulation in the interest of the whole, the internal changes taking place, its "timing" and proportional strength, mean that it is not just the old movement that has been transferred without alteration to a new setting. It is a different psychological event because it has different psychological relations. This is in a way analogous to the chemical combination of sodium and chlorine in producing common salt. Each of the elements modifies the characteristics of the other with the result that the product is not in any sense the mere sum of the properties of each element but a new substance with properties characteristically different from either of its constituents. The new chemical relationships determine the properties of the elements in combination.

Thus the kind of practice in baseball, tennis, or golf which emphasizes isolated fragments of acts, which are later put together into a total pattern of movements, is time wasted. The character of the parts change when they become members of the whole. Acquiring "form" in athletics is not a matter of putting together perfected movements, but of developing precision of part movements through practice of a whole pattern. Even the apparent exceptions prove the rule. Swimming, for example, bears analysis into arm, leg, head, and breathing movements. These are often practiced separately. But the essence of swimming, as every coach knows, is body buoyancy, which is a total behavior pattern. Separate practice of breathing or kicking, under conditions simulating the total act of swimming makes the kinaesthetic cues of "staying afloat" more apparent to the learner. When the total act has been perfected, the "meaning" of the acts practiced separately undergoes a complete change. This illustrates the perceptual aspect of skill.

Perceptual Aspect of Skill. Skill may be considered the motor aspect or correlate of perception. It is executed both with reference to a perceived goal and in the light of the material conditions that have to be taken into account in attaining the goal. Otherwise, the act, even though to outward appearance much the same, will be nothing more than a lifeless mannerism lacking the essential flexibility of skill.

As the goal becomes increasingly more exacting and refined, and is perceived as such by the learner, his responses take on a proportionate graduation and refinement. When we think of the accidental variations in the external situation from moment to moment, the properties and limitations of instruments and machinery, and the existence of bodily structures and functions, we can hardly suppose that a partial, blind neurological mechanism would be equal to the task. Many of these things, it is true, seem to be more or less vaguely "felt" rather than clearly perceived. But this is chiefly because they are so inextricably bound up with the whole act that we are not called upon to give them attention outside their setting. We can find many instances similar to this in visual perception. We may not "see" the color of a person's necktie or even notice that he is wearing one. But it is evident that the presence of the necktie influences the total perception, for we shall "feel" that something is wrong if the necktie is missing, even before we clearly perceive this fact.

There are many aspects of skill for which we lack words. This not only makes it difficult at times for the expert to tell just how he performs an act or how the beginner should be instructed, but it tends as well to conceal the perceptual basis of the act itself. If we watch the young child trying ineffectually to cut with scissors, the paper meanwhile slipping between the blades, we shall find here an interesting example of this. It is clear that he does not have the "feel" of the act. He can perform the individual movements but it is the relation of these that counts. When he apprehends this, which he sometimes does very suddenly, he no longer has any difficulty. Although we, in watching him, know what he lacks, we shall usually find it almost impossible to explain the situation to him. We have no convenient words or expressions for this particular opposing movement of thumb and fingers. It cannot be analyzed into the separate movements for which we may have terms. It is only as all the conditions of an act are apprehended, in relation to one another and to the goal, that the well-adjusted, expeditious, and flexible nature of skill is possible. The ability to perceive in this integrated way is a kind of "intelligence." "Many muscular knowledges have no proper languages. While it is possible to be intelligent about them it is less easy to be intellectual" (expressive in words) (16).

As a perceptual organization, the development of skill shows integration and precision. These two processes do not occur at wholly different periods during the learning. They are really simultaneous, but there are times when one or the other aspect of the whole process seems to be more outstanding. In general, integration corresponds to what is ordinarily regarded as the first organization of the movements or performances, while precision is most clearly seen in the refinement of the act with time.

Integration in Skill Development. The integration of behavior, as opposed to a mere temporal sequence of separate performances, is the prime requisite for the development of an act of skill. It is essentially a matter of the unity of the whole act, and manifests itself in three different ways: (1) in the continuity or persistence of effort toward an end-result or goal; (2) in a form or pattern of the whole act, indicated by such general terms as "writing," "playing tennis," which lays the meaningful setting for the individual or part-movements; and (3) in the scheme of understanding or insight by which the person is aware of these relationships.

1. *Goal activity* is the prime factor in the integration of an act of skill, for it is only with reference to some goal that the

integration can take place. If a child could be put passively through a series of motions that characterize the physical acts of writing, and if through some mysterious power of repetition the series of movements should somehow be permanently connected in the order in which they were first imposed, we should not have an act of skill. The resulting action would be too rigid and invariable to suit any but the original conditions that gave it birth. If we wrote in this fashion on paper we should have to learn all over again before we could write on a blackboard. One of the biggest tasks in teaching skills to children is to bring them to a proper appreciation of the refined and exacting goals of adult behavior. When this is effectively done, the elimination of crudities and awkwardness usually takes care of itself.

2. The form or *pattern* of an act of skill represents the fundamental plan or scheme into which are organized the particular movements or performances, and in the service of which they are individually modifiable. A concrete illustration of the patterning of an act of skill may be found in writing. When due allowance is made for crudities and lack of refinement, it has been noted that a person will write with his left hand in the same general way as he does with his right, and even writing with the toes shows the same general form. There can be no question here of identical movements being involved, for different bodily members are employed. It is only the pattern or form that is the same, which, although learned through the use of the right hand, can also be put into execution with the left hand or even the foot. The pattern determines the specific part-movements of the bodily members. Experiments on "cross-education" show the same thing. Practicing an arm or leg has been found to lead to corresponding, though not of course equal, improvement in use of the opposite member.

3. The conscious correlate of the integrated act is the scheme of *understanding or insight* accompanying the process. This is based upon an apprehension of the relation of means to an end and of the appropriateness of the part movements to the general pattern. Many of these relationships are of a

spatial and temporal nature, and are not usually the kind that can be expressed in words. Because of this fact the integration is more often accompanied and indicated by a "feeling" than by an intellectual appreciation. We get the "knack" of doing something, or "feel" its rhythm, or know "instinctively" what is to be done next. It does not have to be an intellectual affair, but it is a matter of consciously apprehending the act as a whole and the basic relations involved.

This awareness of the act as a whole may serve to produce an original "set" or "disposition," from which will emerge in their proper time and order the specially featured movements. In speaking a sentence, the tone of voice and the stress on various words are "parts" which take their character from the "whole," the whole being the meaning or intent of the speaker. The same effect is apparent in the beginning student of dancing, who in watching the instructor or in saying to himself "One, two, three," is building up his awareness of the act as a whole. In the light of this awareness his anticipated actions will emerge in their proper setting. To give attention to a part movement will often lead to extreme awkwardness. The proper subordination of detail to whole is destroyed through such a shift of emphasis.

The importance of the original "set" in the unfolding of an act of skill, the organization of which is thus determined at the very beginning, is seen in a number of instances. Explaining to the beginner just what is to be done or how it is to be done, or even at times guiding his movements so that he may get the "feel" of the act, are means of enabling the learner to build up in conscious anticipation his scheme of understanding. This functions in the "initial delay," when as is often the case the performer will hesitate a little in order to "set" himself for the act. The initial delay is often seen to be particularly effective in very difficult skills, such as acrobatics, and in the early stages of learning. Going slow and stopping every once in a while may also help the beginner, for this enables him to rehearse the organization of the act in consciousness. The scheme of understanding is both the sign and determiner of the integration.

Skill and Effective Intelligence. Since the integrative aspect of skill is closely linked with insight and understanding, it is evident that we are dealing here with an "intelligent" activity. This may not be strictly of the same kind, however, as we have in "abstract intelligence." It has been suggested that we make "intelligence" broad enough to include both. Because many of the material relations involved in skill are of a concrete, temporal, and spatial nature, our apprehension of them does not depend upon abstract thought. Where these may be expressed in conceptual terms, such as, "move a little to the right," "back and forth," "hold the hand rigid," abstract intelligence may be of considerable help. But when the organizing relation cannot ordinarily be "intellectualized," as in cutting with the scissors or following the syncopated rhythm of music, an ability to think abstractly may be of no immediate value. This distinction is worth keeping in mind because studies of the relation of intelligence to skill are often based on the exclusive use of tests of the abstract kind.

Factor analyses of mechanical abilities, such as the coordinated movements required to assemble various objects in the Minnesota Mechanical Assembly Test, have shown the presence of the more intellectual abilities in these tasks, particularly the spatial factor (12, 19). Simple manual dexterity was not found to play a significant role. An earlier study of mechanical ability revealed two factors, abstract intelligence and spatial ability (7). Spatial ability may not be intellectual in the strict sense of the term, but nevertheless involves integrative understanding.

Precision and Refinement. After the original integration of the part movements takes place by fitting these into a scheme of understanding, the further development of the skill is characterized by its precision or refinement. This takes place with practice and the passing of time. It manifests itself in the progressive reduction of irregular, jerky movements, in a nice adjustment of detail, in correct timing and proportion, and in the increase in speed and facility of the act as a whole. The progress of precision or refinement is fairly well indicated by the so-called *learning curve*. Figure 59 shows learning curves based on Bryan and Harter's classic study of telegraphy (5). There are a number of features of the learning curve worth noting.

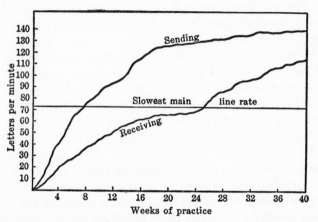

FIGURE 59. The Learning Curve for Telegraphy. The "Receiving" curve shows a conspicuous plateau, while the "Sending" curve does not. (From W. L. Bryan & N. Harter, *Psychol. Rev.*, 1897, 5.)

1. The *initial rapid rise,* due in large measure to the fact that integration or organization is taking place at just this time. The comprehensiveness of integration and the quickness with which it often occurs would imply a rapid rise in performance. The beginning period of learning is the time when the learner is "getting the knack" or the understanding of the goal and the conditions. The beginning period is also usually characterized by strong motivation, indicated by the novelty of the task and the interest aroused. This also would tend to make the rise a rapid one, and give the picture of an "initial spurt." The curve for typewriting is similar (3).

The fairly rapid rise in performance taking place at the beginning of an everyday work period, which is often said to be due to "warming up," may have its counterpart in the beginning of learning. This warming up, if we may judge from a study (17) which found that "the amount of warming-up effect varies directly with the degree of muscular tension," may be largely a matter of release from irrelevant tensions. Getting oneself "set" for an act requires not only an organization of particular physiological and muscular readiness but also a release from those tensions accompanying the different activities with which the person had been previously concerned. Turning from one thing to another naturally requires different sets and attitudes. It may reasonably be supposed that the beginning of learning is similar in this respect to the happenings at the start of each day's work or practice period.

2. *Plateaus.* Many learning curves indicate periods of arrested progress during the learning, which show as a horizontal trend of the curve and are for this reason often called "plateaus." These plateaus represent temporary limits of improvement due to one or more of the following factors:

a) Introduction of *new difficulties,* such as might occur in typing when, after practice had been given only on the letter keys for some time, the use of the number keys would be introduced. This would slow up the performance for a while.

b) Limit of usefulness of a poorer *method* of work. The person learning to type by the "look and pick" method would gradually approach a limit of performance. If he then changed to the touch system, there might soon again be a rapid upward climb of the curve. The intervening period would be marked by a plateau.

c) A difference in the comprehensiveness of the *units of organizations* may also account for a plateau. Thus if we should begin by learning to type letter by letter, that is, a single letter being the unit, we should approach a limit of improvement or plateau, from which we should be able to break away when we began to type words as the unit. This would be comparable to the phenomenon of reading by "words," by "phrases," and so on. That the unit employed by the learner at the start may have considerable to do with plateaus is shown by the fact that the plateau is not found in the typing curve when the pupil learns from the outset to type words rather than isolated letters (1). Again, while there is a plateau in the learning curve for receiving telegraphic messages, there is apparently none in the sending of messages. This difference is probably due to the fact that the matter to be transmitted already exists as a whole, or in large units of comprehension, while the received messages necessarily come singly and favor a more piecemeal attack, at least in the beginning.

Many plateaus may be broken by an increase in the strength of motivation. The fact that improvement may not be as great as was originally expected may give rise to discouragement and a subsequent "going stale." The fact that animals do not show plateaus in their learning curves would point to motivation as a contributing factor. Human motivational life is much richer than that of animals and accordingly tends to result in greater conflict of motives and greater variation and less consistency in performance. The superior organizing ability of humans may also account for a difference of this kind.

Plateaus may also be the artificial result of employing scoring units not suited for showing small degrees of improvement or suited for showing improvement only after a certain critical level is attained. Thus the learning curve of the beginner at tennis might show no improvement for long periods if the scoring was in terms of the number of games won. Until he could improve his tennis up to the point of winning at least one game, the graph would show no progress. This does not mean that he had not been improving in the meantime.

3. The *final limit* of improvement may be regarded as a final plateau. In many cases it marks the operation of the same kind of influences as operate during the temporary plateaus, and may not be strictly final so far as capacity is concerned. It may, for example, be really a method limit, the best that the learner can do with the method of work he now employs. The introduction of a better method of work may lead to further improvement. We may have here also a motivation limit, the best that the learner can do without an increase in motivation. The final limit may of course show an approach to a real physiological or capacity limit, but it is doubtful whether this is ever actually reached. Unless we are dealing with isolated motor activities, such as simple reaction or pursuit, a too ready use of the term "physiological limit" may conceal much that would otherwise be of value in training.

Maturation in Skill Development. When age progress curves show improvement for individuals who have received no special training, or for whom practice has been delayed, the improvement must be due to maturation alone. As we have seen, the genetic development of psychomotor functions is not a matter of practice, but the result of interaction between organic development and the practiced activity. No amount of practice will enable the two-year-old child to control a pen well enough for legible handwriting. On the other hand, the untrained eight-year-old will, once the training is begun, soon catch up in this skill with an equivalent eight-year-old who has practiced since the age of two. Age-progress is thus due partly at least to some internal regulating principle (growth, or maturational effect) and not simply to the number of repetitions of the practiced activity. Is this also true over a shorter period of time? Is it true of learning in adults? We are reminded here of William James' statement that we learn to swim in winter and skate in summer, which indicates that learning goes on to some extent between practice sessions—that something other than practice is controlling the rate of organization and precision.

There is some experimental evidence that this is true of skills. The crucial experiments purport to show that two matched groups, one of which gets considerably more practice than the other during the same time span, will improve equally during the period of training. This would indicate that some kind of internal factor, having to do with the elapsed time rather than with the practice itself, is influencing the learning. Snoddy's study of mirror-tracing shows this effect (18). In this experiment, the subject is required to trace a star-shaped figure viewed in a mirror by moving a stylus through a path around the figure, avoiding contact with the sides of the path. Two groups were given unequal practice for seven days. On the seventh day, Group A had had 31 trials and Group B, seven trials, but the gains in score were equivalent. The two groups learned equally well, apparently as a function of the elapsed time rather than the amount of practice. An experiment by Hilgard and Smith (14) in a different kind of skill task, the pursuit rotor, showed that three groups with unequal practice learned equally well over a much shorter time span, four days.

Whether or not these are maturational effects, similar to the kind of maturation due to growth in the developing child, is in considerable doubt.[1] However, the fact that learning occurs between practice periods as a function of time is at least analogous to age-maturation, in making clear that the development of skill is not merely a matter of repetition and practice. Maturation as a feature of mental development is not limited to an early age, nor is it to be identified with physical growth of the body. Nor is it a wholly internal process in the sense that it is a simple unfolding of some inner isolated mechanism which needs only the passing of time for it to become effective. It is not age alone which makes the child mature, but the trend of vital underlying processes which requires time for its manifestation.

When we turn to learning we find much that is similar. The learner has, in a way, to "grow" to the stimulating situation. His behavior, when he first approaches the task, is not like an unassembled machine which needs only to be put together. He already has certain ways of handling the situation, but they are inadequate, incomplete, inappropriate, immature. The learning is a "becoming," a passing from this earlier stage to a later stage of appropriateness and accuracy. Stimulation and practice set the stage for this transformation, first by attuning him, as it were, to this kind of situation so that he shall be able to profit from it, and secondly by enabling him to reap the special profit of adjustment to the particular learning situation. In the latter phase, stimulation gives and the lack of stimulation may take away.

Physiology of Skill. A movement of any part of the body, such as that of a finger, is not a unitary thing in the sense that

---

[1] Wheeler has expressed an interesting point of view which practically identifies learning and maturation. It would imply that even adult learning over a short time span is due to growth, induced by the stimulation that practice affords, but regulated from within the organism. Although interesting in its implications, crucial evidence is lacking. See R. H. Wheeler, *The Science of Psychology*, New York: Crowell, 1940; and E. R. Hilgard, *Theories of Learning*, New York: Appleton-Century-Crofts, 1948, Ch. 9.

only one nervous impulse and one muscular contraction is involved. Nerves send volleys of impulses to their muscles, and the effect produced depends upon many highly variable features of these volleys, such as their number, their strength, their time relations, and the kind of nerve fibers delivering them. The resulting movement depends not only upon this intricate state of excitation but also upon the corresponding relaxation, tension, and contrary or modifying action of correlative muscles playing upon the same joint or body member. Thus, to move only our little finger really requires that practically all the muscles of the forearm be brought into play. The hand as a whole must be held steady, the muscles acting on one side of the finger must relax while the others contract, and finally the finger must be stopped by the combined action of all the muscles. All this is instigated by a continual volley of nerve impulses coming from the central nervous system and distributed to all the parts concerned. What at first may appear to be a very simple and unitary movement, that of the little finger, is physiologically the result of a very complex interplay of nerve and muscle activity.

Again, if the hand were held vertical, the process would be physiologically different from what it is when the hand is horizontal, because of the changed relations of all the muscles involved. Because it is not physiologically a unitary and consistent thing it would seem impossible for a particular finger movement to be linked up in a mechanical way with other movements. It probably can never happen physiologically in exactly the same way twice.

A quick movement moreover is different physiologically from a slow movement. There is not only a greater number of muscle fibers brought into play but the antagonistic muscles must relax in a different fashion and must act by increased tension to stop the movement. The dynamic setting in the central nervous system must also be different. Gilbreth (11) has shown this difference even in outward action. In his movie-study of the actions of bricklayers at work, he found that fast and slow movements were not performed in the same way. Bricklayers in general employed three different sets of muscular movement: (1) when laying bricks quickly, (2) when laying them slowly, and (3) when demonstrating. Furthermore, experiments designed to measure the physiological cost (e.g., oxygen consumed) of fast and slow movements have shown that under some conditions slow movements are more fatiguing than faster movements (10).

Physiological Changes in Learning a Skill. The development of precision, economy, and smoothness with practice is sometimes assumed to be due to a selective "dropping out" of certain movements. This explanation is misleading, because the changes resulting from practice often result in a greater number of movements with growth in precision. For example Gemelli (9) has shown that the precision of an act of skill, far from being merely the facilitated "running off" of a series of physiologically simple activities, results in an actual increase in the number of such movements. He found that the physiological movements of his subjects in tracing designs were not strictly continuous but that they proceeded by small steps which became more numerous as practice increased. Thus in making what was outwardly the same movement, Gemelli's subjects after practice made about seven times as many of these almost imperceptible spurt-movements as they had made at the beginning.

To illustrate this crudely, drawing a straight line would not be a simple physiological movement at any stage of the process, but after considerable practice and precision there would be seven times as many physiological movements involved in doing this as at the start. Precision results from the refined interplay of a greater number of physiological activities, and the control of these in the central nervous system is a widely distributed and dynamic affair.

It must then be impossible to speak of the refinement of an act of skill as if it resulted from a "selection" of the right movements from out of an original chaos. It would be a strange process of selection that would result in more physiological activities or movements at the end of the process than at the beginning. The development of skill can scarcely be a "simplification" or reduction physiologically, or a mere elimination of incorrect responses. There is a simplification or reduction in energy expended, but not in the complexity of physiological control.

GUIDANCE AND CONTROL OF SKILL

The guidance and control of skill are based upon means of facilitating the integration and precision of the act. Anything that will give meaning to the act, that will help to build up one's scheme of understanding, or that will favor the definite patterning of the act will contribute to its integration or organization. The following principles of teaching skills apply not only to the school situation, but to industrial training as well.

Perception of Goal or Objective. The learner must know what in general is to be done and how he is to do it. It helps if he knows why, that is, has some understanding of the relation between what he does and the objective. While efficient learning is impossible without such an understanding, it is not to be expected that this will extend to such particulars of objective and method as he will be able to appreciate only later on. This point may not be of any great practical value to the instructor of typing, for instance, where the ordinary student has already attained this appreciation. He knows from his general experience what a typewriter is and how it is operated. But we cannot, perhaps, take too much for granted in this respect when it comes to the learning of young children or tasks that are likely to be wholly novel to the learner of any age. It may happen at times that pupils are put through the early rush and crowding of drill periods when they "do not know what it is all about." Learning in such a case is slow. The student of biology can scarcely be expected to show skill in his dissection until he has some understanding of the relative size and delicacy of the organs to be studied.

Methods of Instruction. Verbal instruction may be a means of building up the scheme of understanding. It may contribute to the understanding of the principle or plan of the task as a whole. It can explain the methods of work, the "timing" and spatial ordering of part movements. It can lead to a greater appreciation of the refinement demanded by the tasks. It may assist in the analysis of errors and in seeing how to correct them. It may help, during the period of "initial delay," to build up the anticipated organization by a "mental rehearsing" of the act as a whole.

Demonstrations, models, diagrams, photographs, can also serve in the building up of a scheme of understanding. These practical helps will lose much of their value unless they stress the relationships upon which the pattern of the act is based. Motion pictures and "live" demonstrations, accompanied by verbal instruction, can be quite effective in providing the behavior models and the cues essential to understanding. They are often less effective than they might be, particularly if the teacher assumes that learning a skill is a matter of simple imitation, blind copying, a repetition of movements.

Even mechanical or manual guidance may assist in giving the learner the "feel" of the act and an appreciation of what is to be done. Animal trainers make use of this to give the animal insight into what is required, and humans may also be helped in this way if insight is not to be attained in any other fashion. Such a method of guidance is one, however, to be used sparingly. It tends to decrease the personal activity of the learner, something that is very necessary for learning. Experiments seem to show that this kind of guidance is actually detrimental when introduced into the later or precision stages of learning. The experiments of Gates and Taylor (8) and of Hertzberg (13) may be mentioned here. They agree in finding that, in the learning of handwriting, the tracing of models in grooves, through transparent paper, and so on, is less effective than directly copying the model.

The effectiveness of guidance is related to the stage of learning at which it is given. It is likely to be helpful in the early integrative period, and less helpful or even detrimental in the precision stage. The beginner should receive sufficient guidance so as not to want for an understanding or basis of organization, and not so much that his personal initiative is lessened. If overwhelmed with methodological training in the beginning, the learner may have some difficulty in organizing the instruction into a comprehensive scheme or plan of attack. He may not only be confused as to just what he should be trying to do, but somewhat inhibited in trying. It is important for him to become personally involved in the task—to be moved to attempt to "take hold" in a personal way. A review by Carr (6) of studies on the effect of guidance in the learning of mechanical, manual, visual, graphical, and verbal skills makes the following generalizations: (1) Instruction is sometimes more effective than unguided effort, but sometimes less effective or detrimental. (2) "The most effective results were generally secured by giving a small amount of tuition relatively early in the process of learning." (3) "Detrimental results were generally secured when too much tuition was given or when it was inserted at an inopportune time." (4) For the most part, "the efficacy of the tuition tended to decrease with the amount given and the later the stage at which it was inserted."

These generalizations would apply to the teaching of such skills as golf, tennis, swimming, dancing, football, and track athletics. The correct *form* of the skilled act should be taught in the beginning by demonstration, diagram, or moving pictures, with sufficient analysis or attention to detail to permit an effective scheme of organization. Practice of the movements helps give the learner the "feel" of the act, and manual guidance if not overdone may help at this stage. Verbal corrections of errors may also help, but if overdone may inhibit the learner.

Learning the Task as a Whole. Experiments agree fairly well in showing that the task should be attacked as a whole, and this as early as possible. Formal training on the "elements" of a task has very little to recommend it, unless there happen to be some particularly difficult phases, which may then receive extra practice.

The principle of whole-learning in skills is easily misunderstood. The "wholes" referred to are psychological wholes, and not always logical ones. It might be assumed, for example, that the whole of swimming consists of all the movements observable. If this were the case, we would infer that the best way to teach a person to swim is to heave him into the water (a popular but mistaken notion). Or we might supply floating equipment to allow him to practice the "whole" pattern of responses. In the latter case we would be practicing a psychologically wrong pattern, since the mechanical aid to buoyancy changes the "meaning" of the movements. He has to learn that buoyancy is primarily regulated by the way he breathes, and that breathing must be coordinated in a certain way with other movements. This describes the whole pattern.

But there are subwholes, or modified wholes, of which floating-plus-kicking is one, and arm movements plus "rolling" head and body movements is another. These can be learned separately in stages. This is the modified whole, or *part-progressive* method which has been found to be of value in the learning of mazes. By this method, parts are learned and then combined into subwholes, which are practiced as units and then combined in practicing the whole act or cycle. The "pure-part" method, by contrast, consists in learning each part separately and then combining them into the whole act. The latter has generally been found inferior in the learning of skills. Part-movements practiced separately usually have to be re-learned as part of the whole sequence, thus making the earlier learning uneconomical. One of the writers was first introduced to type-writing by having to memorize the keyboard four ways: forward, backward, down, and up. This was not only a poor substitute for spatial learning, but did not combine with the second step, typing the letters. That is, it did not reduce the "grope and peck" learning of the second step. Once mastered, the latter did not help very much in tackling the larger whole, typing words.

Plateaus were found to be eliminated from the learning when beginning typists were taught to type words from the outset instead of letters. The whole and modified whole methods have also been found to be superior in learning piano music (4). The whole method was superior in two of the three comparisons, ranking second when a very difficult "piece" was learned. The part method was the poorest in all cases. Another investigator (2) compared the effectiveness of training each hand separately and training both simultaneously on a simple task, that of tracing the outline of brass squares attached to a wooden base. He found that the latter method was more effective in the long run. The author concluded from this that movements are essentially different depending on whether they are performed separately or in combination.

Learning the task as a whole enables us to perceive the meaningful relations earlier, thus giving meaning to its parts. Learning a task piecemeal prevents this. The importance of meaning is not confined to verbal materials. Many experiments show that perceptual motor learning poses problems of spatial, part-whole, means-end and other types of relations with which the learner constructs meaningful patterns. Perceptual-motor problems, according to McGeoch, "are not radically different from the logical method in verbal learning. In both cases the learner is seeking to organize meanings to the end of controlling overt response thereby. The persuasive presence of representative devices and meaningful relations in the learning of perceptual-motor acts emphasizes the ubiquity of meaning" (15 p. 168).

Accuracy vs. Speed. The objective of skill should be accuracy first, then speed. The experimental reason for this is that it has been found easier to develop both speed and accuracy by first stressing carefulness than by trying to correct errors after an attitude of careless speedy work has once been acquired. It would seem, however, that speed, where desired, must be made a conscious objective for the learner as early as possible without sacrifice of accuracy. Because of the differences between a slow and a quick action, as motion study has shown, the setting for the two is not quite the same. In the previously cited motion studies of bricklayers by Gilbreth, he found that beginners who learned a slowed sequence of movements during training were handicapped under the normal speeded conditions of the job. The trainees not only had to learn a different set of movements at the faster rate, but were handicapped in doing so by the sequence learned in the first place.

Practice and Drill. There should be adequate spacing of practice periods. "Crowding" the beginner, particularly in the early stages when he is trying to build up his scheme of understanding, may lead to mental confusion or may weaken motivation through fatigue or discouragement. The integration phase needs time to "sink in." In general this will mean that there should be short, well-spaced practice periods at first, though not so short that the beginner will not clearly apprehend the act as a whole. In the precision or so-called mechanization stage, longer and more numerous practice periods may be employed. It has been noted that adequate spacing may help to eliminate plateaus in learning.

Drill is effective and economical only when well motivated and properly spaced. Drill as mere repetition may create unfavorable attitudes toward the task and defeat its own purpose. This is one of the dangers of "overlearning," particularly when practice is carried on indefinitely and the learner is unable to employ his skill in a meaningful practical way. The value of overlearning is dependent upon an optimal distribution of the practice time.

REFERENCES

1. BARTON, J. W. Comprehensive units in learning typewriting. *Psychol. Monogr.*, 1926, **35**, No. 164.
2. BEEBY, C. E. An experimental investigation into simultaneous constituents of an act of skill. *British J. Psychol.*, 1930, **20**, 336-353.
3. BOOK, W. F. *The psychology of skill, with special reference to its acquisition in typewriting.* Chicago: Gregg, 1925.
4. BROWN, R. W. A comparison of the whole, part and combination methods of learning music. *J. exp. Psychol.*, 1928, **11**, 235-247.
5. BRYAN, W. L., & HARTER, N. Studies in the psychology and physiology of the telegraphic language. *Psychol. Rev.*, 1897, **4**, 27-55.
6. CARR, H. Teaching and learning. *J. genet. Psychol.*, 1930, **37**, 189-219.
7. COX, J. W. *Mechanical aptitude.* London: Methuen, 1928.
8. GATES, A. I., & TAYLOR, G. A. The acquisition of motor control in writing by preschool children. *Teach. Coll. Rec.*, 1923, **24**.
9. GEMELLI, A. Recherches sur la nature de l'habilité manuelle. *J. de Psychol.*, 1929, **26**, 163-200.

10. GHISELLI, E. E., & BROWN, C. W. *Personnel and industrial psychology.* New York: McGraw-Hill, 1948.
11. GILBRETH, F. B. *Motion study.* New York: Van Nostrand, 1911.
12. HARRELL, T. W. A factor analysis of mechanical ability tests. *Psychometrika,* 1940, **5,** 17-33.
13. HERTZBERG, O. E. A comparative study of different methods used in teaching beginners to write. *Teach. Coll. Contr. Educ.,* Columbia Univ., 1926, No. 214.
14. HILGARD, E. R., & SMITH, M. B. Distributed practice in motor learning: score changes within and between daily sessions. *J. exp. Psychol.,* 1942, **30,** 136-146.
15. MCGEOGH, J. A. *The psychology of human learning.* New York: Longmans, Green, 1942.
16. PEAR, T. H. The nature of skill. *J. nat. Inst. indust. Psych.,* 1929, **4,** 193-202.
17. RUSSELL, J. T. Relative efficiency of relaxation and tension in performing an act of skill. *J. gen. Psychol.,* 1932, **6,** 330-343.
18. SNODDY, G. S. Evidence for a universal shock factor in learning. *J. exp. Psychol.,* 1945, **35,** 403-417.
19. WITTENBORN, J. R. Mechanical ability: its nature and measurement. *Educ. psychol. Measmt.,* 1945, **5,** 241-260, 395-409.

SELECTED READINGS

COX, J. W. *Manual skill: its organization and development.* New York: Macmillan, 1934.
MCGEOGH, J. A. *The psychology of human learning.* New York: Longmans, Green, 1942. Ch. 5.
PEAR, T. H. *Skill in work and play.* New York: Norton, 1924.
POFFENBERGER, A. T. *Principles of applied psychology.* New York: Appleton-Century, 1942. Ch. 20.
RAGSDALE, C. E. How children learn the motor types of activities. Ch. 3 in *49th Yearbook,* Nat. Soc. Study Educ., 1950.
RYAN, T. A. *Work and effort: the psychology of production.* New York: Ronald Press, 1947.

18

MEMORY

In spite of the best intentions of the educator to make mental development the primary aim of education, the traditional standards of the school, as well as the everyday demands of life require the child to "remember" special facts, events, formulas and expressions. There are many opportune times and places for remembered information and symbols, not only for their own sake, but as a prerequisite for further understanding and appreciation. This is not to be understood as a plea for the primary importance of brute memory work in school. But taking all things into consideration, including school examinations as well as cultural requirements, there is no substitute to be found in other mental operations for remembering, let us say that Columbus discovered America in 1492. To suppose that there can be any appreciable mental development without remembered facts represents as extreme a view as to hold that the first steps in education should be only rote memory work. Both show a misunderstanding of the interrelated nature of mental activities in the divorce of "memory" from the thought processes. There is, however, an economical and an uneconomical use of memory work.

Memory and Thought. Memorizing is a form of learning but it stresses highly specialized features of the learning process. Its orientation and evaluation are based on mental adjustment to the details and specific items of the learning material or content. It will not do, for example, if we are asked to recall the atomic weight of hydrogen, to say that it is somewhere around 1, or 2, or 3. We have to know just exactly what it is if we are "remembering." This is what we expect from the "memory" aspect of learning. If, however, we are "thinking" it will perhaps be satisfactory if we know that hydrogen is one of the lightest elements. This knowledge is the product of the same mental activity that enables us to say that hydrogen has an atomic weight of 1.008, but it is a more general result of the learning. We are not necessarily comparing here the products of two wholly separate mental processes. They can be related to each other as whole to part, or as pattern to detail. This relationship may not only tell us how "memory" works, but it may also enable us to understand how the higher thought processes can affect memory. Both being phases of the same learning activity, the more general features of the experience can determine the setting of the details. The child can "remember" how big "8" is when he learns how it is related to other numbers, that it is bigger than 7 but smaller than 9. A similar remark may be made about our "thinking" of a name which at first we cannot "remember." We are not dealing here with two mere juxtaposed processes when we first think the name is something like "Jordan" or "Johnson" and later recall it correctly as "Jameson." The second is the detailed completion of the first more general phase of the total act of reproduction.

Different Meanings of Memory. The term "memory" is often loosely employed to cover *retentivity, recognition, recall,* or *reproduction,* and is sometimes taken to encompass all learning. We shall limit its use here very largely to the learning of verbal or ideational symbolic material, so far at least as the processes involved in memory can be checked by the reproduction or recognition of such material. It might seem more appropriate to approach our topic through the study of *retentivity,* the characteristic of living beings by which, once having undergone an experience, they are disposed to be influenced by this fact in their future behavior or experience. But our knowledge of the organic changes producing such an effect is very meager, and we have already said enough to indicate that the narrow theory of nerve pathways and synaptic resistance is very unsatisfactory. Our common use of the term "memory trace" adds nothing to the understanding of the phenomenon. It is apparent at least, if such a thing exists, that it is a matter of dynamic organization and not merely a static, structural change in living tissue.

Remembering and forgetting are concurrent processes. The complex mental state underlying a memory performance is in part the result of previous experiences, which affect the learner in two ways: they predispose him to remember some things, and to forget others. The learning process thus involves forgetting as well as remembering. In memorizing experiments, the test of the learner's performance is a test of both learning and forgetting. For practical purposes, we make a distinction here in terminology. A curve is ordinarily called a *learning curve* when it deals mainly with the period of practice during which the responses are being acquired; it is called a *curve of retention* or forgetting when it deals mainly with the period in which the responses are disappearing. The latter is usually taken, then, after a period of lapsed time or intervening activity. The use of terminology sometimes gives the impression that learning and forgetting are independent processes. Actually, both are performance curves representing different aspects of the same mental processes. In the broad sense, both should be considered curves of learned performances. Figure 60 illustrates the continuity of the two curves.

Instead of thinking of "forgetting" and "remembering" as simple opposites, we should bear in mind that some things are remembered at the expense of other things. We also forget some things we have learned because new learning supplants them. In this special sense, learning may be a "cause" of forgetting, and forgetting may be said to facilitate learning. Memory work is very far from being a mere "stamping in" and "fading out" process.

Memory, Motivation, and Understanding. The basic principles of remembering, as well as other forms of learning, are to be found in need or motivation, integration, and precision. We tend to remember those things which are well organized for the purpose of achieving our goals, things which are seen as means to a deeply personal end. Our "memories" become imbedded or incorporated in the self, and this is why we remember them. One's ability to remember a certain kind of material is usually

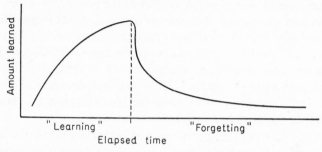

FIGURE 60. The Continuity of Learning and Forgetting. Strictly speaking, the whole curve is a learning curve. "Forgetting" is that period after practice has ceased.

found to be closely linked with his dominant interests. Ordinarily, the person who complains of difficulty in recalling simple facts, such as names or faces, may be set down as one who lacks a vital interest in other people rather than the "ability" to remember. We have a strong tendency to "rationalize" in explaining away our shortcomings, and it usually seems to us better to blame our defects upon some organic cause than upon the more personal and dynamic factors of motivation. The lack of interest or of understanding will perhaps explain many deficiencies in memory that we should like at times to attribute to chromosomes or to nerve cells. Our failure to remember the process of extracting square root, for example, may be attributed to lack of a "mathematical mind," but the more probable explanation may be that we didn't learn it very well in the first place and have little interest in it. It is easier to say "I can't" than "I won't." Hence we have, in the two factors of interest and understanding, two of the most practical suggestions for improving the "memory" and for reducing the amount of drill work in the classroom.

The Integrative Aspect of Memory. We are referring here to what is often called the "association of ideas." While there is a place perhaps in psychology for such a term, it has come to be so colored by certain theoretical overtones that it has lost much of its usefulness. We shall, instead, employ the term *integration* or organization to refer to the process by which our ideas and experiences become so ordered in our mental functioning as to lead to effective mutual reproduction. *Redintegration* is the term referring to the reinstatement or recall of a whole idea or experience upon presentation of a part of the original whole. A taste of mustard, for example, may recall a picnic. The sound of a bell may reinstate the idea of a church, school, a poem, or the story in a novel.

The effective principle of memory is that our particular ideas or experiences can be integrated or organized into larger wholes, patterns, or units. Or, stating the same thought perhaps more accurately, certain things or objects, which on some other occasion might each have its own symbolic representation in consciousness, can come to be perceived as integral parts of a larger schema. They then act on future occasions to reinstate this schema or any part feature or detail of it. It is only by virtue of this fact that one idea, by reinstating the whole unit, can suggest or recall the other. There need be no "bonds" existing between individual ideas in the sense that one, as an independent psychical entity, becomes annexed or externally connected with another independent and unitary idea. They become organically and dynamically connected like the root and leaf of a tree, and for the same reason: they form parts of a larger functioning whole. And they are *reproduced* in consciousness, in a certain order or connection, in the same way that the leaf and root are connectedly *produced*—as features of a larger inclusive system. Whether we try to be specific about the nature of these larger units or whether we designate them, in a tentative fashion, as forms of "belongingness," there cannot be much doubt of their importance. We always remember experiences as patterns, or as members of patterns. Our experience gets organized into relations or meanings, so that the apparent "fragments" of experience subsist in memory, and are recalled, as parts of wholes.

Patterns of Integration

What is the nature of these larger wholes or patterns of organization? Although there can be as many of these as there are fundamental relationships in which things may stand to one another and be apprehended, it will be convenient to speak of a few significant kinds.

Wholes of Instrumentality. Why should "knife" suggest "fork," "needle" suggest "thread," "pencil" suggest "paper," and so on? It is because these ideas represent objects that operate together in reality as wholes of instrumentality to satisfy various needs of ours. And it is simply because we originally apprehended them as serviceable in *pairs,* as complementary units of reality so far as our wants are concerned, that each, in its mental representation, is subsumed under one general pattern of eating, sewing, writing.

It is often said that such instances of our association of ideas may be explained by the principle of "contiguity in space." But this can scarcely be the psychological reason why the ideas are associated. As a principle, it speaks merely of a condition of the outside world, which of course must be realized before any of these pairs can ever function as instrumental wholes. If a fork were never seen in proximity to a knife, if a needle and thread never happened to be in the same room at the same time, then there would of course never be any association of the corresponding ideas, simply because they could never be employed by a person as complementary instruments. While spatial or temporal contiguity is a necessary condition of reality for the association of many ideas, it is hardly a psychological principle at all. That it should be so often violated, moreover, is added proof that it is not a basic principle of mental operation. We do not usually find that "knife" suggests "chair," nor does "pencil" suggest "light," or "mud" suggest "tree," although these may have been experienced together ever so often. They may have been contiguous in time or space, but this does not of itself lead to the association of the corresponding ideas, simply because they do not find their place in any convenient patterns of experience. They do not form meaningful wholes.

⌊The whole of instrumentality is a very important organizing unit of mental development. The merit of "learning by doing," particularly as applied to younger children, is based upon the fact that the personal activity in employing the instruments of education serves to organize these in relation to the vital interests of the individual. They are then remembered in association because they were *used* in association and with reference to some need. ⌋

Logical Wholes. These subsuming wholes or patterns of experiences are based upon what are ordinarily called logical relationships, such as similarity, contrast, cause, and effect. "Lion" may suggest "tiger," "black" suggest "white," "sun" suggest "light," because each of these pairs represents a logical whole or general pattern of experience into which each of the members fits as a feature or detail.

It is not sufficient, if we wish to bring about such an organization of experience, that things actually be similar, contrasting, or one the cause of the other. They must be apprehended as such, at least in a vague way, before they can be integrated into a subsuming thought pattern. This should explain why the child's "associations" are much fewer in number than those of the adult. The subtle relationships forming the basis of the more mature organizations are understood only with difficulty and rather slowly throughout the process of education. The adult's greater facility in memorizing or remembering is due to his superior ability in apprehending relationships existing between things and in integrating the facts in accord with these patterns. Understanding—the understanding of relations—is the second key to efficient memorizing and good memory ability.

If we regard the extensive knowledge of the expert as the single accomplishment of some separate "memory" power, it will indeed be a source of wonder "that one small head can carry all he knows." There would undoubtedly be a "strain" on "memory" if all information had to be retained as isolated facts. But the expert himself probably feels very little strain on his retentive capacity and as a general thing actually does much less real memorizing than the novice. He has systems of knowl edge, generic classifications, principles, and insights which enable him to organize his experiences into larger and more comprehensive wholes. Witness, for example, the greater ease of remembering the facts of chemistry after we are introduced to the periodic table, or the contribution of the Mendelian laws to remembering the facts of heredity.

The use of laws in particular forms of memorizing, as in spelling, is a practical example of the organizing power of relations in memory work. It may seem at first that the child who learns that "*i* comes before *e* except after *c*" is employing rather his ability to think and that this is hardly a case of memory at all. But this is a rather arbitrary distinction. There is probably no pure retentive "capacity" apart from the integrative functioning of the mind. There may be different plans and schemes of organizing experience, some of them more comprehensive and efficient, others less so, but there seems to be always an integrative aspect of memory. Practically, it is a question of whether we shall, in our memory work, stress understanding, logical relationships, schemes, and intelligible rules—the integrative plans of the more efficient sort—or whether we shall be satisfied with the less efficient and more easily disrupted patterns of learning. Memory work is not essentially different from thought, or at least should not be if memorizing is to be done efficiently. Drill work need not be arbitrarily divorced from thinking, but should emphasize as much as possible the processes of understanding and comprehension.

Whatever value a "memory system" may have, apart from increasing one's intention to remember, is usually to be found in the use of logical relationships. These relations are at times rather arbitrary but they may function on occasion with some degree of efficiency. Thus, a person can remember the number of his auto tag, 1582, by regarding it as made up of a number (8) which is the sum of the other three (1, 5, 2), and by considering the scheme, 1 2 5 8, as being slightly transformed into $1 + 5 = 8 - 2$. While relations such as these are in a way artificial, they represent a device that may be of definite assistance at times in remembering. Where possible, however, more natural relations are to be preferred.

An attempt to explain the influence of the higher thought processes on memory, while retaining at the same time the notion of mechanical bonds of association, is represented in the concept of "determining tendency." This name was applied to the mental set or attitude arising in the *"Aufgabe"* or voluntary acceptance of the task of recall. There is little doubt at the present time that "determining tendencies" or their equivalent play a very important role in reproduction. What the word "white" suggests to us will depend upon whether we are asked to give its opposite, its generic name, or the name of an object of this color. The theoretical difficulty with "determining tendency" is that it has usually been interpreted as a separate mental process acting from the outside upon the association itself. Instead, it should be regarded as the broader integrative aspect of the single act of remembering.

Temporal and Spatial Wholes. That "stars" may suggest "stripes" is due to the fact that together they represent a spatial whole, a flag. It is here that the associative principle of "contiguity in space" receives its most plausible conformation. But it is to be noted that, although continuity in space is an essential condition for the existence of a spatial whole or unit, it is really the spatial whole or pattern itself that functions so far as memory is concerned. We do not remember stars in connection with flagpole, contiguous though they may be, but in connection with the stripes with which they constitute a meaningful pattern of experience—a flag. The contiguity in space is not of itself sufficient cause for the association; the "togetherness" by which two ideas are associated is "belongingness" in a whole.

Temporal wholes are those of rhythms, melodies, acts of movement, having a time relation as their foundation. They are the kind that are often brought into play (contiguity in time) when we attempt to memorize nonsense syllables. Early experimenters in the field of memory made great use of these nonsense syllables in the hope of getting rid of meaning and logical relations, and of reducing the process to one of "pure" memory. The outcome of this was not, apparently, the isolation of a pure bond-forming capacity, but rather the restriction of the

study of memory to one narrow kind of patterning—that of a
temporal or spatial kind.

That the learning of nonsense syllables is not merely a matter
of forming bonds with repetition has become evident with more
inquiring studies of the problem.   Says Ogden:

The "meaninglessness" of a series of nonsense syllables is only relative.
Although these syllables are unrepresentative and possess fewer membership characteristics than words or commonly employed prefixes and
suffixes, they can and do enter into a variety of configurations of order
and rhythm, in appearance, utterance and sound. Indeed, it is only
when the series becomes a unified whole . . . that the series can be memorized at all.   (27)

Even nonsense syllables, it would seem, do not eliminate all
meaning, because of their greater variation in significance to
the learner.   One investigation, for example, found that there
is less likelihood of obtaining strictly equivalent lists of nonsense
syllables than when ordinary words are used (4).   Our tendency to organize, it seems, extends even to so-called meaningless
materials.   "Meanings" are introduced to the extent permitted
by the materials and the situation.

Memory for Meaningless Material. Our traditional "secondary laws of association," frequency, recency, and primacy,
seem to be particularly applicable to the memorizing of nonsense material.   Their relative importance in other kinds of
learning has not been sufficiently studied but there is reason to
believe that it would be much less.   The interpretation of their
significance is apparently to be based on the fact that they represent influences that enable the learner, through his own activity, to bring the temporal or spatial pattern to a more advanced
stage of precision or differentiation rather than that they affect
directly any connecting bonds.   The material takes order and
membership within a temporal or spatial configuration through
the organizing processes of the mind.   Repetition, recency, and
primacy are accompanied by changes in this organization as
a whole.

As might be expected of temporal patterns in particular, because of their dependence upon relatively meaningless time or

accent relations, they tend to disintegrate rather quickly. It is for this reason that they are to be considered the least economical forms of memorizing. The closer the memory work of the school approaches the memorizing of nonsense material, the less desirable it must be. We have here something of a paradox. The early experimental psychologists, hoping to contribute to the psychology of education, based their scientific study upon a form of memorizing that has very little to recommend its use in practical life, because it eliminates the most meaningful, comprehensive, and efficient patterns of organization. If, however, there are occasions when we are forced to deal with meaningless material, we may still get helpful suggestions from our knowledge of learning. Arbitrary relationships may be read into the material. Young children will often profit from having the material put in the form of a song or by accentuating its rhythmic character in some other way. It is possible also to motivate the children more strongly, though this is usually more difficult than with meaningful material. The proper spacing of drill periods will also be of considerable help. These are, in a way, only means of trying to "make the best of a bad job." One is tempted to say that the economy of learning demands that children should never be asked to memorize what may be to them more or less meaningless.

Qualitative Aspects of Remembering and Forgetting. Memorizing, it has been said, is not the forming of discrete impressions or traces in the nervous system. The correlative process of forgetting is accordingly not a matter of the simple fading of these. There are qualitative changes taking place in forgetting which apply particularly to the meaningful wholes of remembered experience and which show that we both learn and forget in terms of configurations or patterns.

Experiments in memory have shown what is called a sharpening and leveling effect, which is a way of describing the internal changes that take place in the successive reproductions of visual forms over a period of time (36). An example of this effect is shown in Figure 61. Such experiments purport to show that these changes, either in the direction of emphasis of a cer-

ain characteristic, or in the direction of a leveling down or
understatement of some feature of the figure, are all in the interest of a better, simpler, more normal perception. Most of these
changes could be understood as a trend toward *symmetry* (28).
It would seem that figures with better "forms," more sharply
delimited and more unitary, are more easily and more accu-
ately remembered.

In other words, a person introduces meanings into what he
perceives, and his memory of the perception is a process of
change which emphasizes the meaning. This explains why a
person's memory of an event is often (characteristically so)
distorted and unreliable. The mental process represents an

FIGURE 61. The Reproduction of Memory Figures (Wulf). The figures
the left were the originals, those at the right as these were later reproduced
om memory. The latter show an accentuation of some important feature
the originals, such as angularity or curvilinearity. (From G. W. Hart-
ann, *Gestalt psychology,* Ronald Press, 1935.)

ccentuation or sharpening of those details which are in accord
ith the perceived meaning, and a leveling (or even forgetting)
f these details which are not related to the meaning. Figure 62
ows another case in point. The first drawing in the series
an Egyptian "mulak," a conventionalized art form represent-
g an owl in Egyptian culture, which may have been the basis
f the form of our letter M. A subject studied this drawing, and
as later asked to reproduce it. R1 is his reproduction. An-
her person studied this, and later reproduced R2. A third
produced R3 from his memory of R2, and so on. Careful
xamination of these will show that the successive elaboration
f details follows the perception of the whole. "As a whole
gure was gradually being transformed, certain relatively dis-

connected material was elaborated into some characteristic nat
urally belonging to the new setting" (3). Similar change
occur in the transmission of verbal materials. The processe
involved in remembering and forgetting are in a way dramati
ones, for they delight in contrast, in accentuation, in levelin

FIGURE 62. Changes and Elaborations in the Serial Reproduction
Drawings. Each person in the series draws from memory the reproduction
his predecessor. The unusual Mulak figure becomes elaborated into a fa
liar whole, which progressively becomes simplified and conventionaliz
(From F. C. Bartlett, 3, pp. 180-181.)

and elevating, all to the purpose apparently of emphasizing t
apprehended meaning of the event. Witness the drama
changes taking place in a rumor as it travels through a co
munity (1). These are but exaggerations of the type of chang
taking place within each memory over a lapse of time.

Memory, in the sense of a mere retention of static trac
subject to this or that extraneous influence, does not exist. I
periences are remembered as wholes or patterns, and these p

terns or configurations change over a period of time in accordance with the principle of precision. They tend to become more simple, more balanced, more straightforward, and reduced, as it were, to an "ideal" configuration or pattern.

Memory as a Reorganization Process. The qualitative changes or "distortions" in the original experience, which have been found typical of remembering and forgetting, are illustrations of the general principle of organization in learning. Although earlier work was interpreted as supporting the Gestalt view of a "memory trace" that made progressive changes according to the Gestalt laws of perceptual organization, some recent work (11) challenges this assumption. There is, however, a good deal of experimental evidence to support Bartlett's conclusion that memory is "an active reorganization of past reactions and past experiences which is constantly changing" (3), and that the qualitative changes are determined by the individual's experience, attitudes, and expectations. The original perception, as Postman puts it (29), is organized as a "hypothesis" according to "expectancies or predispositions of the organism which serve to select, organize, and transform the stimulus information that comes from the environment." This is another way of saying that the individual interprets the original experiences according to his needs or preconceptions. Once organized in a meaningful *schema* of pattern, the original experience later goes through a process of "reconstruction." That is, the individual later remembers (or even invents) details that fit the schema, and forgets or eliminates the incongruent details.

Memory is then subject to important social influences. What a person remembers or forgets is related to his cultural background, his group memberships, and other factors. Several experiments have shown that changes in memory are related to the individual's social and political attitudes (6, 19). Not only does a person tend to reconstruct his experiences according to consistent attitudes, but some evidence suggests that when anxiety is aroused by the original experience, the reconstruction takes the form of an attitude that reduces the anxiety (14).

Changes of this kind may, from the standpoint of accuracy, be regarded as "errors" in memory, but they are similar to the errors that characterize many perceptual illusions. They indicate the normal functioning of the mind and not an unnatural one, or one due to influences altogether extrinsic to "memory." Since memory is a process of active reconstruction of percepts, we should expect the changes to be in accord with the general principles of perception and motivation. "Distortions" or "errors" in memory, then, are not extraneous to the learning process, but a lawful and essential aspect of it.

All these facts emphasize the importance of the integrative pattern in the original memorization, for it is this pattern or configuration that will determine the nature of the remembered details. If it is not sufficiently comprehensive, meaningful, or adequate, the qualitative changes of forgetting will probably bring a very great distortion of both figure and details. The school children who memorize poetry, for instance, as a mere temporal sequence of sounds and without understanding may reasonably be expected to recall later on in life only rather absurd "snatches" of the original.

The same principle is illustrated in our forgetting of the more or less irrelevant details of an event. As a rule they add very little or nothing to the experience in its broad outlines, and so are the first to disappear in forgetting. When we come later to recall the original happening, we shall probably find ourselves filling in the details in a fashion unwarranted by the original facts but in line with logical coherency and balanced form.

While emphasizing the distortion or errors in detail produced by the memory process, we must not neglect the good points. This tendency is an aid to learning, as well as a hindrance. Is it not of greater advantage in the long run that we should remember the meaningful patterns of experience than that we should recall merely the detailed impressions of particular things? The person who says that he has forgotten all the history he ever knew may not remember how many ships Columbus had, just where he touched America, or even his name or the year of the discovery. But if he can say that "long ago some one sailed from Europe westward and after reaching a new continent, returned with his report to change the geographical opinions of the world," he really remembers the meaningful whole that history has given him. Though he may not be able to pass a college entrance examination in the subject, he has most certainly not "forgotten all the history he ever knew." When the original learning makes use of the more meaningful plans of organization, the broad significance of these will tend to remain with the individual, to influence his attitudes, appreciations, and organizations of future knowledge, long after the details of fact and experience have slipped away. "Undifferentiated wholes are the first in the genesis of experience. They are the last in the disappearance of experience" (34).

THE RATE OF FORGETTING

The amount of material "retained" over a period of time, or the rate of forgetting it, depends on many factors. Since experimentally retention or forgetting is a measure of performance, memory may be said to have a quantitative aspect. The amount saved or lost is expressed in curves. The shape of the curve we get from experiments in memorizing depends on the kind of material learned, how it was learned, and on the way retention is measured.

The Ebbinghaus Curve of Forgetting. The German psychologist Ebbinghaus did the first experimental investigation of memory in 1885. This well deserves the title of "classic," since it set the pattern for later experiments. It may even be considered the first experiment in educational psychology, since Ebbinghaus intended that his work would serve the cause of education. He summarized a number of sets of nonsense syllables, and after letting a certain amount of time elapse, sometimes hours, sometimes days, undertook to memorize them again. By recording the number of repetitions required for relearning after the lapse of different time intervals, Ebbinghaus was able to construct a "curve of forgetting" which is reproduced in Figure 63. This curve indicated a very rapid loss in the first few hours of the first day and thereafter a gradual tapering off.

The rapid fall in Ebbinghaus' curve was due partly to his manner of measuring retention. This, now widely called the *saving* method, receives its name from the percentage of time or repetitions "saved" in the relearning trials when compared with the original learning. Other methods of measuring retention often give different quantitative results.

Some Methods of Measuring Retention. An old (1922) experiment by Luh compared the effect of various kinds of retention tests on the shape of the curves obtained (20). Up to this time, it had been too often assumed that the Ebbinghaus

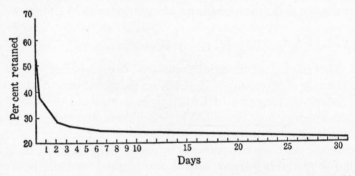

FIGURE 63. The Ebbinghaus Curve of Forgetting for Nonsense Syllables (After Ebbinghaus, *Memory,* Bur. Publ., Teachers College, Columbia Univ.

curve was *the* curve of forgetting. Luh found that the rate of forgetting nonsense syllables depends on what we mean by forgetting, or how we measure it. This has some important implications for study methods. After a sequence of twelve syllables had been learned in special order, the subjects were given five different kinds of retention tests at various intervals.

1. The *anticipation recall* test, in which the person was given a syllable and had to recall or "anticipate" the next one in the series.
2. The *relearning* test, or *saving* method, in which the number of trials necessary to relearn the sequence to perfection was a savings index. This is comparable to the method employed by Ebbinghaus.

3. The written *reproduction* test, which required the person to write out, with pencil and paper, the list originally learned. Here he had to recall not just the next syllable in the list, but the whole list.

4. The *recognition* test, in which the person was given a list of 24 syllables and had to identify or recognize among these the original twelve.

5. A *reconstruction* test, in which he was given the original twelve syllables printed on separate cards and was asked to reconstruct the original sequence, or rearrange the cards in the correct order.

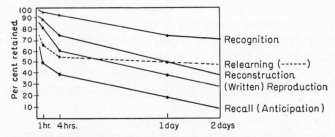

FIGURE 64. Variation in Curves of Forgetting Due to Methods of Measuring Retention. (Adapted from C. W. Luh, The conditions of retention, *Psychol. Monogr.*, 1922, **31**, No. 3.)

We will note here that the different tests give the same kind of quantitative result, that is, the "per cent retained." The quantitative results are therefore comparable. However, the different tests differ qualitatively, in the sense that they require different kinds of organization on the part of the learner. Figure 64 shows the differences in amount retained, as measured by the various tests, at various intervals of a retention period of two days. This is of experimental interest, since the rank orders of the "per cent retained" changes with time; that is, the relearning test ranks fourth after 1 and 4 hours, but at the end of two days ranks second, and actually indicates a 50 per cent "saving" at that time by comparison with the reproduction test which shows less than 30 per cent saved.

Of perhaps greater importance, for our purpose, is the difference in retention as shown by the two recall tests (reproduction and anticipation) and the recognition test. The ability to recognize or identify what one has learned does not "fade" as rapidly as the ability to recall what is learned. This is a matter of common knowledge, since we know that it is easier to recognize a face than it is to recall the name of its owner, and easier to identify his name from a list than to recall the name from cues provided by memory alone.

Implications for Study Methods. The reader will recognize the similarity of these simple memory tests to various kinds of examinations given in school. The essay type of examination emphasizes recall, as in "List and explain the eight causes of the Civil War." The completion or "short answer" type of question demands recall, but often gives additional cues. So does the typical "matching" test. Some objective tests provide more cues and enable the student to get many items right through recognition. (The better objective tests emphasize not only the ability to recall, but knowledge of meaningful relations.)

Basically, studying in order to pass a test is a matter of rehearsing the responses to be made on the test in the form in which the student is expected to make them. Some students study for recognition, not for recall. They do not test themselves by a method that requires recall, and therefore their learning stands the test of recognition only. Indeed, some students (even in college) do not employ self-recitation at all. The one who says "I thought I knew this material, but I just blew up on the test" is ordinarily one who studied for recognition, not for recall.

Recall or reproduction requires the "verbatim" type of response, with or without the assistance of specific cues. With its emphasis on exact detail, the ability to recall material usually shows the greatest amount of loss with time. Students are often vaguely aware of this, and attempt to "restore" their knowledge by ordinary reading and rereading. One experiment showed that simple rereading, even in one sitting, did not raise the recall or comprehension of the average reader very much (7).

Lest we seem to be emphasizing the recall of rote-type learning as the purpose of study, it may be well to remark here that the purpose of study is always comprehension, and that meaningful materials are more easily learned and remembered. The experiments in nonsense syllables, like the one just discussed, are important in showing that there are different kinds of memory performances, not just pure "retentive capacity."

SOME CONTROLLING FACTORS IN MEMORY

The rates of forgetting are influenced by (1) factors in the learning situation or the materials and (2) factors related to the learner's motivation and activity. These factors influence remembering and forgetting through the effect they have on the perceptual organization of the learner.

Meaningful vs. Meaningless Material. Practically all experiments which employ meaningful material show that retention is much better in this case than when nonsense syllables are used. The superiority is even greater when the content is found to be interesting as well. While the disruptive effects of forgetting are probably greater in all cases than we might wish ideally to be the case, they are much greater in proportion to the amount of effort originally expended when the memory work is of the purely rote type.

An interesting study by English and others (7) compares longtime retention for the meaning of a passage read with retention of the exact wording of the same selection. The subjects of the experiment were required to identify a statement as being contained, or as not being contained, in the original passage, first when this was expressed in the exact terms of the original, and second, when the meaning was the same but expressed in very different phraseology. The ability to recognize verbatim statements was found to suffer considerably after two or more days and to show a continuous downward trend with the lapse of further time. Recognition of the paraphrase of the original continued good for periods up to seventy days, with very little decline in the meantime. The authors of the study believe that this kind of "substance learning" shows such marked superiority in retention that we must consider it almost a different process from that involved in the learning of nonsense material and specific items.

A series of significant studies by Katona compared rote memorizing and learning by understanding (16). The materials employed in the experiment were matchstick problems such as that illustrated in Figure 65. The author compared the ability

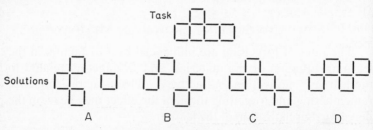

FIGURE 65. An Illustration of Katona's Matchstick Problems. The problem is to make four squares, instead of the five given in the task, by moving three matches. All of the original matches must be used in the solution. (From Katona, 16.)

to retain problem solutions in two groups which had different kinds of practice. One group learned by memorizing; it was shown the same problem in rotated form a number of times, but with the same solution each time. A second group was given practice on a number of examples, i.e., different problems each time; each solution involved the same principle, but the principle was not explained. Successive tests of four problems were then given to both groups, one immediately after practice and one four weeks later. The same tests were also given to a control group, which had no practice. Each test contained one problem familiar to the rote-memory group, but none familiar to the group given varied experience on examples. The rote-memory group did slightly better than the control group on tests, but after all they had seen one problem earlier. The group given practice on examples clearly outclassed the others on both the immediate test and the retest four weeks later.

The conclusions and implications of this and other experiments are of great import for educational psychology: (1) The solution of a problem achieved through the discovery of a general principle does not "fade" like material memorized by rote, but is retained for a long time with little loss. (2) Learning with understanding not only improves retention, but makes the learner more ready for new learning. (3) Rote memory sometimes restricts, rather than widens, the range of problems that can be solved. It is important to note that it was the learning situation itself here, and not any difference in verbal instruction, that made learning with understanding possible in one instance, and reduced its possibility in the other. That is, the varied experience of the group practiced on examples made some degree of insight possible. This was not complete insight, because reports from the subject showed that they could not state the principle clearly. But it was clear enough, apparently, for them to vary their attack, try alternatives, and solve new problems. Furthermore, the insight was not forgotten.

The important difference in these two kinds of learning, according to the author, is the degree of organization on the part of the learner. This gives empirical substance to the statement made long ago by William James, who pointed out that "associations" and "hooks" are in reality *systematic relations:*

In mental terms, the more other facts a fact is associated with in the mind, the better possession of it our memory retains. Each of its associates becomes a hook to which it hangs, a means to fish it up by when sunk beneath the surface. . . . But this forming of associations with a fact, what is it but *thinking about* the fact as much as possible? Briefly, then, of two men with the same outward experiences and the same amount of mere native tenacity, the one who *thinks* over his experiences most, and weaves them into systematic relations with each other, will be the one with the best memory. (15)

Whole and Part Learning. Beside the general principles discussed when this question arose in connection with the learning of skills, there are a few points that we may appropriately make concerning the memorization of verbal material.

Memorizing by wholes is in general superior to memorizing by parts, and for the following reasons:

1. Learning by the whole method makes use of the natural unity of the material to be memorized. The meaning of the details can often be seen only when the material is apprehended

as a whole. We may expect this to be important in both the organization and the future reproduction of these details. What is there, for example, in the first stanza of Longfellow's poem that would give the reason for the "strange device" on the Alpine youth's banner, "Excelsior"? This must come from the story as a whole.

2. Memorizing material as a whole anticipates the way are usually called upon to reproduce. When a poem is first artificially broken up into small units and these learned separately, there is the added task of then putting them together to re-form the whole. The result often resembles a series of bridges, with all of them useless when any one becomes so. The person who learns his material as a unit can often "improvise," substituting here or there for a word, line, or even stanza that may have escaped him. The builder of memorial "bridges" is usually not so adept.

3. Memorizing material as a whole leads to a more facile reconstruction of the story or ideas running through it. After all, is not this really the important thing that we should carry away from our memorizing? To remember the story of Ozymandias, "king of kings," and his broken statue on the "lone and level sands," seems more important than any single line of the sonnet. The single lines, moreover, very often suggest themselves in the light of the story. It might be said that, apart from the question of economy of time and effort in memorizing, stress laid upon the material as a whole seems more consonant with the general aim of memory work.

Some practical *qualifications,* however, of the general statement above should be noted:

1. The more meaningless the material, the less the advantage of the whole method.

2. The greater the difficulty of comprehending the material as a whole, the less the advantage of the whole method.

3. The "whole" or unit of memorization suitable for one person may not be suitable for another, it may be appropriate to a child of one age but not to a younger child. The ideal "whole" of memorization becomes in practice a matter of the

maturity of comprehension of the learner. Those of low intelligence cannot be expected to grasp as large or as complicated a "whole" as the more intelligent. This means that material must sometimes be broken up to fit the mental maturity of the learner, but into units corresponding to the upper limit of his comprehension.

4. If the material is beyond the comprehension of the learner, it is probably inadvisable to employ the whole method. But is is probably inadvisable to ask a child to memorize such material by any method.

5. Young children may more easily become discouraged in trying to memorize long selections, because they look for immediate results from their efforts. The advantage of the whole method is not usually apparent in the first stages of the learning. A proper selection of material would probably go far toward obviating this difficulty without forcing us to give up the advantages of the whole method.

6. The more difficult sections of the material being learned as a whole may be given special attention. This does not mean that we must always separate them from their content and give them extra practice. We may derive much profit from such devices as having them marked out beforehand as difficult, going more slowly over these parts, and stopping at the end of each section and rehearsing it mentally. In so doing the difficult parts may still retain their integral connection with the rest.

The advantage of the whole method is most conspicuous in longtime retention, or "delayed recall." When the time for learning is very short, and the need for some tangible result is urgent, the part method seems superior. The characteristics of the learner is also a factor influencing the relative effectiveness of whole and part methods. Whole methods favor the more intelligent learners, and those of greater chronological age. In other words, the difference in effectiveness between whole vs. part methods is greater with brighter and older subjects (23). This would imply that the whole method is more likely to be superior with increasingly higher levels of mental development.

The Effect of Overlearning. When we carry the memorizing of nonsense syllables to a point beyond that required for immediate errorless reproduction, by doubling or trebling the normal number of repetitions, this extra practice is called "overlearning." Overlearning makes forgetting take place at a slower rate. This result was apparent in the earlier investigations of memory and later studies (18) have confirmed it.

The general effect of overlearning is found to hold with meaningful material also. Studies of the retention of school material such as history show that the rate of forgetting is less

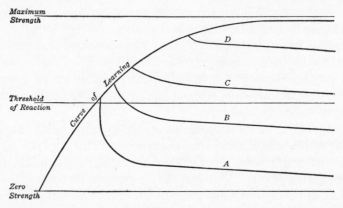

FIGURE 66. The Effect of Overlearning on Rate of Forgetting. With the minimal amount of practice required for immediate reproduction, forgetting is likely to be rapid and extensive after the learning period. When practice is carried beyond this, indicated by higher points on the "curve of learning," forgetting is likely to be less rapid and of smaller amount. This is indicated by the more gradual decline of the upper curves to the right. (From A. I. Gates, *Psychology for students of education,* 1930, by permission of The Macmillan Co.)

for items more easily recalled in the beginning than for those about which the children were originally less sure. The influence of overlearning in retarding the rate of forgetting has given rise to a set of hypothetical curves, shown in Figure 66, indicating the probable relation of the amount of overlearning to rate of forgetting. These curves stress the importance of efficient learning if we would reduce the deleterious effects of time. Any way of improving the original learning will be of advantage here. More thorough understanding of the task, a keener interest in it, and better methods of work are means of bringing about "overlearning." Overlearning is not to be interpreted as "excessive drill." Drill is one of the means of producing over-learning, but unless it is well motivated, mere repetition will produce relatively little effect. It may actually produce a detrimental effect in arousing an attitude of monotony and of distaste for the material itself. Instead of depending on the effectiveness of repetition alone, better results are usually obtained by varying the presentation of the material, by introducing it in new settings, by linking it with definite social and individual interests, and by making use of it in practical situations.

Excessive drill may actually bring about a disruption in the unified pattern, breaking it up into irrelevant details. Parts may lose their proper relation to the whole, resulting in loss of meaning. We have all perhaps noticed the strange character assumed by individual words in a sentence repeated over and over. The word begins to lose its subordinate place in the meaningful whole and develops features peculiar to itself as an isolated sound. The same thing may happen when we review the spelling of a word we have just written. The longer we look at it, the more doubtful we become. It is for a similar reason that recent methods of teaching spelling present words in a context paralleling their actual use. The child who can spell words in lists may often be found to misspell them in his composition.

The Influence of Speed of Original Learning. It has been found that the quick learners are in general the best remem-berers (23). This has been thought by some to cast reflection on the relative importance of frequency and repetition in the association of ideas, for here we have a person repeating a thing less often and yet remembering it longer. The suggestion has been offered that the whole thing is to be set down to differences existing between individuals in the inherent "plasticity" of the nervous system in forming bonds or synaptic connections. There are perhaps more distinctly psychological reasons. In looking a little more deeply into the results of experiments we find what is probably the immediate cause of this relation between facility in memorizing, and tenacity of retention. It can be a matter of the superior methods and the more meaningful integrations that the quick learner employs, a fact accounting not only for the original speed of memorizing but also for the later ease of reproduction.

Lyon (21) found that, of the different kinds of material employed by him in his memory experiments, poetry, prose, nonsense syllables, words and digits, it was particularly in memorizing the less meaningful material, such as digits and nonsense syllables, that the "quick-learners" were least superior, and from some points of view they were actually poorer than the slow learners in retention. In other words, in pure rote memory, or in memorization built upon spatial or temporal patterns, there is less opportunity for the quick learner to bring into play his superior organizing methods. The material is not of itself suited to the more comprehensive plan of integration.

We might expect the faster learners to remember longer, in any case, because the rate of original learning itself requires organization. Learning and retention are continuous processes. The organizing activity that permits faster learning also permits longer retention. The results of experiments merely show that an intervening period of time between the test of original learning and the test of retention does not change this relationship. The major implication to be drawn is that the slower learner does not learn any better just because he is slower. The quick learner is certainly not any worse a learner because of his speed. It is the degree of organization, rather than the time spent in learning, which is the controlling factor in remembering and forgetting.

The fact that intelligence tests are usually successful in selecting the quick learners points in the same direction (10). The more intelligent, being quicker in gaining insight into meanings and relationships, make use of these in organizing their remembered experiences. Intelligence represents a double axe so far as memory is concerned. It furnishes comprehensive schemes or patterns for facilitating the original learning, and this is reflected in turn in better retention. The better the original integration the better the memory.

Retroactive Inhibition. As popular opinion sees it, forgetting occurs through a passive kind of disuse: impressions get traced in the "mind" like chalk marks on the sidewalk, and time causes them to fade away just as the chalk fades from the sidewalk. A correction to this notion is furnished by the experiments in retroactive inhibition. This principle has both theoretical and practical significance. It refers to the fact that when we undertake a second memory task closely following upon another, our ability to recall the details of the first will in general be detrimentally affected. The evidence is that forgetting is not a simple fading with time, but is much affected by the intervening activity.

Experiments in retroactive inhibition show that it is influenced by a number of conditions (31, 23). Some of these are seen to have very practical significance in mental work. (1) If the intervening activity follows immediately upon the original study period, the "interference" effect is greater than if some time elapses before the intervening activity is begun. Relaxation after a learning period is more helpful than immediate engagement in some other mental work. There is much to be said for the common observation that it pays to let a thing "sink in" before turning to something else. (2) Thoroughly learned material is less subject to the "interference" effect than slightly learned material. It pays to overlearn. (3) The more effort or attention required by the intervening task, the greater the memory loss through retroactive inhibition. Easy tasks have less "interference" effect on the original learning than difficult tasks. (4) When the learner is fatigued, the intervening task has a greater retroactive effect than when he is "mentally fresh." A rest period immediately after the original learning appears to favor retention (13). (5) Materials that are interesting or pleasurable to the learner are less subject to retroactive inhibition than neutral ones. The learner's feeling tone is important here. Pleasurable learning appears to resist the "interference" effect of subsequent tasks. (6) Meaningful materials are also less subject to retroactive inhibition than meaningless or senseless materials that are more difficult to organize. (7) If the intervening task is similar to the original learning task, the retroactive inhibition is greater than if the intervening task is quite dissimilar. To reduce forgetting due to intervening activity, it is best to turn to some activity as different as possible from the preceding mental work.

The experiment of Gibson (9) illustrates the importance of task similarity not only on retention, but also in transfer of learning. She had various groups learn a list of names for certain figures, and then gave interpolated practice in learning different lists. This was arranged so that the *degree* of dissimilarity between the interpolated and original material varied from group to group. A recall test of the first list was then given to all subjects. The amount of recall was found to vary inversely with the amount of generalization from task to task; that is, learning a new set of names for *similar* figures disrupted the original learning more than learning a new set of names for *dissimilar* figures. A control group, with no interpolated learning, had of course the best recall. The disrupting effect of the interpolated learning, and the consequent handicap in recall, may be considered *negative transfer*.

The negative transfer, or retroactive inhibition, was seen to be related to the degree of task organization possible. Learning a new or competing set of responses to the *same* figures disrupted the original organization. On the other hand, the individual who learned a new set of names for *dissimilar* figures was able, so to speak, to keep the names differentiated as well as the figures. The dissimilarity of the figures helped him to do so, and thus helped him to keep the original organization intact. The individual who learned different names to similar figures suffered more disruption in the original learning because confusion of figures was a factor in confusing the two sets of names. Melton (24) has shown that the retroactive inhibition is due to two kinds of disorganizing factors: (1) the "unlearning" of the original task which goes on while the second (interpolated) task is being learned, as well as (2) the competition between the original and the interpolated responses during the recall.[1]

[1] The evidence for the "unlearning" factor is that learning the original task tends to slow up the rate of learning the second. This is called *proactive inhibition*. If the interpolated task is later recalled better than the original,

The experimental results, on the whole, appear to be consistent with a theory of retroactive inhibition (or theory of "forgetting") which Hilgard has stated as follows:

Processes with a low degree of internal organization are more susceptible to retroactive inhibition than processes with a high degree of internal organization; and processes with a given degree of organization are interfered with more by interpolated processes with a low degree of organization than by processes with a high degree of organization. (12, p. 169)

Retroactive inhibition seems to point to the fact that all phases of the dynamic process underlying learning are not finished with the end of the period of memorizing. New forms of mental activity interfere in some manner with their going on to completion. With a minimum of mental activity following the learning, as in sleep (33), retention can be better than when the intervening period is filled with waking activities. These facts suggest that forgetting may be the result of interfering mental processes, rather than an outcome of simple fading. The fact that recognition-memory is only very slightly disturbed by an interference of this kind points to the more highly differentiated or detailed features of the learning activity as being most subject to retroactive inhibition. That the more similar interpolated material produces the greater retroactive effect tends to confirm this, for "similarity" is ordinarily taken to refer to the detailed nature of the content.

Interference in the life of interests or motives may also be reflected in poor retention. This is what happens when we grow up or draw away from our childhood associations. We often find that the ability to recall the details of names or places or events is not wholly lost, however, for they may come back to us, if we put ourselves in a certain "frame of mind" reminiscent perhaps of earlier interests. The development of divergent interests is a setting for "retroactive inhibition." On the other hand, the events of our past life may be kept alive, even though we do not refresh our memory through actual recall, through their relation with the active motives of our present life. For-

t must be because the recall of the latter is disrupted by something new ("unlearning") rather than by the response conflict.

getting through "disuse" is very often an instance of the details being of "no use."

Spacing vs. Concentration of Practice. Experimental evidence shows in general that the spacing or distribution of practice periods over a considerable length of time is more saving of the total time and effort spent in memorizing than trying to learn all the material at one or a few sittings. The advantages of spaced learning are especially noticeable for longtime retention.

A number of reasons have been suggested at various times for the relative superiority of distributed learning. While no one of these is perhaps adequate, there are two factors which seem to be of paramount importance. The first is that spaced practice takes advantage of the "maturation" phase of all learning. Practice accomplishes more when given at a higher point on the maturation curve. That distribution is often found to be most effective during the early part of the learning would suggest this. Another reason is to be found in the sphere of motivation. Shorter practice periods may keep the learner working more intensely throughout the whole length of the learning time. Returns from the later moments of a long practice period are apparently diminished because of the concomitant decline of the "work curve." The adverse effects of fatigue are likely to enter here.

A number of conditions, however, are found to call for qualification of the principle, such as the type and difficulty of the material, the length of rest period, and the method of memorizing. While the concentrating or massing of effort seems to be relatively unfavorable to the whole method of learning, it is much less so if stress is placed on detail and immediate recall. "Cramming," in fact, seems to have a good bit in its favor if the only purpose of learning is to pass an examination. If, however, we wish to learn for longtime retention, there is apparently no satisfactory substitute for consistent, day by day work and periodic reviews.

The Value of Recitation. A number of experiments have shown that reading with recitation produces better results than reading alone, whether the material is meaningful or not. In the recitation method, the learner reads, then attempts to recite or recall without looking at it, refers back to the material for cues, and continues to combine recitation with reading in this way. Gates (8) compared the relative value of learning nonsense material and short biographies by mere reading with that of learning by reading plus reciting to oneself. School children were employed as subjects of the experiment. It was clear that to introduce recitation into the learning made for greater economy of time. There was found to be an optimal division of the learning time, somewhere around 60-80 per cent for recitation and 40-20 per cent for reading. An interesting extension of the study of this problem has to do with the stage of the learning at which it will be most profitable to introduce recitation. In general, it has been found that it is most advantageous when introduced not too early. It has been found also that recitation in one's own words, aided by personalized notes or key phrases to serve as cues for recall, is superior to verbatim recitation of the author's words (2). Underlining the words in the text is much less effective as a recitation technique, because it requires less active, personal engagement of the learner and encourages simple recognition, rather than active recall and comprehension.

The advantage of recitation lies partly in the fact that it is a very active form of repeating the material, but its effect extends beyond the actual content repeated. A second recall has often been noted as being superior to a first recall in the number of items reproduced. Apart from the possible influence of reminiscence here, it would seem that the act of recalling certain items makes recall of related items easier in the future. This is perhaps something we might expect if we tend to remember by wholes. The first recall reactivates, as it were, the original whole and this in turn gives greater ease of reproducing other details of this pattern later on. This indicates that a method of study should emphasize the main ideas, and shows the fallacy of "studying for details" rather than for organization of ideas.

Personal Aspect of Memory

What we remember of memorized material, how long we remember it, and in what form we can recall it, depends on how it is organized and integrated in the total personality. Since memory is an organizing process, it depends on the self-involvement of the learner—what he brings to the task in the way of motives and attitudes, and the extent to which these are actively engaged in the learning process. Forgetting, as well as learning, is a function of such features as attitudinal sets, interests, and emotional tone.

The Influence of Emotional Tone. Freud's theory of psychoanalysis stressed the fact that unpleasant, painful, or repugnant experiences tended to be "repressed" or forgotten and buried in the "unconscious." A number of experiments have shown the same trend in the memorization of symbolic materials, namely, that materials accompanied by favorable emotional tone are remembered more easily than unpleasant ones. Thus one of the present writers found that students who had marked occupations and activities on the Strong Vocational Interest Blank as "Like, Indifferent, Dislike" later recalled twice as many of the Like items as those marked Indifferent or Dislike. A study of adolescents' memories of preschool experiences showed a preference in memory for the pleasant experiences (5). Other experiments have shown that students remember pleasantly toned words from a list better than words emotionally regarded as unpleasant or indifferent (25, 35).

Attitudes and Sets of the Learner. The intention to learn depends on the degree to which the learner perceives the task to be related to his goals. Learning for use makes us remember better, particularly if the occasion for using our knowledge is clearly foreseen.

The influence of one's attitude toward the learning material is found also in connection with examinations. Weekly tests are superior to monthly tests so far as retentive power is concerned (17), although there is naturally a limit to which this kind of economy can be pushed. Part of this is probably due to proper spacing of study periods. A more important influence of the examination is to be found in the "examination set." Meyer (26) had his subjects prepare for three kinds of examinations, true-false and multiple choice (recognition set), completion ("recall set"), and the essay type ("recall plus organization"). In spite of the fact that his three groups spent the same amount of time studying the material, an historical account of the Civil War, the "recall set" groups were superior to those who studied for the true-false and multiple choice tests. This was even more conspicuous in delayed memory when the "recognition set" students were found actually to be inferior even in recognition tests (true-false and multiple choice), the kind for which they had originally prepared themselves. The author concludes that it is uneconomical to employ a "recognition set" in studying when, with the expenditure of the same amount of time, a "recall set" produces better all-round results. Greater stress is perhaps in this case laid upon the logical organization of the material.

The form of personal activity we find in review work serves, as we know, to "refresh our memory" and to retard the rate of forgetting. The early rapid decline in some curves of retention suggests that an immediate review might be very helpful. Short review tests, following closely or within a day's time of a lecture or class period, do seem in fact to improve retention to a considerable degree. Later reviews can be more widely spaced, and thus parallel the "curve of forgetting."

Study Skills. Skill in studying is not primarily a matter of rules and methods, but concerns the whole orientation of the student to his task. His motives are of primary importance; attitude plays a more vital role in studying than aptitude or method. The art of study has not as yet been formulated as applied science. However, the principles of memorizing form the basis for programs in training students how to study, and research has shown that these programs result in "increased reading ability, greater skill in organizing work, better use of educational facilities, and more satisfactory personal and social adjustment," as well as higher grades (30). Brighter students, and those with above average grades to begin with, profit most from the training.

On the assumption that study is a rehearsal of those responses the student is expected to make in examinations, methods have been devised which incorporate the principles of memorizing. One example is the *Survey Q3R Method* of study taught at Ohio State University by Professor F. P. Robinson. A brief description of the five steps of this method is given below.

THE SURVEY Q3R METHOD

The title for this new higher-level study skill is abbreviated in the current fashion to make it easier to remember and to make reference to it more simple. The symbols stand for the steps which the student follows in using the method; a description of each of these steps is given below:

SURVEY   1. *Glance over the headings in the chapter to see the few big points which will be developed.* This survey should not take more than a minute and will show the three to six core ideas around which the rest of the discussion will cluster. If the chapter has a final summary paragraph this will also list the ideas developed in the chapter. This orientation will help you organize the ideas as you read them later.

QUESTION   2. Now begin to work. *Turn the first heading into a question.* This will arouse your curiosity and so increase comprehension. It will bring to mind information already known, thus helping you to understand that section more quickly. And the question will make important points stand out while explanatory detail is recognized as such. This turning a heading into a question can be done on the instant of reading the heading, but it demands a conscious effort on the part of the reader to make this query for which he must read to find the answer.

READ   3. *Read to answer that question,* i.e., to the end of the first headed section. This is not a passive plowing along each line, but an active search for the answer.

RECITE   4. Having read the first section, look away from the book
             and try briefly to *recite the answer to your question.*
             Use your own words and name an example. If you
             can do this you know what is in the book; if you can't,
             glance over the section again. An excellent way to do
             this reciting from memory is to jot down cue phrases
             in outline form on a sheet of paper. Make these notes
             very brief!

             NOW REPEAT STEPS 2, 3, AND 4 ON EACH SUCCEEDING
             HEADED SECTION. THAT IS, TURN THE NEXT HEADING
             INTO A QUESTION, READ TO ANSWER THAT QUESTION,
             AND RECITE THE ANSWER BY JOTTING DOWN CUE
             PHRASES IN YOUR OUTLINE. READ IN THIS WAY UNTIL
             THE ENTIRE LESSON IS COMPLETED.

REVIEW   5. When the lesson has thus been read through, *look over
             your notes to get a bird's-eye view* of the points and of
             their relationship and *check your memory* as to the
             content by reciting on the major subpoints under each
             heading. This checking of memory can be done by
             covering up the notes and trying to recall the main
             points. Then expose each major point and try to recall
             the subpoints listed under it. (30, p. 28)

The method of study, in other words, is one of active, purposive reading. We note here the emphasis on the whole-part
approach, and the activation of the learner through (1) the
stress on predicting the examination questions ahead of time,
(2) the selection of *important* points, which requires discrimination and thinking, and (3) self-testing. The Survey Q3R
method is a radical departure from the passive approach of
ordinary reading. It is also strikingly different from the procedures ordinarily used by students in studying, although the
methods of better students may approximate it in some respects.

Survey Q3R may be likened, as Robinson says, to teaching
the crawl stroke to a swimmer whose skill is limited to dog-
paddling. As in swimming, the development of study skills
depends initially on grasping a scheme or model, or in other
words we must first learn what is meant by "study skills."
Further development depends on intensive practice in applying

the principles in order to gain familiarity, smoothness and precision. Development of study skills is too often left to chance in secondary schools, where it becomes extremely important preparation for college work. Guidance in studying can be, and should be, a normal function of teaching.

REFERENCES

1. ALLPORT, G. W., & POSTMAN, L. *The psychology of rumor.* New York: Holt, 1947.
2. ARNOLD, H. F. The comparative efficiency of certain study techniques in fields of history. *J. educ. Psychol.,* 1942, **33,** 449-457.
3. BARTLETT, F. C. *Remembering: a study in experimental and social psychology.* London: Cambridge Univ. Press, 1932.
4. DAVIS, F. C. The relative reliability of words and nonsense syllables as learning material. *J. exper. Psychol.,* 1930, **13,** 221-234.
5. DUDYCHA, G. J., & DUDYCHA, M. M. Adolescents' memories of preschool experiences. *J. genet. Psychol.,* 1933, **42,** 468-480.
6. EDWARDS, A. L. Political frames of reference as a factor influencing recognition. *J. abn. soc. Psychol.,* 1941, **36,** 34-50.
7. ENGLISH, H. B., WELBORN, E. L., & KILLIAN, C. D. Studies in substance memorization. *J. gen. Psychol.,* 1934, **11,** 233-260.
8. GATES, A. I. Recitation as a factor in memorizing. *Arch. Psychol.,* 1917, No. 40.
9. GIBSON, E. J. Retroactive inhibition as a function of degree of generalization between tasks. *J. exp. Psychol.,* 1941, **28,** 93-115.
10. GRANT, M. E. Some theories and experiments in the field of memory. *J. educ. Psychol.,* 1932, **23,** 511-528.
11. HEBB, D. O., & FOORD, E. N. Errors of visual recognition and the nature of the trace. *J. exp. Psychol.,* 1945, **35,** 335-348.
12. HILGARD, E. R. *Theories of learning.* New York: Appleton-Century-Crofts, 1948.
13. HOULAHAN, F. J. Immediacy of interpolation and amount of retention. *J. educ. Psychol.,* 1941, **32,** 37-44.
14. HOVLAND, C. I. Changes in attitude through communication. *J. abn. soc. Psychol.,* 1951, **46,** 424-437.
15. JAMES, W. *Psychology.* New York: Holt, 1908.
16. KATONA, G. *Organizing and memorizing.* New York: Columbia Univ. Press, 1940.
17. KEYS, N. The influence on learning and retention of weekly as opposed to monthly tests. *J. educ. Psychol.,* 1934, **25,** 227-436.
18. KRUEGER, W. F. C. Further studies in overlearning. *J. exper. Psychol.,* 1930, **13,** 152-163.

19. LEVINE, J., & MURPHY, G. The learning and forgetting of controversial material. *J. abn. soc. Psychol.,* 1943, **37,** 507-517.

20. LUH, C. W. The conditions of retention. *Psychol. Monogr.,* 1922, **31,** No. 3.

21. LYON, D. O. The relation of quickness of learning to retentiveness. *Arch. Psychol.,* 1916, No. 34.

22. MARROW, A. J. Goal tensions and recall. *J. gen. Psychol.,* 1938, **19,** 3-64.

23. McGEOGH, J. A. *The psychology of human learning.* New York: Longmans, Green, 1942.

24. MELTON, A. W., & VON LACKUM, W. J. Retroactive and proactive inhibition in retention: evidence for a two factor theory of retroactive inhibition. *Amer. J. Psychol.,* 1941, **54,** 157-173.

25. METZNER, C. A. The influence of affectivities upon learning. *J. exp. Psychol.,* 1939, **24,** 135-142.

26. MEYER, G. The effect of examination set on memory. *J. educ. Psychol.,* 1934, **25,** 641-661.

27. OGDEN, R. M. *Psychology and education.* New York: Harcourt, Brace, 1926.

28. PERKINS, F. T. Symmetry in visual recall. *Amer. J. Psychol.,* 1932, **44,** 473-490.

29. POSTMAN, L. Toward a theory of cognition. In ROHRER, J. H., & SHERIF, M., *Social psychology at the crossroads.* New York: Harper, 1951.

30. ROBINSON, F. P. *Effective study.* New York: Harper, 1946.

31. SKAGGS, E. B. *The major forms of inhibition in man.* Chicago: Univ. of Chicago Press, 1931.

32. SKAGGS, E. B., *et al.* Further studies of the reading-recitation process. *Arch. Psychol.,* 1930, No. 114.

33. VAN ORMER, E. B. Retention after intervals of sleep and waking. *Arch. Psychol.,* 1932, **21,** No. 137.

34. WHEELER, R. M., & PERKINS, F. T. *Principles of mental development.* New York: Crowell, 1932.

35. WHITE, M. M., & RATLIFF, M. M. The relation of affective tone to the learning and recall of words. *Amer. J. Psychol.,* 1934, **46,** 92-98.

36. WULF, F. Ueber die veranderung von vorstellungen. *Psychol. Forsch.,* 1922, **1,** 333-373.

SELECTED READINGS

BARTLETT, F. C. *Remembering.* New York: Macmillan, 1932.
BIRD, C., & BIRD, D. M. *Learning more by effective study.* New York: Appleton-Century-Crofts, 1945.

BROWNELL, W. A., & HENDRICKSON, G. How children learn information, concepts and generalizations. Ch. 4 in *49th Yearbook,* Nat. Soc. Study Educ., 1950.

GARRETT, H. E. *Great experiments in psychology.* (Rev. ed.) New York: Appleton-Century-Crofts, 1951. Chapter on Ebbinghaus experiments in memorizing.

KATONA, G. *Organizing and memorizing.* New York: Columbia Univ. Press, 1940.

KINGSLEY, H. L. *The nature and conditions of learning.* New York: Prentice-Hall, 1946.

MCGEOGH, J. A. *The psychology of human learning.* New York: Longmans, Green, 1942. Ch. 11.

ROBINSON, F. P. *Effective study.* New York: Harper, 1946.

19

THINKING PROCESSES

THINKING, like other forms of learning, doesn't "just happen." It occurs only under certain conditions. In fact, when we consider human behavior in general, good, hard thinking appears to be a rather rare form of behavior. This is perhaps because thinking requires effort, and perhaps because the external and internal (psychological) conditions which prompt thinking may not be too typical of ordinary human life.

All of us are familiar with "thinking" through personal experience, but we do not customarily analyze it as a mental *process*. We do not, for that matter, assign it the same universal meaning; the term is loosely used. Unfortunately, in spite of thousands of years of thought about thinking, all of the conditions for its occurrence are not understood and cannot be specified. But enough is known about the process to contribute something to the problem of teaching students to think. We shall be concerned in this chapter with the psychological nature of the thinking process, and some applications to the work of the school. What are the conditions of thinking? What factors are conducive to thinking, and what are the deterrents? What factors initiate it, and how does it manifest itself in behavior?

The Role of Thinking in Development. There are many kinds of training which can be served only by preparing the child in advance to meet situations in a rather specific manner. There are many other occasions in life, however, for which the child cannot be specifically prepared beforehand. For such situations as these he can be made ready only in a much more general manner, through the development of comprehensive insights, tendencies, and methods of approach. To make these directly applicable to the problem at hand usually calls for "thinking."

The origin of the general patterns of experience also requires thought. Thinking is a phase of the whole of development. There are not two kinds of activities, learning on the one hand and thought on the other, to account for mental growth. As a special form of learning, however, thinking has its own characteristic features. These have their basis in the fact that thought, instead of being directly concerned with the details of actions or events, as are skill and memory, deals immediately with the scheme or plan of organization which holds these details together. Whether thinking plays an important role in learning will depend upon our approach to the field of fact requiring organization. It has occasionally been suggested that from the point of view of the school, with its emphasis on the organization of factual knowledge, learning is a form of thinking. To the educator, this way of putting it may be more meaningful than the psychologist's reverse twist "thinking is a form of learning."

The child's progress in thinking is basically a matter of using previous schemes of organization in new situations. His previous patterns of experience predispose him to organize the unfamiliar situations after the manner of the old ones. But in the course of development these behavior patterns themselves undergo changes.

When we consider the contribution of training and experience to thinking, we are inclined to give first place to the particular knowledge and information helpful in solving a problem. But thinking is not generated out of factual information alone. No one thinks because he knows but because of something he does not know. The occasion for thought is a new situation dissimilar in some respect from the old. It is when we feel our knowledge to be incomplete or inadequate, when we are impelled to bridge the gap between the familiar and the new that we have a sufficient stimulus for thought. More than a vague

"intellectual curiosity" is required, if thinking is to be directed
along certain lines.

It may seem that thinking depends heavily on "memory."
If this were so, then development in thinking would consist in
the accumulation of many remembered facts or details which
could be put to work in new situations. But "memory," as we
have seen, does not work this way. The details of experience,
as we have seen, are soon forgotten, and they undergo "distortions" in accord with new schemes of organization. The details
are most easily lost through the effects of retroactive inhibition.
As "memory" fails, a greater burden is thrown on thought; that
is, on adapting old principles or schemes of organization to new
situations. As they are adapted, and are found to "work" in
new circumstances, the old schemes are themselves transformed.
They become meaningful in new ways, and more widely applicable. This is really a necessary outcome of the advance in
mental development. The more mature intellectually a person
is, the less he can depend on "memory" in the narrow sense of
the term. The significance of this in the education of the child
will be evident.

The "enrichment" of experience through education is to be
sought chiefly in the realm of thinking, because it is principally
through thought that the world of fact is itself extended. Under
the guidance of dynamic integrative tendencies new properties
and relationships appear in objects in the perceptual field. The
child who knows that the jam may be obtained only through
reaching may discover that books have a previously unrecognized property of forming a step. The pupil who has thought
about the story of the Indians will see an arrowhead where another sees only a stone. Dirt will take on a new meaning to the
child who understands the bacterial origin of disease.

Thought, apart from a few instances where immediate or
organic needs may be obstructed, always has a broad social setting, through which the individual's curiosity is directed into
particular channels. To transport "a Newton born among Aus-
tralian bushmen" to a civilized community at the age of twenty-
one would leave him still a bushman intellectually. To teach
him to read and to supply him with encyclopedic facts would

not of itself alter his status. He might be remarkably capable of solving a bushman's problems, but he would have very little interest in the problems of his adopted community. In most cases these problems would not even exist for him.

It may seem that we are dealing here with the question of interest rather than with thinking ability itself. But we cannot divorce the two in any concrete performance calling for thought. The mind is not a mere registering camera but is highly selective of the facts of experience. The school does its part toward creating selective and organizing dispositions in the child but it does this, with varying degrees of effectiveness, on a broader background of home and cultural influences.

The Setting for Thought

A Definition of Thinking. Thinking is a determined course of ideas, symbolic in character, initiated by a problem and leading to a solution.

1. *Thinking is initiated by a problem.* The problem is personal; that is, it must be experienced by the individual. He has a goal, an objective, an end in view. A problem situation arises when progress toward the goal is blocked in some way and when "available, habitual response patterns are not adequate to permit the individual to surmount the obstacle and proceed toward his objective" (19). The essential factors in a problem situation are therefore a goal, an obstacle, and inadequacy of immediate responses. These are essential conditions for thinking. Blocking or thwarting of goal-activity does not provoke thinking if an immediately available response leads to solution. A problem is essentially an incongruity between what is given (details of the situation) and what is required for solution. The need consists not only in the attainment of a goal, but the need to resolve the incongruity, to "make things fit," to organize mental processes to achieve effective solution. There is not only a need for action, but a need understand. In other words, the learner must feel a need do something, but does not know what to do, and finds that the first things that come to his mind won't fit. Hence one chara

teristic of thinking is *search;* he looks to past experience and to details of the situation for cues or meaningful relations. Without a problem, there will be no search.

2. *Thinking is symbolic in character.* Thinking is essentially a flow of abstract ideas, not a flow of muscular movements. The activity is symbolic rather than overt; the individual must "*stop* and think." Instead of running off movements, he symbolizes them with words or gestures. This may be called mental self-talking or self-instruction. We do not imply that all thought necessarily involves words or images, but that it is usually accompanied by some kind of symbols. The learner can thus act out his responses mentally, instead of actually doing them in the physical sense. This mental "acting out" may be expressed by and assisted by movements, but is independent of them. Thinking involves abstraction. When the individual "tries something" he tries it mentally, so to speak, before trying it overtly. The act is seen to fit some sort of hypothesis or concept of a solution before it is physically attempted.

3. *Ideas in the thinking process follow a determined sequence toward solution.* The thinker is not, as one psychologist [1] put it, "an ego sitting upon his throne, interpreting sense impressions at random." The course of ideas must make sense, must consist of "reasonable" relations. We recognize this as a sign of normal behavior; only deranged persons or very young children are not expected to make sense. When we say ideas must make sense, we imply some kind of determination. But this is not mechanistic determination; the thoughts are not blindly run off. We mean here that the mental activity arises from motives of the learner, and one motive is the need for making sense of the situation in terms of what is required. The ideas and "provisional tries" do not suggest themselves, but are suggested by the thinker's conceptual goal. It is this conceptual goal, or what the thinker is trying to achieve, that determines the persistent "carry through" that is characteristic of creative thinking.

The only kind of situation that will induce thinking is a problem situation. However, the setting for thought also includes

[1] Martin Scheerer.

aspects of readiness in the individual. Whether he thinks or not, when faced with a problem conducive to thought, depends on various internal conditions or "sets." Also, the kind of "thinking" he does is a result of these many aspects of readiness. One person may simply give up or withdraw from the problem situation, and is said to "lose interest." Another may "blow up" emotionally due to the frustrating circumstances. A third may wait expectantly for someone else to give him the solution —the result of a learned tendency to expect others to solve problems for him.

There are different kinds of "thinking," or at least different kinds of mental processes commonly described as such. Some thinking is said to be "logical," because the problem-solver searches for facts, causal explanations, or logical relations. There are also modes of thinking which are highly egocentric or "autistic," with ideas springing from emotional attitudes, prejudices, or feelings of being threatened. We commonly speak of some persons as being rigid, as having "closed minds," or "logic-tight compartments." We recognize others as ready to modify their ways of looking at problems, to accept new ideas, to shift gears in their thinking.

Goal Activity. The energy necessary for reorganizing the material of thought arises basically in the internal stress associated with a personal need or motive. There is an important difference in the stress leading to ordinary overt behavior on the one hand and that leading to thinking on the other. It must have what Thurstone (20) called less "urgency" in the second case. This urgency is a matter of the remoteness of the goal. The impulse to get out of a burning building, for example, is less conducive to thought than a more remote benefit. "This leads us to the peculiar but undoubtedly correct conclusion that if the urgency of a situation is reduced to a minimum, we can readily show our best intelligence about it." The transfer from action to thought brings about a shift in accent from the goal itself to the means of attaining it. Instead of being the dominant feature of the behavior pattern the goal-idea is born rather as a guiding influence.

Wertheimer makes the same point about problem solving. "In a sense," he says, "a subject may become virtually blind if he looks only at that goal, and is entirely governed by the urge toward *it*. Often he must first forget what he happens to wish before he can become susceptible to what the situation itself requires" (21). Many of our compulsive and ineffective attempts to solve our problems are in this sense "goal-blinded" responses. A strong goal-drive impels us to follow the shortest, most direct, and therefore the most familiar path to the goal. Reorganization usually involves an attempt to arrive at a fundamentally unfamiliar view of the situation. This transition is difficult and, as Wertheimer says, "is one of the great moments in many genuine thought processes."

A concern with immediate goals thus initiates activity, but overconcern with one's goals prevents the transition from blind activity to the self-detached, objective frame of mind required in creative thinking. Genuine thinkers like Edison and Einstein, says Wertheimer, characteristically forget themselves in thinking. This does not imply that their activity is unmotivated; rather, the need to attain immediate and useful goals is replaced by a larger and more inclusive need to solve the problem in terms of its own intrinsic requirements. The urge to *do* something must first be controlled. We must *stop* and think.

In the school, an excessive concern with "getting the right answer" may be a real deterrent to insight and understanding. Not only is this emphasis more likely to produce goal-blinded responses, but it sets the goal as one of satisfying the teacher rather than learning to think and solve problems.

Activity as a Deterrent to Thought. A certain natural opposition therefore exists between action and reflection. Action prevents reflective thought. Thinking is in a way a kind of "inhibition," an inhibition of impulsive, regressive activity. The child has to learn how to reduce vital goals of behavior to a state of lesser urgency and to inhibit the more ready, regressive forms of action-tendencies. This in its larger setting is perhaps part of the problem of personality development. But it may show its influence in the realm of thought as well. The

excessively busy, bustling household, or the feverish classroom
or impatient teacher are scarcely an appropriate setting for
thought.

Modes of Thinking

Determining Tendencies in Thinking. To say that thinking is initiated by a problem implies that the flow of ideas is
"channeled" in a certain direction. The direction our thoughts
take, however, is seldom if ever determined entirely by what the
problem requires. We are predisposed to respond to an unfamiliar situation as we have in the past, in certain ways which
may have fit other situations but do not fit this one. This is the
tendency toward "reproduction." A "thoughtful" or "problem-solving" attitude requires us to inhibit this tendency toward
reproduction in order to see exactly what this particular situation requires. Our past experiences must, in other words, furnish the pattern for dealing with the present problem, but must
be regulated by the demands of the present situation.

Let us illustrate this by the method which the thoughtful
child would probably employ in one of the Binet test problems.
He has just been asked what are the three main differences between a president and a king, and this, along with the general
tenor of the examination, gives him the "problem-attitude," or
disposition to *search*. He is disposed at the very start to set
himself against the "reproduction attitude." He knows the
problem he is to be given will require organization of the data,
and he is going to solve it if he can. The following is then read
to him: "A man who was walking in the woods near a city
stopped suddenly, very much frightened, and then ran to the
nearest policeman, saying that he had just seen hanging from
the limb of a tree a —— what?" It is evident that the keynote
of this is that it describes a "frightening situation." But what
kind of a frightening situation? Instead of completing this in
terms of some particular event he knows, he holds up its further
definition in the light of conditions of the problem. It next
becomes "a-frightening-with-appeal-to-the-law" situation. But
this is not the end. It becomes still further defined through

analysis of its setting as a "frightening-with-appeal-to-the-law-in-the-case-of-tree-hanging" situation. The answer "dead man" is a particularization of this tendency which can be completed only in this way, of all the possible plans of organizing facts which he potentially possesses.

If we turn to the other extreme of the "thoughtless" child, we find him perhaps manifesting a *reproduction attitude*. He understands that the problem describes a "frightening" situation but this may be completed immediately to produce the answer "bear." There is no inhibition of this while he studies the problem. He acts on the basis of an insight into the most familiar feature of the situation and allows this to go to completion in accordance with the reproduction set. Or perhaps he acts on the basis of a partial insight into the "tree-hanging" aspect of the problem and says, "a monkey."

Provisional Thinking and "Trial and Error." This is the most common form of thinking in everyday life. It represents a kind of compromise between a pure problem attitude and the pure reproduction attitude. If our child should try to integrate "bear" with the other data, he would find that it does not "fit." It does not fit because of the policeman. This leads to a further definition of the problem and he may say "robber." But this does not "fit," either. So he brings in the tree element to further define the problem. The end result however is the same here as in the child with the problem attitude. It is the awareness of the "frightening-with-appeal-to-the-law-in-the-case-of-tree-hanging" situation which produces the final solution. Trial-and-error thinking is not a blind lunge into the unknown which is then conserved if no untoward consequences follow. The trials are *provisional tries,* or genuine attempts to reach a solution. They may appear random or unorganized for several reasons:

1. If the urge to do something is particularly strong, the individual tends to run rapidly through the alternatives suggested immediately by past experience. This may not be simple reproduction, because the process is selective. He rejects some possibilities immediately because they do not fit, and tries those

which seem to be more appropriate. In the example above, "bear" is thus rejected in favor of "robber."

2. The solution or "search-model" may not be well defined. The individual is not sure of just what he is looking for, or is not clear as to just what is required for solution. The problem situation is vaguely perceived, and its details do not hang together very well. Before meaningful relations can become apparent, the individual may have to try several possibilities as a means of clarifying the situation and seeing what is required. From this point of view, trial-and-error is really an effort to define more precisely a vaguely perceived problem by inventing, trying, and rejecting various "search-models."

3. Even when the problem is fairly definite, and the individual knows exactly what to look for as a solution, certain familiar aspects of the situation may dominate and control his perceptions and give him a false sense of direction. This is due to the mental set, as we saw, given by past experience. "Policeman-as-robbery-preventer" is a set which directs attention away from his larger role as custodian of the general welfare, and prompts the response "robber."

Trial-and-error thinking appears to be inefficient, because much of it is essentially unfruitful search. Teachers are therefore often inclined to be impatient with the child's *apparently* disorganized and "off the track" attempts. But he may be on another track. That is, he may have (and often does) an imperfect hypothesis or search-model, which is why his responses are "wrong."

Many of the problems which the child encounters do not have their setting in a definite sequence of thought-steps so that he may solve them in a direct fashion as did the first child of our illustration. Facts that should be known before the problem is attacked are not known, or perhaps only vaguely known. The problem becomes a number of problems which then must be dealt with in a piecemeal fashion.

It is conceivable, perhaps, as some writers have suggested, that the problems of formal education might be so well "paced" in difficulty and sequence that a child need never have recourse to trial-and-error thinking. This must be very difficult to realize in practice. It does seem, however, that we can take advantage of the suggestion to increase the mental efficiency of the pupil. By encouraging him to adopt a problem attitude and to inhibit reproductive tendencies, his method of attack will be more comprehensive and direct. "Crowding" the child with assignments on which he must get something done, right or wrong, tends to favor partial insights and trial-and-error thinking which is never completed. In order to resist the internal and external pressure calling for "results," the child needs to have a wholesome confidence in his own ability and to set a definite value on the products of his own mental life.

Logical Reasoning. In logical reasoning we are concerned more with giving an orderly account of our inferences than with their material truthfulness. This requires the ability to retrace the steps taken during thinking and to make explicit what was only implicitly contained in the original act of thought. The syllogism is a formal expression of the result. To be a practical logician one must study the relation of thoughts rather than the relation of things. Young children are neither sufficiently introspective nor sufficiently capable of generalizing to carry on this kind of thinking in a formal manner. They are more likely to be correct in their conclusions than to be able to tell why they are correct.

Studies of children's reasoning (6) show that they observe the same general patterns as the adult, but their ability to render explicit all the implications of these comes only rather slowly with age. Moore (11) found that it was not until the age of ten or eleven that the average child was able to pick out the error in 50 per cent or more of his simple logical fallacies. A sample of his material was, "All automobiles have four wheels; here is a vehicle with four wheels; therefore it is an automobile." Piaget (12) has suggested that logical reasoning develops in connection with the "socialization" of language and thought. As the child grows older he learns to think and speak partly at least for the benefit of others. He is often called upon to justify his statements, beliefs, and even actions. This is likely to turn his attention to the logical background of his thinking and toward the widely accepted generalizations which make his particular statement or act appear reasonable in the eyes of others. The syllogism is in a way a socialized thought process.

Since we ordinarily regard the ability to give logical reasons for our inferences as a significant and perhaps dominant feature of thinking, it becomes important to give attention to the influences which may favor this. A child may be able to solve actual problems but lack the ability to retrace the steps of his thinking. It is perhaps just here that he is most likely to reflect the cultural influences of his social environment. When greater stress is placed upon action and instrumental responses, as in the home of lower "cultural level," logical reasoning may lag behind other aspects of thought development.

Psychologically, thinking and problem solving do not usually follow logical, formal processes. We are sometimes deceived into believing they do, or at any rate should, because the "steps" in problem solving are often set down in a logical sequence. One familiar analysis of the process, originally suggested by Dewey (3) outlines problem solving into five steps: (1) becoming aware of the problem, (2) clarifying the problem, (3) proposing hypotheses for solution, (4) reasoning out implications of the hypothesis, (5) testing the hypothesis against experience. Such an analysis is actually a retracing of steps taken during thinking and a formalizing of them, not a description of the individual thinker in action. Even Einstein did not follow this formal pattern (21). As R. L. Thorndike says, "actual behavior in response to a problem situation is often confused, illogical, disorderly. Furthermore, each problem solver and each problem to be solved has its own individual characteristics. Diversity rather than uniformity is the rule in the attack upon problem situations. We do not find the problem-solver going neatly and logically through the sequence of steps. . . . Rather, he jumps around, often starting in the middle, returning then to the initial steps, moving back and forth" (19, p. 196). The assumption that thinking is, or should be, formal and logical often results in attempts to teach children the "steps" and eventually to give up teaching them how to think as a hopeless job.

Autistic Thinking. Autistic responses to problems are prompted by a strong emotional self-reference, and are thus likely to be inordinately "egocentric" and nonrealistic. If a child should answer our Binet thought question with "snake" because he once had a very frightening experience with a snake in a tree, that would be an example of what is called "autistic thinking." Although the answer may seem to "spring from nowhere," it really springs from the needs of the individual. The person who approaches social problems with a strong need to redress the grievances of the "underdog" may be thinking so autistically that his interpretation may be quite onesided. His opposite number, a person mainly intent on maintaining a social system that enhances his own status, may also be blind to certain aspects of social problems. Either person may be unaware of his prejudices, his flights of fancy, his blind spots. The problem is defined in a certain way because of a strong, emotionally toned tendency. It is not unusual to find people trying to solve important problems in this manner. They are said to be thinking wishfully, feeling rather than thinking, or showing "more heat than light."

Autism is another illustration of the urgency of motives interfering with the use of reason. Here, however, the urgency does not arise in the objective nature of the situation, but in the dominant character of the individual's motive and the peculiar personal meaning of the situation in relation to this. In fact the real situation has characteristics which, in conjunction with a problem-attitude, would oppose such a definition of the thought. When the opposition increases to the extent that the realities of life effectively block the motive or the thought arising from it, the individual may give up the problem attitude and continue with his "thinking" anyway. The impulse will issue neither in action nor in "realistic" thought, both of which are checked by the nature of the real situation. The thinking will be determined in its nature and definition by the character of the motive and of the previously formed dispositions to organize facts in certain ways. The most conspicuous examples of autistic thinking are daydreaming and revery. The wish-fulfilling nature of these is usually only too apparent.

This type of thinking is relatively ineffective, not because of its emotional coloring but because it is not strictly problem-centered. Autistic thinking never completely loses contact with reality, but it is commonly an "other-time, other-place" reality that functions here. We may relive in fancy the joys of youth or we may imagine ourselves in an environment of wealth and luxury. This is in a way a means of escape from the more unpleasant features of the immediate present. When the escape is complete or when it is more than a temporary retreat, autistic thinking may become undesirable. Dissatisfaction with things as they are furnishes the motive power of much creative and inventive thought but the means of attaining the goal are here sought in the actualities of life. It is only when both the goal and the means of attainment are defined in terms of an "other-time, other-place" reality that thinking becomes wholly autistic and ineffective.

Abstract Thought Processes.   The schemes of organization through which we think are made available through the process of abstraction.   This is easily illustrated by means of problems or exercises typical of school activity.   Symonds (18) mentions the following types of problems which were used in an experimental analysis of thought processes by a group of graduate students in education:

Definition.   What is the meaning of the word metropolis?

Statement of Relationships.   What is the relation between the conditions of labor and the conditions of life in the home?

Classification.   Are the deposits in a bank to be counted as among the resources or the liabilities?

Illustration or Examples.   Illustrate the principle that it is sometimes just to charge more for a short than for a long haul.

Selective Recall.   What rights are guaranteed by the amendments to the Constitution?

Generalizing.   Is banking competitive or monopolistic?

Comparison.   Compare the recreation of boys and girls today with that of boys and girls a century ago.

Evaluating Recall.   What are the weaknesses in our national banking system?

Explanation.   Why has the church great power?

Application. What application should the buyer make of the principle
that demand varies inversely with the price?
Criticism. Criticize favorably or unfavorably the work of the League
of Nations.
Discussion. Discuss capital punishment. (18, p. 9)

These types of problems are seen to be arranged in a kind of
hierarchy, so that the later ones involve combinations of the
mental processes involved in earlier ones. A "discussion" of
capital punishment presumably involves "criticism," which involves selective recall, generalizing, comparison, evaluation,
explanation, etc. All generalizations are based on selective recall, classifications, statements of relationships. If we now ask
"where do thinking processes begin?" it would seem that they
go back to word meanings or concepts. The first step in thinking, beyond simple observation, is the formation of concepts
through the perception of relations. It is also the first step in
teaching the child to think.

LEARNING CONCEPTS AND RELATIONS

Thinking is in many basic ways similar to perception and
memory. But it is of the essence of thinking that a new organization is required, and objects must therefore take on
new meanings. In "remembering" we can be satisfied with old
integrative plans and the staid characteristics of things, but in
thinking it is different. The process by which objects acquire,
under the guidance of a certain mental set, newly differentiated
qualities and attributes is *abstraction.* When the process is
carried to the stage in which this property is apprehended in its
own right, independently of the original perceptual background,
we have a concept. The awareness that this is applicable to a
number of different situations makes it a general concept or
generalization. The wide significance of language is based on
concept formation.

The Nature of Concepts. A word is a symbol for a concept,
but it is not the same thing. We have frequently observed that
much school learning reduces to word recognition, or forming
arbitrary associations between symbols and meanings. The

symbol 4, standing for "fourness," and the word ocean, standing for a large body of water, are purely arbitrary. But as concepts develop, they take on more meanings and associations. A child's association between four fingers and counting things to four contrasts greatly with the mathematician's grasp of the manifold properties of "fourness." The development of "ocean" progresses through many stages from "a large blue area on a map" to a complex symbolization like "oceans of goodness." Conceptual development involves changes from vague, inexact, concrete representations to clear, exact, abstract ones.

At any stage, a concept refers to more than one object or experience, or to one object in relation to others. This is a class concept, which groups a number of particulars so that one symbol (e.g., "ocean") stands for all. An *abstract idea* represents a common aspect or attribute of the class, such as "fourness" or "loyalty." The genetic development of concepts, as we have seen, involves the process of differentiation and integration. Differentiation requires that the learner have many opportunities to perceive the concrete differences between the class attributes which are common and the particular details which vary. This is the basis of generalization and integration, or the process of cognizing properties of things in relation to class (rivers *flow,* all quantities have *four* fourths). These processes are seen to be the essence of thinking.

Concept formation has been extensively studied in the laboratory, and the results are of some importance to our understanding of the thinking process.

Experiments in Concept Formation. One of the classical experiments on abstraction was performed by Moore (10). He exposed to his subjects a group of five geometrical figures, shown in Figure 67, which was replaced after a fraction of a second by another group. This was followed by the exposure of a third group, and so on. The whole process was continued until the subject was able to abstract the figure common to all the groups. Moore found that this came about by the *"accentuation of the`common element at the expense of the surrounding elements."* An early stage in the process was marked by a positive awareness of the existence of a common element which then gradually became defined in terms of the actual characteristics of the figure itself. The two stages may be described as follows:

1. The cue or common element stands out, but not strikingly enough to be identified. This is a low level of awareness. Differentiation is not complete, hence there is no integration.

2. With continued experience, the cue or common element emerges as distinct and explicit. It can be identified and named as the element common to the different figures. Thus perception proceeds from that which is more general to that which is particular. Repetition is accompanied by a detailed differentiation of the perception.

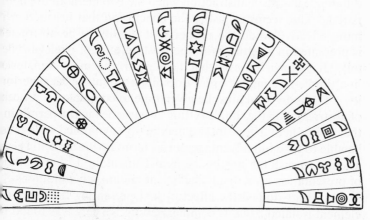

FIGURE 67. Geometrical Designs Employed in Studying Abstraction. Rows containing five figures were exposed to a subject successively until he abstracted the common element, in the above instance a half crescent. Introspections of the subjects revealed the stages in the process of abstraction. From Moore.)

The experiments of Hull (9) are of interest here because he attempted to study the significance of different methods of learning in the evolution of concepts. The experimental material consisted of Chinese written characters, groups of which contained a common element hidden in a more or less complex setting. The subject was to learn to name the whole character

on the basis of the common symbol it contained. Hull's learn
ing curve for the process of abstraction showed this to take place
with considerable suddenness. After an initial plateau in which
practically no improvement in naming occurred, an abrupt and
rapid rise was seen to follow. A final period of diminishing
returns, due perhaps to increase in the facility of giving the
nonsense-syllable name, was usually but not always present
A comparison with the early part of an ordinary learning curve
suggests that insight or organization is the common factor pro
ducing the rapid and upward climb in both cases.

In studying the relative efficiency of the simple-to-complex
and complex-to-simple methods of presenting the material
Hull found the former to be superior. Figure 68 shows the
difference in rate of abstraction when the two methods are com
pared. This seems to justify the conclusion that instruction is
more effective when the property or quality to be abstracted
is presented in a setting with the least amount of irrelevant de
tail. It is shown however that the mere arrangement of materia
in a simple-to-complex order does not account for its superior
ity. The individual must be given time to complete his process
of abstraction in the simple setting "where the factors permitting
the evolution of a concept are maximally favorable." He must
be able to take full advantage of this more favorable setting, an
attempt to rush the process being detrimental. Either method
of presentation is relatively inefficient under such conditions.

Hull also studied the effect of first presenting the common
element isolated from its complex setting. There was found to
be no advantage in this. Even the ability to draw the character
from memory or to define it in isolation was not "a true index
of the functional value of a concept." The best method was
found to be one of presenting the character both in and out of
its natural setting. The importance of linking a concept as
early as possible with practical illustrations is here suggested

The experiments of Smoke (16) bring the laboratory study
of abstraction closer to the real conditions of everyday life
His figured material made the concept dependent upon certain
relationships inherent in the design rather than on the recogni
tion of a common "element" in the narrow sense of the term

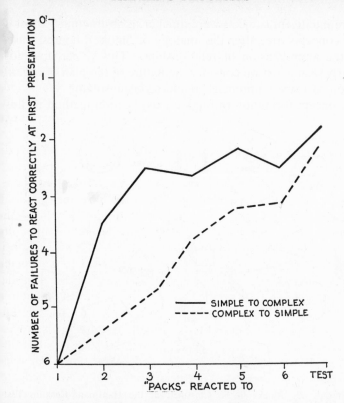

FIGURE 68. The Rate of Abstraction as Affected by the Method of presenting the Material. The upper curve shows the superiority of the "simple-to-complex" method. The subject was required to name a Chinese character on the basis of a more fundamental character contained within it. When presented along with others of a similar nature, these characters were more quickly learned if the element to be abstracted was presented in a simple setting at first, proceeding then to more complex settings. The lower curve shows the rate of abstraction under the complex-to-simple order of presentation. (From Hull.)

Thus a "vec" was an equilateral triangle bisected by a line drawn from an angle to the opposite side. The details of size, position, or color might be very different from one occasion to the next. Smoke found that the subject may learn a concept and yet be unable to define it in words. He also noted the use of "hypothesis" in formulating the concept and the fact that his more intelligent subjects were quicker in abstracting. Most of our concepts are, after the analogy of Smoke's figures, based on the apprehension of relationships. This is perhaps most clearly seen when we consider the nature of the plan of organization basic to comprehension and problem-solving.

Concept formation through a classification method is illus-

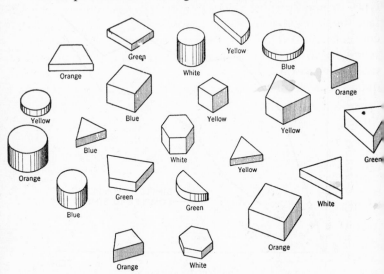

FIGURE 69. Blocks to be Classified in the Hanfmann-Kasanin Test. There are four kinds of blocks, namely "lag," "mur," "bik," and "cev." Which blocks are in each classification? (From Hanfmann and Kasanin, *J. Psychol.*, 1937, **3**, 521-540.)

trated by the problem given in Figure 69. The reader might try this problem, and note his tendency to classify the blocks in terms of such concrete perceptual features as color, shape, size, height. This, like other experimental procedures in concept formation, illustrates the general principle that concepts are formed through problem solving.

There is some evidence that concrete and abstract behavior are qualitatively distinct levels of activity, and that inability to abstract has farreaching implications for problem solving and personal adjustment (5). Hence it is important to understand the psychological processes by which concepts are attained, over and above the external features of materials and methods which facilitate their attainment. This problem was investigated in a series of studies by Heidbreder and associates (7).

The Attainment of Concepts. In preliminary experiments, Heidbreder compared the difficulty of attaining three different types of concepts: (1) concepts of concrete objects such as face, building, tree, (2) spatial forms or figures, (3) number concepts (see Table 22). Each concept was given a nonsense-syllable name. The persons in the experiment were presented with a series of drawings like those in Figure 70 and were required to learn the nonsense syllable name of each drawing.

TABLE 22

OBJECTS, SPATIAL FORMS, AND NUMBERS IN HEIDBREDER'S STUDY OF ATTAINMENT OF CONCEPTS

Concrete Objects		Spatial Forms		Numbers	
Names	Concepts	Names	Concepts	Names	Concepts
Relk	Face	Fard		Mank	6
Silm	Bird	Quan		Joft	3
Glif	Hat	Palt		Perg	4

This was not, however, a simple rote memory performance, because the drawings represented six class concepts, and it was possible to respond to drawings called by the same name as to members of a class. The syllable *Relk,* for example, was always used as the name of a drawing of a human face. The syllable *Fard* was always applied to a circular drawing of some sort, such as a coin, a wheel, a clock, or a circular design. The word *Ling* always applied to drawings which represented two identical objects, such as two bees, two vases; the word *Mank* to drawings of six identical objects. The class concept was said to be "attained" when the subject could without error name the drawings as soon as they appeared. As in other experiments of concept formation, this amounted to identifying the common property. However, the common property never appeared the same way twice; "relk" might appear as a man's face, a woman's face, a child's face, front view, side view, with the drawings differing considerably in concrete detail. In order to learn the name and apply it correctly, the subject of course had to abstract or generalize the similarity from the irrelevant details.

It was found that the concepts were "attained" consistently in the following order: the concrete objects were learned first, the figures next, the number concepts last. But why this order?

FIGURE 70. Some Illustrations of Heidbreder's Drawings Used in Studies of Attainment of Concepts. (From Heidbreder, *J. Psychol.*, 1947, **24**, p. 95.)

If the investigators could discover why, they could learn something of the psychological process in concept formation, as opposed to the mere externals of the performance itself. Because of controlled conditions in the experiment, they could rule out a number of possible explanations: (1) Differences in the familiarity of the figures would be ruled out, since the order is not from the more to the less familiar. Numbers are more familiar than the figures. (2) The order is not due to the presence or lack of conventional names, because the conventionally nameless *pran* and *stod* figures were learned before the number concepts "two," "five," and "six." (3) The nonsense syllables were equally difficult to learn and equal in the helpful associations they might arouse. (4) The relative simplicity or complexity was not a factor, the order of attainment being neither from simple to complex nor vice-versa. Nor could the order be attributed to differences in perceptual "goodness of form" in the drawings. Furthermore, a special effort was made to keep the drawings of a given class from being too uniform. They differed in size, detail, and to some extent in general outline. (5) A "trial and error" explanation, i.e., that the order of attainment was due to a blind guessing, did not seem feasible because the varying detail made a multitude of reactions possible. Thus one subject might have stumbled on the "right" response by chance or lucky accidents, but it is highly improbable that all of the subjects would do so consistently in the order found. (6) Granted that insights of some sort occurred, why did they occur in the order found? It seemed clear that none of the factors named above, or any combination of them, could have accounted for the findings. It might be said that the obvious order is "less abstract to more abstract" but here lies the precise problem. In the psychological sense (not the logical) why should "twoness" be more abstract than "circularity," or "circularity" more abstract than "building"? The question is not "What was presented?" but "What did the subject make of it?"

Subsequent experiments (8) seem to show that (1) concepts were more readily attained when their critical features were arranged in contexts (drawings) so that they could be apprehended at the perceptual, rather than intellectual, level; (2) that at both levels concepts were more easily attained when their critical features were more "thing-like." The thing-character thus would consist of object-properties, such as form or shape, the arrangement of trunk, limbs, and leaves to represent "tree-ness," or an arrangement of features to make a "face." To put it another way, a face or a building or a tree is more nearly a thing than is a mere spatial arrangement of a certain shape or a mere number quantity. This implies that they are more readily perceived as units—not because they are simply more familiar or more simply arranged, but because their very thing-character facilitates a perceptual response. The attainment of the concept of "twoness" or "circularity," on the other hand, requires a greater departure from the direct kind of response we make in first perceiving a concrete object. We can stroke a face, enter a building, climb a tree. These are "thing-like." Spatial designs are less "thing-like," but we can nevertheless trace a design or imaginatively "move around" a circle. The number percept is least like the things of experience. Genetically, we respond to "things" before we respond to "ideas," and the perceptual whole which makes the idea possible depends on its thing-character or its tangibility as an object. In the psychological sense, the ease of concept formation depends on the degree to which the critical feature can be distinguished through the perceptual processes we normally use in identifying objects.[1] One of the goals of mental organization is "thing-ness."

These findings appear to be in accord with what is known of the intellectual development of children. Gestures in response to objects precede language responses. Nouns or names of objects are the first words to appear, and the young child is often unable to distinguish between the name and the thing it stands for. Spatial concepts like "square" or "circle" or "triangle" might be learned through perception of objects to those shapes, but more complex figure-concepts would seem to depend on the development of drawing or writing ability. An analysis of children's number responses (15, 14) shows that children ordinarily approach concepts of numbers through concrete perceptual activities. The results also show why classroom demonstrations and motion pictures provide "object-experiences" and thus facilitate the formation of concepts.

The Role of Perception. Relations between things are not (except as a poor figure of speech) grasped, acquired, retained, since these expressions seem to imply the "container" view of mind which we repudiated earlier. More properly, relations are *cognized*. Cognized relations are not added as a kind of after-thought to our experience of things. We do not first just sense things or isolated sense-qualities and then as a second step throw these sense-impressions into some kind of relation-

---

[1] It was deduced from this principle that color concepts should be more difficult of attainment than spatial ones, but easier to attain than number concepts. Experiments indicated this prediction to be verified.

ship. Relations are contained, at least implicitly, within our experiencing of the world from the very first, and they emerge from it in varying degrees of clearness under the directed activity of our mental life.

This is but another way of speaking of the "structured nature of our consciousness." Many psychologists have stressed this principle, particularly in the field of perception, and they have suggested the terms "Gestalt," "pattern," "configuration," to indicate it. We perceive things as wholes, and the resulting pattern or configuration of consciousness is the mental description of the physical relations as apprehended by us. Thus our perception of an automobile, for instance, is in a way the mental counterpart of the physical relations existing between the several parts of that object, the wheels, motor, and body, which allow it to serve our purpose as a self-propelling vehicle. There must of course be very definite relationships here, such as contiguity in space, reciprocal movement of motor and wheels, and body fastened to frame, before it can *be* an automobile. Minor details of body, wheels, motor, do not matter as long as these fundamental or essential relationships hold. The pattern of our perception accordingly depends upon these essential relations and not upon the details of structure. In fact, the details of structure are of such small importance in the perception of "an automobile" that most of the time we do not notice them, and even when they are most conspicuous they are usually nothing more than features of the total pattern.

Although our most direct and immediate apprehension of the physical world of perception is "figured" and explainable in terms of relationships holding between things, it is necessary to go beyond this in order to arrive at the *eduction* of relations characteristic of thinking. Thought is concerned principally with abstracted relations, with things "in relation," and with kinds of relations not represented in the early undifferentiated perceptions. Certain refinements and developments must take place before a relation can be explicitly known. Because of the genesis of thought out of perception, it will be helpful to understand the connecting links between the two. Various common sayings, such as "knowledge through experience," and "nothing in the intellect that was not first in the senses," refer to this connection, and such educational techniques as object lessons and the project method make practical use of it.

Perception and Eduction of Relations. Concept formation, as we have seen, is a process of (1) perceiving relations by recognizing likeness and differences, and (2) symbolizing the organization or pattern of these relations by means of a name. The "thing-character" of the objects of sense data thus takes on a more abstract character. The fact that we tend to perceive sensory stimuli as objects, to be immediately aware of their "thing-character," to discriminate between them as two separate objects, furnished the necessary setting for the eduction of a relation between them.

The mere ability to differentiate two objects, however, would not in itself appear to be sufficient to educe a relation between them. Even relatively "stupid" animals can perceive likeness and differences, and respond as though they were aware of a relationship. Hens are able to respond to the darker of two gray papers regardless of their absolute brightness, apparently on the basis of a cognized relation of "darker than." Although this was a kind of general rule of choice, however, certain errors or exceptions to this general rule indicate that the hen is not really capable of educing the relationship "darker than." There would be no errors or exceptions if the relation were clearly abstracted. Such a relation is perhaps implicit in the experience of perception, but has not been educed.

The human being, however, is not limited to perceptual knowledge, although this represents a necessary starting point. For many problems of children's thinking we may commonly take it for granted that perceptual discrimination is sufficiently developed so that no difficulty will be encountered here. To ask the eight-year-old child, "If one block of wood weighs five pounds, how much will three blocks weigh?" or "Why do animals have fur?" will require an organization of the data and perhaps a conceptual abstraction of properties and attributes, but the ordinary child has, by this age, already differentiated these in perception.

Some recent experiments dealing with the thought processes of children are of interest here. Dixon (4) found that the ability of children to respond correctly to a ring segment illusion was related to their ability to distinguish between the words "big" and "little." The child who knew the word meanings could usually recognize the "error" in response to the illusion; the child who could not distinguish between the words big and little usually failed to detect the error in the illusion. The eduction of the size relation, and the symbolization of it through words, is a basic factor in "thinking" even about tangible objects.

The work of Piaget (13) illustrates what he calls the "reversibility" of genuine thought processes. In one experiment the child is given various containers and a certain amount of water, and pours the contents of one large container into several smaller ones. If the child when questioned says that the amount of water is the same, he demonstrates a "reversible" thought process. Some young children, however, cannot "see" this, even when the water is poured back and forth several times. Two rods of equal length may be seen as equal in position ══════ but not in position ──────── . Two ribbons of equal length may not be seen as equal when they are changed from ══════ to ⌒ . A collection of poker chips may "increase" when spread out and "decrease" when put in a pile. The child does not "conserve," as Piaget puts it, the notion of size apart from its configurational representation. Form is not differentiated from content. He therefore distinguishes between "habits," and simple "perceptions" on the one hand, which are not "reversible," and *thought* processes, which are. "Reversibility" would seem to depend on the eduction of a relation (like relative size, for example) and the symbolization of it.

It will happen, however, in some instances that the setting for the thought problem is not so well prepared for by an earlier differentiation of perception, and then the child must first "observe" before he can "think." Before we can succeed in bringing home to the child that, say, an apple and a pear belong to the same botanical family (a relation), it would probably be necessary to have him discriminate perceptually a number of features of the fruit, such as its five-fold division and the arrangement of the seeds. Because of similar needs throughout school life, the classroom and the school laboratory, by providing experiences for refined perceptual discriminations, contribute to the development of thinking ability. There is a converse relationship between thought and perception, through which perception is improved. To be aware of a certain relation existing between two things, for example, that the apple and the pear are botanically alike, will often bring about the emergence of perception of many physical features of the object which otherwise would pass unnoticed. Thus the teacher and the school textbook further the perceptual process by pointing out relationships leading to class concepts and abstract ideas. Because its contents are largely statements of relationships, the textbook offers on its part direction to the work of observation in the laboratory. These illustrations of the school application of thought processes are based on the principles of eduction proposed by the English psychologist Spearman.

The Process of Eduction. Spearman's account of the eductive process is based on experimental studies of children (17). According to him, thinking begins with the "fundaments" of perception—what is seen, heard, touched, or otherwise perceived. Fundaments are "the given," or sense data. The second stage in cognition is the active engagement of the self, by which the person goes beyond the sense data presented, and organizes them into relations. Spearman gives two principles of this mental activity:

1. *The eduction of relations.* The mentally presenting of any two or more characters tends to evoke immediately a knowing of the relation between them. Or as expressed by the same author in another place, "When two or more items [percepts or ideas] are given, a person may perceive them to be in various ways related." We may paraphrase this principle as follows: We have a natural tendency to apprehend objects as members or parts of a whole or total pattern, the principle of organization of the pattern being the relation that is educible in the particular instance.

2. *The eduction of correlates.* The presenting of any character together with any relation tends immediately to evoke a knowing of its correlative character. Or as otherwise expressed: "When any item and a relation to it are present to mind, then the mind can generate in itself another item so related." This process is so closely bound up with the preceding, particularly in the concrete case of thinking out a problem, that it is difficult to tell where one leaves off and the other begins.

The visual models in Figure 71 may help to make these clear.

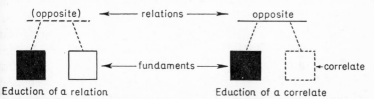

FIGURE 71. Visual Models of the Eduction of Relations and the Eduction of Correlates. Solid lines represent what is given, dotted lines what is to be educed. At the left, presentation of the fundaments "black" and "white" lead to the eduction of "opposite." At the right, presentation of the fundament "black" and the relation "opposite" lead to the eduction of the correlate "white." If the fundaments were two shades of gray, the relation educed would be "darker than" or "lighter than." How would you diagram the process if the fundaments were "apple" and "pear"?

The solid lines represent what the person begins with, and the dotted lines what is immediately educed or known from them. Black and white immediately evokes the relation "opposite" according to the first principle. The presenting of "opposite" and "black" as in the question: "What is the opposite of black?" evokes the correlative character "white." But the relation is the same. How would you show the visual model of *apple-pear* → *fruit*? Of *apple-pear* → *rosaceous tree* (more likely from a botanist)? Note that fruit and rosaceous are names for a complex pattern of relations involving "similarity." Note also the function of language in supplying symbols for complex patterns. The very fact that a student who is verbally given a relationship pattern implied in "The apple is a member of the rose family" will be very curious to observe that the fruit of the rose is indeed very much like an apple and the apple blossom is very much like a "rose."

From such experiences the meaning of verbal symbols and statements is enriched. This is basic to thinking with words. He may also learn coincidentally (and this generalization may be aided by the teacher) that thinking with words may trap the unwary, since words have many meanings and a person exclusively preoccupied with familiar meanings may be word-bound and "one-sided" in his thinking. From many such experiences with words and thing-relations he may gradually form other generalizations like the following: *Reading is a thinking process. A better vocabulary enables a person to think better. People can influence your opinions and attitudes by the words they use.* In this way, the student reaches a higher level of readiness for practical logic, or even for the study of logic, through experiences with words and things. Principles are learned only through a knowledge of facts and relations. Our point is this: it may be of no earthly use to the student to know that an apple and a rose belong to the same family. The "fact" may have no utilitarian value. But if such things are properly taught, by a teacher who knows why she is teaching them, their cumulative value should result in the development of thinking ability.

At first glance, Spearman's principles may appear to be logical rather than psychological. They do, however, furnish a conceptual model for "cognizing relations," and are real aids for analyzing the perceptual and conceptual processes we call thinking. We must not ignore, however, the psychological variables that enter into the eduction of relations and correlates. The most important are these:

1. The relations evoked by what is given clearly depend on previous experience: mental set as related to the goal of action or thought, interest, attention, and the like. All aspects of readiness enter into the eduction.

2. In most cases, the two "characters" presented must be perceived as two separate things. This is certainly true in the classroom. There must be opportunity to differentiate. Spear-

man's principle would seem to imply that a high degree of particularization had already taken place.

3. Lower level relations must genetically precede higher level relations. A higher level relation is dependent on relations which have previously been abstracted. Thus in educing a relation implied in the statement that "Gray is the result of the combination of light waves of many different lengths," the fundaments "light waves" and "wave lengths" would have to be produced by previous eductions.

4. The "correlate" educed from the presenting of a character and a relation arises from a tendency to reproduce past experience, or more crudely, from "memory in the service of thought." But it is not a random reproduction. Mental organization determines what memory is produced; it must fit what is required. The relation and one of its terms determine the appropriateness of any particular bit of experience to complete the pattern or configuration. When the child is asked, "Gold is a precious metal. What's another?" he may answer "tin." It may not be the right answer, but we can be sure it fits *his* comprehension of what is required. He may be attending to "metal" primarily, or precious may mean to him something like "shiny."

SOME FACTORS IN THINKING ABILITY

An individual's ability to think through a problem will depend upon his general mental maturity, his background of experience, certain character or volitional traits, and his facility in the use of language.

The Role of Intelligence in Thinking. Although intelligence is sometimes defined as the ability to think, the two functions are not really the same. A person's thinking is a reflection of his intelligence plus other factors. While we may measure general mental maturity with very little stress upon knowledge, we cannot estimate the quality of a person's thinking apart from the truthfulness and value of the knowledge he attains in this manner. To think is to think about something, and to think well is to attain true knowledge about this something through the reorganization of experience. Thought is a step closer to knowledge than is intelligence. The teacher may be a better thinker than the student, the old man better than the boy, the urbanite better than the farmer, the high school student better than the average youth, in spite of very little difference in IQ.

Since most thinking deals with abstractions, the duller child will approach a problem with fewer of the "materials" of thought. He will lack many of the insights and differentiations which the more mature child will have developed from ordinary experience. Much of the instruction in school assumes the existence of general concepts which ordinarily cannot be taken for granted. The pupil who has not as yet succeeded in discriminating between "a president and a king" will find some of his civics problems much more difficult than they should be. If he has not derived the "symbolization" relation from general experience his progress in algebra will be considerably impeded. Many difficulties in school subjects arise in the immaturity of the student rather than in the inherent relations of the subject itself. The school must after all build on the insights and organizations generated out of the ordinary experiences of life.

When the thinking involves higher-level relations, when the number of fundaments or details is large, when a high degree of generalization is required, or when a premium is placed on speed, the less intelligent pupil will work under a handicap not experienced by the bright. These points suggest how difficulties may be obviated. Breaking up a thought problem into convenient steps and confining these to a few well-chosen fundaments will help the slower learner very much. He can learn his difficulty with generalization more easily if he gets many examples to which the principle applies. The whole process may be approached more leisurely so that the child will not be forced into taking an attitude or mental set unfavorable to thinking. Uniform standards of achievement and uniform methods of teaching will serve only to accentuate differences in thinking between the bright and dull and to deprive the latter of the advantage that should normally be expected from school experi ences as a stimulus to thought. The outcome will be that the slower child will tend to become an inveterate "memorizer" instead of developing whatever ability he has for thinking.

The Role of Language in Thinking. We should be very seriously handicapped without the facilities of spoken or written language. It has already been pointed out that verbal formulation tends to give fixity and stability to the educed relations, and to contribute to their definition. This would be of considerable significance in making more readily available the differentiations and organizations of one's earlier experience. A ready command of verbal formulations of scientific relations, generalizations, and specific items of knowledge may offer an appreciable contribution to one's ability to think in the advanced stages of any science. As Bartlett (2) says, "Nobody ever thinks who, being challenged, merely sets up an image from some specific and more or less relevant situation, and then finds for himself a solution, without in any way *formulating* the relational principle involved. For carrying out this formulation, for utilizing the general qualitative and relational features of the situation to which reference is more or less openly made, words appear to be the only adequate instruments so far discovered or invented by man." It seems clear that language facilitates thought. But it is equally clear that words may on occasion become a substitute for thinking and impede progress in this respect. Many years ago, Dewey pointed out that the premium placed by the school on the attainment of technical facility and external results often makes language a detriment rather than an advantage in thinking:

In manipulating symbols so as to recite well, to get and give correct answers, to follow prescribed formulae of analysis, the pupil's attitude becomes mechanical, rather than thoughtful; verbal memorizing is substituted for inquiry into the meaning of things. (3)

Modes of Thinking and Teacher-Pupil Relationships. Among the complex factors that affect the teacher-pupil relationship are differences in modes of thinking. We are not referring here to differences in maturity, which are important in themselves, but to individual differences in emotional "sets" or "thinking attitudes" which are characteristic of teachers as well as students. If the classroom is to provide a genuine experience of the group process in thinking, discussion and exchange of ideas must be a give-and-take relationship, allowing freedom of expression and contributing to mutual understanding. Differences in modes of thinking can make teacher-student relations, and the relations among students, quite difficult in this setting. The autistic thinker, for example, can seldom be understood; his very egocentricity may often keep him from being aware that he is not understood.

Abel (1) has suggested a number of classifications of the predominant "modes of thinking" and expression of teachers and students, based on one year's observation of classes in two high schools. Of the students and teachers observed, she found some "logical" ones who asked questions of fact and asked for causative or logical explanations, while others were "autistic," giving free reign to imagination. Some were "subjective," showing interest in things that touched them personally but indifferent otherwise, and some were "objective." "Egocentric" speakers were apparently not aware of their listeners, while "socialized" persons tried hard to make themselves understood. Some were rigid, with "logic-tight compartments," others flexible and aware of their prejudices. "Compulsive" individuals relentlessly argued a point, and others were ready to drop an idea and move to something else. Abel also identified such predominant attitudes as the "knowledge" attitude of wanting to know, seeking evidence; the "appreciation" attitude, as illustrated by "That's lovely," "Beautiful work," or calling things good, bad, funny, and the like. Finally, the "use" attitude: utilitarian, concerned with efficiency, the "What's the use of learning that stuff?" approach.

Abel found, of course, that no individual's ideas or expressions fit uniformly into a single category. Although the teacher or student varied somewhat in different situations, he usually showed predominant trends in one direction or another. There are perhaps several points to be made here in relation to teacher pupil adjustment.

1. The nature of the subject matter determines to some extent the mode of thinking expected of the student. Thus the mathematics teacher might expect the student to think in a rigidly logical manner, and be upset by those who do not. In literature or art or music, this kind of thinking would be a handicap; the predominant attitude must be subjective and appreciative.

2. The attitudes of teachers might vary independently of subject matter, and Abel found this to be the case. In one literature section, the teacher's thinking was "logical, unemotion, rigid, and compulsive," and this teacher expected the students to think as she did. Another had mostly appreciative attitudes, and was pleased when students had attitudes like hers. In social science classes, one teacher attempted to develop unprejudiced attitudes in the students. Another was primarily egocentric, did not seem to be aware of whether the students were thinking reflectively, and seemed to be pleased when students expressed appreciative attitudes on topics that interested the teacher (war, militarism, oriental religions).

3. Some students (as well as teachers) may be overly consistent in their approach to thought, and thus find it difficult to adjust to some subjects or classes. The rigid overlogical student with a predominant "use" attitude may please the science teacher but drive other teachers "crazy" with questions about causative explanations. He may also be scornful of students less compulsive or rigid than himself in this respect. Many students may need to develop greater fluidity in their approaches to various kinds of problems and subject matter. This may be done, as Abel suggests, by a more balanced program not only of subject matter, but of different kinds of teachers.[1]

[1] A recent "factorial" study of response patterns in a test of logical inference (Gaier, Lee, and McQuitty, *Educ. and psychol. Meas.*, 1953, **13**, 550-567) indicates that college freshmen also have different styles of reasoning that characterize them as individual personalities. Some rather typically prefer unambiguous or dogmatic statements in jumping to conclusions, some can tolerate ambiguity when the evidence is not clear, some are overoptimistic and like to think that most any kind of inference must be true, some typically like to suspend judgment, etc., all showing personal cognitive attitudes that people bring with them in their approach to a problem.

4. Verbal facility may often be confused with logical think-ing. The verbally facile student finds it easier to repeat the arguments or thought processes of others, but may not have examined them carefully. It is perhaps easier for him to please most teachers and to convince them that he is "thinking." The thought processes of the quiet, more deliberate, less verbally facile student are more difficult to ascertain.

On the whole, it would seem that teacher-pupil relationships might be improved in the classroom if more attention were given to the interaction of varying modes of thinking, or motivational "sets." The teacher's predominant trends in thinking, rather than the subject matter, would seem to determine what kind of behavior or participation she expects or demands of students and how the student's progress is judged. This principle may provide the most suitable frame of reference for evaluating the teacher's often heard remark that students cannot be taught to think.

REFERENCES

1. ABEL, T. M. Modes of thinking and classroom adjustment. *J. soc. Psychol.*, 1938.
2. BARTLETT, F. C. *Remembering*. New York: Macmillan, 1932.
3. DEWEY, JOHN. *How we think*. Boston: Heath, 1933.
4. DIXON, J. C. Concept formation and emergence of contradictory relations. *J. exp. Psychol.*, 1949, **39**, 144-149.
5. GOLDSTEIN, K. *After-effects of brain injuries in war*. New York: Grune & Stratton, 1942.
6. HAZLITT, V. Children's thinking. *Brit. J. Psychol.*, 1929, **20**, 354-361.
7. HEIDBREDER, E., BENSLEY, M. L., & IVY, M. The attainment of concepts: IV, Regularities and levels. *J. Psychol.*, 1948, **25**, 299-329. See also *J. gen. Psychol.*, 1946, **35**, 173-223, and *J. Psychol.*, 1947, **24**, 93-138.
8. HEIDBREDER, E., & OVERSTREET, P. The attainment of concepts: V, Critical features and contexts. *J. Psychol.*, 1948, **26**, 45-69, 193-216.
9. HULL, C. L. Quantitative aspects of the evolution of concepts. *Psychol. Monogr.*, 1920, **28**, 1-86.
10. MOORE, T. V. The process of abstraction. *Univ. of Calif. Publ. Psychol.*, 1910, **1**, 73-197.

11. Moore, T. V. The reasoning ability of children in the first years of school life. *Stud. Psychol. and Psychiat.*, Catholic Univ. of America, 1929, **2**, No. 2.

12. Piaget, J. *Judgment and reasoning in the child.* New York: Harcourt, Brace, 1928.

13. Piaget, J. *The psychology of intelligence.* New York: Harcourt, Brace, 1950.

14. Reiss, A. Numerical quantification vs. number sense. *J. Psychol.,* 1943, **15**, 99-108.

15. Reiss, A. An analysis of children's number responses. *Harvard educ. Rev.,* 1943, **13**, 149-162.

16. Smoke, K. L. An objective study of concept formation. *Psychol. Monogr.,* 1932, **42**, No. 4.

17. Spearman, C. *The nature of intelligence and the principles of cognition.* New York: Macmillan, 1923.

18. Symonds, P. M. *Education and the psychology of thinking.* New York: McGraw-Hill, 1936.

19. Thorndike, R. L. How children learn the principles and techniques of problem solving. *49th Yearbook,* Nat. Soc. Stud. Educ., 1950.

20. Thurstone, L. L. *The nature of intelligence.* New York: Harcourt, Brace, 1926.

21. Wertheimer, M. *Productive thinking.* New York: Harper, 1945.

SELECTED READINGS

Brownell, W. A., & Hendrickson, G. How children learn information, concepts, and generalizations. Ch. 4 in *49th Yearbook,* Nat. Soc. Stud. Educ., 1950.

Dewey, J. *How we think.* (Rev. ed.) Boston: Heath, 1933.

Heidbreder, E. *Studying human thinking.* Ch. 4 in Andrews, T. G. (Ed.), *Methods in psychology.* New York: Wiley, 1948.

Humphrey, G. *Thinking: an introduction to its experimental psychology.* New York: Wiley, 1951. A technical exposition for the advanced student.

Humphrey, G. *Directed thinking.* New York: Dodd, Mead, 1948. An excellent book for general reading.

Leeper, R. Cognitive processes. Ch. 19 in Stevens, S. S. (Ed.), *Handbook of experimental psychology.* New York: Wiley, 1951.

Piaget, J. *The child's conception of the world.* New York: Harcourt, Brace, 1929.

Piaget, J. *The child's conception of physical causality.* New York: Harcourt, Brace, 1930.

Wallas, G. *The art of thought.* New York: Harcourt, Brace, 1926.

Wertheimer, M. *Productive thinking.* New York: Harper, 1945.

20

PROBLEM SOLVING

THE APPLICATION of the psychology of thinking to the school is most apparent when we consider thinking as problem solving. There seems to be no doubt that thinking is the most important goal of education. As Bode says, "the power to think is the educational kingdom of heaven; if we seek it persistently, other things will be added unto us" (2). On the other hand, it has often been pointed out that teachers have more often been interested in the outcome of thinking than in the process of thinking, and that most educational work is really training in following the thought processes of the teacher or the writer of the textbook. The emphasis is chiefly on reproduction, rather than on productive or creative thinking. Wertheimer considers the distinction between productive and reproductive thinking most important in the work of the school. "It is at least an open question whether the way in which [teachers] interpret thinking does not cause serious hindrance, or actual impairment of genuine abilities" (15).

Teaching students to think means first of all providing problem situations. The big question for the teacher is "What kinds of problems?" Many of the "problems" assigned in school require reproduction of something learned, and nothing more. More often than not, mathematics is taught as a process involving "steps." If the student follows the steps, he can solve the problems; but the sequence is very often learned by rote or accepted on faith. Problem solving then is made to depend not on comprehension, but on memorizing and reproducing the steps. In laboratory science, the student is given an experiment and instructions for carrying it out. In biology, he is more often given classifications of plants and animals than he is required to discover why certain organisms superficially dissimilar are classified together. In English, he may be given various ready-made thought schemes for "analyzing" plays, stories, or poems. This information may be useful in developing thinking, but if the work of the classroom goes no further than this there is real danger that the creative abilities of students may be impaired rather than developed.

The art of teaching requires facility in designing and presenting problems that test the student's ability to reorganize his knowledge and apply it to new situations. This requires thinking by the teacher as well as the students. If we understand the dynamic processes in problem solving, we can more easily design problems conducive to thought. What is it that makes a situation a problem? How does a person ordinarily behave in a problem situation? What makes problems difficult, and what makes thinking difficult? What are the characteristics of productive or creative thinking? These questions are considered in this chapter. They are fundamental in helping the teacher to recognize genuine thinking when it occurs, and to discriminate mere reproduction from genuine comprehension. The psychological principles of thinking are best illustrated by experiments in problem solving.

A Problem Situation. The following situation, presumably conducive to thought, is described by Wertheimer:

Two boys were playing badminton in the garden. One boy was twelve, the other ten years old. They played several sets. The younger was by far poorer, he was being beaten in all the games. . . . The loser—let us call him *B*—became more and more unhappy. He had no chance. *A* often served him so cleverly that he could not possibly return the bird. The situation grew worse. Finally *B* threw down his racket, sat on a tree trunk, and said, "I won't play any more." *A* tried to persuade him to continue. No answer from *B*. *A* sat down beside him. Both looked unhappy. (15, p. 127)

Does this situation call for thinking? If so, why? At first glance, the situation may appear to be quite trivial. Psycho-

logically, it is not; it contains all the elements of grave human
problems. It is a problem because there is a goal, obstacles to
the goal, and no clear perception of means to the goal. As
soon as we put the problem in these terms, we have commenced
to think about it; that is, we are using ideas which initiate a
train of other ideas. In order to make our later discussion of
thinking more meaningful, we ask you to STOP RIGHT HERE and
think it out to a solution, making notes on your course of ideas
and the solution you finally propose. What do you suggest?

Problem Attitudes. Wertheimer put the badminton prob
lem to a number of persons and observed their reactions. In
most instances, thinking did not occur at all. Some persons
waited to have the story continued, asked irrelevant questions
like who the boys were, what the boys did, whether it was an
experiment, etc. Some made irrelevant associations of the "this
reminds me of . . ." variety, or recalled things they had read
about child psychology. Some tended to classify the case
with a "this is a case of . . ." response, and embarked on gen
eralities. That is, a train of ideas was initiated by the story
but could not be called thinking because it was not in the direc
tion of solution. We might say that there was no "problem
attitude," no personal involvement in the situation as a problem
Some individuals did some groping and fact-gathering by asking
further questions which were not completely aimless. This
behavior may be regarded as an attempt to get a more adequate
structuring of the problem and might be considered a prelude
to thinking. But it often went no further than this.

Some persons engaged in what Wertheimer has called repro
ductive thinking. That is, they offered proposals which were
simply reproductions of past experience, things they had seen or
heard before. These were ordinarily applications of some rule
of behavior (often, says the author, remembered from courses
in educational psychology) or prevailing ideas about children
human nature, or morals. It was thus suggested that the
younger boy be bribed with a reward like a piece of chocolate
that he be scolded, or reasoned with, or given a handicap. Usu
ally these proposals were offered in a tone of deep conviction

Granted that such behavior often passes as "thinking," we may well raise the question here as to whether it really is. It is certainly an orderly ideational process, involving a course of ideas directed toward a conclusion. The situation is perceived as similar to other situations experienced in the past, and as a member of a class of situations, all handily grouped together under some sort of rule, label, principle, or abstract concept. The response certainly involves transfer through generalization, or an application of old learning to a new situation.

But do we find here any critical examination of the solutions proposed in the light of the demands of this particular situation? We see no attempt to differentiate this situation from others in the past, such as "But maybe a bribe or reward would not work here," or "What behavior am I trying to reward, anyway, and why?" Do we find here any attempt to define the problem by further elaboration, such as: Just what need is frustrated here, and what are the boys' goals? What are the obstacles? In what does an effective solution consist? Do we find any search for a model of a solution, or a comparison between the ready suggestion and some kind of ideal solution? It must be admitted that the "reproductive" behavior does not reveal any kind of search except a search of memory or past experience, that the proposals offered so readily and with such conviction appear to be determined by past experience. The behavior seems to be a relatively blind "running off of habits" with easy recall and no great effort.

Productive thinking, according to Wertheimer, involves more than this. It involves the kind of mental struggle which we find is not typical of the purely reproductive process. The productive thinking process is an attempt to answer this kind of question: What factors, intrinsic to the situation, need to be altered in order to reach a solution? That is, if the situation is immediately perceived to be similar to those encountered in the past, a more or less "ready-made" solution, based on learned relationships, would be immediately available. In a sense, there is no problem or "felt difficulty." It would be apparent, from the ease and conviction with which some proposals were

made, that the individuals did not *feel* it to be a particularl
weighty problem.

We may find, however, that previously learned relationship
are of little help and may actually be a hindrance, because the
cause us to perceive the situation in the wrong way—to defir
the problem in such a way that a really effective solution
obscured. We know, for example, how badminton is playee
we can infer the reasons why the younger boy will not continu
we know why he is being beaten. We have a vague concep
of the goal as "continuing the game." But the solution is elu
sive. Is it possible that the knowledge we have is hinderin
the solution? Let us consider the boys' solution to their ow
problem.

Problem Solution. The solution proposed by the older bo
consisted in changing the game, so that the new purpose wa
to keep the bird going back and forth, and the "score" woul
be the number of exchanges without letting the bird fal
"What score could we make? Do you think we could make
ten or twenty? We'll start with easy serves but then let us mak
it harder and harder. . . ." Why was this solution satisfac
tory? Because the boys themselves thought of it, or because
fits the situation? We must admit that it fits admirably, becaus
it allows the game to continue with satisfaction to both player

It was achieved, we note, by altering an intrinsic factor i
the situation. We may compare the solution for "fitness" wit
other possible solutions: Have the older boy teach the younge
one (not a game); let them play dominoes to equalize the ag
and skill difference (not *this* game); rule out the older boy
wicked serve (less satisfaction to him). We are not, howeve
concerned with the logic of the solution; the point is that it f
the problem as the boys saw it. The solution seems simple—
that is, in retrospect. We immediately see the relation betwee
what is given (details of situation) and what is required (t
continue the game).

The reader may agree that before the solution was identifie
the problem was not so simple. What made it difficult? Th
difficulty was not in the situation, but in the way it was per

eived.   Past experience tricked us into seeing it in the wrong
way, giving us the wrong direction, introducing red herrings.
All we know of badminton tells us that it is a competitive game.
We were mired down, or tangled up, in our unstated assump-
ion that "continuing the game" meant "against each other."
If the reader will go over the notes he made while attempting
o solve the problem, he will probably find that his whole train
of ideas was along this line.)   Since we are not aware of the
assumption, we have great difficulty in seeing the game as a
cooperative enterprise which can nevertheless result in the same
kind of satisfaction to the players.

Seeing the problem in a new way involved what may be
called *recentering,* reorganizing, restructuring.   The details or
parts were rearranged to form a new whole.   What emerges
is a new product, not a reproduction of past learning.   Learned
relations were utilized, of course, but they were utilized in a new
way.   The solution did not come about by a "this reminds me
of . . ." or "this is a case of . . ." type of response.   Productive thinking is difficult for this reason.

The process exemplifies recentering, or transition from a
"one-sided" view of the situation to a center or fundamental
issue; a change of meaning of the parts or details in accordance
with a new whole; a tendency to interpret the details in terms
of their "fittingness" to what is required; a tendency to face the
fundamental issue boldly and draw the consequences.   These,
according to Wertheimer, are the characteristics of productive
or creative thinking.

We note, in the problem of the badminton game, that the
ideas aroused depended entirely on the idea of what was required for effective solution.   The solution required "continuing the game with satisfaction to both players."   This idea,
called a *search-model,* determined what we searched for in the
way of solution, and what means or proposals were suggested.
The search-model not only gives direction to our thinking, but
a model with which to compare or test any proposal we might
hit upon.   We might thus reject the possibility of having the
older boy teach the younger one because it does not fit our
concept of "game," or does not satisfy the boys' need to compete

with some kind of standard. The search-model, whether mor
or less adequate, is an abstract concept that determines wha
cues we look for in the situation or in past experience. Our re
sponses do not come from "out of the blue" but are suggested b
the conceptual goal which defines the nature of the problem
In other words, the search-model defines the problem for u
and determines our behavior.

THINKING PROCESSES IN PROBLEM SOLVING

Thinking often looks easier than it really is because we ofte
view the process in retrospect, rather than from the point o
view of the person actually engaged in struggling with a prob
lem. The logician's analysis of the problem solving proces
into a series of formal steps, for example, appears to disguis
the psychological complexity of the thinking processes. Thi
kind of descriptive analysis, as we have seen, is essentially a
matter of looking backward from the solution to the steps tha
apparently led to the solution. The real difficulty in problem
solving, however, is that the solution or "search-model" itsel
may be obscure or inadequate, and for this reason we may no
make adequate use of certain critical details in the situation
Once the solution is known and the relations of means to enc
are comprehended, all the details seem to "jump into place."
Some consideration of the thought processes in problem solv
ing may help to show why thinking is difficult, and some type
of problems more difficult than others. Why, for example
does a problem look easy to a teacher who knows the "answer"
and very difficult to the student? Why does the student whc
comes up with the "right answer" often convince the teacher
that he comprehends the problem, when as a matter of fact he
may not?

Eduction of Relations in Problem Solving. A study by
Strasheim (13), primarily undertaken to devise a novel methoc
of testing intelligence, illustrates the principles of eduction anc
their implications for verbal problem solving. He presented tc
children between five and ten years a series of ten stories, containing the "fundaments" of a situation. After reading each

tory, he tried to discover by appropriate questioning, if his children had succeeded in educing the proper relations and correlates. All the stories presented a problem which could be solved on the same general principle, that of "tossing" or deciding by chance.

Selected samples of Strasheim's ten stories with his comments on each follow:

First story: One day some boys wanted to play football, and so Tom and Dick, the two biggest boys, were asked to pick sides. As they had no money with which to toss for first pick, they had to find some other way. One saw some pieces of paper on the ground, took *two* and made one *shorter* than the other. He then held the two pieces in his hand, with only the *tops* sticking out so that his friend could not see which piece was the longer. He then said to his friend, "If you draw the *longer* one, *you* shall have first pick."

The first story obviously supplied the rule, i.e., a series of relations which may be applied to the same or similar fundaments on future occasions.

Sixth story: Some time later Tom and some other boys went to the park to play football. When they wanted to pick sides they found they had no money to toss with. They looked about for paper, but there was none to be seen, and all they could see were a few sticks lying on the ground.

This situation forces the testee, if he has not already done so, for the first time to apply the relations he has educed in the previous situation, to entirely changed fundaments. It serves to show therefore whether the relations have so far been "abstracted" from the original fundaments, that they can be readily applied to others. This step is made a little easier by the fact that the old fundaments are definitely ruled out, and the new ones are given, with the added warning that they are new ones.

Tenth story: During the last war two English sailors were captured by the Germans. As it was summer and the water quite warm they decided to escape by swimming. As soon as it was dark, therefore, they undressed and got into the water. When they were near the land they heard shouts and saw a boat coming along. The one said to the other, "Look here, if one swims back to the boat and keeps it busy, the other can escape." So they decided to toss to see who should go back. Of course they had no money, so they had to find another way.

In the earlier stories, the child had to educe relations and appl[y]
them to various situations. Later, he has to find the funda[-]
ments for himself through a process of exploratory search re[-]
calling various details of previous situations in relation to th[e]
present problem, and then selecting appropriate ones from th[e]
"re-products." A close analysis of these mental processes re[-]
veals certain relations, such as spatial, causal, likeness-diffe[r-]
ence, as fundamental to the discovery of certain attributes. A[ll]
these are necessary to the eduction of the higher relation "draw[-]
ing by chance."

The results indicated two genetic stages of eduction, whic[h]
the author called the perceptual and conceptual. Since th[e]
mental activities of the young children were relatively slow, th[e]
thought processes could be followed without great difficult[y.]
The early *perceptual* stage is one in which "the relations ar[e]
in intimate contact with the fundaments . . . with the resul[t]
that they are suitable for future occasions only when the sam[e]
or similar fundaments occur." In other words, the relation i[s]
educed from the more concrete sensory data, and carries ove[r]
to a new situation which is more or less similar in concrete detai[l.]
Choosing sides with paper may transfer to choosing with stick[s.]
This form of eduction, the author points out, is common in ordi[-]
nary life and explains that form of behavior guided by "rule o[f]
thumb." It also explains why people may be able to "do[”]
things, but are unable to explain how or why they do them.

The *conceptual* stage is one of elaborate eduction of a highe[r]
level relation like "deciding by chance." This concept involve[s]
a high level of abstraction. As such it can be applied easily t[o]
the most varied fundaments; the principle applies to the tent[h]
story as well as the others, in spite of their complete dissimi[-]
larity in concrete detail. The higher level eduction is als[o]
clearer, and thus facilitates the eduction of correlates. Find[-]
ing *another* way of deciding by chance is relatively easy, eve[n]
when the familiar things (paper, sticks, matches, money) ar[e]
absent, if the concept is clear. In the transition from the pe[r-]
ceptual to the conceptual stage, says Strasheim, "it is probabl[e]
that the analysis of the fundament into attributes (the eductio[n]
of the attributive relation) plays a very prominent and necessar[y]

part." He believed his study to show that, although eduction was possible without the power to express in words what had been educed, yet those children who were able to express themselves well on the point found the words "a very useful support in that they give fixity and concreteness to the relations" (13). Without the word "chance" we would find the tenth problem difficult.

Some Types of Thought Problems. Many of the laboratory experiments in problem solving have important implications for the work of the school. Most experimental studies of thinking have dealt with problems of the following kinds:

1. The eduction of a relation and its application (correlate eduction) in a new situation when the fundaments are familiar objects and the relation to be educed is of a fairly simple kind. Strasheim's first test situation would be an example of this. The "crucial" feature of the problem was the eduction of relations centering around "choice by chance," and the recall of appropriate correlates with which this scheme could be carried out.

Common arithmetic problems, as encountered in school, are of this sort. If 4 oranges cost 10 cents, how many can be bought for a dollar? This can be done by counting, but the principle of "proportion" may not be educed; hence the difficulty. The correlative numerical calculations necessary are usually of a simple kind. The difficulty of some problems lies in the search for satisfactory factual correlates. The thinking involved in many inventions illustrates this, for just what was needed may have been long known. The use of this type of problem in teaching is largely for the sake of deriving generalizations and extending their sphere of application.

2. The eduction of a higher level relation, that is, one depending upon the prior eduction of lower level relations, and upon their clearness and availability as fundaments. How are poem and statue alike? The difficulty in this type of problem commonly lies in the fact that the lower level relations have not been previously educed, or they have not been sufficiently abstracted to serve as fundaments for the eduction of the higher level relation. Strasheim found that very few of his children

were able to make use of sand or clothing to extinguish a fire when no water was handy. This required the eduction of the relation of "opposite" between two lower level concepts, "fire as air-feeding" and "water as air-excluding." The lower level or attributive relation had not apparently been abstracted. The children could recognize fire and water, but the critical attributes are not essential for recognition. This is the kind of problem in which "analysis" of the nature of objects becomes of such great importance for developing class concepts. Its educational use leads to an extension of the child's conceptual knowledge.

3. Problems demanding the eduction of a number of relations and the organization of these into a temporal pattern. Puzzle-boxes, mazes, and mechanical models exemplify this type of problem. Any one of the relations involved in such a case may be easily educed (e.g., this lever releases this pin) but the difficulty enters when all these relations are to be organized into a temporal pattern or plan. This is the type of thought problem which is particularly likely to show a trial-and-error method of attack.

The pioneer study by Ruger (12) was based on a number of rather difficult mechanical puzzles which his adult subjects were required to solve. In most cases the solution came by accident, but when this did occur there was usually some awareness of the appropriateness of the successful movement or variation. This awareness progressed, during the trials, from a vague feeling to explicit recognition to an image and finally to a verbal formula. A similar description could perhaps be given of the way in which many thought problems become defined for the child.

Thought problems which favor a "puzzle-attitude," namely that the solution is to be hit upon merely by chance, would seem to have many disadvantages educationally. The school can contribute more to the thinking of the child through the use of problems of another kind, by the proper "pacing" of these, and by arousing and strengthening the child's realization that his early experiences contain, at least implicitly, the solutions of many later difficulties. The child's ability to think is in a way inversely related to his tendency to rely upon a mere trial-and-error method of attack.

4. The fourth type of thought problem involves the eduction of a relation which is *arbitrarily* determined in advance by the experimenter. The Hanfmann-Kasanin classification problem in Figure 69 is an illustration of this; the classification is based on the principle of a double dichotomy—large or small *and* tall or flat. There are thus four classifications: tall and large, tall and small, flat and large, flat and small. The crux of the problem lies in discovering the schemes underlying the "class concepts" by which the various drawings were grouped, and applying an arbitrary name to the drawings on this basis. The results and conclusions of such a study are related perhaps to the development of children's thinking over a long period of time. This type of experiment appears to illustrate one source of difficulty in classroom practice. Many scientific relations and methods are presented to students in a form which to them, because of lack of both knowledge and maturity, seems to be thoroughly arbitrary. These concepts may become clear with additional experience. This type of experimental problem resembles the inductive lesson of the classroom, as for example when biology students are given a number of plants and their characteristics and asked to classify them. It differs from a puzzle-problem in that it favors rational anticipation and leads to complete understanding.

√ **Difficulty of Thought Problems.** The difficulty of thought problems arises from three main sources: the nature of the relation to be educed, the nature of the fundaments, and the genetic stage of readiness of the problem-solver. The difficulty of a problem may vary as follows:

1. According to the *number of terms or fundaments* that must be held in mind at one and the same time. Thus the Binet tests show that it takes a mental age of about five to perform three simple "commissions," putting key on chair, shutting door, and bringing box, in the proper order. It would be easier to do two things of this sort in the right order. When the number

of fundaments increases in number, the eduction of the relation seems to be correspondingly more difficult.

2. According to whether they are *lower- or higher-level relations*. Thus, the interpretation of pictures is found at the twelve year level in the Stanford Binet (a higher-level relation required), while description (dealing with lower-level relations) is found at year seven. Conceptual thinking is more difficult than concrete thinking.

3. According to the *kind or quality of the relation*. For example, giving "differences" between common objects is placed at year seven in the Binet test, while giving "similarities" is among the tests for year eight. Again, to be able to distinguish between what is "essential" and what is "accidental" belongs to a relatively advanced stage of maturity. Abstract thinking is based upon a number of such relations. Piaget (11) has given us some very interesting data on the young child's difficulty with the word "because." Abstracting the cause-effect relation of external events is more difficult than educing the relation of personal motive for action. Piaget attributes this to the "egocentric" character of the young child's thinking.

The difficulty of a thought problem may be centered in the fundaments if these are qualities or attributes of things which had not previously been differentiated in perception. The child may not be aware, for instance, of the different physical features of plants, leaves, and fruit, which furnish the basis for many principles and relations of botany. A student may not be able to understand the biological relation of the nucleus to the rest of the cell if he has not first seen it under the microscope. The fundaments may sometimes be objects beyond the ordinary experience of the pupil. Why Arctic animals have thick coats of fur may be a difficult problem for the child living in the tropics if he has never used clothing to keep warm.

Another source of difficulty may be the immaturity of the problem-solver. There is a maturational sequence of development in thinking as well as in motor skills. The child of five defines a chair by saying, "A chair is to sit." It is not until two or three years later that the chair emerges from its personal setting of "use" to become a "thing" apprehended in its own right

A problem dealing with the objective similarity or dissimilarity of common articles would be beyond the maturity of the five-year-old. His thought problems must be very largely concerned with the best way of doing things.

Thus, a boy of eight years was asked, "Is the sun alive?" to which he answered, "Yes." Asked "Why?" he replied: "It gives light. It is alive when it is giving light, but it isn't alive when it is not giving light." Asked, "Is a bicycle alive?" the child replied: "No, when it doesn't go, it isn't alive. When it goes, it is alive." To the question, "Is a mountain alive?" the child answered, "No." The query, "Why not?" brought the reply, "Because it doesn't do anything." It is obvious that for this child the concept *life* means ability to move or do something.

By way of comparison, let us take the more mature concept of a twelve-year-old boy similarly questioned. The boy said that he knew what it meant to be alive. He was then asked, "Is a fly alive?" He said, "Yes," and, upon being asked "Why?" replied, "If it wasn't alive, it couldn't fly." To the question, "Is a bicycle alive?" the boy replied, "No." "Why not?" brought the reply, "Because it is we who make it go." Further questioning verified the fact that this boy attributed life to anything that could move of its own volition. (10, p. 185)

Finer discriminations come only after cruder discriminations of the same kind. The home economics student who is now prepared to handle the problem of "grades of meat" was, perhaps but a relatively short time ago, able to distinguish only two kinds, "good" and "bad." A scale of quality is a refinement and expansion of a pair of opposites. A pupil cannot understand what a "restrictive" clause is in grammar until he has the more general understanding of a "modifying" clause. Difficulties of this kind are to be found at all levels of thinking. The concept of "factor," as employed in psychological discussions of ability, represents a step in the development of the more general notion of "cause" which many students find difficult to take. They do not distinguish the kind of cause that is a "condition" of the change from the "principal-agent" or from the "constitutive-element" type of cause.

Another grave source of difficulty in problem solving is the wrong "direction" frequently given by past experience. This is

a special case of difficulty in seeing relations and has been sin-
gled out for study in the laboratory.

Direction and Recentering. We saw in the badminton
game problem that our past experience created the special difficulty of giving the wrong direction. The problem tended to
center around the familiar concept of badminton as competitive, and the solution required the boys to give up this meaning
and recenter toward badminton as cooperative. What was the
source of difficulty? Eduction was not difficult, since some
persons readily educed the idea of offering a bribe, giving a
handicap, and the like. The total picture, based on familiarity
with badminton as usually played, resulted in the wrong kind
of eductions. An eduction consists, in a sense, of simple "reading off" a relation or a correlate from what is given. But productive or creative thinking, as recent writers have pointed out,
usually involves a recentering or reorganization of the problem,
so that something new, something not "co-contained" in the
original familiar picture, can be educed (4). We present here
a problem to make this clear.[1]

> A shepherd, an inveterate smoker, is tending his flock on
> the western end of a small island, which is entirely covered
> by inflammable brush and grass. The whole perimeter of the
> island consists of a high steep cliff, with the exception of a
> single path to the sea at the eastern end. A fire, fanned by a
> brisk wind, breaks out at the eastern end of the island and
> sweeps rapidly toward the sheep, cutting off their only route
> of escape. The shepherd realizes that they will perish in the
> fire or fall over the cliff to their destruction. How can he
> save the flock?

The reader might try this problem with adult subjects, let
them diagram it, and keep notes on their responses. He will
find that the more able ones usually recall that forest rangers
combat fires by setting fires, or recall some verbalism such as
"fight fire with fire," which leads to the eduction that the shep-
herd (a smoker) probably has a match. "Set a fire," they say.
So much for past experience. The critical aspect of the prob-

[1] Example suggested by Martin Scheerer.

em, testing the adequacy of the search-model, is where the person would set the fire. (Setting it to the east of the sheep is not insightful.) Past experience will ordinarily dictate a false train of thought along the line of "flee the fire" instead of "use the fire." Recentering is required for solution.

A number of experiments by Maier (9) were designed to discover some essential aspects of problem solving. One important question is this: If the individual has all the necessary parts or equipment for solving a problem, has available all the responses necessary, and also knows that the responses and equipment are essential to the solution, will he be able to solve it with this and nothing more? In other words, does complete familiarity with the essential parts make it possible for a person to put them together to make a structural whole?

Maier's results caused him to conclude that something more —an appropriate general *direction*—is also needed. In one of his experiments, college students were given the problem of erecting a T-shaped structure from which two pendulums could be suspended so as to make chalk marks at indicated points on the floor (see Figure 72). Different groups were given different kinds of instruction, but the same material (poles, wire, clamps, chalk) were given each group. One group was shown the details of putting the poles together with clamps to make a *horizontal* T in a doorway, and of clamping the length of wire to a pole to make a plumb line. Another group was given a hint of direction—"how simple this problem would be if we could just hang the pendulum from a nail in the ceiling." A third group was given both direction and training on details. The results clearly indicated that both the part-training and the direction toward the whole were essential; of students given both, 22 achieved the solution, while only one of the 62 students in the other groups was able to do so. "Direction" as Maier uses the term, appears to be a suggestion of the general form of the search-model.

Wertheimer's study of problem solving in the area of a parallelogram brings an illustration closer to the school situation (15). He attended high school class sessions in geometry in which the teacher instructed the class in the usual method of

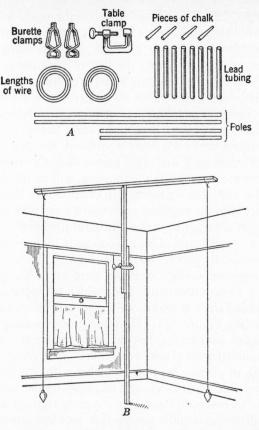

FIGURE 72. Maier's Pendulum Problem. (Figure from Crafts, *et al* *Recent Experiments in Psychology,* New York: McGraw-Hill, 1938.)

finding the area of a parallelogram by dropping perpendicula lines to the base and proving that the triangles are equal, as i Figure 73-I. In this way the teacher demonstrated, with a num ber of examples, that the area of a parallelogram was equal t the base times the altitude, like the area of a rectangle. Th class learned this easily and were able to solve a number o examples independently. They appeared to have "compre hended." Whereupon Wertheimer presented the identica problem in a different way by turning the rectangle around, a in Figure 73-II.   The students dropped the perpendiculars as they had been taught, and said "the area is equal to the base times the altitude," but in the unfamiliar setting could not explain why it was so.   This was a blind reproduction, without real understanding.

In what respect is this finding similar to that of Maier's pendulum study?   Through the teacher's demonstration, the students were given practice in essential *parts* of the problem, dropping perpendiculars to make a rectangle.   They were thus given a search-model of a certain form, having little triangles on each end as in Figure 73-III.   But when given the identical parts in altered form, the solution required a conceptually new search-model.   (Note that Figure 73-II has no familiar little triangles to prove equal.)   The students perceived relations,

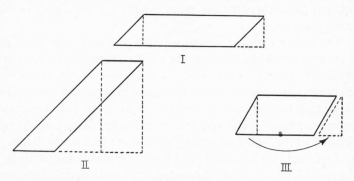

FIGURE 73.   Wertheimer's Problem of Finding the Area of a Parallelogram.   High school students who learned to make a rectangle of the figure by dropping perpendiculars, as in the drawing at the top, could not solve the problem when the parallelogram was presented in another position, as in (II) at left.   To make the transition from the familiar "equal triangle" solution (III) to the unfamiliar situation (II) is a process of "recentering."

but only in the familiar setting.   The relations could not be transferred to the second figure which requires organization of the part relations into a new whole.   Similarly, in Maier's pendulum problem, students who had learned to fit the poles together to make a *horizontal* T in a doorway could not transfer this knowledge to a solution requiring a *vertical* T against the ceiling.   A knowledge of relations, even correct ones, does not result in the solution of a problem when the search-model is inadequate.

It is often assumed that all thinking is reproductive—that students cannot be expected to comprehend the essential structure of the parallelogram problem, but only to reproduce what they had learned through demonstration and drill. To test this assumption, Wertheimer presented the parallelogram problem to subjects who had been shown how to find the area of a rectangle by dividing it up into a number of squares. In one striking but not exceptional instance, a 5½-year-old child given a paper figure of a parallelogram solved the problem by cutting the figure with a pair of scissors. That it was not just memory, or the association of scissors with paper, that led to the solution is shown by the fact that other children given scissors and encouraged to use them usually cut the figure in the wrong places.

The author cites the scissor solution as a case of productive or creative thinking, because the solution depends on the perception of "inner relations," or of what is required by the problem itself. The person completely naive in geometry can apparently grasp the problem as one of "making the parallelogram into a rectangle." This requires recentering. Many adults responded to this problem by saying "I don't like mathematics," or "I learned that in school but I have completely forgotten it." The point is this: learning through demonstration, drill, or other forms of imitative repetition, although depending on perception of relations, often proves a deterrent to the recentering required to solve a new or unfamiliar problem. Creative thinking is not merely a running off of habits or memories or even relations, but a reorganization of past learning to fit a new set of requirements. Psychologically, the act of the 5½-year-old child was quite similar in some respects to the mental process of Einstein in reorganizing the whole science of physics to fit a new concept, relativity (15).

Group Processes in Problem Solving. So far we have been talking as though the solution of problems is the work of one individual acting alone. However, problems are often solved in everyday life by a group of persons pooling their individual contributions into a collaborative effort. This is particularly true of social problems, the solution of which involves the satisfaction of many individuals with differing goals and points of view. It would seem that the effective solution of such problems should be improved by cooperative thinking, since the interaction of individual proposals and criticisms serves to clarify problems and to select more adequate search-models. However, group thinking may also be disintegrating, and there are some types of problems requiring sustained and highly integrated activity which can best be solved by concentrated individual activity. R. L. Thorndike's summary of factors pertinent to cooperative thinking points up both advantages and disadvantages:

1. The group typically brings a broader background of experience to a problem situation than does any single individual.

2. As a reflection of 1, the group is likely to produce more and more varied suggestions for dealing with a problem than will arise from a single individual.

3. The diversity of viewpoints is *likely* to be more representative of the larger population from which they were drawn than is the viewpoint of the single individual.

4. As diversity of background and interest within the group becomes greater, it becomes increasingly difficult to reach a real agreement among the members of the group as to the definition of the problem and the values to be served. Reconciliation of conflicting goals becomes the real problem.

5. Just as a group is likely to produce a greater range of suggestions, so also a group is likely to be more productive in criticisms of proposals and bases for rejecting them.

6. Interstimulation is a distinctive feature of group effort. The suggestion by X, which is criticized by Y, serves as the stimulus to Z for a new and perhaps quite different suggestion.

7. Interpersonal dynamics becomes a significant element. The assertive, the dogmatic, and the persuasive individual—each plays a distinctive role.

8. With increasing size and diversity of group memberships, unity and integration of effort are often difficult to achieve. Group members may show a tendency to "ride off in all directions." (14, p. 209)

In recent years, education has become increasingly aware of the importance of the social factors involved in cooperative problem solving. The school provides an excellent training ground for this particular type of activity, and the modern teacher should make the most of it. It is not so much a question of whether better solutions may result from group discussion, but whether the child will benefit from the give-and-take process just described. It can be an excellent way of motivating the individual to think and will serve to sharpen his concepts as well.

Learning and Teaching to Think

We now come to the important question of this chapter: how can we teach the student to think? The answer largely depends on what we conceive to be the characteristic features of the thinking process. For instance:

1. If thinking is conceived to be a power or "mental muscle" to be strengthened through practice, we should attempt to improve thinking ability through mental gymnastic exercises in difficult problems. We have seen that this concept (formal discipline) is unscientific and that exercise as such would be an educational waste of time.

2. If we hold thinking to be a "logical" process that can be learned by applying rules, we should teach the student rules, formulae, neat but artificial patterns such as syllogisms or other rituals, and drill them in the use of these in solving problems. This misconception of the thinking process, and the educational practices that follow it, have not been fruitful in the classroom.

Children, after reading a problem, are instructed to ask themselves and to answer in sequence the following set of questions: "What am I asked to find?" "What facts am I given?" "What numbers shall I use?" "What process (e.g., addition) shall I use?" "What is the probable answer?" Incessant drill on this kind of formal analysis has failed to produce good problem solvers. On the other hand, some research has demonstrated that better results are to be secured when children are given plenty of verbal problems and left to their own devices. (3, p. 122)

3. If we are unaware of genetic differences in readiness or ability to think and assume that the characteristics of thinking

behavior look alike at all stages of development, we are likely
to expect thought processes in the child which are characteristic of the well educated adult. (The example cited above
shows this approach.) We may also set up thinking problems
which are too difficult or otherwise inappropriate. Or, if convinced that children cannot think at any level, we may simply
ignore this aspect of their development.

4. If we confuse thought and language, which is the vehicle
(and not the only one) of thought, we may tend to overemphasize verbalization, i.e., to reward empty verbalisms in the classroom. This, of course, destroys those very attitudes and tendencies which are basic to thinking activity.

5. If we conceive thinking to be an imitative process, or
one learned by imitation, our teaching may be confined exclusively to the "this is the way to do it" approach, in which the
teacher becomes a demonstrator and the student an imitator.
Demonstration is necessary and important, but can be overdone. If the student is never placed in problem situations which
require originality or reorganization of what he has learned,
he may never develop the "search attitude." In Wertheimer's
study of the area of the parallelogram, the students learned
through demonstration a technique for finding the area (dropping perpendiculars to the base) but did not know *why* the
technique worked. Furthermore, they were not curious about
why it worked.

6. If our concept of "thinking" is inadequate, we may be
in the position of not recognizing thinking when it occurs, and
therefore not rewarding it when it occurs. Children often do
not think in school because they are not encouraged to do so.
Even children, said William James, "can enjoy abstractions,
provided they be of the proper order; and it is a poor compli-
ment to their rational appetite to think that anecdotes about
little Tommies and little Jennies are the only kind of things
their minds can digest" (7, p. 152).

Learning to Think. There is no formula for teaching students to think. The mere assumption that there is, or that we
can invent one, is based on the corollary assumption that think-

ing is a formal process.   The principles of logic provide conceptual models of correct thinking, but they mislead us into the belief that thinking really follows such a pattern.   The psychology of thinking is not well developed, and the thinking process is at best only partially understood.   But such descriptions as we have of productive thinking and problem solving show that it is complex, disorderly, mixed up with false starts and backtracking, and characterized by long periods of apparent stagnation as well as by sudden flashes of insight.   This is as true of Einstein's work in relativity as it is of the child's solution to a mechanical puzzle.

However, the attitudes conducive to thinking are learned, and can therefore be developed.   This is easily misunderstood. We do not mean that if *methods* of thinking are taught, in the form of generalizations and principles, the student will necessarily apply them when he encounters a problem.   Why not? Because the principles of logic and formal analysis are in themselves high-level relations, which must be educed from lower level relations.   The principles of logic are thoughts about thinking, not thinking itself.   To put it another way, you cannot form an adequate concept of "thinking" without knowing, from your own experience, what thinking is.   As with other forms of behavior, you can learn to think only by doing it.   Seen in this light, the attempt to teach the student to think by means of formal rules and patterns is putting the cart before the horse, because he may not have the experience necessary to comprehend the meaning of the concepts embodied in the rules.   Concepts like induction, deduction, analysis, reason, cause, are genetically very complex.   The word "think" is a symbol for a very difficult concept, as the material in this chapter must have convinced you.   The student may learn and use the words, but not understand the concepts.   Thus our formal attempts to teach him to think may boomerang, and result in unthinking verbalisms.

The child learns to think, then, by doing it.   The conditions for learning to think are the same as for learning to spell, typewrite, kick a football, or jump rope, but thinking *activity* is different.   The learner must have a need for thinking, or in other words a goal to initiate activity; an appropriate level of readiness, or interest and ability; a problem situation, or one in which his immediately available responses are inadequate for reaching the goal and require reorganization. There must be mental activity, which involves *search* for interpretations and hypotheses, provisional tries and errors, reformulation of experience in terms of what is required. There must be satisfying consequences, or feelings of "success." If thinking in response to problem situations is rewarded or found satisfying, it will tend to be repeated. Unsatisfying consequences will lead to avoidance of thinking.

We have seen that the problem attitude, or search attitude, is basic to the successful solution of problems. It is a "determining tendency" in thinking. Learning to think, in so far as it can be guided by the teacher, is a process of learning a problem-solving attitude. The school may guide the development of thinking by providing problem situations in which thinking will appear, and by seeing to it that thinking is rewarded. To manage this successfully, the teacher must know what thinking is and be able to recognize it in action.

How to Recognize Thinking. Since thinking originates in a problem, we should expect that this beginning stage should be one of confusion and trial and error behavior. Confusion as such may not indicate a stage of readiness for thinking; we must distinguish between the confusion resulting from no clearly perceived goal (which is not conducive to thinking) and confusion resulting from the blocking or thwarting of a clearly perceived goal, which may initiate thought. What are the signs that a student may be seeking clarification?

The student who doubts, criticizes, or expresses skepticism may be facing a genuine problem: he may be telling us that this fact, that procedure, or some generalization is not consistent with his experience. Hollingworth's bright child was thinking when he objected to the teacher's statement that Gutenberg invented printing and pointed out that the Chinese had printing much earlier. Some teachers feel that such behavior is disruptive and tend to discourage it. Of course, doubts and questions are sometimes mere attention-getting devices, but they may also be genuine attempts to clarify problems. The teacher who would encourage thinking must invite the open expression of genuine problems, no matter how disrupting and unpleasant it may seem to her. Furthermore, problems are personal and concerned with personal goals. We must resist the inclination to scorn or ignore the student who wants to build a better mouse-trap, inconsequential though his scheme may seem.

Thinking is characterized by search. The student's errors may not be stupid, but only seem so because we do not know what his search-model is. The teacher who is impatient with errors, simply because they are errors, completely smothers attempts to think. The distinction between "good" and "poor" errors (functional and nonfunctional) is important here. The student who comes forth with a novel and "logical," but mis-taken, way of solving a problem, based on an inadequate search-model of his own construction, needs to be taken seriously. His creative efforts should be guided toward discovery of the defect in his search-model or assumptions, and toward the selection of a more suitable model. We must often resist the tendency to force the student to "do as he is told" and follow the standard procedures. Exploring a new possibility, no matter how "wrong," may result in the student's discovering the *why* of things. It may pay all teachers to ponder the significant fact that Edison and Einstein were not considered "good" students in school.

Thinking is a delayed response. Action impedes reflection. A person faced with a real problem needs plenty of time, be-cause the clarification of a problem is a slow and rather disor-derly process. We must not only provide problem situations, but encourage the student to "stop and think" and give him time. To encourage thinking, the teacher must inhibit the impulse to move ahead and to place a premium on immediate results.

The fact that thinking is symbolic means that not only words, but gestures, drawings, and diagrams are used in thinking. Self-expression, sometimes even the most bizarre sort, accom-panies and aids genuine attempts at clarification. The student should therefore be encouraged to "talk out loud," use "body

English," draw or sketch his concepts no matter how strange such behavior may seem to a class. If we are to place a premium on thinking, rather than slavish conformity to rules and procedures, we must treat the groping attempts at clarification with respect, as we would any form of artistic performance.[1]

Teaching to Think. We should concentrate on the learner, not on methods of thinking. The contribution of formal education to thinking lies chiefly in motivating the learner, in enriching his experience or broadening his background of information, and in organizing classroom activities in a manner favorable to reflective thought by providing problem situations.

1. *Motivation.* All that has been said of the motivation of learning is applicable to thinking as well. Any teaching devices which aim at an increase in the sense of achievement through the raising of problems of vital interest will serve to supply the mental energy needed for the new organizations of experience. Many of the rules given by educators for training students to think, such as, "children must be permitted to offer suggestions toward solution of problems," "encourage the formation of hypotheses," "cultivate creative imagination," are fundamentally matters of motivation. A teacher may, through inordinate stress upon the factual content of subject-matter, discourage personal initiative in forming hypotheses, which represent one of the first steps in thought. Again, the lack of proper pacing of problems, with the attendant difficulty of thinking and discouragement in the face of failure, may create a predisposition away from thinking. The child may acquire the notion that it is more important for him to know the answers to his problems than it is for him to have obtained these answers himself. The premium which we place upon mere efficiency as such in the

---

[1] A recent study of rote memorization, understanding, and transfer by Hilgard, Irvine, and Whipple (*J. exper. Psychol.*, 1953, **46**, 288-292) shows the kinds of errors or difficulties likely to arise in the full use of the "understanding" method of learning. Some subjects do not resist the "reproductive tendency" but become impatient and adopt rote memorization once the solution is attained. Others become careless in diagramming the order and relations involved in the problem. Still others seem to be satisfied with but partial understanding and then rely on rote memory of the formula as a crutch for later use instead of intelligently reconstructing it in thought.

earlier grades may not infrequently work against the stimulation of personal initiative so necessary for thinking.

2. *Enriching Experience*. Education relies mainly on verbal processes, and necessarily so, because the most effective communication is through language. This must not blind us to the fact that words are just symbols of meaning. Learning through words is a kind of vicarious experience. This implies that in any verbal communication the person on the receiving end must supply his own meaning. Words are bare bones, which must be given flesh, blood, and vitality through personal experience. The important goal of education is the development of adequate concepts, and conceptualization is enriched by sensory experience. We cannot acquire an adequate concept of an egg beater, a sunset, or a piano through verbal description. Teaching concepts means providing situations which facilitate their comprehension, and this implies more than defining a word and giving examples. If we grasp the principles of eduction, it should be clear to us that a concept is not learned, once and for all, as a static thing, but is developed through progressive experience. Consider "mother" or "motherhood," for example. What does "mother" mean to a child, to an adolescent, to a biologist, to a sociologist? The adequacy of the concept, at all levels of development, is limited by the personal experience of the individual. The ability to think is therefore limited in the same way. It is in this sense that "one picture is worth a thousand words."

Enriching experience involves first utilizing that immediate source of first-hand information, the *community*. Its fields, streams, farms and factories provide a natural laboratory for the study of natural and physical science. Its government, industry, and planning problems make it possible for social sciences to become more vital and less bookish. Its theaters, art galleries, music concerts, and other activities provide aesthetic experiences. The student will of course explore his community of his own volition, but many factors place narrow limits on these experiences. The upper and lower social strata, for example, have little opportunity to learn how the other half lives. It is an unpleasant fact that students ready to graduate from high school often do not know the range of occupational oppor-tunities in the community. The job of the school is then to give direction to the student's participation in community life, in order to make his verbal learning more meaningful. Projects, visits, and community studies thus play a vital part in laying a foundation for adequate concepts and productive thinking.

Visual aids such as photographs, models, slides, and motion pictures play an important role for the same reason. They should properly be regarded as supplementary to verbal learn-ing, and not substitutes for it. Visual aids are means to an end, which is concept formation. The danger of visual aids and other means of concrete experience lies in treating them as ends in themselves. When the school gave up the notion of improving thinking through formal discipline, it often went to the opposite extreme of supposing that more visual and auditory experience, "sense-training," and projects would of necessity further thought. Movies make their specific and significant contribution in depicting *action* and *motion* when this is nec-essary for the understanding of the lesson (5). They are often, however, inferior to laboratory or shop demonstrations by the teacher. "Seeing" is not simply a matter of looking, nor is the mental representation of reality, even when tested as a matter of facts or of information, merely a photographic image. To have the pupil draw a feather pictorially, for example, does not lead to such accurate information about the nature or structure of the object as is the case when a schematic drawing has been made (1). The reason for this seems to be that, before the lat-ter type of drawing is possible, the significant relations of the details of the feather must first be appreciated.

There is no satisfactory substitute for direct personal experi-ence of reality, and instructional devices should be appropriate to the nature of the fact or object of thought. Motion pictures and animated drawings may make places, people, events, and processes more real, thus making language more meaningful and thinking more effective. "Children who are lacking in imagination, low in intelligence, or below the average in read-ing ability, are helped especially" (6). But a vivid or realistic reproduction of the objective situation does not substitute for an active mental elaboration of the relationships underlying the sensible details.

REFERENCES

1. AYER, F. C. *The psychology of drawing.* Baltimore: Warwick & York, 1916.
2. BODE, B. H. *Conflicting psychologies of learning.* Boston: Heath, 1929.
3. BROWNELL, W. A., & HENDRICKSON, G. How children learn information, concepts, and generalizations. *49th Yearbook,* Nat. Soc. Stud. Educ., 1950.
4. DUNCKER, K. On problem solving. (Translation by LEES, L. S., from 1935 original) *Psychol. Monogr.,* 1945, **58,** No. 270.
5. FREEMAN, F. N. *et al. Visual education.* Chicago: Univ. of Chicago Press, 1924.
6. HORN, E. *Methods of instruction in the social studies.* New York: Scribner's, 1937.
7. JAMES, W. *Talks to teachers on psychology.* New York: Holt, 1899.
8. LAYCOCK, S. R. *Adaptability to new situations.* Baltimore: Warwick & York, 1926.
9. MAIER, N. R. F. Reasoning in humans. I, On direction. *J. comp. Psychol.,* 1930, **10,** 115-144. II, The solution of a problem and its appearance in consciousness. *J. comp. Psychol.,* 1931, **12,** 181-194. III, The mechanisms of equivalent stimuli and of reasoning. *J. exp. Psychol.,* 1945, **35,** 349-360.
10. MUNN, N. *Psychology.* New York: Houghton Mifflin, 1946. From PIAGET, 11.
11. PIAGET, J. *Judgment and reasoning in the child.* New York: Harcourt, Brace, 1928.
12. RUGER, H. A. The psychology of efficiency. *Arch. Psychol.,* 1910, No. 15.
13. STRASHEIM, J. J. *A new method of mental testing.* Baltimore: Warwick & York, 1926.
14. THORNDIKE, R. L. How children learn the principles and techniques of problem solving. *49th Yearbook,* Nat. Soc. Stud. Educ., 1950.
15. WERTHEIMER, M. *Productive thinking.* New York: Harper, 1945.

SELECTED READINGS

DUNCKER, K. On problem solving. *Psychol. Monogr.,* No. 270, 1945. For the advanced student.

FLESCH, R. *The art of clear thinking*. New York: Harper, 1951. A popular self-help book that presents the meat of psychological research in easily digestible style.

HUMPHREY, G. *Directed thinking*. New York: Dodd, Mead, 1948. For general reading.

JOHNSON, W. *People in quandaries: the semantics of personal adjustment*. New York: Harper, 1946. Presents illustrations of how our words, meanings, and preconceptions throw us off the track. For general reading.

THORNDIKE, R. L. How children learn the principles and techniques of problem solving. Ch. 8 in *49th Yearbook,* Nat. Soc. Stud. Educ., 1950.

WERTHEIMER, M. *Productive thinking*. New York: Harper, 1945. Deserves thorough study by anyone interested in thinking and problem solving.

21

LEARNING AND PERSONAL ADJUSTMENT

A<small>LL</small> <small>LEARNING</small> is adjustive; that is, the outcome is in the direction of relating the self more favorably to the environment. This is another way of saying that learning is purposive, that the learner's activity arises from his personal needs and is directed toward his personal goals. Learning as adjustment consists in the progressive changes taking place in the patterns of our experience and behavior toward better adjustment to the felt demands of life.

Our understanding of educational psychology would be quite incomplete unless we raise such questions as these: What are the forms of personal adjustment? What are the characteristic ways of meeting emotional problems? What psychological principles govern the guidance of adjustment through counseling and other means? To deal with these questions, we must consider some aspects of the learning process which have not yet been discussed.

The Concept of Adjustment. In the broadest sense, adjustment means doing something to solve a problem. It is a form of adaptation to new circumstances, usually circumstances which imply some kind of demand, threat, disturbance, or loss of equilibrium to the self. *Adaptation,* a term used in biology, refers to behavior which keeps the organism alive, in good health, and able to reproduce. The organism seeks food when hungry, water when thirsty, and seeks means of reproducing its kind. Organic behavior is organized internally to ward off various threats; for example, the body attempts to eliminate poisons and to compensate for extreme temperatures. The forms of adaptation are said to have survival value, i.e., they prevent destruction of the organism and make it more effective in dealing with threats of destruction.

Psychological adjustment is similar, but here we must draw a distinction between adaptation and adjustment, because some forms of adjustment are not adaptive. Suicide, for example, is one. It solves a psychological problem (after a fashion) but destroys the organism. The thirsty shipwrecked sailor who drinks sea water also performs a psychological adjustive act which is not biologically adaptive.

We may further define the concept of adjustment as follows: Adjustment is an activity which is motivated by need (either primary or learned) and results in the reduction of tension induced by that need. Suicide and drinking sea water are adjustive because they reduce tensions. These acts are maladaptive, and therefore considered "maladjustive," but they are nonetheless adjustive by the definition just given. Maladjustment *is* adjustment, and follows the same principles of learning. This point is important. Such undesirable forms of behavior as temper tantrums, pathological lying, blaming others, or extreme shyness are adjustive but socially maladaptive; that is, they do not help the individual to get along better with others. Even such apparently self-impairing and self-destructive behavior as neuroticism and psychosis are adjustive, because they serve to reduce some kind of emotional tension and to solve (more or less effectively) personal problems. We may say that all human acts are attempts at adaptation, but not all of them are successful. We may also say that an act may be adaptive to one aspect of a situation, but not to others. Sea water may quench the sailor's thirst, but not effectively.

Note that when we speak of learning as adjustment, we emphasize needs as "tensions," and we focus on one particular aspect of the consequences of behavior—the reduction of tension. Adjustment always implies reward, satisfaction, gratification, need-fulfillment. The term "nonadjustive behavior" therefore describes behavior which is continued without reduction of tension, or without satisfying consequences.

The Adjustment Process. The process of adjustment is shown diagrammatically in Figure 74. The individual impelled by a need (1) is proceeding in the direction of a goal or end-result (4) and is blocked by an obstacle. He then makes varied responses (2) and finally gets around the obstacle by some response or other which leads to "readjustment."

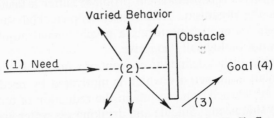

FIGURE 74. The Adjustment Process. (From L. N. Shaffer, 11, after Dashiell.)

Any blocked motive may induce varied behavior. In many ordinary situations, adjustments are made to the blocking of inconsequential goals by habitual responses, i.e., a person with a dry fountain pen fills it or uses a pencil. This is an adjustment. We are concerned, however, with the much less trivial general needs for dominance, affiliation, status, and the like, which are products of social learning and whose thwarting usually results in great emotional tension.

The source of thwarting may be any threatening thing, person, or event. It may be something outside the individual, an environmental obstacle like the command of a parent, the wishes of a girl friend, or a dead battery that will not start the car. Actually, we can draw no fine distinction between obstacles that are within the individual and those that are outside his skin. Thus the parental command or the wishes of the girl friend function as obstacles only because of the individual's attitude—his wish to please the parent, or his fear of punishment or loss of the girl friend's affection. The dead battery, on the other hand, is quite objective.

Some very important sources of thwarting are both subjective and objective, such as personal defects like ugliness, lack of athletic ability, poor speech, or lack of education. These may be "real" or imaginary, but as we have seen they are real to the person who believes they are. An obstacle may be an anticipation of disagreeable consequences. Thus a boy's anticipated disapproval by his girl friend may thwart his goal of taking another girl to a dance quite as readily as her actual expression of disapproval. Two motives are operating here. This source of thwarting is motivational conflict, involving two antagonistic motives which are approximately equal in strength. Conflict is probably the most important aspect of all personal adjustment problems. Practically all sources of thwarting involve motivational conflict; that is, the obstacle in most cases is a second motive or goal drive in an opposite direction to the first.

The major respect in which personal adjustment problems differ from more objective types of "thinking" problems is in the adequacy of the solution. In thinking, the only adequate solution is one that is required by the "inner relations" of the problem, i.e., a rational solution. It must not only "make sense," but must do so in a rational, logical way. This is true of a problem in mathematics, for instance. In the problem of the badminton game, the boys' decision to change the game to a cooperative effort was the "best" solution because it fit what was required, was most logical. From the adjustment point of view, however, the sole criterion of what constitutes the solution of a problem is tension-reduction, or doing away with frustration. By this criterion, the decision of the younger boy to quit the game was a "solution," because it reduced the tension caused by his being constantly beaten. The decision to switch from badminton to checkers or quoits might have been an adjustment solution if it removed the source of frustration. In other words, the adjustment point of view sees the problem only from the standpoint of the learner, his needs and goals. Any act that reduces tension, or results in satisfaction to the thwarted individual, is a solution or adjustment. We do not mean here, obviously, that all adjustments are considered adequate in the moral or social sense. Stealing, lying, and murder are immoral and socially maladaptive, hence "maladjustive." But they are adjustive. The importance of this lies in the psychological distinction between adjustive and "nonadjustive" behavior, in which the individual does not vary his responses, but does the same thing over and over without any reduction in tension. It is important also to distinguish between rational and non-rational solutions to personal problems. Rational solution is one form of adjustment, but it is rare in problems where emotional tension is high. Rational solutions require thinking, and as we saw previously a strong goal drive with accompanying tension is not conducive to thought.

The adjustment point of view is important to the teacher because it leads to an understanding of the student's problem. By contrast, the nonpsychological view dictates that we find out whether a boy is stealing or lying, and punish him for it; that we find out whether a girl is depressed, and try to talk her out of it (usually by appealing to logic, persuasion, or suggestion). This approach ignores the problem. The adjustment point of view is psychological; it focuses on *why* the boy steals or the girl is depressed. The answer is always to be sought in the personal problem of the individual: What need or goal, blocked by what obstacle, is being satisfied by this behavior? It may turn out (although this oversimplifies the matter) that the boy steals because he is depressed, and the girl is depressed because of uncontrollable impulses to steal.

Homeostasis: The Principle of Organization. From the adjustment point of view, we must think of the individual as an active organizer of his behavior. The purpose of organization is to maintain a stable inner equilibrium of the self, to ward off or deal with threats to personal stability. An analogy from physiology may help to show how the individual is organized to deal with threat.

Cannon, a Harvard physiologist, stated the principle of homeostasis after many years of research with the processes by which the body repairs and restores itself to maintain an optimum state of balance (1). The term "homeostasis" means "same state" or "uniform state." The principle is one of self-regulation or self-balance, by which the body wards off invaders from without and within, restores its tissues, and maintains a uniform optimum state which not only enables it to survive, but to grow and develop. The materials of the body, Cannon said, are fragile and remarkably unstable; the body tissues are very sensitive to stimulation and fatigue. They are subject to such wear and tear and such threats of stoppages that life itself would seem to be very precarious. The heat produced by muscular effort, for example, "would be so great that it would cause some of the albuminous substances of the body to become stiff, like a hard-boiled egg" (1).

An example of the body's tendency to maintain stability is its resistance to external heat. In recent tests by the Air Force men were rigged with instruments in various parts of the body for measuring temperatures, blood pressure, rate of respiration, perspiration, metabolism, pulse, and the like. Then they were exposed to intense oven heat for a number of minutes. Temperatures close to skin surfaces rose alarmingly, and most of the physiological measures taken were abnormal during the period of exposure, but the blood temperature rose only slightly. All of the apparently "abnormal" reactions were compensating for the extraordinary threat to the life of the organism, which depends on the maintenance of an optimum blood temperature. In this sense, of course, they were not abnormal at all, but merely aspects of a normal tendency to maintain conditions necessary for survival. The basic tendency to organize external and internal conditions to maintain a uniform state of equilibrium has been called "wisdom of the body," systematic relevance, a state of vigilance.

The analogy applies to psychological adjustment as well. The facts of learning and development fit very well into a principle of *psychological homeostasis,* by which the learner selects and adjusts to environmental conditions in accordance with his need for an effective, stable organization.

Self-Consistency: The Goal of Mental Life. We can think of all the manifold needs of the individual in terms of a single need—the need to maintain and enhance the self-concept. All the activities of the individual can be seen to serve this purpose, because all motives refer to the self-concept. Let us think of the self-concept as a kind of mental picture or idealized image.

All of us are more or less aware of a mental picture of ourselves which we regard as appropriate, an organized composite of our abilities and disabilities, our interests and dislikes, our virtues and defects. That is the "self as perceived by the self" which we strive to maintain and enhance. The self-concept is not so much the way we *think* about ourselves, for thinking implies an objective frame of reference—an ability to see ourselves from someone else's point of view. It is rather the way we *feel* about ourselves.

We can best illustrate what this means by asking what kinds of things annoy us, disturb us, make us angry, or cause us to have feelings of failure. Someone who has never played tennis and who does not conceive of himself as athletically inclined will not be disturbed by a slighting remark with reference to his tennis ability. Provided he can be induced to play, he can take a number of severe drubbings with the utmost composure. By contrast, one who conceives of himself as a "good tennis player" may be annoyed, disturbed, irritated, profoundly depressed by the loss of a tennis match, or even by a slighting remark. The manner of response will depend on still other aspects of the self-concept. He may also conceive of himself as a "good loser," or as a "gentleman," and conceal his feelings. Or he may accept himself as inferior to a highly respected opponent and actually, in this case, interpret a close defeat as a success. Pleasurable feelings accompany experience which is self-maintaining or self-enhancing, and painful feelings accompany experience which threatens the self-concept. The self-concept is thus emotional in character, in the sense that our emotions are engaged in maintaining and defending it. Emotional disturbances are symptoms of the thwarted motive.

All of a person's behavior, whether he is aware of it or not, defends and preserves the self-concept, which sets up expectations for the person as to how he shall behave, what people will think of him, what kinds of things he will find satisfying. His attitude, therefore, towards any thing, person, or event will be relative to his self-concept. He will adjust, in other words, in accordance with a need for what Lecky called an inner *self-consistency* (4). His "resistance" to certain kinds of learning, whether it takes the form of avoidance, inattention, or forgetting, is an outward aspect of inner integration. The seeming perversity with which an individual may thus resist "good" advice, a "helpful" solution to his problem, or the gestures of others who have his own welfare at heart, is psychologically lawful. His refusal to learn the things necessary to his presumed goals and to "adjust to reality" is not perverse, but a normal tendency to maintain his integrity in the face of threats to his very self. This resistance is predictable in all of us; and, since it is emotional and not "intellectual-logical," we cannot easily be argued out of it. In fact, the very arguments used to dislodge us from such an attitude often threaten us so much that they serve merely to reinforce the attitude.

How many times have we noticed that a student may show every sign of understanding what he is told, nod his head in agreement, leave us with every apparent intention of putting our advice into practice—and then promptly forget about it and do the opposite? If we ascribe such behavior to perversity, lack of intellectual grasp, or weakness of will we are missing the point. The child's psychological armor, organized around the self-concept, is tough enough to withstand all of the slings and arrows of advice and instruction from teachers and parents which are at odds with his self-picture.

Changes in basic attitudes involve changes in the self-concept. A new attitude is not a matter of putting on a new garment, but one of literally altering our psychological shape, or reorganizing the self. An individual's attitude towards the objects in his environment always has a self-reference. If he becomes interested in playing the violin, for example, it is because it seems to him that the skill is valuable for the attainment of some personal goal, and thus becomes a subgoal in itself. If a small boy develops a strong antipathy towards his mother, it may be because he perceives her as a threat to the attainment of some goal with which he is strongly identified. If the goal is to join the gang "across the tracks" his purpose is to become something which he perceives as admirable—perhaps to build up his self-concept as a "tough" boy—more masculine, more adequate.

The "goal" is thus an aspect of his self-concept. In order to give up this goal, he must alter the self-concept. It is clear that if his goal is thwarted by his mother his reaction will be either resistance to his mother or reorganization of his self-concept—possibly to include a self-definition of something like a "dutiful son." Resistance would be more likely. If his goal were thwarted by the gang itself, reorganization of the self-concept would be more likely and probably more rapid. Similarly, if the aspiring violinist discovered that he had no ability, he might soon "lose interest," which means not only dropping the goal but also changing his perception of himself. All of a person's likes and dislikes, interests and aversions are "aspects of his self-concept." Also, the adoption of goals or the relinquishment of goals involves changes in the self-concept. A new attitude towards *anything* means a new attitude *towards one's self in relation to the thing*.

Personal Reorganization. Attitudes towards one's self are difficult to change, since there is a strong drive towards maintaining and enhancing the self-concept. Under what conditions, then, do we change? We alter the self-concept when it is threatened by some experience, and when we cannot deal with the threat in any other way. The would-be violinist who has feelings of failure can try harder, practice more, and still fail. He also might blame his teacher and change to another one, or explain his failure as due to poor health, distractions, and other factors. Maybe none of these alibis satisfy him, and he still feels frustrated. Then he gradually alters his self-concept as a last resort. Notice, we said gradually; it usually takes time. As James would put it, he gives up pretensions he cannot gratify. We may describe this process as "lowering his level of aspirations" or "giving up" or "accepting reality," but what he has really done is change the *meaning* of reality by giving up an aspect of his self. He has changed the meaning of the role he is to play, and thus altered a lot of meanings of things in his environment. We may say that he has acquired "insight" into his motives. But altering the self-concept was the *last* thing he did. It was an effective way of dealing with threat but it was the most radical way, since it involved reorganization of his self.

The foregoing discussion states a principle of personal organization which explains not only why the individual resists change, but under what conditions he will actively seek to alter his organization. We may state the principle as follows: personality changes are radical alterations of the self-concept, and occur as a result of experiences which require reorganization of self-evaluative attitudes. As long as the individual's experience is satisfying and fulfilling his needs, the self-concept is adequate and will remain unchanged. The self-concept becomes inadequate and untenable when the individual's experience is at odds with his view of himself. He will change or reorganize it only under two conditions:

1. He must perceive a discrepancy between his experience and the implications of the self-concept. That is, the self-evaluation of "very bright person" will be given up only when he perceives that he fails at something (e.g., getting poor school marks) in which he should succeed.

2. He must be able to perceive the differences between the demands of the situation and the demands his self-concept makes of him. In other words, he must become at least partially aware of what aspect of the self-concept is not tenable. The redefinition that might result is something like this: "I am very bright in most things, but not in school work." This may not be a highly conscious process, but perceptions of this kind do not require a high level of awareness.

When these perceptions are clear, reorganization of the self-concept occurs; when vague or obscure, the result may be anxiety or nonadaptive behavior. Thus the school bully will become docile and cooperative if he is beaten often enough or soundly enough to make the differentiation clear. Conversely, the timid child will gain confidence if he succeeds in mastering the bully at his own game. The new experience, although satisfying, is at odds with the original self-evaluative attitude of timidity or inadequacy. The self-concept, then, "not only influences behavior but is itself altered and restructured by behavior and unsatisfied needs" (11). In terms of learning principles, unsatisfying consequences or consequences not consistent with the self-concept lead to alteration of the self-concept and attendant needs. They result, also, in a readiness to attempt different forms of behavior.

The organized personality is therefore best described as an internally consistent system, with the individual's behavior organized around an attempt to maintain "self-consistency," an effective balance between the demands he makes of himself and the demands society makes of him. The individual maintains self-consistency, when threatened by a discrepancy between personal and social demands, by (1) rejecting or resisting the social demands, which may be crudely described as a "refusal to learn," or (2) altering his self-concept and his demands on himself, which alters his behavior and thus constitutes learning. It is the individual himself, through his perception and interpretation of his behavior and its consequences, who maintains the organizational balance. Adjustment is by no means a passive process.

Learning Theory in Personal Adjustment. In outlining the role of learning in personality development, Mowrer and Kluckhohn (9) list four fundamental principles of behavior. These principles should by now be familiar to the reader, for they have been mentioned in various parts of preceding chapters. We call attention to them here in order to synthesize some broad aspects of learning, and particularly to give meaning to our concept of adjustment. How do these principles fit the case of the sailor drinking sea water, or that of the schoolboy running away from home?

1. Behavior is functional or adjustive. "The view that living organisms make movements when stimulated and that this is the end of the matter is definitely *not* a functional theory of behavior. . . . In its simplest, most basic form, adjustment implies that living organisms tend to go into action and to remain in action until the source of their activity is removed . . . that their behavior tends to result in the elimination of the stimulation, or irritation, which produces it."

2. Behavior always involves conflict or ambivalence. "Conflict is an ever-present feature of behavior, i.e., every act,

however gainful, also entails some sacrifice or loss; no form of adjustment (stimulation reduction) can occur without some disadjustment (stimulation increase)." Choosing one thing always involves giving up something else, so that reducing one kind of tension builds up another tension. From this point of view, all behavior is a continuous attempt to balance tensions or reduce conflict. The individual is constantly striving for unity or equilibrium. To put this another way, the learner in a problem situation will vary his behavior only if forced to by circumstances (conflict). The principle that "all learning involves conflict" means that all variation in response is due to blocked goals, which in the subjective sense is seen to be motivational conflict.

3. Behavior can be understood only in relation to the field, or context, in which it occurs. We can understand what a person is doing only when we know what he is trying to do. The "field or context" is the situation as perceived by the individual. He always does the most appropriate thing in response to the situation as he sees it at the moment of action. This is the meaning of "total response to total situation."

4. Behavior tends to preserve or maintain a state of maximal integration, or internal consistency. "Living organisms show a tendency to select those modes of adjustment which involve the least possible conflict . . ." Behavior is thus self-regulating, both in the biological and psychological sense. Our definition of individual behavior as an organized attempt to maintain and enhance the self-concept is a special instance of this principle.

Since the self-concept has many different aspects, the satisfaction of need is a difficult matter. Satisfaction of one motive often involves deprivation of the other. As Gardner Murphy puts it, it is "actually a curtailment, a mutilation of the self, to give up something on which we have set our hearts; the self is the poorer."

Life is crowded full of these inexorable choices where no decision can be made without renouncing an important value. The child who has been punished wants to strike back but will bring on himself a loss of safety and love. We want power and know how to get it, but we shall lose the respect of those who look on. Macbeth knows the way to be kind, but he will lose the "golden opinion" of "all sorts of people." Children may know how to impress teachers; but they know that if they do as teacher wishes, their classmates will see through it all. (10, p. 300)

Thus conflict may involve not just two different objects, but two antagonistic motives toward the same object. This is the special meaning of *ambivalent* attitudes, both positive and negative attitudes toward the same thing, person, or event. The core of conflict often (and usually) consists of ambivalent attitudes toward the self. One aspect of the self-concept may consist of something like a self-definition of "powerful person," another a definition of "well-liked" person. Literature is full of dramatic instances of conflict, from Oedipus Rex, Macbeth, Hamlet, and Faust to Studs Lonigan and Scarlett O'Hara. We also find in literature, as in life, that the characteristics of an individual often involve a dominance of certain modes of adjustment, or ways of meeting difficulties. These are learned in one kind of conflict situation and tend to transfer to other situations varying in detail; that is, they tend to become habitual.

MODES OF ADJUSTMENT

Meeting Difficulties. What is perhaps one of the most distinctive characteristics of personality is the way in which the individual meets his difficulties; whether, for example, he habitually tries to escape them, whether he withdraws into the safe inner sanctum of his own thoughts, or whether he fights back with a vehemence out of proportion to their seriousness. Mental hygienists and psychiatrists are continually holding up to our attention the great importance of early life in this respect. Clinical experience with problem children and with neurotic adults often produces a story of a constantly recurring theme which runs well back into early childhood and which seems to have its origin in inadequate attempts at adjustment.

Difficulties, as we know, cannot be avoided in life. Only a condition of extreme mental lethargy could hope to be free of them, in which case mental development of any kind would be impossible. Most difficulties are caused by internal conflicts between opposed and sometimes contradictory desires, wishes, and tendencies within the personality itself. There is probably very little after all which we could not have if we were willing to pay the price by giving up something in return. To speak of meeting a difficulty is usually only another way of saying that we are called upon to rearrrange or to bring order into our life of desires. It is for this reason that we can scarcely hope to understand the personal difficulties of a growing child unless we become acquainted with the nature of his wishes and motives. It does not do to judge the seriousness of a child's difficulty from adult standards. An event which is insignificant in the eyes of the grown-up may be very critical in the emotional life of the child.

The most common ways of solving conflicts, or reducing tensions, are (1) rational solution, (2) adjustment by substitution, (3) adjustment by defense, and (4) adjustment by withdrawing. The various forms of substitution, defense, and withdrawing reactions have sometimes been called "mental mechanisms" or "adjustment mechanisms," but they are not mechanical. These ways of meeting difficulties may become habitual and thus acquire a kind of automaticity. But, like all habits, they were originally learned in a problem setting, and tend to persist because they have the same value for the individual in the situations in which they are used. From an external point of view, they appear to be mechanical adjustments, but this means that they have been learned to a degree of precision. Since their function is to deal with threats and solve the problem by changing the meaning of the situation, the more appropriate term might be "adjustment dynamisms."

Rational Solution of Conflict. This demands an insight into the nature of the difficulty; raising it to the level of consciousness if we suspect an unconscious source; facing things as they actually are; a voluntary acceptance of one of the alternative competing desires with a definite rejection or postponement of the other; and the employment of an intelligent plan to attain the desired end. The dissatisfaction which arises from the frustrated desire or tendency may be employed as a motivating force for a new adjustment within the more general field of this tendency. While this dissatisfaction may lead to a good bit of wishful thinking, resembling fruitless daydreaming in quality, it will nevertheless differ from the latter so far as the thinking will be ultimately capable of being converted into fruitful action and behavior. As we said previously, rational solution of conflict is a rare occurrence. Productive thinking is not too common in human behavior, and thinking about one's personal problems is doubly difficult. It requires insights into one's motives, and such insights are often painful to face. Some of the other modes of adjustment are more common because they are self-protective; that is, they keep us from having to recognize and accept the painful fact that our motives may not be entirely worthy. In this way they not only insulate the individual from painful self-recognition, but deter the kind of thinking that leads to rational solution.

Adjustment by Substitution. The distinctive feature of substitution reactions is the replacement of a blocked or frustrated motive with a different motive or activity. The individual, perhaps unconsciously and without any definite plan about the matter, takes advantage of other opportunities offered by his physical and social environment to satisfy a frustrated wish or desire. In *compensation,* the substituted activity or goal is one which has about the same value for social development as the frustrated alternative. A child who desires to excel in a sport that is blocked to him by lack of ability, for example, may compensate by becoming superior in another. The physically unattractive or defective child may compensate by developing a boastful swagger. The person short in stature may develop a decisive manner, a loud voice, and other "masculine" characteristics. These are cases in which one activity substitutes for another in fulfilling the same general need. We also have *vicarious compensation,* in which the activity is carried out by someone else with whom the individual is strongly identified. The poorly educated father may thus get substitute satisfaction for his own frustrated wishes through the college degree of his son, or the socially frustrated mother through the social success of her daughter. *Identification* with another can be a substitute source of satisfaction, as in the case of a crippled boy who identifies with a well-known athlete, or the golf duffer who associates with expert players. Compensation is of course useful as well as limiting, particularly in connection with various forms of childish activity, such as recreations, athletics, and hobbies where the child is allowed to "blow off steam," or to satisfy normal desires not otherwise easily gratified. These activities perform in a way the function of a safety-valve, protecting the child from an accumulation of frustration and disappointments. The child who is pent up in the house or in school on a rainy day often compensates for his restrictions in less desirable ways. Among the less desirable forms that substitution reactions may take are obnoxious attention-getting, delinquency, and nervous habits.

In *sublimation*, the substituted activity or goal represents a higher level of social development. The child is continually sublimating his desires by leaving behind the activities, plays, and games of early years for the satisfactions that come in connection with the more mature concerns of later childhood and early youth. It is said that the somewhat common childish tendency toward cruelty to animals may be sublimated, in the laboratory and dissecting room, into the search for biological knowledge or surgical skill. The fighting "instinct" may be sublimated into the "conquering" of evil, or of the world through knowledge ("knowledge is power"). The possibilities of sublimation will depend very largely upon the number of opportunities offered by the child's social and cultural environment for the progressive fixation of his wishes on more worthy goals, and upon the example set for him by the behavior of his parents, friends, and acquaintances. It suffers slightly in comparison with the rational solution, since it depends less upon insight and personal initiative, and more upon the stimulating character and stability of the social surroundings.

Adjustment by Defense. Defense reactions are elaborate ways of defending ourselves from self-accusations or feelings of guilt. They are active attempts by the individual, through natural and unconscious tendencies, to shield himself from ever having to admit personal defect or defeat, or from the antici- pated unpleasantness associated with a conflict. Defense re- actions may be classified as (1) forgetting, (2) projection, (3) rationalization, (4) defense through ailments. It is important to note that they are unconscious tendencies; their peculiar value as defense reactions depends on the individual's not being aware of them or their defensive function. In other words, the individual must not catch himself at these reactions, or they lose their value for personal adjustment.

1. *Defense by forgetting.* *Suppression,* or complete forget- ting, is one of the convenient ways of protecting ourselves from the thought of an unpleasant experience or duty, or from a wish or desire which is faced with possible frustration. It probably seems so natural for the young child to forget to wash his hands, to do his home work, or to return a borrowed article, that noth- ing very important can be made out of such behavior. Forget- ting, however, is an aspect of learning and is therefore moti- vated. Many things are forgotten because we have no use for them. On the other hand, many things are forgotten be- cause they are unpleasant (mild threats or frustrations) and thus associated with conflict. Forgetting is thus an aspect of the integration of personality, the purpose of which is reduction of conflict.

Repression is a more serious form of forgetting, in which the frustrated desire or the unpleasant experience is banished from consciousness but operates from an unconscious level to influence conduct. What is known as the "inferiority complex" is one example of repression. All persons have feelings of in- feriority about one thing or another, which are consciously rec- ognized as such. The inferiority complex consists in repressed or unconscious feelings of inferiority, produced ordinarily by not being able to handle one's humiliating experiences in a rational manner. The inferiority feelings, and the experiences which produced them, are forgotten and not recognized, but are revealed in various forms of undesirable behavior: self- consciousness, oversensitivity, self-criticism, gnawing little wor- ries about blunders, remorse, regrets, and the like (3). Here the repressed experience has an emotional "carryover" to a wide range of behavior and causes the individual to over-react to situations which the ordinary person might consider trivial. It is as though the person has a bad case of sunburn which is not consciously painful and escapes his notice, but which makes him self-protective without conscious control. The repressed fear or guilt is a kind of psychological damage analogous to sunburn, and by further extension of the analogy the repression is a kind of anaesthetic which deadens the pain but does not remove the behavioral consequences.

The value of repression as a form of adjustment lies in its "anaesthetic" quality. It turns the individual's attention away from any stimulus or situation which suggests the original painful experience. But repression is an unfortunate kind of adjustment, for it has one feature that renders it capable of mischief. Because it always results in avoidance-reactions, it allows the individual no opportunity to reduce emotional tensions aroused by situations. Thus a painful sex experience, although repressed, may cause a girl to avoid the opposite sex without being aware that she is doing so or knowing the reason why. She anticipates and avoids guilt feelings associated with men. This prevents the possibility of learning a different set of reactions to men, because the repressive forgetting puts the source of conflict beyond conscious control.

Furthermore, repression produces tensions. The person with an inferiority complex may avoid putting his abilities to the test (by failing to apply for a job, for example, through fear of being turned down), but all such challenging situations cause tension. The girl who avoids men behaves toward them in a fearful or hesitating way, indicating tension. Since the use of stern disciplinary measures, such as strong punishment, fear, shame, and ridicule are often identified as the cause of repression in the growing child, it would seem that such measures are to be avoided as much as possible if we wish the child to grow up in full rational control of the forces entering into the development of his personality. Because of the strictness with which minor sex delinquencies are sometimes met in children, it is probably not unusual that complexes centering around sex should be found as the cause of certain peculiarities of adult behavior.

2. *Projection.* We are said to "project" when we attribute to others the undesirable qualities of character which we find within ourselves. By projecting our own faults upon others we can avoid the unpleasantness of having to regard ourselves in an unfavorable light, a retreat or defense from facing the difficulty at its real source. Attitudes of hate, cruelty, suspicion, and mistrust may perhaps develop from such a mechanism. The extreme cynic or chronic complainer is one who as a child probably learned to take this way out of difficulties. The militant reformer and officious meddler has probably also come to be such through the nonrational mechanisms of projection. The scrupulously honest student who distrusts others and finds much evidence of cheating among them may possibly be projecting his own feelings of guilt. That is, he feels tempted himself.

3. *Rationalization* is a natural tendency to maintain self-consistency, self-respect, or the respect of others, by offering specious reasons for one's conduct or the issue of events. The "sour-grapes" device consoles us through convincing ourselves that the thing we set our heart upon was after all probably not worth winning. The "Pollyanna" form of this mechanism is often employed to explain away our lack of success by implying that things are better left as they are. This justifies, in our own minds, our not giving any more effort or attention to the problem, and is a form of retreat by which we are saved from any possible future disappointment. The "transfer of blame," or blaming others for our own failure, by maintaining that they were unfair, unjust, or prejudiced against us, protects us from having to face the unpleasantness of admitting that we were unequal to the demands of the occasion, or from giving new effort to the solving of the problem. This mechanism may operate, along with projection, in influencing our attitudes toward particular social groups, of one nation toward another, of capitalists toward laborers, and of one religious group toward others. A great deal of our social, economic, and religious prejudice can often be traced back to these mechanisms.

Children apparently experience a strong tendency to rationalize, partly because of their lack of insight and partly because they are so intent upon preserving their status in the eyes of their elders, parents, and teachers. They are particularly likely to offer reasons which they know will appeal to adults. Many childish "lies" are much less serious as moral problems when we consider them from such a viewpoint. In fact many of these might rather easily be forestalled if the child could be assured that he is not faced with the loss of affection or the good opinion of others as a result of minor everyday incidents. If that assurance or reward is not forthcoming from his elders, we can hardly blame him if these mechanisms keep their appeal much longer than they should. Because of the importance attached to the devices of rationalization and projection in modifying the child's social attitudes, as exemplified in prejudice, cynicism, and snobbery, they are the two ways of meeting present difficulties that are probably most closely related to the child's future social adjustment. When employed in an exaggerated manner, these mechanisms, as do of course all the defense reactions, incline the child away from gaining a rational insight into his difficulties and planning intelligently for an effective way of handling them.

At their worst, rationalization and projection can be manifestations of serious adjustment difficulties. Consistently blaming one's failures on conspiracies of others, for example, is usually a sign of very deep-seated feelings of inferiority. The notion of being conspired against may reduce tensions caused by inferiority feelings, but in turn causes situations in which the notion may assume even more definite form. If we express an impulse to help the "victim," for example, it may be misinterpreted as a further indication of "conspiracy." The pattern may thus "snowball" until the individual adopts this mode of adjustment almost exclusively and finds it an appropriate self-defense in almost any kind of situation. When the pattern becomes rigid, it is often accompanied by aggression. Not content with untiring efforts to accumulate "evidence" against the league of persons conspiring against him, the self-styled victim may actually distort reality to such an extent that his perceptions are delusive. There is thus a shading off of rationalization patterns from a relatively harmless tendency to blame others to the more serious stage in which the person becomes aggressive and arms himself with all sorts of evidence against the conspirators, then to the critical stage in which he fancies that his telephone is being tapped or that he is really a prince being persecuted by his family's political enemies. It is not, however, rationalization itself that produces this unfolding pattern, but the disintegration of personality due to many factors.

4. *Defense by ailments.* We all recognize that nobody blames us for anything when we are sick or injured. Consequently, adopting some kind of physical ailment is a convenient way of reducing tension through an approved self-defense. Ordinary *malingering,* or feigning sickness or injury, is a common form of behavior in children and a source of "alibis" for adults. Also, a person who does have a sickness or injury may use it as a device for explaining failure and reducing tension. This is a form of rationalization.

In *conversion,* conflict is avoided by a physical disability brought on by the conflict itself; the person is said to "convert" emotional tension into symptoms of a physical disorder, as a way out of the difficulty. The disability furnishes an excuse for not putting forth an effort to meet the difficulty or protects us in advance from an anticipated disappointment or frustration. It is often true that the individual gains satisfaction of a frustrated desire through the physical disability itself. Illness will gain for him the sympathy and concern of his friends, which he may not deserve otherwise. The continued use of various forms of physical indisposition, such as headache, weakness, or sore thumb, as a convenient excuse for not doing his work, may eventually lead in the child to an habitual tendency to fall back upon such a device in the face of difficulties. Oversolicitude on the part of parents or others for minor childhood ills, or extreme contrasts in affectionate or sympathetic treatment of the child when sick and when well are likely to favor this mechanism.

In general any conditions that would place a premium, from the child's viewpoint, upon remaining ill, or that would deny him reasonable satisfaction for his desire for sympathy, affection, or recognition when in good health make a fertile soil for the development of conversion. In extreme form, conversion sometimes shows itself in hysteria and "nervous breakdowns." Unconscious imitation of parents may also be a factor here. It has been found (5) that parents who are known for their fainting or headache spells (often symptomatic of conversion) are also likely to have children who faint, experience temper tantrums, or who have periodic headaches. Perhaps some constitutional predisposition is at work here, although it may be doubted that this is the sole cause.

Adjustment by Withdrawing. Withdrawal, as a mode of adjustment to thwarting, is characterized by a complete failure to cope with the difficulty and a tendency to retreat from the tension-producing situations. Like other modes of adjustment, withdrawal is a "normal" or commonly practiced way of reducing emotional tension. Like the others, it can develop into an habitual kind of response, and herein lies the mischief. When practiced more or less rigidly, inappropriately, and as a response to nearly all kinds of difficulties, withdrawing behavior in children is a very serious symptom of poor adjustment. Also, it is much more likely to escape the notice of teachers than the other forms of behavior mentioned. Shaffer (12) classifies withdrawing reactions into seclusiveness and timidity, pseudo-feeblemindedness, negativism, phantasy or daydreaming, retrogression, and the more acute mental disorders known as schizophrenia or dementia praecox. Some of these merit special discussion.

In *retrogression,* the individual retreats from conflict by adopting responses found satisfying or tension-reducing at an earlier stage of development. He thus seeks to satisfy his desires in a more primitive or childish manner. The crying of the grown-up girl, the "childishness" of some people when they cannot "have their own way," the tendency to live in the past and to obtain one's chief satisfactions therefrom, are examples of this form of reaction. The excessive "babying" of older children and the tendency of certain parents to keep their children closely dependent upon them seem to be important factors here.

The *shut-in reaction* is so called because the frustrated individual withdraws from contact with the outer world into the inner sanctum of his own autistic "thinking" and daydreaming, where in imagination he may satisfy his unfulfilled desires. The "sulkiness" or "pouting" of certain children is a budding example of this. Phantasy is a normal form of development in the play of young children, who play various roles and talk them out aloud. In this form, it is not particularly a reaction to frustration, but may easily become so. Daydreaming is a particularly convenient way of playing roles which are deeply desired but not possible in the hard world of reality. It thus satisfies basic motives, and compensates for feelings of failure and inferiority. In the classroom, daydreaming is most common among bright children who learn quickly and are bored with the tedium of routine drill, and among dull children who are bored because the work is too difficult. This points up the necessity of providing for individual differences in ability in the school.

Negativism, unlike the others considered, is an active and often explosive form of withdrawing, characterized by refusal to conform, rebellion against authority, stubbornness, and temper tantrums. It is quite likely to be noticed by teachers, but not as a form of withdrawal. The negativistic child is aggressive, but also often seclusive. The reaction is an adjustment by withdrawal because it represents a tendency to retreat from tension-producing situations. Consistent refusal may appear to be nonadjustive, but as Shaffer says, "if resistance operates to secure the child what he desires, to get him out of unpleasant tasks or to make him the center of attention, it will be learned and employed repeatedly, as will any other form of adjustment that proves to be of value as a tension reducer" (12).

Persistent Nonadjustive Behavior. It is quite difficult to draw a distinct line between adjustive and nonadjustive behavior. In general, these two categories are an attempt to classify the reactions of a person to problem situations: How effectively does the individual confront, attack, and cope with the obstacles? We have seen that the forms of behavior classified as adjustive have one common consequence, namely, reduction of tension. Even "maladjustments" are tension-reducing and satisfying to the individual, although they are not considered effective ways of attacking or coping with problems and are not socially approved. Nonadjustive behavior is the name we give to those reactions which result in neither satisfaction nor achievement; that is, the individual neither reinterprets the problem in a way which will reduce tension, nor does he directly attack or deal with the obstacles in a practical way. He remains in an unadjusted state, with high emotional tension and his responses disorganized. When this state persists for a long period, it is a serious mental condition.

Shaffer (12) gives three characteristics of the nonadjusted state: (1) a persistent *visceral state,* caused by dominance of the sympathetic nervous system which acts in all emotional states as if to prepare the organism to meet an emergency. This is the physiological side of being "keyed up"; there is a heightened readiness for activity, which predisposes the person to very strong reactions to ordinary stimuli. (2) The second characteristic is *diffused motor activity,* which means that he overreacts to situations and shows many random, disorganized, restless movements. This is similar to ordinary "nervousness"; the pencil chewers, nail biters, floor walkers, and excited talkers show the same behavior. The difference here is that such activity is persistent, not merely an excited reaction to a specific situation. (3) A state of *worry or anxiety,* similar to a fear reaction. Worry ordinarily refers to a response to the fairly well-defined situation, as when a student worries constantly about his grades. We call this state anxiety when it "spreads" or transfers to many different kinds of situations, when nearly all the problems of life are reacted to in the same way.

Anxiety is sometimes described as "free-floating," meaning that it attaches to almost any kind of situation and moves around to all the problems of life-adjustment. The state is chronic; without knowing why, the individual seems to look for things to worry about, and inevitably finds them. We see here, then, the picture of heightened tension and disorganized overactivity that solves no problems and does not reduce the tension. From a purely descriptive point of view, nonadjustive behavior may be classified several ways. Psychiatric terms include *neurasthenia* or "nervous weakness" with chronic complaints of fatigue, aches and pains; *hypochondria* or preoccupation with health and imaginary ailments; *anxiety states* characterized by persistent vague fears and forebodings of doom.

Why does nonadjustive behavior persist, since it produces no satisfying consequences? This is one of the puzzles of the psychology of adjustment. May the neurasthenic and the hypochondriac be said to "enjoy poor health," as the saying goes, and their behavior therefore have some adjustive value? It does seem that this is possible, since psychiatrists report that this behavior ordinarily accompanies profound feelings of inferiority. It then seems plausible that the constant physical complaints help to explain away the individual's "failures," and persist because they have an adjustive value similar to conversion and rationalization. The fact that such persons have frequently been coddled as children and have enjoyed past illnesses leads additional support to this view.

The question of why anxiety persists is more difficult. A recent book by May (8) points out that anxiety, unlike ordinary fears, strikes at the very core of personality, and thus is symptomatic of the person's drive to defend himself against a threat to the "whole" person—the internally consistent system of self-evaluative attitudes which we have called the self-concept. Anxiety is a drive to defend the *unity* of the person through which other drives are subordinated, controlled, and satisfied. But the need for personal unity is not satisfied by anxiety. Unlike normal behavior in a problem situation, in which the individual varies his interpretation and responses in the presence of obstacles, anxiety appears to be a fixated or stereotyped response. The person in the grip of an anxiety state does not seem to be aware of alternatives. Actually, he is, but does not seem able to do anything about it.

Although it is not known how anxiety is learned, some experiments with animals may offer an explanation by analogy. These experiments have been successful in producing a "fixated" response in the rat. The fixation was found to be not just a very strong habit, but a response that persisted in spite of all attempts to modify it by ordinary reward and punishment. Two common ways of inducing the fixated response are as follows:

1. The rat is presented with an *insoluble problem*. It is placed on a platform from which it is forced (by blasts from an air hose, for example) to jump toward either of two windows faced with upright pieces of cardboard. A "right" response knocks over the card and leads to food, while in the "wrong" response the animal plunges against a rigid card and drops into a net. The situation is arranged by varying the cards at random so that the rat, no matter what it does, will be "wrong" and get punished half the time. It cannot learn. After a number of trials, the animal develops a fixated "position preference" or in other words always jumps toward the same window or card (6).

2. The rat is punished excessively at the moment of choice. At a "choice point" in a T-shaped alley the animal must decide which wing of the T it will follow as a path toward food. As it approaches the choice point it is given a severe shock. After repeated trials under these conditions, the rat develops a fixated "position habit"—it invariably makes the same response, taking the right turn, for example, over and over again.

After a fixated response is established, the animal cannot seem to learn any other responses. There is no way to reward an alternative response, because the animal will not make any other. Nor can the fixation be removed by punishment. In one experiment, the rat persisted in a position reference even when the response was punished consistently hundreds of times (7). Drugging the animals with metrazol did not help either. There is no point here in attributing anxiety to the rat, but the parallel between the rat's abnormal fixation and human anxiety is striking. Both are nonadjustive; the fixation resists modification, and human anxiety is very resistant to clinical treatment. We have here a suggestion as to how human nonadjustive reactions are learned.

If we apply the rat experiments to human learning, we might infer that nonadjustive behavior is a result of continued frus-

tration. It may very well be that the human child, when placed
continually in insoluble problem situations, becomes so deeply
disturbed and apprehensive that it cannot adapt to any, the result being an habitual anxiety state. It seems plausible also
that nonadjustive behavior (and here we might include *negativism,* because it is in many ways nonadjustive) is not modifiable by punishment. Excessive punishment, we must conclude,
can play no part in effective learning because it destroys the
organized, varied behavior necessary to deal with obstacles
and solve problems. The child who is always "wrong" and
always gets punished no matter what he does undergoes a severe
threat to his total personal organization, and the result may be
persistent nonadjustive behavior. The importance of animal
studies here should be obvious: no such experiments, it is safe
to say, will ever be done with human children.

REFERENCES

1. Cannon, W. B. *Wisdom of the body.* New York: Norton, 1939.
2. Havighurst, R. J. *Human development and education.* New York: Longmans, Green, 1953.
3. Heidbreder, E. The normal inferiority complex. *J. abn. soc. Psychol.,* 1927, **22,** 243-258.
4. Lecky, P. *Self-consistency: a theory of personality.* New York: Island Press, 1945.
5. Levy, D. M., & Patrick, H. T. Relation of infantile convulsions, headbanging, and breath-holding to fainting and headaches in parents. *Amer. J. Neurol. & Psychiat.,* 1928, **19,** 865-887.
6. Maier, N. R. F., Glaser, N. M., & Klee, J. B. Studies of abnormal behavior in the rat. III, The development of behavior fixations through frustration. *J. exp. Psychol.,* 1940, **26,** 521-546.
7. Maier, N. R. F., Glaser, N. M., & Klee, J. B. XII, The pattern of punishment and its relation to abnormal fixations. *J. exp. Psychol.,* 1943, **32,** 377-398.
8. May, M. *The meaning of anxiety.* New York: Ronald Press, 1950.
9. Mowrer, O. H., & Kluckhohn, C. Dynamic theory of personality. In Hunt, J. McV. (Ed.), *Personality and the behavior disorders,* I. New York: Ronald Press, 1944.
10. Murphy, G. *Personality.* New York: Harper, 1947.
11. Raimy, V. C. Unpublished Ph.D. dissertation; quoted by Snygg, D. & Combs, A. W., *Individual behavior.* New York: Harper, 1949.

12. SHAFFER, L. F. *Psychology of adjustment*. Boston: Houghton Mifflin, 1936.

SELECTED READINGS

BLAKE, R. R., & RAMSEY, G. V. *Perception: an approach to personality*. New York: Ronald Press, 1951. Chs. 5 and 8-13 examine the role of perception in personal adjustment.

CARROLL, H. A. *The dynamics of adjustment*. New York: Prentice-Hall, 1951. Chs. 7-9.

JOHNSON, W. *People in quandaries: the semantics of personal adjustment*. See note at end of preceding chapter.

MOWRER, O. H. *Learning theory and personality dynamics*. New York: Ronald Press, 1950. Chs. 13, 16-18.

MURPHY, G. *Personality*. New York: Harper, 1947. Pt. IV, Chs. 20-25.

ROGERS, C. R. *Client centered therapy*. Boston: Houghton Mifflin, 1951.

SHAFFER, L. A. *Psychology of adjustment*. Boston: Houghton Mifflin, 1936.

SNYGG, D., & COMBS, A. W. *Individual behavior*. New York: Harper, 1949.

TRYON, C., & HENRY, W. E. How children learn personal and social adjustment. Ch. 8 in *49th Yearbook,* Nat. Soc. Stud. Educ., 1950.

INDEX OF NAMES

INDEX OF SUBJECTS